KERUX COMMENTARIES

# ECCLESIASTES AND SONG OF SONGS

KERUX COMMENTARIES

# ECCLESIASTES AND SONG OF SONGS

*A Commentary for Biblical Preaching and Teaching*

JORDAN W. JONES
CHRISTOPHER R. PASCARELLA

*Ecclesiastes and Song of Songs: A Commentary for Biblical Preaching and Teaching*

© 2024 by Jordan W. Jones and Christopher R. Pascarella

Published by Kregel Ministry, an imprint of Kregel Publications, 2450 Oak Industrial Dr. NE, Grand Rapids, MI 49505-6020.

All rights reserved. No part of this book may be reproduced, stored in a retrieval system, or transmitted in any form or by any means—electronic, mechanical, photocopy, recording, or otherwise—without written permission of the publisher, except for brief quotations in printed reviews.

Unless otherwise indicated, the translations of the Scripture portions used throughout the commentary are the authors' own English rendering of the original biblical languages.

Scripture quotations marked ASV are from the American Standard Version. Public domain.

Scripture quotations marked CSB have been taken from the Christian Standard Bible®, Copyright © 2017 by Holman Bible Publishers. Used by permission. Christian Standard Bible® and CSB® are federally registered trademarks of Holman Bible Publishers.

Scripture quotations marked ESV are from The ESV® Bible (The Holy Bible, English Standard Version®), © 2001 by Crossway, a publishing ministry of Good News Publishers. Used by permission. All rights reserved.

Scripture quotations marked KJV are from the King James Version. Public domain.

Scripture quotations marked NAB are taken from the New American Bible, revised edition © 2010, 1991, 1986, 1970 Confraternity of Christian Doctrine, Washington, D.C. and are used by permission of the copyright owner. All Rights Reserved. No part of the New American Bible may be reproduced in any form without permission in writing from the copyright owner.

Scripture quotations marked NASB are taken from the (NASB®) New American Standard Bible®, Copyright © 1960, 1971, 1977, 1995, 2020 by The Lockman Foundation. Used by permission. All rights reserved. lockman.org.

Scripture quoted by permission. Quotations designated (NET) are from the NET Bible® copyright ©1996, 2019 by Biblical Studies Press, L.L.C. http://netbible.com All rights reserved.

Scripture quotations marked NIV are taken from the Holy Bible, New International Version®, NIV®. Copyright © 1973, 1978, 1984, 2011 by Biblica, Inc.™ Used by permission of Zondervan. All rights reserved worldwide. www.zondervan.com. The "NIV" and "New International Version" are trademarks registered in the United States Patent and Trademark Office by Biblica, Inc.

Scripture quotations marked NLT are taken from the *Holy Bible*, New Living Translation, copyright © 1996, 2004, 2015 by Tyndale House Foundation. Used by permission of Tyndale House Publishers, Carol Stream, Illinois 60188. All rights reserved.

Scripture quotations marked NRSV are from the New Revised Standard Version Bible, copyright © 1989 National Council of the Churches of Christ in the United States of America. Used by permission. All rights reserved worldwide. https://www.friendshippress.org/pages/nrsvue-quick-faq

Italics in Scripture quotations indicate emphasis added by the authors.

Photos and figures on pages 68, 88, 97, 139, 163, 173, 195, 203, 229, 232, 243, 256, 273, 286, 303, 314, 330, and 341 are public domain.

Illustration on page 115 is by Rachel E. Jones. Used by permission.

The Hebrew font, NewJerusalemU, and the Greek font, GraecaU, are available from www.linguistsoftware.com/lgku.htm, +1-425-775-1130.

ISBN 978-0-8254-2564-6

Printed in China

24 25 26 27 28 / 5 4 3 2 1

# Contents

Publisher's Preface to the Series / 7

Preface to Ecclesiastes and Song of Songs / 9

Exegetical Author's Acknowledgments / 11

Preaching Author's Acknowledgments / 13

Overview of All Preaching Passages / 15

Abbreviations / 29

## ECCLESIASTES

Introduction to Ecclesiastes / 33

### *The Observations of Qohelet (1:1–6:9)*

The Reality of God and the Enigma of Life (1:1–18) / 57

Illusive Pursuits, Authentic Living, and the Gifts of God (2:1–26) / 77

Human Temporality and the Timelessness of God (3:1–15) / 93

The Fear of God and the Evil of Inequity (3:16–5:7 [HB 6]) / 105

The Impermanence of Wealth and the Providence of God (5:8 [HB 7]–6:9) / 123

### *The Admonitions of Qohelet (6:10–12:14)*

The Works of God Are Unsearchable, So Be Wise and Fear Before Him (6:10–8:13) / 135

The Works of God Are Unsearchable, So Live Joyfully Before Him (8:14–9:10) / 159

The Works of God Are Unsearchable, So Avoid Folly and Live Freely Before Him (9:11–11:6) / 171

Life Is Short, So Enjoy It and Remember God (11:7–12:7) / 189

Human Endeavor Is Futile, So Heed the Wise and Follow God (12:8–14) / 201

# SONG OF SONGS

Introduction to the Song of Songs / 211

## *The Rudiments of Love (1:1–2:17)*

The Lovers Invite One Another (1:1–8) / 227

The Lovers Affirm One Another (1:9–2:7) / 241

The Lovers Anticipate One Another (2:8–17) / 255

## *The Acts of Love (3:1–5:1)*

The Lovers Pursue One Another (3:1–11) / 267

The Lovers Embrace One Another (4:1–5:1) / 281

## *The Renewal of Love (5:2–8:5)*

The Lovers Renew Their Pursuit (5:2–6:13 [HB 7:1]) / 295

The Lovers Renew Their Embrace (7:1 [HB 2]–8:5) / 311

## *The Lessons of Love (8:6–14)*

Love Is Supreme (8:6–7) / 327

Love Is Rewarding (8:8–14) / 337

References / 347

# PUBLISHER'S PREFACE TO THE SERIES

Since words were first uttered, people have struggled to understand one another and to know the main meaning in any verbal exchange.

The answer to what God is talking about must be understood in every context and generation; that is why Kerux (KAY-rukes) emphasizes text-based truths and bridges from the context of the original hearers and readers to the twenty-first-century world. Kerux values the message of the text, thus its name taken from the Greek *kērux*, a messenger or herald who announced the proclamations of a ruler or magistrate.

Biblical authors trumpeted all kinds of important messages in very specific situations, but a big biblical idea, grasped in its original setting and place, can transcend time. This specific, big biblical idea taken from the biblical passage embodies a single concept that transcends time and bridges the gap between the author's contemporary context and the reader's world. How do the prophets perceive the writings of Moses? How does the writer of Hebrews make sense of the Old Testament? How does Clement in his second epistle, which may be the earliest sermon known outside the New Testament, adapt verses from Isaiah and also ones from the Gospels? Or what about Luther's bold use of Romans 1:17? How does Jonathan Edwards allude to Genesis 19? Who can forget Martin Luther King Jr.'s "I Have a Dream" speech and his appropriation of Amos 5:24: "No, no, we are not satisfied, and we will not be satisfied until 'justice rolls down like waters, and righteousness like a mighty stream'"? How does a preacher in your local church today apply the words of Hosea in a meaningful and life-transforming way?

## WHAT IS PRIME IN GOD'S MIND, AND HOW IS THAT EXPRESSED TO A GIVEN GENERATION IN THE UNITS OF THOUGHT THROUGHOUT THE BIBLE?

Answering those questions is what Kerux authors do. Based on the popular "big idea" preaching model, Kerux commentaries uniquely combine the insights of experienced Bible exegetes (trained in interpretation) and homileticians (trained in preaching). Their collaboration provides for every Bible book:

- A detailed introduction and outline
- A summary of all preaching sections with their primary exegetical, theological, and preaching ideas
- Preaching pointers that join the original context with the contemporary one
- Insights from the Hebrew and Greek text
- A thorough exposition of the text
- Sidebars of pertinent information for further background
- Appropriate charts and photographs
- A theological focus to passages

- A contemporary big idea for every preaching unit
- Present-day meaning, validity, and application of a main idea
- Creative presentations for each primary idea
- Key questions about the text for study groups

Many thanks to Jim Weaver, Kregel's former acquisitions editor, who conceived of this commentary series and further developed it with the team of Jeffrey D. Arthurs, Robert B. Chisholm, David M. Howard Jr., Darrell L. Bock, Roy E. Ciampa, and Michael J. Wilkins. We also recognize with gratitude the significant contributions of Dennis Hillman, Fred Mabie, Paul Hillman, Herbert W. Bateman IV, and Shawn Vander Lugt who have been instrumental in the development of the series. Finally, gratitude is extended to the two authors for each Kerux volume; the outside reviewers, editors, and proofreaders; and Kregel staff who suggested numerous improvements.

—*Kregel Publications*

# PREFACE TO ECCLESIASTES AND SONG OF SONGS

In the context of the ancient Near East (ANE), a world replete with its own literature on creation, law, prophecy, history, worship, wisdom, etc., the Hebrew Bible speaks with a voice uniquely its own. And yet, for all the similarity of genre, style, and subject matter within the literary corpora of the ANE, we find in the Hebrew Scriptures both a familiar mode and an unfamiliar message. Most kinds of texts we encounter in Scripture have analogs from nonbiblical literature; yet, while Scripture was also written by human beings, its truth and power are uniquely the product of the Holy Spirit's inspiration. For example, it is well known that Egypt and Mesopotamia had their own pessimistic literature with its own messages. But in the biblical book of Ecclesiastes, Qohelet (the author) wrote "the words of truth" (דִּבְרֵי אֱמֶת; Eccl. 12:10). Egypt and Mesopotamia likewise had their own love poetry, but Israel's love lyrics, inspired by the Spirit, constitute "the most excellent Song" (שִׁיר הַשִּׁירִים; Song 1:1).

The book of Ecclesiastes has been interpreted in a great number of ways over the millennia, but what readers will find in this volume is a commitment to Qohelet's brutal realism as the backdrop against which his prescription of joy is set. He goes to great pains throughout his teachings to expose the harshness, unfairness, and unpredictability of life. This he does to disabuse his readers of their many delusions—that is, their false beliefs that through wisdom one can hack the system of life to attain a truly satisfying degree of wealth, knowledge, social status, and longevity. He does this by dragging them through the turmoil of his own internal anguish to offer up, in the words of Uncle Screwtape from Lewis's classic satire, "that particular kind of clarity that hell affords." Only when his readers understand the world for what it is will they be able to find gratifying joy in the simple pleasures we commonly take for granted: food, drink, work, and family—all of which come not from the futility of human ambition but are the "gift" of God (2:24–26; 3:12–13; 5:18 [HB 17]; 8:15; 9:7–9).

If, in Ecclesiastes, we see the evil of the world in all its unfiltered ugliness, in the Song of Songs we encounter starry-eyed lovers who view one another and the natural world around them through rose-tinted glasses. This collection of love songs should be understood as a loose, sequentially imprecise storyline of a man and a woman in love, singing to one another with otherworldly language. Adulations like "you're pretty" and "nice hair" are insufficient praise to express how these utterly smitten lovers truly feel about one another. And these terms go well beyond praise as the lovers actually pursue and embrace one another, but ever with a view to the Shulammite's powerful refrain to engage in love only at the appropriate time, one that accords with nature's rhythms and, by extension, the desires of God (2:7; 3:5; 8:4). The books of Ecclesiastes and Song of Songs teach modern believers a lot about how to live wisely in God's world.

When was the last time you heard a sermon on a passage from Ecclesiastes or Song of Songs? Maybe you have recently heard a sermon on the seasons of life from Ecclesiastes 3 at a funeral or the unquenchable love from Song of Songs 8 at a wedding. But consider if you have ever heard a whole sermon *series* on these books. Ecclesiastes and the Song can unfortunately often be neglected for Christian worship because of the many difficulties they present to pastors in preaching them. First, there are thematic issues. How does a pastor preach the erotic language of the Song? How should pastors tackle the negative or despairing comments of Qohelet? Second, there are structural issues. These books are not easy to outline. The Song is poetry and does not fit into a neat and tidy predetermined structure. While scholars are more confident that Ecclesiastes is laid out in two major sections (1:1–6:9; 6:10–12:14), there is no broad agreement on how each half should be broken down. Hopefully, when reading this commentary, such challenges from the text provoke excitement rather than avoidance.

Due to the uniqueness of Ecclesiastes and the Song, the homiletical sections of this commentary seek to capture the wild and untamed nature of these books, while also providing a path forward for preaching them during Christian worship services. Consider the insights, illustrations, and outlines of the homiletical sections as suggestions and guidance from someone who has tried to preach these passages in worship services before. You may disagree with some of the interpretations found in the homiletical sections. That is fine. It is often by working through disagreements and coming up with alternatives that the shape and scope of a sermon will come into focus. Most importantly, may these sections—and the commentary as a whole—seek to increase your appreciation for and delight in these amazing books of the Bible!

# EXEGETICAL AUTHOR'S ACKNOWLEDGMENTS

*In gratitude to my wife and children—Rachel, Kelsie, Kohen, and Kennan.*
*May we live joyfully in the ever-changing present,*
*learning therein to delight in the otherworldly beauty of our world.*

The texts of Ecclesiastes and the Song of Songs are deep waters—saying anything about them requires a lot of focus. Accordingly, I have many people to thank for providing me with the time and feedback needed to complete this project.

My wife and kids have been very supportive as I worked in my study over the last few years, wrestling over the right words to convey the emotional weight of both Qohelet and the lovers. When the kids were out of school for summer and winter breaks, the task of writing meant I would have to get up well before the sun so that I could still get my regular work done, spend time with my wife, help my daughter solve the world's social complexities, and humiliate my sons at pickup basketball—for that last part, I am not sorry. My parents, siblings, and in-laws have also kindly cheered me on. The same goes for my Sunday school class at First Baptist Church of Suffolk, Virginia, whose love and wisdom were an encouragement to me as we read through Ecclesiastes together. I also want to thank the faculty, staff, and students of Regent University's School of Divinity for continually supporting me and asking about the project, even if it just meant picking my brain about a difficult passage in either text. Two such students, in particular, were immensely helpful: Kristen Wilson, who read and commented on the Song portion, and Joseph Green, who did the same for Ecclesiastes. Both were excellent Hebrew students in the MDiv program at Regent. Kristen also soared through a year of Akkadian with me; and I have it on good authority that Joseph was outstanding in Greek. Ecclesiastes and the Song are hard to interpret, so I'm sure I did not have satisfying answers to every question posed to me, but I gave what I could and what I felt the text allowed me to give. I am also indebted to my good friend, Chris Pascarella, with whom I have had many conversations about these texts and the numerous complex interpretive issues contained in them. Our long friendship has resulted in great trust, which meant that it was easy to work with him over the past few years. His rich homiletical commentary has been challenging to me, and I'm deeply grateful for it. Furthermore, I want to thank Shawn Vander Lugt and the staff at Kregel Publications, all of whom have been very encouraging and insightful while Chris and I worked on this volume—I am indebted to them for the wisdom and direction they provided.

Finally, I'm thankful to the Lord who, by the Spirit, worked through human authors to produce the powerful words of Scripture. I am among those who think that Qohelet is a good teacher, a sage who should be given enough wiggle room to express the full range of his emotions, and one who repeatedly points his readers to good things: acceptance of realism, joyful living, and reverence for God. Qohelet's teachings have greatly impacted how I think about life and my own futile efforts to control various outcomes; it has also helped me to better appreciate many things I normally take for granted. The Song likewise has redefined how I think about romantic love, the majesty of creation, and the role of the natural world in pointing us continually to the beauty of God. That said, I do not read the Song typologically nor allegorically; rather, the text is an ancient Israelite love song, inspired by the Holy Spirit, and broadly instructive on the topic of romantic love. Nevertheless, all the stunning beauty it conveys is grounded in the beauty of its Creator and the love that goes forth from him.

For His Glory,<br>
Jordan W. Jones

# PREACHING AUTHOR'S ACKNOWLEDGMENTS

*To my wife, Heather,
and children, Roman and Ruthanne*

All glory must be given to God first!

This endeavor would not have been made possible without the love and support of my wife, Heather. I cannot think of a greater gift the Lord has given me than her. She has always encouraged me to pursue the various opportunities the Lord has opened up for me, including this commentary. She embodies not only the fierce love and commitment depicted in the Song of Solomon, but also the wisdom and guidance that comes through in Ecclesiastes.

I would also like to thank my parents, Joe and Linda Pascarella. They too have embodied the fierce commitment and unquenchable love exhibited in the Song. They have supported my decision to pursue ministry and have continually invested in me and my family.

Some of my biggest thanks must go to Dr. Paul Fink, who passed on to his heavenly reward some years ago. Dr. Fink was my homiletics professor at Liberty University. He taught me how to exegete the Greek text, how to move from exegesis to developing a homiletical outline, and finally, how to stand and deliver a message from God's Word. I will always be indebted to him for the training I received.

I must thank the congregation at Lincroft Bible Church (LBC). LBC was my home church growing up and has been my only place of employment since graduating seminary. It is truly a privilege to deliver God's Word to my church family on a consistent basis. I must also thank the LBC youth group for challenging me and forcing me to continually grow in how I communicate God's Word. As I've said before, if you can hold the attention of a sixth-grade boy during a sermon, you can hold anyone's attention!

I would also like to thank those who have shaped me through spiritual and theological formation during my time at The Southern Baptist Theological Seminary, particularly Dr. James M. Hamilton and Dr. Peter J. Gentry. While they may have different interpretations of these books themselves, I have learned so much from them about how to read the Old Testament texts.

Finally, I am indebted with gratitude for my friend Jordan Jones, with whom I was able to collaborate on this commentary. It would not be without his influence and encouragement that I am a published author. This has been a partnership and friendship that began in the residence halls of Liberty University in 2005 and continues to this day! For that, I am so thankful.

Thank you to everyone else who has believed in me and encouraged me along the way. I would not have been able to produce this work without you.

In Christ,
Chris Pascarella

# OVERVIEW OF ALL PREACHING PASSAGES

## Ecclesiastes 1:1–18

**EXEGETICAL IDEA**
The book's narrator reveals Qohelet's sobering thesis: all human effort is ephemeral and inconsequential in light of the endless, enigmatic rhythms of nature. Qohelet's formal introduction (starting in 1:12) and initial investigations reveal a more specific indictment of human effort: the very process of investigating all knowledge (which includes both wisdom and folly, 1:17) brings only anxiety and sorrow.

**THEOLOGICAL FOCUS**
Embracing the harsh realities of life's brevity and human ineffectuality can be sobering, but it is a necessary embrace to achieve a fuller, healthier understanding of human existence in the light of God's sovereign and transcendent design.

**PREACHING IDEA**
Trust God even when life seems vain.

**PREACHING POINTERS**
Ecclesiastes opens with the declaration that life is vanity. In excruciating detail and with impeccable logic, Qohelet backs up his thesis by pointing out that nothing really changes. People might think they're getting ahead, but in reality, it's all been done before. Even worse, the quest for wisdom in the face of an incomprehensible life leads only to frustration for Qohelet. Yet, Qohelet still believed that somehow God was behind it all—all the mysteries, difficulties, and vanities of life.

Although Ecclesiastes features very ancient wisdom, its message resonates through the ages and is especially relevant for our modern world. While Western culture has become more prosperous than ever, there has been a rising poverty of meaning and significance. The abundance of wealth, availability of all kinds of pleasure (particularly sexual pleasure), and the West's obsession with work has led us all down the path described by Qohelet. The only question is: Will we turn to God, or will we continue our dead-end pursuits at all costs?

## Ecclesiastes 2:1–26

**EXEGETICAL IDEA**
Qohelet finds that the human pursuit for lasting satisfaction or gain in one's pleasure, wisdom, and work is a futile endeavor; instead, one ought to live authentically before God.

**THEOLOGICAL FOCUS**
Become disillusioned with the vain pursuits of pleasure, wisdom, and work apart from God; resolve instead to live authentically before him.

**PREACHING IDEA**
Find your satisfaction in God alone, because everything else will disappoint you.

**PREACHING POINTERS**
Qohelet embarked on a quest to find fulfillment through human endeavor. He pursued pleasure, wisdom, and work. Yet all those things disappointed him. He realized they could not provide the satisfaction he was looking for. His journey of futile discovery was not solely negative, however. He came to realize that trusting in God's sovereign control over all things could free his heart to enjoy the simple pleasures of life. Good things were meant to be good things, not God things.

We live in a time of human history when so many things compete for our attention. Glowing screens fill our minds with endless entertainment. We can have exposure to all kinds of sexual immorality, whether digital or in person. We have access to more information than at any other point in human history. We can now work anytime, anywhere with our smartphones and laptops. And yet, a thick sense of despair sits over us. Human beings are not more satisfied in our culture of abundance than in ancient times of scarcity. That's because lack of fulfillment is ultimately a theological problem, as Qohelet points out. We were made for God. And seeking fulfillment in anything else is a dead end, as St. Augustine so eloquently said in his classic prayer to God from the *Confessions*, "Our hearts are restless until they find their rest in you."

# Ecclesiastes 3:1–15

**EXEGETICAL IDEA**
Qohelet demonstrates that the temporality of human life and limitations of human knowledge stand in stark contrast with the timelessness and omnipotence of God. In response, he resolves that humans should live authentically within the limits set by the Sovereign Gift-Giver.

**THEOLOGICAL FOCUS**
Acknowledging human life's brevity and divinely ordained limitations is necessary for embracing a proper vision of God, one that drives humans into a state of authentic living before him.

**PREACHING IDEA**
Embrace God-given limits.

**PREACHING POINTERS**
Qohelet taught his students that all their efforts would not stand before the relentless march of time, exemplified in the steady rhythm of nature. Qohelet even declared that one of the greatest perceived human efforts—acquiring wisdom—was a grievous task. But such grief did not prevent Qohelet from testing other areas of life, such as pleasure and work, to see if they

could provide fulfillment and satisfaction. He found that they could not. Qohelet eventually came to see that a path to fulfillment comes from putting God at the center of life and then enjoying the life he gives.

The world is a big, incomprehensible, and ultimately uncontrollable place. Humans respond by attempting to tame the world and bend it to their will. They strive to transcend the limits of the world, especially the constraints of time. But such efforts are foolish, according to Qohelet. Attempting to break barriers of the world will only lead to frustration and despair. Instead, people can live authentically before God by embracing the limits he has given.

## Ecclesiastes 3:16–5:7 (HB 6)

### EXEGETICAL IDEA
Qohelet, in mournful reflection over the many injustices and inequities of the world, resolves that people should take joy in their work while rightly revering God.

### THEOLOGICAL FOCUS
Since the human experience is one full of inexplicable injustices and unfairness, the only worthwhile path for people to take is to do their work joyfully and revere God rightly.

### PREACHING IDEA
Stop pretending and face reality: God is sovereign over a broken world.

### PREACHING POINTERS
Qohelet observed all manner of injustice and tragedy in the world. He had seen instances where the wicked triumphed over the righteous. Although he hoped for God's future judgment, he also recognized the tragedy of the human condition: People die just like animals. Wherever he looked, he saw the strong taking advantage of the weak. He saw the misery that rivalry and discontentment produced. In a world filled with inequity, he proclaimed a path of authentic living before God. He discouraged rashness of speech and attempts at bargaining with God. Instead of advocating for a new way of living, he reached into the past and emphasized a common theme in the Hebrew Scriptures: the fear of the Lord.

Qohelet's realistic description of the state of the world, as well as his admonition to live authentically before the Lord, is a necessary splash of cold water on the face of modern life where curation is the norm. Digital technologies and the internet have given people the ability to screen out the parts of life they would rather ignore. Moreover, these technologies provide a powerful way to present a certain image of oneself, an image of one's own making. But God is not fooled. He sees the intent and motives of our hearts.

## Ecclesiastes 5:8 (HB 7)–6:9

### EXEGETICAL IDEA
Qohelet asserts that wealth is fleeting, uncertain, and cannot satisfy, but God's providential care for humanity is sufficient for human joy.

**THEOLOGICAL FOCUS**
The problem with wealth is that humans trust in it for something it can never provide: satisfaction and joy, both of which are the rewards of the person who delights in God's simple gifts.

**PREACHING IDEA**
Serve God, not money.

**PREACHING POINTERS**
Qohelet undertook his own search for significance and fulfillment, only to find that everything "under the sun" led to disappointment and disillusionment. His experience must have influenced his teachings as he observed the vain strivings of those around him. He routinely pointed out the folly of pursuing work and wealth as one's source of fulfillment. Wealth, in particular, presented an allure to those he observed. Yet those who pursued riches always ended up in the same place as he did: craving something of substance, yet never finding it.

The message of Ecclesiastes concerning wealth is vitally important for believers today. Despite recent economic uncertainties in many places, most are still enjoying the most affluent and prosperous era in world history, and Americans are the greatest beneficiaries at this time. Yet, according to Qohelet, the pursuit of wealth is a fool's errand. Wealth cannot satisfy. In fact, wealth doesn't just *not* satisfy, but pursuing it is like drinking salt water; it creates a more intense craving. To live wisely, believers must approach wealth in a cautious and contented manner. They must put away their constant craving and simply enjoy the gifts God has given them.

# Ecclesiastes 6:10–8:13

**EXEGETICAL IDEA**
Qohelet acknowledges that God's works are unsearchable and concludes that one of the best things a human can do is live wisely in the fear of God.

**THEOLOGICAL FOCUS**
The "work of God" (7:13), which includes the enigmatic ways of the world, cannot be found out such that life could be manipulated or controlled by humans; therefore, one ought to live wisely and fear God.

**PREACHING IDEA**
Grow wise.

**PREACHING POINTERS**
Qohelet began his investigation into the vanity of life by observing the world around him (1:1–6:9). He recognized that pursuing typical avenues of human fulfillment like work or money could never satisfy. In light of his observations, Qohelet begins admonishing his students. If they are to survive and thrive in this "vain" world, they should follow his prescriptions. He first speaks to the limits of human knowledge (6:10–12). He then moves on to speak about how to have a "better" life (7:1–14), the limits of wisdom (7:15–29), how to relate to those in authority (8:1–9), and what to do when you observe injustice in the world (8:10–13).

Sitting behind all of Qohelet's proverbs and admonitions is the larger command to be wise. Qohelet recognizes that wisdom, even with all its limitations, provides one of the best ways to navigate through life. Qohelet clearly exposes the incomprehensibility of the world, which is felt so keenly today as it seems like the modern world gets faster and more complex with every passing day. The only hope we can have to make our way through such complexity is the stabilizing force of wisdom.

# Ecclesiastes 8:14–9:10

**EXEGETICAL IDEA**
Qohelet acknowledges that God's works are unsearchable and concludes that one of the best things a human can do is live joyfully before him in a world afflicted by death.

**THEOLOGICAL FOCUS**
The work of God, which includes the enigmatic ways of the world, cannot be figured out such that life can be manipulated or controlled by humans; therefore, one ought to live joyfully before him.

**PREACHING IDEA**
Enjoy your life.

**PREACHING POINTERS**
Qohelet recognized the unpredictability of the world and the limits of human knowledge. Even human wisdom has limits. If the world, and the God who made it, could not be fully understood, Qohelet concluded that the best course of action would be to live wisely and joyfully before the Lord. Instead of striving for knowledge and accomplishments greater than the world can bear, Qohelet taught that human beings should be content with their lot in life and enjoy the simple gifts God gives to them.

Enjoying life is easier said than done, especially with the onset of modern culture. Digital advertising presents a near-constant stream of discontentment-inducing content before our eyes. Social media gives off the impression that everyone else in the world is doing better than we are. On the opposite end of the spectrum, cable news programs can make it seem like the whole world is a complete disaster, about to fall apart at any minute. Consuming such messages and images can breed despair and discontent in our hearts, making it difficult to enjoy what God has given. Qohelet's messaging, then, is a breath of fresh air, for it honestly acknowledges the tragedies and difficulties found in the world but offers a hopeful path forward to enjoying life.

# Ecclesiastes 9:11–11:6

**EXEGETICAL IDEA**
Qohelet acknowledges that God's works are unsearchable, just as his world is unpredictable. In light of this, he instructs his pupils to avoid the dangers of folly while living life freely and generously.

**THEOLOGICAL FOCUS**
The world is full of unpredictable danger, so it is best to avoid folly and live one's life in freedom and generosity, acknowledging that humans do not have control over life's outcomes.

**PREACHING IDEA**
Prepare for the future, but don't try to predict it.

**PREACHING POINTERS**
Qohelet admitted that the ways and works of God were beyond human comprehension. He counseled against human beings exhausting themselves for exhaustive knowledge. Not only was the world incomprehensible from Qohelet's point of view, but it was also unpredictable. The future defies being figured out. Instead of making vain attempts to control the future, Qohelet advised his students to live with wise preparation for whatever may come.

Despite the advances in technology, human beings are still incapable of predicting the future. Attempting to predict the future may do more harm than good, inflating someone's perceived control over the world when, in reality, they have none. Instead of fruitlessly trying to predict what may or may not happen, Qohelet's counsel is much wiser: prepare for, but don't try to predict, the future. Adequate preparation equips people to encounter a range of unexpected outcomes, whereas prediction locks them into believing only one conceivable future will occur, rendering them helpless in the face of unexpected circumstances.

# Ecclesiastes 11:7–12:7

**EXEGETICAL IDEA**
In his final admonition, Qohelet directs his pupils to fix their thoughts on God while they live, knowing that old age and death come sooner than one thinks.

**THEOLOGICAL FOCUS**
The certainty of death brings the value of life itself into perspective, directing Godfearers to enjoy their lives free from vexation and to prioritize God in their hearts while they still can.

**PREACHING IDEA**
Don't wait until it's too late. Remember God when you're young.

**PREACHING POINTERS**
Because of the inscrutability of God's ways, Qohelet concluded that one of the best ways for people to live is to pursue wisdom and trust in God's sovereignty. As Qohelet wrapped up his teaching, he reminded his students of the importance of being mindful of God in one's youth. Instead of pursuing a vain life, he advised those he taught to fear God and keep his commandments.

"Youth is wasted on the young," the adage goes. Although a cliché, the saying resonates with many people as they look back on their younger years with regret. Instead of pursuing the things of God, they pursued the things of the world, only to be left disappointed. Qohelet's admonition to the young is an important message to relay to the younger generations today, so that those coming behind us can be spared the pain and heartbreak of vain pursuits—although such wise counsel will only stave off foolishness if it is heeded.

# Ecclesiastes 12:8–14

**EXEGETICAL IDEA**
The narrator of Ecclesiastes returns to summarize the teachings of Qohelet, noting that while there is always more to learn under the sun, including many things that cause confusion and vexation, the simplest truth also happens to be the most profound: people must follow God.

**THEOLOGICAL FOCUS**
The legacy of the Hebrew sages is in their wisdom, as collectors of proverbs and teachers of life, but that wisdom finds its center in their admonition to fear God as the ultimate judge, whose commandments are the only lasting thing in a world otherwise plagued by *hevel*.

**PREACHING IDEA**
Fear God.

**PREACHING POINTERS**
In his final teaching, Qohelet instructed his students to remember God while they still lived. Old age and death would come upon them before they knew it, so Qohelet desired for them to have a strong foundation in God to face those things. In the final section of the book, the frame narrator summarized Qohelet's main teaching point: even though the world seems incomprehensible, irrational, and vain, the best thing someone can do is fear God and obey his commandments.

In a complex and often unpredictable world, it can be tempting to overcomplicate and overthink our existence. Human beings can undergo an endless search to figure out the mysteries of the universe and the meaning of life. The frame narrator of Ecclesiastes advises us to keep things simple. Instead of stressing ourselves out by attempting to know the unknowable, we must stay focused on the most important thing: fearing God and doing what he says. If we follow this simple, but hard, advice, we will make our way wisely through a world of vanity.

# Song of Songs 1:1–8

**EXEGETICAL IDEA**
The lovers' desires for one another lead them to initiate the process of courtship through invitation, welcoming all subsequent joys the courtship may bring.

**THEOLOGICAL FOCUS**
Truthfully acknowledging one's affections and initiating the process of courtship can echo and affirm, when done in accordance with God's standards, the divine authorship of love.

**PREACHING IDEA**
Cultivate a passionate relationship.

**PREACHING POINTERS**
The author of this book did not just write a song, but he wrote the "Song of Songs," the best song. He wrote the best song on the best theme: love. He was not shy in extolling the beauty and passion of human love. He carefully constructed an intricate song detailing the exploits of a man and woman in love. He began his song by showing how the man and the woman longed for and pursued each other.

The message of the Song of Songs is desperately needed in the church today. The enticements of a culture awash in sexual immorality can lure believers away from the purity God demands. On the other hand, some believers may see the licentiousness of the culture and respond by unintentionally denigrating God's good gift of marital sexual intimacy. Consequently, the beauty and power of God-sanctioned romance needs to be emphasized. The Song provides the proper understanding of love, romance, and sexual desire for the church. Strong desire comes from God and should be cultivated for marriage. When the Holy Spirit directs our desires, we can experience the wonders of God's love both in our marriages and in our churches.

## Song of Songs 1:9–2:7

**EXEGETICAL IDEA**
The man and the woman affirm one another with elegant language, further intensifying their desire to be together.

**THEOLOGICAL FOCUS**
Verbal affirmation in romantic relationships engenders confidence, vulnerability, and intimacy.

**PREACHING IDEA**
Use words wisely to build flourishing relationships.

**PREACHING POINTERS**
The man praised the woman as if she were royalty, although she was a humble worker of the land. The woman reciprocated his affirming words by proclaiming he was royalty too. The man and the woman continued to trade compliments back and forth, demonstrating that the bond of their love had led them to a blossoming and fruitful relationship. Yet the woman recognized the power of romantic love and encouraged others to wait until the right time to fulfill the desires for romantic love.

The characters of the Song provide the paradigm for how we can improve our relationships. We must speak words of affirmation to one another, generally, in both marriage and friendships. For married couples, these words will include comments about one another's beauty. For those who are not married, these words will include affirmation of the work God is doing in each other's lives. In romantic relationships, though, we must be careful not to stir up desires for love before the appropriate time. Couples who pursue courtship before they are ready for the commitment of marriage invite considerable difficulty into their lives.

# Song of Songs 2:8–17

**EXEGETICAL IDEA**
The man and the woman eagerly anticipate one another as they seek to remove every obstacle to their love.

**THEOLOGICAL FOCUS**
Healthy romance involves both longing for the other person as well as a willingness to address known obstacles that could hinder the relationship.

**PREACHING IDEA**
Overcome alienation through intentional effort.

**PREACHING POINTERS**
The lovers encountered many different obstacles during their relationship. At times, the relational alienation between them seemed like they were separated by a vast mountain range. Even when in close physical proximity, the lovers sometimes felt as if there was a wall between them. In other moments, they were vexed by smaller problems. While these smaller issues might have seemed insignificant, if left unattended, they could have wreaked havoc on the harmony of the relationship, just as foxes can destroy an unattended vineyard. They had to put forth intentional effort to overcome the relational isolation and separation they felt.

The existential alienation people feel is rooted in their estrangement from God through sin. Even the best relationship has times when each person feels estranged from the other. Human beings can feel isolated and lonely even when sitting in a crowded room. Therefore, we should not be surprised when we experience relational distance from friends, relatives, and even our own spouses. The reality of relational separation should lead us to take action to overcome the distance and be close to those we care about.

# Song of Songs 3:1–11

**EXEGETICAL IDEA**
The lovers seek and find one another to make preparations for their wedding.

**THEOLOGICAL FOCUS**
God honors the honest pursuit of a mate at the right time, which at the very least includes being guided by the wisdom of his word and the witness of his word in creation.

**PREACHING IDEA**
Channel intense desire toward marriage.

**PREACHING POINTERS**
The Song has captured the intense desire of love through its poetic descriptions of a man and woman who have pursued one another in a romantic relationship. The intoxicating power of love has caused the woman to warn others against awakening love until the right time. She understood that the intense desire that moved her toward her beloved needed to be directed toward an appropriate end. The proper end of sexual desire in the Song, as in the rest of the Scriptures, is marriage.

Both the church and the world need to hear the message that marriage is the proper destination for the fulfillment of intense romantic longing, particularly sexual longing. While all manner of sexual activity outside of marriage is promulgated by the culture, the church can provide a picture of true human flourishing by pointing to God's design. The Bible teaches us that the safest and most liberating context for true sexual fulfillment is the covenant of marriage. Therefore, all people should channel their intense sexual desires toward the pursuit of marriage.

# Song of Songs 4:1–5:1

**EXEGETICAL IDEA**
The lovers embrace one another in marital intimacy.

**THEOLOGICAL FOCUS**
Sexual intimacy in marriage is a good gift from God that is designed for human pleasure and for God's glory.

**PREACHING IDEA**
Enjoy God's gift of marital intimacy.

**PREACHING POINTERS**
The man and the woman pledged themselves in marriage to one another. Then, on the verge of their wedding night, they continued to pursue each other with lovely words. The man repeatedly reminded his wife how beautiful she is. He worked his way down her body with dramatic metaphors to express his desire. He beckoned her to come down from her place of isolation and be joined to him in body and soul. His pure bride responded to him, making herself accessible so that they might enjoy all the fruits of intimacy together in unashamed joy.

Sexual intimacy is a very important aspect of a godly marriage. While many outside of the church may believe that God is against sex, the reality is that God created sex as a gift to be enjoyed within marriage. Only within a committed covenant marriage can a couple experience being naked but not ashamed. Married couples can enhance the intimacy of their sexual encounters by complimenting one another's beauty.

# Song of Songs 5:2–6:13 (HB 7:1)

**EXEGETICAL IDEA**
The lovers renew their pursuit of one another in the face of obstacles.

## THEOLOGICAL FOCUS
When believers experience marital hardships that create distance, they must passionately renew their pursuit of one another to restore the relationship.

## PREACHING IDEA
Perseverance and commitment are necessary to build lasting love.

## PREACHING POINTERS
Even after the man and the woman are married, they still find themselves separated from one another. The man knocked on the door of the house to be with his wife, but when she answered, she found that he had already left. The woman embarked on another nighttime search to find the man. The journey was treacherous, however, as the guards of the town physically assaulted her. The woman beseeched others to send a message to her beloved if they found him: she was lovesick. She then praised the man, likening him to a great statue. After an exchange with the chorus again, she came to realize where he was: in his garden. She returned to the man and he was delighted to be with her, for he spent considerable time praising her beauty again.

Getting married does not solve all of a couple's problems, as this portion of the Song shows. And while we cannot know the reason for the couple's separation in this passage, we do know the kinds of things that impede our own marriages. After the honeymoon, couples must continue to work on their relationship. One area of struggle for couples can be a difference in libido. Generally, men desire sexual intimacy more frequently than do women, although this varies among couples. One spouse may approach the other for intimacy, only to feel like they are being rejected. The pain of rejection, whether it manifests as emotional neglect or denied sexual advances, can cause rifts between couples. No matter what the problem is, however, perseverance is needed to build long-term, healthy relationships.

# Song of Songs 7:1 (HB 2)–8:5

## EXEGETICAL IDEA
The lovers renew their embrace of one another.

## THEOLOGICAL FOCUS
Believers ought to renew their embrace of one another throughout the many seasons of marriage.

## PREACHING IDEA
Pursuing sexual pleasure with your spouse has no expiration date.

## PREACHING POINTERS
After their time of separation, the couple renewed their pursuit of each other. Their pursuit for one another did not stop there; they renewed their embrace in sexual intimacy. The man praised his wife's beauty once again and determined to make love to her. The woman responded to the

man by expressing her own feelings of sexual desire. She took the initiative to think of exciting ways to make love to him. She intensely desired him, even longing to cast off all ancient societal norms so that she could be close to him.

No matter how long a couple is together, pursuing sexual pleasure with one's spouse never expires. Of course, older couples will face challenges that come with aging. But even older couples can still be exclusively devoted to one another and pursue each other in a myriad of ways. Nothing is greater than an enduring love.

# Song of Songs 8:6–7

**EXEGETICAL IDEA**
The woman proclaims that love is more powerful than any earthly force, even as powerful as death itself.

**THEOLOGICAL FOCUS**
Believers should acknowledge the inimitable power of romantic love, driving them to revere it as divinely given rather than as a mere tool for manipulation and pleasure.

**PREACHING IDEA**
Love is supreme.

**PREACHING POINTERS**
After writing many chapters of imaginative poetry, the author provided the clearest exposition of love in the whole book. The author explained that love is a force as strong as death, backed up by the repeated lovesickness the woman felt when separated from the man. The power of love crashed over the woman like a wave. Love burned in their lives fierce like lightning. Love was so valuable as to be priceless, such that if anyone tried to buy it they would be criticized as a fool.

If love is the most important thing in the world, believers should do everything in their power to grab hold of it. Human love provides a dim picture of God's fierce love for his people. As great as human love is, human life becomes meaningless without the love of God. Once people experience God's love, they learn to love everything, and everyone, properly.

# Song of Songs 8:8–14

**EXEGETICAL IDEA**
The woman proclaims the ways in which love is rewarding.

**THEOLOGICAL FOCUS**
Those who pursue love honorably, prioritizing the romantic relationship over competing forces, are granted pleasure, longevity, and peace.

**PREACHING IDEA**
Pursue love the right way and reap the rewards.

**PREACHING POINTERS**
Wrapping up the Song, the woman provided poetic lessons on how to handle love. She spoke of the importance of proper sexual conduct and its resulting rewards. She described how love works. Love must be freely given. She emphasized the important role community played in the preparation for love. After her lessons on love, the man beckoned the woman away to himself again, indicating that the cycle of longing, estrangements, and pursuit never ends.

The Song is love poetry that bears some resemblance to wisdom literature since at least part of its purpose (see most clearly in 8:6–14) is to instruct others in how to rightly navigate the power and complexities of love. As the book ends, the woman rightly reminds us to pursue love the right way. If we abide by God's standards and follow his will, certain rewards will come to us. They may not be worldly rewards of sexual fulfillment or a life of ease and prosperity; instead, we will receive a harvest of peace, contentment, and a lifelong partner to pursue.

# ABBREVIATIONS

## GENERAL ABBREVIATIONS

| | |
|---|---|
| A.D. | in the year of our Lord (*anno Domini*) |
| ANE | Ancient Near East(ern) |
| B.C. | Before Christ |
| EBH | Early Biblical Hebrew |
| HB | Hebrew Bible |
| LBH | Late Biblical Hebrew |
| LXX | Septuagint |
| NT | New Testament |
| OT | Old Testament |
| SBH | Standard Biblical Hebrew |

## TECHNICAL ABBREVIATIONS

| | |
|---|---|
| cf. | compare (*confer*) |
| ch(s). | chapter(s) |
| e.g. | for example (*exampli gratia*) |
| et al. | and others (*et alii*) |
| etc. | and so forth, and the rest (*et cetera*) |
| i.e. | that is (*id est*) |
| p(pp). | page(s) |
| § | section |
| v(vv). | verse(s) |
| trans. | translation |

## BIBLICAL SOURCES

*Old Testament*
| | |
|---|---|
| Gen. | Genesis |
| Exod. | Exodus |
| Lev. | Leviticus |
| Num. | Numbers |
| Deut. | Deuteronomy |
| Josh. | Joshua |
| Judg. | Judges |
| Ruth | Ruth |
| 1 Sam. | 1 Samuel |
| 2 Sam. | 2 Samuel |

*Old Testament (continued)*
| | |
|---|---|
| 1 Kings | 1 Kings |
| 2 Kings | 2 Kings |
| 1 Chron. | 1 Chronicles |
| 2 Chron. | 2 Chronicles |
| Ezra | Ezra |
| Neh. | Nehemiah |
| Esther | Esther |
| Job | Job |
| Ps./Pss. | Psalm(s) |
| Prov. | Proverbs |

## Old Testament (continued)

| | |
|---|---|
| Eccl. | Ecclesiastes |
| Song | Song of Songs |
| Isa. | Isaiah |
| Jer. | Jeremiah |
| Lam. | Lamentations |
| Ezek. | Ezekiel |
| Dan. | Daniel |
| Hos. | Hosea |
| Joel | Joel |
| Amos | Amos |
| Obad. | Obadiah |
| Jonah | Jonah |
| Micah | Micah |
| Nah. | Nahum |
| Hab. | Habakkuk |
| Zeph. | Zephaniah |
| Hag. | Haggai |
| Zech. | Zechariah |
| Malachi | Malachi |

## New Testament

| | |
|---|---|
| Matt. | Matthew |
| Mark | Mark |
| Luke | Luke |
| John | John |
| Acts | Acts |
| Rom. | Romans |
| 1 Cor. | 1 Corinthians |
| 2 Cor. | 2 Corinthians |
| Gal. | Galatians |
| Eph. | Ephesians |
| Phil. | Philippians |
| Col. | Colossians |
| 1 Thess. | 1 Thessalonians |
| 2 Thess. | 2 Thessalonians |
| 1 Tim. | 1 Timothy |
| 2 Tim. | 2 Timothy |
| Titus | Titus |
| Philem. | Philemon |
| Heb. | Hebrews |
| James | James |
| 1 Peter | 1 Peter |
| 2 Peter | 2 Peter |
| 1 John | 1 John |
| 2 John | 2 John |
| 3 John | 3 John |
| Jude | Jude |
| Rev. | Revelation |

## EXTRABIBLICAL SOURCES

| | |
|---|---|
| b. B. Bat. | Babylonian Talmud, tractate Bava Batra |
| Sir. | Sirach |

## PERIODICALS

| | |
|---|---|
| *AcT* | *Acta Theologica* |
| *AfO* | *Archiv für Orientforschung* |
| *BBR* | *Bulletin for Biblical Research* |
| *Bib* | *Biblica* |
| *BibInt* | *Biblical Interpretation* |
| *BSac* | *Bibliotheca Sacra* |
| *CBQ* | *Catholic Biblical Quarterly* |
| *CTM* | *Concordia Theological Monthly* |
| *HS* | *Hebrew Studies* |
| *HTR* | *Harvard Theological Review* |
| *HUCA* | *Hebrew Union College Annual* |

# Abbreviations

| | |
|---|---|
| *IEJ* | *Israel Exploration Journal* |
| *JBL* | *Journal of Biblical Literature* |
| *JBQ* | *Jewish Bible Quarterly* |
| *JCS* | *Journal of Cuneiform Studies* |
| *JSOT* | *Journal for the Study of the Old Testament* |
| *JSS* | *Journal of Semitic Studies* |
| *RB* | *Revue Biblique* |
| *SEÅ* | *Svensk Exegetisk Årsbok* |
| *SJOT* | *Scandinavian Journal of the Old Testament* |
| *SJT* | *Scottish Journal of Theology* |
| *Them* | *Themelios* |
| *TynBul* | *Tyndale Bulletin* |
| *VT* | *Vetus Testamentum* |
| *ZAW* | *Zeitschrift für die alttestamentliche Wissenschaft* |

## SERIES

| | |
|---|---|
| AB | Anchor (Yale) Bible |
| ABS | Archaeology and Biblical Studies |
| AIL | Ancient Israel and Its Literature |
| ANETS | Ancient Near Eastern Texts and Studies |
| ApOTC | Apollos Old Testament Commentary |
| BZAW | Beihefte zur Zeitschrift für die alttestamentliche Wissenschaft |
| CC | Continental Commentaries |
| FAT | Forschungen zum Alten Testament |
| HACL | History, Archaeology, and Culture of the Levant |
| HCOT | Historical Commentary on the Old Testament |
| IBC | Interpretation: A Bible Commentary for Teaching and Preaching |
| ICC | International Critical Commentary |
| JSOTSup | Journal for the Study of the Old Testament Supplement Series |
| LHBOTS | Library of Hebrew Bible/Old Testament Studies |
| NAC | New American Commentary |
| NCB | New Century Bible Commentary |
| NICOT | New International Commentary on the Old Testament |
| NIVAC | NIV Application Commentary |
| OLA | Orientalia Lovaniensia Analecta |
| OTL | Old Testament Library |
| OTS | Old Testament Studies |
| SBLDS | Society of Biblical Literature Dissertation Series |
| SBLMS | Society of Biblical Literature Monograph Series |
| TOTC | Tyndale Old Testament Commentaries |
| WAW | Writings of the Ancient World |
| WBC | Word Biblical Commentary |
| WeBC | Westminster Bible Companion |

## REFERENCES

| | |
|---|---|
| *ANEP* | Pritchard, James Bennett, ed. *The Ancient Near East in Pictures: Relating to the Old Testament*. 2nd ed. with supplement. Princeton, NJ: Princeton University Press, 1969. |
| *ANET* | Pritchard, James Bennett, ed. *Ancient Near Eastern Texts Relating to the Old Testament*. 3rd ed. Princeton, NJ: Princeton University Press, 1969. |
| *CAD* | Gelb, Ignace J., et al. *The Assyrian Dictionary of the Oriental Institute of the University of Chicago*. 21 vols. Chicago: Oriental Institute of the University of Chicago, 1956–2010. |
| *COS* | Hallo, William W., and K. Lawson Younger Jr., eds. *Context of Scripture*. 4 vols. Leiden: Brill, 1997–2016. |
| *GKC* | Gesenius, Wilhelm. *Gesenius' Hebrew Grammar*. Edited by Emil Kautzsch. Translated by Arthur E. Cowley. 2nd ed. Oxford: Clarendon, 1910. |
| *HALOT* | Köhler, Ludwig, Walter Baumgartner, and Johann J. Stamm. *The Hebrew and Aramaic Lexicon of the Old Testament*. Translated and edited under the supervision of Mervyn E. J. Richardson. 2 vols. Leiden: Brill, 2001. |

## BIBLE TRANSLATIONS

| | |
|---|---|
| ASV | American Standard Version |
| CSB | Christian Standard Bible |
| ESV | English Standard Version |
| JPS | Jewish Publication Society translation of 1917 |
| KJV | King James Version |
| NAB | New American Bible |
| NASB | New American Standard Bible |
| NET | New English Translation |
| NIV | New International Version |
| NJPS | *Tanakh: The Holy Scriptures; The New JPS Translation According to the Traditional Hebrew Text* |
| NLT | New Living Translation |
| NRSV | New Revised Standard Version |

# INTRODUCTION TO ECCLESIASTES

## OVERVIEW OF ECCLESIASTES

**Title:** Ecclesiastes

**Authorship:** An inspired scribe in the tradition of the Israelite monarchy whose teachings are presented by a narrator

**Date:** Uncertain; possible preexilic origin for Qohelet's teachings with a later exilic to postexilic compilation in the Persian period (550–332 B.C.)

**Readers:** Pupils in an instructional setting in ancient Israel, though intended for the broader Israelite (later "Jewish") community and possibly beyond

**Historical Settings:** Uncertain; possibly preexilic Judah with relevance for exilic and postexilic Jewish communities following final compilation

**Occasion for Writing:** To disillusion readers from unrealistic assumptions about the world in order to promote authentic living in the fear of God

**Genre:** Realistic wisdom (traditionally construed as "pessimistic wisdom")

**Literary Structure:** A collection of observations (1:3–6:9) and admonitions (6:10–12:7) framed by a narrator (1:1–2; 12:8–14)

**Theological Emphases:** The eternality of God and the futility of human endeavor, the works of God and their incomprehensibility, future judgment, and holy disillusion

## TITLE

"Ecclesiastes" is how the title appears in the Latin Vulgate, translated from the Greek (Ἐκκλησιαστής), which appears in 1:12 of the LXX, itself being a translation of the Hebrew "Qohelet" (קֹהֶלֶת), typically rendered in the English versions as "Preacher" (e.g., ESV, KJV, NASB) or "Teacher" (e.g., CSB, NET, NIV, NLT) or left untranslated as "Q/Kohelet(h)" (e.g., JPS, NAB). This latter approach is best since neither "Preacher" nor "Teacher" are really appropriate designations for the term "Qohelet," a noun derived from the verb (קהל) "to assemble" (see Schoors 2013, 35; technically, a feminine participle, see notes in Holmstedt, Cook, and Marshall 2017, 48).

Though feminine, the term "Qohelet" is consistently used with masculine verbs, indicating that this term was a frozen title referring to a male speaker: "Hebrew words of this type were sometimes used to denote offices or functions, and might then acquire a secondary meaning of the holder of such an office or the performer of such a function" (Whybray 1989, 2; see Neh. 7:45, esp. Ezra 2:55 with "the sons of Hassophereth" בְּנֵי־הַסֹּפֶרֶת). Functionally, Qohelet may be someone who assembles people for the purpose of leading them in some capacity, which could involve giving a speech (see the many attestations of the verbal form in *HALOT* s.v. "קהל"). He could also be someone who collects wisdom. For purposes of this commentary, the book itself will be referred to as "Ecclesiastes," but the main speaker of the text will be called "Qohelet." Canonically, the book of Ecclesiastes belongs in the third section of the Hebrew Bible (HB) titled *Ketuvim* (כתובים) or "Writings," and more specifically is one of the five scrolls comprising the *Megillot* (חמש מגילות), along with Song of Songs, Esther, Lamentations, and Ruth.[1]

## AUTHORSHIP

Compared to other biblical literature, Ecclesiastes is unusual. And that recognition is fairly standard in biblical studies (see Davis 2000, 159). Its content betrays a keen awareness of the biblical Hebrew texts, but its form is unlike any other. The book's inclusion into the canon was not at first smooth according to the Mishnah, and this is likely due to Qohelet's seemingly unorthodox statements and supposed contradictions of thought. But by the end of the first century A.D., following the Council of Jamnia, it was accepted. Notes Seow, "Ecclesiastes was clearly a book on the margins of the canon, but in the end its authority was acknowledged by the majority of Christians and Jews" (1997, 4; see also Dell 1994, 301–29). Indeed, a careful, spiritually sensitive reading of Ecclesiastes reveals that it is not here by accident.

The term "Solomon" never appears in the text. Nevertheless, authorship has traditionally been attributed to Solomon for several reasons, one being the use of the verb (קהל) in 1 Kings 8:1 where Solomon "assembles" (יַקְהֵל) the people (see title). The term "Qohelet" (קֹהֶלֶת), typically translated "Preacher/Teacher," is from the same verbal root. Also, aside from David, only Solomon was "king over Israel in Jerusalem" (Eccl. 1:12). Nearly all early Jewish and Christian writers promoted Solomon as the author. However, in a foreshadowing of modern critical scholarship on the topic, Martin Luther asserted that the author had to have come later, possibly Ben Sira during the time of the Maccabees (Bartholomew 2009, 44). And most modern scholars now likewise assert that Solomon's persona was adopted by a later author for rhetorical purposes, though there is disagreement about when exactly everything was written down (on the adopted persona interpretation, see Forti 2021, 517–18; Longman 1998, 5; Sneed 2015a, 346; and many others). This commentary follows the thread that Ecclesiastes is Solomonic in the sense that it exists within the tradition of wisdom first promoted by Solomon, but that it was penned by a later, Spirit-inspired scribe who used Solomon's identity in order to say things Solomon never did. Qohelet wishes

---

1 Throughout this commentary, verbal roots are unvocalized when referring to their lexical forms, as here with קהל. In general, Hebrew may appear if a grammatical or exegetical point warrants its inclusion, but also, and admittedly much more subjectively, when its inclusion might satisfy the curiosity of readers who wish to glance at the unaccented Masoretic Text behind a particular English translation; more obvious expressions containing entry-level Hebrew vocabulary may not be included. Masoretic accentuation has been removed, but may also appear in a few places, where relevant. Furthermore, if quotation marks are used around English terms that are unaccompanied by Hebrew, these represent a translation of a Hebrew term or terms in the passage and are not scare quotes used for emphasis, which is the function of italics in this volume. Finally, unless otherwise indicated, all translations are the authors'.

to use Solomon's voice to say things the king presumably could have said had he grown in wisdom rather than idolatry (see notes on 1:1 and 1:12). Those things include the fact that the extreme overindulgences of Solomon's life deeply contradicted the wisdom he espoused (chs. 1–2), and that there is much more to say about life and "the work of God" (8:17; 11:5) than can be found in the action-consequence teachings of Proverbs alone (chs. 3–12). Qohelet's Solomonic persona is not explicitly continued after chapter 2 but lingers in the background nonetheless, having been established as his identity for the sake of argument.

### Solomon, Some Other Davidic King, or an Inspired Scribe?

The traditional view of assigning the book to Solomon is based upon several lines of thinking, like (1) the assumption that the elder king is looking back over his reign and is now repentant of so many vanities; (2) the attribution of the book to "the son of David" who self-identifies as "king over Israel in Jerusalem"; (3) the author's seemingly intimate knowledge of incredible wealth and wisdom; and (4) the fact that the verb "to assemble" (קהל), related to "Qohelet" or "Assembler" (קֹהֶלֶת), is used in conjunction with Solomon in 1 Kings. Tremper Longman notes, "Thus, the 'Assembler' may be an intertextual reference to 1 Kings 8 and a subtle hint that Solomon is the referent" (1998, 2). Longman further explains the desire among traditional Jewish and Christian circles to see some kind of repentance from the renowned king and famed author of so much wisdom (3). Nevertheless, he and many others point out the problems with identifying Solomon as its author, a summary of which includes: (1) the adoption of the nickname "Qohelet" rather than Solomon using his own name; (2) the past tense "was king" in the first verse describing Qohelet (Solomon died as king, but see Murphy [1992, 11] and others who offer as possible the present perfect translation "I still am king," though this suggestion is less likely); (3) the assertion of Qohelet that he was wiser than all who ruled in Jerusalem before him (but only David preceded, and it seems unlikely that Qohelet means to include prior Canaanite rulers as well); (4) Qohelet's bemoaning of the injustices of the wealthy upon the poor despite Solomon's own participation in such oppressions; (5) the obviously later style of Hebrew in Ecclesiastes (see "Date"); and (6) statements about the king in the third person that seem awkward coming from Solomon himself (Longman 1998, 4–6; see also the helpful list of internal and external evidence for non-Solomonic authorship in Bartholomew 2009, 46–54). For these reasons, scholars commonly assert that Qohelet is a much later scribe who adopted a Solomonic persona for the sake of argument (so Dell 2020, 145; M. Fox 1999, 372. Fox sees the frame narrator, who wrote 1:1–2 and 12:8–14, as the inventor and secret identity of Qohelet, which itself is a nickname for Solomon). But Solomon was not the only wise and powerful king capable of writing this text, and the intentional, rhetorical choice of Qohelet to leave out the name "Solomon" opens interesting possibilities.

The objections to Solomonic authorship are daunting, and the circumstantial evidence used to attribute the text to Solomon could be used of other righteous/wise kings, like Josiah or Hezekiah, especially when we consider that several others have preceded them as king in Jerusalem, a description that does not fit with Solomon (1:16; 2:7, 9). This same argument can be made for the authorship of the Song of Songs. The Talmud (b. B. Bat. 15a) claims it was Hezekiah who wrote both books (Schoors 2013, 2). Given the claim of Jerusalemite kingship in the book, the lack of Solomon's name, and the noted difficulties with attributing the text to Solomon, it is possible that the wisdom of Qohelet was first conceived within the court of a later Davidic king, like Hezekiah (see Quackenbos's arguments in favor of Hezekiah [2019, 168]). Even if this is true, the teachings appear to have been compiled later by a scribe (see "Date"). But in 1:12, Qohelet is referred to as "king over Israel" (מֶלֶךְ עַל־יִשְׂרָאֵל), a title reserved for David and Solomon in the united kingdom of Israel-Judah. Is it possible to refer to Hezekiah or some later Davidic king (like Zerubbabel? See Weinberg 2003, 166) as "king over Israel"? This can happen only if Qohelet adopts Solomon's persona, which he does (M. Fox 2004, x).

### *The Work of a Frame Narrator*

But what about the prologue (1:1–2) and epilogue (12:8–14) of the book? While the body of Ecclesiastes could be the words of a king or other scribe nicknamed Qohelet, it appears the bookends represent the efforts of a later scribe to present the words of the author in biographical form. The suggestion that just one person wrote the entire text, including the prologue and epilogue, seems unlikely given that the narrator speaks about Qohelet in the third person (e.g., 1:1–2; 7:27; 12:8–14; however, some scholars [e.g., Garrett, M. Fox, etc.] see even this as the rhetorical technique of a single author). Yet, it seems the intention of the frame narrator is to present Qohelet's words as separate (though not distinct in content) from his own. If Qohelet is just a stage name for the frame narrator, meaning that the narrator is speaking about himself, then the endorsement given to Qohelet in 12:9–10 is oddly egotistical and not in keeping with the overt humility of Qohelet throughout the book. Hence, just as Proverbs presents itself as written by more than one hand, so Ecclesiastes presents itself as the work of Qohelet compiled and presented by an unnamed narrator who bookends the text.

Despite the presentation of the text as a product of more than one writer (that is, one writer quoting another), some scholars dismiss the third-person incursions (1:1–2; 7:27; 12:9–10) as simply a level of narration along with two other levels: the wisdom passages in the book and the Qohelet sayings—all this, writes Duane Garrett, is a clever "literary technique" used by a single writer, Solomon. He states that the reason the various levels of narration "flow together so well is that they are all part of a single perspective of a single author," but since there are no comparable examples of biblical and ancient Near Eastern (ANE) authors narrating/presenting their own first-person speeches in the third person, he cites an example of this phenomenon from modern English literature, which may not be a sufficient comparison (Garrett 1993, 263 n. 54; see also M. Fox's comparable suggestion [1977, 94–96]; the epilogue of the Egyptian Instruction of Any, while perhaps comparable in purpose to Eccl. 12:8–14, is not sufficiently comparable in form). Indeed, the frame narrator's message does not diverge in content from that of Qohelet, but that in no way implies that they are the same person. The model of a narrator presenting the writings of a sage is in keeping with the citation practice known from Proverbs and Job (e.g., "the words of Agur" in Prov. 30:1). The words of the frame narrator (1:1–2; 7:27; 12:8–14) are presented in the manner one would expect from a biographer.

A modern analog for the structure of Ecclesiastes might be the format of a guest lecture at a university or conference, given in absentia. The substitute presenter (i.e., the frame narrator) briefly mentions the paper's actual author and title, reads the author's paper in his/her absence, and at the end of the lecture offers a few closing comments in conclusion (or attempts to answer audience questions). Similarly, at the conclusion of Ecclesiastes, the narrator reflects positively on Qohelet's words, life, and contributions to wisdom (see also Heim's view on Qohelet as a performer [2019, 8]). Nevertheless, Garrett concludes that "there is no reason" to think that the writer speaking in first person (Qohelet) and the writer speaking in third person (the presenter of Qohelet's teachings) "are two different people. Otherwise, we would expect the frame narrator to have given us the Teacher's actual name" instead of saying

"I, the Teacher" (Garrett 1993, 263). However, if a frame narrator is faithfully recording the words of a past sage who called himself "Qohelet," then that is precisely what has happened.

In sum, to suggest that the teachings of Qohelet were the product of some later Davidic king or inspired scribe, and that these teachings were compiled and presented by an even later scribe (the frame narrator), is not a contradiction of biblical authority; rather, it merely parts from one of several Jewish and Christian traditions regarding the composition of the book—namely, that Solomon wrote the entire thing by himself (see Dell 1994 for how early Jews and Christians wrestled over these same issues but still came to regard the text as inspired Scripture).

## DATE

The question of precise dating cannot be satisfactorily answered. And in many ways, the content of Ecclesiastes, like Job, by its very nature resists being pinned down to one time period, which is perhaps a rhetorical technique to present the teachings of Qohelet as timeless. This commentary views the ideology of Qohelet's teachings as stemming from an earlier period (possibly late monarchic Judah), though the linguistic updating of his teachings may have taken place later by the frame narrator, perhaps in the Persian period (550–332 B.C.) or later.

Many recent scholars set Ecclesiastes in the Ptolemaic period (305–30 B.C.; e.g., Heim 2019, 4–5; Sneed 2015a, 348). The debate over dating usually hinges on issues of language and ideology. The dominant scholarly view is that "the language of the book is close to Mishnaic Hebrew—and hence characteristically Aramaizing" (Young 1993, 140; a point made most famously by Delitzsch 1982 [1877], 190). Ian Young and Daniel Fredericks, however, argue in favor of a monarchic date (see below). Beyond this, the ideas communicated in the book seem, according to many scholars, consistent with later Greek philosophical thought tied to the historical circumstances of Jewish life under Ptolemaic Egypt. However, these two lines of reasoning (late language and Greek ideology), commonly used to promote a Hellenistic dating, are not absolute barometers since they may not adequately account for the linguistic arguments of others (like Seow [1996], who sets the text in the Persian period, or even Fredericks [1988], who sees the text as preexilic). In light of the many complexities herein and the lack of historical context provided by the book itself, it is best to approach these issues eagerly but humbly.

### Qohelet's Hebrew

Concerning the book's language, Seow makes the daunting assertion that "there is perhaps no other book in all of the HB where the language has received more attention from scholars than Ecclesiastes" (1997, 11). Acknowledging this at the front should constitute flexibility (as in a lack of dogma) among serious exegetes. The discussion below will cover some of the major reasons why scholars consider Ecclesiastes to be the product of either the monarchic period or a later setting.

### Monarchic Dating

Young offers a robust defense of the monarchic dating of Ecclesiastes: "The internal evidence fits more easily with a preexilic rather than a postexilic setting" (1993, 148). However, there are problems with this assertion. Some of Qohelet's style of Hebrew is similar to the style of the Mishnah, which came much later—"Driver, whose work for a long time was about the last word on the linguistic question in Qoheleth in the English language, lists some thirty-nine words and expressions related to Mishnaic Hebrew and Aramaic (Driver 1913: 474f)" (Young 1993, 148). For example, the relative pronoun (שֶׁ) frequently occurs alongside (אֲשֶׁר), "an excellent example of how 'classical' and 'non-classical' elements are mixed together in Qoheleth" (Young 1993, 148). The greatly simplified syntax of Qohelet is similar to the Mishnah and is marked by, among many things, the absence of the *waw* consecutive and the presence of the personal pronoun plus participle to construct tense along with the frequent use of (יֵשׁ) and (אַיִן) (Young 1993, 149). Overall, concludes Young, the Mishnaic feel of Qohelet brought on by Aramaisms, the particle שֶׁ, the demonstrative pronoun זֹה, and other linguistically late features are confronted by the fact that "Qohelet contains more of an admixture of 'classical' Hebrew than does the later-attested Mishnaic Hebrew" (p. 149). Young does not wish to cast doubt on S. R. Driver's list as evidence that Qohelet is certainly Aramaizing, but "the issue at stake is whether these characteristics of Qoheleth's language are necessarily post-exilic" (p. 152). His key argument is that the so-called Mishnaic style found in Ecclesiastes is a reflection of the vernacular Hebrew spoken in preexilic Israel. For example, while nominal formations with the suffix וֹן appear on several words in the Aramaic style, Young points out the same phenomenon in Moabite forms like "Eglon" (עֶגְלוֹן) in Judges 3:12 as well as the cities "Heshbon" (חֶשְׁבּוֹן) and "Samaria" (שֹׁמְרוֹן; p. 150). Many consider the higher concentration of such forms evidence of a later composition, but it could equally be the influence of a particular dialect or, as Young asserts, simply Qohelet's unique style (p. 150). Furthermore, colloquialisms come in the form of "incongruence of number and gender" as well as "the irregular use of the definite article"—this, he argues, is just Qohelet's style of "a less formal variant of Hebrew than the Standard Literary Language" (p. 150; see p. 154, where he compares the "low" Hebrew of Qohelet with low German; see also Rendsburg 1990, 16–17).

Young concludes then, "The chronological sequence of the development of Biblical to Mishnaic Hebrew is not related to the language of Qohelet. Qohelet is not Standard Biblical Hebrew. It represents a literary genre (the personal monologue style) and a type of language (analogous if not related to Mishnaic Hebrew) which is unique in the ancient Hebrew tradition" (p. 151). Though Young argues for a monarchic dating, he asserts that Qohelet's style is not clearly early nor clearly late:

> we have found that behind Driver's lists Qoheleth exhibits an individuality which not only separates it from LBH [Late Biblical Hebrew] but from the whole tradition of SBH [Standard Biblical Hebrew]. As we have shown earlier, Qoheleth must be allowed to stand alone. It cannot be put into any linguistic slot, and therefore dating the book on linguistic grounds is to proceed from the wrong basis entirely. (1993, 154)

However, Young *does* use linguistic grounds for his dating schema (i.e., his suggestion that Qohelet is writing in the vernacular of the monarchic period, a style that eventually becomes the common form of Hebrew in the Mishnah).

In a final attempt to cast doubt on the late dating of Ecclesiastes, Young suggests that just as the Mishnah was handed down as oral law and only eventually written, so the writing of Qohelet may have been the last step on a long journey of oral transmission in a local dialect that the eventual writers wanted to preserve. This last theory is the most plausible offered by Young since it does not ignore the obvious presence of late Hebrew in the text. It is an attempt to make the best sense of the fact that Qohelet is neither perfectly late nor early linguistically (see Fredericks 1988, 244).

### Exilic or Postexilic Dating

Robert Holmstedt, John Cook, and Phillip Marshall assert that the arguments of scholars like Young are self-defeating since such arguments conclude both that (1) the development of ancient Hebrew is unrecoverable due to the difficulties posed by textual transmission, and that (2) there are such things as EBH and LBH in existence in the biblical literature (2017, 34–35). Consequently, Holmstedt, Cook, and Marshall—and many others (most notably,

Schoors 2004 and 2013; see also Seow 1997, 20–21)—continue to look for loanwords and later linguistic features (pronouns, verbal system, syntax, etc.) as evidence for dating biblical texts (see esp. Holmstedt, Cook, and Marshall 2017, on the relative pronoun, pp. 23–26 and 37–39, and the verbal system, pp. 26–33 and 39–40). At the conclusion of his masterful work on the language of Ecclesiastes, Antoon Schoors notes, "The lexical study of this book shows again that the language of Qoh is definitely late in the development of BH and belongs to LBH" (2004, 499). While late features could be the result of dialectical peculiarities (Fredericks 1988), the overwhelming presence of these features points to a composition after the fall of the Judean monarchy; in other words, Fredericks "disregards the frequency and distribution of the traits under consideration" (Schoors 2013, 5). He concludes, "C. L. Seow rightly points out that Qoh's vocabulary should be dated no earlier than the second half of the fifth century, because of the Persian loanwords פַּרְדֵּס and פִּתְגָם and the Aramaisms. I agree that this language is postexilic or LBH. It is, however, not easy to be more accurate in fixing its date" (Schoors 2004, 501; see also Seow 1996, 643–66). Schoors goes further than Seow, seeing the Graecisms in the text as evidence supporting a date of composition in the Hellenistic period (2004, 502).

This commentary follows the linguistic arguments offered by Seow. After his extensive review of prior scholarship, Seow goes on to identify the language of Ecclesiastes as the Jewish vernacular of the Persian period, "with its large number of Aramaisms and whatever jargons and dialectical elements one may find in the marketplace" (1997, 20–21). The text has too many preexilic features to be confidently labeled LBH or Mishnaic Hebrew, but Persian loanwords and the awkward transitional nature of Ecclesiastes's Hebrew suggest a setting in the Persian Empire (Seow denies the existence of Greek loanwords and, as such, denies the Ptolemaic setting). Likewise, Anson Rainey (1964, 152–53) situates Qohelet rather in Mesopotamia during the Persian period. He refers to Akkadian linguistic and cultural influence, a possible allusion to Darius in Qoh. 4:15, and Qohelet's familiarity with the business climate of that area. He concludes that "there is much in favor and nothing against the assumption that Qohelet wrote his book in Achaemenian Mesopotamia before Alexander the Great" (see Schoors 2013, 3 Rainey also rejects the suggestion that Qohelet's joy statements [aka *carpe diem* statements] are Epicurean in nature [1964, 153]). Schoors, of course, considers this an exaggeration since it does not account for proposed Hellenisms. There is more to be said, though, on how Qohelet's teachings reflect much older Mesopotamian and Egyptian thinking.

### Qohelet's Timeless Teaching

Those who propose a third-century Ptolemaic setting for Ecclesiastes will view Qohelet's teachings through the lens of that period. Hellenism was certainly considered something "new" (1:10) to which Jewish people had to respond. However, if Qohelet is responding to the community's reaction to Gentile incursion, that phenomenon need not be limited to the circumstances of the third century B.C. and later. The encroachment of non-Hebrew ideas and the threat of syncretism have always plagued the Israelites. Accordingly, we find in Scripture a concerted effort by biblical scribes throughout the centuries to elevate the ideas of their cognitive environment (the ANE) to Yahwistic standards and spiritual renewal (concerning "cognitive environment criticism," see Greer, Hilber, and Walton 2018, xvii–xix). As such, the basis for Qohelet's ideas is not totally unknown in much older Egyptian and Mesopotamian literature (Sneed 2015a, 348, though he sets the text in the Ptolemaic period). Dru Johnson demonstrates convincingly that ahead of Hellenistic influence, "Judaism already had its own philosophical style" with similarities to ideological constructs found throughout the fertile crescent of the ANE, though with important distinctions (2021, 81–115, 151). Fredericks would, of course, agree with this, noting that the supposed connections to Hellenistic thought in Ecclesiastes could naturally appear in preexilic Israel (1988, 249; see Buhlman [2000], who argues for a few key places of Hellenistic thought). The linguistic arguments of Young and Fredericks aside, there is a valid case for posturing an early date for the ideology of Qohelet himself, whom I take to be a distinct person from the frame narrator, the latter being more likely a Persian period Jewish scribe who collected and immortalized Qohelet's teachings on a scroll, updating the Hebrew as he went.

By preserving Qohelet's words, the scribe was also carrying forward concepts from the broader cognitive environment of Iron Age Israel. The ideological world of which ancient Israel was a part was not so limited by the types of chronological and geographical boundaries one might expect. Shared motifs, concepts, and religious beliefs were able to span millennia and cross territorial boundaries thanks to trade, warfare, the oral transmission of stories, religious syncretism, and the enshrinement of knowledge through the Sumerian invention of the world's most important and transformative technology: writing. Through writing, we are able to observe these shared cultural ideologies that help inform our understanding of the world out of which God called his people.

For Ecclesiastes, scholars point to several texts from Mesopotamia, Ugarit, and Egypt. But the most often cited text is the Epic of Gilgamesh. It is also the world's oldest written story, featuring a royal protagonist who sets out on a journey to obtain immortality. In the Old Babylonian version—an excerpt from which is featured below (*ANET*, 90; Gilgamesh X:III:1–14)—Gilgamesh mourns the death of his friend Enkidu, after which the ale-wife says to him:

Gilgamesh, whither rovest thou?
The life thou pursuest thou shalt not find.
When the gods created mankind,
Death for mankind they set aside,
Life in their own hands retaining.
Thou, Gilgamesh, let full be thy belly,
Make thou merry by day and by night.
Of each day make thou a feast of rejoicing,
Day and night dance thou and play!
Let thy garments be sparkling fresh, (10)
Thy head be washed; bathe thou in water.
Pay heed to the little one that holds on to thy hand,
Let thy spouse delight in thy bosom!
For this is the task of [mankind]!

Gilgamesh is told that he will not succeed in his quest for immortality because the gods have set a boundary for human life. Consequently, he ought to realize the futility of his quest and determine to live life to the fullest now, embracing life's simple joys of food, drink, and family.

As in line 2 from the excerpt above, Qohelet is also on a journey, but an intellectual one: "to seek" (1:13), "know" (1:17), and "figure out" (7:25) the mysterious ways of God's world and the folly of humanity. As in line 4 of Gilgamesh, Qohelet acknowledges throughout his teaching that God has appointed death for humankind (e.g., 1:13; 2:15; 3:18–22; 9:1–6). And anyone familiar with the joy or so-called *carpe diem* sections in Ecclesiastes will recall how after Qohelet reckons with death's inevitability and life's unfairness, he too resolves (as Gilgamesh is told in lines 6–9 above) that the only thing worthwhile is to "eat and drink and find joy" in one's work (2:24–26; 3:12–13, 22; 5:18–20 [HB 17–19]; 8:15; 9:7; 11:7–12:1). Qohelet directs his pupil to put on the garments of celebration (9:8; Gilgamesh lines 10–11) and embrace one's wife with love (9:9; cf. Gilgamesh lines 12–14).

The similarities between the two texts continue (e.g., the futility of human endeavor being compared to chasing "wind," etc.; see Anderson 2014, 157–75). In all, though, the two texts are radically different types of literature that share *some* ideologically related themes. The major difference emerging in Ecclesiastes is the repeated focus on God as sovereign (1:13; 3:11, 14–15; 7:14), creator (12:1), judge (3:17; 5:1–7 [HB 4:17–5:6]; 8:13; 11:9; 12:14), and gift-giver (2:26; 3:13; 5:20 [HB 19]; 7:14), as well as the injunction that people must fear him (3:14; 5:7 [HB 6]; 8:12–13; 12:13). The books of Job and Ecclesiastes start to mirror aspects of the Babylonian tales of the Righteous Sufferer and the Epic of Gilgamesh, respectively, but the biblical texts veer away from meaninglessness and hopeless ignorance and toward a faith-centric resolve in the God of Israel. This is one key feature of the HB in its ANE context that marks it as literature of spiritual renewal—that is, God's written project to renew creation through his chosen people, using known constructs from the human experience (i.e., the cognitive environment of ancient Israel) as channels through which to reveal new, Spirit-inspired truths.

Themes related to those found in the Gilgamesh excerpt above and in Ecclesiastes can also be found in the Babylonian texts A Dialogue About Human Misery (*ANET*, 439) and A Pessimistic Dialogue Between Master and Servant (*ANET*, 438), among other ANE parallels. For a further discussion on the ANE ideological background to the teachings of Qohelet, see the "Genre" and "Literary Structure" sections of this Introduction (see also the sidebar "Futility in the Epic of Gilgamesh" p. 70). There is insufficient space here to work through each of these texts to demonstrate that the ideology of Qohelet is older than the proposed Hellenistic setting. Ideas can carry forward through the centuries, so this line of reasoning alone is not sufficient to prove an early date; rather, it is observed that the sheer volume of parallel thinking between Ecclesiastes and much older ANE material should lend credence to the position that Qohelet's teachings were first conceived in the late-monarchic or at least Persian periods.

## Conceived Early, Presented Late

Arguments for an early dating of Qohelet's language are often reduced to a claim that it is impossible to recover the development of the Hebrew language, and so those who favor a monarchic date have to rely on the ideology of Qohelet's message as representing the concerns of an earlier period in Israelite history. Of course, those who prefer an exilic or postexilic setting for Qohelet will see his concerns as consistent with those of the Persian or Ptolemaic periods. Perhaps a better suggestion would be to assert that the ideas of Qohelet are in fact early, but that the linguistic updating and publication of these ideas in their extant form is the work of an inspired scribe from after the exile.

We acknowledge that the language of Ecclesiastes is late, meaning Persian period or later, though Seow's reasoning keeps us on the earlier end of that spectrum, as in pre-Hellenistic. However, this does not perfectly address the original age of its conception and ideas. If Qohelet is in fact a historical figure from an older time whose words were copied and presented later by the frame narrator in the late transitional Hebrew known to him (or by affecting a transitional Hebrew of his own by mixing Qohelet's Hebrew with later Hebrew), then we may have an explanation for the mixture of grammatical features. We may also then have a better explanation for the heavy presence of ANE literary and ideological motifs throughout the text. As the following section will demonstrate (as well as the sections "Genre" and "Literary Structure"), we understand the conceptual world of the ANE as more dominant in Ecclesiastes than the supposed Hellenistic influence.

The reality is that the concerns raised in Ecclesiastes could fit in more than one place historically, and once a scholar determines its placement in a particular time period, all the other pieces tend to fall into place (see Anderson 2014, 157 n. 1 on the importance of remaining measured when dating the book given its many ambiguities). Given the lack of concrete evidence, it would be better to remain measured in one's approach, acknowledging the mixture of early and late linguistic features and the debates surrounding such features, the presence of both very old (e.g., Gilgamesh, Egyptian wisdom) and perhaps later ideas (the suggestion of influence from Hellenistic philosophy), and the fact that Ecclesiastes, like Job, appears to have been written as an intentionally timeless piece of literature. Furthermore, the ideas in Qohelet even appear in future foreign contexts far removed from the influence of Israel, Hellenism, and the ANE (Longman 1998, 10). In other words, the wisdom of Ecclesiastes is well-suited for any age!

## HISTORICAL SETTING AND READERS

After the fall of Jerusalem to Babylon, the following centuries featured an encroachment of Gentile culture that interrupted eschatological expectations, pushing the promises of Isaiah 65–66 (that the wicked nations will be judged, and God's people rewarded with new heavens and a new earth) far into the future. "In view of the distance to a possible eschaton," what could still be realized from such hopes other than that people should enjoy life's simple things (eating, drinking, rejoicing; cf. Isa. 65:13; Krüger 2004, 54)? The same level of urgency appears to be lacking or at least less prominent in Solomon's day, but increasingly relevant with the future invasions of Assyria and Babylon. This would hold true of course for the Persian and Ptolemaic periods as well. The majority of scholars hold the Ptolemaic view, given the presence of LBH, suggested Greek loanwords, Qohelet's supposed response to concerns over later Greek imperialism, and more (e.g., Krüger 2004). However, "the absence of any explicit mention of historical circumstances or reference to formative national-historical events makes it difficult to contextualize Ecclesiastes within any Israelite historiographical setting" (Forti 2021, 515). The timelessness of Ecclesiastes allows for multiple proposals, but its indirect allusions to Solomon and parallels with ANE literature draw this commentary in the direction of an older historical setting, pre-Alexander.

As for its readers, a direct address is made to "my son" (12:12), a strong indication that a teacher-pupil relationship is in view, geared toward a young man or young men (11:9) in the scribal world (Sneed 2015a, 347). But Qohelet's wise observations are universal in nature; his words would appear to apply to anyone, though they may have originally been intended for those living in Jerusalem or other exilic city centers where wisdom could be traded in the streets, in homes, and between scribes. These could be the "sons of businessmen, bankers, minor court officials—the next generation of 'movers and shakers'" (Davis 2000, 160), but that does not exclude the general populace as well since Qohelet's role is a public one (1:12; 12:9), and his observations are relevant to both the lowly farmer and the royal vizier (note also the Egyptian wisdom motif of a father addressing his son, and yet such texts were clearly meant for a broad audience). So, his readers were not merely members of a wisdom class or school, but people in the mainstream of society who were interested in learning about wisdom and God (see the general argument of Whybray 1974). The reasons for thinking that Qohelet's message would be especially poignant to a younger readership are expressed below in "Theological Emphases."

## OCCASION FOR WRITING

The thoughts expressed in Ecclesiastes are deeply personal and some of them do not, at first, sound orthodox (e.g., 2:15–17; 7:13; etc.). Hence, the consensus is to see Qohelet's words as a counterbalance to the established Jewish school of thought encapsulated in Proverbs. However, depending on when the text was written, some see this as a movement from within Israel's already-diverse thought world, and others look to the potential Hellenistic influences of the Second Temple period: "The book of Qohelet can only be understood as an attempt to profit as much as possible from the Greek understanding of the world, without forcing Israel's wisdom to give up its status" (Lohfink 2003, 6). It is important, though, to observe that the diversity of thought expressed by Qohelet was already part of the biblical world (consider Job, Psalms, Lamentations) and present in texts from the broader ANE of which pre-Alexander Israel was a part. It is, then, not at all necessary to view the ideology of Qohelet as an attempt to bridge Jewish theology with Hellenistic philosophy.

Qohelet is responding to a caricature of established wisdom, as evinced by his citation of what appear to be commonly received proverbs from his world, some of which are found in the book of Proverbs, though others that he may have composed himself (Dell 2020, 138, 145; for more on this point, see "Holy Disillusion" below). The epilogue (12:8–14) affirms that Qohelet is a good, legitimate teacher, though some scholars think the epilogist is intent on discrediting or correcting the sage, warning the reader to beware of misleading, self-proclaimed wise men (e.g., Longman 1998; see Shields 1999, 2006, who asserts that the epilogist is using Qohelet's words to discredit the wisdom tradition represented by Proverbs). The lens one chooses for reading the text obviously influences one's interpretation throughout the book. Is Qohelet a good, wise teacher who wishes to push through the fluff in order to give his readers a realist's perspective on life, death, and God? Or is he a false teacher uploading errant notions into the heads of naive youths? My position is to affirm the frame narrator's evaluation of Qohelet as a good teacher, which he does not state tongue-in-cheek, and to presuppose that the content of Qohelet's teaching is useful, good, and in keeping with the fear-of-God standards of Proverbs (so Dell 2020, 143). As such, Qohelet is not subverting Proverbs but simplistic assumptions about the world that may have resulted from people interpreting Proverbs as absolutes—that is, apart from the lived-in reality that things do not, in fact, always work out the way one expects. This is how Job and Qohelet can affirm Proverbs on the one hand but still express honest angst over life's incongruities on the other. Qohelet wants to bring his students into the same headspace, to disillusion them from an unnuanced commitment to the retribution principle in order to highlight the only perfectly reliable truth in the universe: God must be feared.

## GENRE

Ecclesiastes bears greatest resemblance to, broadly, the kind (but not the style) of writing featured in Job, Proverbs, and various chapters and smaller sections of the HB. This kind of writing has been traditionally identified as "wisdom literature" (Dell 1994, 303–4; on current discussions related to the genus "wisdom" in the Bible, see Kynes 2021; Sneed 2015b; and the more nuanced classification "Solomonic collection," as in, e.g., Dell 2021, 321–36).

While the Hebrew of Ecclesiastes appears to be late (see "Date"), much of its content is more closely related to ANE literature than to Hellenistic thought. It is most comparable to Job and other pessimistic self-loathing and society-loathing texts from Egypt (e.g., Dialogue of a Man with His Soul; The Eloquent Peasant) and Mesopotamia (The Righteous Sufferer). The Ugaritic Stories of Kirta could also fit into this family. In each of these texts, there are complaints of injustice either inflicted by the gods on the protagonist or inflicted by some part of society onto another part. While the action-consequence proverbs of Israel, Egypt, and Mesopotamia promote a retributive principle whereby the righteous are always blessed and the wicked always suffer—both by God's/the gods' hand(s)—the wisdom of Ecclesiastes, Job, and related ANE texts portray humanity in turmoil over life's most difficult questions, a turmoil brought on by physical and/or psychological anguish. The sufferers question God (or the gods) for why things seem so unjust, or why they are suffering even though they have lived righteous lives. Hearing little or nothing in response from God (or the gods), the speakers turn either to a form of faith (in the case of Israelite wisdom) or to despair (in the case of certain ANE analogs). There are some overlaps, though, with the positive resolutions found in these texts. For example, the Egyptian Dialogue of a Man with His Soul gets especially bleak as the man repeatedly longs for death ("Open the door of death to me. Is that too much to ask?"; cf. Job 6:9) but resolves that the only worthwhile thing to do is to "Enjoy living as if every day were a feast day. Stop worrying" (Matthews and Benjamin 2016, 241). While the longing for death as a relief from suffering better parallels Job, the Egyptian author's resolution sounds much like Ecclesiastes 3:12: "I perceived that there is nothing better for them than to be joyful and to do good as long as they live" (e.g., 5:20 [HB 19]; 7:14; 8:15; 9:7). But on what basis should the Egyptian stop worrying? One key difference in the biblical text is the fear-of-God principle and the admonition to keep his commandments (esp. 12:13)—a high view of God throughout the book of Ecclesiastes forms the basis for why people should not vex themselves (e.g., 3:12–15; 5:20 [HB 19]; 7:10–14). There is another clear structural relationship between this Egyptian text and Ecclesiastes: the concept of a person working through their struggle by conversing back and forth "with my heart," a personified character in both texts. Others have pointed out this similarity (e.g., Seow 1997, 123), but Holmstedt, Cook, and Marshall understand it to be a key interpretive device for Ecclesiastes whereby Qohelet sets out to pursue foolishness while his heart is tasked simultaneously with pursuing wisdom (2017, 23). This parallel between the two texts is striking, but the concept of heart/soul as conversation partner is much more apparent in the Egyptian text than in Ecclesiastes; so, while there is a similar motif at work between the two, it is not nearly as fully fleshed out in Ecclesiastes (however, Holmstedt, Cook, and Marshall would rebut that the reason the conversation does not consistently continue beyond Ecclesiastes 2 is because it has already been established and can be assumed moving forward, likely having been dropped by the author to avoid repetitiveness).

Some of the circumstances and ideologies in the ANE texts are paralleled in the biblical texts of Job and Ecclesiastes, but there are unique differences in the Israelite group. This includes the authors' repeated appeals to the fear of God and their resolutions to trust in God's justice despite all the injustice they perceive. The book of Job has a richer resolution than its Babylonian counterpart, and Qohelet is not just desperately flinging himself toward pleasure in light of meaningless suffering; rather, he is embracing authentic living, which entails enjoying the simple things as gifts from God (2:24; 3:13; 6:19) while living in the fear of God (8:12).

## LITERARY STRUCTURE

Ecclesiastes resembles autobiographical texts from Egypt and Mesopotamia. Egyptian tomb inscriptions feature a threefold layout that comprise (1) a list of accomplishments of the deceased, (2) affirmations of ethical behavior and wisdom, and (3) admonitions to those who read the text that they too live ethically (see Burkes 1999, 171–208; Davis 2000, 174). Longman's presentation of similarities between Akkadian autobiographies and the text of Ecclesiastes 1:12–12:7 is convincing (1991; 1998, 8, 15–20). In light of these similarities, especially to the Cuthean Legend of Naram-Sin, he identifies Ecclesiastes as "framed wisdom autobiography" (1998, 17). Three of the fifteen texts he analyzes in *Fictional Akkadian Autobiographies* (1991) bear special resemblance to Ecclesiastes in form (not content), as they contain: (1) a first-person introduction (1:12), (2) a narration of the speaker's accomplishments (in the case of Qohelet, this includes his observations;

1:13–6:9), and finally (3) a concluding section "with wisdom admonitions, instructions on how to behave (6:10–12:7)," giving advice to the reader in the form of a parting lesson of sorts (Longman 1998, 17–18). One mark of this switch at 6:10 is the presence of the second-person "you" either embedded in the verbal forms or appearing as an independent pronoun (the second person actually starts appearing with 5:1, but more often from 6:10 onward). Accordingly, several commentators break up the text into two major halves starting at 6:10 (e.g., Seow, Longman), but the rationale for doing so is merely adequate rather than entirely convincing. For that reason, others find the division at 6:10 to be an arbitrary one, resigning that no proposed structure for Ecclesiastes works perfectly (e.g., Holmstedt, Cook, and Marshall 2017, 2). One thing upon which nearly everyone agrees is that the narrator's incursions appear at 1:1–2; 7:27; and 12:8–14.

I follow Longman's assessment of the genre and, consequently, the structure, viewing Ecclesiastes as a wisdom-centric autobiography (1:12–12:7) bracketed by the framework of a narrator's prologue (1:1–11) and epilogue (12:8–14). A frame narrator is not featured in the Akkadian texts, only here in Ecclesiastes (I part slightly from Longman's approach by identifying 1:1–2 as the prologue, viewing 1:3–11 as an informal and poetic introduction by Qohelet before formally introducing himself in 1:12). The parallel to Akkadian autobiography is sensible and a helpful way to understand the structure of the text just as Hittite suzerain-vassal treaties model a pattern roughly paralleled in the Mosaic covenant's stipulations, blessings, and curses. In all such cases where ANE literary structures are paralleled in the Hebrew Scriptures, the point of departure comes with the content of the compositions. As Don Fowler so eloquently explained to countless students taking his Old Testament Backgrounds course over many years at Liberty University, "God often used *known constructs* in order to reveal new truths to his people," that is, concepts and models taken from their cognitive environment, the ANE (Fowler 2008). These "new truths" from the Lord to his people were packaged inside familiar literary structures that had themselves developed over millennia in their respective contexts.

This commentary follows the English versification while providing the Hebrew in brackets when the Hebrew differs in chapter 5 (e.g., Eccl. 5:10 [HB 9]). The text begins with a prologue (1:1–2) in which Qohelet is introduced in the third person by an unnamed narrator. Following this, the main body of the text (1:3–12:7) features Qohelet's teachings in the first person (with one incursion from the narrator in 7:27). Immediately after is the epilogue where the narrator returns, speaking of Qohelet once again in the third person (12:8–14). The bookends were written by a "frame narrator" who comments on the body of the text and its author, Qohelet. Naturally, then, the text was composed by two different hands (and I would say only two—see "Authorship"). Beyond the prologue and epilogue, the teachings of Qohelet themselves can be divided into two major sections: the observations of Qohelet (1:3–6:9) and the admonitions of Qohelet (6:10–12:7). In the case of Ecclesiastes, however, *any comprehensive exegetical outline would need to be redesigned to serve homiletical purposes*. For this reason, we have included the prologue (1:1–2) with the observations of Qohelet (1:1–6:9), and the epilogue (12:8–14) with the admonitions of Qohelet (6:10–12:14).

We have broken up the text of Ecclesiastes into several homiletical units, though these rough divisions cannot do justice to recurring themes interspersed throughout (e.g., the call for joy, fearing God, life's unpredictability; see "Outline of Ecclesiastes"). At the conclusion of their section on structure in Ecclesiastes, Holmstedt, Cook, and Marshall note, "For the usability of this volume, we have included smaller section headings in the commentary. The reader should note, though, that these headings are intended to be a convenience for using the volume and do not reflect any formal position on a structure within the book" (2017, 3). Likewise, for the preachability of this very complex and multistructured biblical text, we offer a suggested homiletical outline that is condensed in order to take the expositor through the text in ten sermons rather than many months; accordingly, what we have provided in the outline section below should not be taken as a strict exegetical outline of the text.

## THEOLOGICAL EMPHASES

If the book of Proverbs highlights almost exclusively the retribution principle known to Job and his interlocutors—that God causes good things to happen to the righteous and bad things to happen to the wicked (e.g., Prov. 3:33; 12:21)—then Ecclesiastes overcompensates in the other direction, emphasizing the parts of life that are unpredictable, unjust, confusing, and enigmatic, as when the righteous suffer and the wicked prosper (Eccl. 8:14). Proverbs is, however, aware that the wicked can achieve enviable levels of success in life, though temporary it may be (Prov. 3:31–35; 23:17). Likewise, Qohelet acknowledges the general principle that things do not end up well for those who do not fear God (3:17; 8:13; 11:9; and the frame narrator in 12:13–14). So, it is not true that Qohelet's wisdom is meant to obliterate the teaching of Proverbs or stand against it; rather, Qohelet exists as the opposite side of the same coin, pointing out the exceptions to the retribution principle and even exaggerating those exceptions to make his point. Proverbs and Ecclesiastes complement one another in order to round out the human experience in light of the fear of the Lord (Dell 2016, 49; see also Estes [2014, 118–29], who ties Ecclesiastes to Proverbs through observation of the shared themes of seeking and finding). Job achieves this balance in a dialogical story form that acknowledges both the topsy-turvy reversals of life, where the wicked go seemingly unpunished and the righteous suffer, without abandoning allegiance to God, and the general acknowledgment that he will settle the score: "For what is the hope of the godless when God cuts him off, when God takes away his life?" (27:8).

The major theological emphases in Ecclesiastes revolve around Qohelet's various applications of the term "vanity" *hevel* (הֶבֶל) in contrast with how God is described in the text. The term can refer to futility/emptiness, as in lacking substance. Qohelet applies the term to (1) human endeavors, where the term is best understood as "superficial/empty/futile" (1:2; 1:14; 2:1, 11, 15, 17; 4:4, 7–8; 5:7 [HB 6], 10 [HB 9]; 6:4, 9, 11; 7:6; 11:8, 10; 12:8); and (2) to the enigmatic ways of the world or God, where the term is best understood as "incomprehensible" (1:2; 2:19, 21, 23, 26; 3:19; 4:16; 6:2; 8:10, 14; 12:8; see note on 1:2). Notes Seow, Qohelet "does not mean that everything is meaningless or insignificant, but that everything is beyond human comprehension" (1997, 59). If Qohelet's focus is said to be on meaninglessness, that term should at least be further defined as incoherence or incongruence. See Arthur Keefer's psychological approach in defining meaning in Ecclesiastes—though purpose and significance are important aspects of meaning, "'coherence' remains the book's unquestionable focus," noting that Qohelet "concentrates most on the (un)reliability and (in)comprehensibility of patterns in life" (2019, 449).

The theological emphases in Ecclesiastes cover the following topics: the eternality of God and the futility of human endeavor, the works of God and their incomprehensibility, future judgment, and holy disillusion.

### *The Eternality of God and the Futility of Human Endeavor*

God is portrayed as wholly outside of the created order, yet fully in control of it. He "made everything," but he has made it impossible for human beings to figure it all out (3:11; 8:17). This is aptly demonstrated by Qohelet's poetic prelude (1:3–11). God's actions are immutable and meant to invoke reverence in the heart of humanity (3:14–15). By contrast, humans are a breath (1:3–11). Humans are powerless, but God is sovereign (7:13–14). Humans are ignorant (3:11; 7:23–29), but God knows all (3:11; 7:14; 12:14). God does good work, but humans twist everything with their scheming (7:29). The clear allusions to Genesis in the book of Ecclesiastes demonstrate Qohelet's theology of creation and fall—that is, humanity's fall into sin (Gen. 3:1–24) following God's "good" creation (Gen. 1:31; Eccl. 7:29), and how humanity is now appointed to return to the dust (3:20; 5:15–16 [HB 14–15]; 12:7; also, Gen. 3:19; Job 34:14–15; see also sidebar: "Life After Death in Ecclesiastes" p. 108). The certainty of this leads him to the observation that human endeavor is ultimately vain.

Human endeavors are seen for what they are: temporary and lacking in substance. In practice, Qohelet does not actually promote a view among his disciples that what one does is irrelevant or does not matter, for he consistently preaches wisdom, generosity, enjoyment of life's simple things, and the fear of God. Why then does he call human endeavor "futile"? Key to understanding Qohelet's technical contradiction here is to embrace his role as a teacher who employs the rhetorical strategy of overcompensation and hyperbole to make his point. So many of Qohelet's opposing observations can be understood in light of this pedagogical strategy. This is not to say that Qohelet is optimistic or immune to the harsh results of his investigation, but that his approach now (as he is writing) is pedagogically centered and not exactly the same as it was when his investigation was in progress. For that reason, there is evidence throughout his teaching of how the investigation affected him personally; so, it is expected that readers should see his internal turmoil and how he uses that as a sharp edge (12:11) in his rhetoric (see excursus "Contradictions in Ecclesiastes").

Qohelet stared straight into the darkness and embraced it; yet his awareness of the pervasive injustices and bleak realities of life still "coexists with a firm belief in God—whose power, justice, and unpredictability are sovereign" (M. Fox 2004, ix). As such, Qohelet "refuses to impose pat and reassuring 'meanings' on" inexplicable suffering; nevertheless, "he maintains a faith in God's rule and fundamental justness, and he looks for ways to create a meaningful life in a world where so much is senseless" (M. Fox 2004, ix). Qohelet, like Job and the psalmists, vacillates between overly negative and even theologically incorrect views and what he knows to be true about wisdom and the sovereignty of God. Ethan the Ezrahite, the writer of Psalm 89, was cut from the same cloth. Ethan accuses the Lord of abandoning his covenant with David, "casting his throne to the ground," asking "How long, O Lord? Will you hide yourself forever? How long will your wrath burn like fire? Remember how short my time is! For what vanity you have created all the children of man! What man can live and never see death? Who can deliver his soul from the power of Sheol?" (Ps. 89:39–40 [HB 40–41], 46–48 [HB 47–49] ESV; here "vanity" is שָׁוְא, expressing the nuance of human mortality). Aside from the psalm's closing expression of blessing to the Lord (Ps. 89:52 [HB 53]), the fact that this complaint and address are before God is evidence of a heart committed to trusting in the Lord despite all circumstances. Like Job's accusations toward God (40:8; cf. 7:17–21; 9:17; 10:3; 34:9; 36:17–25; but see 16:19), the psalmists' lamentations, and all other scriptural representations of God's people teetering on the edge of orthodoxy in the midst of suffering, Qohelet's investigation into life's seeming futility has led him down a dark road for which there is no satisfying answer apart from an enjoyment of God's simple gifts *and* a final resting on the justice and sovereignty of God.

# Introduction to Ecclesiastes

## Contradictions in Ecclesiastes

The effort to attribute the body of the text to multiple redactors to account for contradictions of thought risks ignoring how parts of Job, the Psalms, and other biblical passages feature various attitudes/feelings expressed in a single passage by a single author. Human beings are complex, strongly feeling one way and then another as they are working through problems in their own heads or out loud (see Dell 2020, 144). Caution is warranted, though, when reading supposedly contradictory statements by Qohelet and concluding from that that he is teaching opposing principles. In a number of cases, we find that only one of his two views is consistent with his final word on the matter, while the other is an expression of his anguish as he works things out—we must give Qohelet the same latitude we give all lamenters in Scripture as they vacillate in their perspectives before arriving at a place of trust in God. Scholars may, for example, cite Qohelet's opposing views on pleasure, but we must decide whether these are true contradictions of thought or if he merely has different applications of pleasure in mind. For example, sinful pleasure is not an appropriate application of "pleasure/joy" in light of Qohelet's repeated injunction to fear God. Qohelet furthermore found that "pleasure" (שִׂמְחָה) was ultimately unsatisfying as a life goal (2:1–11), yet "to enjoy" (שׂמח) life and experience "joy" (שִׂמְחָה) is what he recommends to his readers as one of the only good things a person can do (3:12, 22; 5:17 [HB 18]; 8:15). As in the book of Proverbs, so here in Ecclesiastes we must consider how a sage's terminology should be understood within the specific context provided, meaning that a different context may warrant a different application of the same terms. If we understand Qohelet as rejecting hedonistic joy and pleasure as an ultimate end, but promoting the kind of authentic joy that receives freely from God and is interwoven with a fear of God, we find a simple resolution.

Though it should be observed that Qohelet uses "joy" (שִׂמְחָה) differently in his description of hedonistic pleasure in 2:1–11 than in later passages where he commends "joy" (שִׂמְחָה), the complexity of Qohelet's thought life should not be disregarded. The emotional pendulum is an ordinary human experience, which is why it is so clearly represented in Job and Ecclesiastes. It is certainly possible to both affirm orthodox theology and at the same time possess feelings that seem to contradict what you believe, feelings often brought on by difficult circumstances, doubt, or unresolved questions about God and his world. Neither Job, Qohelet, Habakkuk, nor other lamenting or imprecatory voices of Scripture back away from the notion that God is sovereign and good, even if they *feel* otherwise in the moment; in other words, their faith is intact in the end, but their pain still takes full expression on the page.

At times they are as utterly hopeless as Heman in Psalm 88, before whom God is hidden (88:14 [HB 15]), who feels the crushing weight of God's wrath (88:16 [HB 17]), and whose "only companion is darkness" (88:18 [HB 19]). Unlike similar psalms of grief, there is no happy ending to this psalm, where Heman might be expected to convey his resolve to trust God; rather, the psalm simply ends in darkness. However, it is still true that Heman's prayer is *to* the one whom he calls "the God of my salvation" (88:1) at the start of his prayer (see Hab. 3:17–19, where the prophet's response to certain destruction and death is to trust "in the God of my salvation"). Asaph is also given space to question God's allegiance to his own promises, whether he has cast off steadfast love forever (Ps. 77:1–10 [HB 0–11]), but Asaph forcibly turns his heart in the next verse toward the faithful "deeds of the LORD" in the exodus and wilderness wandering as a means to restore his own faith (Ps. 77:11–20 [HB 12–21]; cf. the comparable shift in tone in Psalm 22 between v. 16 [HB 17] and v. 22 [HB 23]).

Qohelet is likewise permitted to express unsavory views in the course of figuring things out and as an expression of his frustration and anguish (2:15–17). When the text is read as a whole, however, it is revealed that Qohelet clings to orthodoxy, but that does not prevent him from venting his thoughts, employing hyperbole for rhetorical purposes to make his ultimate point that the *only* thing that matters in life is living authentically in the fear of the Lord. The frame narrator claims that Qohelet taught knowledge and sought to write "the words of truth" (Eccl. 12:10), so his objective in the epilogue is not to correct Qohelet but to echo his conclusions. Qohelet's ultimate message is a true one, but the path he takes to get there is, as with other wisdom texts, not paved with the stone tablets of the Law but with the thorns, rocks, potholes, and tripwires of a fallen creation—a world imbued with the beauty and wisdom of God but deeply marred by sin (7:20, 29). If the Song of Songs exalts the former, then Ecclesiastes bemoans the latter.

### The Works of God and Their Incomprehensibility

A distinct theme emerging from the foundational observation that human endeavors are futile is the realization that humans are desperately ignorant. We cannot satisfactorily figure out a single person (see notes on 7:23–24 where Qohelet claims to have figured out only one man out of a thousand) or unravel the most routine mystery of God's creation (11:5). If moderns object to Qohelet's prescientific analysis of human ignorance with, "Well, we've learned a few things since the Iron Age," they need only think of the infinite number of things human beings still do not know and how what we currently know is not fully understood. But Qohelet intends to undercut all that was already known and all that would ever be known when he asserted the following: "Just as you do not know how the spirit comes to the bones in the womb of a pregnant woman, so also you do not know the work of God who makes everything" (11:5). How does an infant obtain its breath (or better yet, its spirit! The Hebrew term can mean either)? Even if we were to give an impressive answer, Qohelet would find a way to undercut that with a yet deeper question that cannot be answered. His point stands—we do not know.

According to Qohelet, we do not know even the things we think we know (aside from the fact that we must fear God; 3:14; 5:7 [HB 6]; 7:18; 8:12–13; 12:13). Qohelet exposes the hopeless ignorance of humanity in order to disillusion his disciples, young people who may suffer from sophomore syndrome. Qohelet applies this same ignorance to himself in more than one place (esp. 7:23–29; and anywhere he uses "incomprehensible" *hevel* [הֶבֶל] to describe God's world and works). His investigation led to the resolution that when one puts all his/her effort into unraveling the universe so as to understand it, one ultimately fails: "Then I observed all of God's works, how a human being is unable to figure out the work that is done under the sun. Even though he strives for it, he cannot figure it out. Even if a wise person says he knows, he [actually] was not able to figure it out" (8:17). Admitting ignorance pushes humanity away from hubris and toward trust (as in Job), so Qohelet wishes for his disciples to admit their ignorance (that their so-called knowledge is *hevel*), so that they can start living authentically in the fear of God.

## *Future Judgment*

Qohelet looks ahead to a time when God will judge all people (3:17; 8:12–13; 11:9), but he lacks a well-formed idea of life after death. Concerning the afterlife, Qohelet writes, "Who knows?" (3:21–22). The concepts of heaven and hell are not more fully revealed in the canon of Scripture until Jesus speaks of them in the New Testament though Jews already had an understanding of the eschaton and future judgment as evinced by early Jewish literature and the portrayal of the Pharisees' theology in the Gospels. In the Hebrew canon, the repeated and dominant view is that there is only Sheol. Nevertheless, a few passages do hint at life after death (e.g., Ps. 49:15 [HB 16]; Isa. 26:19; Dan. 12:2; see commentary notes on 3:17; 8:12–13; 9:5–6; 11:9; 12:7 and 13; passages in the Psalms about being rescued from Sheol are typically references to God saving someone from death, not resurrecting that person). This is not to say that the HB denies the existence of an afterlife, but that it was not always understood or fully communicated by biblical authors since, as noted, it had not yet been more fully revealed.

Qohelet observes the wicked going to their death unpunished (8:10–11), justice never having been served in life. Yet, in the next pair of verses (8:12–13) he asserts that things will not go well for the wicked. Oftentimes scholars interpret this as merely the confusing, conflicted thoughts of a wise man who is trying to reconcile the pervasive injustices of the world with the truths about God's justice that he has grown up learning. But Qohelet's claims regarding judgment are cast as indicative statements about a future reality that would satisfy the present reality of injustice: "God *will* judge the righteous and the wicked" (3:17). Qohelet is not willing to let go of his faith. His hope for future judgment may be, partly, that God will, over time, settle the score in favor of the righteous (by affecting succeeding generations of wicked and righteous people; Job 21:19), eventually manifesting universal justice. This would be consistent with the Israelite concern for the community and the "hope of the resurrection and continued survival of the nation," which "becomes their hope" though they may not live to see it (Routledge 2008, 306). This does not, however, satisfy the notion that God will judge every "deed" (11:9; 12:14), an intensely personal judgment from God. Qohelet may have hoped for the judgment of individuals beyond the grave, even though he could not state for sure how that would happen (3:21) since for now all he observes is that everyone and everything dies. Notes Franz Delitzsch, "It cannot surprise us if Koheleth finally decides that the way of the spirit of man is upwards, although it is not said that he rested this on the ground of demonstrative certainty" (Delitzsch 1982, 271; though "spirit" in 12:7 likely just means "breath"; see note on this verse). The afterlife is much discussed in the Second Temple period, and if in fact Ecclesiastes had been written that late (and many propose it was), perhaps he would have addressed it more fully, but he appears to have the same understanding of Sheol as many older HB writers. Still, though never explicated, there are hints among the HB writers of a future beyond death, as would be expected if such theology was being progressively revealed (rather than "developed"—eternal truths are not developed by people) leading up to the time of Christ (Routledge 2008, 309; note also the debates over a possible hint at the afterlife in Job 19:25–27; see Routledge 2008, 258 n. 50).

## Holy Disillusion

Roland Murphy warns against trivializing Ecclesiastes since the book "has suffered from excessive summarizing" by interpreters who often reduce the text's theological message to something like "just fear God because everything is vanity" (1992, lviii). Reductionism should be avoided in biblical scholarship; however, we cannot start by assuming (as some have) that Qohelet's teachings are so complex that they are incommunicable to us. Qohelet intends to teach his pupils; after all, "the goal of wisdom is the formation of character" (Crenshaw 1998, 3). And we must acknowledge that Qohelet makes clear, repeated statements throughout his work that lend themselves toward the formation of a thesis or proposition. If we hear all he says and we still cannot form a sentence, however imperfect, that grasps his major, repeated points, then we have not heard him carefully enough. No such thesis could perfectly encapsulate everything he discusses, but the repeated joy-refrains (so-called *carpe diem* statements) and admonitions to fear God are provided as resolutions throughout the book for how to respond to injustice, inequity, powerlessness, ignorance, delusions, the transience of life, and the reality of death, in order that we should live authentically (i.e., joyfully and wisely) in the fear of God.

A propositional summary like the one just provided could be expanded in the following way: In light of life's unpredictability and incomprehensibility, and its seemingly incurable sorrow, injustice, and folly, one ought to live joyfully and wisely in the present, thankful for one's work and life's simple pleasures, walking in the fear of God. One should not worry about solving every problem since that is impossible. Also, satisfactory joy cannot be found in futile ambition, and life has a sinister way of confounding one's expectations. Knowing all this, what better thing is there to do than to live life freely with an open hand (11:1–6), accepting from God whatever may come, knowing he will one day make all things right in judgment (though it is never specified by Qohelet how or when God will do this; see "Future Judgment").

Qohelet is also a realist. His hyperfocus on the evil of the world betrays such a commitment. By focusing on life's contradictions, injustices, and the many enigmatic ways of the world, Qohelet wishes to emphasize how very little we know, how ineffective we are, and how often things do not meet our expectations. Qohelet does not deny the wisdom of Proverbs, and does not stand opposed to the retribution principle, generally, but is "defending the Israelite doctrine of God against a corruption of it—found in such texts as Psalm 37 and parts of the Book of Job—which made the righteousness of God into a rigid principle but in doing so implicitly denied his freedom" (Whybray 1989, 30; I part with Whybray's suggestion that the principles found in Psalm 37 are really different from that of Proverbs, which Qohelet accepts, but I affirm that the words of Job's friends present an exceptionless/absolutist version of the retribution principle that Qohelet teaches against). By embracing his realism, Qohelet's pupils will be disabused of false assumptions they have about the inviolable prosperity of the righteous, and thereby they will come to the place where all they know are life's simple gifts along with a command to fear God. Upon realizing that they know next to nothing (7:23–24; 11:5), that they cannot fix the world (7:13), and that life is terribly brief, there will be nothing left to them except for the choice to live authentically and fearfully before God. By throwing a bucket of cold water into the faces of his sleepy sophomores, Qohelet affects a holy disillusion in them whereby they disbelieve false promises, including the religious reductionism of an unflinching commitment to retribution theology.

The term "holy" (קָדוֹשׁ) appears only in 8:10, so it is not Qohelet's term of choice to describe God or human allegiance to God (not that he would disagree with those notions). But his chosen expression, "fear God," is related (see Ps. 34:9) and refers to the activity of people walking in keeping with God's holiness. Hence, the term is chosen here to describe the state of mind proposed by Qohelet, who wishes to strip away all of life's superficialities so that only the good, God-fearing (by implication: holy) parts remain. Qohelet wants his readers to develop a deep disaffection for the false promises of earthly ambitions given how very empty these masters actually are—"The goals that humans pursue to find happiness are mirages, optical illusions of the mind" (Heim 2019, 39)—and adopt a more sophisticated and spiritually coherent view of the world that would replace the delusions of life, be they delusions of material or spiritual grandeur (through rote adherence to the retribution principle).

Beginning in the garden of Eden, when they rebelled against their creator, humans brought curses to the ground as well as banishment from God's intimate presence. Many delusions have since arisen in the human heart. This is the picture Qohelet paints of the present world, a place full of futility. And though humans cannot return to Eden on their own, they can at least return to the simplicity of God's garden commands to Adam and Eve (Gen. 2:15–25), commands represented by Qohelet's joy statements (2:24–26; 3:12–13, 22; 5:18–20 [HB 17–19]; 8:15; 9:7–10; 11:7–12:1; see Clemens 1994, 7–8). Today, this return is accomplished through the finished work of Christ, whose sacrificial death brought forgiveness of sins and whose resurrection brought justification before God for all who believe in him (Rom. 4:25). It is in Christ that a believer can embrace the holy disillusion that Qohelet teaches.

The principles of Qohelet's writing are apparent in Jesus's own life and teaching (e.g., Matt. 6:1–6; Luke 12:13–20; see esp. Matt. 6:25–34), and they are critical for the success of a believer's daily life in Christ. The believer must recognize first that the world is full of evil, slander, "and constant disagreement among people whose minds are depraved and deprived of the truth," but that in Christ we can have contentment—"But godliness with contentment is great gain. For we brought nothing into the world, and we can take nothing out. If we have food and clothing, we will be content with these" (1 Tim. 6:3–10, CSB). The apostle Paul's teachings more than once echo (intentionally or not) Qohelet's frustration over futility and resolution to embrace an authentic simplicity in the fear of God (e.g., the following texts feature forms of the Greek term for "futility" ματαιότης used in the LXX as the equivalent of the Hebrew "vanity/futility" [הֶבֶל] in Ecclesiastes: Rom. 1:21; 8:20; 1 Cor. 3:20; 15:17; Eph. 4:17; see also 1 Peter 1:18). This is not to assert that the apostle Paul always had Ecclesiastes in mind whenever he wrote the term "futility," but that the "truth" of Qohelet (Eccl. 12:10) survived the centuries and made an impact on early Christian thinking, affecting the very way the gospel was communicated by the apostles.

A disaffection for the world's false forms of salvation is required when coming to Christ (1 John 2:15–17), but the process of stripping off such false things continues throughout a believer's life. Salvation does not come through hedonism, intellectualism, professionalism, greed, or other delusions of control; it comes through Christ alone. In other words, a degree of holy disillusion accompanies salvation, and this reorientation of the mind continues throughout a believer's life as they work out their salvation reverently and by the power of God (Rom. 12:1–2; Phil. 2:12–13). In sum, Qohelet teaches of holy disillusion, but the gospel has revealed that this mindset cannot be achieved in one's own strength apart from God in Christ.

## Conclusion

Ecclesiastes is part of the broader stream of orthodox biblical theology, but this is not because the frame narrator smoothed things over at the end (12:8–14); rather, the very message of Qohelet, while hyperbolically negative, speaks to hope in a hopeless world. His positive statements do more than shruggingly offer a way forward (a *modus vivendi*, as Murphy puts it) in the midst of life's incomprehensible absurdity (Murphy 1992, lix); they, in fact, point to the only hope one truly has in life, a hope echoed by the frame narrator at the end. The two men stand at odds in their means of delivery, but they stand together in their final resolution. Does that mean that we do not need both speakers? Does the latter cancel out the former? Not at all. Qohelet's unique contribution is to pull readers through the harsh realities of life, through how it feels to honestly observe and experience the chaos all around. He affirms that the wisdom extolled by Proverbs is indeed better than folly, but such wisdom is not the full story. For that reason, he provides a perspective that supplements the simplified approach of Proverbs but does not ultimately contradict it. For the sages of Proverbs, the glass is half full, but for Qohelet, the glass is half empty. Both agree, however, that there's water in the glass—"Both ways of looking at the world have value, and, as the OT writers recognized, they need to be held together" (Routledge 2008, 224).

## OUTLINE OF ECCLESIASTES

The Kerux Commentary Series presents an exegetical commentary of the biblical text followed by a homiletical guideline suggesting helpful ways to preach and teach the text. While a purely exegetical outline is helpful for seeing the whole text at a detailed level, a homiletical outline will need to factor in the practical concerns of how one might preach/teach the text in a reasonable amount of time, giving consideration to the book's repetitive themes and numerous, loosely related pericopes. Preaching or teaching through the book of Ecclesiastes can take one week or many. The difficulty of formulating a homiletical outline of the book is chiefly due to the book's resistance to a strict structure, much like Song of Songs and the sentences of Proverbs. There will always be random aphorisms or asides that do not seem to fit perfectly within what is perceived to be a larger unit of text.

There is more than one way to approach the preaching of Ecclesiastes. Particular occasions or preferences may result in treating the entire book as the basis for a single sermon, while others may prefer to divide the book into multiple sermons along thematic lines, pulling from several places for each sermon. The model presented in this volume works through the text from beginning to end, assuming an authorial purpose behind the arrangement of the text in its final form, but with consideration to clumps of themes as they appear in the text. This requires a departure from any strictly exegetical outline whenever related themes run over from one section to another. The "preaching units" (meant to represent individual sermons) in the outline appear as bold bullet points, there being ten total. It should be noted again, though, that no outline that follows the sequence of the text will be able to sufficiently account for the recurrence of themes appearing throughout.

### THE OBSERVATIONS OF QOHELET (1:1–6:9)

- The Reality of God and the Enigma of Life (1:1–18)
  - The Triviality of the Human Experience (1:1–11)
  - The Sorrow of Deep Knowledge (1:12–18)
- Illusive Pursuits, Authentic Living, and the Gifts of God (2:1–26)
  - The Emptiness of Pursuing Pleasure (2:1–11)

- The Emptiness of Pursuing Wisdom (2:12–17)
- The Emptiness of Pursuing Work (2:18–23)
- The Joy of Authentic Living Before God (2:24–26)
- Human Temporality and the Timelessness of God (3:1–15)
  - An Ode to Human Temporality (3:1–9)
  - An Exposition on Divine Eternality (3:10–15)
- The Fear of God and the Evil of Inequity (3:16–5:7 [HB 6])
  - Inequity and Death (3:16–4:3)
  - Inequity and Labor (4:4–12)
  - Inequity and Legacy (4:13–16)
  - Rightly Revering God (5:1–7 [HB 4:17–5:6])
- The Impermanence of Wealth and the Providence of God (5:8 [HB 7]–6:9)
  - Wealth Cannot Satisfy, but God's Gifts Are Delightful (5:8–20 [HB 7–19])
  - Wealth Cannot Satisfy, but God's Gifts Are Sufficient (6:1–9)

## THE ADMONITIONS OF QOHELET (6:10–12:14)

- The Works of God Are Unsearchable, So Be Wise and Fear Before Him (6:10–8:13)
  - The Powerlessness and Ignorance of Humanity (6:10–12)
  - God's Works Are Unalterable, So Live Wisely Before Him (7:1–22)
  - Humans Suffer from Many Limitations, So Conduct Yourself Properly in the World (7:23–8:9)
  - Death and Justice Are in God's Hands, So Fear Before Him (8:10–13)
- The Works of God Are Unsearchable, So Live Joyfully Before Him (8:14–9:10)
  - Respond to Life's Enigmas with Joyful Living (8:14–17)
  - Respond to Death's Certainty with Joyful Living (9:1–10)
- The Works of God Are Unsearchable, So Avoid Folly and Live Freely Before Him (9:11–11:6)
  - Life Is Unpredictable, but Wisdom Is Helpful (9:11–18)
  - Avoid Folly and Choose Wisdom, Though It Is Not Invincible (10:1–20)
  - Life Is Unpredictable, So Live Freely (11:1–6)
- Life Is Short, So Enjoy It and Remember God (11:7–12:7)
  - Enjoy Life While You Can (11:7–10)
  - Remember God While You Can (12:1–7)
- Human Endeavor Is Futile, So Heed the Wise and Follow God (12:8–14)
  - Heed the Wisdom of the Wise (12:8–12)
  - Above All, Follow God (12:13–14)

# THE OBSERVATIONS OF QOHELET (1:1–6:9)

The book of Ecclesiastes opens with the narrator introducing the teacher of the book in 1:1, whom he calls "Qohelet." Qohelet then begins with a stirring monologue that summarizes some of his key observations regarding the enigmas of the natural world, the ephemerality of human life, and the futility of human endeavor. Beginning in 1:12, Qohelet introduces himself and summarizes his own investigation into deep knowledge and how his many queries led him to a place of sorrow and vexation over life's futility, concluding that the investigation was itself "a striving after wind" (1:17). In this first large unit of Ecclesiastes (1:1–6:9), Qohelet makes a series of observations about life and how it is so enigmatic, inequitable, and transient, leading to the resolution that all a person can do is live authentically—that is to say, living simply, joyfully, gratefully, and reverentially before a sovereign God.

The first major section, The Observations of Qohelet (1:1–6:9), is broken into five preaching units: The Reality of God and the Enigma of Life (1:1–18); Illusive Pursuits, Authentic Living, and the Gifts of God (2:1–26); Human Temporality and the Timelessness of God (3:1–15); The Fear of God and the Evil of Inequity (3:16–5:7 [HB 6]); and The Impermanence of Wealth and the Providence of God (5:8 [HB 7]–6:9).

# Ecclesiastes 1:1–18

**EXEGETICAL IDEA**
The book's narrator reveals Qohelet's sobering thesis: all human effort is ephemeral and inconsequential in light of the endless, enigmatic rhythms of nature. Qohelet's formal introduction (starting in 1:12) and initial investigations reveal a more specific indictment of human effort: the very process of investigating all knowledge (which includes both wisdom and folly, 1:17) brings only anxiety and sorrow.

**THEOLOGICAL FOCUS**
Embracing the harsh realities of life's brevity and human ineffectuality can be sobering, but it is a necessary embrace to achieve a fuller, healthier understanding of human existence in the light of God's sovereign and transcendent design.

**PREACHING IDEA**
Trust God even when life seems vain.

**PREACHING POINTERS**
Ecclesiastes opens with the declaration that life is vanity. In excruciating detail and with impeccable logic, Qohelet backs up his thesis by pointing out that nothing really changes. People might think they're getting ahead, but in reality, it's all been done before. Even worse, the quest for wisdom in the face of an incomprehensible life leads only to frustration for Qohelet. Yet, Qohelet still believed that somehow God was behind it all—all the mysteries, difficulties, and vanities of life.

Although Ecclesiastes features very ancient wisdom, its message resonates through the ages and is especially relevant for our modern world. While Western culture has become more prosperous than ever, there has been a rising poverty of meaning and significance. The abundance of wealth, availability of all kinds of pleasure (particularly sexual pleasure), and the West's obsession with work has led us all down the path described by Qohelet. The only question is: Will we turn to God, or will we continue our dead-end pursuits at all costs?

# THE REALITY OF GOD AND THE ENIGMA OF LIFE (1:1–18)

## LITERARY STRUCTURE AND THEMES (1:1–18)

For purposes of the homiletical outline, the prologue (1:1–2), informal introduction (1:3–11) and formal introduction (1:12–18) are all included in this first preaching unit. The text's prologue (1:1–2) is given by an unnamed narrator who introduces the wise teacher named "Qohelet," noting also that this sage was a descendant of Jerusalem's first great king, David, and was himself a king of Jerusalem. He then gives Qohelet's thesis: "Vanity of vanities, says Qohelet, vanity of vanities! All is vanity" (1:2). Following the prologue, Qohelet's informal introduction (1:3–11) summarizes much of his teaching, concluding with the brutal realities of his discoveries—that everything in life is endlessly cyclical and that nothing is ultimately satisfying nor truly new (1:9; 4:8; 5:10 [HB 9], 12 [HB 11]; 6:3, 7). Nature survives while generation after generation of human life passes into oblivion, as people work their whole lives to make and say and do things that have already been done by previous generations and will be done again by future generations.

After the shock treatment of 1:3–11, Qohelet introduces himself formally in 1:12 and describes the process of his research: he attempted to acquire great wisdom in order to make sense of the world (1:13). The investigation, however, led him to an unhappy conclusion: that God has subjected humanity to live a severely limited life on earth, one filled with futility and powerlessness (1:14). Qohelet's investigation was itself exhausting and deeply unsatisfying, leading him to the conclusion that efforts to understand everything (represented by "wisdom, "madness," and "folly," 1:17) lead one to deep "vexation" and "sorrow" (1:18).

- *The Triviality of the Human Experience (1:1–11)*
- *The Sorrow of Deep Knowledge (1:12–18)*

## EXPOSITION (1:1–18)

By insinuating that the identity of Qohelet was King Solomon (1:1), the author drew the attention of an ancient audience that was intrigued with the history of the wise king and his reputation as a master songsmith and sage (1:1; see 1 Kings 4:32). However, the summary of Qohelet's teachings that immediately follows is jarring for its readers, coming across as the opening sonnet of a Shakespearean tragedy wherein the player cries from center stage the gloomy proclamation that "Everything is futile!" The entire section is a rhetorical technique meant to shock the reader to attention. Following the blunt force of the narrator's proclamation in 1:2, Qohelet's informal introduction (1:3–11) uses universal observations to effectively prove the aforementioned thesis. Both the pedigree of Qohelet (1:12) and the comprehensive breadth of his investigation into life (1:13–14) leave the reader stunned at his initial conclusions—not only is the world totally enigmatic and human endeavor futile and ephemeral (1:3–11), but the pursuit of ultimate understanding is *itself* like chasing the wind (1:17); it brings only "vexation" and "increases sorrow" (1:18).

## The Triviality of the Human Experience (1:1–11)

The narrator of Ecclesiastes introduces a sage called "Qohelet" who proceeds to summarize the content of his own teachings: that the march of time and the cycles of life make human existence seem trivial by comparison.

**1:1.** The wise teacher of Ecclesiastes is a sage of significance within the tradition of Solomonic wisdom. The narrator of the text opens his prologue (1:1–2) by introducing the "words of" (דִּבְרֵי; as in "teachings of") this person (cf. Prov. 30:1; 31:1), much like the opening line of an Egyptian wisdom text (e.g., The Instruction of the Mayor and Vizier Ptah-Hotep; see *ANET*, 412), though the content of such texts differs significantly from Ecclesiastes (see Seow 1997, 95, 99). The main speaker of Ecclesiastes is introduced as "Qohelet," which is a participle (7:27 and 12:8) in use as a noun. English versions translate the term variously as "Preacher" or "Teacher," or leave it untranslated as "Q/Kohelet(h)," the latter of which is preferred (see "Title" in the Introduction). The verbal root (קהל) "to assemble" appears thirty-nine times in the HB and is typically used to call an assembly or gather people and/or things together. Michael Fox points to the comparable soapbox style presentation of Lady Wisdom in Proverbs 1 and 8, a public teacher who wants to wrangle fools together in hopes of saving their lives (2004, 3; Krüger 2004, 41). The finite verb is also used of Solomon in 1 Kings 8:1 when he gathers the elders of Israel to witness the ark of the covenant being brought into the temple.

To further identify the sage, the narrator labels him "the son of David, king in Jerusalem." The LXX includes the words "king of Israel" (βασιλέως Ἰσραήλ), which parallels both the Hebrew and Greek of 1:12 below, though with the added preposition (ἐπί/עַל). As noted in the section on authorship in our Introduction, most modern commentators understand the book to be written much later than the days of Solomon, perhaps by a Jewish sage who wanted to appropriate the name "Solomon" as the spirit behind Qohelet's teachings. The text seems to move beyond even what we know of Solomon's experiences to function as a commentary on all the famed king's vanities. As greatly as Solomon is revered in the Judeo-Christian tradition, it is acknowledged that his sins of immorality and apostasy brought great pain into Israel and precipitated the division of the kingdom into the northern and southern territories. Would a person whose spiritual legacy was to abandon exclusive worship of the Lord, use forced labor to compound his wealth and possessions, and anger the Lord to judge the nation write humbly about the futility of his own life (see 2 Kings 9–11)? Perhaps. Some contend that it would take a person as experienced as Solomon to speak properly about the evils of such a life; however, Solomon's life ends in 2 Kings 11 with no sign of repentance. And though some interpreters have assumed that Ecclesiastes is his expression of repentance, it should be observed that Qohelet *does not repent of anything in his teachings*; rather, he expresses anguish over the ephemerality, incongruence, and ineffectuality of human life, resolving how to best live in light of those realities.

Furthermore, why would the book insinuate that Qohelet is Solomon without expressly stating as much by including the term "Solomon"? After all, a clear attribution could only help readers understand the true identity of the author. But an observation of the text as a whole (with its late Hebrew and incongruities with Solomon's life) suggests that its actual author avoided the term "Solomon" intentionally as a rhetorical technique in order to assert that Qohelet's teachings are on par with Solomon and should be considered part of the Solomonic wisdom tradition, and/or that they speak ironically to the futile life of wickedness led by the once wisest king of Israel. Hence, Qohelet may be a later, inspired scribe, perhaps a Davidic king like Hezekiah, but not likely Solomon. The assertion of the frame narrator in 1:1 is echoed in the rhetorical strategy of Qohelet expressed in 1:12 and throughout chapter 2.

> ### The Meaning of "Vanity" (*hevel* הֶבֶל)
>
> There are two main ways we view the term in Ecclesiastes: to express what is futile (which may include the idea of illusion) and what is incomprehensible/enigmatic. To capture these senses under one roof, the translation "vapor" may be used at times in the commentary. Hebrew terms are known to carry more than one nuance depending on how they are being used (e.g., חָכְמָה meaning "moral wisdom" or "practical skill" depending on the context). *Hevel* foundationally means something like "breath" or "vapor," as further evinced through Semitic cognates, but is deployed metaphorically throughout Scripture to refer to something lacking in substance—such as idols and, consequently, those who create and then worship idols (2 Kings 17:15; Isa. 44:9–11).
>
> It is clear from the term's usage in the HB that being *something* is better (practically and/or morally) than being *nothing* (הֶבֶל). There is play with the conceptual/metaphorical use of the term and its tangible effect. For example, idols are so cheap and porous (and by implication, powerless; 1 Kings 17:15) that it only takes a mere "breath" (הֶבֶל) for them to be blown away (Isa. 57:13). Like translucent clouds, they are so airy that they cannot withstand other, barely moving air (Isa. 40:24). Qohelet's shocking assertion is that idols are not the only thing incapable of withstanding a light breeze—human life in general is a "breath/vapor" (הֶבֶל) that disappears in a moment (cf. Pss. 39:6 [HB 7]; 62:10 [HB 11]; 144:4). By extension, all things human are transient. No one lasts and nothing a person does will last forever. More specifically, though, the most common assertion is that nothing to which human beings ascribe value is lastingly valuable in itself. Not only are all human endeavors temporal, but it is especially what *humans* do that accounts for the most fleeting, futile, and incomprehensible things—"vapor of vapors!" (הֲבֵל הֲבָלִים)—known to exist (1:2, 14).

**1:2**. Everything Qohelet observes in life is "vanity" (הֶבֶל), which, depending on how it is used throughout Ecclesiastes, can refer to the futility of human life or to the incomprehensible world God has created (it may also refer to the transience/ephemerality of human life in certain contexts, e.g., 3:19?; 11:10?; even 12:8? given its proximity to 12:1–7, but that is not a use of the term featured elsewhere in the HB). Given that the meaning fluctuates, it may be best just to read the line as "'Vapor of vapors,' says Qohelet, 'Everything is a vapor!'"

In Isaiah we read, "A voice says, 'Cry!' And I said, 'What shall I cry?' All flesh is grass, and all its beauty is like the flower of the field. The grass withers, the flower fades when the breath of the Lord blows on it; surely the people are grass. The grass withers, the flower fades, but the word of our God will stand forever" (Isa. 40:6–8 ESV). The message of the "voice" in Isaiah 40:6–8 is consistent with the message of Qohelet in Ecclesiastes: humans do not last, but God does (see esp. Eccl. 3:9–15). The thesis of Ecclesiastes (1:2) is felt abruptly, like a splash of cold water on the face of the sleeping reader: "Vanity of vanities, says Qohelet, vanity of vanities! All is vanity!" And unlike elsewhere in the book where there are hints of hope, the entirety of this opening passage remains dark and dreary, in order to hold the reader in the grip of gloom for more than a moment. It is as if the author knows the human tendency to run in the other direction, toward the sunshine and roses, so he wants to corner his pupils quickly in order to throw life's harsh realities right into their faces.

Options abound for the term "vanity" (הֶבֶל), such as "vanity" (Brown 2000; Davis 2000; Loader 1986; Murphy 1992; Ogden 1987; Seow 1997; Whybray 1989), "meaningless" (Garrett 1993; Longman 1998), "futility" (Crenshaw 1987; M. Fox 2004; Krüger 2004; Sneed 2015a, 352), "a breath" (Alter 2010; Lohfink 2003), "absurd" (M. Fox 1989; Schoors 2013), "evanescent" (Burkes 1999, 46), "mirage" (Heim 2019), "illusory" (Weeks 2012, 3, 119), "enigmatic" (Bartholomew 2009, 106–7), and others. Some even suggest that Qohelet's use of the term *hevel* (הֶבֶל) is an intertextual connection to "Abel" (הֶבֶל) in Genesis 4, meaning that everywhere Qohelet looks he sees the incongruities of life as a reflection of the inequity in Abel's story; hence, he groans over the vanity—that is, the "Abelness"—of all things (Meek 2013, 256). This list is far from comprehensive, and not every scholar mentioned here consistently sticks to one definition throughout their work. Many of these terms are interchangeable, but some fit a particular context within Qohelet's teachings better than others. How one interprets the range of the term's meaning is consequential for how one interprets the book as a whole. If the term is to be translated consistently as "meaningless/pointless" or even "absurd," then Qohelet is calling the works of God meaningless or absurd, and yet he shows great respect for God throughout the text. Regarding the activity of humans, if all their deeds are meaningless or absurd, then how does that leave room for Qohelet's exhortations to enjoy one's work, family, and simple pleasures while fearing God?

Just as the Hebrew construction "Song of Songs" (שִׁיר הַשִּׁירִים) functions as a superlative for "the most excellent song," the phrase "vanity of vanities" (הֲבֵל הֲבָלִים) means "the most vain thing." Throughout his teachings, Qohelet calls many things "vanity" including unresolved conundrums in life that cause him vexation. But of all these things, which might he consider "the most enigmatic thing"? It could be his very investigation into the fact that "all is enigmatic" (1:17), or merely the fact itself. Practically, Qohelet applies the term "vanity" (הֶבֶל) to (1) human endeavors (where the term is best understood as "superficial/futile" primarily, but possibly also "ephemeral/transient"; 1:14; 2:1, 11, 15, 17; 4:4, 7–8; 5:7 [HB 6], 10 [HB 9]; 6:4, 9, 11; 7:6; 11:8, 10; 12:8), and (2) to the "work of God" (8:17; 11:5) and the operations of his world (where the term is best understood as "incomprehensible/enigmatic"; 2:19, 21, 23, 26; 3:19; 4:16; 6:2; 8:10, 14; 12:8). These lists are not strict designations since an argument could be made for moving one reference into the other category and vice versa. Some scholars prefer not to break up the term "vanity" in this way, or at all, and see Qohelet's use of it throughout Ecclesiastes as a reference to all that is "illusory" or a "delusion" in the world (Weeks 2012, 118–19). The definition "illusion" is very helpful when Qohelet refers to human pursuits, like his foray into hedonism (2:1–11), and it fits well with Qohelet's efforts to disillusion his pupils; however, the single-definition approach for *hevel* "vanity" fails to satisfy every occurrence of the term (e.g., in my opinion, "illusion" does not make good sense in 2:23; 6:2, and a couple of other places where "incomprehensible" works better). For that reason, it seems best to understand Qohelet's use of the term as varied and situationally specific.

The immediate context of each passage will help the reader decide whether "vanity" has primarily anthropological or cosmic implications (for further discussion, see Murphy 1992, 4). With regard to Qohelet's application of the term "vanity" to the ways of God, it would be erroneous to think of him as impious or interested at all in confronting the Creator (he is not as bold as Job), which is why it is important to understand his use of "vanity" (הֶבֶל) in reference to God as "inexplicable" or "incomprehensible" due to God's transcendence and inaccessibility (cf. Isa. 55:8–9). After all, not even the "heaven of heavens" (another superlative meaning "highest heaven") can contain God, much less a temple, even less a human mind (1 Kings 8:27). The choice of "incomprehensible" for הֶבֶל follows a similar line of reasoning as Fox's choice of "absurd" in that it admits that the world and its goings-on are "counterrational, a violation of reason" (M. Fox 2004, xix). If Qohelet sees the incongruent realities of injustice and reversals of outcome (where the wicked get what the righteous deserve, and *vice versa*) as "absurd," that evaluation must also take into account Qohelet's expressed belief in God's sovereignty and justice, which produces in him an "essential humility" (Davis 2000, 164) in the face of absurdity; hence, Qohelet does not evaluate God's world as "absurd," but rather takes the limitations of human cognition into account, which is why I think "incomprehensible" is a better translation for when *hevel* (הֶבֶל) refers to God's ways and world. Throughout the commentary, the term "enigmatic" may be used alongside "incomprehensible."

**1:3**. Human life is brief; hence, human endeavors are futile. The informal introduction (1:3–11) summarizes Qohelet's teachings, wherein he uses aspects of nature as a contrast against which to set humanity's ephemerality. As proof of his thesis that "all is vanity" in 1:2, Qohelet points to the perpetuity of time and nature, which outlast everything. The natural world is an enigma, something that simply cannot be adequately understood by humans. And it is against one form of vanity/enigma (nature's rhythms) that he sets another form of vanity/transience (human life and endeavors). To understand Qohelet's use of hevel, we must place all things human against the eternality of God and the relentless, erosive onslaught of creation.

Qohelet defends his position that every human endeavor is superficial by asking what "gain/profit" (יִתְרוֹן) comes from all human "toil/anxiety" (עָמָל) in life. A survey of the term "toil" (עָמָל) in the HB reveals it to be more specific than just work. It carries instead the nuances of striving and suffering throughout life to get ahead, to make life better, and to stave off death. The term for "gain/profit" יִתְרוֹן (verbal root: יתר "to be left over") appears only in Ecclesiastes (ten times) and here represents not economic advantage per se, but the potential for humans to flourish and enhance themselves. As Ellen Davis puts it, "What is the human value? Is there any meaning? Will it make me any more of a person?" (2000, 172).

The expression "under the sun" appears twenty-nine times in twenty-seven verses throughout Ecclesiastes (1:3, 9, 14; 2:11, 17–20, 22; 3:16; 4:1, 3, 7, 15; 5:13 [HB 12], 18 [HB 17]; 6:1, 12; 8:9, 15, 17; 9:3, 6, 9, 11, 13; 10:5), but nowhere else in the HB. By using the phrase so frequently, Qohelet is constantly pitting human endeavor against the immovable presence of nature and time. Just as in the present summary of his teachings here in 1:3–11, so throughout the book, Qohelet wants to remind readers that there is no activity a person can do that will change the fact that he or she is standing directly under the sun. Humans may delude themselves into thinking that what they are up to permanently changes anything on earth, but if they were only to look straight up into the sky they would realize that the sun (and by implication, all of creation) has not moved one bit (however, Heim, in keeping with the Ptolemaic dating, sees the expression "under the sun" as a "cypher for foreign rule under Egypt" [2019, 4]). So, Qohelet implies, whom are we fooling when we attribute to our work such great significance? It is all a vapor that will blow away; meanwhile, the sun is busy doing its work and cares not an iota for what goes on down below. Seow clarifies that "under the sun" essentially means "the realm of the living," similar to the Akkadian expression "to see the sun" (1997, 105). The expression does not point to a lack of divine revelation on earth, but to the transient human experience (and, hence, the futility of human endeavor) as contrasted with the immoveable forces of God's creation. The permanent rhythms of nature are the constant/control in Qohelet's experiment, and human experience is the variable. Nature has remained a loyal expression of God's unmoving power in a way that humans have not. It was not the earth that plotted rebellion against God in Genesis 3, but humans who, through their scheming, have complicated how God has made them (see notes on 7:20, 29).

**1:4**. Stone, soil, and sea never seem to die, though all humans do; accordingly, nature is used in verses 4–8 as a foil for human output. Ecclesiastes 1:4 is about the transience of human life against the permanence of the physical earth, from which three examples follow: the sun (1:5), the wind (1:6), and the waters (1:7). The earth stands as the object of comparison against which all human effort crumbles into insignificance, for the earth is immovable (1 Chron. 16:30; Pss. 33:8–9; 93:1; 96:10; 104:5; 119:89–90). The seasons, the days, the nights, the weather patterns, and the agricultural cycles will continue for as long as the earth continues (Gen. 8:22). The two most formidable bodies of creation, the earth and the sun, never go away. Sure, human beings can dig pits and build palaces, but given enough time the earth will fill in every hole and topple every monument.

**1:5**. The sun is as predictable as it is permanent. The transience of human life is emphasized by means of contrast, here placed against the backdrop of three natural elements known to be immutably and perpetually repetitive in the pattern they follow on the earth. To start, the sun is described as completing the same journey over and over again, monotonously taking the same path day after day with no apparent change. Nothing affects it on its journey. It "longs" or "pants" (שׁוֹאֵף) to get back to its starting point the way someone might "long" for shade in the wilderness (Job 7:2) or an animal might "pant" like a famished, wild donkey (Jer. 14:6). This term "metaphorically evokes the strain of the trek" (M. Fox 2004, 5; also Seow 1997, 107). But why is the sun in such a hurry? Why does it labor in this way? Does it have somewhere novel or important to be? Of course not, and this is the point Qohelet wants to make. The sun is going nowhere special or unexpected, yet its pace never relents. It is in a hurry to go where it already is. Scholars cannot help but point out how Qohelet's morose perspective is contrasted with the psalmists' ebullient vision of the sun, which "comes out like a bridegroom leaving his chamber, and, like a strong man, runs its course with joy. Its rising is from the end of the heavens, and its circuit to the end of them!" (Ps. 19:5–6a [HB 6–7a] ESV; e.g., M. Fox, Murphy, Davis). Egyptian hymns likewise praise Osiris, personified as the sun: "you rise for us daily in heaven! We cease not to see your rays!" (Lichtheim 1973a, 118). But Qohelet is not among those who sing, "Here comes the sun!" Rather, for him the sun is a testament to the incomprehensibility of all things and the transience of human existence. Qohelet is not interested in *how* the sun reaches its starting point, scientifically speaking. He may have his assumptions based on what we know of ANE cosmology (Seow 1997, 108), but that is irrelevant for him here. If we focus on his scientifically inaccurate assertions in 1:5–7, we fall prey to a chronological snobbery that misses Qohelet's point entirely—the fact the moderns *know* better about how the earth works does not change our experience of its phenomena one iota. What Qohelet describes is precisely what we experience.

**1:6**. The wind is as tireless as the sun. Qohelet the naturalist turns his focus from the east–west slog of the sun to the south–north bounding of the wind. The wind, as it turns out, also swirls endlessly on a loop from start to finish and back again. The BHS suggests that the repeated סֹבֵב is an accidental repetition, but it is likely an intentional feature of the text, conveying the sense of something going "around and around and around" without end. The repetition of sibilants (שׁ, ס, ס, ס, צ, ס) creates onomatopoetic "s"-sounds that mimic the wind's swirling activity in a continually hissing pattern around the earth. Furthermore, the subject of the sentence, "wind" (רוּחַ), appears nine words deep in the verse, which may be meant to portray the wind's "unrelenting pull forward" (M. Fox 2004, 5).

**1:7**. The final element of comparison is water. While the sun and wind run in circles above, the rivers run endlessly into the sea below. Streams or rivers flow into other streams and dump into the sea, but the sea is never full. Streams also never seem to run out, but every generation of human life comes to an end. Qohelet is not interested in exceptions to his assertions (like dry spouts with barren wadis) and would not entertain any if they came to mind. He is simply contrasting the temporal (humanity) with what seems eternal (nature). Humans rest in death, but the waters of the earth are restless. He is also expressing bewilderment over this natural phenomenon—the fact that water never stops flowing and yet the sea is never full! In comparing the impermanence of humanity to the permanence of nature, what he discovers is that even the most innocuous natural phenomena escape his understanding: "All is incomprehensible!" If simple things like this are an enigma, how much more the ways of the world he plans to discuss later in the text (see notes on 3:11 and 11:5)?

Here is a man who sits on the edge of the beach, watching the waves crash for hours, but rather than feeling peace, he feels despair. What the psalmists note as evidence of God's faithfulness (the natural world and its courses; Pss. 33:6–9; 93:1; 104; see Davis 2000, 172), Qohelet sees as proof of human futility. Medieval Italian theologian St. Bonaventure assumed Qohelet meant the same thing the psalmists did, understanding his focus to be not on "an oppressively monotonous universe which shows humans how pointless their own movement is, but rather humanity's failing to treat the cosmos as a book which speaks of God" (Atkinson 2015, 16; for a medieval commentator, Bonaventure surprisingly relies more on the literal sense in his discussion of Ecclesiastes than on the spiritual; see Bonaventure 2005, 9). But all the evidence of the Hebrew text here points to Qohelet's frustrations, not his supposed enlightened and optimistic contemplations of nature. One might be tempted to laugh at Qohelet's overt pessimism or become annoyed with his negative perspective in these first few verses, seeing it as an inappropriate response to God's creation; however, we at the same time acknowledge the value of "holy restlessness" and how Qohelet's approach may well fit in this category (Davis 2000, 171). It is important, after all, to remember the purpose for which he made these observations about nature; he was not dragged begrudgingly to the beach by an obnoxiously talkative friend, nor getting away from the grind of the office in order to blow off steam; rather, he was actively investigating whether human endeavors had any lasting purpose. He is a realist more than a pessimist, and he was tired of all the half-answers and cheery delusions. He was tired of pretending that everyone's accomplishments really accomplished anything. So, he went to the beach where his bias was confirmed—the waves roll in eternally, as they always have.

**1:8**. Listing every recurring natural phenomenon (e.g., the moon, the stars, the seasons) would be utterly exhausting; it is actually an impossible task. "All things," sampled in the types of natural phenomena mentioned in 1:5–7, are "wearisome" such that no one could "utter them" all without quickly tiring out. In other words, Qohelet could go on for hours pointing out how different aspects of nature are on an endless loop, but what use would that be? Even if he did take the time to do it, his hearers would discover that there is always more to see and hear. It still all leads nowhere. The point is not that the human race goes on meaninglessly just like the rivers fail to satisfy the sea—which points to a failure of human comprehension, not a lack of meaning—but that human endeavor is fragile and impermanent and, for those reasons, futile when compared to the relentless march of nature (see note on 1:4 above). In sum, Qohelet is in a sour mood here as he contrasts concrete realities with human frailty, and he wishes to transfer that mood onto his pupils for the sake of a wakeup call (see "Holy Disillusion" in the Introduction).

**1:9**. Just as the natural world is full of predictable sameness, so human endeavor is hopelessly unoriginal. In this way, the immovable patterns of nature serve both as a point of comparison for repetitive human behavior and as a contrast (see 1:4, 11) to human impermanence. Both nature and humans repeat their respective activities over and over again, but only nature sticks around; from the human perspective, the same sun and the same rivers and the same mountains are here today as they were thousands of years ago, but the same people are not—"a generation comes, and a generation goes" (1:4).

Ecclesiastes 1:9–11 serves as the conclusion of Qohelet's informal introduction (1:3–11). What began as a question (1:3) has now become a string of confident assertions (1:9–11). Qohelet started by asking what man had to gain from all his toil "under the sun" (1:3). He followed this with a comparative investigation that pitted nature's permanence against humanity's ephemerality. Having seen the evidence in 1:4–8, he now asserts, rather than asks, that "there is nothing new under the sun" (1:9). Whatever existed before will keep on existing, and whatever happened before will keep on happening (see 3:15). His statement links up with the modern sentiment that "history repeats itself," sometimes spoken by someone mid-sigh after seeing their kids make the same mistakes they made at that age. Qohelet observes that the cycles of nature always have "been" and always will "be," but that humans never "do" anything truly new (see the verbs in 1:9). Someone may plant a potato where one has never been planted, but that does not constitute newness—the fact remains that humans just keep planting potatoes.

Fox paraphrases Qohelet's view of humans as "figures in a computer game, whose actions seem to vary with each play but are really just ephemeral variants of possibilities dictated by software"—that their "achievements are an illusion, mere echoes of archetypal events" (M. Fox 2004, 7; Whybray and Blenkinsopp also see Qohelet advocating for a mixture of necessity and free will). Rudman, however, views Qohelet as having a more deterministic understanding of God's control over human action (Rudman 2002, 97–98, which is the conclusion of his broader discussion of 3:1–15). Fox's approach accurately conveys Qohelet's idea that humans have a measure of experiential freedom within a defined field of possibilities; however, I would add that these parameters are set by God (3:1–15), though only partially known to us through observation of repetitive human behavior throughout time. Throughout the book, God is identified as the one responsible for ordering natural phenomena in a predetermined way (e.g., 3:1–15; 7:13–14), but Qohelet does not fully answer the question of how far God's sovereignty extends into matters of the human heart. He consistently places blame for human behavior on humans (7:20, 29), but would likely agree with the sages that God can direct human actions and outcomes (Prov. 16:1, 9; see notes on 3:1–15; see also Jewish history of interpretation on the determinism of Ecclesiastes in Rudman 2002).

**1:10**. Continuing from verse 9, Qohelet notes that there is nothing new, and those who claim to see something new are fooling themselves: "The limited perspective of humans *misleads* them to think that they can break the cycle" (Heim 2019, 44, emphasis original; for more on the hubris of human knowledge, see 8:17). Whether English versions render this line as a question (cf. LXX) or a statement does not matter much for the point that Qohelet would like to make: that only a naive person says, "Look at this! It's new!" (רְאֵה־זֶה חָדָשׁ הוּא) since it was already in the forever-past that came before it. There is essentially nothing humans produce "of value that pierces the monotony of life" (Murphy 1992, 9).

**1:11**. There are no new "things," only forgotten things. Qohelet asserts that none of the old things are remembered; furthermore, no one will remember anything that is now happening, nor will anyone remember any future thing that has yet to be accomplished. Every generation will naively declare, "Look at this new thing!" Nonetheless, it is only new to them—the sun has seen it countless times. The question of "gain/profit" *yitrôn* (מַה־יִּתְרוֹן) in 1:3 is here contrasted with the lack of "remembrance" (אֵין זִכְרוֹן) *zikrôn* of 1:11 (note the rhyming of the two nouns); "The soundplay links research question and poetic reflection, and this suggests that *yitrôn* (*success*) is difficult to find for those who lack *zikrôn* (*memory*)" (Heim 2019, 44, emphasis original). We could go beyond Heim's adjective "difficult" here to express Qohelet's fuller sense of "impossible": "There will be no remembrance" (v. 11).

Ecclesiastes 1:11 represents the thoughts of Qohelet at the end of his disillusionment and foreshadows what is to follow throughout the book. This opening poem (1:3–11) is a dark prelude that, on the one hand, jumps ahead to Qohelet's initial conclusions (that all is vanity), but on the other hand does not yet give his final, hopeful prescription for how to live in light of that futility. There is no silver lining to 1:11, which is likely a rhetorical technique to keep the audience startled and locked in for more, hanging on in suspense for a positive resolution, believing that the lack of one could lead his pupils to anarchy and lawlessness in light of human futility. But Qohelet will continue withholding hope for all of chapter 2, dragging the reader through his despair until 2:24–26 where he will provide the first glimmer of light. For now, Qohelet refuses to even mention God. And when he eventually does, it will not be a reference to God's love but to his transcendent sovereignty—that his ways are impossible to understand, and that he will one day judge all people.

In 1:3–11, all human endeavor helplessly erodes one generation at a time, giving in to the eternal beating of the wind and waves until everything we have built or thought becomes sand. From where Qohelet sits, all humans will one day vanish without a trace, leaving behind little to no evidence that they were ever here (eventually, no evidence at all). Everything about them will disappear, except perhaps for a little bit of damage they left behind, or some other unprovenanced relic. Cormac McCarthy's novel *No Country for Old Men* illustrates this point well. As he hiked across the barren West Texas terrain, rifle in tow, Llewelyn Moss saw a few Native American drawings on stones: "The rocks there were etched with pictographs perhaps a thousand years old. The men who drew them hunters like himself. Of them there was no other trace" (McCarthy 2005, 11). Llewelyn is just the latest model of a seemingly never-ending rotation of hunters who all patrolled the same land. One day he too will die and be replaced (see note on 9:5–6).

### The Sorrow of Deep Knowledge (1:12–18)

Qohelet shares his qualifications, though ironically given what follows, and then tells of how he has investigated all of life only to discover that the deeper his knowledge of the world went, the more sorrow it compounded for him.

**1:12**. He declares, "I, Qohelet have been king over Israel in Jerusalem." Murphy points out the Talmudic tradition that Solomon was deposed at the end of his reign, an explanation for the conjugation "was" (הָיִיתִי) here, for why would Solomon ever say he "was" king as if that happened in the past? However, according to the biblical text, Solomon died as king (Murphy 1992, 13). Still, some argue that because it is possible to translate "was" as "have been" (a Hebrew present perfect), the claim of kingship need not *necessarily* be taken as a past and completed event (GKC §106; Seow 1997, 119).

The only new information here that we did not get in 1:1 is the prepositional phrase "over Israel" (עַל־יִשְׂרָאֵל), though the LXX does supply the phrase in the expression "King of Israel" (βασιλέως Ἰσραήλ) in 1:1. This is the clearest confirmation that Qohelet is cast as Solomon, for no other descendant of David was "king over Israel in Jerusalem." Already on two occasions the text has refrained from using the name "Solomon" (1:1, 12) to identify Qohelet, likely to spark interest in the reader who will soon discover, if it was not apparent from 1:3–11, that this version of Solomon is, tonally, a stark contrast from the sage of Proverbs. Is that because here we have an aged Solomon looking back critically over the many futilities of his life? How would that accord with the evidence against Solomonic authorship? It is better to see Qohelet as a later sage or Davidic king who has adopted the Solomonic persona in order to parody the life of the once great king, a rhetorical angle that supports his didactic goal of holy disillusion (see "Authorship," "Holy Disillusion," and especially the notes on 1:1, 16; 2:9–10, 12). Notes Heim, "Qoheleth's implicit argument is: if I can show that even someone like the legendary King Solomon could not obtain true success, no-one can" (2019, 47).

We can engage with arguments over authorship, but it is not helpful to get too hung up on a specific historical association. Whether the author is Solomon, a later Davidic king, or some other scribe, the great wisdom of Solomon spoken of here is a setup for the disappointments that follow as his life is exposed for its many futilities (2:1–23) and his tone is transformed into one of greater humility: "I thought to myself, 'I will be wise,' but it was far from me" (7:23b).

**1:13**. Qohelet applied his heart to search out, by means of wisdom, "all that is done under heaven," which is a way of referring to all human and divine activity (see Solomon's request for this very ability in 1 Kings 3:9). While he is happy to reflect on nature (1:3–11), his specific focus is on animate agents: God and humanity. And Qohelet wishes not to be quickly dismissed as the village idiot who hangs out by the city gate and pontificates aloud all day, running his mouth to whoever is too polite to keep walking (he has a category for such people; see 7:4–6; 10:3). A man like that would not have the capacity or willingness to think deeply about his own conclusions. Qohelet, however, unlike our hypothetical babbler, drew conclusions about the world only after careful deliberation "by wisdom."

The main question that emerges next is what is meant by the pronoun "it" (הוּא) when Qohelet says, "It is a contemptible business that

God has set before humanity with which to be troubled." Does "it" refer to human endeavors in general or, more specifically, to Qohelet's investigation? God is credited with creating an enigmatic world that human beings are now desperately trying to understand, and it is this "contemptible business" to make sense of things that Qohelet here (and later in the book) laments. This verse should be held alongside 3:11, where Qohelet notes that God has put "eternity into their hearts" but has made it such that they "cannot figure out what God has done from the beginning to the end." The world is incomprehensible, and while God is ultimately sovereign over its creation and human limitations (1:13), humans have nonetheless taken something good and complicated it through their scheming (see note on 7:29).

**1:14.** Having been exposed to all human and divine activity, he concludes that it is all vanity. But "vanity" should be understood as multivalent, taking on the meanings of "futile" and "ephemeral" with regard to human activity, and "incomprehensible" regarding divine activity (see note on 1:2). Qohelet's key assertion that "all is vanity" serves also as an abstract or summary of his long investigation to follow, one marked by the repeated expression "I have seen" (רָאִיתִי), a term appearing in many places throughout the book (1:14; 2:2, 12–13, 24; 3:10, 16, 22; 4:1, 4, 7, 15; 5:13 [HB 12], 18 [HB 17]; 6:1; 7:15, 27, 29; 8:9–10, 16–17; 9:11, 13; 10:5, 7; see note on 10:5–7). He conveys that he has seen everything he needs to see in order to arrive at the conclusion that human endeavors are futile and that God's ways are incomprehensible (on the latter point, see 7:23 and 8:16–17).

"Wind," like human endeavor, is everywhere and constantly changing directions, so where would you even begin to chase it? There is too much of it. The task of collecting it is exhausting, pointless, and impossible. Some scholars claim that here in 1:14 Qohelet is putting the deeds of humanity under the same umbrella as the "works of God" (7:13; 8:17), arguing that Qohelet sees both as equally vain (M. Fox 2004, 9; Murphy 1992, 11–13). Though Qohelet indeed uses the term to describe both human and divine activity, he means something different when thinking of humans than when thinking of God. Again, Qohelet's use of "vanity" throughout the book deserves a bit more nuance. His reverence for God throughout insinuates that the "vanity" of divine activity is actually an observed "incomprehensibility." The meaning "futile," on the other hand, is applied only to humanity (see note on 1:2). For some, *hevel* here means "incongruous," as in defying expectations (e.g., Ortlund 2014, 283), which is helpful and close to M. Fox's "absurd" (2004, xix), but both "absurd" and "incongruous" imply "incomprehensible" at the very least. I consider this final term best since it lacks any hint of judgment toward God's works and activity, which would be inconsistent with Qohelet's positive attitude concerning God throughout his teachings.

**1:15.** Humans cannot control, order, manipulate, or fix the world. Ecclesiastes 1:15 serves as Qohelet's example of the futility of human action. He claims that it is impossible for human beings to straighten out or adequately account for the "crooked" ways of the world, with "crooked" referring to how things are backward or the opposite of human expectations ("crooked" does not necessarily refer to moral evil, but can, depending on the context). In fact, in 7:13 this verse is paraphrased and explicitly attributed to God: "Look at the work of God, for who can straighten out what he has made crooked?" The term "to make crooked" or "to bend" (עוה) almost always refers to sinful human activity in the HB, like attempting to deceive someone (Amos 8:5). So Bildad asks rhetorically, "Does God bend justice?" (Job 8:3; cf. 34:12). "Of course not," Bildad would answer, but what Job was experiencing seemed to suggest that God does in fact bend circumstances to create unexpected outcomes. Near the beginning of the book, Job would accuse God of being an unjust judge (Job 9:13–24), but by the end of the book it has become clearer that God's sovereign ways are incomprehensible, leaving room for the possibility that God is somehow involved in manipulating evil for the sake of his ultimate purposes (Job 42:1–6; consider Acts 4:24–28). Qohelet follows Job in this second sense: that God's way of making some things straight and making other things crooked simply cannot be reconciled by humans in any satisfactory way. What Qohelet does understand, though, is that humans are incapable of undoing the work of God: "What is crooked cannot be made straight and what is lacking cannot be counted." The root verb "be counted" (מנה) appears in other very recognizable passages in the HB, as when God makes a covenant with Abraham and says that no one will be able to count his offspring (Gen. 13:16; see Num. 23:10), and when the psalmist states that God counts the stars (Ps. 147:4). Perhaps Qohelet is here drawing upon these very famous occurrences of the verb as a way of shocking the reader with an equally negative truth, as if to say, "Remember when God said that Abraham's offspring cannot be counted? Well, guess what else cannot be counted—the amount of dysfunction in the world!"

**1:16.** Qohelet claims to be the wisest king who has ever reigned over Jerusalem (see sidebar "Royal Identity in the Ancient Near East" p. 69). He is Hercule Poirot, Sherlock Holmes, and Miss Marple all rolled into one—no one surpasses his investigative skill because no one has more experience or accomplishments (2:7, 9). In 2:1 and 2:15, Qohelet "says/thinks" (אמר) "in" (בְּ) his heart, most likely meaning that he had a conversation partner throughout his investigation—his own heart! This use of the term "heart" (לֵב) is distinct in Ecclesiastes from elsewhere in the HB: "Rather than לֵב used with verbs of speaking to express the idiom for internal speech (i.e., someone thinking or speaking to himself), it is used as a full-fledged character in Ecclesiastes" (Holmstedt, Cook, and Marshall 2017, 21). Here in 1:16, both the verb "said" (דבר) and the preposition "with/in" (עִם) are different than in 2:1 and 2:15 (בְּ/אמר), but it is not clear that a distinct meaning is intended. The irony of his claim in this verse is seen immediately in the two verses that follow, as well as in other places where he openly admits his failure to acquire the level of wisdom desired (e.g., 7:23; 8:16–17). But for now, Qohelet is engaging in total self-aggrandizement by muttering to himself the equivalent of "I'm

Pritchard: "This autobiographical account, composed in connection with the dedication of a palace, was discovered in 1902 in modern Zinjirli in northwest Syria. It dates from the second half of the ninth century B.C." (Pritchard 2011, 296; see also *ANEP* §455). Autobiography of King Kilamua of *Y'dy-Sam'al*. Public domain.

the greatest!" His repeated use of the independent personal pronoun "I," along with the claim that no one greater preceded him as king over Jerusalem (there was only David before him), is an effective parody of Solomon, and a clever setup for the disappointment that follows (see Heim 2019, 49).

> **Royal Identity in the Ancient Near East**
>
> In Ecclesiastes 1:12–16, Qohelet identifies himself, his role, his royal heritage, and his sage calling. And he asserts that his accomplishments in wisdom exceed that of all who came before him (also in 2:7, 9–10). It was important for the kings of Egypt, Mesopotamia, Hatti, and the Levant to communicate their identity effectively since a clear patrilineal pedigree (e.g., "my father was") along with a list of past accomplishments (almost always military campaigns and building projects) were used to legitimize the king's right to reign, reducing the likelihood of naysayers and coups (see Ellis 1989, 176; see also Sennacherib's claim to have received great knowledge and wisdom from the gods; Elayi 2018, 19). They employed royal propagandistic measures, like monumental inscriptions and massive artistic reliefs, to promulgate belief in their greatness throughout the kingdom.
>
> Royal inscriptions chronicling military campaigns or building dedications would begin by listing the name, titles, and divine loyalties of a particular ruler. For example, in his palace dedication inscription, King Sargon II of Assyria had written, "Palace of Sargon, the great king, the king of the universe, the king of the land of Aššur, viceroy of Babylon, king of the land of Sumer and Akkad, beloved of the great gods" (my trans.; for text, see Borger 1963 §38).
>
> In addition, kings would often cite their affinity for justice and how they served as protectors of the people. Sennacherib called himself "beloved of the great gods, guardian of justice/stability, lover of justice, who creates help, who goes to the assistance of the weak" (my trans.; see Grayson and Novotny 2012, 172). A similar pattern is observed in King David's epic self-description at the close of his life in 2 Samuel 23:1–7 where he lists his father and a number of titles associated with his God-ordained role as king and exactor of justice in Israel. At times, rulers would assert that they were better than all who came before them, such as the Phoenician Kilamuwa, King of Yaudi (*Yʾdy-Samʾal*), whose accomplishments overshadowed those of his predecessors: "Gabbar became king over *Yʾdy* but he was ineffective. There was *Bmh* but he was ineffective. There was my father Hayya but he was ineffective. There was my brother Shaʾil but he was ineffective. But I, Kilamuwa, the son of *Tm*, what I achieved, the former (kings) did not achieve" (*ANET*, 654).
>
> Like Ozymandias (see note on 2:11), and like a great many real ANE kings, Qohelet pronounces his name, rank, and great qualifications at the head of his inscription. Like Kilamuwa, he claims to have exceeded the accomplishments of all who came before him (1:16; for more examples of the motif of the "unworthy predecessor" in ANE biography, see Knapp 2015, 52–53). However, two interesting distinctions are observed in Qohelet: (1) his accomplishments are focused only on wisdom and wealth (1:12–16; 2:9), not military success, and (2) Qohelet is self-critical in admitting that the sum total of his wisdom ended up causing nothing but headaches (1:18) and amounted to "a striving after wind" (1:17; 2:11). Furthermore, Qohelet actually "uses the motifs of royal inscriptions to reflect upon the failure of kingship" (Suriano 2017, 305), an important distinction between Ecclesiastes and Near Eastern analogs.

**1:17.** Not only are all human endeavors vain, but the pursuit of ultimate understanding is "also" a chasing after wind. I say "ultimate" regarding Qohelet's pursuits (esp. in ch. 2) to make a distinction between the kinds of ordinary pleasure, wisdom, and work that he sees as good gifts from God (2:24–26) and the reckless pursuits of fulfillment in these things, pursuits that produce only disappointment and vexation (see sidebar "Ultimate Satisfaction versus Temporary Value" p. 85). The contrast between "wisdom" and the pair of terms "madness and folly" is like the contrast between "good" and "evil" elsewhere in Scripture. Wisdom serves here as the functional equivalent of "good," and folly as the functional equivalent of "evil." Qohelet intends readers to recall that the historical Solomon had requested God give him the ability to understand people and the ability to discern between "good and evil," an expression that is not just morally centered but actually refers to ultimate wisdom and understanding (1 Kings 3:9). Also, given the intertextual connections to Genesis later in the book (e.g., 12:7; Gen. 3:19), there is likely a reference here to the creation story and the prohibition against eating from the Tree of Knowledge of Good and Evil (Gen. 2:16–17). All that came from Adam and Eve's disobedient pursuit to "be like God, knowing good and evil" (3:5) was the pain of childbirth and working the thorny ground (3:16–17). While Qohelet was never given a command by God *not* to plumb the depths of knowledge, what he ends up with is not better than what Adam and Eve got, as Ecclesiastes 1:18 shows.

**1:18.** The LXX was unsatisfied with the notion that collecting wisdom leads to "grief" or "vexation" (כַּעַס), so they amended the term to what seemed like a more logical reading, "knowledge" (γνώσεως)—"For in a multitude of wisdom is a multitude of knowledge" (ὅτι ἐν πλήθει σοφίας πλῆθος γνώσεως). However, the contextually superior reading is "vexation" (כַּעַס), especially given the parallel line. Sure, Qohelet will concede that there is some value in wisdom (1:13), but not so much that it is ultimately satisfying or persists beyond a person's death. More than that, the amassing of knowledge about the world will only make one more aware of its injustices, atrocities, and vanity, such that the reward of the very wise is that they become very sorrowful. Of course, later in Ecclesiastes, Qohelet commends wisdom and talks about the dangers of folly. So, is wisdom good or is it bad? The difference seems to be in the effort "to know" wisdom comprehensively on the one hand (1:17), and merely to behave wisely (e.g., 2:13; 7:1–12) on the other. The former is deeply wearisome (1:18), but the latter is useful (2:13). The business of collecting wisdom by means of studying how humans behave is deeply draining and like chasing after wind, but that does not mean that wise behavior, in general, should be rejected.

> **Futility in the Epic of Gilgamesh**
> This first chapter of Ecclesiastes demonstrates that the book is close to the ideology known to us from the ANE in the Iron Age and prior and does not need to be philosophically linked to the Hellenistic age. The text most often cited in this regard is the Epic of Gilgamesh, written first in Sumerian but later developed and expanded in Akkadian. Gilgamesh, a villain turned hero, embarks on an epic quest for eternal life but discovers that "humans are not defined by immortality, but by their ability to build great cities like Uruk and to make good friends like Enkidu" (Matthews and Benjamin 2016, 38). It is not the action sequences in this story that bear the greatest resemblance to Ecclesiastes but the philosophical musings about life, such as when Gilgamesh uses the sobering reality of human mortality to encourage his friend Enkidu when they both face death: "Who can climb to heaven and become immortal? Only the members of the divine assembly live forever. The days of humans are numbered; human deeds are like a breath of wind" (Matthews and Benjamin 2016, 44). Qohelet likewise points to the great distinction between God's immutable deeds (Eccl. 3:14–15) and the fact that human deeds are only a "breath" (1:14). After the death of Enkidu, Gilgamesh nevertheless searches for immortality but is advised along the way that he

should eat, drink, and be happy, taking joy in his wife and children (see Matthews and Benjamin 2016, 46; cf. Eccl. 3:12–13; 9:7–10). With the help of a living ancestor, Utnapishtim, Gilgamesh is told about a plant that can make one immortal, though it is at the bottom of the sea and nearly impossible to retrieve. Gilgamesh succeeds in acquiring the plant, but after all his efforts to get it, a serpent comes along when he is not looking and steals it away, leaving Gilgamesh to lament: "for whom have my hands toiled, for whom has my heart pounded? I have nothing to show for my work. I have worked for this snake" (Matthews and Benjamin 2016, 52; on a similar unpredictable circumstance, see Eccl. 10:8, 11). Similar feelings are expressed also by Qohelet who mourns the "great evil" of someone toiling all their lives for wisdom and possessions only to leave it all to someone who did nothing to earn it, who may even turn out to be a wasteful fool (2:18–21). While the Epic of Gilgamesh and Ecclesiastes share some similar lines of thinking regarding the futility of life, and while both provide the maxim that one should live life with joy, Ecclesiastes goes beyond this to prescribe joy within a specific spiritual context—one's reverence for the only just, sovereign, and gracious God (1:13; 2:24–26; 3:10–18, 17; 5:1–7 [HB 4:17–5:6], 18–20 [HB 17–19]; 7:13–14, 18, 26–29; 8:12–17; 9:1, 7; 11:5, 9; 12:13–14).

## THEOLOGICAL FOCUS

Ecclesiastes is not Proverbs, nor the Song of Songs. Accordingly, the author of our text does not welcome the reader into an elegant, warm sitting room, take their hat and coat, and offer them a cup of tea while Vivaldi plays softly in the background. On the contrary, the reader is thrust out into the snow naked in the dead of night while the evictor screams "Useless!" to the dissonant sounds of Schoenberg. Then, after the blast of 1:2 comes the cascade of hail from 1:3–11, a psychological pummeling that cannot be avoided because it is all so observably true. Qohelet is not just a naysayer in a bad mood. He is grief, futility, and piercing realism disembodied and scratched into letters on a scroll. The effect is intentional—to put the God-fearing reader on his or her heels with a cliff behind them and no theological rope to grasp. The book of Ecclesiastes invites this kind of raw discomfort. He is eager to hear the faithful young woman or man quote from the sagacious words of Solomon, "The righteous is delivered from trouble, and the wicked walks into it instead" (Prov. 11:8) just so that he can pity their naivety by rebutting, "Who cares? You will all be forgotten" (see 1:11).

Yet hidden in chapter 1 of our text is an acknowledgment of God's reality and role in the universe. He is the one who has placed toil in the path of humanity, even the ever-itching desire to understand the world he has created (1:13; 3:11), yet he has hidden the coveted result of that quest for knowledge. In the absence of satisfying answers, we have the sorrow and the disappointment of discovering that we as human beings are helplessly ignorant (1:17; 3:11; 8:14–17). To make matters worse, God is behind the many things that confuse us. He is the one who makes some things straight and other things crooked without any clear, discernable reason (1:15; 7:13). We may think he has a reason, but we do not get to know it. Like Adam and Eve, we crave what we cannot have and are miserable as a result. Through this insatiable longing, we invite sorrow, vexation, and pain into our lives.

Already in chapter 1 we see that there is at least the possibility of hope by the mention of "God" in 1:13. And having read Lamentations, Job, the Psalms of lament, and several like passages scattered throughout the Scriptures, we know that in the darkest times, when God seems totally absent and the reality of suffering threatens to contradict all we have learned from our training in orthodoxy, faith must prevail. Qohelet, however, has not yet in chapter 1 furnished hope or given any prescription for our condition; yet, in several places in the coming chapters he will offer up the balm of joy in the fear of God. For now, though, it is important to embrace the cold we have abruptly entered and welcome the snow on our skin, honoring Qohelet's perspective by leaving ample room for his many disappointments. Otherwise, holy disillusion will not be achieved (see "Theological Emphases" in the Introduction), for we will not know the beauty of Qohelet's prescriptions until we understand the real pain of our condition. Notes Eric Ortlund, "Only after we have been truly vexed, only after we see our illusions for what they are and mourn their passing, only after we fully acknowledge our place in a creation subjected to frustration, only then can we rejoice" (2014, 282). By analogy, we observe that the gospel likewise does not begin with the resurrection and exaltation of Christ, but with the "man of sorrows" who first suffered in a world made futile through sin (Isa. 53:3; Mark 9:12).

## PREACHING AND TEACHING STRATEGIES

### Exegetical and Theological Synthesis

The book opens with the declaration of a mysterious "Preacher/Teacher" named Qohelet. He exclaims that life is vanity (1:1–2). All human endeavor seems ultimately futile. Human life is a mere breath, with the forces of nature outlasting all human achievement (1:3–11). Yet the seemingly inconsequential nature of human life did not deter Qohelet from attempting to figure out the mystery of existence (1:12–13a). But despite his best efforts, Qohelet came to realize that even the pursuit of wisdom is vain, leading to frustration (1:14–18).

So, does Qohelet have anything encouraging to say? Yes, in fact, he does. Qohelet subtly acknowledges the sovereignty of God over human affairs by admitting that it is God who gives people the task of trying to figure out life (1:13). Therefore, the text invites us to contemplate the mysteries of life but to also recognize our finitude and lack of understanding. We are not God. And our only hope is to rest in his control of the world that can often seem so out of control to us. But our perspective is not the final word on life.

### Preaching Idea
Trust God even when life seems vain.

### Contemporary Connections

*What does it mean?*
The smoke rising from a campfire can be deceiving. From a distance, it looks permanent, solid. But a gust of wind exposes the fragility of the smoke, wiping it away in an instant. If you walked closer to the fire, the smoke might even look like something you could grasp with your hand. And yet, attempting to close your hand around the smoke only makes it slip through your fingers more easily.

Such is life, according to Qohelet. It looks permanent. In the foolishness of youth, it may even feel like you will live forever. But life is *hevel*. It passes by quickly. Those reading this commentary might be able to easily remember their teenage years, thinking they would be "forever young" as the song says. You may only now realize you are in your fourth or fifth decade. Even more jarring is the fact that life is like "breath," exhaled—expired—in a moment (Ps. 144:4). We've all known people who have died way too young, taken too early, in our opinion. We've known the tragedy and pain of seeing someone living for the Lord, only to have their life cut short through illness or accident. We have also seen the wicked and those who squander their precious lives away survive for years, decades even. Life feels unfair. It is *hevel*.

Like the smoke that curls and wisps in the wind, enticing us to grasp it, life is an enigma. It cannot be figured out. You may have great success in your life for a moment, only for things to turn sour in the next one. You may have started to get your life together, to build something special, to gain momentum in a career or relationship, only to have a worldwide pandemic bring everything to a crashing halt. You may have finally returned from an injury after a long rehab only to get injured in the very next game. Vanity of vanities; all is vanity.

*Is it true?*
Where is God in all of this? Where is God when life hurts? Even more pointedly, where is God when life feels unfair? Like a mystery? *Hevel*? The teaching of Qohelet seems to begin quite depressingly, pointing out how life seems like a vapor or an enigma (1:2). Life is like running on an imaginary treadmill without going anywhere (1:3–11). Trying to research it and figure it out only brings more pain (1:12–18). So, is God absent?

As Ecclesiastes opens, the book reveals to us the reality of God. It is tempting to look out on the absurdity and tragedy of life and conclude, "There's no God in it." It is even tempting to take Qohelet's opening words to imply God's absence in the world. If we look closely enough, however, we can see God's presence in Qohelet's first section. Qohelet obliquely references God when he speaks of human life being lived "under the sun" (1:3, 9, 14). By pointing out the futility of life "under the sun," Qohelet is subtly pleading with the audience to turn their eyes to the heavens (Ps. 121:1–4). In other words, Qohelet is driving us to the edge of the cliff of human despair in order to shock us awake to the reality of God. Life can be tragic . . . without God. With God, however we can live wisely in this broken and bent world.

*Now what?*
To navigate the complexities of life, people must trust God's sovereign hand over their circumstances, even when everything *feels* out of control. Trusting God does not come natural to those apart from Christ, for they observe the created order but deny that there is a creator (Rom. 1:18–23). They can become what the psalmist predicted: "The fool has said in his heart, 'There is no God'" (Ps. 14:1). While sinful human beings cannot reason their way to God, believers who have embraced the revelation of God in Christ have their eyes opened to a good and gracious God who is guiding all things toward their proper ends (Rom. 8:28). Christians must trust the Lord in all things, even when they suffer.

While suffering brings its own challenges to faith, believers must also contend with pressure to give into the complete secularization of life. The wider culture rejects a transcendent reality of God by default. People in Western cultures now live in the "immanent frame" where only the cares and concerns of this life dominate our minds, according to philosopher Charles Taylor. We live in a world where the default position is to live life "under the sun." Therefore, Qohelet has quite accurately diagnosed our modern malaise when he speaks of living life "under the sun." He's talking about our lives when we limit our gaze to this solar system, without ever lifting our eyes to see the beauty and glory of God in heaven (Ryken 2014, 21). Therefore, believers must always call themselves back to experiencing the reality of God, which occurs most clearly through word and sacrament every Sunday in church.

**Creativity in Presentation**
The only thing you need to do to illustrate the truth of this section is to have people think about their past week. A brief moment of reflection will be more than enough to prove the point that our world is broken, often feeling repetitive, mundane, and irrational. If you'd like to take things further, you could quickly scan the day's news stories on the internet—and then, to be reminded of the even further depths of life's seeming vanity and human depravity, read the comments.

As mentioned before, smoke is almost like a visible manifestation of the word *hevel*.

While smoke seems substantive and solid, it is actually ephemeral and easily blown away. Like smoke, life is easily disposed of, whether through tragedy or the sheer passage of time. Like smoke, life entices us to try to get a handle on it and to control it; and yet, the harder we try to control it, the more easily it slips through our fingers. Our attempts at mastering life are *hevel*.

Our delusions are not confined to only trying to control life. Another misguided notion is believing that we can make permanent progress. Qohelet reminds us "that which has been is that which will be, and that which has been done is that which will be done" (1:9). Human life can feel like being stuck on a spiritual Peloton bike (a company that produces stationary bikes). To use its bikes, the company requires a video subscription to its training classes and workouts. Watching the classes gives the rider the illusion that they are going somewhere, like up a mountain, but the reality is they are just peddling away in their living rooms, dripping sweat on their newly cleaned carpets.

Throughout our lives, we can think we're making progress, only to realize that we're right back in the same place that we started. We may believe we're growing in sanctification, only to see the same sins we struggled with as teenagers rear their ugly heads. We may believe that we've made significant progress in mending a relationship, only to have the annoying quirk of the other person's personality send us spiraling into a fit of frustration and caustic words. The only hope we can have to make real progress is to trust in God's control of the world. When we trust in God, we can make progress according to *his* plan, which is conformity to his Son (Rom. 8:29).

The big idea for the text is, "Trust God even when life seems vain." The opening section of Ecclesiastes provides an opportunity to speak frankly about the difficulty and tragedy of life, while at the same time encouraging the congregation to see God's hand at work. Based upon the big idea, your outline points could provide reasons why believers should continue to trust God despite the hardships of life. An outline for the sermon could be:

- Even when life feels like a vapor, God is sovereign (1:1–3)
- Even when life feels futile, God is faithful (1:4–11)
- Even when life feels beyond comprehension, God is wise (1:12–18)

## DISCUSSION QUESTIONS

1. What general statement about life does Qohelet begin with (1:2–3)?

2. What natural phenomena does Qohelet reference? What point is he making about life (1:4–7)?

3. How does Qohelet describe the human condition (1:8–11)?

4. Why is seeking wisdom so wearisome (1:12–18)?

5. Do you think it's important to acknowledge that life is broken? Why or why not?

6. How can we as Christians have hope in the face of a world that is *hevel*?

# Ecclesiastes 2:1–26

## EXEGETICAL IDEA
Qohelet finds that the human pursuit for lasting satisfaction or gain in one's pleasure, wisdom, and work is a futile endeavor; instead, one ought to live authentically before God.

## THEOLOGICAL FOCUS
Become disillusioned with the vain pursuits of pleasure, wisdom, and work apart from God; resolve instead to live authentically before him.

## PREACHING IDEA
Find your satisfaction in God alone, because everything else will disappoint you.

## PREACHING POINTERS
Qohelet embarked on a quest to find fulfillment through human endeavor. He pursued pleasure, wisdom, and work. Yet all those things disappointed him. He realized they could not provide the satisfaction he was looking for. His journey of futile discovery was not solely negative, however. He came to realize that trusting in God's sovereign control over all things could free his heart to enjoy the simple pleasures of life. Good things were meant to be good things, not God things.

We live in a time of human history when so many things compete for our attention. Glowing screens fill our minds with endless entertainment. We can have exposure to all kinds of sexual immorality, whether digital or in person. We have access to more information than at any other point in human history. We can now work anytime, anywhere with our smartphones and laptops. And yet, a thick sense of despair sits over us. Human beings are not more satisfied in our culture of abundance than in ancient times of scarcity. That's because lack of fulfillment is ultimately a theological problem, as Qohelet points out. We were made for God. And seeking fulfillment in anything else is a dead end, as St. Augustine so eloquently said in his classic prayer to God from the *Confessions*, "Our hearts are restless until they find their rest in you."

# ILLUSIVE PURSUITS, AUTHENTIC LIVING, AND THE GIFTS OF GOD (2:1–26)

## LITERARY STRUCTURE AND THEMES (2:1–26)

After making his initial observations about life and describing the process of his investigation in 1:13–18, Qohelet now turns to address the plight of human endeavor in a more detailed, case-by-case (or vanity-by-vanity) way in 2:1–26.

Humanity's chief pursuits in life (pleasure, 2:1–11; wisdom, 2:12–17; work, 2:18–26) are addressed one at a time, though shared themes run throughout. The investigation into pleasure begins in 2:1 and is followed by a description of Qohelet's forays in wine, women, and wealth. He speaks also of building projects, which are expressions of his prowess as a wise craftsman (note: pleasure, wisdom, and work are not strict, unrelated categories). Finding that pleasure is only pleasing for a moment, he moves on to consider whether wisdom will gratify him in a more lasting way (2:12–17). For the reader, it is a shock that pleasure was worthless, but an even greater shock that wisdom is deemed to be only a little better off (2:13). However, by the time Qohelet turns to consider "all" his toil in 2:18–23, the reader rightly anticipates that this too will turn out to be a futile pursuit. There is truly nothing a human can do that is ultimately satisfying in a lasting way (see note at 1:17 for what I mean by "ultimately"). Human ambition falls flat in the face of death. All that is left is to live authentically before God, which entails pleasing him and enjoying his sovereignly bestowed gifts (2:24–26).

Generally speaking, most scholars follow the minor divisions as set forth below (e.g., Davis 2000, 176–85; Schoors 2013, 18), though they may not envision all of 2:1–26 as a single unit of text, a decision we made for purposes of constructing a homiletical outline of Ecclesiastes (see "Outline of Ecclesiastes" in Introduction).

- **The Emptiness of Pursuing Pleasure (2:1–11)**
- **The Emptiness of Pursuing Wisdom (2:12–17)**
- **The Emptiness of Pursuing Work (2:18–23)**
- **The Joy of Authentic Living Before God (2:24–26)**

## EXPOSITION (2:1–26)

Should anyone doubt Qohelet's opening assertions that all is vanity, he proceeds to explain in blistering detail how none of life's pleasures (and he believes he has experienced them all) satisfy a person for more than a moment (2:1–11); how none of life's wisdom (and he thinks he has known it all) keeps one from eventually dying (2:12–17); and how none of the world's professions (and he has done or at least seen them all) can fulfill the human appetite for ambition (2:18–23). The *only* worthwhile thing a person can do is enjoy the simple things in life as gifts sovereignly bestowed by God (2:24–26).

### The Emptiness of Pursuing Pleasure (2:1–11)

Qohelet discovers that the unfortunate consequence of having everything is that once one does, he/she has nothing left to look forward to, materially; hence, fulfillment must be located elsewhere.

## Illusive Pursuits, Authentic Living, and the Gifts of God (2:1–26)

**2:1**. Like Dr. Watson and Sherlock Holmes, Qohelet and his own heart team up as coinvestigators on a quest to see whether there is any lasting value and fulfillment to be had in pleasure. Qohelet's formal introduction and explanation of his investigation back in 1:12–18 reached forward to the conclusion that such an investigation is worthless. But here in chapter 2, he is backtracking to take us through that process to a time prior to his revelation that such investigations only bring sorrow. He presents his past experiences with pleasure, wisdom, and work as if they were a test or an active investigation consciously undertaken at the time of their consumption, though they were really just the ordinary behavior of a powerful king spanning decades. It is only after having experienced all these things that the disappointment of his soul sets in and he, posing as Solomon, can look back at it all in hindsight, construing it as an investigation for rhetorical purposes.

He personifies his heart, "I said in my heart," treating it as "an external conversation partner" (Holmstedt, Cook, and Marshall 2017, 21). He challenges his heart politely with, "Come on, let me test you. Pursue pleasure" (לְכָה־נָּא אֲנַסְּכָה בְשִׂמְחָה וּרְאֵה בְטוֹב). Jumping ahead somewhat anticlimactically, we learn right away that even pleasure is "futile." This first verse serves as Qohelet's procedural statement for what follows in 2:2–11, where he provides several specific examples of how he went about "testing" his heart with pleasure only to find that pleasure was vanity.

Elsewhere in his teachings, Qohelet commends simple pleasure or "joy" as the only good thing a person can do in a wild, unpredictable world (3:12, 22; 5:18; 8:14); however, in these passages there is a different sense attached to "joy" than is communicated by the hedonism of 2:2–11 and passages like 7:3–6 where the mirth of partying fools is decried. The specific meaning of a Hebrew word is contingent upon the context in which it is used.

**2:2**. Qohelet questions the value of laughter and pleasure. Depending on how the translator treats the *lamed* (לְ) preposition on "laughter" and on "pleasure/joy," Qohelet could be speaking *about* these two entities, or he could be speaking *to* these two entities as personified participants in his experiment (see Heim [2019, 51], who takes the latter approach). If Qohelet is speaking *about* these entities, then he is making a judgment call on their lack of value. If he is speaking *to* these entities, then he is coaxing them to join in on the investigation. Since his heart is his only conversation partner elsewhere in the book, I take the former approach, that Qohelet is speaking *about* these things and asserting at the start that they are useless.

When considering what Qohelet means when he derides things that seem good, it is important to keep in view both the immediate context of the passage and Qohelet's tendency toward hyperbole. In the case of laughter, it is not bad (see 3:4) and it would occasion the simple joy commended by Qohelet in a number of places. So, what does he mean by calling laughter "folly" or "mad"? Just as "joy" is understood in 2:1–11 in the negative sense of hedonistic pleasure, so laughter is caught up in the negative sense here and refers to the frivolous, mirthful idiocy of a person whose only pursuit is shallow revelry (see Qohelet's condemnation of this state of mind in 7:1–6). In contrast, the "laughter" or "merrymaking" that results from the return of exiles in Psalm 126:2 is different in that it is purposeful and validated by the circumstances, not an expression of mindless and incessant cackling (contra M. Fox, who does not sharply distinguish contexts for "joy" or "laughter" in Ecclesiastes but sees Qohelet as contradicting his views on the topic [2004, 12]). Being a king or assuming the role of king, Qohelet was privy to the superficial way some wealthy people live their lives, and he found it detestable. More than that, though, he denounces any notion that satisfaction can be found in pleasure-seeking, even if the pleasure comes from accomplishments (2:4–8).

**2:3.** Qohelet tried using alcohol as a catalyst for joy, to see if living life in a cheery stupor is the best way to go. Thankfully, throughout this drunken experiment, he kept one foot in wisdom, seizing folly, so as not to go too far.

If one is to test the limits of hedonism, perhaps the best way to do it is with one foot stuck firmly in the world of wisdom. This way, one could theoretically attempt both to indulge in pleasure and keep one eye open, compartmentalizing one's mind so as to evaluate the experience of pleasure from the outside, through an objective lens. This is hypothetical, of course, and absurd. No such experiment is successfully held where it does not cost the experimenter and their friends and family dearly. Qohelet's point here is not to recommend others to follow in his footsteps, but to expose hedonism for the vanity it is. Qohelet "explored" (תַּרְתִּי) with his heart (the same verb appears in 1:13), meaning that he went about his next task thoughtfully, not just engaging in total recklessness. This is not to say he did not get drunk in the process—after all, his heart was "carried away" with wine (see Seow 1997, 127)—but that he clung to some degree of sober-mindedness throughout the process so that he would be able to assess his experience afterward. Is this even possible to do? Since his experiment is not real but only a hindsight reflection of past indulgences, the answer to that question is irrelevant. His so-called experiments are really a creative construal of past indulgences in light of present wisdom, but he has joined the experiences of pleasure and introspection in the same scene for rhetorical effect.

His heart was still "guiding with wisdom" through the trial as he sought to "take hold of folly," meaning to keep it in handcuffs so that he could learn something from his indulgence. The *BHS* suggests a possible reading, "not behaving foolishly" (וְלֹא אֹחֵז), which would fit the previous line about keeping wisdom nearby throughout his drunken experiment, but the explicit negation is not necessary (see commentary note in *BHQ* on confusion in the Greek versions featuring "to take hold of joy" τοῦ κρατῆσαι ἐπ' εὐφροσύνῃ). Qohelet is not embracing folly or "irrationality" as if to adopt it; he consistently rejects folly throughout his teachings. Rather, he is restraining it since he assumes from the outset, like the sages of Proverbs, that there is no value in folly.

Finally, it should be noted that his explanation of these experiences in 2:2–11 does not smack of some clever attempt at reverse psychology, as if he could convince the kids to stay away from drugs, alcohol, and sex by telling them how awful it is; on the contrary, his disillusion with superficial pleasure is real and deeply felt. He wants his students to feel it as well.

**2:4–7.** Qohelet's monumental projects were another avenue by which exploring whether pursuing pleasure as a chief end was worthwhile. This led him to do what all ANE kings did as a way of conveying their prowess and wisdom—build. Just a casual survey of ANE building inscriptions would make apparent to the reader that kings attained great gratification from building temples to their patron deities, palaces for themselves, and other structures such as Qohelet here describes. He does all this "for myself" (לִי), an expression appearing eight times in 2:4–8, which "exposes a sort of consumerism, an obsessive striving to fill an undefined but gnawing spiritual need by material goods" (M. Fox 2004, 13).

The infinitive construct (לְהַשְׁקוֹת) from שׁקה ("to water/irrigate") also appears in Genesis 2:6 to describe a mist coming up from the ground to water the land, in Genesis 2:10 to describe the river flowing from Eden that watered the ground, and in Joel 4:18 to describe the eschatological temple in Jerusalem from which would flow a stream that would water the Valley of Shittim. The imagery is of a king not only creating life, but providing the means by which it could be self-sustained to produce even more on its own (see sidebar "Ancient Near Eastern Building Inscriptions" p. 80).

Qohelet's list of acquisitions includes slaves bought, slaves born in his house, and many livestock. Just as the orchards, gardens, and forests self-perpetuate through irrigation, Qohelet's human and animal possessions procreate, thereby multiplying his wealth more than any ruler who came before him in Jerusalem (see sidebar "Royal Identity in the Ancient Near East" p. 69).

**2:8.** He also acquired the treasures of other kingdoms, either through trade or war. Among these spoils were the "pleasurable delights of men." The term "delight" (תַּעֲנוּג) is used of the woman in the Song of Songs 7:6 (HB 7). The "delights of the sons of man" are described as שִׁדָּה וְשִׁדּוֹת, possibly meaning "a fine woman, and fine women!" This translation is conjectural but is based on comparative and etymological data that give the possible nuance of "fine" or "dainty," or possibly even "breast." If "breast," then the term may be a metonymy for "woman" (see the notes on this verse in NET). The queen and royal harem of a foreign enemy were certainly part of the spoils of war for any king (as were other non-royal women—think of Esther's story). The *BHS* invites for comparison Judges 5:30, where part of the spoils of war are graphically described as "a womb/woman, wombs/women for every man!" (רַחַם רַחֲמָתַיִם לְרֹאשׁ גֶּבֶר). In sum, Qohelet has described part of his acquisitions as war or trade spoils that include the sensual pleasures of fine women. Such acquisitions, as horrible as they are to Christian sensibilities, were the pride of such kings. It should be recalled, though, that Qohelet is donning the wig of Solomon and listing these things not as an actual point of pride, but as a setup for the foil that follows: all of it was vanity (see Schreiner and Compson 2022, 95–96, on the description of Solomon's possessions in 1 Kings 4:21–28 [HB 5:1–8] as a possible "criticism of Solomon's opulence, reputation, and military might.").

**Ancient Near Eastern Building Inscriptions**
It was an essential part of an ANE king's resume to demonstrate his productivity, wealth, and creative prowess through the construction of impressive structures, whether they be palaces for himself; temples for his patron deities; or vineyards, groves, and pools of water that symbolized his prosperity and benevolence through the imagery of growth and life. Part of Qohelet's resume touches on his building projects (2:4–6), and the imagery provided echoes similar royal texts from Semitic kings in the East and West. Mesha, king of Moab, after describing how he defeated Israel in battle, notes, "It was I (who) built Qarhoh, the wall of *the forests* and the wall of the citadel; I also built its gates and I built its towers and I built the king's house, and I made both of its reservoirs for water inside the town" (*ANET*, 320, emphasis original). King Ashurnasirpal II of Assyria, after introducing himself in glorious fashion (see sidebar "Royal Identity in Ancient Near East" p. 69; see also *ANET*, 558), describes how he planted orchards and how he "[. . .] collected and planted in my garden] from the countries through which I marched and the mountains which I crossed, the trees (and plants raised from) seeds from wherever I discovered" (*ANET*, 559). In the Tell Sīrân bottle inscription discovered in Amman, Jordan, an Ammonite king's works are immortalized, having built "the vineyard and the garden and the tunnel" (*Aḥituv* 2008, 363; for Eccl. 2:8 see also the City of David ostracon No.1, line 2 "silver collector," *Aḥituv* 2008, 26).

When a king conquered another king's territory, cutting down their buildings and gardens was symbolic of the defeated king's inability to sustain

> life in that region. The conquered king is shown to be weak and ineffectual, as when Shalmaneser III defeated Hazael of Damascus: "(There) I cut down his gardens" (*ANET*, 280). Hittite prayers include pleas to the god that he would curse his enemies, namely those who seek to "burn your temples; (iv) others seek to obtain the rhyta, the cups (and) the utensils of silver (and) gold; others seek to lay waste your plowland and pasture, vineyards, gardens (and) groves; (5) others seek to capture your plowmen, vinedressers, gardeners (and) millwomen—give evil fever, plague, famine (and) *misery* to these enemy countries" (*ANET*, 397, emphasis original). Qohelet states, "I even collected for myself silver and gold and the property of kings and provinces" as well as "singers" and harem girls (Eccl. 1:8), just like many ANE kings who boasted of defeating their enemies and carrying away spoils of silver, gold, livestock, produce, and people (see Sennacherib's boast in *ANET*, 288).

**2:9–10.** For the third time (1:16; 2:7) Qohelet states his superiority to all who ruled in Jerusalem before him (see sidebar "Royal Identity in the Ancient Near East" p. 69; some take this to be a reference to all Jerusalemites [royal and non-royal] who came before Solomon, but the claim is made in a royal context and is consistent with propaganda from other royal, monumental inscriptions). The importance of this superlative is to show that there is no other Israelite king who could speak more authoritatively about these things than he could. And if all other Israelite kings "who came before" him are unqualified, then the same must be true for all non-royals. The extreme boastfulness of such a claim should not be lost on the reader. In his parody of Solomon, Qohelet is portraying the great king negatively in order to set up the reader for the shocking conclusion of 2:11: that it was all vanity.

According to 2:10, his investigation into pleasure was so comprehensive that he denied himself no delight that passed before his eyes, nor any pleasure that entered into his mind. Just as Solomon had given the queen of Sheba all that she asked (1 Kings 10:13), so Qohelet gave himself "everything his eyes asked for" without restraint. The noun "joy" and the verb "to rejoice" appear in the same verse here in 2:10, but not in the same clause. Nevertheless, their close proximity is rare in the HB. The two are joined syntactically in 1 Kings 1:40 when the people were "rejoicing with great joy" at the anointing of Solomon as king, and in Jonah 4:6 when the prophet "rejoiced with great joy" because of the plant the Lord "appointed" to give him shade from his discomfort. The very next morning, though, the Lord "appointed" a worm to eat the plant, leaving Jonah sunburned and windburned and wishing for death like Job (Job 7:16; Jonah 4:7; cf. Eccl. 4:2). Perhaps Qohelet would interpret the "rejoicing with great joy" of Jonah's relief from the sun as futile when set against matters of much greater importance in that context, like the sovereign purposes of God.

**2:11.** Qohelet concludes by sharing the results of his investigation into pleasure: "All was futile and a striving after wind." The "toil" of Ecclesiastes 2:11 refers to the construction works and other accomplishments mentioned in 2:3–10, all of which fall under the umbrella of his investigation into pleasure. These works could easily be included in Qohelet's treatise against "toil" in 2:18–23 where he likely returns in his mind to the construction of said palaces, vineyards, and other such endeavors.

"There is no gain/profit/reward" to be had under the sun. To Qohelet, an elegant palace is no more than a sandcastle; given enough time, it too will erode into nonexistence (1:11). Pleasure's inability to satisfy Qohelet echoes many passages where the prophets declare judgment on Israel and other nations who put their trust in pleasure and extravagant wealth (too many passages to mention but see esp. Isa. 47:8–15, where the pleasures and "wisdom" of Babylon will eventually turn to "stubble" when "the fire consumes them"). The emptiness of what humans produce is related to their own ephemerality, such that what we end up with is nothing producing nothing. The nations are "nothing" before God and are counted as "nothing and emptiness" (Isa. 40:17, 23), like the makers of idols who themselves are "nothing" and hence produce idols that are "nothing" (Isa. 44:9–11). All such unworthy sources of satisfaction and trust ultimately fail, proving how superficial and ephemeral they were (see Rom. 6:21).

With Ecclesiastes 2:11, Qohelet has concluded his investigation into pleasure and found it severely lacking; in fact, it is ultimately devoid of substance beyond momentary fulfillment, for "the eye is not satisfied with seeing" all the beautiful things one can amass, and "the ear is not satisfied with hearing" the elegant voices of the kingdom's best singers (1:8). Humans will always want more. Naturally, then, ultimate satisfaction must be found elsewhere—perhaps in wisdom (2:12–17; see note at 1:17 for what I mean by "ultimate").

The verses stretching 1:12–2:11 relay Qohelet's self-introduction and self-aggrandizement (in parodying of Solomon), a theme common among ancient kings (see sidebar "Royal Identity in the Ancient Near East" p. 69). Percy Shelley's stirring poem "Ozymandias" also comes to mind, which tells of a traveler who found the statue of a long-dead despot jutting out of the sand with an inscription reading: "My name is Ozymandias, King of Kings; / Look on my Works, ye Mighty, and despair!" Anyone familiar with monumental royal inscriptions from the ANE will recognize the exalted tone of Ozymandias, though perhaps a bit caricatured by Shelley for effect. The irony of such stones is multilayered, marked by their sheer number, their megalomaniacal language, their dilapidated state, and the fact that they are so old and so long forgotten that it takes specialists to decipher what they say. As the poem continues, the traveler (a sort of frame narrator him/herself) notes somberly: "Nothing beside remains. Round the decay / Of that colossal Wreck, boundless and bare / The lone and level sands stretch far away" (Shelley 2012, 326). References to this poem could fit beautifully in several sections of this commentary since it so effectively captures the futility of human achievement, seemingly understood by Qohelet, though perhaps not by the contemporaries he wished to reach.

### The Emptiness of Pursuing Wisdom (2:12–17)

Qohelet's investigation moved on from pleasure into the topic of wisdom where he found that the perceived advantages of intellect were merely an illusion in the face of death.

**2:12**. The next stage of his investigation led him to wisdom and madness/foolishness. Having put aside pleasure as the prism through which he views experiences, finding it useless, he now dons his wisdom-folly bifocals to compare and contrast these two ways of living. He is investigating "wisdom," "blindness" (הוֹלֵלוֹת), and "folly" (סִכְלוּת), the latter two conveying a joint mode of thoughtlessness and wicked living (cf. 1 Sam. 13:13; 2 Sam. 24:10). The term "wisdom" (חָכְמָה) in Ecclesiastes primarily means "skillful living" or "knowledge," but can also carry the connotation of morally upright living (e.g., 7:4–5; 10:2) as it often does in the book of Proverbs (see note on 2:13).

Qohelet then asks, "For what [can] the person [do] who comes after the king? They do what has already [been done]!" He is asserting more than the fact that those who come after him will only repeat the same mistakes he has made (see 1:10). He is insinuating, by means of a rhetorical question, that his inquiry into wisdom and folly will serve for all time, such that his conclusions will stand long after he is dead. There will be no new kinds of wisdom and folly that come after him, at a time when the king is no longer around to investigate them.

## Illusive Pursuits, Authentic Living, and the Gifts of God (2:1–26)

Everything that is done now has already been done in the past and nothing will change in the future. This statement by Qohelet serves to legitimate his inquiry into wisdom and folly as a once-for-all-time study, in the same way that 2:7 and 2:9 were meant to legitimate his inquiry into pleasure. No one has been greater than Qohelet, so no one can speak more authoritatively about pleasure than he can (2:1–11); likewise, all the wisdom and foolishness a person can do has already been done and will be done again, so Qohelet's insights on this matter are comprehensive and final. He would not want his pupils wasting their time trying these things out for themselves.

Since I have suggested in the Introduction and notes thus far that Qohelet may be a later Davidic king or scribe assuming the persona of Solomon in order to parody the wise king, should Qohelet's assertion that he is the best-suited investigator for this task be taken seriously or as tongue-in-cheek? In other words, does Qohelet wish for his pupils to see such claims as real or as a mockery of Solomon, not to be taken seriously? The answer is a little of both: Qohelet is cleverly playing both sides—he does not wish to contradict the claim that Solomon was as wise as Scripture says he was (1 Kings 4:30), but at the same time, he wants to expose the hubris of Solomon by demonstrating the extreme limits of even the wisest king. This is only made easier by the fact that Solomon lived such a rebellious life at the end. Hence, the version of Solomon we get in Ecclesiastes is "Qohelet's Solomonic anti-hero" (Heim 2019, 56).

**2:13**. Wisdom is better for a person than folly. This is the first positive thing Qohelet has said about anything, but before the reader gets too hopeful, he/she should keep reading. Though Proverbs does a masterful job of contrasting the wise person with the fool such that they could not be more different from one another, there is one thing the two have in common: death.

Wisdom cannot save a person from eventual death, but at least it is useful. Concerning "wisdom" (חָכְמָה), there is not always a clear-cut distinction in Scripture between wisdom's morally upright sense (e.g., fearing the Lord, helping the poor) and its skillful/intellectual sense (e.g., being artistically gifted and knowledgeable, like an excellent stone smith). The dominant nuance of "wisdom" intended in each place is dependent upon the immediate context. In 2:12, "folly" (סִכְלוּת) was paired with "blindness" (הוֹלֵלוֹת), the latter sometimes translated as "madness"; the idea is walking through life in a morally negligent way, not prioritizing good things. Since both ignorance and wickedness are featured on the negative side of the ledger in this verse, both righteousness and intellect/skill could be implied by Qohelet's view of "wisdom" (חָכְמָה) here.

**2:14**. As indicated by the previous verse, you can get much more done in the light than in darkness. Light and darkness are used throughout Scripture as corresponding images for righteousness (e.g., Prov. 4:18; 6:13) and wickedness (e.g., Prov. 2:13; 4:19). Qohelet perceived, though, that while wisdom is more helpful in the short term, it does not change everyone's ultimate deathward trajectory (Eccl. 2:16). For Qohelet, the reality of death eclipses any positive notions he has about wisdom's usefulness for the living. His reaction to death's universality is that there is no point in pursuing *ultimate* wisdom since we all die (2:15 clarifies that he valued wisdom more than he should have: "Now why have I been so exceedingly wise?"). This makes him sick to his stomach (2:17). As the rest of his teachings show, death puts wisdom's worth into proper perspective, highlighting its limitations. For the living, death is still relatively useful (see 7:11–12).

**2:15**. Qohelet's investigations are so deeply felt because they are so very personal. While his teachings as a whole address the state and fate of all human life, he is running these experiments on himself. He is his own test subject to determine whether there is any lasting value to pursuing ultimate fulfillment in pleasure, wisdom, and work. In 2:11 he concluded, with great emotion expressed through the repetition of "all," that every bit of good he had ever done for himself had been a colossal waste: "All was vanity and a striving after wind!"

With pleasure deemed a bust, surely the sages of Proverbs were right that there is something redeemable about wisdom—but it turns out that wisdom is only useful if you are alive. Perhaps the "son" sitting at his father's feet in Proverbs 1–9 was under the delusion that wisdom rescues a person from every harm; however, Qohelet's anticlimactic realization is that wisdom cannot save a person from death. You can escape death in the short term by making good use of wisdom, but you have only pushed it off to a later date (7:11–12). Eventually, old age or an unfortunate accident (9:11) will prevail (12:1–7). This revelation is deeply and personally felt by Qohelet, who exclaims, "Why have I been so wise?" Given his nod to wisdom's usefulness both here in 2:13–14 and elsewhere (e.g., 1:16; 2:3, 9, 26; 7:10–12), Qohelet's specific question here goes beyond, "What use was it to be wise at all?," and asks more deeply, "Why have I been *so exceedingly* wise?" (וְלָמָּה חָכַמְתִּי אֲנִי אָז יוֹתֵר) or as the NET puts it, "Then what did I gain by becoming so excessively wise?" Qohelet is bemoaning his lifelong obsession with wisdom as if he had formerly deluded himself into thinking that it would bring greater degrees of satisfaction. He had overinvested in the wrong area, but given the reputation of wisdom, this had seemed like a reasonable decision at the time. He is learning though that pleasure, wisdom, and work cannot bring lasting "gain" (1:3) or make a person truly "satisfied" or "full" (cf. 1:9; 4:8; 5:10 [HB 9], 12 [HB 11]; 6:3, 7). Whatever satisfaction a person has in wisdom will be abruptly terminated at the moment of death, if not before. So Qohelet groans that "even this" is vanity.

**2:16**. Here, he finally states explicitly what he has insinuated in 2:14–15: "O how the wise person dies just like the fool!" (see the similar grief expressed in Ps. 49:10 [HB 11]; perhaps Qohelet is among the sons of Korah!).

Qohelet's students may rebut that at least death cannot remove the public memory of the wise. But Qohelet is prepared for this attempt to rescue wisdom and has already addressed it broadly back in 1:11: given enough time, nothing will be remembered! The concept of remembrance is important in modern cultures, and it was very important in the ANE setting of biblical Israel. To be forgotten is a great tragedy (e.g., Job 19:14; Pss. 9:18 [HB 19]; 31:12 [HB 13]; 42:9 [HB 10]; Eccl. 1:11; 9:5), which is why it is so comforting that God has not "forgotten" his people nor his covenant with them (e.g., Isa. 44:21; Jer. 50:5). People forget. God does not.

**2:17**. If Qohelet's sour psychological state is not already apparent, it becomes most clear here in 2:17. Discovering that pleasure was ultimately unsatisfying was a burdening realization (2:11), but to find that wisdom is in the same class causes Qohelet to fall into a deeper loathing of life and everything in it. He "hated life" because it was all so "contemptible" (רַע) to him. The adjective "evil" (רַע) has a range of meanings: NET reads "awful"; other options include "worthless," "injurious," and such (see *HALOT* s.v. "רַע" 1251–53). It is not just that Qohelet *considers* all human activity worthless, but that he is grieved by its worthlessness (see his similar reaction to the worthlessness of "toil" in 2:20). In his formal introduction (1:12–18), he had already given a preview of his mental state regarding wisdom (1:18), but here we have the reason for his sorrow: death usurps everything, even wisdom! Salvation/fulfillment must come from elsewhere.

Whatever was done under the sun was "distressful upon me" (רַע עָלַי). The NJPS renders the expression idiomatically, "For I was distressed," and the ESV reads "was grievous to me." The construction (רַע עָלַי) appears in Psalm 109:20 where the psalmist desires judgment on those who speak "evil against me" (רַע עַל־נַפְשִׁי). Here, though, the preposition עַל here simply means "to," given its use in Late Biblical Hebrew (see Seow 1997, 136).

> **Ultimate Satisfaction versus Temporary Value**
> Throughout the book of Ecclesiastes, Qohelet grieves the discovery that so many good things in life are annulled by the existence of inexplicable suffering, loss, and above all, death. His frustrations with pleasure, wisdom, and work throughout chapter 2, for example, are not that these things are altogether worthless or that death completely invalidates them; we must bear in mind that the joy statements (aka *carpe diem* statements) throughout the book preach of the relative, temporary value of all three things for those who are yet living (2:24–26; 3:12–13, 22; 5:18–20 [HB 17–19]; 8:15; 9:7–10). What death invalidates is the pursuit of pleasure, wisdom, and work as *ultimate ends* in life. Any abstract notions that these things can fully save a person from insignificance, boredom, or even death are merely delusions in light of several harsh realities. Rather than jumping to conclude that Qohelet is contradicting his views on the value of pleasure, wisdom, and work in these passages, it would be better to understand the contexts in which he addresses them. If they are viewed as one's chief end in life, then they will invariably fail to satisfy (see note on 2:24), but if they are viewed as gifts of God to be enjoyed temporarily, then they will fulfill the purpose for which God has given them (notice the role of God as gift-giver in the joy statements).

### The Emptiness of Pursuing Work (2:18–23)

Qohelet's investigation leads him to the concept of one's efforts to work, build, create, and amass wealth in this life—all aims that fall short of the ultimate satisfaction one seeks.

**2:18**. The third test begins. This time Qohelet will investigate to see if it is possible to be fully satisfied in life by one's work or "toil." This section features the first of a few instances in Ecclesiastes where Qohelet will bemoan the fact that all of a person's hard work is left behind to someone else who did nothing to earn it (5:15 [HB 14]; 6:1–2; cf. 4:16; 10:16; see note on 2:20–21). At the start of his investigation into pleasure (2:1), there was a bit of a delay before he arrived at the full despair of his conclusion in 2:11. For wisdom (2:12), there was less of a delay (2:14). Now with toil, there is no delay; he steps straight into anger and sorrow over the uselessness of burying oneself in work in order to find "gain" (1:3). For Qohelet, toil was only worthwhile if he could keep its proceeds forever, which is akin to making one's work an ultimate end in life, but death takes everything away and puts it all into the hands of a successor.

**2:19**. His successors will never be able to appreciate all the hard work, investment, and toil it took to have everything he has. This, he says, is "incomprehensibly stupid" (a paraphrase of this particular occurrence of *hevel* "vanity"). The term "vanity" is best understood as "incomprehensible" in several places, and since "this" (זֶה) refers to the perceived injustice of a successor inheriting all the hard work of his/her predecessor, then "incomprehensible" would be a better fit than "ephemeral" or "futile." Adding the word "stupid" is in keeping with Qohelet's assessment of this scenario in 2:20 where he calls it "an immense evil," and of a nearly identical scenario in 6:2 where Qohelet goes beyond the description "vanity" to call the situation "horrifically sick" or "a grievous evil" (ESV). Qohelet expresses not joy (as in Prov. 13:22) but grief at the thought of losing control—for such vain, obsessively controlling people, "letting go of their achievements for the sake of someone else, even their own flesh and blood, is just not their thing" (Heim 2019, 60).

**2:20–21**. Qohelet's investigation has led him into misery, just as he had said back in 1:17–18. It should be noted, though, that the text presents him as having done this to himself. It does not portray him as the victim of an unfortunate circumstance or some other cause for depression. The verb "to despair" (יאשׁ) in the HB gives the sense of hopelessness that Qohelet felt, though his reasons for feeling this way are not comparable to the real suffering described by other verses where the verb also appears (for example, Job 6:26; Isa. 57:10; and Jer. 2:25; 18:12).

This concept (leaving one's hard work behind to be consumed by others who did not work for it) is known elsewhere in Scripture. In Deuteronomy 20:5–8, the law stipulates that before the people go into battle, the commanders of the army are to gather their soldiers together and discharge any men who fit into the following categories: (1) men who have just built a house but have not yet dedicated it, "lest he die in battle and another man dedicate it"; (2) men who have just planted a vineyard but have not yet seen it through to harvest, "lest he die in battle and another man enjoy its fruit"; or (3) men who are betrothed to a woman, but have not yet married her, "lest he die in battle and another man take her." There is a final condition for release that is less relevant to our point: (4) men who are fearful and might spread their fear to others. However, in the first three cases, the reason given for why these men should return now from battle is that they might die "and another man" take their house, vineyard, or betrothed wife. It was perceived as an injustice for someone who has not earned a thing to take it from someone who has put in the hard work to have it but has died too young. Qohelet might delight in this legal principle, but would add,

"You can be released from battle, but no one can be released from death!" Qohelet (mimicking Solomon) does not want to leave his belongings and accomplishments to anyone, even in the most desirable scenario of an inheritance that follows a long life and a natural death (e.g., Genesis 49; Prov. 13:22).

**2:22–23**. Having realized the ineffectiveness of pleasure (2:1–11), wisdom (2:12–17), and work (2:18–23) to fully satisfy a person or bring "gain" (1:3), Qohelet now asks, "What gives?" (my paraphrase). Where is the "gain" in all this? Specifically, regarding work, what is the point of living a life where your days are filled with labor, which brings "pain/suffering" (מַכְאֹבִים) and "vexation/grief" (כַּעַס)—both terms appearing in 1:18—and your nights are filled with anxiety-induced insomnia? The problem of sleeplessness comes up again in 5:12 (HB 11) regarding the anxious, possessive Scrooge and in 8:16 regarding the exhaustion of one who tries to figure out God's world.

### The Joy of Authentic Living Before God (2:24–26)

Qohelet's initial investigation now over, he turns to those things in life that no human achieves through toil but are considered gifts of God, resolving that a person should take joy in such things rather than live a life of futile craving.

**2:24**. Embrace authentic living before God. Qohelet's conclusion wraps up all three sections on pleasure (2:1–11), wisdom (2:12–17), and work (2:18–23). Some scholars prefer to see 2:24–26 (and all the other joy [*carpe diem*] statements in the book) as Qohelet's negative, begrudging resolve to just get on with life because God has made it so miserable that all we have left is to seize the day out of spite; however, that is not the sense conveyed here. Qohelet is rather drawing upon a scriptural principle of taking delight in God and the simple things provided by him rather than putting the hope of satisfaction—see the verb "to satisfy" (שׂבע) in 4:8; 5:10 (HB 9); and 6:3 (cf. 6:7) and "gain" (e.g., 1:3; 2:11, 13; 3:9; 5:16 [HB 15])—in the futile pursuits of ultimate pleasure, wisdom, and work. The psalmist declares that the Lord "satisfies the longing soul" of those wandering through desert wastes, "filling them with good" (Ps. 107:4, 9; cf. Ps. 22:27 [HB 28]). In a parallel context from Isaiah 58:11, the prophet declares that the Lord will "continually lead and satisfy the soul" of his desperate servant. The Lord declares, "My people will be satisfied with my goodness" (Jer. 31:14). These visions of satisfaction in the Lord entail God giving his people all they need physically, but the idea of God satisfying the person's inner being is closely related.

Indeed, Qohelet prescribes eating, drinking, and "embracing joy" (my gloss of וְהֶרְאָה אֶת־נַפְשׁוֹ טוֹב) in one's work (my reading of 2:24 as comparative—"there's nothing better for a man than"—follows the parallel sense in 3:12 as well as the Syriac and targumic variants listed in *BHS*, also preferred by *BHQ*). He understands these simple things as coming "from the hand of God." He states this in a rhetorically clever way. Concerning wisdom (2:15) and toil (2:21, 23), he had declared, "This also is vanity" (גַּם־זֶה הֶבֶל). Accordingly, one would expect his use of "this also" (גַּם־זֶה) here in 2:24 to be followed by "vanity" (הֶבֶל), but it is not; instead, he declares, "This also I saw: that it is from the hand of God" (גַּם־זֹה רָאִיתִי אָנִי כִּי מִיַּד הָאֱלֹהִים הִיא). He uses the familiar pattern as a rhetorical technique to make the following point: "The only thing that is *not* vanity is to find enjoyment in simple, authentic living as a gift from God."

> **Qohelet: Preacher of Joy or Begrudging Ingrate?**
> R. Norman Whybray (1982) calls Qohelet a "preacher of joy," which some take as too positive and, hence, not doing justice to the foreboding style of the text; nevertheless, Whybray's summary of the holistic view (taking the good of Qohelet with the bad) within the stream of scholarship is very helpful. A number of scholars have argued on the basis of such passages as 2:24–26; 3:12–13; 5:18–19 (HB 17–18); 8:15; 9:7–9 and of the recurring references to human life as God's gift, that Qohelet believed that despite all its frustrations and pain, life could be a joyful experience for the person who "fears God." For them, Qohelet's religious faith was all the stronger for his refusal to shut his eyes to the bad things in life and for his unflinching realism (Whybray 1989, 24).
>
> So, while some reduce these positive statements from Qohelet as his begrudging resolve to just take what one can from this miserable existence since that is all anyone can do (see Murphy [1992, lix], who offers up the possibility that Qohelet's approach is dialectical in nature), "it is equally possible to argue that it is just this series of positive statements, punctuating the book, which expresses Qohelet's true conclusions: that it is only the person who has taken full account of the vanities of this world and faced up to them who is free to receive the divine gift of joy in simple things" (Whybray 1989, 25). Qohelet has nothing positive to say about what he finds under the sun except when he references God, who is in fact not "under the sun" but outside it. Toil by itself and for itself is futile, but if a person receives his or her toil thankfully as God's good gift, then simple toil can be a means for joy (2:24; 5:19 [HB 18]).

**2:25**. Ecclesiastes 2:25 makes the point that no one can enjoy the simple things in life apart from God since all such good things come from God (the MT's "apart from me," מִמֶּנִּי, is likely a scribal copying typo for the original "apart from him," מִמֶּנּוּ. The MT reading is possible given other grandiose statements from Qohelet, but less likely given the focus on God in 2:24–26). This is meant to contrast all human ambition for ultimate satisfaction in pleasure, wisdom, and work (2:1–23, where all the glory goes to humanity) with the free gifts of God. Already back in 1:13, Qohelet had hinted at one of the recurring theological themes of his teaching: the sovereignty and providence of God. Here in 2:25–26, that principle is fleshed out further. Both the giving of life's simple things and the power to enjoy them (see 6:2) are the result of divine providence. But given the "for" (כִּי) at the head of the next verse, it is clear that Qohelet wishes not only to make a comment on divine sovereignty but to assert that trying to live "apart from" God, practically speaking, means seeking to please oneself rather than pleasing God, which is spiritually disastrous.

**2:26**. Qohelet prescribes living in a way that pleases God. Access to life's simple pleasures of "wisdom, knowledge, and joy" come through pleasing God, not through blindly groping for them like the men of Sodom searching for Lot's door. Such people live a miserable, anxious, toil-filled existence on the hamster wheel of life, "gathering and collecting, only to give to the one who is good before God." This is the ironic reversal of 2:18–21 above, where a person works their whole life only to die and leave it all to someone who did nothing for it. In the present scenario, Qohelet does not blame the inheritor; in fact, it seems the person who simply trusts God ends up with unexpected blessings of God that are funneled away from the vain materialists and into the hands of those who are simply obedient. In this way, Qohelet starts to sound like the sages of Proverbs, though with less of an absolutist delivery. In sum, Qohelet presents two paths: (1) please God and enjoy the simple things in life as gifts from him, or (2) pursue lasting satisfaction through your own toil only to die with the realization that it is unattainable, your belongings sovereignly redirected into the hands of those who please God.

Qohelet concludes with his refrain that "this also is vanity and a striving after wind."

To what exactly is he referring, though? The immediate context of 2:26 suggests that his refrain applies to the activity of the "sinner" who is uninterested in pleasing God. In that sense, "vanity" here should be understood as "futility."

The "flood tablet" (Tab. XI) from the Epic of Gilgamesh. Public domain.

## THEOLOGICAL FOCUS

Qohelet the sage, posing as Solomon, looks back over a life filled with wasted energy and bemoans the fact that it never actually brought lasting "gain" (1:3; 2:11, 13). For rhetorical purposes, he has portrayed Solomon's life experiences as an investigation into "madness and folly" (1:17), an experiment that proved that pleasure, wisdom, and work are unable to satisfy the human heart in any ultimate way (2:1–26). His conclusion appears as a recurring theme in Ecclesiastes (note his use of "to satisfy," שׂבע, and related terms, e.g., 4:8; 5:10 [HB 9], 12 [HB 11]; 6:3, 7; see note on 2:24). Qohelet thus bemoans that no one achieves contentment/fulfillment through these things before the inevitable interruption of death.

Hence, there is nothing better for a person to do than to live an authentic life that pleases God, something achievable whenever he/she receives the simple things in life (eating, drinking, and working with joy) as gifts from the Sovereign Provider (2:24–26).

In the Sermon on the Mount, Jesus exhorted his disciples not to worry about tomorrow or what they would eat or drink or wear, asking, "Isn't life more than food and the body more than clothing?" (Matt. 6:25 CSB). Qohelet's prescription of taking simple joy in eating, drinking, doing one's work, and pleasing God coincides well with this. The anxious toiler does not sleep (Eccl. 2:23); nor does the vexed rich man who fears losing all he has (5:12 [HB 11]); nor the weary man desperately trying to understand all of God's world (8:16). Jesus likewise asks, "Can any of you add one moment to his life span by worrying?" (Matt. 6:27 CSB). Qohelet would shout in response, "No one can!" Jesus even makes references to the great wealth of Solomon and how his glory was surpassed by flowers that own nothing and live very short, ephemeral lives. If the Father cares for flowers that live only the length of a day, how much more does he care for people? Those who "eat the bread of anxious toil" (Ps. 127:2a) are out to please themselves but are never pleased (Eccl. 2:26b; cf. Isa. 55:2). By contrast, those who receive God's good gifts seek to please him (Eccl. 2:26a); for them, there is rest, "for he gives sleep to his beloved" (Ps. 127:2b). These essential teachings from Qohelet, Jesus, and the Psalms are bound up in the present peace (Col. 3:15) and future rest afforded by the gospel (Heb. 4:8–11).

# PREACHING AND TEACHING STRATEGIES

## Exegetical and Theological Synthesis
After proclaiming his thesis that all is vanity (1:14), Qohelet recounted his quest to find fulfillment and satisfaction in this life (2:1–26). Unfortunately, every pursuit left him empty. The pursuits of pleasure (2:1–11), wisdom (2:12–17), and work (2:18–26) did not lead to lasting significance or satisfaction. Yet amid the dissatisfaction, Qohelet gained glimpses of what truly mattered: God. "Who can have enjoyment without him [that is, God]?" Qohelet mused (2:25). The answer: no one.

All people, everywhere, are looking for meaning and significance for their lives. What Qohelet exposes is the utter futility of trying to find satisfaction in the things of this world. Only God satisfies. Yet the good news is that if people can find satisfaction in God, they can also truly enjoy life's simple pleasures because they are no longer importing into them cosmic significance. They become merely God's good gifts to be enjoyed, which is exactly what God intended them to be.

## Preaching Idea
Find your satisfaction in God alone, because everything else will disappoint you.

## Contemporary Connections

### What does it mean?
God created human beings in his image to love and worship him (Gen. 1:26–27). The priority of worship for human beings is expressed by Jesus in his retort to the devil: "Go Satan! For it is written, 'You shall worship the Lord your God, and serve him only'" (Matt. 4:10). Humanity finds its wholeness and completeness in relationship with God through worship. True satisfaction, then, only comes from putting God at the very center of your life. Unfortunately, when Adam and Eve fell into sin, they chose to pursue other things rather than God, namely, their own will for their life (Gen. 3:1–7). They chose to put something other than God at the very core of their lives. Because sin infects all people, everyone naturally attempts to build their lives on other things instead of the Lord. Yet all those other things will inevitably disappoint.

Qohelet exposes the absurdity of pursuing other things rather than God for satisfaction. Pleasure disappoints because after a weekend of partying, Monday always comes (2:1–11). All pleasures enjoyed by human beings eventually come to an end, and most end much earlier than we would like. Surprisingly, Qohelet makes the case that even wisdom will disappoint (2:12–17). We're all headed to the same place, so who cares if you've figured out the mysteries of the universe? Some may pursue more practical things like work. Yet work disappoints because we're never able to fully enjoy the fruits of our labor (2:18–26).

*Is it true?*
In a podcast episode entitled "Work as Identity, Burnout as Lifestyle," the host interviewed two writers about American workers' relationship with their work. Why are so many Millennials and Generation Z Americans "burning out" at work? One author, Anne Helen Peterson, surmised that capitalism is to blame. According to her theory, younger Americans must constantly work just to keep up with the work and economic demands on their lives. They have internalized a capitalistic mentality where they must work all the time. The other writer, Derek Thompson, had a far more compelling theory: he proposed that the decline in religion among Millennials could be one of the leading causes of burnout. Because religion provides a sense of transcendent meaning and significance for its adherents, it helps to keep work in its proper place and prevents it from becoming an all-consuming reality.

Thompson exposed a truth that Qohelet knew long ago: work does not, indeed cannot, satisfy the human soul. While the Bible declares work good—it was, in fact, instituted before the fall (Gen. 2:15; Keller 2016)—it was never meant to fill the human soul. Only God can do that. Every other thing mentioned in the passage, as well, is a good gift of God. Pleasure is good, including sexual pleasure found in a covenant of marriage as the Song of Songs so eloquently communicates. But it is not ultimate. Sexual pleasure in marriage is meant to point us to our union with Christ (Eph. 5:22–33). Wisdom is good, but wisdom by itself is not ultimate. It is meant to point us to the true wisdom of God (1 Cor. 1:24).

*Now what?*
How do we stop putting things that will not satisfy us at the very center of our lives ? Do we need to become ascetic Christians who shun all pleasure, activity, and fun? St. Augustine reflected on these kinds of questions in his work *City of God*. Augustine taught that the virtuous life is one of "rightly ordered love" (*City of God* XV.23). In other words, Augustine knew that a growing Christian life puts God number one on the list of life's priorities. Putting God first does not mean that he is the *only* thing on the list. Other things matter too (family, work, pleasure, etc.). But all these things must be subordinated to him.

Recalibrating our hearts to put God number one begins with worship. In worship, we experience a taste of God's goodness and beauty. In worship, we take the focus off ourselves, our concerns, and our lives to put our attention on God. When concentrating upon the Lord in worship, we obey the exhortation of the author of Hebrews when he tells us to be "fixing our eyes upon Jesus" (Heb. 12:2). To break the power of other "centers," we must worship.

Worshipping, then, entails a commitment to a local church. It is in the gathered assembly that God addresses his people through the word preached and through the word demonstrated in the sacraments of baptism and the Lord's Supper. The baseline commitment for all Christians, then, must be to attend gathered worship every week (Heb. 10:24). Of course, extenuating circumstances always come up in life such as illness, vacation, and other things. But for Christians, the general inclination of their hearts should be to gather weekly in worship.

Besides worship, another way to avoid overemphasizing other things in life is to embrace limits. Comfort and pleasure are narcotics, dulling us to the hard life of cross-carrying that Jesus demands (Luke 14:25–35). So, setting limits on how much TV we watch, how much time we spend online, how much online shopping we do, can be a way to keep these things in their proper place. Setting limits with our work is vital as well. God created the world to operate on a pattern of work and rest (Gen. 1:1–2:4). So, practicing the art of Sabbath can help keep work from consuming every aspect of our life.

## Creativity in Presentation

*The Good Place* (2016–2020) is a TV show that explores what happens to us after we die. The series builds to a climax when the main characters finally reach the "Good Place," the show's concept of heaven. Unfortunately, the characters are underwhelmed because the Good Place is merely a place of unending pleasure. They can do whatever they want to do, but what they find is that a life of unending pleasure is not satisfying. To combat their boredom, the characters are tasked with building a new system for how people can get to the Good Place. Their new system now focused on rewarding moral growth. Yet, after spending significant time together and seeing the moral growth of others, many of the characters are still left dissatisfied. Consequently, they build a doorway that leads to the cessation of existence. Eventually, most of the characters pass through the door. The subtle messaging is that even in the face of pursuing growth as a human being, life loses meaning. After all is said and done, after experiencing all that life has to offer, they walk through a door where they cease to exist.

Thankfully, a TV show is not the final word on finding meaning and happiness in life. What if there is an eternal reality that is always satisfying? What if there is a reality better than ceasing to exist? The Bible indicates that there is such a reality. Eternal satisfaction is found in the infinitely satisfying God. While Ecclesiastes exposes the bankruptcy of satisfaction in lesser things, the book of Psalms expresses the profound truth that "In Your [God's] presence is fullness of joy; In Your right hand there are pleasures forevermore" (Ps. 16:11 Amplified Bible).

The big idea for the passage is "Find your satisfaction in God alone, because everything else will disappoint you." Throughout the passage, Qohelet engages in a thought experiment, or better yet, a pursuit experiment to see if different things can bring him meaning, purpose, and satisfaction. But each utterly fails. An appropriate outline for the text would be to focus on how each of the things that Qohelet pursues disappoints:

- Pleasure will disappoint you (2:1–11)
- Wisdom will disappoint you (2:12–17)
- Work will disappoint you (2:18–23)
- But God will not disappoint (2:24–26)

## DISCUSSION QUESTIONS

1. Why is pleasure fleeting (2:1–11)?

2. Why does wisdom disappoint just like pleasure (2:12–17)?

3. Why is pursuing work as the center of one's life a futile endeavor (2:18–26)?

4. If all human pursuits ultimately do not satisfy, how can we wean our hearts off them?

5. What gives real satisfaction?

# Ecclesiastes 3:1–15

**EXEGETICAL IDEA**
Qohelet demonstrates that the temporality of human life and limitations of human knowledge stand in stark contrast with the timelessness and omnipotence of God. In response, he resolves that humans should live authentically within the limits set by the Sovereign Gift-Giver.

**THEOLOGICAL FOCUS**
Acknowledging human life's brevity and divinely ordained limitations is necessary for embracing a proper vision of God, one that drives humans into a state of authentic living before him.

**PREACHING IDEA**
Embrace God-given limits.

**PREACHING POINTERS**
Qohelet taught his students that all their efforts would not stand before the relentless march of time, exemplified in the steady rhythm of nature. Qohelet even declared that one of the greatest perceived human efforts—acquiring wisdom—was a grievous task. But such grief did not prevent Qohelet from testing other areas of life, such as pleasure and work, to see if they could provide fulfillment and satisfaction. He found that they could not. Qohelet eventually came to see that a path to fulfillment comes from putting God at the center of life and then enjoying the life he gives.

The world is a big, incomprehensible, and ultimately uncontrollable place. Humans respond by attempting to tame the world and bend it to their will. They strive to transcend the limits of the world, especially the constraints of time. But such efforts are foolish, according to Qohelet. Attempting to break barriers of the world will only lead to frustration and despair. Instead, people can live authentically before God by embracing the limits he has given.

# HUMAN TEMPORALITY AND THE TIMELESSNESS OF GOD (3:1–15)

## LITERARY STRUCTURE AND THEMES (3:1–15)

The passage is broken into two sections: the poem on human temporality (3:1–9), and an exposition on divine eternity (3:10–15), both of which include the notion of divine sovereignty. The first covers 3:1–9, with verses 1–8 comprising the best-known passage in all of Ecclesiastes and one of the best-known passages in all of Scripture (thanks especially to how frequently the poem is read in Christian funeral services). Ecclesiastes 3:1 and 9 serve as a prologue and epilogue to the poem proper (3:2–8). The implication of verse 1 is that humans are bound by time and by divine appointments outside of their control. Ecclesiastes 3:9 concludes with the logical question: so, what do humans actually "gain" (cf. 1:3) from their endeavors, given that patterns of life and boundaries of time are externally set and determined well outside of human control? The poem proper begins in 3:2, which sets the tone with its mention of death. This is what drove Qohelet to despair in 2:17, having acknowledged in 2:11 that all his toil was superficial in light of it. Death also hangs in the background of the question in 3:9.

Ecclesiastes 3:10–15 states explicitly what the poem implied: God has set boundaries of time and knowledge for human beings. Qohelet's treatise on God's sovereignty and eternality is interrupted by his prescription of what humans should do in light of all this (3:12–13). It closely echoes 2:24–26 where he also recommended authentic (that is, simple and grateful) living before a providential God. The final two verses (3:14–15) pick back up on his description of God's eternal nature and inalterable actions, noting that the divine modus of sovereign decree serves as an impetus for human worship: "God has acted so that people fear before him" (3:14). These divisions (vv. 1–9 and 10–15) are followed by Schoors as well (2013, 227–82), though most scholars will end the first unit at 3:8 (see Samet 2019, 580).

- *An Ode to Human Temporality (3:1–9)*
- *An Exposition on Divine Eternality (3:10–15)*

## EXPOSITION (3:1–15)

Nothing a human being does during their lives can change the course of creation in any lasting way. The times and seasons have already been set by forces outside of their control. These forces were alluded to in chapter 1 by way of pointing to the sun, the wind, and the streams, but their master is now shown to be God himself. Qohelet's prescription for humanity in light of all this (3:12–13) echoes what he taught in 2:24–26, but with the added nuance that we should recognize God as sovereign (3:14–15).

Ecclesiastes 3 reveals that the reason humans can do anything in this life is not because God has given them total independence and individual sovereignty, but because he has afforded them a measure of freedom within strictly set boundaries (see note on 3:1). He has subjected humanity to the rule of a superior force called "time" (3:1), which serves as a limiting agent for all human activity. The poem in 3:1–9 speaks abstractly about categories of time, which is explained later as the work of God 3:10–15. The topic of the entire unit (3:1–15) is a contrast between the temporality (and, hence, ineffectuality) of humanity, and the eternality and sovereignty of God in ordering and performing all things. The final set of verses serves as a comfort to Qohelet for the malaise left over from his disappointing revelation that humans have no control. God's sovereignty is a rescue from the delusion that human beings have the power to thwart his will or manipulate the universe to their gain.

### *An Ode to Human Temporality (3:1–9)*
Qohelet teaches that the various categories of human life, arranged here by times and seasons, are not set by humanity but come from elsewhere, the implied source being God.

**3:1**. "For everything there is an appointed season, and a time for every matter under heaven." Though labeled a "prologue," this should be read as the first line of the poem (see Linafelt and Dobbs-Allsopp 2010). This portrays all human endeavors as falling into chronologically arranged slots within a preset framework. It could be fairly surmised that the one who established this structure is God, but that is not stated until 3:10. The section as a whole (3:1–15) pits the futility of human endeavor against the immovable, sovereign will of God. In this way, 3:1–8 echoes themes from 1:3–11, where the ephemerality of all things human is set against the backdrop of nature's seemingly eternal rhythms. The tone of the poem reminds one of the Gezer Calendar, a stone inscription found at Tel Gezer that reads, "His two months are (olive) harvest, His two months are planting (grain), His two months are late planting; His month is hoeing up of flax, His month is harvest of barley, His month is harvest and *feasting*; His two months are vine-tending, His month is summer fruit" (Pritchard 2011, 287, emphasis original; *ANET*, 320). Times of the year are ordered by farming activities that are themselves ordered by natural phenomena created by God.

By asserting that there is an allotted time for every *kind* of thing, Qohelet does not in this poem go so far as to say that every minuscule event is predetermined by God, though that *may* be implied by 3:14–15 (see Samet 2019); instead, he only goes so far as to assert that what goes on in the world is much bigger than individual actions and can all be sorted into broader categories—categories that cycle perpetually from age to age (see note on 1:9 and see the history of Jewish interpretation on the determinism of Ecclesiastes in Rudman 2002).

> **The Extent of God's Sovereignty in Ecclesiastes**
>
> The book of Ecclesiastes is not a systematic theology, so readers ought not draw many hard-and-fast conclusions about the extent of God's sovereignty based on Qohelet's teachings alone. His presentation of the facts is a reflection of what he observes in the world, which is extremely limited (7:23). What he can say for certain is that God is sovereign, but he does not take things much farther than that. Ecclesiastes 3:1–15 reveals that God has arranged human life into fields of experience, setting chronological boundaries for these things. We might call this "sovereignty-lite" since it does not make assumptions about how (and the extent to which) God controls things at the level of human choice, but that humans are not in ultimate control. Sovereignty-lite is all that is needed for Qohelet to make his point. How exactly it all works is not a concern of his. He is only interested in pitting the powerlessness of humanity against the sovereign power of God, a contrast that is meant to affect holy disillusion in his pupils who, like most people, harbor delusions of control over their own lives and circumstances.

**3:2–8**. Ecclesiastes 3:1–8 is one of the most well-known poems in the HB. It is made up of fourteen consecutive pairs of events, twenty-eight events total with each event serving as the opposite of its paired event. The symmetry of its design is afforded by the repetition of "time" (עֵת) followed by an infinitive construct, which may be intended by the author as a way of simulating a rhythmic beating, like the clacking of hooves or the striking of tools. Anachronistically, we may associate the poem's pattern with a metronome or a ticking clock. Most of the events described in 3:2–8 are, in the broadest sense, self-explanatory in the most popular English translations, but difficulty arises with attempt to find specific applications for some of the actions Qohelet describes.

**3:2a**. Born/die: The pair may have started off this list since they are the most universally relatable experiences. Though everyone knows about war, not everyone has personal experience with it (3:8), but everyone can relate intimately to the phenomena of birth and death. Qohelet is simply referring to these categories as appointed by God (cf. Job 39:1–2), and is not necessarily going so far as to say that God has predetermined the exact second of one's birth and death, though one may infer that from 3:14–15.

**3:2b**. Plant/uproot: "To uproot" (לַעֲקוֹר) means to "tear out" as in "to remove" (see Zeph. 2:4 regarding the "uprooting" of Ekron), rather than "to harvest" (contra Heim 2019, 67). It is the act of clearing a field to prepare it for some other use, though Qohelet is likely just using agricultural imagery here as a metaphor for concluding one enterprise or stage in life in order to begin another (see M. Fox 2004, 21).

**3:3a**. Kill/heal: The verb "to kill" (לַהֲרוֹג) here is a general term that does not necessarily imply murder, though it can be used in that way (Gen. 4:8). Who/What does Qohelet have in mind? Humans killing humans? Humans killing animals? Animals killing either? And does the "healing" refer to one or both? The answer is "yes" to all. The line is intentionally ambiguous and simply refers to the oft-repeated phenomena of killing and healing.

**3:3b**. Tear down/build up: It is best to understand this generally, but a helpful illustration might be the act of breaching a city wall in order to invade it (2 Kings 14:13) and tear down its structures, only to follow that with resettlement and the building of new structures. Occupation levels in ancient Israelite settlement mounds are frequently stacked atop one another like a layer cake (good examples include Megiddo, Beth-Shean, and Lachish), serving as helpful illustrations of the phenomena described in this line.

**3:4a**. Weep/laugh: The "weeping" (לִבְכּוֹת) could be out of joy (Gen. 33:4) or sorrow (Gen. 23:2), but since this term is paralleled with "mourn" in the line that follows, the meaning of sorrow is preferred. The "laughing" is left unqualified, but it is probably not the kind decried by Qohelet as the maniacal cackling of fools (7:3). Rather, it is paralleled with the positive activity of "dancing" in the next line (see 2 Sam. 6:21; Ps. 114:4). Again, since Qohelet is not stopping to make value judgments on the activities listed in these verses, it is best to understand them as generally as possible.

**3:4b**. Mourn/dance: The "mourning" is reserved for funerary mourning in the HB, and the "dancing" for celebratory dancing like David before the ark of the covenant (1 Chron. 15:29) or the "skipping" of a young calf or goat, a symbol of life (Ps. 29:6; Isa. 13:21).

**3:5a**. Throw/gather stones: Many contexts may apply as an explanation for these activities (e.g., removing stones that were ritually impure as in Lev. 14:40, though with שׁלך). Several commentators have seen in this verse a sexual metaphor. For this interpretation, they rely partly on the "embrace" of the parallel line (3:5b), but the two halves of the verse do not need to be conceptually related (e.g., 3:7); furthermore, the identification of a sexual metaphor here seems "arbitrary" (M. Fox 2004, 21; see also Debel 2014) and ignores more likely meanings, like those conveyed in Isaiah 5:2 (also a poem), which describes the act of clearing a plot of stones in order to build a vineyard and then erecting a watch tower in the midst of it.

**3:5b**. Embrace/refrain: To "embrace" (לַחֲבוֹק) can simply mean to hug a friend or relative (Gen. 29:13; 33:4; 48:10), but it can also refer to sexual embrace, as in Song 2:6; 8:3, and Proverbs 5:20. The idea that one must "refrain" (לִרְחֹק) from sexual embrace for a period of time (during ceremonial uncleanness, Lev. 18:19, or during warfare, 2 Sam. 11:11), supports the possibility that the sexual context is what Qohelet has in mind.

**3:6a**. Seek/lose: What was lost? What is being sought? It is unspecified, but seeking and losing are universally relatable phenomena. Usually the verb "lose" (אבד) means "destroy," but in the *qal* stem it can mean "become lost," "go astray," or "be carried off," senses that might be borrowed by the *piel* here and confirmed by the parallel with "seek" (בקשׁ). *HALOT* prefers the meaning "give up as lost" for this verse (s.v. "אבד I" 3). Qohelet is not arguing that anyone would consciously schedule a time to lose their wallet and car keys, or the loosely equivalent seal, cord, and staff (see Gen. 38:25), but that this sort of thing inevitably happens. More serious matters may include the search for understanding, like Qohelet's quest to figure out everything under the sun (1:17; 7:23a; 8:16), but there is a time when one must accept some things as lost or unsearchable (1:18; 7:23b; 8:17).

**3:6b**. Keep/throw: One may keep an excess of something, like leftovers at a meal (Ruth 2:18; 1 Sam. 9:24, or leave it out until it stinks, Exod. 16:19–21). But there are times when it is best to throw things out, like worthless idols (Isa. 2:20; cf. Matt. 13:48).

**3:7a**. Tear/stitch: Many kinds of tearing and mending can be found in Scripture. As with the activities mentioned in 3:2a–6 above, Qohelet has left the meaning intentionally ambiguous for the sake of pointing to universally shared experiences. One well-known example of tearing in Scripture is the tearing of clothes as an expression of grief (e.g., 1 Kings 21:27). The rare verb "stitch" (תפר) only appears in a few places (Gen. 3:7; Job 16:15; Ezek. 13:18) but should also be understood generally for mending.

**3:7b**. Keep quiet/speak: There's a time to "shut up" (Judg. 18:19; 2 Kings 2:3) and a time to speak up (Isa. 62:1). The theme of guarding one's mouth as an expression of humility and prudence appears elsewhere in Ecclesiastes (5:1–7 [HB 4:17–5:6]; 6:12; 7:5–6; 8:2–4, 17; 9:3, 17–18; 10:3, 12–14, 20) as well as many other places in Proverbs, Job, and other HB texts (esp. wisdom texts, like Prov. 15:1–2; reflected also in the NT, esp. James 3:1–12), and in ANE texts, particularly in wisdom literature. In the Egyptian Satire on the Trades, a young man is warned to keep his mouth shut when in the presence of an elder: "When you enter a man's house, and he's busy with someone before you, Sit with your hand over your mouth. Do not ask him for anything, only do as he tells you" (Lichtheim 1973a, 190; for a fuller discussion on the biblical and ANE gesture of shielding one's mouth to symbolize silence, see Jones 2022, 66–67; and parallel occurrences in Judg. 18:19; Prov. 30:32; Job 21:5; 29:9; 40:4; Mic. 7:16). Wisdom often calls for its adherents to keep quiet or else risk getting a bloody nose (see Prov. 30:32–33; M. Fox 2009, 881–82; see sidebar "The Gesture of Silence in the Hebrew Bible" p. 115).

**3:8a**. Love/hate: In Isaiah 61:8, the Lord declares that he "loves justice" and "hates looting and iniquity," and his loyal people feel the same way (Pss. 45:7 [HB 8]; 97:10). Qohelet, however, is not so much presenting what is appropriate to feel as the fact that there are times when either feeling can occur (see note on 9:1). Love and hate can lead, respectively, to the outcomes listed in the next line.

**3:8b**. War/peace: The relationship to the previous line is apparent. The emotions of the first half of the verse (3:8a) precipitate the actions of the second half of the verse (3:8b) but are presented in reverse order. Again, specific applications are not in view here, but one does come to mind: on his deathbed, David recalled to Solomon how Joab, during a time of peace, had shed the blood of Abner and Amasa for things the two men had done during times of war (1 Kings 2:5). Joab had crossed the accepted boundary points between war and peace, and as such was perceived by David to be a loose cannon and a future threat during Solomon's reign.

Pritchard: "An inscription, probably a school exercise tablet, on limestone, written in verse" (see note on 3:1; *ANEP* §272). Gezer Calendar. Public domain.

**3:9**. The worker has no lasting "gain" from his toil. The adjective "lasting," though not appearing in the Hebrew text, is an important reminder that Qohelet does see "gain" (יִתְרוֹן) in some things (2:13; 5:8 [HB 7]; 7:12; 10:10?), but it is relative gain since death undermines any possibility for lasting gain (e.g., 1:4–11; 2:15, 18; esp. 9:5). In light of the poem (3:1–8) and Qohelet's eyewitness testimony in the next verse that God is the one who appoints all humanity's toil (3:10), verse 9 is meant to highlight the utter ineffectuality of all human activity by asking rhetorically, "What lasting or satisfactory profit is there in human endeavor?" (my paraphrase). The problem with viewing this as a genuine question is that it has already been asked rhetorically back in 1:3, answered by way of illustration in 1:4–11, answered in the negative in 2:11, asked and answered (though differently) in 2:12 and 2:15, and asked rhetorically again in 2:22. To this we could add every conclusion made so far by Qohelet that "everything is futile" (e.g., 1:2). Lasting gain in pleasure, wisdom, work, and other such human pursuits is unattainable (2:1–23).

Qohelet puts authentic living in a separate category from the pursuit of "gain" that he is confronting in his teachings. By "authentic living," I refer to Qohelet's repeated prescriptions to eat, drink, enjoy one's toil, please God, enjoy one's wife, live generously, and so on (2:24–26; 3:12–13, 22; 5:18–20 [HB 17–19]; 8:15; and 9:7–9). In none of these texts does the term "gain" (יִתְרוֹן) appear. That may be because the simple things of the authentic life are taken for granted by Qohelet's readers and not considered "gain," as in worthy life goals or sources of ultimate satisfaction.

### *An Exposition on Divine Eternity (3:10–15)*

Qohelet contrasts the eternity and power of God with the temporality and limitations of humanity, resolving that the best thing to do is to pursue the authentic life.

**3:10**. A new section begins here as Qohelet shifts to discuss God's role in all this. God is portrayed throughout as sovereign, but more specifically as the one who orders life (3:10), the one who creates all things (3:11a), the one who limits human understanding (3:11b), the one who provides life's simple blessings (3:13), the one who acts omnipotently for the sake of human worship (3:14), and the one who sustains all things (3:15; for clarity, see note on this verse). Ecclesiastes 3:10 echoes Qohelet's opening statement back in 1:13 where he indicates that the plight to which God has assigned humanity is a contemptible one in light of life's many futilities (1:14–15). This attitude from Qohelet is honest, but one that is confronted and corrected repeatedly by his resolution to embrace the joy of authentic living (see the many verses listed in the note on 3:9).

**3:11**. It is God who does the really permanent, meaningful things in this life. In contrast with the superficiality and ephemerality of human endeavor is God's sovereign determination of times and seasons, having made everything "fit beautifully in its appropriate time" (NET). God has even put "eternity" (הָעֹלָם) into the human heart. Scholars have long debated the meaning of "eternity" here and the whole expression in 3:11 (for a helpful breakdown of the various interpretations, see Gault 2008). The arguments of Seow fit best with the surrounding verses: "It means simply 'eternity'—that which transcends time. It refers to a sense of that which is timeless and, as such, stands in contrast to *'ittô* 'its time.' Qohelet's point is ironic: God who has made everything right in its time has also put a sense of timelessness in human hearts" (1997, 163). This sense of eternity implanted in the human heart may explain humanity's hunger to "figure out" God's world (3:11b; 7:23–24; 8:17), that "contemptible business" (1:13) that causes "vexation" and "sorrow" (1:18; see note on 1:13). Is this related to Blaise Pascal's notion of an abyss in the human soul that longs to be filled with what is infinite and immutable, later referred to as a God-shaped hole in the human heart (see Pascal 1958, 113)? The expression translated by the ESV "yet so" (מִבְּלִי אֲשֶׁר) in 3:11 appears only here in the HB, and *HALOT* renders it "without the possibility of" (s.v. "בְּלִי" mng. 4, 133). God has ordered everything but has not given human beings the ability to "find out" or "figure out" (מצא) God's works from beginning to end.

> **Divine Mystery in Ecclesiastes**
> The idea of divine mystery is not unique to Scripture. This concept in 3:11 and later in 11:5 has parallels to Egyptian wisdom where the scribe admits he does not know how the sun and moon come and go or where the elements of nature really come from other than to say it is all "the hidden work of the god, he makes it known on the earth daily" (Lichtheim 1973a, 210; see Qohelet's similar quandaries about the elements of nature in 1:4–7). Such admissions have not kept humanity from attempting to decode the mysteries of the universe, mysteries that have been concealed by God himself and that cannot be acquired through human wisdom (3:11; 8:17; see also 1 Cor. 1:21; 3:18–20). By contrast, God fully understands human thoughts and considers them mere folly (1 Cor. 3:20)—he knows the machinations of the wise, "that they are futile" (ὅτι εἰσὶν μάταιοι; note: the root form of Paul's adjective "futile" μάταιοι here is from the noun "futility" ματαιότης, which is the term used in the LXX of Ecclesiastes to translate the Hebrew noun "vanity" הֶבֶל). When human limitations are taken into account, pursuing wisdom and knowledge is a good thing (e.g., Eccl. 2:13; 10:2), but pursuing it as an *ultimate* thing is delusional like chasing the wind (2:15–17) because it does not account for the limitations God has set on humanity (e.g., ignorance, but most importantly death).

**3:12–13**. People ought to enjoy life and "do good" as long as they are alive. If this is merely a *carpe diem* statement, then "to do good" (וְלַעֲשׂוֹת טוֹב) would mean "have fun" or "live it up!" But here Qohelet's recommendation is to engage in right moral behavior before God, corresponding to "pleasing" God back in 2:26. Similarly, the prescription to eat, drink, toil, and enjoy in 3:13 corresponds to the same activities back in 2:24, just as the nod to God's providence in 3:13 corresponds to the same in 2:25. To "do good" as a reference to pleasing God is an ancient, covenantal command: "when you do what is good and right in the eyes of the LORD your God" (Deut. 12:28).

**3:14**. There is a time for everything under heaven (3:1), but God's actions, by contrast, are timeless. God's determinations and appointments on the earth are immutable. This notion is communicated elsewhere in Scripture by reference to the immovable "word of God," which "stands forever" as contrasted with common flora, which quickly succumbs to death (Isa. 40:8). God's edicts are "irrevocable" (דִּי־לָא תֶעְדֵּא), like those of a mighty emperor (Dan. 6:12 [HB 13]), and also eternal, outliving any king (Ps. 33:11). You cannot add or take away from whatever God has done or appointed, and this principle exists so that people will "fear" (meaning "revere") him. The suggestion by some that Qohelet's admonitions to fear God, given throughout Ecclesiastes, are merely pragmatic (as in "do it or die!") and do not intend the sense of reverence and honor implied by this term elsewhere (most notably, Prov. 1:7) is unfounded (see Whybray's defense of "fear" as "revere" and rejection of the definition "be horrified/terrified" [1989, 75]). The construction "so they'll fear *before* him" (שֶׁיִּרְאוּ מִלְּפָנָיו) may warrant a more nuanced understanding of what Qohelet means to revere God, but it does not warrant an *opposite* understanding of what it means to fear God throughout Scripture, such as "be horrified of." In light of New Testament doctrine, Davis notes that when believers see the magisterial works of the Creator, they "stand still before God in awe (v. 14) and trust, resting on the gospel promise that nothing of substance perishes eternally, nothing of value is forgotten by the God who seeks and saves the lost" (Davis 2000, 185; see note on 8:13 and sidebar "The Fear of God in Ecclesiastes" p. 117).

**3:15**. There is nothing new under the sun because God himself sustains/perpetuates the world's repetitive processes. The chapter so far (3:1–15) has reflected the principles of the informal introduction (1:3–11) of the book, where Qohelet's overarching ideas about human endeavor are conveyed—namely, that the immovable forces of creation (implied in which is God's creative and sustaining power) are both a foil and a contrast to the fickle, ephemeral, and superficial endeavors of humanity. In chapter 1, it was the circuitous routes of the sun, wind, and streams that illustrated the point that "What has been is what will be" (1:9). Here in 3:14–15, God is specifically named as the one who sovereignly operates all these forces and, by implication, all things that happen. Qohelet never specifies what exactly God controls, but that his control is comprehensive. Ecclesiastes 3:15 restates 1:9 but adds the explanation that it is actually God who is doing all "that is." The line reads, "And God seeks what has been pursued," which is an idiomatic way of stating that God is seeking to repeat what has already been done before. In other words, God is keeping the engine of the universe going, sustaining its processes, and appointing its "times" (3:1–8). The NET translates the line with greater clarity than many other versions: "God will seek to do again what has occurred in the past." The natural processes of the earth are not simply the unwinding of a clock set by an abstract deistic force but the active work of God's sovereign agency in all things: "God has not just made the world the way it is (and will be) then left it to run, but continues working to ensure its future without help or interference from others" (Weeks 2020, 508).

> **Responding to Divine Omnipotence and Human Powerlessness**
>
> Some may prefer to see Qohelet in 3:9–15 as deeply disdainful, throwing his hands in the air and resolving that we should just put on our blinders to enjoy life in blissful ignorance since that is the only option God has given us in this miserable existence. On the contrary, the sense in 3:12–13 is that there is something positive to take away from the acknowledgment that human endeavor is ephemeral and God's determinations eternal: that humans should not fall for the delusion that they can control outcomes or change God's design; rather, they should find enjoyment in the simple things as already noted in 2:24–26. Qohelet wants them "to enjoy" life "and to do good." If Qohelet's conclusions in 2:24–26 and here in 3:12–13 were coming from a heart that is unflinchingly bitter, it seems unlikely he would advise humans to please God, do good, and receive the simple pleasures of life as "God's gift." He often starts out negative in his thinking, but that leads him to these positive resolutions. Humans are powerless next to God's ordained design, so they should aspire to "see good" (וְרָאָה טוֹב), meaning "take pleasure" (ESV), "find enjoyment" (NET) in, or "enjoy" (CSB) all their work. The simple enjoyment of simple things here prescribed by Qohelet is not the same as when he tested himself to "see good," meaning to "embrace pleasure" back in 2:1. Though the Hebrew construction is the same, the context of 2:1–11 was one of diving headfirst into hedonism in hopes of finding lasting gain (2:11). Here the associated activities are eating, drinking, and toiling joyfully, but there is no suggestion that a person should pursue ultimate satisfaction in these things the way Qohelet sought it and could not find it in chapter 2.

## THEOLOGICAL FOCUS

In Ecclesiastes 3:1–15, the transience and limitations of humanity (3:1–9) are contrasted with the eternality of God and the permanence of his deeds and decrees (3:10–15). Accordingly, humans are only under the illusion that they understand their world and can control its outcomes. The ode to time in 3:1–9 has the effect of reducing the reader to a grain of sand blown haphazardly across the surface of the beach with no will of its own. It is not that humans do not have a will, but that their will is irreducibly insignificant when compared to the all-encompassing sovereignty of God expressed through time. The poem conveys that "embedded into the created order itself is a kind of equilibrating tendency, a drive toward 'zero'" in which "every 'doing' gets 'undone'" (Peterson 2022, 460, 469). Furthermore, "Humanity cannot create, subtract, stop, or deviate from time. There is no way to stop the clock—no universal referee who can blow a whistle or call a timeout"; rather, all people are subject to God's *divine economy* of time" (Wood 2022, 90, emphasis original). Hence, the planting, uprooting, killing, healing, breaking, building, weeping, laughing, mourning, dancing, scattering, gathering, embracing, abstaining, seeking, losing, keeping, discarding, tearing, sewing, silencing, speaking, loving, hating, warring, and peacemaking of human beings are all preordained strata into which God sorts earthly activity. Individual actions are hence exposed for their superficiality on the incomprehensible timeline of eternity. Given all this, and what was stated back in 1:11 ("There is no remembrance of former things"), what does any human activity amount to?

Qohelet's rhetoric is effective, driving readers to ask, "So what's the point of living, then?" (my paraphrase of 3:9). While the actions of humans are insignificant when contrasted with the march of time, the appointments of God are called "beautiful" (3:11). Humans are imbued with this beauty and they hunger for more of it, but God has limited their ability to have or know it all. By raising these issues, Qohelet has effectively primed his students for the kind of holy disillusion that leaves them looking for anything redeemable in life, at which point Qohelet swoops in with the only thing bearing real value—be happy and do good (3:12)! Added to this in 3:13 is the acknowledgment that all the simple pleasures of life are gifts from God, which calls for both authentic and grateful living. Admitting human temporality (3:1–9) and ignorance (3:11) enables people to contrast their mortal smallness with the unreachable, transcendent power of God in the universe, a perspective that leads to reverence (3:14). Only his actions last, making him the highest possible being and, hence, the only one worthy of worship. He will continue to do the things he has done before well into the future (3:15) and nothing can stop him.

Small children look up to older siblings, cousins, and adults with awe because they are stronger, more knowledgeable, and more capable in every way. They can drive, go where they want, and do what they want. To kids, "grownups" do the real things, the things that seem to matter in life. Children, on the other hand, can only pretend to do these things in their Fisher-Price equivalents. But from Qohelet's perspective, and from a divine perspective, adults and kids have a lot in common. Many of the so-called real things adults think they are doing are actually futile in light of the infinitely surpassing power of a timeless God (see the exceptions in 3:12–13).

## PREACHING AND TEACHING STRATEGIES

### Exegetical and Theological Synthesis

After testing various areas of life to see if they could provide fulfillment, Qohelet reflected on the nature of time and God-given limits (3:1–15). Qohelet understood that God had made an "appointed time" for all things (3:1). With a poem of opposing pairs ("a time to give birth and a time to die"), Qohelet provoked his students and readers to discern what season of life they would have found themselves in (3:1–8). Since time marches on, his readers could have rightly questioned, "Does anything I do matter?" (3:9). Yes, Qohelet answered. But the answer only makes sense because God is sovereign and human beings are not (3:10–15).

In the face of a large, incomprehensible world, people could be tempted to despair. Certainly, reading Ecclesiastes could lead them to question the meaning of their own lives! However, Qohelet is not on a quest to cultivate despair in his readers, but humility. Human hubris led Adam to transcend the limit God had placed in the garden. And human hubris leads people in the present time to grasp for more control over their lives than is warranted. God is the One who is ultimately in control of all times, even time. So, the humble human response to the world's inscrutability is to trust God and embrace the limits he gives.

### Preaching Idea
Embrace God-given limits.

### Contemporary Connections

*What does it mean?*
Qohelet declares that there are "appointed times" for things (3:1). Life has seasons. The wise person then discerns what season of life they are in and what the appropriate ways to live in that season are. Some seasons of life call for an upheaval: a time to "uproot," "tear down," "give up as lost," "throw away," and "tear apart" (3:2–7). These seasons may involve cutting back on activities in life, moving to a new place, or establishing painful but necessary boundaries in a relationship. Some seasons call for a time to "plant," "heal," "embrace," "search," "keep," and "sew together" (3:2–7). These times of life are moments when we set down roots, invest deeply in our most important relationships, and persevere in our careers.

During any season of life, the wise person must recognize that God is sovereign over all things (3:10–15). Even though we have a "divine relentlessness" in our hearts, there is no way for us to fully figure life out (3:11). Therefore, we should live according to God's commandments: "do good in one's lifetime" (3:12). People should also enjoy the simple pleasures of life, such as good food and drink, without striving to peer into things only God knows (3:13). God's works, not ours, will remain forever (3:14–15). Therefore, rather than being filled with anxiety, always being stymied from accomplishing some grand plans, we can rest easy, knowing that God is in control, and he is guiding all things.

*Is it true?*
Oliver Burkeman, in his book *Four Thousand Weeks* (2022), advocates for a dose of "cosmic insignificance therapy" to recalibrate our expectations in life. Too often, Burkeman argues, we go around living as if we are the center of the universe. We believe that we need to "make a dent in the universe" (to quote iPhone creator Steve Jobs). Such lofty aspirations can lead people to accomplish great things. Yet sometimes we will fail. And the price of failure is a crushing sense of worthlessness. Burkeman points out that we can overcome our feelings of failure by recognizing that we are really not that significant. We are actually quite "small," given the immensity of the universe and the longevity of time. Recognizing how small we are can be quite empowering, because it lowers the stakes of what we are trying to do. Instead of anxiously toiling away, we can live with a certain ambivalence. In this regard, Burkeman channels his inner Qohelet.

While Burkeman gets quite a lot right, he's missing one important thing from his therapeutic prescription: God. If there is no God, does it really matter whether we're shouting or calmly reciting poetry into the void? The result is the same: we cease to exist, and nothing *truly* matters at that point. The problem is that if nothing matters *then*, does life even matter *now*? While Christians can embrace certain aspects of Burkeman's theory, they acknowledge that there is a sovereign God who is in control over the universe. Therefore, we can relax, knowing that he sits firmly on his throne. Real *holy* ambivalence comes from not just realizing how small we are but from recognizing how big God is.

*Now what?*
Wise people discern what season of life they are in. The text speaks of "appointed times" or seasons. Life comes to us in seasons. Are you in a planting, building up, and keeping time? Or are you in an uprooting, tearing-down, and throwing-away time? Misdiagnosing your season could have disastrous effects in your life. The temptation when confronted with the limits of a particular season of life is to try to pick what season you are in. But the text does not allow us any wiggle room here. We do not pick these seasons; they come to us. The rhythmic flow of the text—a time for this and a time for that—sucks us into its flow, forcing us to recognize that we are presented with these seasons. Instead of resisting the seasons of life, we must embrace them and seek to live in a way that is consistent with them.

Wise people also know the flow of time. The first line of the poem speaks of a "time to give birth and a time to die" (3:2). All people have a birthday and a death day. We do not know when our time to die will come, but time flows in only one direction. Physicist Stephen Hawking writes, "Time flows like a river and it seems as if each of us is carried relentlessly along by time's current."[1] How much time do you have left? There's no way to know. Thus, each person should pray along with Moses, "Teach us to number our days, that we may present to you a heart of wisdom" (Ps. 90:12).

Wise people acknowledge God's sovereignty over all things. God has instilled in all of

---

[1] https://www.dailymail.co.uk/home/moslive/article-1269288/STEPHEN-HAWKING-How-build-time-machine.html.

us a longing for eternity (3:11). The "divine restlessness" we might feel is not license to attempt to transcend the barrier of time. Instead, the longing for eternity should move us to long for God because eternity is where God is. God sits "above" the world and rules over it (Isa. 40:22). Acknowledging his sovereignty, then, is a path to contentment and peace because we refuse to accomplish more than what he has set out for us. We instead trust in his timing and plans.

*Creativity in Presentation*
Most of us would probably like to stop time or travel back in time at some point in our lives. We may wish to stop time to soak up an experience with family or friends, hoping it could last forever. Or we may look back over our lives with regret, wishing we could go back and make things right. The desire to make things right is captured powerfully in the movie *Avengers: Infinity War*. In the movie, the Avengers—a team of superheroes made up of the likes of Iron Man, Captain America, and Thor—suffer a terrible defeat at the hands of the archvillain, Thanos. Thanos had been able to wipe out half of the living things in the universe. The Avengers who were left struggled to cope with losing and loss. All seemed hopeless until Tony Stark (Iron Man) figured out time travel. Because of his discovery, the remaining heroes could travel back in time and undo the damage Thanos had done.

But this life is not like the movies. Time travel is not real and so we do not have the opportunity to go back and undo the mistakes we have made or the calamities we have suffered. Because we only have one mortal life, we must live wisely. We should aim to live in such a way that we will minimize our regrets. And yet, all of us will fumble our way through life at times, even wasting precious moments of time that we could be savoring. But the hope that Christians have is that we serve a God who is timeless. He created time and stands above it. He is not subject to it but the one who exists "from everlasting to everlasting" (Ps. 90:2). Therefore, we can trust in his good plan and that he is guiding our lives. The mistakes, sins, and tribulations of this life are not the last word.

The big idea for this section is "Embrace God-given Limits." A key question that can be asked of the big idea is "what." What kinds of limits do we need to embrace in life?
- Embrace the reality of time (3:1)
- Embrace the seasons of life (3:2–8)
- Embrace God's ordering of life (3:9–15)

## DISCUSSION QUESTIONS

1. Why is it important to recognize the various "seasons" of life (3:1)?

2. Which pairs in the poem resonate with you the most (3:2–8)?

3. What has God set in the human heart (3:11)? What does this mean?

4. How should people live in the face of marching time and a sovereign God (3:12–15)?

5. How can you use your time more wisely this week?

6. How does reflecting on God's sovereignty help us overcome anxiety?

# Ecclesiastes 3:16–5:7 (HB 6)

**EXEGETICAL IDEA**
Qohelet, in mournful reflection over the many injustices and inequities of the world, resolves that people should take joy in their work while rightly revering God.

**THEOLOGICAL FOCUS**
Since the human experience is one full of inexplicable injustices and unfairness, the only worthwhile path for people to take is to do their work joyfully and revere God rightly.

**PREACHING IDEA**
Stop pretending and face reality: God is sovereign over a broken world.

**PREACHING POINTERS**
Qohelet observed all manner of injustice and tragedy in the world. He had seen instances where the wicked triumphed over the righteous. Although he hoped for God's future judgment, he also recognized the tragedy of the human condition: People die just like animals. Wherever he looked, he saw the strong taking advantage of the weak. He saw the misery that rivalry and discontentment produced. In a world filled with inequity, he proclaimed a path of authentic living before God. He discouraged rashness of speech and attempts at bargaining with God. Instead of advocating for a new way of living, he reached into the past and emphasized a common theme in the Hebrew Scriptures: the fear of the Lord.

Qohelet's realistic description of the state of the world, as well as his admonition to live authentically before the Lord, is a necessary splash of cold water on the face of modern life where curation is the norm. Digital technologies and the internet have given people the ability to screen out the parts of life they would rather ignore. Moreover, these technologies provide a powerful way to present a certain image of oneself, an image of one's own making. But God is not fooled. He sees the intent and motives of our hearts.

# THE FEAR OF GOD AND THE EVIL OF INEQUITY
## (3:16–5:7 [HB 6])

### LITERARY STRUCTURE AND THEMES (3:16–5:7 [HB 6])

Scholars break these verses into various sections and subsections based on what they perceive to be grammatical or topical transitions, but no set of suggestions is free of difficulty, and there are several disagreements. This is partly due to Qohelet's rapid topic-switching and terse, proverbial content, which is also a dominant feature of chapter 10. It is sometimes possible to group such verses together based on a common theme, but not perfectly. Qohelet's overall focus on inequity is discernible in 3:16–4:16, but he also covers a number of subtopics and quickly moves from one to the next before getting to his treatise on how to properly revere God in 5:1–7 (HB 4:17–5:6).

The first small unit (3:16–22) is generally agreed upon, but Qohelet's discussion of injustice and death really extends down to 4:3. From 4:4 to 4:12, he shares a collection of thoughts on labor and how people sometimes work with or against one another. The following section (4:13–16) features his observations on royal succession and how no king's legacy will last long before he is utterly forgotten. The following section addresses how one ought to rightly fear God (5:1–7 [HB 4:17–5:6]), but it feels like an unnatural shift given the underlying theme of inequity running from 3:16 to 6:9. The hard transition into 5:1 (HB 4:17) is also the first time in the book of Ecclesiastes that the second person "you" appears. Up to this point, Qohelet's observations have all been in first or third person. Here, however, he makes a direct address to the reader, similar to how he admonishes the reader in various places throughout 6:10–12:8, which we have labeled "The Admonitions of Qohelet" (see Introduction). Though the sudden introduction of "you" in 5:1 (HB 4:17) feels unusual, switching from third to second person abruptly is a recurring feature of the book of Proverbs (e.g., Provrbs 20, esp. vv. 13, 19, 22), and Qohelet's sudden shift to the topic of rightly fearing God is an appropriate reminder at the midway point of a longer discussion on injustice and inequity in the world (3:16–6:9).

- *Inequity and Death (3:16–4:3)*
- *Inequity and Labor (4:4–12)*
- *Inequity and Legacy (4:13–16)*
- *Rightly Revering God (5:1–7 [HB 4:17–5:6])*

### EXPOSITION (3:16–5:7 [HB 6])

Of the many themes addressed by Qohelet throughout the book, inequity is perhaps the largest. The term "inequity" is our way of coupling Qohelet's observations on unfairness (where no human, it seems, is to blame) together with his observations on injustice (where humans are at the center of blame). In his mind, unfair and unjust things are topsy-turvy, or the opposite of what one expects, given the teachings of the sages, most notably the retribution principle in Proverbs.

Concerning unfairness in life, Qohelet's observations extend beyond broken expectations to a place of felt loss, as if there is something improper about the fact that humans die just like animals (3:18–22) or that all kings are eventually forgotten (4:16). But who can be blamed for these seemingly unfair things since such matters extend beyond human control? Qohelet would suggest that God is the one sovereignly behind all of it (1:13; 2:25–26; 3:10, 14–15; 6:2, 10; 7:13–14; 8:17). But Qohelet is loyal to God, as evinced by his insistence upon fearing him, pleasing him, and living wisely. So, he never claims that God has done something wrong; rather, he simply resolves that (1) God is sovereign (see passages listed above) and (2) humanity is incurably ignorant concerning such inexplicable matters (3:11, 22; 6:11–12; 7:23; 8:16–17, and every instance where "vanity" could be read "incomprehensible"). The latter truth serves as a cause for human sorrow since it means we do not get fully satisfying answers to our questions. In his sovereign appointments, God has committed no injustice, but that does not change the fact that humans *feel* some sense of inequity regarding how things happen. This sense of loss is real, and while God sovereignly orders this broken world, the ultimate source of its brokenness is not in God himself, who made all things "beautiful" (3:11) and humans "upright" (7:29a); rather, its brokenness is the result human rebellion: "This is the only thing I've figured out: that God made humans upright, but they have sought out many schemes" (7:29).

The book of Proverbs has much to say about the justice of God, his judgment against the wicked, and how he exalts the righteous. Qohelet does not reject the sages (3:17; 8:12–13, etc.) but perhaps views their observations as generalities, noting that the world also features case after case of inexplicable evil. He never suggests that God does not care about humanity, nor that God perpetuates this evil; nor does he question or accuse God the way Job does in his grief (e.g., Job 10:3). Instead, he simply groans over the backward way in which circumstances flesh themselves out. How can we adequately explain why the wicked so often prevail in this life? What answer can we give to the fact that human beings die just like cattle and that no one can speak with certainty about what happens after death (from Qohelet's limited theological perspective)? What good answer is there for the fact that one's legacy, accomplishments, and wealth can all be destroyed in an instant, never mind the fact that all of it will be eventually forgotten? Qohelet has no answer for these questions. The questions themselves are a form of answer as he grabs his pupils by their collars and stares unflinchingly into their eyes while shouting, "The world is malignant with evil" (see 5:13 [HB 12]; רָעָה חוֹלָה). He hopes to disabuse them of the naive, "vain" outlook on life that is so typical of youth, one that puts hope in hedonism, intellect, materialism, or even one's own sense of what *should* happen. But humans cannot control God or his world. Real life is brutal and untamable, so Qohelet's pupils should stay focused on the joy of their own God-appointed work (3:22; see also 3:13, where one's "toil" is shown to be a gift from God).

Halfway through his long tirade on the injustices and unfairness of life (which really extends to 6:9, though we have broken up this larger passage for the sake of smaller homiletical units), Qohelet shifts topics to observe a crucial principle. Lest his pupils think that irreverence, anarchy, and reckless living are the appropriate response to life's seemingly random inequities, he reminds them that there is one eternal entity who can guarantee ultimate justice on earth, and that entity is God. Accordingly, they should recognize that while the world is disorderly, God is quite orderly. When you enter his presence, he will not tolerate the insincere foolishness or recklessness of the world. It is true that in life, "there is vanity; but God is the one you must fear" (5:7 [HB 6]).

### *Inequity and Death (3:16–4:3)*

Qohelet grieves that injustice so often prevails over the righteous and oppressed, and that human and animal fate seem indistinguishable; hence, he resolves that the only way forward is to have a heart of joy.

**3:16**. Where justice should prevail, injustice thrives. Qohelet begins his series of complaints about injustice by pointing to the fact that he saw wickedness where justice should have been, and vice versa. One way this is often manifested is in "the judicial acquittal of the guilty in exchange for bribes" (M. Fox 2004, 25). He will have more to say about this later in 5:8–9 (HB 7–8), but for now, 3:16 serves as a thesis statement for everything that is to follow as Qohelet pairs the topic of inequity with death (3:16–4:3), labor (4:4–12), legacy (4:13–16), and wealth (5:8 [HB 7]–6:9). In Psalm 94, the psalmist asserts that corrupt judges and rulers who write laws in order to oppress the righteous are no match for the holiness of God (Ps. 94:19–20; many similar passages decry the evils of bribery, corruption, and injustice toward others, e.g., Exod. 13:8; 18:21; Lev. 19:15; Deut. 10:17; 16:19; 27:25; 1 Sam. 8:3; 12:3; 2 Chron. 19:17; Job 6:22; Pss. 15:5; 26:10; Prov. 13:23; 15:27; 16:11; 17:23; 20:23; 21:14; Eccl. 7:7; Isa. 1:23; 5:23; 33:15; Ezek. 9:9–10; 22:12; Amos 2:6; 5:12; Mic. 3:11; 7:3).

**3:17.** In his own appointed time, God will bring justice to the righteous and the wicked (Eccl. 3:17). In the midst of his disappointment over the findings of his investigation, Qohelet continues to place his hope in the justice and sovereignty of God. Here we get a glimpse into Qohelet's stubborn faith, a faith that persists despite the realities of the world that threaten to contradict it. He is confident that God will one day judge the righteous and the wicked, but he never asserts when God will do this or how it will even be possible after a person dies; remember that Qohelet does not assume the existence of an afterlife. He also does not confidently deny it like the later Sadducees. He simply does not know fully about the theological realities of life after death. All he knows about is "Sheol" (9:10), the grave, and the fact that humans are incapable of feeling or knowing or doing anything after they die (9:5–6). Accordingly, God's judgment of human beings must happen now, under the sun, while people are still alive. This faith, however, is confronted by the observation that humans seem to die just like animals (3:18–20), without a perfect resolution to their lives, which would include the score-settling justice of God (8:10–11). Even so, Qohelet's faith remains intact as he provides a pilot light of hope for an afterlife (3:21) and a bullish commitment to God's eventual justice in all matters (see Introduction and notes on 3:20–21; 8:12–13; 9:3, 5–6; 11:9; 12:7, 13, and sidebar "Life After Death in Ecclesiastes" p. 108).

**3:18.** God is "testing" human beings in order to see "that they themselves are beasts" (שְׁהֶם־בְּהֵמָה הֵמָּה לָהֶם). This last clause creates the sounds *shehem beheymah heymah lahem* (this is not a technical transliteration, just a simplified representation of the Hebrew sounds). The collection of "h" and "m" sounds produce alliteration, and the recurring "e" sound makes for assonance. Qohelet may have been quoting a common expression in some circles, or he could be simply waxing poetic. The phonetic beauty of this line is contrasted by the grimness of what it is conveying (see notes on 9:5–6; 7:1–2; and 10:8–11).

The Hebrew of 3:18 is very difficult, and it is not entirely clear what is meant by the notion that God is "testing" human beings. In light of Qohelet's statement on judgment here in 3:17 and elsewhere, though, perhaps the idea is that God has created life in such a way that humans may wonder whether they are anything more than animals. After all, there is no justice among animals, which is often true for humans as well (3:16; from a human perspective); also, humans and animals are born and die the same way (3:20). So, are humans really any different than animals? Qohelet himself is not asserting that he believes humans and animals are actually the same, but that visual evidence leads humans to that conclusion (Weeks 2020, 544). Qohelet's repeated calls for humans to fear God and exercise wisdom demonstrate that he, like Elihu, actually does see the difference (Job 35:11). The test then would be for everyone to see the difference between animals and humans. Failure to maintain that there is a difference could lead to full-blown anarchy and evil since the wicked believe that "the LORD does not see" their many injustices against humanity (Ps. 94:7; Ezek. 8:12; 9:9). The threat of God's watchful eye is just an urban legend, they think, for "there is no God" (Ps. 14:1). For example, David's lackadaisical attitude about Uriah's death reveals a heart that had devalued human life to the level of an animal, saying, "For as the sword devours one, so it devours another" (2 Sam. 11:25). It is as if David is quipping, "Oh well, death happens."

**3:19**. Humans will take note of the fact that both they and animals share the same fate, so what lasting advantage do humans have over animals? Death is the great equalizer. It is the "ultimate *hebel* which embraces all the other manifestations of *hebel* and expresses life's overarching irrationality" (Burkes 1999, 48). As the psalmist notes, man is "like the beasts that perish" (Ps. 49:12 [HB 13]). They have the same breath. Humans, therefore, have no "advantage" over animals in the arena of death. Jewish tradition reinterpreted these verses to make it the wicked man who dies like a beast, not just people in general, since neither animals nor evil people are able to enter into "the World to Come" (Burkes 1999, 64 n. 118, citing Midrash Rabbah Ecclesiastes). But Qohelet has not singled out the wicked; rather, he points out that *all* humans suffer the same fate as animals. This recognition leads to the expected refrain at the end of 3:19: "For everything is incomprehensible."

**3:20–21**. After life, Qohelet explains, "all go to one place . . . the dust" (Gen. 3:19; Job 34:14–15; Eccl. 12:7; see also 5:15–16 [HB 14–15] and sidebar "Life After Death in Ecclesiastes" p. 108). There is a raw honesty to Qohelet's question in 3:21. He is not being disingenuous; rather, he is trying to hold reality together with hope. It is a matter of grief for him that humans die like animals, so the very question of an afterlife is an expression of hope. However, the lack of proof has left Qohelet somewhere in the middle, hoping for something better, even asserting that God will enact judgment against evil somehow (3:17; 8:12–13). In 8:12–13, he states confidently that he knows God will bring the wicked and the righteous their just deserts, but he appears to be lost on how exactly that will happen since he has witnessed more than one funeral for wicked people who never got what was coming to them during their life (8:10). The sages of Israel were well aware that the wicked at times "go down to Sheol in peace," so they offer up the possibility that God will maintain justice by judging the children of the wicked, but Job appears unconvinced by this (Job 21:13–21). No complete answer is given in the Hebrew Scriptures for how the wicked get their just deserts after death, but the lack of an answer is used as an occasion for faith in both Qohelet and in Job, despite all the unchecked wickedness they see on the earth (recall that Job never totally abandons the fundamentals of the retribution principle—e.g., ch. 27—but perhaps he has learned that God does not *always* operate in this way).

Qohelet hopes there is a distinction between man and beast, and he hopes for God's justice, perhaps believing that "the only solution which would be possible would have to come after death," though he cannot confirm the reality of life hereafter (Burkes 1999, 80; Ogden 1987, 63).

### Life After Death in Ecclesiastes
Qohelet could not know for certain whether or how the human life force, represented by "breath" but often translated as "spirit," ascends to God (3:21; 12:7). He is not speaking from the theological perspective of the Pharisees, who had a more well-formed idea of the afterlife. He has also not been given the insight of new covenant revelation such that he could speak with

clarity about future resurrection like the apostle Paul (1 Cor. 15). A survey of the topic of the afterlife throughout the HB reveals a startling lack of information. The dominant understanding expressed by authors is that there is only Sheol, the place of the grave from which no one can return nor praise the Lord (Isa. 38:18).

Qohelet's theology of death is consistent with Psalm 88:8–12 (HB 9–13), where the psalmist depicts Sheol as a place from which no one returns, where God's steadfast love and faithfulness are not declared, and where his wonders are not worked—a land of utter forgetfulness. There are places in the HB that may represent glimpses into the afterlife, or at least a hope for it (e.g., Job 19:25–27; Ps. 49:15 [HB 16]; Isa. 26:19–21; Dan. 12:2–3), but these texts are debated and do not present a fully fledged understanding of the afterlife. The concept of life after death was known to the Israelites due to the influence of Egyptian, Mesopotamian, and Canaanite religions, but it does not show up as overtly in Scripture, except perhaps in a few places mentioned above (many other passages that refer to salvation from Sheol, especially in the Psalms, are contextually about protection from death, not resurrection *after* death). Of course, later New Testament authors saw, by the Spirit's inspiration, the fuller application of certain references to Sheol in light of Christ (e.g., the use of Ps. 16:10 in Acts 2:27). The forbidden practices of ancestor worship and mediumship were predicated on the popular idea that there is something going on beyond death, but perhaps not much. The spirit of Samuel claimed that he was undisturbed down there before being summoned, which may imply he was doing nothing (1 Sam. 28:15).

In any case, Qohelet is not comfortable making a confident assertion. It is notable, however, that he does not deny the possibility of an afterlife but that humans (from his vantage point in salvation history) cannot speak confidently about it.

Such things must be left to God who gave life in the first place and sovereignly controls all things (see note on Eccl. 3:14–15 concerning the afterlife in the HB; see also Introduction and notes on 3:17, 20–21; 8:12–13; 9:3, 5–6; 11:9; 12:7; and 12:13).

**3:22.** Since these issues cannot be resolved perfectly from Qohelet's perspective, the best thing to do is to take joy in one's work, a callback to 2:24–26 and 3:12–13 where he also prescribed authentic living in the face of human futility, transience, and life's unresolvable mysteries.

One's work is "his portion" (חֶלְקוֹ). He had used the term back in 2:10 to describe the momentary pleasure of enjoying one's possessions and accomplishments, stating that this fleeting feeling of enjoyment was his consolation prize for having indulged in pleasure. He then, of course, said that it was futile. The term is used again in 2:21 for the unfortunate task of having to leave all of one's portion to someone who did not earn it. Here, in 3:22, Qohelet prescribes that one should simply enjoy his work, receiving it as his "lot" in life (see also 5:18–19 [HB 17–18] and 9:6, 9 where the term is also used). The term appears one other time, but only in the conventional sense (11:2).

One should resolve to live simply and authentically because one's knowledge and power are only useful for the present—"For who can bring him to see what will be after him?" From Qohelet's perspective, death keeps us from seeing any future activities under the sun, so live more fully *now*.

### The God-Ordained Boundaries of Human Knowledge

Inquiring of the Lord concerning future outcomes is not universally condemned in the HB. However, raw faith is seen as superior. The young David had no assurances outside of his own faith in God that he would be able to defeat Goliath (1 Sam. 17). However, in several places, kings and armies sought knowledge of future outcomes

> through prayer by asking prophets (e.g., Judg. 18:5; Jer. 32:3), by engaging in approved practices that bear similarity to divination (e.g., casting Urim and Thummim, Gideon's fleece) or by partaking in forbidden divination (e.g., 1 Sam. 28; 2 Kings 21:1–9). God has created a barrier between divine knowledge and human knowledge (Gen. 2:17), and at least one outcome of that barrier is the need to trust in God by faith. Ironically, even when God does reveal a bit of his knowledge for human good, it is often despised and ignored (again Jer. 32:2; but also, e.g., Deut. 31:20; Job 21:14–15; Prov. 1:7; Isa. 1:2–3).

**4:1**. Under the sun, the mighty mercilessly oppress the weak, and no one comes to their aid. The theme of injustice and death in the previous set of verses (3:16–22) continues here in 4:1–3 but is restarted. As in the previous passage, Qohelet will move from a statement about injustice (4:1; cf. 3:16–17) into a brief discussion on its relationship to death (4:2–3; cf. 3:18–22).

Qohelet is "morally outraged" by the injustice he sees (Heim 2019, 77). The term "to oppress" (עשק) appears in Amos 3:9 where it refers to the people of Samaria, who have become a spectacle for the nations. It appears also in Job 35:9 where Elihu claims that oppressed people cry out for help because of their oppressors, but God does not answer because the victims are themselves evil. The fact that the oppressors are much stronger is an enigma (aka "vanity") in itself, and though he does not use the term here, its presence is felt. The wicked should be weak and the righteous should be strong, but the opposite is too often true. And the might of the wicked only emboldens them. Twice he states concerning the oppressed, "there was no one to comfort them." By this, Qohelet is not only speaking to the unjust suffering of the weak, but more broadly to the extent of unchecked evil on the earth (unchecked from a limited, human perspective—no one knows how God deals with these things in his own way, only that he does—8:13).

**4:2–3**. The verb translated "considered fortunate" (וְשַׁבֵּחַ) in the English versions (e.g., ESV, NET) elsewhere means "to praise" in reference to God (1 Chron. 16:35; Pss. 63:4 [HB 5]; 106:47; 117:1; 147:12; 145:4). The only other appearance of it in the HB is in Ecclesiastes 8:15 where Qohelet states, "I commend joy." Given its limited and specific use elsewhere in praise of God or of good things, the inclusion of the term here is likely meant to cause shock in the reader since the thing being "praised" or "commended" is not God, but the dead. Qohelet stands in the cemetery clapping to congratulate the dead that they no longer have to endure the rampant injustices of the world. It is as if Qohelet envies them (cf. 2:17). In his mind, they are at rest from the multitude of inequities that plague the earth. We should allow room for Qohelet to make an emotional outburst or rhetorical expression like this without taking his words too far or assuming that this is his final position on the matter, especially in light of all the good things he says about life, for example, "It is pleasant for the eyes to see the sun" (11:7). He, of course, also commends joyful living (see 2:24–26; 3:12–13, 22; 5:18–19 [HB 17–18]; 8:15; 9:4–5, 7–10; 11:1–10).

However, in reflecting on circumstances of unmitigated injustice, such as when people suffer inexplicably and indefinitely with no comfort, he considers death better. This is *not* an admonition from Qohelet that anyone should give up on life or attempt to die as a way of escaping pain. He is simply observing that the already-dead and those who were never born (4:3) do not have "to witness/experience the evil deeds that are done under the sun." They do not have to suffer through life's injustices and unfairness (cf. 6:3–4).

### Inequity and Labor (4:4–12)

In a string of proverbs and observations on daily labor and its inequities, Qohelet reinforces the point he made in 4:2–3 but at least offers a positive comment on the value of working with others (4:12).

**4:4.** Qohelet claims, hyperbolically, that the motivation behind all toil and every achievement is the envy or jealousy one person feels for his neighbor. Ecclesiastes 4:4–6 does not address inequity directly but confronts the motivations and practices in one's labor that can lead to it. Qohelet elsewhere commends work and states that one should be satisfied in his or her labor, understanding it to be one's God-given lot in life (e.g., 2:24–26; 3:12–13). Here, however, his focus has shifted to the general observation that people are motivated by jealousy. The sages identified the fear of the Lord as the stimulant for contentment in life, as contrasted with envying one's neighbor (Prov. 23:17), a vice that "rots the bones" (Prov. 14:30). Envy is vanity, and it will one day perish with everything else (9:6).

In the modern English of the West, especially in the United States, metaphors abound to convey the sentiment shared here by Qohelet. The idea of choosing a simple life is synonymous with escaping the "rat race" of constantly trying to get ahead, that is, the superficial and greed-based path so many choose in order to build their own miniature empires here on earth. Qohelet's expression "striving after wind" is comparable to the modern expression "running on the hamster wheel of life," a reference to how people work incredibly hard but actually get nowhere meaningful. Such toil is born out of envy and not an expression of grateful, authentic work, which Qohelet commends (2:24; 3:13).

**4:5.** Yes, envy and vain ambition abound in the workforce, but avoiding work altogether is not a viable option. The theme of this verse appears to function as a safeguard against the premature conclusion, based on 4:4, that one should avoid work altogether since it is all vanity. On one extreme exists the envy-driven workaholism condemned by Qohelet, but on the other extreme is the path of the sloth (Prov. 12:24; 18:9; 19:15; 20:4, 13; 21:25; 24:30–34). Both paths are futile.

Back in 2:18–23, Qohelet bemoaned the futility of trying to find lasting satisfaction in work, but he still commended work in general (2:24), so long as it was not built on the superficial foundation of greed and obsession (the sense of 2:18–23). Similarly, after pointing out that human beings are incapable of effecting lasting change in the world that could in any way alter what God is already doing (3:1–11), he still commended simple enjoyment in one's work (3:13).

**4:6.** Again Qohelet sets a boundary to show what kind of work is acceptable and what is not. Two handfuls of toil are as useless and harmful as two handfuls of rest. Envy-based, greed-driven, and anxiety-inducing toil is vanity (4:4, 6), but so is the opposite extreme, laziness (4:5). The implication is that one should split the difference by living more modestly and authentically before God.

**4:7–8.** A childless, brotherless man who works tirelessly without enjoyment does so in vain. He spends his whole life amassing wealth, never enjoys his work or the reward of it, and ends up leaving it to no one he loves. Qohelet twice calls this "vanity," once at the beginning of the pair of verses and once at the end. He adds that this is a "contemptible business" (עִנְיַן רָע), the same Hebrew expression from 1:13.

The theme of inequity picks back up again here, more overtly than in 4:4–6. The lonely man described here is not blamed by Qohelet for his loneliness. It is not the man's fault that he has no son, even if, in hindsight, it was folly for him to work joylessly his whole life. Qohelet is not interested in condemning the man but in highlighting an unfortunate circumstance. The scenario he describes contrasts the scenarios in 2:18–21 and later in 6:1–2. In those places, Qohelet bemoans the phenomenon of people working their whole lives just to leave all they have amassed to an heir or a stranger, one who might even be a fool (2:19). However, the present passage deals with the opposite extreme of having no heir, which is also bad, perhaps worse. Qohelet considers it an "unfortunate/unfair circumstance" for a person to work only for themselves without the opportunity to care for children and siblings. With one's parents normally passing away first, a person is typically left with his/her own siblings, spouse, and offspring, but the individual here has no one who can inherit their estate. He is like everyone else in that he has pursued pleasure (cf. 2:1–11), wisdom (cf. 2:12–17), and work (cf. 2:18–23) in hopes of satisfaction. But, as Qohelet has shown, these things do not bring lasting satisfaction (e.g., 5:10 [HB 9]; 6:3). The "workaholic loner" (M. Fox 2004, 29) here in 4:8 never stops toiling and is never satisfied with the wealth he acquires. He works and deprives himself all his life only to realize, in a moment of sobering self-reflection, that he has wasted it. This is the dictionary definition of futility, and a miserable enterprise (see the Lord's instruction to Moses in Num. 27:8–11 for what to do with a man's inheritance if he dies without children, brothers, or uncles).

**4:9–10.** When two people work together, they can accomplish exceedingly more than if one works alone. This is Qohelet's resolution for the misfortune of loneliness expressed in 4:7–8. Companions are able to help one another when one of them is in a bind, like when someone is trapped under the weight of a heavy load. The relationship described here may be practical rather than familial, but it is still better than isolation. According to the sages, if companionship extends to friendship, then it could be more valuable than family (Prov. 18:24).

**4:11–12.** The answer for loneliness that began in 4:9–10 extends here to the scenario of sleeping in the cold. Two companions can keep one another warm enough to sleep, but someone who attempts to sleep alone, in the cold of the outdoors, may be met with the same insomnia afflicting the anxious workaholic (2:23), the paranoid scrooge (5:12 [HB 11]), or the restless investigator (8:16).

So far, companionship has been shown to be useful for greater profits (4:9), safety in one's endeavors (4:10), and warmth in the cold night (4:11). Finally, companionship can rescue a person from ambush (4:12). When it comes to a fight, the more allies, the better. Herein traditional wisdom is confirmed, that "life in community is far superior in every way to a solitary existence. There is no place for individualism and self-reliance in the thought-world of Qohelet" (Heim 2019, 82).

### Inequity and Legacy (4:13–16)
Qohelet relates how the legacy of a once noble king will one day be long forgotten; he calls this "vanity and a striving after wind" (4:16).

**4:13.** Qohelet switches topics quickly, but he is still commenting on the inequities of life as he sees them. Varying interpretations abound for 4:13–16, and I have taken the following approach as a possibility: A poor, wise young man lives in the realm of a foolish king (4:13). Over time, the young man rises from the status of prisoner to eventually replace the foolish king. As more time passes, the new king is replaced with yet a newer king ("the second youth"; 4:15). This latest king's reign was expansive, but he will one day be forgotten by all the people over whom he ruled, just like the two kings who preceded him; this is incomprehensible and/or futile, according to Qohelet.

One would think that an older, experienced king is the best kind, but this is not the case if he is a fool "who still does not know how to heed warning." Such an attribution was applied to Nabal, the wealthy shepherd of Maon whom David encountered while fleeing from Saul. Nabal's servants said concerning their master, "He is such a worthless man; you can't even speak to him" (1 Sam. 25:17). The motif of foolish and braggadocious leaders is well known from ancient literature and modern life (see note on 9:17). A society's elders and their wealth serve as traditional emblems of power, handed down dynastically from generation to generation; however, a poor, unconnected, but wise young man can disrupt societal expectations (see note on 4:15 regarding court stories and the underdog motif in Scripture).

**4:14.** These verses (4:14–16) may represent a specific historical circumstance in Qohelet's memory, but details have been left out, making the scenario more relatable to audiences over time. The elder, foolish king mentioned in 4:13 is not discussed in the remainder of the passage; he was only mentioned in order to draw a contrast that would elevate the younger man, who is the subject of this verse. The "he" of 4:14 is the poor, wise youth who, for whatever reason, started at the bottom of the socioeconomic ladder in 4:13, yet somehow rose to incredible prominence, eventually becoming king.

**4:15.** The "second youth" is yet another young man (likely the prince) who will succeed the new king, the latter being the first youth mentioned above in 4:13 (M. Fox 2004, 31). The whole scenario has parallels with court stories from Scripture (e.g., Joseph, Daniel, Esther) and other rags-to-riches biographies like those of Ruth and David. Readers easily relate to such stories, even if the reader is not him/herself poor or particularly disenfranchised in any way. They relate out of a desire to see the righteous underdog (e.g., David) succeed against the powerful antagonist (e.g., Saul) or in the face of insurmountable odds: "Saul has killed his thousands, and David his tens of thousands!" (1 Sam. 18:7 CSB). Such tales are romantically captivating and have happy endings, generally speaking. As 4:16 will show, though, Qohelet, ever the realist, is unimpressed and eager to obliterate this Hallmark-esque fantasy in 4:15 with raw truth.

**4:16.** The tragedy that undercuts the expected fairytale ending is that one day *no one will remember this dynasty*. Despite all the pomp and circumstance of the prince's public crowning (see the Lord's instruction to Moses in Num. 27:8–11 for what to do with a man's inheritance if he dies without children, brothers, or uncles) and the laud afforded him and his father during their reigns, there is coming a time when no one will "rejoice" in them, for "there is no remembrance of former things!" (Eccl. 1:11). Qohelet wishes to interrupt our warm, fuzzy feelings at the inauguration with a proclamation of "ashes to ashes." If we fast-forward just a little, argues Qohelet, we will see dust return to dust, and memories evaporate until they are lost forever (see 3:20; 5:15–16 [HB 14–15]; 12:7; also, Gen. 3:19; Job 34:14–15; see also sidebar "Life After Death in Ecclesiastes" p. 108).

Qohelet is speaking to the cycles of life as he does in many places throughout the book (Eccl. 1:3–11; 3:15; etc.), hoping to disillusion his readers from the notion that something new or exciting will ever happen (like a new young ruler with a great approval rating). Ecclesiastes 4:16 shows that there was no end of all the people (his present supporters), and of all who came before them (supporters of the previous king), yet future generations will not rejoice in him. Qohelet's point is that this circumstance repeats itself over and over again in human history, so it should be demystified before our eyes. The triumph of a lauded royal ascension never lasts because no king is immortal, and the crowds of supporters praising him will also die and be replaced with different crowds, generations later, who barely remember the heroic story of the prison-to-palace king, or that he ever existed. Just give it enough time (100,000 years? a million?), Qohelet argues, and it will all be forgotten.

Though he is eager to feed these bitter realities to his readers, he does so for the purpose of saying that something is amiss. It is just *not right* that the majesty of a righteous, wise, beloved king should erode away into utter forgetfulness. Something about this is unfair or inequitable.

The tragedy of generational forgetfulness is inherently evil. So rather than participate directly, Qohelet prefers to stand dejected and at a distance while the crowds chant, "Long live the king." But who is to blame for this endless cycle of human exaltation followed by human forgetfulness? Qohelet believes that God orders all things (3:1–15), and that his decisions are immutable (1:15; 3:14; 6:10; 7:13–14), so God is the one maintaining and overseeing these processes (3:15). However, Qohelet's repeated allusions to Genesis 1–3 and his acknowledgments of human sinfulness (7:20), including the fact that humans have a way of ruining whatever God makes good (7:29), point in the direction of human culpability for life's many futilities.

It is not assumed by Qohelet, as it should not be assumed by his pupils, that the "work of God" (7:13; 8:17; 11:5)—a reference to all the inexplicable goings-on under the sun—is somehow inconsistent with his righteous character, enigmatic though it may be. One sentiment with which Qohelet would agree (based on his repeated claims regarding God's justice) is that "all the works of God *are done* in faithfulness" because "he loves righteousness and justice" (Ps. 33:4–5, emphasis added). For this reason, at the declaration of God's judgment against Babylon and consequent salvation of Israel, the prophet exclaimed, "Come let us make known in Zion *the work of the* LORD *our God*!" (בֹּאוּ וּנְסַפְּרָה בְצִיּוֹן אֶת־מַעֲשֵׂה יְהוָה אֱלֹהֵינוּ; Jer. 51:10, emphasis added).

### *Rightly Revering God (5:1–7 [HB 4:17–5:6])*
Qohelet teaches his pupils that the inequities of the world, expressed in the passages that surround 5:1–7 (HB 4:17–5:6), do not change how one must approach God with the utmost reverence and order.

**5:1 (HB 4:17)**. Watch your step. Qohelet is speaking literally (slow down) and metaphorically (slow your mind and mouth) here. It is unclear what physical structure for worship he has in view; those in favor of a monarchic date would point to Solomon's temple, but those in favor of an exilic or postexilic dating will see this as a reference to "any local worship site" (Longman 1998, 150). The point Qohelet is making is not dependent on a certain historical identification; rather, he wishes to express a timeless principle of pacing oneself carefully when approaching God. Temple structures from the ancient world reflect this very concept. Long after the writing of Ecclesiastes, King Herod rebuilt the temple in Jerusalem, the same temple featured in the New Testament Gospels. The southern steps leading up to the Temple Mount in Jerusalem feature alternating widths for each step, which would slow the worshipper down as he/she approaches the house of God. Monumental or otherwise unique staircases leading up to the deity's "house" are a common feature of ANE and Hellenistic temples (e.g., the great ziggurat at Ur and the Parthenon at Athens; see Jacobson and Gibson 1995, 169–70).

In the middle of this extensive section on life's inequities (3:16–6:9) comes an unexpected switch of topic—from inequity to fearing God. For the last twenty-three verses (3:16–4:16), Qohelet has been addressing various examples of inequity, but for the following seven verses (5:1–7 [HB 4:17–5:6]) he breaks the fourth wall to admonish his pupils directly on the topic of fearing God, only to return for twenty-two more verses on the topic of inequity (5:8 [HB 7]–6:9), a section I have labeled "The Impermanence of Wealth and the Providence of God" (see "Outline of Ecclesiastes" in the Introduction).

As mentioned in the exposition at the start of this preaching unit, what appears at first to be an unrelated sideroad may actually serve to redirect the reader's thought process in the middle of an otherwise negative onslaught, thereby affecting the very guardedness Qohelet commends in 5:1 (HB 4:17). Qohelet's prescriptions serve as borders that keep his students from descending into total disenchantment with God. He wants his students to be disillusioned with

# The Fear of God and the Evil of Inequity (3:16–5:7 [HB 6])

what he considers the cheap, superficial vanities of the world so that they will embrace the only thing that is *not* vanity—authentic living in the fear of God (2:24–26; 3:12–13, 22; 5:18–20 [HB 17–19]; 8:15; 9:7; and 11:7–12:1). These passages are also meant to protect against total, unmitigated despair in light of life's vanities, against immoral living under the pretense that God is not watching, never intervenes, and does not care: for the wicked think, "the LORD does not see!" (Ps. 94:7; Ezek. 8:12; 9:9; see note on 3:18–20). Our present passage (5:1–7 [HB 4:17–5:6]) serves this same purpose.

It is better to "listen" than to make the kinds of sacrifices fools make, for they open their mouths to make rash vows before God (5:2–7 [HB 1–6]). Obedience is not the correct nuance for the verb here, but "to listen," as the rest of the passage makes clear (see Seow 1997, 194).

**5:2 (HB 1).** It is important to orient oneself properly before God. Do not speak too quickly or recklessly. When the prophet Isaiah stood before the glorious throne of God, the only thing he could utter was "Woe is me! I'm silenced/destroyed!" (see *HALOT* s.v. "דמה III" 225), "for I am a man of unclean lips and I dwell in the midst of a people of unclean lips" (Isa. 6:5). The aura of God's presence left him speechless (see Job's action of putting his hand to his mouth in response to God—Job 40:4; see sidebar "The Gesture of Silence in the Hebrew Bible" p. 115).

Scripture is, of course, filled with examples of spontaneous pleas to God, even accusations against God or complaints that reveal a lack of faith in the supplicator. In other words, there is clearly a place for such prayers, but Qohelet is teaching his pupils to approach God more cautiously. Unlike Job, Qohelet is unwilling to place blame on God for life's inequities (Job's attitude on this changes, of course). While Qohelet believes that God is the one operating the world behind the scenes (7:13–14), that appears to be distinct in his mind from God bearing any moral culpability. Accordingly, he cautions his pupils to keep their mouths shut when stepping into God's presence in light of the chasmic distance between heaven and earth, which represents the difference between God's heavenly status and humanity's earthly status (on the HB concept of common/profane versus holy and how Christ affects these realms, see Longman 1998, 150). When you speak with God, Qohelet cautions, do not use "many words" (cf. Matt. 6:7), but "let your words be few" (see also Prov. 10:19).

> **The Gesture of Silence in the Hebrew Bible**
> In biblical and ANE texts, remaining silent in certain circumstances is considered wise. One may wait quietly upon the Lord while enduring suffering (Ps. 39:1–2; Lam. 3:25–30) or choose silence to avoid speaking evil (Ps. 141:3; Prov. 13:3; cf. Mic. 7:5). A person entering into the presence of someone of higher authority (typically a god or king) will signal their status and attitude of deference by placing their hand over their mouth (Judg. 18:19; Job 21:5; 29:9; 40:4; Prov. 30:32; Mic. 7:16), a gesture typically expressed by variations on the Hebrew construction "place hand over mouth" (שִׂים יָד עַל־פֶּה). When the Danites conscripted the services of Jonathan in Judges 18, they preempted his objections with, "Shut up! Put your hand on your mouth! And come with us so that you can be our father and priest" (Judg. 18:19). In Micah 7:16, the nations will be awed into silence, placing their hands on
>
>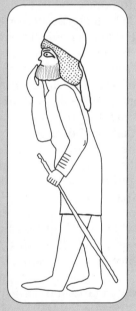
>
> A dignitary raises his hand to his mouth in the presence of Darius I. Persepolis Relief. Throne Room of Darius I. (see *ANEP* §463). Illustration by Rachel E. Jones.

> their mouths when they witness the judgment of God. In Proverbs 30:32, the sages advise that the wicked should put their hands to their mouths to stop foolishness from spilling out, perhaps even as an expression of disgust at one's own evil. Job orders his friends to use this same gesture in amazement at his wretched state and how injustice has befallen him (Job 21:5). His elders and friends put their hands to their mouths in the hearing of his wisdom (Job 29:9). Finally, Job puts his hand over his mouth when God starts to speak (Job 40:4). This gesture also appears in ANE texts and art, often with shared connotations (see note on 3:7; see Jones 2022).

**5:3 (HB 2)**. As dreams are full of silly, hurried activity, so a fool's mouth is full of many words. The reference here is to literal dreams, not one's aspirations (contra Garrett 1993, 311; the term "dream" חֲלוֹם is not used in the HB in the English metaphorical sense of one's "hopes and dreams"). It may be here that "much business" (too much toil in one's daily life) is the cause of vivid, restless dreaming at night (Schoors 2013, 387). Some scholars read the first clause in reverse, suggesting that vivid dreams are what cause "much business" in one's sleep (see Weeks 2020, 641). There are good reasons for both approaches, and both work well to make Qohelet's point: that fools are marked by their many words, or that many words make one a fool (see 10:3 where the fool tells everyone he's a fool). In sum, Qohelet pities the fool who runs his mouth before God.

The term "business"/"affair" (עִנְיָן) appears only in the book of Ecclesiastes (1:13; 2:23, 26; 3:10; 4:8; 5:3 [HB 2], 14 [HB 13]; 8:16) and is used only in negative contexts. Here in 5:3 (HB 2), "dreams" and "much business" are not just a convenient analogy for fools and their busy mouths; the excessive toiling itself points to how humans delude themselves into thinking that their work is more important than it actually is, which causes them to forget their place before God. A flurry of human plans and human striving causes a person to fixate on vanities that, consequently, trick them into thinking their endeavors are important, thus diminishing the priority of God in their minds.

**5:4–5 (HB 3–4)**. When you *do* decide to speak, make it count and follow through with whatever you say. In Jonah 2:9 (HB 10), the prophet declares while in the belly of the fish, "Whatever I vow, I will fulfill!" Practically speaking, vows are transactional, meaning that the supplicant promises to dedicate something to the Lord in exchange for deliverance or some kind of blessing. That does not mean, however, that vows are merely bribery to gain God's favor, though they can be abused in this way (Judg. 11:30; Prov. 20:25). The various examples of vows in Scripture indicate that those made in sincerity are honored (e.g., Gen. 28:2). But the reason it is good to keep one's mouth shut before God is to avoid improperly promising or overpromising—something a fool does (see note on 9:2). As Qohelet states, God "takes no pleasure" in them; in other words, "the God who dislikes such behaviour will hold such airheads to account" (Heim 2019, 91)! The implication here is that vows are often made too rashly, likely due to attempts to manipulate God into ordering certain outcomes (see Jephthah's vow in Judges 11:29–40; and note God's nonparticipation in the passage). This approach toward making vows can quickly slide from genuine worship into a form of ritual bribery whereby people attempt to control the actions of God. But Qohelet has shown that there is nothing a person can do to alter the outcomes God has already determined (3:1–15). In sum, either vow piously and fulfill the vow, or keep quiet.

**5:6 (HB 5)**. The theme of watching one's mouth continues. Words are not just words—they are not inconsequential; rather, they can lead to sin, which results in retribution (see Gordis 1971, 248). This happens whenever a person makes a vow to God but is unwilling to fulfill it. Such a person tells the temple "messenger" that "it was a mistake." The "it" (הִיא) refers to the rash vows of 5:4–5. The term "mistake" (שְׁגָגָה) can refer to unintentional or inadvertent sins (e.g., Num. 15:24, 28). Perhaps the activity described here in 5:6 (HB 5) is of a person attempting to diminish the severity of their sin when speaking to "the messenger" (likely a priest or other temple attendant), taking less than full responsibility for their unfulfilled vow. This type of behavior prompts God's anger and risks him ruining the "work" of the person who vowed falsely. This might involve loss of property or a lack of success in the vower's various enterprises, likely the *very* endeavors that were brought before God in connection with the vow. Hannah made a vow to God that if he would give her a son, she would dedicate him to tabernacle service (1 Sam. 1:11; see "Theological Focus" in this section). God honored her request, and she honored her vow.

**5:7 (HB 6)**. The point made back in 5:3 (HB 2) concerning dreams, busyness, fools, and their many words is revisited to conclude the unit. The syntax is difficult, but the broader sense is not: Human endeavor, with its many delusions and verbosity, stands in stark contrast with the transcendent, unmovable reality of God from whom a single spoken word outweighs everything on the timeline of eternity. So, rather than run one's mouth, it would be better to "fear God."

### The Fear of God in Ecclesiastes
Some scholars argue that Qohelet's talk of fearing God is understood not in the conventional HB sense of worshipful reverence but as actual terror, or possibly even a utilitarian choice to just stay out of trouble. In 5:7 (HB 6), "Qohelet encourages his readers away from a familiarity with God and toward a relationship characterized by fear" (Longman 1998, 155; on the utilitarian approach, see Sneed 2015a, 256). However, there is insufficient evidence in the text to justify this unusual interpretation of "fear" with respect to God (Whybray 1989, 25, 75). Regarding "fear" in Ecclesiastes, Katherine Dell writes, "Surely Qohelet would have known the nuances of its reference? He would probably have known Deuteronomy's use of it (e.g., Deut. 6:2; 10:12). He would probably have agreed with Proverbs 15:33, 'The fear of the LORD is instruction in wisdom' (NRSV), which may not use the language of commandment but still links the fear of God with a concrete practical outcome" (Dell 2020, 142; see Davis 2000, 193; Krüger 2004, 110). Indeed, Qohelet's use of "fear" is not a departure from its dominant use throughout Scripture, where it contains both reverence and practical concern for God's judgment (see notes on 3:14 and 8:13).

## THEOLOGICAL FOCUS
Qohelet has covered a variety of topics under the umbrella of inequity/injustice, including an admonition for how to approach God rightly:

- Inequity and Death (3:16–4:3)
- Inequity and Labor (4:4–12)
- Inequity and Legacy (4:13–16)
- Rightly Revering God (5:1–7 [HB 4:17–5:6])

Life is deeply inequitable, observes Qohelet. Sometimes that inequity is the result of injustice, and sometimes it is merely the characteristic unfairness of life. Qohelet and all believers have an idea in their heads of how things *ought to* turn out in accordance with God's goodness, but too often the opposite happens in life. This reversal of expectations is unsettling and even a cause for doubt in some, as it leaves everyone with that uneasy feeling that something is just *off*. But what are found to be *off* are human presumptions about the world and how God moves in it. Life is not programmed by him to ensure that the right kinds of things (from a human point of view) always happen (1:15; 7:13–14). This is demonstrated by the fact that injustice and death are inevitable (3:16–4:3), that inequities persist in human labor (4:4–12), and that honorable leaders are too quickly forgotten (4:13–16). Furthermore, in the next preaching unit, we see that the wealthy can be bereaved of everything in a moment without notice or explanation (5:8 [HB 7]–6:9]; see Job 1:13–22).

Tucked in the center of all these inequities listed by Qohelet is his own excursus on the fear of God (5:1–7 [HB 4:17–5:6]). Though it represents a jarring change of topic, this is not a misplaced insertion; rather, it is a fitting reminder of God's stable character in the midst of an unstable world. The passage also reminds the reader that human endeavor is as vain in life as it is before God. Do not vow many vows or pray loudly and eloquently to be heard by others or to manipulate God; the currency of vainglorious human effort is not accepted in his temple. God takes "no pleasure in fools" (5:4 [HB 3]), because he "is in heaven and you are on earth" (5:2 [HB 1]). Therefore, fear him and come before him in humility, resisting the kind of careless verbosity that mirrors the vanities of an overly active and, hence, dream-laden life (5:3 [HB 2]). Affix your hand to your mouth when in his presence and acknowledge your weakness as someone who lives in a world that is out of your control, but firmly in his. To march arrogantly into his presence with a list of presumptuous demands or "vain repetitions" (Matt. 6:7) is a very dangerous business. By contrast, one ought to have the right posture (5:2 [HB 1]) and the right state of mind/heart (5:4–6 [HB 3–5]) when entering God's presence. Events in life may unfold erratically, and people may respond in kind, but do not bring such chaos, irrationality, and hubris with you when approaching God.

In 1 Samuel 1–2, Hannah was deeply burdened with how life's inequities had affected her personally. She could not have a son, and her husband's other wife, who had children, taunted her relentlessly "because the Lord had closed her womb" (1:6). Hannah's barrenness was not an injustice perpetrated by a human, but a feeling of unfairness for which she had no explanation. Like the blind man of John 9:3, there is no indication that she is suffering punishment for sin; rather, the Lord had made her barren for reasons only he knows. Her suffering deeply distressed her, so she brought it before God and made a sincere vow to dedicate her son to tabernacle service if God would open her womb. Based on his teaching in 5:1–7 (HB 4:17–5:6), Qohelet would affirm that Hannah approached God the right way and followed through with her word. After receiving the gift of a son, her subsequent praise to God reveals a heart that trusts in his justice and sovereignty in an otherwise inexplicably unfair and unjust world. She indicates that thanks to the secret, unrestricted workings of God on the earth, the mighty are brought low, but the weak are strengthened (1 Sam. 2:4); the hungry are now full and the full are now hungry (2:5a); the barren are bearing children, but those with many children cannot bear more (2:5b); and the poor are made rich (2:8). This is all possible because God is sovereign, able to give life and take it away, and able to make some prosperous and others poor (2:6–7). The fact that God is in control and the only one capable of changing anything was a source of hope for Hannah in the face of life's inequities, and that hope was further confirmed through God's gift of a son.

Qohelet likely read and heard this story more than once, and in that way sat at Hannah's feet as her pupil, learning from a wise believer whose felt suffering with inequity was confronted by bold faith in God's sovereignty. Qohelet would have seen how she, having experienced God as the sovereign "Rock" (1 Sam. 2:2) in an otherwise unstable world, admonished those hearing her victory song to guard their tongues before him—"Do not boast so proudly, or let arrogant words come out of your mouth, for the Lord is a God of knowledge, and actions are weighed by Him" (2:3 CSB).

## PREACHING AND TEACHING STRATEGIES

### *Exegetical and Theological Synthesis*
Qohelet exposed rampant injustices in life to his audience (Eccl. 3:16–4:16). All people will end up suffering the same fate—death (3:16–21). The strong will regularly take advantage of the weak (4:1–6). Even good things, like work and community, are often twisted by humanity's sinfulness (4:7–16). The only resort, Qohelet counseled, was for people to live by the fear of God. They must stop pretending the world is fine, but also they must stop pretending in their relationship with God (5:1–7).

Authentic living before God is the antidote to a world filled with inequity. We cannot control the world, but we worship a God who does. If God is in control and sees all things, what good does it do to pretend before him? Instead of blabbering like a fool, wise people should embrace measured maturity, speaking honestly before God.

### *Preaching Idea*
Stop pretending and face reality: God is sovereign over a broken world.

### *Contemporary Connections*

*What does it mean?*
In the beginning, God created a world he declared "good" seven times (Gen. 1:4, 10, 12, 18, 21, 25, 31). Yet God's good world did not last due to Adam's sin (Gen. 3:1–7). The sin of humanity wrought destruction upon the whole world, which now labors under a curse of corruption (Gen. 3:17–19). What was beautiful is now broken. Ecclesiastes, then, can be thought of as an extended meditation on the brokenness of the world. Throughout 3:6–5:7 (HB 6), Qohelet exposes many ways the world is broken. The wicked triumph over the righteous (3:16). The strong oppress the weak (4:1). In places where people should join hands in unity to accomplish a goal, there is petty jealousy and rivalry (4:4). Instead of contentment with one's labors, there is a constant craving for more (4:7–8). In addition to Qohelet's examples, each one of us could supply our own list of troubles that we have seen in this world.

In a world of such inequity—unfairness and tragedy—how should believers live? Should they just give up and accept that evil will win the day? Should they just close their eyes and live a life of myopic naivete?

Qohelet provides us with the answer by rejecting both pessimism and optimism. Instead, Qohelet argues for a clear-eyed *realism* about the state of the world. Yes, it is filled with injustice and tragic circumstances. We must stop pretending that everything is OK with the world. But the world is also ruled over by a sovereign God who is in heaven (5:2 [HB 1]). Therefore, we must also stop pretending in our relationship with him, and instead, authentically live before him (5:1–7 [HB 4:17–5:6]). The authentic life before God is one that listens to his Word, rather than taking the advice of fools (5:1 [HB 4:17]). It does not attempt to manipulate God with rash vows or bargaining (5:4–5 [HB 3–4]). It is also measured in its speech so that it does not provoke God's wrath (5:6–7 [HB 5–6]).

*Is it true?*
While the advances that humanity has made in the last two hundred years have been astonishing, most people on the earth would admit that the world is tragically broken. Theologian Reinhold Niebuhr agrees with the *London Times Literary Supplement*'s evaluation of human life: "The doctrine of original sin is the only empirically verifiable doctrine of the Christian faith" (Niebuhr 2012, 24). Indeed, while Christians put their faith in God and believe the truths of his Word, at least one reality should be evident to all people: the corruption of the world through sin, oppression, injustice, and tragedy.

In 2010, Foxconn, a manufacturing company of iPhones for tech giant Apple, had to install suicide nets to keep employees from killing themselves (Merchant 2017, 264). Those employees faced harsh bosses and working conditions. An investigation into a competitor of Foxconn that also made iPhones reported that employees often worked hundred-hour weeks and as many as eighteen days in a row. Poor working conditions exemplify the oppression of these corporations.

In the modern world, injustice can even extend into the womb. While the United States Supreme Court struck down *Roe v. Wade* in 2022, eliminating abortion as a constitutional right, some politicians still advocate for permissive abortion policies. Those who support abortion, however, seem to be violating important tenets of the American political system. Many political policies are enacted to protect and support the most vulnerable of society. Who is more vulnerable than unborn children? They are literally defenseless.

Even a quick perusal of our own lives, or the lives of those around us, will reveal deep dysfunction. Addictions, crumbling families, and "deaths of despair," like suicide, are all too common. What are we to do in the face of this inequity?

*Now what?*
When living a world plagued with inequity, the call of the text is clear: we must fear God (5:7). Fearing God looks like refusing to pretend in our relationship with him. Qohelet advises us not to be "hasty in word or impulsive in thought to bring up a matter in the presence of God" (5:2). We should not speak to God casually or carelessly. While God is our loving heavenly Father, he is not our "pal" or "buddy." He is not to be esteemed lightly. He is not to be trifled with as if we can deceive him. He is the Sovereign God of the universe, and we should not try to "play" him. Qohelet tells us that it is foolish to hide or pretend before the Lord because he "is in heaven and you are on the earth" (5:2b). He is so much greater, smarter, and wiser than we are (Isa. 55:8–9). He sees and knows the very depth of our hearts (Ps. 139:1–12). Therefore, we must put away all pretense and hypocrisy, and authentically approach him.

Just like Qohelet, Jesus speaks of the importance of cultivating an authentic relationship with God (Matt. 6:1–6). If we attempt to look and act holy in front of others to gain recognition, we will actually gain nothing (6:1). Instead of calling attention to ourselves, Jesus admonishes us to practice our faith "in secret," that is, before the watching eyes of the Lord and no one else (6:2–6).

Besides admonishing us to fear God, Qohelet also provides some other practical advice for us making our way through this fallen world. He encourages us to develop strong relationships because "two are better than one" (Eccl. 4:9a). Having a team around you allows you to accomplish more and acts as a buffer against tragedy. If you do not have a strong community around you, you may fall and never get up, or be easily overpowered by another (4:10, 12). Community helps you to be resilient and battle through the brokenness. Developing real relationships takes time and effort, however. We do not develop six years' worth of community in six months. Yet the investments we make to build relationships are worth it because "a threefold cord is not quickly broken" (4:12 KJV). We are stronger together.

### *Creativity in Presentation*
Consider all the ways that we attempt to subtly downplay the reality of death. We describe people as having "passed away" or having "gone to a better place," rather than saying, "they died." In recent times, it has been common for the families of those who die to host a "celebration of life" rather than a traditional funeral. The problem with ignoring death is that it cuts us off from deeply understanding who Jesus is. As author Matthew McCullough writes in his book *Remember Death*, "When the reality of death is far from our minds, the promises of Jesus often seem detached from our lives" (2018, 19).

Maybe we also recoil from considering death because it humbles us. It reminds us that we're not as big, or powerful, or important as we'd like to think. McCullough again writes, "Death makes a statement about each of us: you are not too important to die" (p. 54). In the face of death's trivializing power, believers can have hope through Christ's sacrifice. The New Testament testifies that believers were redeemed with "precious blood," the blood of Jesus (1 Peter 1:19). If Jesus shed his precious blood for his people, then they too are precious to him. We are not merely dust, but those Jesus came to save. Remembering death, then, is about remembering Jesus and what he has done to save us.

Not only should we stop pretending about death, but we must face the reality of our work: it cannot give us (ultimate) satisfaction. Qohelet advocates for a better balance of work and rest than modern capitalistic societies often encourage: "One hand full of rest is better than two fists full of labor and striving" (4:6). In 2013, a Japanese news reporter died suddenly from something the Japanese call *karoshi*: death by overwork. The man clocked 159 hours of *overtime* the month before he died (Newport 2021). While most of us will probably not work ourselves to death, each of us can fall prey to a modern work culture that prizes quick responses, never-ending productivity, and ever-expanding ambitions. Certainly, employers can place unrealistic demands upon the shoulders of their workers. But how many times do we overwork because of our own ambition? How many times do we deceive ourselves into believing that we are limitless, refusing to acknowledge reality? Work cannot give us ultimate satisfaction; only God can.

We must also stop pretending in our relationship with God, especially with how we use our words. Qohelet's emphasis on our words is not so much speaking about what we *literally* say. But he recognizes that a chattering, overly informal speech reveals a casual and flippant relationship with God. When we attach "swear to God" at the end of our promises, we undermine our own trustworthiness. It is like when Hollywood producer Harvey Weinstein would swear on the lives of his children to abuse actresses and coerce them into performing sexual acts (as of 2024, Weinstein is currently in prison for his crimes). Instead of airless words, we should desire to speak with measured maturity that indicates a level of depth of communion with the Lord.

The preaching idea is "Stop pretending and face reality: God is sovereign over a broken world." The outline of the text can call the audience to stop pretending in certain ways:

- Stop pretending that death doesn't exist (3:16–4:3)
- Stop pretending that work gives ultimate significance (4:4–12)
- Stop pretending that your name will last forever (4:13–16)
- Stop pretending that God doesn't see your heart (5:1–7 [HB 4:17–5:6])

## DISCUSSION QUESTIONS

1. How should we live in light of approaching death (3:16–22)?

2. Why should we not be shocked by oppression (4:1–4; 5:8–9)?

3. Why is community so important for living wisely in a broken world (4:9–12)?

4. What instructions does Qohelet give when approaching God (5:1–7)?

5. How can believers in Jesus avoid constantly craving the things of this world?

6. How would your life change if you approached God more authentically?

# Ecclesiastes 5:8 (HB 7)–6:9

## EXEGETICAL IDEA
Qohelet asserts that wealth is fleeting, uncertain, and cannot satisfy, but God's providential care for humanity is sufficient for human joy.

## THEOLOGICAL FOCUS
The problem with wealth is that humans trust in it for something it can never provide: satisfaction and joy, both of which are the rewards of the person who delights in God's simple gifts.

## PREACHING IDEA
Serve God, not money.

## PREACHING POINTERS
Qohelet undertook his own search for significance and fulfillment, only to find that everything "under the sun" led to disappointment and disillusionment. His experience must have influenced his teachings as he observed the vain strivings of those around him. He routinely pointed out the folly of pursuing work and wealth as one's source of fulfillment. Wealth, in particular, presented an allure to those he observed. Yet those who pursued riches always ended up in the same place as he did: craving something of substance, yet never finding it.

The message of Ecclesiastes concerning wealth is vitally important for believers today. Despite recent economic uncertainties in many places, most are still enjoying the most affluent and prosperous era in world history, and Americans are the greatest beneficiaries at this time. Yet, according to Qohelet, the pursuit of wealth is a fool's errand. Wealth cannot satisfy. In fact, wealth doesn't just *not* satisfy, but pursuing it is like drinking salt water; it creates a more intense craving. To live wisely, believers must approach wealth in a cautious and contented manner. They must put away their constant craving and simply enjoy the gifts God has given them.

# THE IMPERMANENCE OF WEALTH AND THE PROVIDENCE OF GOD (5:8 [HB 7]–6:9)

## LITERARY STRUCTURE AND THEMES (5:8 [HB 7]–6:9)

This final long section of Qohelet's observations in the book (1:1–6:9) contrasts wealth's impermanence and inability to satisfy with God's providential appointments, which do satisfy. "Providential appointments" refers to God's decision to assign *most* people life's simple sustenances (5:18 [HB 17]; 6:9; i.e., food, drink, work), which we have already seen are sufficient for joy (2:24–26; 3:12–13, 22), and *others* with greater wealth and power (5:19–20 [HB 18–19]), which is more than enough for joy. This entire preaching unit is a part of Qohelet's larger discussion of inequity in the world (3:16–6:9).

The unit is broken into two sections, the first (5:8–20 [HB 7–19]) focusing a bit more on wealth's transitory nature and how the unpredictability of life can steal away, without notice, all a person has. This perceived unfairness or inequity leads the wealth-trusting man to a place of deep misery (5:17 [HB 16]). But joy is still possible if a person will resolve to delight either in the bare necessities God has provided (5:18 [HB 17]) or the abundance he has provided (5:19–20 [HB 18–19]).

The second section (6:1–9) centers around the theme of God's sovereignty to give and take away (6:2), and how a person should respond to this uncontrollable and unpredictable reality with satisfaction in life's simple things (6:9), a theme we have seen throughout Ecclesiastes so far (2:24–26; 3:12–13, 22; 5:18 [HB 17]).

- *Wealth Cannot Satisfy, but God's Gifts Are Delightful (5:8–20 [HB 7–19])*

- *Wealth Cannot Satisfy, but God's Gifts Are Sufficient (6:1–9)*

## EXPOSITION (5:8 [HB 7]–6:9)

As indicated in the literary structure and themes above, the concern of this passage is wealth's impermanence as contrasted with God's providence, but there is more to say about Qohelet's reaction to these realities. When a person who trusts in wealth loses all they have, Qohelet does not portray this as a just reward for that person's misplaced faith but as a "debilitating evil" (5:13 [HB 12], 16 [HB 15]). Involuntary forfeiture of one's savings is seen as inequitable, as something unfair. Qohelet does not delight in the fact that decades of hard work can be lost suddenly in a bad business venture (5:14 [HB 13]) or as the result of premature death (6:2), even if the person who lost it deserved to do so; the moral component is not under consideration. It is important to remember that while Qohelet is a teacher of the "truth" (12:10), that does not mean he drew his material from a temple-sanctioned textbook written by the prophets; rather, his principles derive from observations he has made, or from the school of hard knocks, as evinced by how deeply he feels the losses he describes (this approach is consistent with how the sages of Hebrew wisdom taught from their observations of God's world, from the book of creation). Either he experienced these tragedies personally or witnessed them happening—in either case, it has grieved him deeply (6:2). In his grief, he concludes that one cannot trust wealth and, hence, must resolve instead to delight in God's simple gifts. This involves delighting in "the sight of the eyes" (6:9), that is, life's simple sufficiency that is right before us (eating, drinking, and working with joy). This he finds superior to the "gaping appetite" (6:9) that constantly craves but is never satisfied.

## Wealth Cannot Satisfy, but God's Gifts Are Delightful (5:8–20 [HB 7–19])

By way of exposition and illustration, Qohelet exposes the futility of trusting in wealth, offering up the only worthwhile alternative to such delusions: authentic living before a generous God.

**5:8 (HB 7)**. Having concluded his strategically placed sermon on fearing God (5:1–7 [HB 4:17–5:6]), Qohelet here picks up where he left off in 4:16, resuming his discussion on the inequities of life, but by means of contrast: the impermanence and insufficiency of wealth against the joy-bringing simplicity of God's gifts.

"Do not be astonished!" captures the spirit of Qohelet's teaching as he attempts to disillusion his pupils by exposing them to the many injustices of the world. If you see the oppression of the poor and corruption at the street level, just know that this corruption also extends up the hierarchical ladder of government all the way to the king. Everyone answers to someone; everyone is paying someone. It is not just the poor who are extorted—provincial governors and aristocrats are also victims of the very corruption they perpetuate. The sentiment from Qohelet in this verse could be paraphrased to, "You think this is bad? Well, it's *even worse* than you could imagine!" The construction "do not be amazed" is rendered μὴ θαυμάσῃς in the LXX, similar to the expression used by the apostle John in 1 John 3:13 when he writes that believers should "not be surprised" (μὴ θαυμάζετε) that the world hates them. In both cases, an older figure is speaking to disciples who are younger and more naive. Qohelet's students only see the tip of the iceberg; what lies below is more than they could imagine.

The "high one" (גָּבֹהַּ) spoken of here refers to a high official, but this may also be a veiled reference to the motif of the proud/arrogant person (e.g., Prov. 6:17; 8:13; 11:2; 16:18; 21:4; 29:23; 30:13). In Isaiah, such persons are identified as "haughty/high ones" (גָּבֹהַּ) who will be brought low by God (Isa. 5:15). In the next verse, the character of the haughty is contrasted with God's character as one who is "high/exalted" (from the same root: גבה) in justice (Isa. 5:16).

**5:9 (HB 8)**. Blessed is the land whose king is focused on the just acquisition of wealth through honest labor. This verse has many different interpretations across English translations and commentaries. It seems that Qohelet is trying to point out the one redeemable thing in the corrupt system just described in 5:8 (HB 7). I take the verse to read "a king *devoted to* [לְ] cultivated fields" (see ESV, emphasis added) rather than "a king who is served by the field" (see NET). Qohelet intends to contrast the systemic corruption of 5:8 (HB 7) with wholesome, authentic work, which is represented by the agriculture mentioned in 5:9 (HB 8). A king may demonstrate this commitment by upholding justice, one form of which was to prevent abusers from moving boundary stones and thereby robbing others of land (Prov. 23:10–11; Bartholomew 2009, 218).

### Qohelet and the Gain of the Good Earth

Throughout Ecclesiastes, Qohelet goes to great pains to expose the lack of "gain" (יִתְרוֹן) in human endeavors, accusing human beings of constantly plotting to get ahead, attempting to manipulate outcomes for their own ends. Such behavior betrays a delusion that people have more control over life than they actually do, a delusion that can manifest in morally repugnant ways when human scheming (7:29) involves not just planning for the future but plotting to cheat and oppress others (5:8 [HB 7]). In contrast, a focus on the land and what it does and does not render is considered a purer form of "gain," and is contrasted with the despicable behavior of defrauding others

# The Impermanence of Wealth and the Providence of God (5:8 [HB 7]–6:9)

(see 5:8–9 [HB 7–8]). Notes M. Fox, "This natural and productive way of life stands in contrast to the self-serving bureaucracy in verse 7 [Eng. v. 8] and the compulsive consumerism of verse 9 [Eng. v. 10]" (2004, 35). In this way, Qohelet again points to authentic living in the face of life's unsatisfying endeavors (2:1–26), human powerlessness (3:1–22), and systemic injustice (5:8–9 [HB 7–8]). One must turn away from these delusions and toward a focus on the simple things of life that come as a "gift" (3:13; 5:19 [HB 18]) from the hand of God. For Qohelet, working the ground is a useful example of that (see also 11:4–6, but note that even in farming a person can fall prey to delusions of control). The beauty of this kind of simple living and wholesome aspiration is illustrated in J. R. R. Tolkien's well-known fiction *The Fellowship of the Ring*. In describing hobbits and how they live, he writes that they "love peace and quiet and good tilled earth: a well-ordered and well-farmed countryside was their favourite haunt" (Tolkien 1954, 1). This could be contrasted with the evil scheming of other species and, ultimately, the series's chief antagonists—Saruman and Sauron.

**5:10 (HB 9)**. Loving money is like chasing after the wind. Just as a person cannot catch or capture the wind, so there is never enough money to make one fulfilled. Hence, the person who loves money is a perpetually unsatisfied person. Qohelet reminds us of his investigation back in 2:1–11 where he concluded that the pursuit of pleasure does not satisfy, and money is just one manifestation of that. Money and "abundance/wealth" do not fill a person or bring ultimate gratification. This is not only true in the long run, as when death strips away all a person's possessions and accomplishments (cf., e.g., 2:16, 21; 3:3:18–22; 6:1–3; 9:1–6); it is also manifested during one's life as anxiety over wealth keeps one awake at night (5:12 [HB 11]).

**5:11 (HB 10)**. The verse makes the point that the more wealth one amasses, the more mouths there are to feed: "The thing pursued, namely wealth, takes on a life of its own and starts to control the person pursuing it. All the owner can do is stand and watch as the problems gather momentum" (Bartholomew 2009, 219). The man who toiled restlessly to acquire this wealth now sees it slipping through his fingers as mounting responsibilities begin perforating the hull of his financial ship. There are too many leaks to plug and, accordingly, no actual time to enjoy the wealth. Qohelet quips that the only thing a hoarder of wealth can do with all of his/her wealth is *look* at it (5:11 [HB 10]), which is pretty "pathetic" (Heim 2019, 97). The old Disney cartoons of Scrooge McDuck come to mind, particularly when his favorite pastime is shown to be swimming gleefully through a sea of gold coins he keeps locked away in a towering safe. While it is a fact of life that those who have more will have more to lose, the person who *loves* money is the biggest loser of all.

**5:12 (HB 11)**. The laborer does not fret over losing control of his wealth or his underlings since he has neither. For this reason, he sleeps with ease. In the final line of 5:12 (HB v. 11), the rich lifestyle is again contrasted with the simple lifestyle of the "laborer," a term organically related to all of Qohelet's calls for authentic living before God (2:24–26; 3:12–13, 22; 5:18–20 [HB 17–19]; 8:15; 9:7–10). Sleeplessness is the fate of those who fret over their work (2:23), are anxious over their wealth (5:10 [HB 9]), and try in vain to unravel the mysteries of God's world (8:16).

**5:13 (HB 12)**. One would think that keeping wealth only helps and never hurts, but Qohelet found the opposite to be true in certain cases. He mentions a few "sickening evils" along his way—two of which he presents in this passage, at 5:13 (HB 12; רָעָה חוֹלָה) and at 5:16 (HB 15; רָעָה חוֹלָה), and the other presented in a parallel passage in 6:2 (וָחֳלִי רָע). Grief and disgust merge in Qohelet as he evaluates (1) the greedy man who hoards his wealth to his own detriment (5:13 [HB 12]), (2) that same scrooge returning to his grave as penniless as he was at birth (5:16 [HB 15]), and (3) the man who is wealthy but not able to enjoy his wealth (due to premature death; 6:2).

**5:14 (HB 13)**. To compound the once rich but now poor man's misery, he will now face the dishonor of leaving his son nothing for an inheritance. Had he always been poor, this would not be nearly so great a tragedy. Back in 2:19, Qohelet bemoaned the fact that he would one day have to leave all his wealth to a descendant who did nothing to earn it. That prior, selfish sentiment is here met with an ironic reversal in the form of a far more visceral grief—the phenomenon of losing everything such that you *cannot* leave an inheritance to your children. According to Qohelet, is one thing to not *want* to hand over an inheritance, but another not even to be *able to* hand it over. It started with the man hoarding his wealth "to his misfortune." In other words, he stockpiled wealth his whole life only to lose it all "in a bad business deal," also rendered "a bad venture" (ESV) or "bad luck" (*HALOT* s.v. "עִנְיָן" 857). Regardless of the circumstances of the loss, it came unexpectedly and left him utterly broke so that he had no inheritance "in his hand" to leave to his son (cf. Luke 12:13–20). Qohelet views both the random, unpredictable misfortune of the man *and* his own greed under the same umbrella: "a sickening evil" (5:13 [HB 12]).

**5:15–16 (HB 14–15)**. He came into the world with nothing, and he will depart with nothing. To be clear, though, that was going to happen anyway at the moment of death; so, the statement about going to the grave naked is not showing the consequences of hoarding but is giving us even "further reason why the act of hoarding wealth for its own sake is in itself a reason for misery" (Heim 2019, 101). Greed is doubly futile: it robs one and others from enjoyment in the present and it makes the sting of death even worse since so much more is lost in that final moment. Living greedily is like chasing after wind.

**5:17 (HB 16)]**. Unlike the laborer from 5:12 (HB 11) who seems generally content in life and able to sleep peacefully, the wealthy man now has to face life with so much less than he once had, which stirs up "vexation and sickness and anger" (ESV) in his heart as he sits in the dark without even enough shekels to buy oil for his lamp. If the darkness is not literal, then it is figurative for the state of his soul. Rather than consuming to the point of a "full stomach" (5:12 [HB 11]), he is consumed by "his grief and anger" at having lost it all.

**5:18 (HB 17)**. There are lessons to be learned from the life of the miserable rich man in the previous verses. One is implied (that a person should not hoard wealth), but the other is stated explicitly and is positive in nature (that a person ought to live authentically before God). I have used the term "authentic" to summarize Qohelet's repeated directive to eat, drink, and find enjoyment in one's toil (see Introduction and note on 2:24). Qohelet has not left his pupils with a mere list of "don'ts" but has provided an alternative to the countless futilities one can get oneself into. The solution is to have joy in life's simple things, like eating and drinking and doing one's work (see 2:24; 3:12–13, 22; 8:15; 9:7–10). Qohelet has "seen" that the lifestyle of living in the present and being grateful for God's gifts is "good and beautiful." This authentic style of living, promoted throughout Ecclesiastes, is here contrasted with the Scrooge-like behavior of those who anxiously covet every dime and, consequently, live in total misery.

# The Impermanence of Wealth and the Providence of God (5:8 [HB 7]–6:9)

> **Humanity's God-Given Lot in Life**
>
> In 3:22, Qohelet remarked that to rejoice in one's work is one's "portion" (חֵלֶק) in life. The term appears also in 2:10, 21; 5:18 (HB 17); 9:6, 9; and 11:2. In a few places it refers to a person's lot/share/portion as assigned by God (3:22; 5:18 [HB 17]; 9:9). How one understands Qohelet's reporting on humanity's lot/share/portion depends on whether the interpreter thinks Qohelet is being negative or positive. In other words, is Qohelet saying that the only thing God has given us is the drab misery of daily work and a short life? Or should the act of God giving gifts be understood in light of 3:13, 22, 8:15, and 5:19 (HB 18), where it is attached to the concept of "joy" in one's station? If we allow the authentic-living passages to influence our understanding of the human lot/share/portion, we come away with a more positive view of the Hebrew term when it is connected to the things God ordains. The verb "enjoy" implies that Qohelet is viewing things positively despite all of life's futilities (Whybray 1989, 25–26, 102). To read it any other way one would have to understand Qohelet's words as sarcastic in nature as if to say, "Oh boy, we get to work and then die! Thanks for nothing!"

**5:19 (HB 18).** Everyone who is able to secure wealth, consume wealth, and find contentment in their wealth and station "can only do so through divine providence" (Heim 2019, 106). When Qohelet, donning his Solomonic wig, listed all his accomplishments back in 2:1–10, there was no mention of God "giving" him things or putting him in that position of power; rather, his focus was on his own human accomplishments wrought from human toil. Following that episode, his message has consistently been one of fearing God and receiving life's pleasures as gifts from God. In the present passage, we observe that the main difference between Qohelet's portrayal of Solomon and Qohelet's story of the rich man of 5:10–17 (HB 9–16) is that the rich man just happened to lose it all; what unites them is that both men lived life in a futile way.

In 2:24, 3:12–13, 5:18 [HB 17], and here in 5:19 [HB 18], the notion is repeated that life's simple enjoyments are all gifts from God as opposed to the delusion that a person can control his/her own outcomes, amass possessions impervious to loss, or find ultimate satisfaction in temporal things. All of that is the work of human hands and, as such, is vanity; however, the best things come directly from the hand of God.

**5:20 (HB 19).** What is the outcome of the person who lives life authentically before God? That woman or man is not preoccupied with overthinking the days of their lives, drowning themselves in daydreams of how good things used to be—which, if we are honest, are often delusional thoughts over misremembered times. Rather, God has empowered them to live with an awareness and appreciation of the present; he has preoccupied their hearts with joy.

## Wealth Cannot Satisfy, but God's Gifts Are Sufficient (6:1–9)

Qohelet contrasts wanton craving with the simple pleasure of delighting in the sustenance one already possesses.

**6:1–2.** The same God who gives good things to a person has equal right and power to take that very person's life in accordance with his divinely concealed purposes and timing. The theme of life's inequities and misfortunes continues, here with an example much closer to Qohelet's complaint in 2:18–21 where a man amasses wealth all his life just to leave it to someone who did nothing to earn it. This is a serious concern for ancient men of means (see 2:18–19; 4:8; 6:2; also Ps. 39:6). God gives this archetypal rich man everything his soul desires, so that he is lacking nothing, but God does not allow him to enjoy any of it; rather, all of his possessions are left to a "stranger." Qohelet does not assert that God has done something wrong, but simply observes the phenomenon; sometimes people only work but never enjoy what they have until one day they are dead and lose any opportunity to enjoy it. The fact that this happens is "vanity and a grievous/sickening evil."

It is important to remember that the term "evil" (רָע) in Hebrew has a broad range of meaning and is not limited to its most common use in English, which is morally centered (think Job 1:1). Here, however, Qohelet speaks of it as calamity, like the many "evils" that befell Job (2:10–11). For Qohelet, God is sovereignly behind the scenes and cannot be removed from the equation so as to avoid the problem of this calamity finding its source in him. God gave the wealth and then for reasons known only to him, took it away (see Deut. 8:17–18; 1 Sam. 2:7; Job 1:21; Fredericks 2010, 153–54). Later rabbinic thought regarding the giving and taking powers of God mirrors the Joban sense cited here, but the sage Beruriah clarifies that since God is the owner of all things, all things must return to him (see the profound story of Beruriah and her husband, Rabbi Meir, in Bialik and Rawnitzki 1992, 242; Midrash Mishlei 31). Krüger and others see Qohelet's grief here as extending beyond a universal principle to a specific scenario in the Ptolemaic period toward the end of the third century, where wealth was redirected from Jewish people and into the hands of foreign elites (cf. a similar scenario in Neh. 9:36–37 and the covenant curse of Deut. 28:30–33; Krüger 2004, 125).

**6:3–6**. In an impossible hypothetical scenario, a man lives so long that he is able to father one hundred children and have an unfathomable lifespan (these verses are "clearly fictitious and fabricated: no man sires one hundred children or lives two thousand years"; Krüger 2004, 125). Qohelet takes the fiction even further when he indicates that the man is never even buried, possibly implying that he never dies (see Krüger's allusion to Enoch [2004, 126]). But great progeny and immortality do not bring satisfaction. The entire scenario here is hyperbolic—any Israelite man would want a hundred children and an impossibly long life, but not even *that* would make him happy. Other commentators believe Qohelet to be saying that the man lived a long life but never received a proper burial, which would be a tragedy in ancient Israel (M. Fox 2004, 39; see Isa. 14:20); however, "it is hard to see how the Teacher would regard a joyless life as vindicated by virtue of a good burial" (Garrett 1993, 315). Indeed, Qohelet is not bothered that the man has not had a funeral, but that the man was never "satisfied with pleasure." Another possibility is to see the clause about burial as a reference to the stillborn child in the next line (Garrett 1993, 315; Crenshaw 1987, 120), though the hyperbole of the previous lines about longevity favors the idea of the man never dying (see NET).

Immortality on earth could never happen, and that is the point. Qohelet wishes to paint the most exaggerated picture possible in order to show how meaningless it is to pursue ultimate satisfaction in these things. Immortality, remarkable progeny, and all the pleasures of life could not satisfy this man. It would be better if he had never been born alive than to live a life pursuing fulfillment in those things. A stillborn child never has to "see the sun" (שֶׁמֶשׁ לֹא־רָאָה) or "know anything" (וְלֹא יָדָע), phrases chosen intentionally by Qohelet in light of how much grief "seeing" things "under the sun" has brought him, and how much his great "knowledge" (1:18) has vexed his soul. Unlike the man who lives an impossibly long time and has all an Israelite man could want, the stillborn child has "rest" or "calm" (נַחַת). "Even if he [the old man] lives two thousand years" (וְאִלּוּ חָיָה אֶלֶף שָׁנִים פַּעֲמַיִם), and still is not satisfied with pleasure, it would be better that he was never born (cf. 4:3; Jer. 20:18; Job 3:10). At this point, Qohelet lays down his rhetorical toolkit to acknowledge that death is inevitable for both the seemingly immortal man and the child of the womb: "Do not all go to the same place?" At some point, everyone dies and loses everything they once had under the sun, so the implied lesson is that one should live authentically, joyfully, and presently before God (Eccl. 2:24–26; 3:12–13, 22; 5:18–19 [HB 17–18]; 9:7–10; for the commendation to live life with an acceptance of the present, see 11:1–10).

**6:7**. In 6:7–9, Qohelet shares a series of proverbs that are in keeping with his observations about life, death, and vanity elsewhere in the book. Here in 6:7, he points out how trivial human endeavor is since a person works just to feed themselves, but the process continues indefinitely (see notes on 1:1–11). He will soon get hungry again. This of course works on both literal and metaphorical levels since his "appetite" (נֶפֶשׁ) can refer to both his gullet and his inner self—neither can be perfectly satisfied under the sun, so he must find an alternative to ceaseless craving.

**6:8**. The healthy, wealthy, and wise man cannot escape death. The self-afflicted fool cannot escape death. And no mixture of these two kinds of people (i.e., a poor man who at least knows how to behave himself) can escape death. It eventuates for every kind of person.

**6:9**. It is better to enjoy what is before you, in the present, than to daydream, pine, and lust for things that you cannot see, do not have, and in many cases, should not have.

## THEOLOGICAL FOCUS

As with life and all human endeavor, wealth is plagued with impermanence. Still, to suffer loss is an occasion for sorrow, whether the loss came from a deal gone wrong (5:14 [HB 13]) or from some other unspecified cause (6:2), though both ultimately are from the hand of God (7:14). Such realities drive Qohelet mad with grief and are a sickening evil to him (5:13 [HB 12]). He does not take delight in the suffering of those who have lost everything. He wishes to convey to his students the real sorrow of such circumstances for the purpose of saying something more: sorrow can turn to joy if a person will resolve now to burrow their delight deep into the simple provisions of God (5:18–20 [HB 17–19]).

Less is more if "less" results in joy, and more is less if "more" requires relentless, soul-sapping hunger. In other words, those who delight in what they have (5:18 [HB 17]) are the same as those who are content with what their eyes see (6:9; notice the references to "seeing" in both verses). And those who "love money" (5:10 [HB 9]) are the same as those who have an endless appetite for more (6:9). It was a love for money that led Gehazi, the servant of Elisha, to lie to Naaman and take for himself some of the wealth Elisha had refused. For this, Gehazi and his descendants suffered tremendous loss (2 Kgs. 5:15–27). It was a love of money that drove Achan to sin against the Lord and take silver that the Lord had devoted to destruction. For this, he lost everything (Josh. 7:20–21). Any righteous king ruling over Israel was to abstain from amassing "excessive silver and gold," among other possessions, so that he would learn to fear the Lord (Deut. 17:17, 19). The HB is filled with many more examples of the dangerous allure of wealth.

God has appointed that humans should eat, drink, and enjoy their work in the fear of God (5:18–20 [HB 17–19]). In this way, a person can be guarded from "overthinking" (הַרְבֵּה יִזְכֹּר) everything and becoming mentally weighed down, because God "keeps him busy with joy in his heart" (5:20 [HB 19]). When someone embraces Qohelet's holy disillusion over the fool's gold of human pursuits, then he/she will be taking their first steps toward living a simple, authentic life in the fear of God.

Many things Jesus said in the Gospels directly correspond to the truths shared by Qohelet. In Luke 12:13–20, the parable is told of the rich man who decided to tear down his barns to build bigger ones in order to amass greater possessions so that he can "relax, eat, drink," and "be merry," to which God exclaims: "Fool! This night your soul is required of you, and the things you have prepared, whose will they be?" Qohelet prescribes the same enjoyments, but the difference in Jesus's parable is that the fool has vainly grounded these delights in the unstable foundation of his great wealth. Jesus concludes with, "So is the one who lays up treasure for himself and is not rich toward God." Qohelet would have found in Christ a teacher after his own heart. It was because of Christ that the apostle Paul found contentment in abundance or lack (Phil. 4:11–12). His circumstances did not control the state of his soul; rather, faith in Christ did: "I can do all things through Christ who strengthens me" (Eph. 4:13). Grounded in the gospel, a believer will learn to turn their eyes away from life's vain ambitions and to Jesus.

Jesus warned against a love for money, as did his apostles after him (Matt. 6:24; Luke 16:13; 1 Tim. 6:10; Heb. 13:5). If money is one's master, then God is not (Matt. 6:24; Luke 16:13). In fact, a love of money is the source for so many evils that it can drive one entirely away from faith in God and into a place of deep suffering like the man here in Ecclesiastes 5:17 (HB 16). In 1 Timothy 6:10, Paul specifies that this downfall happens due to one's "craving" for more wealth. For this reason, the writer of Hebrews admonishes, "Keep your life free from love of money, and be content with what you have, for he has said, 'I will never leave you nor forsake you.' So, we can confidently say, 'The Lord is my helper; I will not fear; what can man do to me?'" (Heb. 13:5–6, ESV).

It is difficult to think of Ecclesiastes apart from these later biblical texts that contain a shared ethos regarding money. As Spirit-inspired Scripture, all of these texts speak to and with one another on a topic very close to the human heart: one's trust in wealth versus one's trust in the sufficiency of God.

## PREACHING AND TEACHING STRATEGIES

### Exegetical and Theological Synthesis

Qohelet sought to disabuse his pupils of idealistic visions of life. To do so, he pointed out to them the regularity of oppression (5:8–9 [HB 7–8]). He also demonstrated the vanity of pursuing wealth in painstaking detail (5:10–17 [HB 9–16]). Instead of accumulating money, he advised that people should enjoy the simple gifts God gives. The wise person is content with the lot God has given him (5:18–20 [HB 17–19]). Contentment is key for Qohelet, because money cannot quench craving (6:1–9).

Jesus echoes Qohelet's basic point: those mastered by money cannot live for God (Matt. 6:24). But to break wealth's hold on us, it is sometimes important to stare at the consequences of life lived for the almighty dollar, euro, or yen. A life pursuing wealth is a life that can contribute to cycles of oppression. It is a life of restlessness and insomnia. It is a life of never-ending striving because the hunger and the hustle just won't stop. Ultimately, it is a life of misery.

### Preaching Idea
Serve God, not money.

### Contemporary Connections

*What does it mean?*
Money cannot provide comfort to us. In fact, the pursuit of money often motivates us to cause discomfort to others, which is why economic oppression is so common (5:8–9 [HB 7–8]). The more a person has, the more people who come out of the woodwork to consume it (5:10–11 [HB 9–10]). Many who have a lot also have a lot of sleepless nights, for they are worried about their wealth (5:12 [HB 11]). Money is not always a soft pillow of comfort for our heads, but can be like shackles on our feet, binding us to a life that makes us miserable. Our misery is compounded when we lose what we have (5:13–16

[HB 12–15]). The only thing that awaits the formerly rich person is "great vexation, sickness, and anger" (5:17 [HB 16]).

The reality is that money cannot make us happy; only contentment with God and his gifts can (5:18 [HB 17]). Instead of ceaseless striving, wise people eat, drink, and enjoy themselves with the work that God has given. The relentless chase of wealth does not allow someone to "rejoice in his work" because there is always more to do so that more can be earned (5:19 [HB 18]). Wise people gratefully receive God's gift and do not "overthink" their lives (5:20 [HB 19]).

Money likewise cannot provide satisfaction to the deepest longings of the human heart (6:1–9). Qohelet draws our attention to a few hypothetical scenarios of rich men who never receive ultimate satisfaction (6:1–5). What good does it do to be rich and famous but never actually get to enjoy good things (6:6)? Too much craving is "vanity" and "striving after the wind" (6:7–9). Material things cannot satisfy, particularly wealth, so it is pointless to pursue it as the ultimate goal.

*Is it true?*
Supposedly, famous oil baron John D. Rockefeller (1839–1937) was asked by a reporter, "How much [money] is enough?" It would have been a logical question because Rockefeller was the wealthiest person in America at the time. Some economists believe he would have been worth more than 300 *billion* dollars in today's value. It's difficult to know if this story is true or legendary, but Rockefeller's alleged response was, "Just a little bit more."

Just a little bit more…A little bit more may not seem like a lot, but it is *craving* for more that destroys souls. The apostle Paul warns us of the seduction of wealth, stating, "Some people by their longing for [wealth] have wandered away from the faith and pierced themselves with many griefs" (1 Tim. 6:10). The pursuit of affluence corrodes the soul. God himself warned Israel concerning the prosperity of the Promised Land: "When you have eaten and are satisfied, and have built good houses and lived in them, and when your herds and your flock multiply, and your silver and gold multiplies, and all that you have multiplies, then your heart will become proud and you will forget the LORD your God" (Deut. 8:11–12). God knew that prosperity, wealth, and affluence are major sources of temptations for his people.

Should it surprise us then that as prosperity has risen in the West, it has also become more secular? Should it surprise us that as Americans have become wealthier, rates of church attendance are shrinking?

*Now what?*
Qohelet challenges us to approach our wealth wisely. We need to rein in our ambitions and appetites and pursue God instead. How do we authentically serve God and resist the allure of money? The first way to break wealth's grip on our hearts is to look to Jesus Christ. Jesus, who was rich in heavenly glory, "become poor so that you through his poverty might become rich" (2 Cor. 8:9). Jesus eschewed a life of wealth and comfort in order to accomplish the work that God had given to him, redeeming a people for himself. When we turn our eyes upon Jesus and his sacrifice for our sins, we will avert our gaze from the shiny glow of gold.

A life shaped by the gospel will also be a life of generosity. Now that believers are "rich" in Christ, they can give generously to others in need. Paul contends that there is great blessing in giving generously for "he who sows sparingly will also reap sparingly, and he who sows bountifully will also reap bountifully" (2 Cor. 9:6). Paul is not advocating for a prosperity gospel, as if we will receive money back for money given. Instead, Paul points out that we will receive back *spiritual* blessings from God for money given. A closer sense of God's presence is worth more than a padded 401K.

Another way to combat the lure of wealth is to build limits into our lives. Qohelet tells us to enjoy the simple pleasures of life, such as food, drink, and just the right amount of work. We will never take time to enjoy those things if we are constantly working to make more money so that we can spend more on ourselves. Instead of looking for the "next thing," Qohelet advises us to enjoy the "now thing."

***Creativity in Presentation***

Deceased rapper Notorious B.I.G. accurately summed up the state of the wealthy in his title track, "Mo' Money, Mo' Problems." Too often, we deceive ourselves into thinking that just a little bit more wealth will solve our problems, when it may actually compound our problems, for "when good things increase, those who consume them increase" (5:11 [HB 10]). Long-lost relatives can come out of nowhere, demanding support when we become wealthy. Even more alarming can be the rapid pace at which we spend our money, leading us to destitution. Examples abound of famous athletes going broke, despite making millions of dollars in their careers. Former heavyweight champion Mike Tyson earned more than 300 million dollars, only to declare bankruptcy in 2003. Former all-pro football defensive tackle Warren Sapp earned more than 80 million dollars in his career, only to go bankrupt. Financial peril is not reserved for the famous, however. How many "regular" people spend more than they make, amassing large amounts of credit card debt?

The folly of pursuing riches is so clearly illustrated in Jesus's parable of the rich fool (Luke 12:16–21). A rich man had land that was very productive, just like investing money in the stock at just the right time (12:16). The man had so much extra that he tore down his perfectly good structures to build new ones, just as when we are wasteful and overspend in a home renovation project or other endeavor (12:17–18). The man eventually felt like he could retire, thinking to himself, "You have laid up for many years to come; take your ease, eat, drink, and be merry" (12:19). Right when he was supposed to enjoy his golden years, the Lord exposed his folly (12:20). Nothing the man had earned, built, or produced could spare him from death or God's coming judgment: "This very night your soul is required of you; and now who will own what you have prepared?" (12:21). The pursuit of wealth cannot insulate us from the realities of life.

The big idea for this section is "Serve God, not money." A compelling question to ask of this big idea is, "Why should I serve God instead of money?" The outline of the sermon would then give the reasons why we should serve God instead of money:

- Money cannot comfort you (5:8–17)
- Money cannot make you happy (5:18–20)
- Money cannot satisfy your deepest longings (6:1–9)

## DISCUSSION QUESTIONS

1. Why will those who love money never be satisfied (5:10–12)?

2. When people love money, what happens to them when they lose it all (5:13–17)?

3. How can we have joy in this lifetime (5:18–20)?

4. What is better than never being able to be satisfied, according to Qohelet (6:1–6)?

5. How does the gospel of Jesus Christ loosen money's grip on our souls?

6. How can you grow in generosity and contentment this week?

# THE ADMONITIONS OF QOHELET
## (6:10–12:14)

A change of tone begins the second half of Qohelet's wisdom, as it transitions primarily from observations to admonitions, marked by the use of the second-person "you" as he speaks directly to his pupils. He starts with a brief introduction in 6:10–12, where he describes the state of human ignorance in light of the sovereign determinations of God. The key observation of Qohelet in the midst of his many exhortations is that humans "cannot find out" (7:14, 24, 28; 8:17; cf. 3:11) and "do not know" (9:1, 5, 12; 10:14–15; 11:2, 5–6) "the work of God" (7:13; 8:17; 11:5), which includes the enigmatic ways of the world. The only thing humans can know for certain is that they will eventually die (8:8, 10–13; 9:2–6, 10–12; 10:14; 12:1–7); therefore, the only worthwhile thing to do is to live an authentic (wise, simple, joyful, and grateful) life in the "fear" of God (7:14, 18; 8:10–15; 9:7–9; 11:1–10; 12:11–14).

The introduction in 6:10–12 is followed by a series of five sections contrasting the transcendent qualities of God with the futilities and enigmas of the human experience. The first three sections (6:10–8:13; 8:14–9:10; 9:11–11:6) are centered around the unsearchable works of God, and the remaining two sections (11:7–12:7; 12:8–14) focus on the brevity of life and the certainty of judgment. Each section addresses a main theme with many others interspersed throughout: The Works of God Are Unsearchable, So Be Wise and Fear Before Him (6:10–8:13); The Works of God Are Unsearchable, So Live Joyfully Before Him (8:14–9:10); The Works of God Are Unsearchable, So Avoid Folly and Live Freely Before Him (9:11–11:6); Life Is Short, So Enjoy It and Remember God (11:7–12:7); and Human Endeavor Is Futile, So Heed the Wise and Follow God (12:8–14).

# Ecclesiastes 6:10–8:13

## EXEGETICAL IDEA
Qohelet acknowledges that God's works are unsearchable and concludes that one of the best things a human can do is live wisely in the fear of God.

## THEOLOGICAL FOCUS
The "work of God" (7:13), which includes the enigmatic ways of the world, cannot be found out such that life could be manipulated or controlled by humans; therefore, one ought to live wisely and fear God.

## PREACHING IDEA
Grow wise.

## PREACHING POINTERS
Qohelet began his investigation into the vanity of life by observing the world around him (1:1–6:9). He recognized that pursuing typical avenues of human fulfillment like work or money could never satisfy. In light of his observations, Qohelet begins admonishing his students. If they are to survive and thrive in this "vain" world, they should follow his prescriptions. He first speaks to the limits of human knowledge (6:10–12). He then moves on to speak about how to have a "better" life (7:1–14), the limits of wisdom (7:15–29), how to relate to those in authority (8:1–9), and what to do when you observe injustice in the world (8:10–13).

Sitting behind all of Qohelet's proverbs and admonitions is the larger command to be wise. Qohelet recognizes that wisdom, even with all its limitations, provides one of the best ways to navigate through life. Qohelet clearly exposes the incomprehensibility of the world, which is felt so keenly today as it seems like the modern world gets faster and more complex with every passing day. The only hope we can have to make our way through such complexity is the stabilizing force of wisdom.

# THE WORKS OF GOD ARE UNSEARCHABLE, SO BE WISE AND FEAR BEFORE HIM (6:10–8:13)

## LITERARY STRUCTURE AND THEMES (6:10–8:13)

There is considerable disagreement over how to divide up the rest of Ecclesiastes, particularly 6:10–8:13. Exegetical commentaries often delineate numerous subsections to acknowledge the many times Qohelet switches from one topic to the next. The homiletician, however, must think more broadly in order to preach this section in one or only a few weeks. For this reason, larger units have been imperfectly drawn based on major themes encountered within those units, all while acknowledging Qohelet's various topical interjections throughout.

We observe an overarching theme of human inability and ignorance in the face of God's unknowable ways/works (7:13; 8:17; 11:5). Given that humans are so limited, such that God's works "cannot be found out" (7:14, 24; 8:17), the only thing over which people have control is their own behavior. Humans can choose to live wisely or foolishly, wickedly or righteously. They can either fear God and enjoy a simple life or toil aimlessly in hopes of figuring things out and becoming the master of their own fate, both of which are futile and impossible-to-satisfy objectives, according to Qohelet.

Qohelet's thesis is given in 6:10–12 and is followed by a long selection of proverbs that contrast the usefulness of wisdom, the danger and futility of folly, and the sovereign determinations of God (7:1–22). This is followed by Qohelet's profound admission of ignorance (7:23–8:1a) and how one ought to live in the face of that reality (8:1b–9). He concludes with an expression of grief over how the wicked unfairly prosper, determining nonetheless that God is just and that people should still fear before him (8:10–13).

- *The Powerlessness and Ignorance of Humanity (6:10–12)*
- *God's Works Are Unalterable, So Live Wisely Before Him (7:1–22)*
- *Humans Suffer from Many Limitations, So Conduct Yourself Properly in the World (7:23–8:9)*
- *Death and Justice Are in God's Hands, So Fear Before Him (8:10–13)*

## EXPOSITION (6:10–8:13)

Qohelet begins this unit with a thesis statement that serves to summarize not only the present section (6:10–8:13) but the book as a whole. Humanity under the sun is hopelessly ignorant; people are utterly incapable of understanding "God's work" (7:13). His ways are unsearchable. These human limitations provide a helpful perspective. Since humans cannot "figure out" God (7:14, 24; 8:17) such that they can manipulate him to change the course of history in any way, all that is left for them to control is their own behavior. Accordingly, Qohelet admonishes his pupils to live wisely rather than foolishly, which includes fearing God.

### The Powerlessness and Ignorance of Humanity (6:10–12)

Qohelet sets the tone for the remaining chapters of Ecclesiastes by asserting that human knowledge is severely limited, which he contrasts with the unmatched strength and knowledge of God.

**6:10**. A summary of 6:10–12 would be: humans can no more determine their destinies than they can win an argument with God, so they should never presume to know the future. These verses are rendered in a stylistic but cryptic way in Hebrew. Starting with 6:10, we notice that everything present and past (including humans) has already been "named/called," which is a way of saying that the nature of all things has been defined (Whybray 1989, 110). To say that things have already been named is also a creative way of saying that there is nothing new under the sun.

Furthermore, the concept of naming things is a possible reference to the creation narrative in Genesis 1–2 where God named all things, including Adam, whom he imbued with the authority to name and rule over the animals (Gen. 2:19). God's sovereignty has already been expressed in similar terms earlier in Ecclesiastes (see 1:9 and 3:14–15). Qohelet further asserts that nature and natural limitations of humanity are "known" (6:10). Humanity's chief limitation is that it cannot overpower, manipulate, or control God, for his nature is "mightier" than theirs. If God is indeed the one who has named all things past (and there are no other qualified persons who could do this), then God is also the best candidate to be the "stronger one" mentioned at the end of the verse. Some scholars assert that this stronger contender is anything in life that is more powerful than a human (Fredericks and Estes 2010, 164), but others see God as the one against whom humanity cannot fight (M. Fox 2004, 42). The frequent contrast between divine power and human limitation throughout Ecclesiastes further supports the latter thesis. Humans can thwart other humans (8:9), but they are "not able to contend" with God. Fox sees Qohelet's advice as standing in contrast with the attitude of Job who thought, at least at first, that he could contend with God (M. Fox 2004, 42; see Isa. 45:9—a pot cannot fight with the potter). Qohelet does not expect humans to win or get a perfectly satisfactory answer for their pain.

**6:11**. As we saw back in 5:7 (HB 6), humans are prone to "many words," a practice they should put away in favor of fearing God (see the end of that same verse).

Another clue that God is the unnamed other in these verses is the return of "many words" mentioned earlier in 5:7 (HB 6; however, cf. Fredericks and Estes's very different reading of 6:10 [2010, 158]). Humans use many words to try to control, manipulate, or make sense of their surroundings, but this is all futile. Many words cannot save a person or alter the course of things in any ultimately satisfying way. Only God has that power.

**6:12**. Ecclesiastes 6:12 continues the notion of human ignorance by providing an example. There is no one person who is capable of telling another what exactly is best for them in this life. This seems to undercut the role of the overly confident sage while still leaving room for the general advice offered by Qohelet throughout the book. There is no one capable of giving perfect advice on how to handle the various situations that fall into another person's path. As chapter 10 makes clear, with its many references to the unpredictable nature of life, no one really knows what is going to happen next. It follows, then, that no one knows what will come "after him" on earth. Life is short, and humans live it out hurriedly while it flees "like a shadow." The only things we can confidently assert are the things right in front of us—no one should presume to know what will happen after he/she dies, not even the sages who confidently assert that certain outcomes always follow certain actions (an absolutist take on the retribution principle). The question left hanging in the air is, "What then is good to do during our brief days on earth?" In keeping with this principle, Qohelet would not presume to give advice that is too specific about the individual circumstances of others, but he will provide general wisdom on how people ought to live (see, e.g., 2:24–26;

3:12–13, 22). He continues this trend by contrasting wisdom with folly in 7:1–22.

## God's Works Are Unalterable, So Live Wisely Before Him (7:1–22)

Qohelet promotes wisdom over folly, but the kind of wisdom that accepts human limitations in light of divine sovereignty, an acceptance that leads to joy.

**7:1–2.** From Qohelet's perspective, death results in one's reputation being sealed and one's woes ceasing, but birth is the beginning of both hardships and countless opportunities to sully one's name through folly. It seems he is making the point that it is better for a person's soul to spend more time at the funeral home than at bars and restaurants—perhaps the former helps you better appreciate the latter. The elegant arrangement of words in this verse "glide like oil" (M. Fox 2004, 43)—*tov shem mishemen tov* (טוֹב שֵׁם מִשֶּׁמֶן טוֹב). The second half of the verse similarly features a cluster of assonance and alliteration: *weyom hamawet miyom hawaledo* (וְיוֹם הַמָּוֶת מִיּוֹם הִוָּלְדוֹ). These are not technical transliterations but simplified representations so that the English reader can hear the elegance of Qohelet's poetry in this verse—a verse about death! (See other interesting wordplay in the notes at 3:20–21; 9:5–6; and 10:8–11.)

Ecclesiastes 7:1 introduces the topic, while 7:2–4 expands on this thought. Ecclesiastes 7:5–6 provides a specific example. Qohelet discusses the dichotomous states of mourning and mirth, states embodied by funerals and banquets. He draws this contrast in order to show how the mindset of the sober, realistic, wise person is superior to that of the blissful, shallow fool who parties continuously. Ecclesiastes 7:1 begins with "a good name is better than perfume/oil." Both Proverbs 22:1 and Song 1:3 echo this principle. The term "name" (שֵׁם) frequently refers to a person's reputation in the HB—a reputation one risks losing if he/she leads a fool's life (e.g., Job 18:17). The implication is that a good reputation, one of honor, is better to have than all the indulgences of life that could risk hampering it.

Qohelet means to be shocking in his statement that the day of death is better than the day of birth. One's birth brings celebration, but one's death brings mourning, so how can the latter surpass the former? After all, is it not better to be a living dog than a dead lion (9:4)? Qohelet is certainly capable of contradicting himself, but it is too easy to accuse him of that here. Rather, it is important to consider his statements in context, understanding that his advice, like the advice of the sages in Proverbs, is not perfectly monolithic but can be adjusted to fit various scenarios—"conflicting counsels may be appropriate in different circumstances" (M. Fox 2004, 44; e.g., Prov. 26:4–5).

Despite all death's disadvantages, the "day of death" itself—meaning the time of one's death and the subsequent funeral—represents a time of fond remembrance, appreciation, and a sense of loss in one's community. The day of death also represents a departure from life's many woes, whereas the day of birth is an invitation to the woes. Qohelet could be picturing death as the achievement of reaching the top of the mountain, and birth as the daunting experience of looking up from the bottom before taking the first step. The journey of every human ends at death, "and the living should take it to heart" (וְהַחַי יִתֵּן אֶל־לִבּוֹ). The verb "give" (נתן) followed by "heart" (לֵב) appears elsewhere in Ecclesiastes and refers to deep, weighty thought (1:13, 17; 3:11; 7:2, 21; 8:9, 16; 9:1). This pair of verses (7:1–2) smacks of Proverbs and the dichotomy that is drawn between the wise person (who in this case thinks deeply and carefully about life) and the fool (who in this case drinks and parties seemingly without end). The sobering reality of death has a way of quickly organizing a person's priorities, centering their focus on what really matters. The prophet Isaiah identified this funerary attitude as appropriate for repentance, which he contrasts with the mindless merrymaking of fools who blindly ignore their transgressions against God (Isa. 22:12–13).

Qohelet's advice to spend more time in the funeral home than at the banquet hall may be both a call to repentance as well as a call for pensive acknowledgment of life's transience and the futility of pursuing fulfillment in vaporous things. In fact, the "house of mourning" mentioned in Ecclesiastes 7:2 and 4 may itself be a metaphor for Qohelet's state of mind in this investigation, that is, for the book of Ecclesiastes as a whole.

**7:3–4.** Sorrow is greater than laughter, "for dejection of face" (כִּי־בְרֹעַ פָּנִים) or "being in a state of sadness" will "do the heart good" (יִיטַב לֵב). Seeing the brutalities of the world for what they are forges a path to being joyful over the right things for the right reasons (as opposed to the artificial joy brought from abusing life's good things and hopping from one party to the next, as do the fools described in these verses; cf. 2:1–11). By "does the heart good," Qohelet could also be referring to the physical experience of grieving; for example, we may turn in our minds to the modern expression, "I just need a good cry," by which we mean a moment of emotional unraveling followed by the body's release of healing agents. Grief does not answer all of our questions, but it has a way of bringing things into perspective.

Proverbs 14:13 teaches that outward laughter may conceal an aching heart, and grief may be what comes after joy. Proverbs 15:13, however, teaches that if a person's heart is happy, then it shows on their face, but if their heart is sad, they will seem defeated. Both scenarios are relatable, and either can be true in the right circumstance. Neither verse calls for humans to force a smile through logic, like the inane children's song, "If you're happy and you know it then your face will surely show it; if you're happy and you know it, clap your hands!" (it should be noted that clapping can be a sign of hate!; Lam. 2:15; N. Fox 1995, 54 n. 21). In 7:3, Qohelet makes a third observation to go along with Proverbs 14:13 and 15:13 above, noting that when one chooses the path of sorrow, one is led to a place of deeper happiness. In this scenario, the sadness of one's heart results in sadness on one's face, which leads to greater gladness. This he contrasts with the mirthful idiocy of fools in Ecclesiastes 7:4.

> **The Usefulness of Death**
> Throughout Ecclesiastes, death is portrayed as the ultimate evil of the universe that undermines everything. This deeply vexes Qohelet; yet, in 7:1–4, he reveals that there is something useful about death, specifically in how the living get to experience the death of others. Death can be a helpful tool for maturing those who still see the sun. Death, in general, is crushing, but for the living, it can provide fresh perspective like nothing else can. In an attempt to maintain this realistic perspective, the wise dwell on sobering things ("the heart of the wise is in the house of mourning"), while fools are always searching for their next fix of fun ("the heart of fools is in the house of mirth"). This call to embrace sorrow may seem to contradict the joy statements provided elsewhere in Ecclesiastes, potentially leaving the reader confused as to which of the two paths Qohelet wishes his pupils to take. Does he want them to be happy or sad? The answer is, of course, "Both!," but an overapplication of either is unhealthy. Joy can be taken too far and become a shallow life-focus, like the drunk cacklers of 7:4b; likewise, sober-mindedness can overfixate on unsolvable problems and negativity to the point of emotional paralysis (1:18; 2:17). Qohelet wants neither depressed disciples nor disciples who attempt to bypass life's sorrows through incessant partying; rather, he wishes for his pupils to become realists like himself—people whose acknowledgment of life's sorrows keeps them grounded in life, free from lofty delusions, and occasions the joy of authentic living (2:24–26; 3:12–13, 22; 5:18–20 [HB 17–19]; 8:15; 9:7; 11:7–12:1).

# The Works of God Are Unsearchable, So Be Wise and Fear Before Him (6:10–8:13)

Egyptian funerary scene. Public domain. Pritchard: "Group of women and girls stand with raised hands mourning for deceased, painting from Theban tomb" (*ANEP* §638).

**7:5–6.** What we hear affects us, and what sounds bad at first (the stinging rebuke of a wise person) may be good in the long run. Vice versa, what sounds appealing at first (the cackling of fools) may be total vanity in the end. Qohelet advises that it is better to listen to the rebuke of wise people than to listen to the laughter of fools. Fools are busy laughing at evil (Prov. 10:23), but a wise person receives the "rebuke" (גַּעֲרַת) of other people who are wise (Prov. 17:10). But when a scoffer hears rebuke, he rejects it (Prov. 13:1). As with heavy drinking and incessant merry-making, so laughter is viewed as an escapist behavior exercised by those who cannot stomach healthy confrontation, especially if they are the one in need of correction. It is always easier to turn something into a joke, or otherwise quickly make light of one's selfish behavior.

Ecclesiastes 7:6 describes a whole chorus of fools laughing together at evil things or at their own wicked behavior. Fox points out the onomatopoeia of the Hebrew expression, where a repetition of s-sounds, k-sounds, and i-sounds in the Hebrew text simulates the sound of thorns popping in the fire but producing no useful heat (M. Fox 2004, 45). So, the laughing of fools is a form of false advertising—it looks appealing but is ultimately counterproductive, unhelpful, and even damaging.

**7:7.** Ecclesiastes 7:7–13 is a collection of only loosely related proverbs, if they are related to one another at all. Each verse sees an abrupt change of subject. If these verses have anything in common, it is that wisdom in all aspects of life is better than folly.

Ecclesiastes 7:7 makes the point that financial malfeasance can turn a wise person into a fool. The term "oppression" (הָעֹשֶׁק) could more specifically refer to "extortion" given its other uses in the HB (cf. Lev. 5:23; 18:18) and given the fact that it parallels "bribe" (מַתָּנָה) at the end of the line. This "oppression/extortion makes a wise person look foolish" (הָעֹשֶׁק יְהוֹלֵל חָכָם; see *HALOT* s.v. "הלל III" 249; cf. Job 12:17; Isa. 44:25). Going back to Ecclesiastes 7:1, a person's name/reputation is at stake when he/she accepts a bribe. The sages taught that dishonest wealth troubles a person's household, but those who despise "bribes" (מַתָּנֹת) will live (Prov. 15:27).

**7:8–9.** A humble person is cool-tempered and patient, but an arrogant person is hotheaded and hurried. The notion that the end is better than the beginning echoes Qohelet's assertion that death is better than birth (see note on Eccl. 7:1–2). Just as the end is better than the beginning, so it is better to be humble/patient ("long of spirit" אֶרֶךְ־רוּחַ) than to be arrogant ("tall of spirit" גְּבַהּ־רוּחַ). In a similar construction, Proverbs 16:5 notes that "all who are tall of heart" (כָּל־גְּבַהּ־לֵב), as in "arrogant," are an abomination to the Lord (Prov. 16:5). By contrast, God is "longsuffering" (אֶרֶךְ אַפַּיִם; Exod. 34:6).

> **The Folly of Anger**
>
> In Ecclesiastes 7:9, Qohelet associates "anger/vexation" (כַּעַס) as something that goes hand-in-hand with being a fool. Fools harbor such feelings in their "lap." One's "lap" (חֵיק) or the fold of one's garment is where a person may rest their hand or keep precious belongings (e.g., Ps. 74:11), just as a modern person carries their identification or money in a pants pocket. But this general region of the body refers to one's midsection more than just the base of the torso. It refers to the place where an infant is held (e.g., Ruth 4:16). In another sense, it is the location where one embraces a lover (e.g., Prov. 5:20; see *HALOT*

> s.v. "חֵיק" 312–13 for other examples). It is in this same place that a fool keeps his anger. He feeds his pride because it is precious to him; he keeps it as close as he would a lover or newborn baby. This ease of access makes him "quickly provoked" (NET). The arrogant man's relationship to anger may be contrasted with how "wisdom rests in the heart of the discerning" (בְּלֵב נָבוֹן תָּנוּחַ חָכְמָה) in Proverbs 14:33. Its greatest contrast, though, is with the longsuffering temperament of God who, never losing sight of the transient, breath-like quality of his people, "often restrained his anger and did not excite his wrath, because he remembered that they were mere flesh, a breeze that passes on and does not return" (Ps. 78:38–39). The "breeze/wind" (רוּחַ) frequently appears in conjunction with הֶבֶל ("vanity/breath") in Ecclesiastes: 1:14; 2:11, 17, 26; 3:19; 4:4, 16; 6:9; see also Isaiah 57:13.

**7:10.** Continuing on the theme of how we can never know the future and hence should not jump to conclusions (Eccl. 3:11, 22; 6:12; 7:14; 8:7; 11:2), Qohelet confronts the heart that lingers on "the good ole days." He calls such a person a fool, but in the nicest way possible: "It is not from wisdom that you ask this" (7:10b). An outburst of frustration over better days gone by will not lead one to a present state of contentment. Perhaps the old days *were* better than this very moment, but dwelling on the past gives one's mind no space for hope in what God may do in the present or the future—the story of the present has yet to be told. The elders in Ezra's day rejoiced to see the rebuilding of the temple, but they also wept for how its splendor paled in comparison with the glory of Solomon's temple (Ezra 3:12). Accordingly, Haggai exhorted the returned exiles, who remembered the magnificence of the past, to move forward in new strength, giving them a word from the Lord: that one day he will shake the heavens and the earth, thereby funneling all the treasures of the nations into Jerusalem, making "the latter glory of this house greater than the former" (see Hag. 2:2–9).

**7:11–12.** Wisdom is more valuable than wealth. Before making this point at the end of Ecclesiastes 7:12, Qohelet first elevates wisdom's value to match wealth: "Wisdom, just like an inheritance, is good" (טוֹבָה חָכְמָה עִם־נַחֲלָה). Some translations understand Qohelet to be saying that having wisdom and possessions at the same time is good (e.g., KJV, NASB; also M. Fox 2004, 47, citing Eccl. 9:16). However, given the comparison between wisdom and wealth in 7:12, it is better to understand Qohelet to be saying, "Wisdom, *like* inheritance, is good" (see, e.g., ASV, NIV; also, Murphy [1992, 60], "is as good as"). The point of these proverbs is not that money is valuable, which is obvious for Qohelet's readers. The focus is on wisdom, which is an advantage to those who "see the sun"—those who are yet living.

The term "shade" (צֵל) is metaphorical for "protection" in many places in the HB. The Israelites more than once placed their hope "in the shade of Egypt" (בְּצֵל מִצְרָיִם) rather than trusting in the Lord (Isa. 30:2). Qohelet highlights the greatest point of comparison between wisdom and wealth: both are a form of protection; however, wisdom can do something wealth on its own cannot—wisdom "preserves" (תְּחַיֶּה) one's life. Wealth, on the other hand, is only as useful as its bearer is wise (see Prov. 11:4; see Qohelet's real-world example of this principle in Eccl. 9:13–15).

**7:13.** Humans cannot confound the work of God (see 6:10); humans are incapable of unraveling the things God has "twisted" (מְעֻוָּת; see 1:15). Is it right, though, to assert that God makes things crooked? This verse certainly would have stunned its original readers, as it may yet stun us, since the verb "to make crooked" (the *piel* stem of עות) is primarily used to describe the perversion of justice or twisting of the truth (Job 8:3; 34:12; Lam. 3:36; Amos 8:5). In fact, in Job 34:12, Elihu declares that "the Almighty will not pervert justice" (וְשַׁדַּי לֹא־יְעַוֵּת מִשְׁפָּט). However, God does "twist the path of the wicked"

# The Works of God Are Unsearchable, So Be Wise and Fear Before Him (6:10–8:13)

(וְדֶרֶךְ רְשָׁעִים יְעַוֵּת) in Psalm 146:9, and Job himself declares that God has "wronged" (עִוְּתָנִי) him (Job 19:6 NET). Translations may soften Job's complaint to "God has put me in the wrong" (ESV); however, the sense coming from Job in this verse is that God has done so unjustly. That, of course, is not Job's final assessment of the Lord, whom he considers just (Job 42:1–6), but merely an outburst of his felt experience in the moment (see Job's speech in 12:23–25, which is comparable in tone to Eccl. 7:13). Qohelet, on the other hand, is not crying out from a place of equivalent torment when he asks this question, nor does he deny the justice of God (e.g., 3:17; 11:9; 12:14); rather, his view of God's sovereignty allows for all the seemingly unbalanced happenings on the earth (3:1–15). Though Qohelet would never accuse him of injustice, God is still somehow behind the goings-on of the world. God himself is not evil nor the perpetrator of evil, yet he is depicted in the HB as the sovereign source of "light and darkness" (Isa. 45:7) in the sense of "good and bad" circumstances (Lam. 3:8; see also Amos 3:6). Given the nuances of Qohelet's ideas of God and the world, one should not read too much into the agency of God in the term "made crooked" (עִוְּתוֹ). The fact is that humans are incapable of "fixing" (לְתַקֵּן) what God has determined or perhaps allowed to be crooked (we cannot know Qohelet's conception of the precise extent of divine agency). But the primary focus here, as elsewhere in Ecclesiastes, is on human limitations rather than on what Qohelet assumes is an already accepted fact—that God is sovereign.

Qohelet does not put himself in the position of Job, meaning that he does not comment negatively on God's activity in an accusatory way. He simply accepts as fact the notion that God's agency in all things accords somehow with his justice. Qohelet is more oft to accept such theological conundrums than perhaps others of his day. This is, after all, part of what is asked of the Lord's people: that they should believe by faith despite certain unresolved hang-ups, knowing the incredible limitations of human cognition and the fact that God has intentionally hidden things from us such that we "cannot figure out what God has done from the beginning to the end" (Eccl. 3:11).

**7:14.** Embrace the joy of the good times, and do not get overly perplexed when things are bad; God has made it impossible for us to make sense of life's unpredictable circumstances. In keeping with the sentiment from 7:13 above, Qohelet views God as the ultimate agent behind good days and bad. This is not just a fact to be observed, but a prescription to apply whenever humans are beset by times of evil. Qohelet prescribes that humans should "look" (רְאֵה), often translated "consider" (e.g., ESV, NET), "that God has made one as well as the other." In other words, if God is behind it, what can you do to change it? Absolutely nothing. However, a person *can* redirect their heart and the way they think about things. If the conundrum of evil pushes a person toward vexation, anger, and a stuck mental state as they try to resolve the unresolvable (see the harboring of vexation/anger in 7:9), then they should be liberated from that. The key to freedom is an awareness that you *cannot* figure it out because God has placed limits on human knowledge (see 3:11; 6:10–12).

The latter half of the verse gives a reason behind God's seeming randomization of our good and bad seasons (from a human perspective): "so that man will not find out anything [that comes] after him." Seow (1997, 240) points out this sole occurrence of "so that" (עַל־דִּבְרַת שֶׁ) in Hebrew, noting its appearance in Aramaic (עַל־דִּבְרַת דִּי) in Daniel 2:30 and 4:14. In both Daniel passages, what immediately follows "so that" is the revelation of some knowledge, which accords with the use here in 7:14. God has randomized our days (or so it seems from our limited perspective) *so that* we will not entertain the hubris of thinking we can determine our fate. Though Qohelet does not mention faith by name, we could infer that God does this in order to keep us on our toes and constantly trusting in him.

**7:15**. Humans cannot crack the code of how God operates, so we cannot understand why our expectations are often unmet. The righteous sometimes die young, and the wicked sometimes live to old age; accordingly, we should not assume that it is possible to work the system in such a way that we could manipulate our outcomes. Only God is in control and he has not revealed how or why he does everything he does.

Ecclesiastes 7:15–18 is bound together on the same theme: the dichotomy of righteousness and wickedness. Qohelet here writes to those who have read the words of the sages in Proverbs, words that may leave the reader expecting things to *always* go well for the righteous and poorly for the wicked (the principle of retribution). Qohelet, however, observes that life often does not always unfold in this ideal way. The righteous sometimes suffer. The wicked sometimes prosper. It should be noted, however, that the book of Proverbs often directs its readers toward generalities; not everything stated in Proverbs is intended to be understood as a universal, unalterable fact. In other words, there is more nuance among the sages than the style of retribution touted by Job's friends implies. Regardless of how Proverbs should be properly read, Qohelet is addressing the notion that many Israelites in his day clearly held (as some Christians still hold in the modern world), that God does not allow harm to fall on the heads of righteous people undeservedly (the book of Job addresses this issue, but to what extent did Qohelet's readers understand and apply the principles of that text?). Based on Qohelet's writing, it seems that the prevailing ideology among his hearers was that God operated by a predictable system of retribution.

Qohelet reports on what he has seen in "the days of his vain [life]" (בִּימֵי הֶבְלִי), an expression that might be another confession of his own ignorance, of his own inability to unravel the enigmas of life. At the very least, the expression is evidence of his self-awareness regarding the ephemerality of his own life. Though he is "wise" (12:9), he still speaks out of the limitations afforded by his mortality (see 7:23–29). He has seen a righteous man perish "in his righteousness." The man Qohelet describes did not die *because* of his righteousness, but *while in the state of* righteousness or perhaps even *in spite of* it (Seow 1997, 252). Likewise, Qohelet has seen a wicked man "prolong" his life in spite of that man's wickedness. For some of Qohelet's readers, this observation may be something they too have noticed but not allowed themselves to dwell on, clinging instead to the principle of retribution. Qohelet's mission, though, is to harp on awkward realities until his pupils experience a holy disillusion from their false presumptions so that the only thing left in the end is what is authentic (2:24–26; 3:12–13; 5:18–20 [HB 17–19]; 8:15; 9:7–10).

**7:16**. Do not pursue fulfillment in your own righteousness and wisdom, or you will end up deeply discouraged. The warning here seems strange, especially since chapter 7 is full of admonitions to pursue wisdom and righteousness over folly (e.g., 7:19). But Qohelet's instruction is not totally different from the point he made back in 2:12–17, that wisdom cannot ultimately satisfy a person or change their destiny—death. The wise/righteous and fools die alike; accordingly, we ought not fall under the delusion that wisdom has the power to change more than it is meant to. It cannot rescue a person from every trouble (see note on 10:11), especially not the trouble of eventually dying. The phrase translated "and do not be overly wise" (וְאַל־תִּתְחַכַּם יוֹתֵר) may seem to contradict Qohelet's admonitions elsewhere to *be* wise. But here he is warning against the temptation to overexert oneself in the pursuit, or to "present yourself as wise" (note the *hithpael* stem), possibly suggesting inauthenticity or self-aggrandizement. Back in 2:15 he also paired the verb "wise" together with the term "more/exceedingly" (יוֹתֵר) to point out the absurdity of overexerting oneself given the inevitability of death, in light of which he asked, "Why have I been so wise?" (וְלָמָּה חָכַמְתִּי אֲנִי אָז יוֹתֵר). The sense contained in this question is echoed at the end of our present verse: "Why should you be disappointed" (לָמָּה תִּשּׁוֹמֵם). Most English translations render the verb "destroy yourself," which seems too broad since other uses of the verb (שׁמם) in the *hithpoel* refer to a person being appalled/disgusted by something (Ps. 143:4; Isa. 63:5; see NET: "be disappointed"). To work hard all your life toward an unattainable goal (i.e., ultimate satisfaction in anything this life has to offer), only to realize at the end of your life that your efforts were vanity, would cause great disgust.

**7:17**. Pursuing fulfillment in folly has an even less appealing result (a shorter life) than pursuing fulfillment in wisdom (disappointment; see Eccl. 7:16 above). Following 7:16, Qohelet anticipates the wisecrack from the back of the classroom, "Well, if we're all going to die, then let's keep on sinning!" Antinomianism is not the solution to the problem of death (or the blessing of grace, cf. Rom. 6:1), because God is still judge. So why go headlong into wickedness and foolishness, knowing the consequences that could befall you? That would be like setting a trap for your own feet (Ps. 9:15 [HB 16])! And while Qohelet has seen *some* wicked people prosper, he never indicates that *most* do. Given his acknowledgment of the certainty of God's judgment of the wicked throughout the book, it is clear that Qohelet still holds to a general, though heavily nuanced, principle of retribution. If the prophets and sages are worth listening to, and Qohelet would say they are, then the general rule holds true that God's hand of protection is on the righteous and his hand of judgment is on the wicked. With our human eyes, we see what we think are exceptions to the rule when the wicked get away with evil and are buried in honor (8:10–11); nevertheless, Qohelet's stubborn belief in God's justice leads him to determine that *somehow* God will take care of the righteous and will judge the wicked (8:12–13). He concludes this even without a fleshed-out theology of the afterlife! All this is to say that if a person is leveraging bets on which is the best way to live one's life (wickedly or righteously), the safer bet is always to live righteously (for notions of the afterlife in the HB, see Introduction, the notes on 8:12–13; 9:5–6; 11:9; 12:7, and 13, and the sidebar "Life After Death in Ecclesiastes" p. 108).

Qohelet, who fears God and admonishes his pupils to follow wisdom, does not reject the book of Proverbs. What he rejects is the false notion by some of its readers that there are no exceptions to the principle of retribution. It is still true that being a fool could result in your untimely death: "Why should you die when it is not your time?" And anyone familiar with the history of Israel in the HB knows that God has the right to judge a person whenever and however he chooses. We do not know everything, and we cannot hack the system. Rather, we must resolve to work with what little knowledge we have. Wisdom outweighs folly, but not to the extent that we should delude ourselves into becoming "overly wise."

**7:18**. Hold on to both pieces of advice just given in 7:16–17 (to not be overly righteous or overly wicked), since fearing God actually looks like neither of those two things. Keeping both principles, though they may appear to contradict one another, is essential for the person who fears God (see excursus "Contradictions in Ecclesiastes").

Interpreters have debated the meaning of this verse due to its difficulty, but the preferred reading is conveyed by Seow: "It is good that you grasp the one but also not let go of the other, for the one who fears God goes forth with both of them" (1997, 252). By "both of them" is meant both of the instructions given above in 7:16 and

17 (the term "go forth" יֵצֵא could also mean "escape" in the sense of avoiding trouble). In all, Qohelet presents three options:

1. Pursue wisdom and righteousness vaingloriously, and wind up crushingly disappointed (7:16).
2. Pursue hedonism and wickedness, which is a fast track toward death (7:17).
3. Avoid both such extremes by living authentically in the fear of God (7:18).

The latter option is preferred.

**7:19**. Wisdom can make a person more capable than ten urbanite elites. In other words, do not be easily fooled by robes, titles, other signs of socioeconomic prestige—wisdom outweighs them all. This principle is given a real-life example in 9:13–16.

Commentators see this verse as an interruption of Qohelet's stream of thought, and so opt to place it elsewhere, like after 7:12 (M. Fox 2004, 49, citing Ginsburg). It could be, though, that Qohelet is simply slipping in and out of longer and shorter proverbial formats, all generally related to the broader theme of wisdom's superiority over folly. So, while 7:19 may not belong to the neatly packaged unit of 7:15–18 or even 7:20, the topic has not really changed here.

**7:20**. Qohelet is not denying the existence of righteous people (cf., e.g., 3:17; 7:15; 8:14), but the existence of a person who is so righteous that he/she *only ever* does what is good. Qohelet does not need to include the qualifier "only" for us to understand the line this way, given all he has said elsewhere. The conjunction at the head of 7:20 (כִּי) could mean "but" or "for/because." If it means "but," then the idea of 7:19–20 is that wisdom makes one capable (7:19), *but* no one is perfectly righteous/wise (7:20; the terms are used interchangeably in places). The asseverative use of (כִּי), "surely" or "indeed," could just mean that the proverb stands on its own (see Arnold and Choi §4.3.4i).

**7:21–22**. The fact that no one is without error (7:20) should affect both the way we process the errant speech of others (7:21) and our own errant speech (7:22). In the micro, the example used to highlight the culpability of all people is that of errant speech. Jesus's famous expression "Judge not lest you be judged" (Matt. 7:1) echoes these verses. Qohelet warns his pupils not to internalize every cross word they hear others saying unless they (the pupils) would like to be held under the same level of scrutiny. In the macro, Qohelet is calling for profound humility in light of universal human imperfection.

The expression is "also, concerning all the things that they say, do not put it to your heart" (גַּם לְכָל־הַדְּבָרִים אֲשֶׁר יְדַבֵּרוּ אַל־תִּתֵּן לִבֶּךָ), which is similar to the English expression "don't take it to heart." The idea is that one should take such criticisms lightly. The combination of the verb "give/put" (נתן) and "heart" (לֵב) appears several times in Ecclesiastes as Qohelet describes how he "applies his heart" or "carefully examines" the various matters that he observes under the sun (1:13, 17; 7:2; 8:9, 16; 9:1). This practice many times led him to vexation. Qohelet teaches that taking things too seriously (other than fearing God) is a problem. One more thing he recommends is not overthinking "all" the things people say, some of which may involve cursing you harshly. If you do take too much interest in everything a person says, then it may shatter or overly enrage you when you hear someone in your own house cursing you or your mother.

The other rationale for not taking the words of others too seriously is that "you know that many times you yourself have cursed others." The implied question may be, "Have *you* always meant it when you cursed others under your breath?" The answer is likely no. Such cursings are often just foolish outbursts of frustration. If we have a sensitive conscience, then it would horrify us to know that the person who is the object of our cursing overheard us.

## Humans Suffer from Many Limitations, So Conduct Yourself Properly in the World (7:23–8:9)

In his most profound admission of ignorance, Qohelet reinforces the point that humans are severely limited in terms of what they can figure out, but they should at least know how to behave properly.

**7:23–24.** The humility Qohelet calls for in the previous verses is one he also employs in his own self-reflection. He could not achieve wisdom (ultimate understanding of things) because the knowledge of the past is irretrievable. And as we have seen from other places in his teaching, knowledge of the future is also unattainable (e.g., 3:11; 6:12). Nevertheless, Qohelet "tested" (נסע) all this, which is a way of saying that he applied cognitive pressure to life's conundrums in an attempt to figure them out, just as the queen of Sheba tested (also *piel* נסע) Solomon to ascertain the extent of his wisdom (1 Kings 10:1). But just as the queen of Sheba was unable to put Solomon into a rhetorical vice, so Qohelet could not overcome life's varied puzzles. And just as the queen was left astounded by the mind of Solomon, so Qohelet is befuddled by the unreachable depths of God's world (see 8:17).

This section (7:23–8:9) is broken down into two subunits: (1) the ignorance of humanity and their vain attempts to obtain ultimate wisdom, as told through Qohelet's personal experiences (7:23–8:1a), and (2) how humans should instead appropriate wisdom for its practical benefits (8:1b–9). Combining the end of chapter 7 with the first nine verses of chapter 8 is not an obvious choice, but it does follow a loose pattern in Ecclesiastes of Qohelet commenting on the delusions of humanity and/or the enigmatic nature of the world and then offering practical advice for how humans ought to live in light of these realities.

The first subunit (7:23–8:1a) focuses on how humans have perverted the simplicity and authenticity given them by God in creation (see note on 7:29), which has resulted in delusion and the realization of human ignorance. Humans have convoluted things through their own reasoning and have attempted to manipulate the world around them, including God. A consequence of this activity is that humans have become clouded in their judgment, overly complex, and difficult to understand. For this reason, Qohelet admits that he cannot "figure out" (מצא) people. This section opens in 7:23–24 with a question ("Who can figure it all out?"), a question about plumbing wisdom's depths. It is met with a negative answer: no one can figure it all out. The section concludes with a parallel question in 8:1a ("Who is like the wise?"), one that anticipates a similarly negative answer.

The second subunit (8:1b–9) begins by addressing wisdom's relative usefulness: it at least makes a person's face shine. In other words, there is something to redeem about wisdom (after all, wisdom was never the problem in the first place; rather, trouble came when humans attempted to master it, e.g., 2:12–17). In sum, a pursuit for ultimate wisdom is illusory because it is unattainable, but wisdom, in general, is at least still useful.

In a sobering admission of his own limitations of knowledge as a human being, Qohelet reveals his inner thoughts: that he wants to be wise (אָמַרְתִּי אֶחְכָּמָה), but sadly it was "far" from him. If ultimate wisdom is far from this wise, careful, truth-seeking teacher (12:9–10), then how much further away is it for everyone else? A mere awareness of all that has happened in the world, never mind a reasonable explanation for it all, is so "far" and "deep, deep" (וְעָמֹק עָמֹק), that he asks, "Who can find it out?" Humans are incapable of "finding out" (7:14, 24; 8:17) all that God has done or the reasons why God has done it.

# The Works of God Are Unsearchable, So Be Wise and Fear Before Him (6:10–8:13)

**7:25**. In 7:23–24 he mentions that he had tested all things by wisdom, but here in 7:25–29, he explains a bit more of how that journey unfolded. Qohelet enters into dialogue with his heart, going through the paces (סבב) cognitively, "to know, to spy out, and to seek out wisdom and a resolution" to his quandaries (לָדַעַת וְלָתוּר וּבַקֵּשׁ חָכְמָה וְחֶשְׁבּוֹן). Surely there is some explanation for all the delusions of humanity. But his efforts are unsatisfied; his attempt to comprehend the complexity of evil and what motivates it makes him akin to the historian or sociologist who searches aimlessly for a rationale to explain ethnic prejudices and the violence that results from those prejudices. In the end, the historian finds that there is no boogeyman lurking in the shadows, no rational justification for hating other ethnic groups. Likewise, Qohelet will have to conclude that humans by nature plot evil—it is just what they do (7:29).

**7:26**. In the process of investigating all things wicked and foolish, Qohelet does not manage to resolve any mysteries, but he *is* able to identify an evil worse than death: the wicked seductress. But why this particular evil? Perhaps the temptation to follow a wicked woman is a weakness of his and one he predicts will affect his male pupils as well. It is clear that Qohelet's warning is not against all women (consider, at the very least, his commendation to love one's wife in 9:9), but specifically against "the woman whose heart is snares and nets, whose hands are prison shackles." This language describes a distinct *kind* of woman. There is no evidence in the text to support the thesis that Qohelet is referring to women in general (see note on 7:28). The woman of whom he speaks must fit this sinister description. And even though the enticement of the wicked seductress is primarily in view, she is not the only problem he identifies—the male "sinner" (חוֹטֵא) who goes after her is also implicated. After all, it takes two to tango.

## Qohelet and Women

The principles Qohelet teaches apply to both men and women, but he does specifically mention women a few times (2:8; 7:26–28; 9:9; 11:5). The first mention (2:8) comes in his parody of Solomon, when he acquired female singers and concubines in a vain pursuit of fulfillment through pleasure. In 7:26–28 the wicked seductress is used as an example of the only thing Qohelet could figure out in his investigation into madness and folly, that there actually *is* something worse than death: being trapped by such a woman. In 9:9 he commends loving one's wife as an expression of authentic living, which appears in one of his joy statements. Finally, in 11:5 women are mentioned with regard to pregnancy as an example of the mystery of God in putting "breath/spirit" into a womb. The passage that has received the most attention regarding women is 7:26–28, where Qohelet is often accused of misogyny. However, he talks much more about wicked men *throughout* his teaching, contrary to the claim that he has a misogynistic outlook on the basis of a few verses alone. Nevertheless, why does Qohelet focus on the evil seductress as the one thing that is worse than death?

The only reasonable answer is that the wily woman has more to do with Qohelet's (and his pupils') sinful proclivities in their own context than it does the wicked woman herself. After all, those who are not behaving like a "sinner" (7:26) will not be threatened by such a woman. This archetypal lawless woman is mentioned more than once in Proverbs (e.g., Prov. 5, 7), but the male seducer is not similarly addressed in Scripture (the context of Exod. 22:16 is quite different). The reason for this, though, is far less sensational than some may think; in a society where women had little to no choice in selecting a mate, admonitions to avoid seduction primarily worked one way. Add to this the fact that most Scripture is written by male authors, and it is no wonder that its category-crossing principles are often explained from a male vantage point (as in

> Prov. 1–9, from a father to a son). The Holy Spirit's inspiration of Scripture does not remove the humanness of its authors whose frames of reference or personal concerns are captured in their writing (see esp. Paul's personal notes in the epistles, e.g., 1 Cor. 7:25). Qohelet's warnings apply to women and men alike who must be careful to use discernment in life. Finally, interpreters have frequently seen 7:27–28 as Qohelet's condemnation of women, but the textual evidence suggests that Qohelet is not making a statement on women here but about his own ignorance (see note on 7:27–28 regarding the function of מצא throughout the book; see also sidebar "The Human Inability to Figure It All Out" p. 148). Based on my reading of these verses, it seems that Qohelet's chief contribution to the topic of women is that he, as a human male, is incapable of "figuring" (מצא) them out (7:28).

**7:27–28.** Qohelet can only figure out one out of a thousand men, but he cannot figure out even one woman. Ecclesiastes 7:27 is the only time outside of the prologue and epilogue where we hear from the narrator as Qohelet is referred to in the third person: "says Qohelet."

Certain interpretations of these verses have led to accusations of misogyny as if Qohelet were searching the world over for at least one righteous woman. This interpretation, however, is uncalled for and unsupported by the text, which nowhere mentions a search for "righteous" or "upright" people, but only an effort on Qohelet's part to "figure out" (מצא) people. Other interpretations have Qohelet searching for wisdom among women but finding that there is none; however, this also requires going beyond what is written here in the text (e.g., Fredericks and Estes 2010, 185–86). What has contributed to the confusion, though, is (1) the mention of the wicked woman in the verse prior, (2) the feminine form of the cardinal number "one" (אַחַת) here in 7:27, and (3) a mistranslation of the term "figure out" (מצא) as "find" in 7:28.

As for the first piece of circumstantial evidence, it is important that 7:26 be read as a tangential interjection rather than a north star for the conversation. The thesis statement for these verses is clearly 7:25. Qohelet figures out that there is something worse than death (the wily woman), but that does not truly satisfy his stated investigation in 7:25; rather, 7:26 is a non sequitur warning he feels must be conveyed to his pupils.

Regarding the second piece of evidence, the masculine form of the cardinal number "one" (אֶחָד) appears seventeen times in Ecclesiastes. The feminine form (אַחַת) appears only twice, and both of them are here in 7:27, "[adding] one to another." The assumption may be that Qohelet is sorting through women one by one (as in, e.g., Deut. 21:15; 1 Kings 3:25; see also Weeks 2022, 286); but actually this expression is meant to describe Qohelet's mental pacing (see סבב in 7:25) as when Elisha paced about the room "once here and once there" (אַחַת הֵנָּה וְאַחַת הֵנָּה) in ritual contemplation before raising the Shunammite's son (see also Schoors's suggestion, following Delitzsch, that Qohelet's expression is an "arithmetic and dialectic formula" at work [Schoors 2013, 581]). Qohelet is likewise going through the paces cognitively, moving through matters one at a time (not one women at a time). Hence, the feminine form of "one" is not related to the wily woman of 7:26, nor women generally.

The final piece of circumstantial evidence regards Qohelet's conclusion in 7:28, and it is here that interpreters can err the most by putting words into Qohelet's mouth. For example, following 7:26 Fox believes Qohelet has failed to find one "satisfactory" or "good" woman out of a thousand, and that he is thereby guilty of misogyny (however, Qohelet supplies no such adjective for the woman). Fox also calls Qohelet's words "hyperbolic," though, pointing to the sage's acknowledgment elsewhere that there are good women (see 9:9), and admitting that Qohelet's antiwoman statement "is the only such remark in the Hebrew Bible" (M. Fox 2004,

# The Works of God Are Unsearchable, So Be Wise and Fear Before Him (6:10–8:13)

51–52). Qohelet is certainly capable of hyperbole, but these final two caveats provided by Fox actually work against the claim that Qohelet is being misogynistic. Key to understanding this passage is Qohelet's free admission in 7:22–23 that he is ignorant. He is not especially ignorant compared to others, but as a human he is severely limited in his knowledge (e.g., 3:11, 22; 6:12; 7:14; 8:7; 11:2). In 7:27–28 he continues this admission by demonstrating that he could only "figure out" one man out of a thousand, which is to say that he does not understand why most men do what they do. To compound his ignorance, he admits that he could not figure out even one woman. The potential for misogyny is occasioned only by taking the verb "to find" (מצא) literally (as if he is on the hunt for an upright/righteous woman) rather than figuratively ("to figure out"), which is how it is used elsewhere in the book. People, after all, are *not* hard to find, but they are nearly impossible to figure out. Nowhere in these verses is there an indication that Qohelet is looking for "upright" people; rather, that he is trying to figure out people in general. The word "upright" does not appear in the Hebrew text of 7:26–28, though some translations (e.g., NET, NIV) include it.

---

### The Human Inability to Figure It All Out

The verb "to find" (מצא) is used to express what Qohelet can and cannot "figure out" (as in solving riddles—Judg. 14:18). It is introduced in 3:11 where it is used to describe how human beings cannot "figure out" what God has done in the past and cannot figure out what God will do in the future. The next time the verb appears is in 7:14, where, once again, Qohelet claims that God sovereignly oversees good things and bad things so that human beings cannot "figure out" the future, since every day is unpredictable. The next example comes in 7:24, where again he claims that human beings cannot "figure out" all that has happened on earth. In 7:26, Qohelet "figured out" something more bitter than death. In every example so far, the sense has been figuring out rather than searching to find a particular thing, so why in 7:27–28 would the term suddenly imply that Qohelet went on an exhaustive hunt for a single upright man and a single upright woman, but could only find a man?

As before in 3:11; 7:14, 24, and 26, so in 7:27–28, the term means to "figure out" as in "come to know" or "understand." Given Qohelet's humility and admitted limitations, the fact that he could only understand one man out of a thousand is believable. Because Qohelet is a man, it is equally believable that he could not "figure out" even one woman. Notes Whybray, "The commentators, in interpreting [verse 28], have failed to notice that it does not state what it is that the speaker has sought, and which he has, or has not, found" in his investigations (1989, 127). No matter how much effort a person applies to decode "the work of God" (7:13; 8:17; 11:5; the *what* and *why* of everything that happens), they will not succeed. In the end, some may, through self-delusion, claim that they have succeeded in figuring it all out (8:17). Qohelet gives us the inside track, though—they "cannot figure it out" (לֹא יוּכַל לִמְצֹא; see note on 8:16–17).

---

**7:29**. Qohelet has figured out only this: God has made human beings "upright," but humans have "sought out many schemes." Humans have complicated their own existence by trying to unravel things too lofty for them, trying to manipulate the world into serving only their desired outcomes. The NJPS translation provides an interesting reading: "God made men plain, but they have engaged in too much reasoning." But reasoning alone does not seem to be the problem so much as the presumption that they could figure it all out in the first place, that they could bend the world to fit their ends. Then, having caved to such delusions, they assume that they have accomplished what they had set out to do. But as Qohelet reminds us, "Even if a wise person says they understand, they are not actually able to figure it out" (8:17b). Here

# The Works of God Are Unsearchable, So Be Wise and Fear Before Him (6:10–8:13)

in 7:29 Qohelet's complaint about the human tendency to seek out reasonings or schemes or devices (חִשְּׁבֹנוֹת) is self-referential, since he himself has been guilty of this and has suffered the consequences of it (see esp. chapters 1–2, but also his admission here in 7:23). M. Fox goes so far as to say that Qohelet is "poking fun at himself, for he is the one who undertook such calculations" (2004, 53).

**8:1a**. The first half of this verse concludes the prior section that began in 7:23, making the entire unit 7:23–8:1a. The question that kicked off the prior section, "Who is able to figure it out?," is mirrored here by similar questions: "Who is like the wise?," and "Who knows the explanation for a thing?" In this way, Qohelet bookends the passage (7:23–8:1a) with his thesis couched in rhetorical questions. And his thesis is simple: No human has ultimate knowledge (see note on 7:23–24). In 8:1a, the ideal image of the ultimate wise man is raised up merely for the purpose of being cast down, for no one is really like that; that guy exists only in our imaginations. Hence, for a person to pursue such an ideal of wisdom for him/herself is like "chasing the wind" (2:17).

**8:1b**. Wisdom, when not the object of delusional obsession, does possess some value for everyday life. The new subunit (8:1b–9) concerns the topic of practical living in light of human limitations and begins with the thesis statement in 8:1b. While the ultimate wisdom pursued by Qohelet in 2:12–17 is unachievable, as evinced further by the previous subunit (7:23–8:1a), wisdom is still useful and can help a person guard his/her steps. It can even change a person's countenance (see note on 7:3–4).

**8:2**. A person should obey the words of the king as fastidiously as they would an oath made before God. The first word in the MT is "I" (אֲנִי), which seems out of place and may be a scribal typo for the definite direct object marker (אֵת) according to *BHS*, though that too has its problems (see note in *BHQ*). Some translations, like the ESV and NJPS, try to make sense of the pronoun, but in every case that involves including a verb in the English translation that does not appear in the Hebrew text.

The line reads, "Keep the word of the king according to the oath of God." The "oath of God" (שְׁבוּעַת אֱלֹהִים) is understood primarily as either (1) an oath Qohelet's readers have made to God (NET, NIV), or (2) an oath God has made to the king (ESV; Krüger 2004, 150). Given the uses of the term "oath" (שְׁבוּעָה) in the HB, it does not refer to general allegiance to the Lord but to some special promise to/from God to do something (e.g., Num. 30:3). Since no such oath between God and the readers of the text has been specified, option 1 seems less likely. Option 2 is a possibility given Qohelet's respect for authority and acknowledgment that God appoints all things, including kings. Yet another possibility is to understand the expression "according to" (וְעַל דִּבְרַת) as "in the manner of" (Seow 1997, 279). Seow points to Psalm 110:4 where the expression is used for "according to the manner of Melchizedek" (עַל־דִּבְרָתִי מַלְכִּי־צֶדֶק). This sense is preferred and avoids the confusion of trying to figure out who is making oaths to whom, an exchange not specified by the context. The entire expression "oath of God" is best understood as an oath *before* God, as in an oath between two people that invokes the name of God (see 2 Sam. 21:7 for the line עַל־שְׁבֻעַת יְהוָה אֲשֶׁר בֵּינֹתָם בֵּין דָּוִד וּבֵין יְהוֹנָתָן בֶּן־שָׁאוּל "according to the oath of Yahweh that was between them, between David and Jonathan, son of Saul"). In sum, Qohelet is saying, "Keep the word of the king as you would an oath to God."

**8:3–4**. Be patient in the presence of the king, but not when it comes to doing the king's bidding. An intriguing possibility is to take option 2 above (see note on 8:2) and read the end of verse 2 ("because of the oath of God") as the reason for the command in verse 3; in other words, 8:2b–3a would read: "Because of the oath of God, do not tarry," meaning that God appointed the king, so people should be eager to obey the king. The expression "Do not tarry (stand) on an evil matter" refers to procrastination, negligence, or intentionally withholding bad news or a negative situation from the king. In 1 Samuel 20:38, Jonathan had arranged to fire arrows into a field as a sign to David concerning the murderous intentions of King Saul. Jonathan uses the verb "stand" (עמד) to order his servant boy, who was to collect the arrows, "Hurry! Make haste! Do not stand/delay" (מְהֵרָה חוּשָׁה אַל־תַּעֲמֹד). Likewise, Qohelet warns those in proximity to the king not to sit on an evil matter, but to deal with it promptly. Why is it a good idea to obey the king expediently? "Because he [the king] does whatever he pleases." In other words, his authority is unchecked by human beings—they cannot even question it (8:4); so, the judgment he casts on incompetent servants is final and can be severe.

The type of wisdom offered here is not necessarily a high philosophical concept but simply practical advice on how to stay alive in a world ordered by powerful authority figures. Qohelet uses the example of "the king" here not because he expects the average person to have dealings with the monarch, but because kingship is the highest rank in a land and thus represents all other ranks beneath it. In other words, the principle put forward in this passage is relevant when dealing with other authority figures as well, such as governors who represent the king in a district. Qohelet is not concerned with whether a given ruler is wicked or righteous (Qohelet assumes corruption and tells us to assume it as well; 5:8–9 [HB 7–8]), but that such figures hold a position of authority given them by God through the mystery of his sovereign appointing, and that authority outranks the authority of their underlings. Qohelet is also not interested at this juncture in potential exceptions to the rule like, "What if the king tells me to do something that violates God's law?" We could surmise Qohelet would double down on our responsibility to "fear God" in such cases (3:14; 5:7 [HB 6]; 7:18; 8:12–13; 12:13), but that is not the focus of 8:1b–9. As 8:4 makes clear, the king's authority is unmatched. No one can question his actions.

It is important to remember that the teachings of Qohelet are subversive, but not toward worldly authority. Rather, Qohelet is waging war against human delusions of grandeur. This manifests as delusions of wealth, wisdom, pleasure, or power in some ultimate sense. The harsh unpredictability of life and the reality of death are Qohelet's allies in his quest to disabuse his pupils of such delusional tendencies. Accordingly, it is in full keeping with his ethos to order his pupils to obey the forces of authority that have been placed in their lives. In sum, Qohelet is a philosophical rebel but a dutiful citizen.

**8:5–6**. Those who keep the commandments and do not rebel evince that they are wise in their hearts, having achieved a degree of social and emotional intelligence that serves to protect them, informing them intuitively of the proper time for a thing and the appropriate measure of action.

The proverb of 8:6 echoes the teaching of 3:1–8, that there is a proper time and an appropriate measure of action to deploy for every circumstance, "for the calamity of mankind is great upon him." In other words, the potential exists for immeasurable trouble to enter one's life, so it is best to operate in a measured way. Since trouble is bound to come eventually, why hurry it along or make it worse by rebelling against authority and incurring the wrath of rulers?

**8:7**. No one knows what the future holds (e.g., 3:11, 22; 6:12; 7:14; 8:7). The intense desire of the ancients to know the future is evinced by the widespread practice of divination in the ANE (Maul 2019, 1–16, 20, 219). People wanted to know or manipulate outcomes in advance so that they could live their lives in the most expedient way possible (see sidebar "The God-Ordained Boundaries of Human Knowledge" p. 109; Hilber 2020, 368). People fell under the delusion that they could manipulate fate to serve their ends, so they would attempt to read the stars, the patterns of birds, the internal organs of animals, and even attempt to speak to their dead ancestors. According to Qohelet, the entire notion that a person can know the future is a delusion (apart from the kinds of knowledge God has already revealed, e.g., that he will judge humanity; 8:12–13; 12:14).

**8:8**. Just as humans are severely limited in their knowledge (8:7), so humans are powerless against the forces of death. In the immediate context, this is a statement about how the common man is defenseless against governmental authorities; however, this principle can be applied universally, since humans in general cannot overpower death, not even through wicked scheming.

Qohelet presents the analogy of a human trying "to restrain the wind" (לִכְלוֹא אֶת־הָרוּחַ), though some take this as "retain the spirit" (ESV), as in to keep oneself alive forever. Both meanings could be at work simultaneously, but the idea of restraining the wind is more natural, especially given the repeated references to the futility of "chasing the wind" throughout the book. Just as a human cannot restrain the wind, so he cannot overpower death. And just as there is no deliverance from war, so one's wickedness will not deliver him. The HB lists the conditions under which Israelites can be excused from wartime military service (Deut. 20:5–7), but this would not apply in a later historical context under foreign rule, which might be why Qohelet says this (Whybray 1989, 134). Nevertheless, just as Qohelet is not elsewhere interested in exceptions to his hyperbolic assertions (see note on 8:3–4), so here he simply draws an analogy between the powerlessness of the common man, who can do nothing more than respond to the whims of monarchs and the edicts they issue.

**8:9**. Having seen all the corruption and human convolution that occurs on earth, Qohelet observes that time spent "under the sun" is time spent suffering from and participating in the systemic hardships of human rule. Humans dominate and harm other humans, sometimes under the pretense of doing good, sometimes to perpetuate evil, and sometimes under the seemingly neutral assumption of authority that comes from having superior power and resources (of course, such is not truly neutral given Scripture's repeated commands to care for the poor). Qohelet's desire is not to fix the system but for his pupils to be disillusioned from the notion that they have power only God has. Hence, they cannot change universal principles of inhumane domineering; they can only learn to live wisely within it while fearing God.

This concludes Qohelet's long discussion on the importance of wisdom and the unalterable works of God on earth, some of which he attributes directly to divine activity, and some he simply describes as the evil happenings of the earth that God somehow oversees (7:13–14). In all, humans are self-defeating and others-defeating creatures who, though they were made "upright" (7:29), have found countless ways to mess things up. In light of all this, Qohelet admonishes his readers to live wisely.

### Death and Justice Are in God's Hands, So Fear Before Him (8:10–13)

Qohelet finds it incomprehensible that wicked people go to their graves in honor—people who should be publicly shamed and judged by the courts and by God. Yet, his faith in God's justness remains.

**8:10**. Qohelet presents another enigma (הֶבֶל) in life: that the wicked are able to feign holy lives and go to their graves in honor because no one holds them accountable for their wicked deeds.

The wicked are, to make a modern Western analogy, like mafia dons, gangsters, and corrupt politicians who cross themselves at mass, taking the sacraments to placate their consciences; meanwhile, everyone knows they deal in blood. Nevertheless, such men too often receive a pope's funeral.

There are several competing interpretations of this verse, but nearly all depict Qohelet as discouraged over the fact that justice under the sun is perverted. The MT has the term "to bury" (קבר), but some suggest that the word was originally "to approach" (קרב), believing that the final two letters were accidentally transposed. However, the MT's rendering of "buried" fits best with the following lines where Qohelet bemoans that the wicked are not properly judged. In his view, it is as if they got away with being wicked their whole lives and were never punished for it. As 8:12–13 below demonstrates, though, Qohelet's faith in God's justice remains resolute.

The first subject introduced in 8:10 is "wicked ones" who are entering and exiting "from the holy place," which could refer to a synagogue coexisting alongside the temple in the postexilic period (Seow 1997, 286); however, if Ecclesiastes was written in the preexilic period (see Introduction), then "holy place" could possibly refer to the temple or part of the temple. Those same wicked people used to go about and "boast" about "what they did." Instead of "boast" (שבח), the MT supplies the similar-looking (שכח) "to forget," but several versions (e.g., ESV, NET, NIV) assume the middle radical (כ) was intended to be (ב), resulting in (שבח) "to praise" or "to boast" in the *hithpael* (see note in NET). This suggested emendation of the MT accords with the LXX's reading, "They were praised in the city" (ἐπῃνέθησαν ἐν τῇ πόλει). Are the wicked boasting about or being praised for their outward holy acts, or for their wickedness? Any of these possibilities would be unpleasant for Qohelet, who believes that the wicked do not deserve a distinguished burial or the right to boast/be praised.

Other interpretations choose to stick with the main use of (שכח) in the HB, "to forget" (e.g., KJV, NASB), as if their wicked deeds are too quickly forgotten. Others assume a new subject is being introduced, taking "thus" (כֵּן II) as "righteous" (כֵּן I, see both in *HALOT* 482–83), a reference to the righteous ones whose deeds are too quickly forgotten. Under this interpretation, Qohelet is discouraged that the unlauded righteous ones are being "*forgotten* in the city." It seems strange, though, for the subject of the verbs to suddenly switch from "the wicked ones" to "righteous ones" who are being "forgotten"; nevertheless, the NJPS maintains this reading: "*such as had acted righteously* were forgotten in the city" (emphasis added; so, M. Fox 2004, 58; and Seow 1997, 286). Schoors, however, maintains that the absurdity Qohelet observes is that the wicked were being praised for doing wicked deeds (2013, 625), like the fools who perish and go to Sheol but whose actions are praised (Ps. 49:13 [HB 14]). In the prophet Jeremiah's day, the Lord forbade people from attending the funerals of the wicked (Jer. 16:5).

**8:11**. Because the wicked frequently do not face judgment in a timely fashion, they persist in their wickedness. The psalmist is likewise frustrated by the prosperity of the wicked, noting that the only suffering such people ever face is death (Ps. 73:3–4). Qohelet prefers to see judgment executed speedily and would prescribe that human judges do so; however, the subtext of Qohelet's complaint is that God himself does not see to it that judgment comes swiftly. This concern is likewise conveyed by the prophet Isaiah: "But if the wicked man is shown favor, he does not learn righteousness. In a righteous land he acts unjustly and does not see the majesty of the Lord" (Isa. 26:10 CSB). God's servants call upon him to exact judgment on the wicked lest their evils continue unabated.

Qohelet would not dare to judge God on this point, but the reality of what the sage "sees" under the sun frustrates and confuses him. So, he must resolve to maintain the seeming contradiction between what he sees with his own eyes (the wicked going unpunished) and what he believes in his heart about the righteousness of God manifested through judging the wicked.

However, Qohelet would not need reminding that God's longsuffering toward sinners is a major theological theme in the HB. His mercy toward the wicked is the preferred catalyst for repentance rather than severe punishment. For this reason, he allowed the Judeans to prosper while they worshipped "the queen of heaven," though they mistakenly took their prosperity as a sign that they were pleasing the fertility goddess (Jer. 44:15–19). However, according to the prophet Jeremiah, their prosperity during that time was not a sign that they were doing the right thing, for the Lord was fully aware of their evil the whole time they were doing it (Jer. 44:21), and now his judgment would be manifested in the war-hungry nation of Babylon.

**8:12–13**. Like Qohelet, Asaph observed the prosperity of the wicked and how they seemingly go to their graves unjudged by God, full of riches and honor (Ps. 73:3–12; Eccl. 8:10–11), but both men resolve anyway, *against all physical observations*, that God will one day judge the wicked and honor the righteous (Ps. 73:16–28; Eccl. 8:12–13)! But if they cannot be confident that there is an afterlife, how will God do this? They do not know for sure *how* he will do it, only *that* he will do it. Statements like Ecclesiastes 8:12 display the complexity of a devout Israelite's thought life. Qohelet cannot be atomized into a caricature or given a reductionistic label, such as "blind traditionalist" on the one extreme or "pessimistic deist" on the other; rather, he acknowledges *both* the unresolved injustices of the world *and* the immutable nature of a just God. In this way Qohelet walks by faith *and* by sight, holding incredible tensions in balance. In the end, though, his approach does not leave him totally paralyzed since his faith in God repeatedly wins out and becomes his final word on all matters. Accordingly, we can say that Qohelet's approach is theologically consistent with the style of faith taught throughout the HB (e.g., Prov. 3:5–6) and with those famous "walk by faith and not by sight" statements of Christ and Paul (John 20:29; 2 Cor. 5:7), but Qohelet chooses to live in a greater degree of tension than perhaps other Israelites of his day, so as not to deny the physical realities around him while on the way to faith. After all, how rich is a person's faith if he/she is not first willing to acknowledge the realities of evil and death?

Since his discussion of death throughout the book leaves little room for an afterlife in his thinking, verses like 8:12–13 have become fodder for debate over the extent of his beliefs on this topic. It should be noted, though, that the authors of the HB in many places convey a lack of awareness of an afterlife (e.g., Ps. 88:10–12; see Introduction and notes on 3:17, 20–21; 9:3, 5–6; 11:9; 12:7, 13, and sidebar "Life After Death in Ecclesiastes" p. 108). Even though the wicked prolong their lives through their wicked machinations and go to their graves in honor (8:11), Qohelet "indeed also knows" that it will go well for those who fear God and that it will *not* go well for those who do not fear God. Qohelet even adds that the wicked will not prolong their days, *even though* he has just finished complaining that the wicked do, in fact, prolong their days through evil scheming (8:11). What we are witnessing in the heart of Qohelet is not foreign to the sages and prophets of the HB, that is, a stubborn commitment to faith in God and his character despite the many incongruities and injustices one may "see" (8:10).

The psalmists many times cry out in complaint like Job at the afflictions befalling them at the hands of the wicked, bemoaning how it *feels* like God is elsewhere and unconcerned with them, but the same psalmist will throw his chariot in reverse to express the notion: "Nevertheless, I trust you!" (e.g., Job 19:23–29; Ps. 22:21–22 [HB 22–23]). Likewise, Qohelet's own self-awareness of his limited understanding as a human propels him to both trust and distrust his own eyes. He must trust, for what can a human do other than believe what their own body and mind are telling them? At the same time, what can the Spirit-filled person do other than trust God wholeheartedly despite the mind-boggling contradictions one sees under the sun? After all, as Qohelet has rightly noted, the dead do not come back to life (9:5–10). This is a fact he has observed with his eyes many times and is indeed a fact of the natural order of life under the sun. But for those who "fear before God," there is always a sliver of divine possibility, a crack in the shut door of human impossibility.

## THEOLOGICAL FOCUS

The present section covers a large selection of text, from 6:10 to 8:13, and while Qohelet addresses several issues less extensively, it appears that the thrust of his focus goes to the inscrutability of God's ways (e.g., 6:10–11; 7:13–14), an unresolvable fact that leaves humans with the only options available to them: live wisely and fear God (the general theme of 7:1–8:13). What can a person do that is better than this?

As noted, there are several interesting concepts addressed in the unit, from the futility of unending, mindless merry-making (7:1–7), to the value of wisdom in a religiously hypocritical or morally repugnant world complicated through human schemes (7:8–29), to the importance of observing God-ordained structures (8:1–9), and finally to faith in God's justice despite the unmitigated injustices one observes under the sun (8:10–13). That final pericope may serve to summarize all that precedes it in this unit since it addresses the dual reality that people can get away with a lot of evil and even prolong their lives through it *and* that God is still just and will settle the score both for those who fear him and those who do not.

In 8:11, Qohelet's call for swift justice rings true for modern ears. A simple internet search for "instant karma" will pull up hundreds of videos and stories of people behaving badly only to have justice served right away either because the victim fought back, a police officer was just around the corner, or the perpetrator accidentally injured him/herself. The popularity of such stories is due to the deeply satisfying sense of justice felt by the viewer to see things actually working correctly in the world. More frequently, justice is prolonged or somehow abrogated. The feeling expressed by many who are denied justice is precisely what Qohelet expresses, calling it "befuddling/enigmatic" (הֶבֶל). Though it escapes his comprehension how such evil can persist unpunished, Qohelet's faith in God causes him to "know" (8:12) that judgment is coming for the wicked (see notes on 3:20–21, 22; 8:12–13).

Isaiah 26:8–11 likewise reveals that unless God chooses to intervene, which he does often to fulfill his hidden purposes on the earth, the wicked can go about unpunished, receiving praise and abundance throughout life; however, when the Lord displays his justice in the earth, the whole world sees it and flees from wickedness. The passage also describes the people of God witnessing the proliferation of evil and praying for the revealing of God's justice. They long for the time when the exalted Lord fills "Zion with justice and righteousness. There will be times of security for you—a storehouse of salvation, wisdom, and knowledge. The fear of the LORD is Zion's treasure" (Isa. 33:5–6 CSB). In Christ, this hope will one day be fully manifested, but for now, the calling on God's children is to live wisely and fear the Lord.

## PREACHING AND TEACHING STRATEGIES

### *Exegetical and Theological Synthesis*

God's works and ways are inscrutable. They are so far beyond our comprehension that human beings must not deceive themselves into thinking that they know more than they do (6:10–12). Instead of attempting to control the uncontrollable, people must cultivate wisdom by seeking "better" alternatives (7:1–14). But even wisdom has its limits, especially when compared to the all-consuming power of sin (7:15–29). Qohelet still commends wisdom, however, particularly when facing social issues like politics and injustice. Wise people submit to authority (8:1–9). They continue to fear God even when his justice may be called into question by the success of the wicked (8:10–13). Although it may seem like evildoers get away with their evil, Qohelet trusts that God will eventually bring all of them to justice.

In the face of a world that is complex and incomprehensible, the best thing people can do is to live wisely in the fear of God. Wisdom provides us with the tools necessary to navigate through a complex world where we do not know the future. We may not always get everything right, but we can make better decisions than if we give ourselves over to foolishness. The fear of God takes the focus off ourselves and places it on the one who is worthy of all worship. It was worship that brought back the psalmist from the ledge of despair when he observed injustice in the world (Ps. 73:17–18). And it will be worship—the fear of God—that helps us endure injustice in our lives as well.

## Preaching Idea
Grow wise.

## Contemporary Connections

### What does it mean?
Qohelet seeks to humble his students by pointing out that human beings can only understand such a small amount of life. Their situation is like a husband who often stares slack-jawed at his wife after failing to understand her feelings (7:28). Therefore, instead of trying to figure everything out on their own, human beings should rely upon God and his wisdom (6:10–12). Growing wise entails choosing the "better" way: sorrow is better than laughter (7:1–4), rebuke is better than flattery (7:5–6), patience is better than haste (7:7–10), wisdom is better than foolishness (7:11–12), and contentment is better than striving (7:13–14). Sitting in sorrow, hearing rebuke, exercising patience, growing in wisdom, and practicing contentment may all feel extremely difficult at the time, but committing ourselves to these things will reap the reward of being able to make our way through the vanity of life.

While Qohelet sees wisdom as better than foolishness, he also acknowledges its limits. Wisdom cannot overcome the unpredictability and tragedies of life, exemplified in circumstances where good people die young while the wicked live long lives (7:15–18). Wisdom is also very elusive, so giving your life to find it can be an arduous task you might never actually achieve (7:23–25). Moreover, wisdom cannot free people from the all-pervasive stain of sin (7:26–29). While trying hard to be wise is good, it is not ultimate. Something more powerful than human wisdom is needed to save us from sin.

Continuing his discourse on the application of wisdom, Qohelet guides his students through social issues such as politics and injustice. He calls for obedience to those in authority alongside a commitment to always do what is right (8:1–9). Furthermore, he calls on his audience to trust God in the face of injustice, especially when the wicked succeed (8:10–13). Nothing could call into question God's goodness and fairness faster than evildoers getting away with it, but Qohelet clings to God's future judgment setting the world right.

### Is it true?
Even with the advent of modern technology, human beings know so little about the world. In fact, we seemingly know more about outer space than about the deepest recesses of our own oceans. Yet, it can be tempting for modern "enlightened" people to disdain those who existed in earlier times for their lack of sophistication or

progress. Even our own parents are not exempt from our contempt: *"I'd never do it their way!"* we think to ourselves. Even with all the technological advances and impressive findings we've made in the past fifty years, we must seriously ask ourselves, "Are we really able to control life?" If the global pandemic of 2020 should have taught us anything, it is that life is beyond our control. Living wisely in an opaque and contingent world must involve admitting the fallibility of our own intellect.

If our world seems incomprehensible, then what of God? His ways are inscrutable: "For as the heavens are higher than the earth, so my ways are higher than your ways" declares the Lord (Isa. 55:9). Since only God is big enough and powerful enough to control life and alter its course, human beings should give up trying to control life and instead pursue wisdom. Life cannot be reduced to a set of "best practices" or optimized and turned into a systematic checklist for superior performance. Only the prideful think they can know every contingency or come up with every plan B. Eventually, they will be wrong, and their miscalculations will cost them. A wise person, on the other hand, acknowledges the limits of their knowledge.

By humbly acknowledging their limits, the wise person can make better decisions and give better advice. They make better decisions because they know they cannot predict the future, so they prepare as best they can but then submit the rest into God's hands. Wise people give better advice because they do not oversell the effectiveness of their guidance. They know their knowledge is partial. Wise people focus more attention on their character, *being* a certain kind of person, rather than on accomplishments or success.

### Now what?
Wise people admit their fallibility (6:10–12). They entrust themselves to God, calmly resting in his providence. They also choose the "better" path, the path of wisdom. Wise people will reflect on their mortality, recognizing the limited time God has granted them on the earth (7:2–4). They also submit themselves to evaluation from trusted friends. They do not write off rebuke but instead embrace it when it comes from valued sources (7:5). Who in your life can speak honestly and forthrightly about your flaws? It is important for all of us to have people in our lives who can tell us, "No, don't do that." The presence of wise counselors is particularly important for pastors and other ministry leaders. Otherwise, unaccountable pastors can use their power and influence to abuse others.

Besides choosing the better path of wisdom, wise people pursue contentment. Contentment applies to a wide variety of areas, from our circumstances to our finances, to even our place in history: "Do not say, 'Why is it that the former days were better than these?'" (7:10). We must not give in to the sin of nostalgia, pining for the "good ole days." Instead, we must remain content right when and where God has placed us. Qohelet provokes reflection on our level of contentment when he asks: "Who can straighten out what God has made crooked?" (7:13). God puts limits in our lives, so why do we strive so hard to overcome them? Attempting to liberate ourselves from our current conditions can often lead to frustration and despair. Are you content where God has you right now? Or are you looking for the next best thing? Are you always changing jobs? Do you bounce from relationship to relationship, hoping that the next person will fill the hole in your heart? Being wise means being content.

### Creativity in Presentation
The Netflix documentary *Jimmy Savile: A British Horror Story*, a two-part series that aired in 2022, chronicles the life and many accomplishments of one of the most praised, most popular celebrities in the United Kingdom for many decades spanning from the 1960s through to the time of his death in 2011 at eighty-four years old. Savile was a renowned

BBC presenter who was endlessly praised by the media for his charitable efforts in hospitals and a girl's reform school, becoming a favorite of prime minister Margaret Thatcher, a darling of the British Royal Family, and a universally loved celebrity by people of all working classes. He received an honorary doctorate, saw buildings dedicated in his name, and was knighted by the queen. His funeral was so magnificent that many compared it to the passing of royalty. Though there had been accusations of crime throughout his life, the various powers at the time believed they were false flags. It was only after his death that his predatory savagery as a serial child molester was proven. He died with great honor and was never made to face the justice system while on earth. Following the global exposure of Savile's crimes, the English people felt disillusioned and angry. One participant in the documentary noted, "There was a feeling that there hasn't been a day of reckoning. There hasn't been a day of judgment. And I think that's where the anger comes from."

The problem of injustice can vex even the wisest person. Why do the wicked win? Why do evildoers triumph while those who follow God die ignoble deaths? When confronted by the Jimmy Saviles of the world, we must cling to God's future justice. Those who do evil will not get away with it ultimately, but in actuality, they are "storing up wrath for [themselves] on the day of wrath and revelation of the righteous judgment of God" (Rom. 2:5). Paul further speaks of God's retributive justice at the end of time, when he explains the vindication of God's people involves God "repay[ing] with affliction those who afflict you" (2 Thess. 1:6). The wise endure the hardship and suffering of injustice by patiently waiting for God's justice.

The big idea is to "Grow Wise." We can use this text to explain different ways for how to grow wise:

- Admit your ignorance (6:10–12)
- Choose the better way of wisdom (7:1–22)
- Conduct yourself prudently in the world (7:23–8:9)
- Fear God above all else (8:10–13)

## DISCUSSION QUESTIONS

1. Why should human beings be humble about how much they can know (6:10–12)?

2. What things make up a "better" life for us (7:1–14)?

3. What are the limitations of wisdom, according to this passage (7:15–29)?

4. How should we deal with those in authority over us (8:1–9)?

5. What should we do when we observe injustice (8:10–13)?

6. Where do you find your wisdom lacking? How can you grow wise in that area of your life?

7. How is Jesus the perfect fulfillment of wisdom?

# Ecclesiastes 8:14–9:10

**EXEGETICAL IDEA**
Qohelet acknowledges that God's works are unsearchable and concludes that one of the best things a human can do is live joyfully before him in a world afflicted by death.

**THEOLOGICAL FOCUS**
The work of God, which includes the enigmatic ways of the world, cannot be figured out such that life can be manipulated or controlled by humans; therefore, one ought to live joyfully before him.

**PREACHING IDEA**
Enjoy your life.

**PREACHING POINTERS**
Qohelet recognized the unpredictability of the world and the limits of human knowledge. Even human wisdom has limits. If the world, and the God who made it, could not be fully understood, Qohelet concluded that the best course of action would be to live wisely and joyfully before the Lord. Instead of striving for knowledge and accomplishments greater than the world can bear, Qohelet taught that human beings should be content with their lot in life and enjoy the simple gifts God gives to them.

Enjoying life is easier said than done, especially with the onset of modern culture. Digital advertising presents a near-constant stream of discontentment-inducing content before our eyes. Social media gives off the impression that everyone else in the world is doing better than we are. On the opposite end of the spectrum, cable news programs can make it seem like the whole world is a complete disaster, about to fall apart at any minute. Consuming such messages and images can breed despair and discontent in our hearts, making it difficult to enjoy what God has given. Qohelet's messaging, then, is a breath of fresh air, for it honestly acknowledges the tragedies and difficulties found in the world but offers a hopeful path forward to enjoying life.

# THE WORKS OF GOD ARE UNSEARCHABLE, SO LIVE JOYFULLY BEFORE HIM (8:14–9:10)

## LITERARY STRUCTURE AND THEMES (8:14–9:10)

Qohelet's thoughts drift to and fro through chapters 7–10 of Ecclesiastes, like loose crates in the belly of a waterlogged ship (see also "Literary Structure and Themes" for 6:10–8:13). And though these miniature treatises bob about somewhat haphazardly, we at least enjoy the comfort of staying on the same boat/theme throughout this central portion of the book: that the world is inexplicably evil and God is incomprehensibly sovereign. It is in how humans ought to respond to these realities that we observe the greatest difference between the two sections. The resolution in the previous section (6:10–8:13), to be wise and fear God, is substituted in this new section (8:14–9:10) with a resolution to embrace joy and authentic living before God (8:15; 9:7–10).

The remainder of chapter 8 (vv. 14–17) is not totally dissimilar from the verses that come immediately prior regarding the inequitable treatment of the godly and ungodly (8:10–13); however, beginning in 8:14 and continuing through 9:10, the theme of joy becomes prominent. Twice in the midst of his musings, Qohelet prescribes the enjoyment of life's simple things (8:15; 9:9) as the only distraction from the conundrums of life and the fact that humanity "cannot find out" God's ways (8:17). While in 6:10–8:13 there persisted a greater frequency of admonitions to be wise and fear God, here there is a return to the enjoyment of simplicity as first expressed in 2:24–26. That return appears most readily in 9:7–10, where Qohelet offers up the delights of eating, drinking, and enjoying one's spouse while we still can, "for there is no work or planning or knowledge or wisdom in Sheol where you are going." Some take this final statement in 9:10 as a depressing resolve, but Qohelet is finding a way to balance the reality of the situation (the fact that all people die) with the opportunities of the present to enjoy the short life we have. He is a realist, and he does not mind stating the facts. These joy statements (8:15; 9:9) bear pedagogic weight for believers living in a fallen world.

- ***Respond to Life's Enigmas with Joyful Living (8:14–17)***
- ***Respond to Death's Certainty with Joyful Living (9:1–10)***

## EXPOSITION (8:14–9:10)

Qohelet has not changed topics from the verses immediately preceding this section (8:10–13), neither from the overarching topic of God's unsearchable works (human life in general), nor the immediate context of the righteous and wicked not getting their just deserts. However, his solution to the world's perplexities and God's unsearchability has now shifted from "be wise and fear God" in 6:10–8:13 to the overlapping commendation to "live life joyfully while you still can" in 8:14–9:10 (my paraphrase).

The unit begins with Qohelet's continued gripe over the inequities of life, particularly in how bad things sometimes happen to the righteous and good things sometimes happen to the wicked (8:14–17). This phenomenon is the opposite of what one might expect after reading Proverbs since it does not seem to accord with the retribution principle. Straight away, though, Qohelet "commends" (ESV), "recommends"

(NET), or "praise[s]" (NJPS) joy. A human being living in this topsy-turvy world ought to find enjoyment; it seems to be the one constant that "goes with him" or "will accompany him" throughout his life (8:15). Toil by itself can be miserable or even futile (if one expects ultimate satisfaction from it; see 2:18–23), but when delusions are replaced with joy, then one's work can hold value for the present. The alternative is to toil day and night anxiously and sleeplessly, hoping to acquire sufficient wisdom and knowledge in an attempt to fully understand the world of the incomprehensible Creator. In the end, one may resolve to lie or deceive him/herself by saying, "I understand God and his ways," but Qohelet warns us that "even if a wise man claims to know, he is not able to figure it out. (8:17). It would be better to admit one's limitations and embrace joy.

In the following section (9:1–10), Qohelet begins by lecturing on death as the great equalizer over humanity (9:1–6). He then follows that observation with an admonition for joy (9:7–10). Despite all humanity's scheming (see note on 7:29), no one is clever enough or righteous enough to escape death. The one positive statement he makes in these verses, if you can call it positive, is that the living have at least one thing the dead do not have: the knowledge that they too will one day die (9:5). Meanwhile, the dead can know nothing. Qohelet's hyperbole is effective at stripping away the reader's ego about what they know in life and what they think they can accomplish. His objective from the beginning of the book remains evident: to affect holy disillusion in the hearts of his pupils so that they will put their energy into the only things that matter, which he here reiterates in 9:7–10.

Qohelet's recommendation is one that should sound familiar to his pupils since it finds parallels in 2:24–26; 3:12–13; 5:18–20 (HB 17–19); and most recently, 8:15. In this latest version of the joy statement, he includes the already-encountered pleasures of eating, drinking, and working with joy, to which he adds the enjoyment of one's spouse. The impending reality of death is used by Qohelet as an incentive for his pupils to enjoy life's simple things to the fullest.

### Respond to Life's Enigmas with Joyful Living (8:14–17)

In the face of apparent injustices and humanity's inability to figure it all out, Qohelet recommends that his pupils live authentic lives filled with joy.

**8:14.** Doubly enigmatic (הֶבֶל) to Qohelet is the fact that the righteous are sometimes getting what the wicked deserve, and the wicked are sometimes getting what the righteous deserve. Familiar material appears in all four verses of this unit (8:14–17), but Qohelet finds new ways to make some of the same points. The first idea expressed in this verse is not a novel one given what the reader has seen so far in Ecclesiastes, especially after the long section from Qohelet on life's inequities (6:10–8:13). The repetition of the now well-known term "vanity" or "enigma" (הֶבֶל) bookending this verse, however, makes it clear that this particular point of frustration is uniquely distressing to him. It contradicts a strict understanding of the retribution principle taught in Proverbs (the traditionalists who held to it absolutely, e.g., people like Job's friends, represent how many would take the generalizations of the sages and turn them into absolutes). The book of Proverbs, in context, is not so ruthlessly binary.

**8:15.** In a world where everything is variable and unpredictable, human beings can, if they so choose, stake claim on the one thing they can carry with them for the rest of their lives—joy. For Qohelet, such joy is not what anyone makes it; rather, it must be an expression of authentic living (eating, drinking, working joyfully) in the fear of God. For Christians, Christ is the hidden reason for the joy Qohelet commends, a joy made effectual through the Holy Spirit: "I have spoken these things to you so that My joy may be in you and your joy may be complete" (John 15:11; 1 Thess. 1:6 CSB).

Immediately following the disturbing (though not shocking) statement of 8:14 is Qohelet's prescription: enjoy life's simple things. This is best paralleled in 2:24–26; 3:12–13; and 9:7–10, and it follows Qohelet's pattern of presenting painful, inalterable realities and then providing a resolution for how to behave in the face of those realities. Such simple enjoyments can be taken with a person throughout their life. Joy becomes a valuable companion that "accompanies him in his toil" all the days of his life, as many as "God has given him."

### Insomnia in Ecclesiastes

The phenomenon of lying awake at night appears in a few places in Ecclesiastes. In chapter 2, Qohelet discussed how one is not able to find lasting satisfaction in pleasures (2:1–11), wisdom (2:12–17), and toil (2:18–23). There, in 2:23, it was *toil* that caused insomnia; in 5:10–12 (HB 9–11), it was *pleasure* that caused insomnia; and in 8:16, it is the pursuit of ultimate knowledge that keeps him from rest. His observation in 8:16—that people are not sleeping due to their futile efforts to unravel things too lofty for them—is a subtle admission that he is one such person. He may refer to people generally—"He doesn't see rest in his eyes!"—but his personal experience with this bleeds through: *he* is the insomniac! As he said earlier, "In much wisdom is much vexation, and he who advances in knowledge advances in sorrow" (1:18), a sorrow that keeps him up at night.

**8:16–17.** Qohelet exhausted himself by his attempts to understand the world, experienced the insomnia that such a task would inflict upon its master, and concluded that humans cannot figure out "the work of God" on earth, no matter how wise they seem to be or how ardently they claim to have done so.

The final verse (8:17) of this short unit reflects a familiar theme known from 6:10–8:13: human beings are not able to "figure out" (מצא) things. Perhaps it would not be a shock to learn that humans cannot unravel the least of the mysteries of God, but Qohelet goes further to indict the "wise man" who claims "to know," revealing that *even he* is not able to figure it all out! The profoundness of this statement is reached by reading it within the broader context of wisdom literature, especially Proverbs. Qohelet's pupils had likely grown up with a near-reverential awe of the sages, their heroes, so to hear that they are just as incapable of solving God's mysteries as everyone else is intended to shock (see notes on 10:8–11, esp. v. 11, where Qohelet again undercuts the mythos surrounding wisdom's supposedly inviolable power). As a wise man himself (12:9), Qohelet falls into the same pot along with everyone else on earth whose knowledge has been severely limited by God (see note on 3:11). Wisdom has made his life better in a practical way that supports his ethos to "fear God," but it has not brought him an inch closer to answering the question "Why?" about virtually everything that happens on earth.

What humans cannot figure out is pretty all-encompassing: namely, everything that happens under the sun and why it happens the way that it does; this he abbreviates by means of the expression "all the work of God" (see 7:13 and 11:5). The reader will recall texts like 3:9–15; 7:13–14, and others where God is depicted as the sovereign worker in varying degrees responsible for all the goings-on here on earth (see notes on those verses).

### Respond to Death's Certainty with Joyful Living (9:1–10)

Qohelet bluntly conveys the darkest reality to his disciples—the finality of death—and follows that with the brightest possible prescription: joyful, authentic living in the fear of God.

# The Works of God Are Unsearchable, So Live Joyfully Before Him (8:14–9:10)

**9:1**. In contrast to the extreme incapability of humanity to figure things out and control their circumstances is the matchless ability of God to hold everything in his hand (7:13–14). Humans do not know whether their futures will be marked by love (good things, generally speaking) or hate (bad things, generally speaking).

The love and hate spoken of here are not God's emotions but those of humanity. Human beings do not know when and how their futures will intersect with passions of love and hatred from within themselves or from others. But God knows everything, a sentiment expressed by the construction "in the hand of God." For "the earth is the LORD's and all its fullness, the world and all who live in it" (Ps. 24:1). This is to be contrasted with humans, who neither know anything (in an ultimate sense, see 8:17) nor have control over anything. As Qohelet puts it, "No one knows what is before them." In sum, humans cannot figure out what is happening now (8:16–17), and they cannot know the future (3:11, 22; 6:12; 7:14; 8:7; 11:2), but God possesses both; a classic children's song states it best: "He's got the whole world in his hands."

> **The Knowability of God**
> The problem confronted by Qohelet's investigation into "the work of God" (7:13; 8:17; 11:5) is not that God is unknowable in every sense, though some commentators take this approach, seeing the emotions of love and hate in 9:1 as God's seemingly fickle, unpredictable mood changes: "The righteous and the wise and their deeds are in the hand of God. Whether it is love or hate, man does not know; both are before him" (9:1 ESV; these emotions refer to humans; see note on 9:1). The God of Israel was, rather, clear about who he is and what he expects of his people (Lev. 19:2). The unknowability of deities was, however, a frustration experienced by neighboring peoples—one expressed by the righteous sufferer of Akkadian literature (the so-called Babylonian Job) who could not ascertain what it took to please or enrage the gods: "What seems good to one's self could be an offense to a god, / What in one's own heart seems abominable could be good to one's god!" (*COS* 1:488). On the contrary, Qohelet has already instructed his pupils to do what pleases God (e.g., 2:26; 8:10–13). So, the expression "even love, even hate" in 9:1 refers to human emotional futures that are, like the "deeds" of the righteous and wise, also in the hand of God (see Seow 1997, 298; contra M. Fox 2004, 61). The "work of God" (7:13; 8:17; 11:5) on earth cannot be figured out by human beings, and there is much we do not know about the nature of God, but what he *has* revealed to humanity is his righteous character and the desire that humanity live in accordance with that character, which Qohelet expresses to his disciples through admonitions to live wisely and fear God.

**9:2**. Death is the destiny of all humanity here under the sun, and there is no class of person who can escape it. The syntax of the first clause is difficult to follow, leading some scholars to suggest an emendation of the MT. The LXX understood "everything" (הַכֹּל) to be a mistake for "vanity" (הֶבֶל), and if the first word of 9:2 is included as the last word in 9:1, then the end of 9:1 would read "everything before them is vanity/enigmatic." This fits the context fine and helps clean up the confusion of the MT's syntax, which is why some scholars prefer it (M. Fox 2004, 610); however, the expression at the start of 9:2 "Everything is the same for everyone" (הַכֹּל כַּאֲשֶׁר לַכֹּל), while awkward, is not impossible to maintain since it also fits the context well (see Seow 1997, 299). It is this last sense I follow here.

We take the end of 9:1 to mean "no one knows all that lies before them," so it is easy to see that Qohelet is expounding upon human limitations here (in 9:2) by addressing the universal fate of humanity—death. He presents five pairs of people, the first person in each pair serving as the righteous individual and the second person in each pair serving as the unrighteous (the expression "as for the good person, so for the sinner" כַּטּוֹב כַּחֹטֶא should not be counted as separate category since it is a summary of the ledger, like column headings). Whether one is on the righteous side of the ledger or the unrighteous is irrelevant when it comes to death—all die (though it is not irrelevant when it comes to judgment; 12:14).

Incense altar from Megiddo (see 9:2 regarding sacrifice). Public domain (see *ANEP* §575).

### Swearing Oaths

Ecclesiastes 9:2 features several pairs of people, each distinguished by whether they are righteous or wicked (see note on 9:2). The final pair features the one "who swears an oath" versus the "one who fears an oath." If the pattern from the previous pairs is followed, then the first of these two is the righteous person. But there is some debate over whether the order of good/evil paradigm is reversed here, making the one who swears an oath the unrighteous person. Both expressions can mean "to keep an oath" in the HB. The only other place in the HB where people "fear" an oath is 1 Samuel 14:26, where the soldiers of Saul were afraid of violating Saul's oath that whoever ate honey before his enemies were avenged would be cursed: "For the people feared the oath." In this example, fearing the oath meant keeping it, which is thought to be a good thing, generally speaking. However, Saul's hasty swearing of the oath is criticized by Jonathan (and, by that, the prophets) since it was a foolish oath that increased the likelihood of perjury among his men. To this we could include the admonition not to swear by God's name falsely (Lev. 19:12).

Consider also how the sages of Proverbs decried the practice of striking one's hand in pledge with another since it was a sure way to get oneself in trouble (Prov. 6:1; 11:15; 17:18; 22:26; see Jones 2019, 71–92). Seow even points out "a bilingual inscription in Akkadian and Hurrian found at Ras Shamra [that] contrasts the reverence for the sacred oath with the readiness to commit perjury" (1997, 299). For Qohelet, though, perhaps none of these things come to mind and he simply means to contrast the righteous person who is willing to swear an oath to God with the unrighteous person who is afraid to commit himself to God. Looking ahead to the New Testament, Jesus's instruction not to swear oaths in Matthew 5:38 must be read within the context of first-century Judaism (Blomberg 1992, 112), but it reflects a tendency in Scripture to steer Godfearers away from oath-taking and toward simple truth-telling, especially given the tendency of humans to break their word and the severe consequences of doing so. Accordingly, the entire enterprise of oath-taking should be considered in light of Qohelet's stern instructions in 5:1–7 (HB 4:17–5:6).

**9:3**. Human life is full of evil, from cradle to grave, until one day all join up in Sheol with the assembly of the powerless and forgotten who preceded them. Ecclesiastes 9:3 is a reiteration of the previous verse with the added note that the human heart is full of evil and folly throughout their lives. This is consistent with Qohelet's statement back in 7:27–29 where he revealed that human beings are incomprehensibly evil. Yet, while we know that no one is perfect (7:20), Qohelet still believes that some people are righteous Godfearers and that they should be contrasted with the wicked (see 7:2 above, 8:10–13, and other verses in Ecclesiastes). Nevertheless, here he has cast off all efforts at classifying people relative to their righteousness. His eyes are overwhelmed with all the "evil that is done under the sun" and how it seems to persist unabated throughout a person's life—a life that culminates in death: "and after it [life], *to the dead!*" (וְאַחֲרָיו אֶל־הַמֵּתִים; emphasis added). Their status will all be changed one day from those who are capable of doing evil to those who are capable of doing nothing. Readers should remember that Qohelet is speaking from a perspective of limited revelation since he does not have a clear view of the afterlife, much less the promises of Christ fulfilled through the gospel. In his approach, Qohelet is consistent with the widely held belief in the HB that death is the end of the road, meaning that there is no general, well-formed knowledge of an afterlife (e.g., Job 7:9; Pss. 6:5 [HB 6]; 30:9 [HB 10]; Isa. 38:18); exceptions are rare (e.g., Isa. 26:19; Dan. 12:1–2) and do not reflect general knowledge. Passages that speak of people being rescued or brought back from Sheol (e.g., Pss. 30:3 [HB 4]; 49:15 [HB 16]; 86:13) are not, in the minds of their authors, references to physical resurrection from the dead, but to deliverance from present suffering. Such passages may, however, be understood within the broader canon as containing eschatological hopes of resurrection that extend beyond the contemporary understanding of their original authors (see esp. Ps. 16:8–11 and Acts 2:27; see note on 3:20–21 and sidebar "Life After Death in Ecclesiastes" p. 108). This does not mean that Qohelet is absolutely certain that nothing happens after death (3:21), as the Sadducees were, but that death is as far as his eyes can see.

**9:4**. The person who is among "all the living ones" has at least some kind of "hope/confidence" (בִּטָּחוֹן), a term that appears only elsewhere in the parallel passages of 2 Kings 18:19 and Isaiah 36:4. In these texts, the term is used by the emissary of King Sennacherib who taunts the people of Jerusalem by asking them where they get their nerve: "What is this *confidence* [בִּטָּחוֹן] you have?" (emphasis added). Put another way, "What is the source of your hope?" Qohelet claims that the living have at least some kind of "confidence," but this is merely a setup, a bit of false advertising—the next verse will reveal the true nature of this "confidence."

For Qohelet, "A living dog is better than a dead lion," by which he means that it is better to be a disgusting, ceremonially unclean scavenger that still has breath than to be a stately, regal, but dead superpredator. For the Israelites, dogs were a pariah of the animal kingdom, which helps to contextualize Jezebel's demise and the taunting speech of Goliath (see also, e.g., 1 Sam. 24:14 [HB 15]; 2 Sam. 3:8). But for Qohelet, if it is alive, then it at least has some value, if only for itself.

**9:5–6**. So, what is the singular "confidence" of the living spoken of in 9:4? Answer: it is the knowledge that they too will one day die. For Qohelet, to live is to have the privilege of knowing only a few things for certain (e.g., that God will judge all people, that humans are flawed, etc.). In this set of verses, though, the only thing the living can know for certain is that their demise is inevitable. For Qohelet, if someone is a dog in some socially denigrated sense, at least they are still living and capable of knowing things, for "the dead know nothing." Not only do the dead know nothing, but it will also not be long until the dead are no longer *known* by anyone—"their memory is forgotten." Some make it their business to be remembered long after they are gone, but Qohelet has already explained that forgottenness is an eventuality (1:11; 2:16; see also 9:15). Qohelet is of course not unique in this belief; rather, his thinking is consistent with that of his theological context. Consider David's prayer to the Lord, "What gain is there in my death (lit. 'my blood') if I go down to the grave? Will the dust praise you? Will it proclaim your faithfulness?" (Ps. 30:9 [HB 10]). The dead no longer have a "reward" or something to gain in life (שָׂכָר *sachar*), and their "memory" (זִכְרָם *zichram*) is "forgotten" (נִשְׁכָּח *nishkach*). The assonance and alliteration of this line produce *we'eyn 'ōd lahem sachar, ki nishkach zichram*! "And there's no more reward for them; even the memory of them is forgotten!" As in the note on 7:1–2, these are not technical transliterations but simplified representations so that the English reader can hear the cleverness of Qohelet's rhyme in this verse—a verse that is, again, about death (see also note on 1:11; for other interesting occurrences of alliteration and assonance, see notes on 7:1–2; 9:5–6; and 10:11). The expression "even their love, even their hate" is a call-back to 9:1; love and hate bookend this pericope of 9:1–6. Only God holds the present and future in his hand (see note on 9:1); humans can hold onto nothing (see note on 1:11).

**9:7.** While you live, live authentically. The new pericope begins here (9:7–10) and serves as Qohelet's concession that there is something redeemable for the living beyond just the ability to know that they will one day die (9:5–6). In fact, it should be understood that Qohelet's obsession with death, which is really just his commitment to reality, is an attempt to put his pupils in the ideal mindset for enjoying life to its fullest: "The integral link between death and the enjoyment of goods suggests that Qohelet considers meaningful living to be dependent on one's ability to face, and reflect on, one's mortality" (Rindge 2011, 280). At first, he lists the simple pleasures of eating and drinking, commendations already encountered in 2:24–26; 3:12–13; 5:18–20 (HB 17–19); and 8:15. To this, he adds the line "For God has already accepted your works" (כִּי כְבָר רָצָה הָאֱלֹהִים אֶת־מַעֲשֶׂיךָ). The verb "to accept" (רצה), when God is the subject, refers most frequently in the HB to God taking pleasure in or favoring the offerings and deeds of his people. What precisely does God approve of here in 9:7? It is stated: the simple pleasures of life listed here along with any comparable such things that accord with authentic living in the fear of God. Any suggestion that God approves of whatever a person does (both good and evil things) is not in keeping with Qohelet's admonitions throughout the book to be wise and fear God.

**9:8–9.** Live life in a celebratory way, expressing joy over the *real* pleasures in life, like one's spouse. Recognize such things for what they are—God's gifts to you in this life. The term "oil" (שֶׁמֶן) is better understood as "ointment" that represents perfume. The color white is actually less prominent than the idea conveyed by it: clean clothes. Qohelet wishes for his pupils to live their lives in a celebratory way, enjoying life's simple things (not to be confused with the mindless, drunken partying of 7:4–6). These good things represent a person's "portion/share" in this life, which is called "God's gift" in 3:13.

Qohelet admonishes his pupils to "See life with the wife whom you love" with the verb "see" serving as an idiom for "enjoy/take pleasure in" (רְאֵה חַיִּים עִם־אִשָּׁה אֲשֶׁר־אָהַבְתָּ) (see 2:24; 3:13; and 6:6). Interestingly, the verb "to see" (ראה) appears forty-seven times in Ecclesiastes, and most of the things Qohelet "sees" are the cause of considerable consternation both for him and for his readers. And although the imperative "see" here means "enjoy," one cannot help but consider a connection to all the awful things Qohelet has "seen" throughout the book. If so, this is one of the very few things in Ecclesiastes that Qohelet "sees" and considers good (see also 11:7). In 2:24; 3:13; and 9:8, Qohelet suggests that man forcibly turn his eyes away from the futilities and enigmas of life to have them rest instead on the simple, beautiful gifts God has placed in his path during the few days he is given on earth (not unlike the Pauline admonition in Phil. 4:6–8). As the sages remarked, "He who finds a wife has found a good thing and has obtained favor from the LORD" (Prov. 18:22).

**9:10**. Fully acknowledge death, and by that concession, become empowered for authentic living. The concluding verse for this pericope (9:7–10), its larger section (9:1–10), and this preaching unit (8:14–9:10) is one that combines a positive affirmation with a sobering reality. "Work," Qohelet insists, "with all your might," knowing that no one can work in Sheol. What he stated back in 9:5–6 he repeats here: there is no faculty of thought that exists in the grave, no ability to work there (see note on 9:3). Qohelet's final word does indeed seem negative, but it should not be taken as such. He is unwilling to let go of the reality of death and has, in the face of it (nay, *because of it*), found joy.

Though we conclude this preaching unit on a positive note (9:7–10), it is essential to remember how we got here. Qohelet's rhetorical technique has been to drag his pupils kicking and screaming into a state of holy disillusion, disabusing them of the distracting, unsatisfying futilities of life. If they do this, as he has, they will be able to see the few things that are *really* worth living for.

## THEOLOGICAL FOCUS

The question Qohelet asks has not changed: What about life is redeemable since all is enigmatic and/or futile (הֶבֶל), given that everyone eventually dies? But his answers are expanding. In the previous preaching unit (6:10–8:13), the answer to this question was that people should live wisely and fear God. Here in 8:14–9:10, the positive directives are that humans should pursue joy (8:15; 9:7–9) and work heartily while they still can since death affords no such privilege (9:10).

The first six verses of chapter 9 convey the impartiality of death over all the living. The living have "hope/confidence" (בִּטָּחוֹן; ἐλπίς in the LXX) that the dead are incapable of having (since there is no thought or work in Sheol;

9:4), but this confidence turns out to be nothing more than the awareness that they too will someday die (9:5). An enticing possibility for intertextuality may be observed between this passage and the apostle Paul's magisterial letter to the Romans. In Romans 8:18–25, he discusses the "futility" (ματαιότης; the term used by the LXX of Ecclesiastes for הֶבֶל) imposed upon creation and how God's children and creation itself long for redemption; this is their "hope" (ἐλπίς), according to 8:24. Interestingly, Paul then goes on to define "hope" as something beyond what someone can "see" here on earth; rather, hope is what believers and creation cannot see but are confident will come—redemption (8:25). By contrast, Qohelet's field of view is limited to what he can see on earth, so from his perspective the only hope/confidence a living person has is that they will one day die. The apostle Paul is expanding the term "hope" in light of the recent advent of Christ and how God will, through him, glorify creation along with all who are found in him.

In Qohelet's world, this gospel has not yet been revealed. Nevertheless, what he prescribes for humans living in a fallen world is still immediately relevant for Godfearers of all ages: that they should enjoy life's simple pleasures and live to the fullest in response to a sobering awareness that they will one day pass on from earth. In this vein, believers ought to work "in their might" (9:10).

## PREACHING AND TEACHING STRATEGIES

### Exegetical and Theological Synthesis

Qohelet once again points out the injustice, absurdity, and inscrutability of life (8:14, 16; 9:1–6). The good are often punished, and the wise are often left bewildered because no one can figure out what God is doing in the world. People do not know whether they will receive blessing from the Lord or not (9:1–2). Qohelet's message is essentially, "Life sucks, and then you die" (9:3–6). But his advice takes a surprising turn—in the face of a life that is *hevel*, he recommends that people "eat, drink and enjoy life" (8:14; cf. 9:7). God himself approves of this because he has given us these good gifts (9:7). Therefore, instead of vainly striving after great accomplishments, foolishly attempting to predict the future, or pointlessly pursuing pleasures that will never satisfy, wise people will fear the Lord and be content with his good gifts.

## Preaching Idea
Enjoy your life.

## Contemporary Connections

### What does it mean?
Qohelet points out the unfair reversals that occur in the world: sometimes good people are treated like bad people, while bad people are treated like good people (8:14). Sometimes the good will take the blame upon themselves for the good of the community. Many times, the good do not get to make the decision to take the blame for something; rather, it is just thrust upon them by the wicked. Qohelet sees the unfair treatment of the good and evil as another example of the vanity of life. As Qohelet attempted to observe everything that was happening on the earth, all he found was ceaseless activity and human striving day and night (8:16–17). People were wearing themselves out! And for what? Nothing, really. Because no one can ever figure out everything that God has done or will do (8:16). Not even the wisest people can know everything.

Qohelet's observations on the unfairness of life and the inability of people to figure it out crescendo to one tragic truth: all people, whether good or bad, rich or poor, will die (9:2–3). The "same destiny ultimately awaits everyone" (9:2 NLT). The tragedy of life is compounded by the fact that death wipes away everything someone knows and being remembered by others (9:5–6). In the light of such a bleak prognosis of human destiny, Qohelet offers a surprising admonition: enjoy your life (8:15; 9:7). But why? Because there's no use fretting about the inevitable; death comes for all of us. Rather than anxiously attempting to avoid that fate, we should embrace the truth and get on with living our lives. There is a certain liberation that comes from accepting our fate and then living as best we can, given the time we have left.

### Is it true?
Growing up, I was always perplexed by my mom's immense enjoyment at going to and throwing parties. All kinds of parties: birthday parties, holiday parties, and some parties for no other reason than to get together with friends. When I would ask her why she spent so much time planning and decorating for these parties, she embodied Qohelet's wisdom. She would respond: "Life is hard enough. You have to take every opportunity to celebrate." My mom understood that a wise Christian life is lived enjoying God's gifts amid a broken world.

Qohelet's admonition to enjoy life stands in marked contrast to how Western culture treats pleasure. Living in a time of such great abundance, people often give themselves over to hedonism, the pursuit of pleasure in things like material objects, sex, or digital entertainment. Hedonism abuses enjoyment, for it makes pleasure the end goal of human existence. True enjoyment must be placed in the larger context of living wisely in the fear of the Lord. The opposite of hedonism is "hustle culture," a phenomenon found on the internet. Hustle culture propounds a simple philosophy: people must always be "on their grind," working harder and longer than anyone else. Only if someone will give themselves to grinding it out will they become wealthy. But to what end? By constantly working, they put themselves on a never-ending treadmill of performance without any real time to enjoy life.

Both views discount how difficult life really is. A hedonistic pursuit of pleasure will ultimately disappoint and lead to despair because nothing "under the sun" truly satisfies (cf. 2:1–26). A life given over to hard work will also lead to disillusionment because life cannot be tamed by our efforts. One moment we may be on the verge of a career breakthrough, and in the next we may be unemployed. Those who do not take the time to enjoy their lives may just end up embodying Rabbi Harold Kushner's famous saying, "Nobody on their deathbed has ever said 'I wish I had spent more time at the office!'"

*Now what?*
In the face of a life that is unfair, untamable, and tragic, what are we to do? Enjoy the simple pleasures God has given us. The apostle Paul tells us that it is those inspired by demons who forbid enjoying God's good gifts (1 Tim. 4:4). Christians can enjoy all things because "everything created by God is good, and nothing is to be rejected if it is received with gratitude" (1 Tim. 4:5). Relishing God's good gift is a sign of Christian maturity.

The practice of Sabbath provides a context for believers to enjoy God and his gifts. In the Old Testament, God commanded his people to honor the Sabbath day, to stop working and take time to rest (Exod. 20:8–11; Deut. 5:12–15). The people were to put away their work and enjoy the simple pleasures of life that God gave them. Many Christians reject the idea of keeping the Sabbath because, they argue, Jesus fulfilled the Sabbath (Col. 2:16–17). The rejection of keeping the Jewish law is certainly correct, for believers are no longer under the Mosaic covenant (Rom. 10:4; Gal. 3:19–26). Moreover, physical rest is typological of finding spiritual rest in Christ (Heb. 3:10). Yet, while the legal aspects of Sabbath-keeping are no longer in force, God still wove a pattern of work and rest into the fabric of creation (Gen. 2:1–4).

Therefore, the question we must ask ourselves is not necessarily, "Do I have to keep the Sabbath?" Instead, we should ask, "Is it wise *not* to set aside time every week to rest?" God is not calling the Church to set aside a specific day filled with elaborate rules to rest, but he does desire that we spend extended time every week to worship him and enjoy life. Maybe taking a twenty-four hour break can help you put work in its proper place and enjoy the life that God has given you. Maybe it's time to embrace Sabbath. For a great resource on Sabbath, check out Peter Scazzero's chapter on Sabbath in *Emotionally Healthy Spirituality* (2006), which interprets the practice of Sabbath through a Christ-centered perspective.

### *Creativity in Presentation*
Qohelet acknowledges the unfairness of life where good people are often treated like they are wicked (8:14). Christopher Nolan's movie about Batman, *The Dark Knight*, exemplifies these dynamics. In attempting to clean up the streets of Gotham, Batman knows he needs an ally who works within the system; his brand of vigilante justice will not bring about change on the scale he longs for. To foster real change, he aligns himself with hotshot district attorney Harvey Dent. Dent is the "white knight" of Gotham, a man of incorruptible character in a city filled with corruption at the highest levels of government. If Dent can be held up as an icon, Batman reasons, then the city will rally around Dent and pursue justice in its streets.

The importance of Dent as an exemplar of virtue and justice is precisely why Batman's nemesis, the Joker, seeks to take him down. Joker attempts to turn Dent evil by convincing Dent that no matter how much good he attempts to do in the world, chaos and injustice will prevail. Dent eventually breaks and becomes the villain Two-Face. In the final showdown between Two-Face and Batman, Dent espouses his new morality: "The world is cruel. And the only morality in a cruel world is chance." Dent then flips a coin on whether to kill the police commissioner's son. Before Dent can pull the trigger, Batman swoops in, saving the boy but killing Dent. The Dark Knight had killed the city's "savior." What would happen now?

Batman, standing over Dent's dead body, states that "Gotham needs its true hero," referring to the uncorrupted Harvey Dent. So Batman takes the blame for all the destruction that Dent as Two-Face caused. "You either die a hero, or you live long enough to see yourself become the villain," Batman says. He continues, "I can do those things, because I'm not a hero, not like Dent. I killed those people, that's what I can be. . . . You'll hunt me. You'll condemn me, set the dogs on me." The true hero of the story takes the blame for what the villain has done.

In Batman's example, we have a faint echo of the gospel, for the apostle Peter describes Jesus's death representing "the just for the unjust" (1 Peter 3:18). Jesus, the completely righteous one, received the punishment for the sins of humanity, so that human beings might be forgiven (cf. 2 Cor. 5:21). In the gospel, there is a glorious exchange whereby Jesus receives our corruption, and we receive his perfect righteousness by faith.

The big idea for Ecclesiastes 8:14–9:10 is "Enjoy your life." We can use this text to exhort our congregations to find appropriate and God-honoring joy in life. But why? Why should we enjoy our lives? In this passage, Qohelet provides three (rather surprising!) reasons:

- Life is unfair (8:14–15)
- Life is untamable (8:16–17)
- Life is tragic (9:1–10)

## DISCUSSION QUESTIONS

1. How does Qohelet describe life in 8:14–17?

2. What destiny awaits all people (9:1–6)?

3. Why should people enjoy their lives amid so much suffering and difficulty (8:14; 9:7)?

4. How does the gospel of Jesus Christ help us enjoy life? How does it keep the pursuit of pleasure in proper perspective?

# Ecclesiastes 9:11–11:6

**EXEGETICAL IDEA**
Qohelet acknowledges that God's works are unsearchable, just as his world is unpredictable. In light of this, he instructs his pupils to avoid the dangers of folly while living life freely and generously.

**THEOLOGICAL FOCUS**
The world is full of unpredictable danger, so it is best to avoid folly and live one's life in freedom and generosity, acknowledging that humans do not have control over life's outcomes.

**PREACHING IDEA**
Prepare for the future, but don't try to predict it.

**PREACHING POINTERS**
Qohelet admitted that the ways and works of God were beyond human comprehension. He counseled against human beings exhausting themselves for exhaustive knowledge. Not only was the world incomprehensible from Qohelet's point of view, but it was also unpredictable. The future defies being figured out. Instead of making vain attempts to control the future, Qohelet advised his students to live with wise preparation for whatever may come.

Despite the advances in technology, human beings are still incapable of predicting the future. Attempting to predict the future may do more harm than good, inflating someone's perceived control over the world when, in reality, they have none. Instead of fruitlessly trying to predict what may or may not happen, Qohelet's counsel is much wiser: prepare for, but don't try to predict, the future. Adequate preparation equips people to encounter a range of unexpected outcomes, whereas prediction locks them into believing only one conceivable future will occur, rendering them helpless in the face of unexpected circumstances.

# THE WORKS OF GOD ARE UNSEARCHABLE, SO AVOID FOLLY AND LIVE FREELY BEFORE HIM (9:11–11:6)

## LITERARY STRUCTURE AND THEMES (9:11–11:6)

As noted in previous discussions of literary structure and themes in Qohelet, chapters 7–10 present several challenges to the interpreter who wishes to view Qohelet's teachings sequentially, in longer cohesive units. This is due to Qohelet's repeated volley from topic to topic throughout the text, at times presenting short parable-style lessons, at times general observations about the evil he sees, and at times proverbs that admonish his pupils to live wisely and not foolishly.

When we observe the content of 9:11–11:6, taking note of these scattered styles of teaching, two primary headings emerge: (1) wisdom versus folly and (2) the unpredictable nature of life. The section begins with an introduction that appears to address both topics (9:11–18) before settling first into the wisdom/foolishness discussion (10:1–20) and then into the unpredictability-of-life discussion (11:1–6). The introduction of 9:11–18 begins with a brief set of propositions on life's unpredictability in 9:11–12 (a topic that will be picked up later in 11:1–6), followed by an illustration (9:13–16), and then a final set of propositions (9:17–18) regarding wisdom's relative value. The whole section of 9:11–18 *may* serve as a protracted thesis for 10:1–20 (where the topics of life's unpredictability and wisdom's relative value are worked out), but that is only a suggestion among other possibilities.

In the first large unit (10:1–20) following the introduction (9:11–18), Qohelet is once more addressing the dichotomy of wisdom versus foolishness. In the second large unit (11:1–6), he addresses the unpredictable nature of life and how one ought to respond to it.

- *Life Is Unpredictable, but Wisdom Is Helpful (9:11–18)*
- *Avoid Folly and Choose Wisdom, Though It Is Not Invincible (10:1–20)*
- *Life Is Unpredictable, So Live Freely (11:1–6)*

## EXPOSITION (9:11–11:6)

The first eight verses (9:11–18) of this unit may serve as an introduction to the two major areas of teaching ahead: wisdom versus folly and the unpredictability of life. Qohelet begins by mentioning the familiar themes of life's inequity and human ignorance, but with the added notion that unexpected things can happen to anyone at any time: "for time and chance happen to all of them" (9:11). He then shifts in 9:13 to introduce his next set of teachings on wisdom with a story (9:13–16), concluding that wisdom is more effective than swords and spears, but one fool ("sinner") can destroy everything (9:17–18).

For the next twenty verses (10:1–20), Qohelet trumpets a long list of proverbs that teach the avoidance of folly and the helpfulness of wisdom, but also the limits of wisdom. His counsel is familiar and predictable, but no less important. This instruction takes many shapes as he navigates through various circumstances where wisdom brings life and health. However, an important point is made in 10:8–11 (esp.

v. 11) that wisdom cannot protect a person perfectly; it cannot make one invincible.

There is a shift of tone and topic at the beginning of chapter 11, one that may startle the reader after going through the long list of wisdom sayings that made up chapter 10: "Toss your bread in the river!" (my paraphrase of 11:1). This counsel is given in the broader context of life's unpredictability and the human need to live freely in response to it. By "live freely," I mean to convey Qohelet's instructions in 11:1–6 to embrace generosity and free-spiritedness in light of life's unpredictable hurdles over which humans have no control. There is no way to perfectly predict the weather (11:3–4) or the outcome of your crops (11:6). No one understands the mystery of pregnancy such that they can perfectly predict when it will happen or know all its outcomes in advance (11:5a). In the same way, humans "do not understand the work of God who makes everything," for, as previously noted, his works are unsearchable (11:5b; see 7:13–14; 8:17).

### *Life Is Unpredictable, but Wisdom Is Helpful (9:11–18)*

By means of proposition and illustration, Qohelet teaches the relative value of wisdom in confronting a capricious world.

**9:11–12.** Things do not happen the way one would expect them to happen; there is this unpredictable factor called "chance" that interferes with the fastest runner winning the race or the most intelligent negotiator striking the sure deal. You cannot bet on things happening the way you think they should, since wisdom does not always win one bread. By "chance," Qohelet is not denying the things he has already affirmed about the sovereignty of God (e.g., 3:14–15; 7:13–14), but that from the human perspective it often seems that problems crop up randomly and unexpectedly, radically altering what seemed like certain outcomes. The supposed guarantees of swiftness, strength, wisdom, or knowledge—qualities meant to protect one from undesirable ends—are found to be false promises against the unforeseen winds of "chance." This point may find company in the inequities previously discussed (primarily in 3:16–6:9), but here the sense is less overtly one of injustice and more one of life's irregularities and seeming chaos. As mentioned in the exposition above, 9:11–12 and 17–18 are the propositional sections of a longer thesis/introduction (9:11–18) that governs 10:1–11:6. The point made here in 9:11—that various forms of "wisdom/skill" do not guarantee protection and success will be demonstrated in the story just below (9:13–16) and picked up again in 10:8–11.

Ecclesiastes 9:12 provides a bit of explanation for 9:11, an explanation that harks back to previous comments made by Qohelet regarding the limited intellect of humanity, including their lack of foreknowledge (see, e.g., 6:12; 8:7): "For indeed, man does not know his time!" Like fish caught in a deadly net, and like birds caught in a trap, human beings are ensnared "suddenly" at an unfortunate time. The comparison with animals may remind Qohelet's pupils of his words back in 3:16–22 where he explains that God is testing humans to show them that they are just like the beasts (see notes on those verses). Qohelet will pick up later on the theme of life's unpredictability and how humans ought to respond to it in 11:1–6, but for now he moves on to introduce the topic of chapter 10: avoid folly by choosing wisdom.

**9:13–14.** The sentiment expressed in the first line by "great" (וּגְדוֹלָה) is not one of shock at how horrible the following story is but at how delightful it is to see wisdom prevailing in an evil circumstance. We could paraphrase: "This is a great example!" There is an important life lesson in the story of the besieged city and its unlikely rescuer.

A very "small" city, practically a hamlet with walls, was surrounded by the army of a "great" king who, in besieging it (surrounding it and thereby disallowing people to enter or exit the city for an extended period of time, hoping for a surrender) built "siegeworks" against it. The siegeworks could be a reference to a massive ramp built up the side of the hill upon which the city rests, giving the invading army easier access to the city wall against which they could apply pressure until they successfully break through. An excellent visual example of this is seen in King Sennacherib's invasion of the Judean city of Lachish circa 701 B.C., which was later depicted in a massive wall relief in his palace at Nineveh. Lachish, however, was not rescued. Jerusalem, on the other hand, was delivered. And while Jerusalem does not qualify as a "small city with only a few men," an analogy could be made in how Hezekiah dug out a water access ahead of Sennacherib's invasion so that Jerusalem would not die of thirst during the siege (2 Kings 20:20).

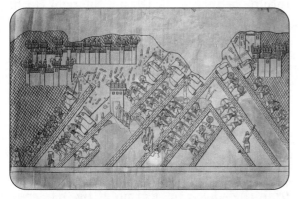

Relief found in Nineveh depicting the Assyrian siege of King Sennacherib on the Judean city of Lachish in 701 B.C. Public domain (see 2 Kings 18:13–19:37; *ANEP* §§372–373).

**9:15–16**. Qohelet's dual thesis in 9:11–18 is that wisdom is helpful (the city is saved), but that it cannot guarantee the best possible outcome (the wise man was not memorialized; see 9:11–12). The city had few men who could fight, but a lack of soldiers does not necessarily mean defeat. Though these verses (9:13–18) are about the victory won through wisdom and the folly of forgetting that wisdom, this very story is an example of the principle shared in 9:11 regarding unexpected outcomes. The almost certain outcome of this invasion was that the invading king would win, but there was an unpredictable factor that he could not possibly have prepared for: the wisdom of a single poor man. By his wisdom this "poor, wise man" delivered the city, though we do not know how. This verse is not expressing a possibility of the city being saved, as in "he could have saved it," but an indicative reality—"he saved the city through his wisdom." As Fox notes, the entire point of wisdom's superiority in 9:13–18 falls apart if we are talking about a poor, wise man who *could* have done something great though it never actually happened; "If the wise man had not actually saved the city, how could anyone know that he *could* have done so?" (M. Fox 2004, 66). Sadly, however, what should have been a significant lesson to the people involved was too quickly forgotten since "no one remembered that poor man." The verb "to remember" (זכר) can mean "pay attention to" as in "listen to" (see, e.g., NET, NJPS), but the point of this story is *not* that no one heeded the words of the poor man in the moment, but that people quickly forgot him afterward. Wisdom succeeded in one sense (saving the city) and failed in another (memorializing the wise man; see 4:16). The sages of Proverbs were right that wisdom is helpful, but we must dispense with any delusion that wisdom guarantees *only* good outcomes.

Wisdom is valuable, as evinced by this very story, but it is not valuable in the eyes of fools who quickly forget it. Had a valiant warrior swooped in to rescue the small city, perhaps there would be legends of his might told to future generations, and his name certainly would not be forgotten. However, "the wisdom of the poor man is despised and his words are not heard." By "heard," Qohelet may mean that the tale of the pauper's wisdom has been lost to the sands of time, not repeated in the oral memory of the community he rescued (see 1:11 and 9:5).

**9:17–18**. Wisdom is immensely helpful, but it is not invincible (see 10:11); it cannot prevail when fools have their way. This concluding pair of verses summarizes the aforementioned episode in 9:13–16. Wisdom is superior to might, and an illustration of this principle is observed in the contrast between the bombastic, egotistical declarations of a conceited ruler with the meek, careful wisdom of a quiet sage (see 5:1–7 [HB 4:17–5:6]). But no matter how much good one can do through wisdom, it only takes one megalomaniacal king/governor/overseer/ruler to "destroy" everything (9:18).

### *Avoid Folly and Choose Wisdom, Though It Is Not Invincible (10:1–20)*

In a long string of proverbs, Qohelet reveals the consequences of living like a fool in a world already fraught with unpredictable dangers; accordingly, he espouses the relative value of wisdom to increase (not guarantee) one's chances of success.

**10:1**. The stench of a little folly is stronger than the fragrance of abundant wisdom. All of chapter 10 addresses the trope of wisdom's superiority to folly, but more from the angle of avoiding folly than from the angle of pursuing wisdom—these are two sides of the same coin (cf. 7:1–8:9 where the directive is more to *pursue* wisdom). This first verse sets the tone for chapter 10 by comparing the damage done by a few dead flies (or NET: "one dead fly") with the damage done by just "a little folly." In this way the verse mirrors the final line of 9:18, which serves as a transition into this new section devoted to the avoidance of folly. The sense connoted by "perfume" may be in how a pleasant aroma is powerful enough to alter the moods and feelings of people nearby; it is distractingly pleasant. One dead fly, however, is all it takes to turn that aroma into an awful stench (one wonders whether this illustration comes from personal experience—if Qohelet had applied cologne one morning before testing it first, leaving him smelling like Beelzebub all day). In the same way, one fool running his/her mouth can ruin an altruistic, communal sense of positivity felt by any group of people.

**10:2**. Wisdom is not just about skillfulness but about moral rightness. Qohelet shares a series of wisdom-sayings (really these are "folly-sayings"; see note on 10:1) in rapid-fire succession, one proverb not necessarily related to the other. In this verse his general observation is that while the wise lean to the right, fools lean to the left. A handful of verses in the HB mention how a person (or animal) should not (or does not) turn to the right or the left but should remain on the straight path (Prov. 4:27; illustrated in Num. 22:22–32). That was how the Israelites were to respond to the covenant, turning neither to the left nor the right (Josh. 23:6). However, the idea conveyed by 10:2 is that there is something sinister about "the left." Ehud's assassination of King Eglon was successful in part due to the secretive nature of his left-handedness (Judg. 3:21). That there is some sense of superiority associated with the right hand is seen in Genesis 48:12–20. Most interesting, though, is what Seow points out in the final verse of Jonah (4:11), where God explains that the Ninevites lacked a moral compass such that "they could not tell their right from their left"; he also notes the tendency in postbiblical Hebrew to associate "the left" with doing what is wrong (1997, 313).

**10:3**. Even in the execution of mundane, ordinary activities, like walking down the road, the fool is "mindless" (לִבּוֹ חָסֵר). He presumably does not literally shout "I'm a fool," but his actions and other words are sufficient evidence for passers-by to conclude as much about him. Perhaps the appropriate image is of drunken fools stumbling down the street from house to house, from party to party, like the cackling idiots of 7:4–6.

**10:4.** Do not jump too quickly to defend yourself or respond in rash anger. Merely remaining "calm" has a better chance of garnering sympathy or favor. Mirroring the sentiments of 5:1–7 (HB 4:17–5:6) and especially 8:2–5, this verse calls for the wisdom of restraint when a powerful figure is angry at you for "great offenses," either real or imagined.

**10:5–7.** Too often in life, the wrong people are placed in positions of authority, while the more capable and qualified go unnoticed (see 9:15–17). Admittedly, this interpretation adds layers to the bare bones that 10:5–7 provides the interpreter, but the enigmatic nature of these lines requires a degree of creativity. It is not surprising that scholars have debated from extremes on what Qohelet means here.

Picking back up on the theme of foolish rulers (cf. 9:17), Qohelet identifies an "evil" (in the sense of "misalignment" more than "wickedness") on the earth that involves inept rulers installing other inept rulers into positions of authority: "An error going forth from a ruler: fools are set in many high places." This he contrasts with the "wealthy" who are found in an unlikely and unfortunate position of being "in low estate." Some take Qohelet to be demonstrating his class bias in favor of the wealthy (e.g., M. Fox 2004, 68), but others deny that the contrast here is one of class distinction (e.g., Garrett 1993, 335) or even "wealth" necessarily (e.g., Seow 1997, 315). In fact, it would be inconsistent with the rest of Ecclesiastes to understand Qohelet as exalting others simply because they have wealth; he had just elevated the wisdom of a poor man back in 9:13–16, and had plenty to say about the vanity of trusting in riches back in 5:8 (HB 7)–6:9. Whether the terms "rich" and "poor" refer to righteous and unrighteous persons in the HB is entirely dependent upon the context in which those terms occur. Take the rich man of Proverbs 10:15, for example, whose wealth is a sign of his wisdom. He could be contrasted, however, with the rich man of Proverbs 22:16 or 28:6–11 whose wealth is a sign of his wickedness. God is the maker of both the rich and the poor (Prov. 22:2), but how people use their riches will be judged (see sidebar "Qohelet and Wealth" p. 175). What troubles Qohelet in 10:5–6 is the dysfunction of a society that has cast off order and replaced nobles with those who have no business being in office (see sidebar "Qohelet and Order" p. 180). If not literally nobles, then it is possible that the "princes/rich" versus "slaves/poor" paradigm is merely a clever analogy to represent the wise versus fools, especially given the larger theme of wisdom versus folly in 9:11–10:20.

Ecclesiastes 10:7 is the final time in the book where Qohelet utters some variation of the phrase "I have seen" as relates to the observations he has noted throughout his investigation of all that happens under the sun (1:14; 2:2, 12–13, 24; 3:10, 16, 22; 4:1, 4, 7, 15; 5:13 [HB 12], 18 [HB 17]; 6:1; 7:15, 27, 29; 8:9–10, 16–17; 9:11, 13; 10:5, 7). This investigation began back in 1:14 and is now nearing its conclusion (see note on 1:14).

> **Qohelet and Wealth**
> In his earlier parody of Solomon's wealth (2:1–11), Qohelet conveyed how futile it is to amass excessive riches that essentially just sit there in the bank and remind you that you are rich (5:11 [HB 10]). It will all one day go to someone else, presumably one's children, and they may waste it all in an instant (2:18–21). Money cannot go with a person to Sheol, so what gain is there for the wealthy to continuously collect so much of it? It would be better to be "poor" and "wise," like the imprisoned lad of 4:13 or the elder sage of 9:15, than to be a rich fool. The person who views wealth as an ultimate achievement may lose it all in an instant, like the hoarder of 5:13–17 (HB 12–16) who, in a stroke of bad luck, lost everything and was resigned to a state of vexation and anger for the rest of his life. He is like the impossibly rich but still unfulfilled man of 6:1–6; according to Qohelet, it would be better that such a man was never born!

> Life is so unpredictable and inequitable that princes may find themselves wallowing in the mud while slaves sit on their thrones (10:5–6). If a person has wealth, they should enjoy it as God's gift (5:19 [HB 18]; 6:7, 9), not desperately and selfishly pine for ever more of it. Wisdom is not perfect, but it is a more worthwhile pursuit since it at least provides a layer of protection, kind of like money (7:11). For these reasons, a person should not "love money," for they will never "be satisfied" with it (5:10 [HB 9]); instead, it will turn a person into an insomniac who cannot buy rest because they will not let go of the very wealth that is keeping them awake (5:12 [HB 11]). Knowing the futility of pursuing wealth as an ultimate end, it is best to live one's life freely and authentically before God, which means to enjoy life's simple pleasures as gifts from him while emulating God's generosity in one's treatment of others (11:1–2).

**10:8–11.** Wisdom does not make a person invincible; it cannot rescue a person from all harm (see notes on 9:11–12). The first two verses form a pair (10:8–9), as do the following two (10:10–11), and all four verses work together chiastically: serpent (10:8), cutting logs (10:9) // cutting (10:10), serpent (10:11; see Garrett 1993, 335).

Scholars have debated the meaning of these verses. The majority view is that Qohelet is praising the value of wisdom while relativizing it. Most believe that he does this by listing calamities that *may* take place in an unpredictable world if one does not properly apply wisdom (M. Fox 2004, 69–70). Most also believe that 10:10–11 provides two scenarios wherein the laborer has neglected to use his wisdom/skill. A few scholars, however, understand 10:11 as describing the lack of an opportunity to use one's wisdom/skill in the first place rather than the failure of the laborer (because the snake catches the charmer off guard and bites before he has a chance to charm it; Longman 1998, 246). So, is the snake charmer of 10:11 at fault for not applying his skill quickly enough? Or is he not to blame since he did not even notice the snake was there? In either case, wisdom/skill was unapplied and hence damage was incurred. The takeaway of 10:8–11 is that wisdom can help curb the frequency of unpredictable danger in life, but wisdom is useless if it is not applied. Another possibility is to understand wisdom itself, or at least an unrealistic view of wisdom's value, as the real target of Qohelet's criticism (see excursus: "The Relative Value of Wisdom in Ecclesiastes 10").

The climactic final verse (10:11) features yet another instance of clever wordplay from Qohelet: "If the serpent bites before it is charmed, there's no success for the charmer." The combination of sound in this verse (note the l-sounds and s-sounds, especially) may be an imitation of the hissing "whisper/incantation" (לָחַשׁ) of a snake charmer, who him/herself imitates the snake: *im yishōch hanachash belōʾ lachash, weʾeyn yitrōn livaʿal halashōn* (not a technical transliteration, just a simplified representation of the Hebrew sounds as in the notes on 3:20–21; 7:1–2; 9:5–6).

### The Relative Value of Wisdom in Ecclesiastes 10

Rather than viewing 10:8–11 as Qohelet's recommendation that we apply wisdom in life, one possibility is to view the pericope as his criticism against those who hold to an absolutist view of the retribution doctrine (e.g., the likes of Bildad, Zophar, Eliphaz). In this approach, Qohelet is criticizing their way of thinking by mimicking the style of their speech in 10:8–10, applying the act-consequence form to a discussion of ordinary, amoral chores. He then makes their point that wisdom solves all problems ("wisdom brings success," 10:10c). Qohelet, however, says this tongue-in-cheek—he does not actually believe that wisdom can always save a person, as the very next verse (10:11) and the rest of his teachings demonstrate. If these verses are read the way most scholars do, as basic advice from Qohelet, then his speech is overly simplistic and, for that reason, odd. Notes Heim, "[W]hy [does Qohelet] spend so much effort on stating the obvious? The answer lies in the proverbial string's contextual function. Qoheleth is making a pointedly funny yet subversive point" (2019, 167). While Heim believes the target of Qohelet's criticism is the ruling elite, my interpretation is closer to what I believe Qohelet's overall purpose is in the book—to disabuse his pupils of their delusions, a common one being the inviolability of wisdom. Hence, the snake charmer of 10:11 is not neglectful and too slow to act, nor caught off guard and unable to apply his wisdom/skill quickly enough. Rather, fault lies with wisdom/skill itself. In this view, the charmer has encountered "the uncharmable snake" (הַנָּחָשׁ בְּלוֹא־לָחַשׁ) that no amount of wisdom can quell, regardless of how effectively it can be deployed (see Seow 1997, 327, and my reading of הַנָּחָשׁ בְּלוֹא־לָחַשׁ below). The point then is not that we ought to be more diligent in our application of wisdom, but that there are circumstances in which wisdom is utterly useless. Most scholars take בְּלוֹא to mean "before," as if there is a temporal sequence in view. And, while a temporal reading is possible, it is an interpretation and is not necessitated by the Hebrew text (Weeks 2022, 519). Furthermore, if the problem with the charmer is that he did not properly apply wisdom, then 10:11 is redundant, making the point already made about the lumberjack in 10:10. Qohelet's point, rather, is to demonstrate the limits of *wisdom*, not the limitations of human beings and their poor timing or misapplication of wisdom. The translation "uncharmable snake" does require the interpreter to disregard the disjunctive *tiphchah* accent on "snake" (הַנָּחָשׁ) so that the entire phrase could be read, "If an uncharmable snake [הַנָּחָשׁ בְּלוֹא־לָחַשׁ] bites, then there is no advantage for the charmer." This snake will not be affected by charms no matter when they are given.

Noting this emendation, the context of the entire unit of 10:8–11 could be understood in the following way: Qohelet begins by listing a number of ordinary occupations or chores that he claims *will* result in eventual disaster (taking the *yiqtols* as indicatives). By doing so, Qohelet is mimicking the retribution topos that can be seen in passages like Proverbs 26:27, where one's wicked behavior *will* result in sure repercussions (though Qohelet parodies this by substituting amoral chores). Certain Israelites (e.g., the friends of Job) understood the generalities of Proverbs as absolutes, developing the false notion that this retribution principle is always the way things play out in life. It is against this backdrop of inevitable calamity that Qohelet, satirizing such absolutists, props up the value of applying wisdom/skill to one's work

> (10:10c). His brief exposé on labor is only a setup, though, for his main contribution to the topic is when he asserts that wisdom is utterly useless in certain circumstances (10:11). Qohelet's claim is jarring and arguably new among the Hebrew sages, and yet his entire presentation betrays a traditional ring.
>
> Situated in the center of chapter 10, which otherwise focuses on the avoidance of folly, this pericope briefly repudiates the view that wisdom makes one invincible. Furthermore, scholars' readings of 10:11 as a critique of the snake charmer's laziness, incompetence, or failure to act quickly enough do not provide an adequate corrective for the overstatement of wisdom's value in the previous verse. Rather than view the snake charmer as unprepared, Qohelet sees the conjuror's wisdom/skill as useless before a serpent that cannot be charmed in the first place (see the uncharmable serpents of Jer. 8:17 or the "uncharmable snake" ṣerri la šipti in Akkadian; *CAD* Š/3 s.v. "*šiptu* A" mng. g.2', 91). By this assessment, *wisdom itself* is shown to be inadequate rather than the worker. In sum, Qohelet assumes a known literary topos from Hebrew wisdom texts to mock the absolutists' dogma on retribution and the invincibility of wisdom, asserting instead that suffering is for everyone, not just the wicked/foolish, and that not even wisdom can save you from it.

**10:12.** The content of one's heart (10:2) comes out through the lips and into the ears of others, which affects the hearers and/or how they view the speaker (10:12). Though the previous section (10:8–11) is certainly intended to be distinct from the present section (10:12–14), scholars sometimes connect the "charmer" (lit. "master of the tongue"; בַּעַל הַלָּשׁוֹן) from the end of 10:11 with the wise and foolish speech here in 10:12. Qohelet also likely meant for the related "tongue" (10:11), "mouth" (10:12), and "lips" (10:13) of these verses to at least bridge the two units of thought. Tova Forti argues that 10:11–12 should be read together to make the point, "No spell exists that can counter the damage inflicted by the fool" (2014, 91).

Ecclesiastes 10:12–14 centers on the theme of the fool's words and how they often get him into trouble. The virtue of keeping one's mouth shut was discussed briefly back in 5:1–7 (HB 4:17–5:6), though it appeared in the context of the "house of God." However, the principle is very easily applied to all of life. The sages taught that the words of the wicked wait cunningly behind a boulder in order to "ambush" an innocent passerby, "but the mouth of the righteous delivers them" (Prov. 12:6). Qohelet gives the proverb in reverse order, starting with the words of the wise which are "gracious," but the lips of a fool "consume him." The ESV, NET, and others supply "win him favor" or "bring him favor," though the verb is not provided in the Hebrew text; it is rather assumed. The KJV, NASB, and others do not supply an additional verb, but understand the first line as an expression of how other people are affected: "The words of a wise man's mouth *are* gracious" (KJV). This parallels Proverbs 12:6 nicely since in both texts line 1 communicates how innocent third parties are affected, and line 2 communicates how the speaker of wisdom or folly is affected. In either interpretive track, though, the concept of the fool's destructive behavior is present.

**10:13**. From start to finish, the fool's tongue carves a path of destruction for everyone, including him/herself. One can imagine Qohelet shaking his head from side to side in shame while uttering the pejorative "stupid fools" concerning those whose words are self-destructive and others-destructive. There is an elevation from the folly in the first half of the verse to the "wicked madness" (NET) in the second half, a description applied to "his mouth." The term rendered "madness" (הוֹלֵלוּת) is derived from the verb הלל (*HALOT* s.v. "הלל III" 249) and may be roughly equivalent to the modern English pejorative of calling someone "crazy," "insane," or "a lunatic"; however, this very Hebrew verb was used to describe how David "pretended to be crazy" (וַיִּתְהֹלֵל) to avoid capture by Saul's allies, making random markings on a door and letting saliva dribble down his beard (1 Sam. 21:13 [HB 14]). It is likewise used to describe the crazed state of a drunkard who stumbles around and behaves erratically (Jer. 25:16). The verb is used in Ecclesiastes 2:2 to describe the nonsensical cackling of fools, and in 7:7 to describe the state of mind of the righteous when confronted with corruption, which is probably connected to the idiotic laughing of the prior verse (7:6). The nominal form appears several times in Ecclesiastes (1:17; 2:12; 7:25; 9:3), though with the slightly different spelling (הוֹלֵלוֹת). Part of Qohelet's original investigation in 1:17 (also 2:12) was to understand or make sense of all the "madness" he saw in the world, which must refer to the human delusions he describes throughout the book. This "craziness" is at home in humanity, from Qohelet's perspective (7:25; 9:3), and the result of their continual scheming (7:29). With the addition of the term "evil/wicked" (רָעָה), he makes the point that the insanity he observes in the mouths of fools is not some kind of neutral stupidity, but in fact depravity (see his use of "wickedness" [רֶשַׁע] in 7:25).

**10:14**. The blabbermouth-braggart gives off the impression that he knows more than he does, even more than a person is able to know (see 8:17). He never took seriously the wisdom that there is a time to be silent (see note on 3:7b). As noted already, no one can say what the future holds (3:11, 22; 6:12; 7:14; 8:7; 11:2). Only God knows these things and he has chosen not to reveal them to humanity. The fool is surging with presumption, believing that his many words will correct and fix the situation, but the more he talks, the less useful he becomes. If he would simply shut his mouth, people would think he is wise (Prov. 17:28). After all, "a man of understanding remains silent" (Prov. 11:12; see Eccl. 5:1–7 [HB 4:17–5:6]).

**10:15**. In contrast with what he pretends to know (10:14), the fool reveals that he actually knows *less* than the average person. This verse seems to stand alone in chapter 10. There is utter futility in toiling when you have no idea what you are doing. The fool's toil "wearies him" because there is no knowledge or purpose in it. One imagines that the man has been tasked with carrying something to the city but has no idea how to get there. So, he ends up wandering aimlessly until he wears himself down to nothing, like Saul searching blindly for his father's donkeys (1 Sam. 9:5); without the intervention of the prophet Samuel's wisdom, there would have been little chance of success (1 Sam. 9:20). Towns and cities in the Iron Age typically sat on high hills and were major landmarks for travel, connection points between the ancient roadways. Just as Qohelet made a clever transition from 10:11 to 12 (see note on 10:12), so in 10:13 the term "city" prompts the reader for the topic of 10:16–17.

**10:16–17**. Waking up just to consume is the feral behavior of an untrained young man and does not reflect the dignity of a wise leader. Qohelet's indictment is not against breakfast, per se, though it was not likely an ordinary meal for the average Israelite (cf. Judg. 19:5; Perkin 1988, 772–73). Eating in the morning may have seemed strange to Qohelet, though some modern cultures today think nothing of it. That may be what inspired the translation "feasting" (e.g., ESV, NASB, NIV) since this would be an equivalent excess.

This pair of proverbs reflects a phenomenon known to many in the world: living under the leadership of an immature, self-indulgent ruler. Sometimes these kinds of rulers come into power illegitimately, which accords with Qohelet's imagination here (consider 10:5–7 and the contrast in 10:17). Whether it be the CEO of a company or the prime minister of a nation, the people are cursed when their leader is an incompetent hedonist who starts his day with drinking and overeating. Celebrations should be observed at appropriate times, but a young, unwise ruler may take full advantage of the privileges of his office whenever he feels like it. One thinks of Absalom's sedition against David and brief usurpation of the throne, an act symbolized by his public fornication with his father's concubines atop the palace roof in the sight of all the people (2 Sam. 16:22). This act was not merely symbolic; it also betrayed a heart of impulse and indulgence. He came into too much power and authority too quickly, and illegitimately. His reign would have doubtless been one of extreme indulgence, conspicuous consumption at the expense of and in the sight of the people.

This is contrasted with 10:17 where the land is blessed by a rightful heir who understands the rhythms of his own culture and respectfully observes the established norms, perpetuating the sense of order or propriety that the people have come to love or, at the very least, accept. When he drinks and eats, it is "for strength" or possibly "in success/victory/ for accomplishments" (בִּגְבוּרָה), as the term is used in the books of Kings to eulogize the mighty deeds of a king (e.g., 2 Kings 10:34). The idea here is not that eating and drinking should only be done for sustenance, but that feasts should take place at the proper times and for the right reasons, such as at the conclusion of a battle, to celebrate a victory, or to worship God (e.g., Gen. 14:18; Num. 28:17; 1 Sam. 14:32; Ps. 23:5).

> **Qohelet and Order**
> Like the sages of Proverbs, Qohelet speaks to his desire for an ordered society. He is someone who values authority, as well as proper behavior before authority (5:1–7 [HB 4:17–5:6]; 8:2–5; 10:20). Even when rulers are corrupt (4:13; 5:8 [HB 7]; 9:17; 10:16), he does not advocate rebellion. Instead, he wishes for a society in which those now in positions of authority were not previously lawless vagabonds (10:5–6), haphazardly pulled off the street and set into positions of great consequence based only on the fickle whims of a tyrannical ruler, presumably one who does not know how to take good advice (see 4:13). In an ordered society, slaves are not sitting on the throne (cf. Prov. 30:22; Lam. 5:8) and nobles are not traipsing through the mud (Eccl. 10:7). The wealthy envisioned by Qohelet in 10:5–6 are not merely rich, but likely nobles who are supposed to be holding the noble office rightly appointed to them, sitting on thrones, and bearing the responsibility afforded by that office. When nobles stand up from their seats, their servants should not presumptuously sit down in their absence.
>
> This ideology is reflected in both Egyptian (e.g., The Admonitions of Ipuwer) and Mesopotamian proverbs, such as one Sumerian text that, for a few lines, decries the inappropriate behavior of palace servants: "When (the lady) left the house, / and (the slave girl) entered from the street, / in the absence of her lady the slave girl sat down at a banquet" (*COS* 1:564 §41). The desire for proper order is found across cultures in ancient wisdom texts, and it often involves honoring superiors in social settings; however, calls to honor the king are more commonly seen in monumental inscriptions commissioned by kings who claim to have been appointed by the gods. In the Hebrew Scriptures, specifically here in the wisdom of Qohelet, fearing the God of Israel likewise includes

honoring those to whom he has given authority (Jer. 29:7; cf. Rom. 13:1–7 and 1 Peter 2:17), be they good rulers (5:8 [HB 7]; 10:17) or powerful fools (9:17).

**10:18.** Just as the laziness of the rich endangers his kingdom (10:16–17), so the slothfulness of a man endangers his house. Ecclesiastes 10:18–20 is a collection of three proverbs related only by the chapter's general observation of the value of wisdom versus the consequences of folly. It begins with a principle known from Proverbs (sloth; e.g., 12:27; 19:15). Low points on the flat roofs of an Israelite house may collect water during a rare deluge or begin to cave in due to heavy supplies sitting atop them. If one of the horizontal "beams" (הַמְּקָרֶה), as in ceiling joists, is not repaired in a timely fashion, this could result in tragedy. Cracks in the lime plaster also provide passage for water to leak into the home's interior.

**10:19.** Feasting is fun and itself not a bad thing. The improper execution of this fun is what makes it good or bad (see note on 10:16–17). The translation "money answers everything" (ESV), though a possible rendering of the Hebrew (וְהַכֶּסֶף יַעֲנֶה אֶת־הַכֹּל), can be misleading. In several places in Ecclesiastes, the term "all" (כֹּל) should be understood as "both" (e.g., 7:18). Here in 10:19, Qohelet is conveying that access to money is needed to provide "both" food and wine.

**10:20.** It has been noted how dangerous it is to defy the king (8:1–5), but make sure you guard even your thoughts lest you let something slip from under your breath and that minor dissension be brought by unexpected means to the ears of the authorities. In a treaty between Hittite King Mursilis and Duppi-Tessub of Amurru, the latter is instructed: "If anyone utters words unfriendly toward the king or the Hatti land before you, Duppi-Tessub, you shall not withhold his name from the king" (*ANET*, 204). Qohelet is not a political rebel and does not condone rebellion. His rebellion, rather, is against the delusions of life to which nearly all fall prey. In Qohelet's political context, the wise thing to do is keep one's mouth shut and fear God. But what if fearing God means disobeying the king? This question goes unaddressed, perhaps because such a phenomenon would be unusual in Qohelet's setting, whatever precise historical context that may be.

### Life Is Unpredictable, So Live Freely (11:1–6)

In one of his final admonitions for how his pupils ought to conduct themselves in their daily affairs, Qohelet emphasizes how life's unpredictable nature should drive one away from delusions of control and toward expressions of freedom and generosity.

**11:1.** Human generosity is the proper response to divine generosity (after all, the bread was a "gift" from God in the first place; see God's role in the joy statements: 2:24; 3:13; 5:18 [HB 17]; 8:15; 9:9). Ecclesiastes 11:1–6 constitutes a new topic for Qohelet. Here he provides a way forward for those who, in response to life's unpredictable and often violent, despoiling changes, have chosen to hold onto every shekel too tightly, falling under the delusion that they can control life's outcomes and prepare for every storm. Life is inequitable and unfair, leading some to react with extreme caution in every aspect of their lives, but the tactic of the paranoid, distrusting, misanthropic miser is not a healthy one. It betrays a delusion that we as human beings can accurately predict life's problems and thereby control life's outcomes. Almost everyone would agree that humans cannot do this, but almost all live as though they can. It would be better to live freely, with an open hand, giving and receiving from God.

"You will find it," claims Qohelet. If taken literally, Qohelet's statement is false; you will not likely find bread several days after you toss it into the lake or river. Instead, casting one's bread on the water is a metaphor for not being too tight-fisted with your possessions (the principle of throwing good deeds in the water to have them return to you, already known in Egyptian wisdom, is not likely a reference to beer production, contra Homan 2002, 275). Fox points out a parallel proverb from the Egyptian Instruction of Ankshehonq: "Do a good deed and throw it in the water; when it dries you will find it" (M. Fox 2004, 72; Lichtheim 1980, 174). Let go of some things and you will be surprised by the fact that other good things will come your way. This is not an action-consequence statement as in Proverbs where the righteous and wicked get what they deserve, nor is it in keeping with the modern notion that "what goes around comes around"; rather, Qohelet is noting that in life, good things and bad things come drifting by on the stream and there's no way of knowing when either will come: "Wisdom should not be so optimistic as to regard reward as something that could be reasoned" (Whitwell 2009, 94; see notes on 10:8–11). So, give freely and receive freely. Advantage in life is not the result of performing good deeds (contra certain midrashic interpretations; see Magarik 2000, 270). God's common grace reveals this truth the world over. A gift for all people in this life is that we are often surprised by good things from God; consequently, we likewise ought to surprise others with good things.

**11:2**. Be generous since all you have could be taken away from you in a moment—at which point you will have nothing left to give. There is always the possibility that some "disaster" (ESV)/"misfortune" (NJPS)/"calamity" (NET) could befall your crops, storehouses, livestock, or other things. Just as a bad business venture can leave a person broke (5:14 [HB 13]), so a strong wind or a deluge can wash away all a person has. Jesus had both natural disasters and man-made problems in mind when he admonished his disciples (perhaps with the text of Ecclesiastes in mind) against storing up treasures on earth "where moth and rust destroy and where thieves break in and steal" (Matt. 6:19 CSB). Qohelet does not say that the reason one should be generous is so that generosity will be repaid, but that there is more wisdom in generosity. It is better to be open-handed than to live in constant vexation and frustration over acquiring and keeping possessions (2:23; 5:17 [HB 16]; 6:3).

**11:3–4**. These verses are an exposition on the end of the previous verse (11:2b). The natural disasters alluded to there are now exemplified by a storm that brings heavy rainfall and, presumably, strong enough winds to push over trees. The latter may be understood as an unrelated phenomenon. In any case, the point is that nature is not tame and does not take your life and plans into consideration.

Nature has no regard for human life nor human endeavor, so it is senseless for a person to think they can hack the system and avoid losses altogether (5:14 [HB 13]). It is precisely the moment when a person's guard is let down that something unexpected happens. Even in the twenty-first century, meteorologists are frequently incorrect about weather predictions. Those who fixate on finding the perfect moment to plant their crops (or engage in any endeavor) will exasperate themselves trying. It is better to simply find a good enough time and to remain open to the possibility that things will not work out how you expect.

**11:5**. Humans know very little about what is going to happen in life; hence, they cannot justify stingy and controlling behavior as if that will ensure only good outcomes. Qohelet uses the image of natural disasters and storms in 11:3–4 to make a point about this ignorance, and then states that just as we do not know where the wind goes, and cannot understand the mystery of fetal gestation, so "you do not know the work of God who makes everything."

# The Works of God Are Unsearchable, So Avoid Folly and Live Freely Before Him (9:11–11:6)

The "work of God" appears in 7:13 and 8:17 and refers to all that God does and oversees—which is everything. Attempting to understand perfectly why any particular phenomenon happens precisely the way it does is what it means to try to figure out the work of God; no one can (see the end of 8:17).

**11:6**. An awareness of our inability to control life's outcomes should drive us to live life to the fullest (hedged by wisdom, of course; 10:2). The possibility of things falling apart or failing can make some people overly cautious or paralyzed with fear, thinking that if they do nothing, then nothing can go wrong (see Jesus's kingdom of God analogy to this line of thinking in Matt. 25:24–30). That is *not* the proper way to respond to life's unpredictable nature, and it is not the attitude Qohelet wants his pupils to adopt after hearing him lament over the many inequities of life. Doing nothing is not the correct response. In fact, the opposite is true: "Everything your hand finds to do, do it with your strength" (9:10)! Just as the proper way to respond to death's inevitability is to work heartily, with one's might, so the proper way to respond to life's unpredictable losses and tragedies is to "withhold not your hand."

## THEOLOGICAL FOCUS

Qohelet is concerned with promoting the relative value of wisdom for a good life and the ethos of living freely in the face of life's calamities. For those who have determined to keep on living and to do so authentically in the face of life's enigmas and futilities, there is great value in wisdom, particularly when it comes to the avoidance of trouble. Among the many principles of wisdom shared by Qohelet throughout 9:13–11:6, one important theme that appears both in 9:17–18 and in 10:12–15 is that of guarding one's mouth. Wisdom is rarely associated in Scripture with loud, boisterous speech (there are exceptions, e.g., Prov. 1:20–33). Consequently, wisdom is often heard only when one listens carefully to the right sources, like the wise man who rescued his city in 9:13–16. The words of the wise not only rescue people, but they give grace (10:12) to those who hear. The raucous fool, however, shouts uproariously to assert control or make a show of his perceived abilities and knowledge. Inasmuch as Saul's physical height was a false indicator for leadership ability, so the aggressive dictates of an overly confident ruler may deceive some into thinking that he is wise and fit for duty (10:18). In reality, his words are "evil madness" (10:13), likely because he is wise in his own eyes and does not know how to take advice (4:13). The more he talks, the more he reveals his ignorance (10:14). It would be better to offer wisdom humbly (10:17) and to otherwise remain silent in order to hear from God (5:1–7 [HB 4:17–5:6]).

Qohelet's other concern is with how we respond to life's unpredictable nature. When confronted with life's many futilities along with the fact that the world is unfair, some may choose to respond with anarchy, others sloth, and still others paranoia, but none of these responses is appropriate according to Qohelet. Throwing one's hands in the air to give up on life, to quit trying, is not an option for the wise nor for those who fear God. Qohelet is certainly sympathetic to feelings of desperation, anxiety, and grief over the innumerable vanities of a world twisted by human scheming (7:29) and otherwise totally enigmatic, and he has expressed such feelings throughout the text, but he never consents to the nonsolution of giving up.

Regarding paranoia and the false notion that it is possible for a person to be so careful that they successfully control all or even most outcomes, Qohelet offers up a point of disillusion and a point of advice, which follows his typical pattern of teaching throughout the book. To disabuse those who think life can be hacked and micromanaged, he points to the dark clouds swirling overhead and wonders what on earth human beings can do to stop what is coming (11:3). Not only are humans incapable of adequately predicting when the storms of life come, but there is often little they can do to avoid the impact once it is here. Rather than buy into the false god of control—and here is the advice—it would be better to live one's life freely with an open hand. For example, the generosity of the virtuous woman in Proverbs 31 is symbolized by the fact that she opens her hand with gifts to the poor (Prov. 31:20). She is indeed wealthy and very capable, but her status is not the result of stinginess or hoarding. In kind, Qohelet instructs his pupils to give generously to others (11:2–3), offering the hyperbolic directive to "toss your bread out onto the water" (11:1). Give now, on your own terms, and do it both because life has a way of snatching things away suddenly *and* putting obstacles in your path when you least expect them. Of course, the unnamed agent in all of life's activity is God, whose works are indiscernible (8:17; 11:5).

For Godfearers of the new covenant, Christians are challenged by Qohelet and the New Testament to live freely before God, which means giving generously (11:1–5) and working wholeheartedly (11:6). Generosity manifests itself both in the giving of money/goods and the performance of honest labor. Both these qualities must come from a heart that is free, not bound up with the anxiety of trying to control all the outcomes. Once a Christian is able to divorce from the delusion that this is even possible, they will be empowered to let go of things more easily and to give of themselves liberally. So much of the beauty in Qohelet's teaching is mirrored in Jesus's Sermon on the Mount where he instructed his disciples to give more than is expected and go farther than is required, especially when dealing with one's enemies. The apostle Paul likewise instructed the believers in Colossae to honor their superiors by doing their jobs well, to "work heartily, as for the Lord and not for men, knowing that from the Lord you will receive the inheritance as your reward. You are serving the Lord Christ" (Col. 3:23–24 ESV). Qohelet's call to Godfearers everywhere is to live life authentically, which means living freely.

## PREACHING AND TEACHING STRATEGIES

### *Exegetical and Theological Synthesis*
Qohelet continues his admonitions to his students in this section. His teaching style resembles a basketball passing drill: sometimes it touches on one topic before passing off onto another topic only to return to the original topic shortly thereafter. Binding all the disparate sections together is an overarching emphasis on wisdom and the unpredictability of the world (9:11–11:6). One thing Qohelet notices about the world is that things don't always turn out as expected. Sometimes the slow runner wins. At other times, the wise words of a poor man can deliver a city from the assault of a great foe (9:11–17). While wisdom may not fully insulate someone from the unpredictable tragedies of life, foolishness will certainly make a person more vulnerable to being destroyed by them. Qohelet advises us to stay away from foolishness and pursue wisdom (10:1–20). Even the wisest people, however, can have their joy and determination worn away by the chaotic nature of life. To combat an overly cautious or fearful disposition toward life, Qohelet commends his audience to boldly step out and take calculated risks (11:1–6).

### *Preaching Idea*
Prepare for the future—but don't try to predict it.

### *Contemporary Connections*

#### *What does it mean?*
Often in life, what we think should happen does not actually happen. The most prepared team does not always win, nor are wise people always honored (9:11–16). Qohelet still acknowledges that wisdom is better than foolishness. Wisdom

overcomes "weapons of war," meaning that insurmountable challenge can be conquered by wisdom (9:18). People who commit themselves to growing wise have a distinct advantage over fools, especially since life is so unpredictable.

Even the wisest people can be undone by life, so they should avoid making things even more difficult for themselves by avoiding foolishness (10:1–20). A little foolishness can ruin a life (10:1). Foolish people do evil and are easily identified (10:2–3). Rulers who give foolish people power bring countries to ruin (10:5–6). Fools are undone by their own words (10:12). Fools deceive themselves and make self-defeating arguments (10:13). Fools claim to know the future but actually know nothing (10:14). A little work wears out fools and keeps them from being successful (10:15). A king who is a child (i.e., naïve and foolish) brings his land to ruin (10:16). Fools are lazy, which brings widespread consequences into their lives (10:18). Fools make fun of those in authority indiscriminately, which then comes back to bite them (10:20).

A foolish person, to use a cliché, will "put all their eggs in one basket." If the basket falls over, they lose everything. Instead of relying on only one source of security, Qohelet tells his audience to diversify their assets (11:2, 6). Wise people divide their gifts (their talents, resources, and efforts) to reduce risk. Since perfect conditions to act never come, people should make smaller investments to see what pays off (11:6). Ultimately, diversifying assets helps to manage risk because unpredictability is inherent in life due to the mysteriousness of God's plans (11:5). People cannot know the future, so they should be well prepared with a wide variety of skills and assets to face whatever comes their way.

*Is it true?*
Throughout his teaching, Qohelet emphasizes how life is beyond human control (1:3–11; 6:12; 8:7–8, 17). The human experience demonstrates this to be true as well. Yet many modern people seem bent on attempting to control the uncontrollable. The human thirst for control is why the Bible warns against "divination" and "witchcraft" (Lev. 19:31; 20:6, 27). Such practices were attempts to know the future. If people could know what was coming, they could control it. While going to a soothsayer or witch-doctor is not a widespread practice in the West, the people of modern Western societies still love predictions and prognostications of the future. Sometimes a desire to control the future is smuggled under the guise of goal setting. Setting goals is not necessarily equivalent to witchcraft, of course. Making plans is even good to a degree (Prov. 16:9). But we must be careful that we are not attempting to control life on our own terms rather than submit to the Lord's will (James 4:13–16).

Just because we cannot, and probably should not, try to predict the future, that does not mean we should not prepare for it. Qohelet supports the preparation for an uncertain future through the pursuit of wisdom, the avoidance of foolishness, and the diversification of our assets. The book of Proverbs also speaks regularly about preparing for the future (6:6–11; 22:3; 27:12). Preparing for the future (instead of trying to predict it) is founded upon humility. We acknowledge that we cannot know what will come around the bend, but we trust God to be with us as we faithfully apply efforts to prepare.

*Now what?*
The Bible tells us that we pursue wisdom by searching the Scriptures. We must read it, meditate on it, and apply it. It is through searching the Scriptures that we grow wise. How committed are you to taking in God's Word? How many other forms of media do you consume? How many podcasts do you listen to? How much TV do you watch? Are you consuming God's Word in a similar way? We also grow wise through feedback and evaluation: "Better is open rebuke than hidden love. Faithful are the wounds of a friend" (Prov. 27:5–6). Getting feedback from trusted friends is one of the best ways to grow

wise, even if they have painful words to speak. It is through hard conversations with people who love and care for us that we grow the most.

We can avoid foolishness by listening. In Proverbs, Solomon repeatedly exhorts his son to "hear" or "pay attention to" his wise instructions (Prov. 1:8; 4:1, 20; 5:1, 7; 7:24). To live and learn is good, but according to Proverbs, to listen and learn is better. We can hear stories of foolish people ruining their lives and learn to avoid their pitfalls.

How do we diversify our assets? Be curious. Seek to learn and try new things. Don't pigeonhole yourself with negative thinking that you will always be a certain way or are too old to try something new. Don't become overoptimized in any one thing: so good in one area that you begin to grow worse in others. Overoptimization is why so many geniuses and advanced academics have underdeveloped social skills. They have focused so much time in only one area of their life that they have neglected others. Are you so focused on your work that you are neglecting your family? Are you so focused on other areas of life that you have forgotten about the Lord?

### *Creativity in Presentation*

Nassim Nicholas Taleb made his fortune from stock market crashes. From the 1980s to the late 2000s, Taleb repeatedly insulated himself from these crashes by pursuing financial mechanisms that go up if the market goes down. Large, unpredictable crashes Taleb dubbed "black swan events." Black swan events are hard to predict and extremely negative. Not being ready for them can be catastrophic. The problem is that human beings are generally terrible at predicting the future. So how do human beings make good decisions and thrive in their lives when their lives are filled with uncertainty and risk? In 2012, he recorded his thoughts on living a thriving life in the face of uncertainty in a book called *Antifragile: Things That Gain from Disorder*. According to Taleb, certain things get better from stress and disorder. Unfortunately, human beings routinely grow significantly weaker from chaos, but Taleb desires people to grow during these difficult but hard-to-predict times.

An important principle from *Antifragile* that comports with Ecclesiastes is Taleb's "barbell method." Just as a barbell has weights on each end that balance each other, so we must approach life in an opposite but balanced way. On one side of the barbell, you make extremely safe and conservative decisions. For example, you may keep a well-stocked "emergency fund" for your finances. On the other end of the barbell, you take a lot of small but risky actions (cf. Eccl. 11:6). These actions are certainly risks, but they are small so they will not cause a catastrophe if they do not work out. For example, pursuing a side hustle of becoming a fiction writer (a risk) while maintaining a steady job as a schoolteacher (a safe choice) would be an example of the barbell method.

A vivid example of those who did not live according to Qohelet's wisdom is found in the movie *The Big Short*, a fictional account of the financial crisis precipitated in 2008 by the housing bubble. The movie chronicles how big banks gave out many unreliable loans, often approving risky mortgages for people who had no business obtaining one. Eventually, the bubble burst and many people found themselves financially ruined. Overextending oneself financially can lead to disaster.

How do we live well when life is unpredictable? The big idea instructs us to avoid arrogant predictions and to choose a better way: "Prepare for the future (but don't try to predict it)." What does adequate preparation for the future look like, though? Qohelet unpacks three principles for preparing for the future:

- Pursue wisdom (9:11–18)
- Avoid foolishness (10:1–20)
- Diversify your assets (11:1–6)

# The Works of God Are Unsearchable, So Avoid Folly and Live Freely Before Him (9:11–11:6)

## DISCUSSION QUESTIONS

1. What examples does Qohelet give to show the unpredictability of life (9:11–18)?

2. How are the foolish described (10:1–20)?

3. Why should people diversify their assets (11:1–6)?

4. How can we pursue wisdom in everyday life?

5. What kinds of people do you regularly surround yourself with: the foolish or the wise?

6. How can you diversify your skills, experiences, and resources?

# Ecclesiastes 11:7–12:7

**EXEGETICAL IDEA**
In his final admonition, Qohelet directs his pupils to fix their thoughts on God while they live, knowing that old age and death come sooner than one thinks.

**THEOLOGICAL FOCUS**
The certainty of death brings the value of life itself into perspective, directing Godfearers to enjoy their lives free from vexation and to prioritize God in their hearts while they still can.

**PREACHING IDEA**
Don't wait until it's too late. Remember God when you're young.

**PREACHING POINTERS**
Because of the inscrutability of God's ways, Qohelet concluded that one of the best ways for people to live is to pursue wisdom and trust in God's sovereignty. As Qohelet wrapped up his teaching, he reminded his students of the importance of being mindful of God in one's youth. Instead of pursuing a vain life, he advised those he taught to fear God and keep his commandments.

"Youth is wasted on the young," the adage goes. Although a cliché, the saying resonates with many people as they look back on their younger years with regret. Instead of pursuing the things of God, they pursued the things of the world, only to be left disappointed. Qohelet's admonition to the young is an important message to relay to the younger generations today, so that those coming behind us can be spared the pain and heartbreak of vain pursuits—although such wise counsel will only stave off foolishness if it is heeded.

# LIFE IS SHORT, SO ENJOY IT AND REMEMBER GOD (11:7–12:7)

## LITERARY STRUCTURE AND THEMES (11:7–12:7)

Beginning at 11:7 and continuing until 12:7, Qohelet puts all his scribal energy into one of the main concerns of his teaching, into the immovable, inevitable force that has inspired so much of his writing—death. However, rather than talk as he has before about the gloomy certainty of death and its power to quench everything (in scattered verses throughout, but esp. 9:1–6), Qohelet's approach to the topic here is centered on how a person ought to go about redeeming the short time they have been given on earth. This requires that they both enjoy their lives free from vexation (11:7–10) and live conscientiously before God while they still can (12:1–7).

These sections are not difficult to delineate, and the choices made here are similar to those made by other commentators (e.g., Garrett 1993, 339; Seow 1997, 346). The first section (11:7–10) deals with the attitude and emotional experiences of Qohelet's young pupils. They should do what they can to avoid the unnecessary "vexation/anxiety" he has spoken of throughout the book (e.g., 1:18; 2:23: 5:16 [HB 15]). The second section (12:1–7) begins with an admonition to "remember" God while still young and not yet beset by the difficulties of physical decay that come to everyone who lives long enough.

- *Enjoy Life While You Can (11:7–10)*
- *Remember God While You Can (12:1–7)*

## EXPOSITION (11:7–12:7)

Qohelet desires that his pupils not be like those who drink and party their lives away in blissful stupidity, always putting off or ignoring what matters in life (7:4–6). He also rejects the opposite end of the spectrum, where a man/woman obsesses over negativity, grinding anxiously over every potential misfortune and how to avoid it in order to maximize wealth (5:13–17 [HB 12–16]). He rather wishes for his pupils to hold two seemingly disparate things in balance: the imperative to live freely and joyfully on the one hand, and the acknowledgment on the other that "the days of darkness" are coming. By "days of darkness," Qohelet is referring both to the final stages of a person's life where their physical and mental capacities are all but gone, and to the finality and eternity of death. As he has noted previously, there will be no more knowledge, love, hate, envy, or reward once a person dies (recall that Qohelet does not have a clear understanding of the afterlife). But for those who live to an old age, mental and physical abilities often begin to fade long before the moment of death, as illustrated by 12:2–6.

The first subunit (11:7–10) addresses the need for people to enjoy life to its fullest, "for youth and adolescence are a vapor." In light of this, Qohelet releases a string of five imperatives and a jussive in 11:9–10 alone whereby he admonishes the young man to "rejoice" (שְׂמַח), "let your heart delight you" (וִיטִיבְךָ לִבְּךָ), "walk" (וְהַלֵּךְ), "know" (וְדָע), "remove" (וְהָסֵר), and "put away" (וְהַעֲבֵר). The verbs relate variously to the removal of harmful things and the pursuit of healthy things. His concluding statement is not that youth is meaningless, but that one's youth goes by so quickly that it is like a "breath" or a "vapor" (see Job 7:16; Pss. 62:9 [HB 10]; 144:4).

The second subunit (12:1–7) also features an admonition, which serves as Qohelet's final bit of advice in the body of his teaching (12:8–14 is not part of Qohelet's teaching, but the words of the frame narrator). The injunction is that students should "remember" (זכר), as in "give careful thought to," "your Creator" (בּוֹרְאֶיךָ) while they still can, before the maladies of old age come. The signs of old age are then referenced allegorically throughout this passage (however, not all commentators read this passage allegorically, e.g., Schoors 2013, 783; see Seow 1999, 212, who takes the passage to refer to the eschaton). In the verses that follow, Qohelet uses images of nature and domestic activities to serve as emblems of life's certain, eventual end when one's "breath returns to the God who gave it. (12:7).

### *Enjoy Life While You Can (11:7–10)*

Life is fleeting, Qohelet reminds his pupils, so there is only a small window of time in which to maximize joy before it is all over. He encourages them not to waste their lives in vexation.

**11:7**. It is sweet to be alive! The term "sweet" (מָתוֹק) also appears in 5:12 (HB 11) to describe the sweet sleep of the laborer who is not lying awake paranoid over riches and how to keep them. Throughout his teaching thus far, Qohelet has mentioned "the sun" many times (thirty, to be precise), and the term is predominantly used in negative contexts (exceptions: 5:18 [HB 17]; 7:11; 8:15; 9:13). The present verse (11:7) is by far the most positive use of the term "sun" throughout his teaching. As miserable as Qohelet's musings have been over all the evil he has seen under the sun (e.g., 5:13 [HB 12]; 6:1; 10:5), he *still* considers it "pleasant for the eyes." This insight is remarkable given all the bad press planet Earth has gotten throughout the book of Ecclesiastes. In spite of all the inequity, injustice, futility, pain, and certainty of death, it is still a good thing to be alive. But how does a person achieve the "goodness" of life here referenced by Qohelet? The answer is given in 11:8–10.

**11:8**. People ought to possess a measured joy in life. In contrast to the man who lives the hyperbolic span of two thousand years and is incapable of enjoying any of it because he is never satisfied (6:1–6), Qohelet prescribes that a man choose to enjoy his life. This seems like a deceptively simple principle whenever it is given throughout Ecclesiastes, but honest readers will know how difficult such an admonition is to follow. Life's many trials are effective for putting the human heart into regular anxiety if not checked by faith in God. To be clear on just what is meant by the enjoyment prescribed by Qohelet, he immediately counterbalances joy with an acknowledgment of darkness; the goal, then, is not to possess the brand of joy sponsored by hapless, drunken dolts (7:4–6), but to possess the sobriety of mind that allows one to delight in the sun and fully appreciate its beauty, knowing that soon it will descend over the horizon. After that, there will be only dark nothingness (from Qohelet's limited perspective on what comes after death; see note on 9:5–6).

Given the reference to judgment (11:9) and the metaphor for dying and death in 12:1–7, the "days of darkness" here do not refer to the many lousy days a person may experience in ordinary life (7:14) but to the end of life altogether. That is an important consideration for contextualizing Qohelet's use of the term "vanity" (הֶבֶל) here. As discussed in the note on 1:2, the term means either "futile" or "ephemeral" when referring to human endeavors, or "enigmatic"/"incomprehensible" when referring to life and the world in general, which Qohelet refers to as "the work of God" (8:17; 11:5; also implied in many places throughout, e.g., 7:13–14). Since death means the end of humans thinking or doing anything (9:6), the term cannot mean futility or ephemerality. The point beyond death is Sheol, and it belongs to the category "the work of God," for only he has full view of it and sovereign control over its gates (e.g., Job 26:6; Ps. 31:17 [HB 18]; Prov. 15:11; Isa. 7:11). Therefore, "all that comes" after life "is an enigma." We could translate *hevel* as

# Life Is Short, So Enjoy it and Remember God (11:7–12:7)

"nothingness," but that is too confident an assertion for Qohelet, who is not sure about what happens after a person dies (see 3:21 and the motif of man not knowing what will come after him; see also introduction and notes on 3:17, 20–21; 8:12–13; 9:3, 5–6; 11:9; 12:7, 13, and sidebar "Life After Death in Ecclesiastes" p. 108). Qohelet is more likely to say "I cannot figure it out" than to say he knows for certain what will be. After all, one of the very few things about which he is confident is that God will somehow judge all people, and if that happens after the moment of death, then it is more than "nothing."

**11:9.** The prescription of joy continues. The intent of this verse is similar to 9:7 where Qohelet told his pupils to eat, drink, and be merry "for God has already approved/delighted in your works." The command at the beginning of 11:9 is morally unqualified, mostly. It is neither a command to follow one's heart into sin nor explicitly a command to pursue only God-ordained pleasures. It is just a command to live joyfully. The qualification comes at the end of the verse, where pupils are reminded of the judgment of God. But does that judgment come on earth or in the eschaton? Qohelet assumes the former and may hope for the latter (see "Future Judgment" in Introduction). That knowledge should inspire a particular kind of enjoyment (see sidebar "Qohelet's Brand of Joy" p. 191).

### Qohelet's Brand of Joy

Throughout the book of Ecclesiastes, Qohelet has promoted a brand of joy that embraces life's simple pleasures but never forgets the source of those pleasures: "this is the gift of God" (5:19 [HB 18]; see also 2:24–26; 3:12–13, 22; 8:15; 9:7–10). So, when Qohelet tells his disciples to pursue joy in 11:8–9, it must be understood in the context of his other statements on the topic. In other words, when Qohelet tells them "walk in the ways of your heart," he is not rejecting the Torah command stating that one should *not* follow one's heart and eyes into sin (Num. 15:39; contra Sneed 2015a, 343). The command here is rather to embrace life's joys and pleasures liberally *within* the fear of God. Those pleasures have already been defined in the joy statements throughout the book.

The freedom propagated here by Qohelet cannot be understood apart from his repeated instruction to fear God, as well as his reminders that God will someday and somehow bring all people into judgment. To walk "in the sight of your eyes" (בְּמַרְאֵי עֵינֶיךָ) is the kind of generous freedom afforded Adam and Eve in the garden, God having created "every tree that was pleasant to the sight and good for food" (כָּל־עֵץ נֶחְמָד לְמַרְאֶה וְטוֹב לְמַאֲכָל), an unimaginable bounty from which the image-bearers may freely eat (2:16) so long as they observe but one small boundary (2:17). There is likewise a bounty of good things to see and do in the world that, if properly appreciated, will keep one from the "evil" deeds of the wicked (8:11). But what if they are not *properly* appreciated? It is possible to follow one's heart into sin. Adam and Eve, for example, pursued a counterfeit form of enjoyment, which resulted in judgment. Likewise, Qohelet's pupils must live within the lines of divine commands concerning joy, not straying to the left like a fool, for all people will be judged for their deeds, "whether good or evil" (12:14).

**11:10.** In conclusion, relax and live well! Qohelet wishes for his pupils to consider whether any of today's stressors will matter in five years' time. Many commentators understand the two items the pupil should expel from his life as anxiety/care/vexation and physical pain/malady. The first is easy to concede, given Qohelet's use of that term throughout the book, beginning in 1:18. It seems unlikely, however, that the second clause is about removing bad health and physical pain from one's body (there was, after all, no Tylenol® in the old world). A better parallel to the first line would be to understand this "trouble" (רָעָה) as perhaps "sorrow" or, given the mention of God's judgment at the end of

11:9, "evil." The only other time in the HB where the terms "trouble/evil" (רָעָה) team up with "flesh" (בָּשָׂר) is in Jeremiah 45:5, where God declares "I am bringing disaster upon all flesh" (רָעָה עַל־כָּל־בָּשָׂר). In Jeremiah, the term refers to the judgment of physical suffering, which may lend support to the thesis that the youth is to put away "pain" from his body. But, in a world before modern medication, how would one actually go about doing this?

Concerning this second thing the pupil is to avoid, then, we can make the following observations: (1) We have seen throughout the book that it is impossible to avoid random "trouble" because life is unpredictable (see 9:11–11:7), so why would Qohelet warn his pupil to avoid something he cannot avoid? (2) We recognize that it is almost equally impossible to "put away" physical pain. (3) "Sorrow" is a better possibility for רָעָה and parallel to the first thing he is to avoid: "vexation." Youth passes by quickly, like a vapor, so why spend it in emotional turmoil?

### Remember God While You Can (12:1–7)

The brevity of life should inspire not only enjoyment of the present, but *rightful* enjoyment, meaning that people should spend their days dwelling on God while they still have the ability to do so.

**12:1.** The final admonition from Qohelet is that his pupils prioritize God in their youth. The difficulty with the term "creator" is its plural spelling (בּוֹרְאֶיךָ), literally "your creators," and the *BHS* lists no textual variants that put the term in the singular (though unlisted, the LXX reads: τοῦ κτίσαντός σε "who created you"; the *BHQ* notes that other versions understood this as singular, the MT presenting a plural of majesty [GKC §93ss] or "merely a matter of late Hebrew orthography," 110). This opens possibilities, noted by various scholars—the term "creators" here could be "well(s)" (from בְּאֵר), as a metaphorical reference to one's wife or birth, or to one's "grave/pit" (בּוֹר), or to all three meanings at the same time (creator, well, pit) as clever wordplay (Heim 2019, 191–92). But given Qohelet's other references to the fear of God throughout his teaching as well as the imperative to "know" that God's judgment is one day coming (just as above in 11:9), it may be best to understand the term בּוֹרְאֶיךָ as a misspelling in the MT for the singular "your Creator" (e.g., CSB, ESV, NIV) rather than "your vigor" (NJPS) or "well" or "pit" (see Whybray 1989, 153). To this we may add other commands in Scripture to "remember the LORD your God" (Deut. 8:18). The righteous are "those who remember the LORD" (Isa. 62:6; cf. Pss. 20:7 [HB 8]; 77:3 [HB 4]; Isa. 63:7; Jer. 2:7).

The importance of putting one's energy into God "in your youth" (which, in this passage, refers to all of life leading up to the very end) is that the day is coming when one's physical and mental maladies will be so numerous that it will be difficult to enjoy God in quite the same way. The "days of evil" (יְמֵי הָרָעָה) are really "days of malady," since the term "evil" (הָרָעָה) here must refer to the inevitable decline of one's mental state that accompanies the decline of one's physical state. "Evil" has a wide range of meanings in the HB that can include everything from moral wickedness to natural disasters, depending on the context in which it is used. If a person lives long enough and suffers enough irreversible physical malady and/or psychological pain, they may come to the place where they consider death a better alternative than life. Over the millennia, countless elderly (or younger, but very ill) believers have uttered the words, "I'm just ready to be with the Lord now." Qohelet likely witnessed this attitude among some of the elderly of Israel and perhaps considered it an inevitability for himself as well, which is why he assumes its certainty here at the end of 12:1.

**12:2.** Whether this is a reference to diminishing eyesight or a more general point about the looming approach of death, or both, Qohelet wishes to express that the days of darkness are coming (11:8).

The metaphors used throughout 12:2–7 employ common imagery from nature and domestic life to describe the decline of the human body near or at the time of death. The scene is one of townsfolk and animals scurrying to safety ahead of a looming storm. Commentators suggest that the passage has eschatological overtones since it employs imagery typically associated with the motif of the divine warrior (Seow 1997, 353–54, citing 2 Sam. 22:12; Job 36:29; 37:19; Ps. 18:12 [HB 13]; Judg. 5:4; Isa. 19:1; M. Fox 2004, 78). The images are indeed relevant, but the connection should not be taken too far. Qohelet is likewise borrowing familiar imagery from the eschatological "day of the LORD" motif (see, e.g., Isa. 13:6, 9; Ezek. 13:5; 30:3; Joel 1:15; 2:1, 11) to suit his rhetorical purposes. The "day of the Lord" in Scripture depicts an undoing of creation that sees the light of Genesis 1 replaced with darkness: "The sun and the moon are darkened, and the stars withdraw their shining" (Joel 2:10; cf. Ezek. 32:7–8). As Heim notes, "Every important word in Ecclesiastes 12:2a appears in the narrative about these two days of creation" (2019, 193). In sum, the eschatological language of global uncreation is employed in this passage to describe how a town reacts to the encroachment of an ominous storm, the townsfolk and animals themselves being metaphors for the declining body of an elderly person. The admonition in 12:1 to "remember your Creator" is amplified by the severity and finality of what comes at the end of one's life. For those near death, it might as well be the day of the Lord since, for them, this is the end.

**12:3**. Bones and eyes eventually grow weak. As old age enters its latter stages, the human body begins to fail in a number of ways. Qohelet lists different types of people found in a town setting, each by their occupation. He envisions a time when they become somehow impaired, implying that they can no longer do the work they used to do. The various groups of workers are meant to serve as metaphors for the failing body of old age. The "keepers of the house," as in the servants, will one day "tremble/shake" (שֶׁיָּזֻעוּ) in fear at the approaching storm, a term that appears in Esther 5:9 in reference to the fact that Haman did *not* tremble in fear before Mordecai but was filled with rage. Metaphorically, the shaking "keepers of the house" may represent the trembling or lack of mobility that accompanies old age (see M. Fox 2004, 79; Garrett 1993, 341–42; Longman 1998, 270).

Some take a more literal approach to the passage as a whole, denying the metaphor for old age and viewing the shaking here as simply "the fearful reaction of those who guard the house" in the eschaton (Seow 1997, 355; see also Heim's interpretation of the passage as describing a city under siege [2019, 194–96]). Invaders are known to use storm imagery to describe their invasions, such as how Sennacherib "roared loudly like a storm (and) thundered" against the Babylonian troops (Elayi 2018, 23). However, given that the immediately preceding context of 11:7–12:1a was focused on what one should do while a "youth," and the reference to burial at the conclusion of this passage (12:7), it is more likely that the entire unit is addressing the topic of the human body by means of metaphor. The "mighty men" may refer to the laborers of the household, and metaphorically the limbs of an elderly person, growing weaker with age. The "grinders" (teeth?) are decreasing in number and the women who peer out the windows (eyes) are growing dim, presumably because all are heading in to avoid the storm (see Longman 1998, 270).

**12:4**. Hearing eventually fails. As the allegory continues, the villagers shelter quickly before the mass of dark clouds swoops over the town. Doors along the street are shut and the women cease grinding at the mill and "the daughters of song are muffled," the latter being either a reference to literal singers, as in hired entertainers or simply the sound of young women playing

# Life Is Short, So Enjoy it and Remember God (11:7–12:7)

(one wonders if this is meant to parallel the royal singers Solomon hired in the prime of his life; 2:8). The first activity in 12:4 is the shutting of twin doors, which is likely a reference to the ears since the following three metaphors have to do with the decrease of sounds. A town can become eerily quiet just before a storm; likewise, the storm of death is precipitated by a loss of hearing in the weakening body of an aged man or woman. Barzillai the Gileadite complained about his old age to David: "I'm now eighty years old. Can I discern what is pleasant and what is not? Can your servant taste what he eats or drinks? Can I still hear the voice of male and female singers? Why should your servant be an added burden to my lord the king?" (2 Sam. 19:35 CSB).

A more difficult line to interpret in the context of storm preparation is the activity of one who "rises up at the sound of a bird" (ESV). To what household or village enterprise could this refer? It could be that "the sound of the bird" (לְקוֹל הַצִּפּוֹר) is actually the subject preceded by the preposition *lamed* (לְ) as is known to happen in Late Biblical Hebrew, hence Seow's translation: "the sound of the bird rises" (see his related suggestions; 1997, 358). If their volume is rising, this seems out of place since the other two images in the verse refer to sounds dampening (i.e., doors shutting, grinding ceasing as metaphors for the decreased hearing of an elderly person). Furthermore, while the verb "to rise" (קוּם) and the noun "sound/voice" (קוֹל) are not syntactically related elsewhere in the HB, the term "sound/voice" (קוֹל) does appear with the conceptually related verbs "to lift" (נשׂא, e.g., Isa. 52:8) and "to raise" (*hiphil* of רום, e.g., 2 Kings 19:22), both of which refer to an increase in volume. Another possibility emerges, though: the sound of the bird rising may refer to the phenomenon of its squawking growing more distant as it flies away in response to the storm. The further the sound rises, the dimmer its sound becomes. This interpretation would fit better with the metaphors of decreased hearing in the verse.

**12:5.** As the body grows weaker, fear and danger may increase. The opening line refers literally to the townsfolk or a household preparing for a torrent. They are "fearful of what is on high [the storm clouds] and the terrors in the street." It has become dangerous outside. The thunder, lightning, rain, and hail that originate on high come down to affect the ground. Metaphorically, this could refer to the worries that can accompany the elderly who are not as able-bodied as they used to be, resulting in a greater caution over what they are willing to expose themselves to or whether they are going to leave the house to begin with.

Though the townsfolk have shut themselves inside and ceased all their labors, hunkered down in preparation for the storm, the flora and insects seem undisturbed, as the former continue to blossom and the latter scurry about. The Hebrew of 12:5 is difficult. Regarding "the caper berry," it may be better to understand the verb "shrivels/fails" (פרר) as a misidentification for "sprout" (פרח); hence the emendation to the MT would be "the caper berry sprouts" (וְתִפְרַח הָאֲבִיּוֹנָה; M. Fox 2004, 81, citing the *NJPS*). However, others will understand all three of the activities in this verse as negative: "the almond becomes revolting, the locust droops, and the caper comes to naught" (Seow makes a formidable case; 1997, 361–63). Is the imagery in 12:5 asserting that nature will go on unaffected while man decays into oblivion (a point Qohelet has made elsewhere; 1:3–11)? Or is this imagery a continuation of the metaphor of man's declining body, where the decay of locusts and plants represent his failing faculties? Or is it a mixed bag?

The most likely explanation for the activities of the almond tree, the locust/grasshopper, and the caper berry are that they are all three unfazed by the death of humans. They, like the sun on its circuits, will continue long after the humans have passed on (cf. 1:3–11). The almond tree and locust are common enough in the HB, but the choice of the caper berry (a known aphrodisiac in the ANE) may be to signal that human procreation will continue long after the death of this hypothetical "man who is going to his eternal home." The funeral is set at the end of the verse. Funerary scenes from ancient Egypt show mourners overcome by grief as they put their hands up to their faces while they sob (see Dominicus 1994, 66).

The ancient Israelite town of Beersheba. Public domain. Note the main street and adjoining buildings: "And the doors on the street are shut and the sound of the grinding is low" (Eccl. 12:4a).

### Sheol: The Land of No Return

According to Qohelet, all people, righteous and unrighteous, the wise and fools, the rich and poor, are headed to the same place (9:3), and the name of the place is "Sheol" (9:10). In 12:5, it is referred to metaphorically as the "eternal home" (בֵּית עוֹלָם). In a nonbiblical Aramaic inscription about the prophet Balaam, it is said that the god El will travel to the "eternal home" (בית עלמן), which Shmuel Aḥituv notes is a reference to the realm of the dead (2008, 456, 459). The phrase occurs nowhere else in Scripture, though. In Mesopotamia, the underworld was similarly referred to as "the land of no return" (*ANET*, 107; see "Descent of Ishtar to the Nether World"). For Qohelet, who has no clear conception of resurrection or the afterlife (though he is not so confident as to say he knows for certain what happens after death; see 3:21), death is final and for that reason incomparably weighty. He would agree that Sheol is the land of no return, but he would disagree with ANE and Mediterranean conceptions of the afterlife found in Egyptian, Canaanite, Mesopotamian, and Greek literature. Instead, he would argue that the faculties of an aging man or woman continue on their path of decline until the point of death where there is no "thought or knowledge or wisdom in Sheol" (9:10). There is at least a symmetry to death (12:7), and because of that an extent to which it makes sense, but that in no way makes its reality less grim. Nevertheless, Qohelet's hope remains in God (8:12–13).

**12:6.** Remember God before life is broken into a thousand pieces, well beyond repair. Qohelet's admonition in 12:1 was to remember the Creator in the days of one's youth, "before" (עַד אֲשֶׁר) the evil days come and "before" (עַד אֲשֶׁר) the storm of old age (12:1–2). Here the force of the imperative returns with the prepositional phrase "before" (עַד אֲשֶׁר), only this time the pupil ought to remember his Creator before life is shattered altogether. The "snapping/removal" of the cord, the "breaking" of the golden bowl, the "smashing" of the pitcher, and the "breaking" of the wheel all point to death. Seow posits that the imagery is of a ceramic lampstand made to look metal, with arms extending outward to symbolize the tree of life. Accordingly, he translates the first line "before the silver tendril is smashed," noting that "cord" (חֶבֶל) "may refer to anything that is long and twining" (1997, 364–65). The lampstand may be like the lamp described in Zechariah 4:2, where a bowl sits atop it. The image of a bowl held by a cord, though, is unknown in Scripture and remains unattested in the archaeological record. If the images are to be understood independently of one another, then we are less certain of the meaning. In any case, it is minimally evident that when silver and gold objects break, something precious and valuable has been lost.

The next metaphor involves the shattering of a pot at a water source, which may practically occur when the strength of a flowing stream yanks the jar from one's hand or a full jug slips from the weight and smashes on the ground. If the jar and the "wheel" are to be understood together, then the idea may be that a pulley breaks, dropping the jar down a cistern, smashing against the walls as it makes its sudden descent (Longman 1998, 273). Notes Fox, "Deliberately broken vessels are often found in Jewish tombs of the Second Temple period. They were perhaps smashed as part of a funeral rite symbolizing the shattering of life" (M. Fox 2004, 82; see esp. Seow 1997, 336–37). Humans are made of dust (Gen. 2:7); in creation, God brought particles together into a collected whole that could be shattered back into particles. Similarly, humans are often compared to pottery (e.g., Job 10:9; 33:6; Isa. 29:16; 45:9; 64:8; Jer. 18:6).

**12:7.** The cycle of life culminates in the curse of death, a promise once made by God to Adam in the garden, and it is the fate of all living things: "For you are dust, and to dust you must return" (Gen. 3:19; see Job 34:14–15; Eccl. 3:20, 5:15–16 [HB 14–15]). Working off the imagery of a shattered earthen vessel in Ecclesiastes 12:6, Qohelet now brings the metaphor home: "And dust returns to the earth from which it came," which is certainly an allusion to Genesis 2:7 where God forms man from "the dust of the ground." And just as God had breathed the "breath of life" (נִשְׁמַת חַיִּים) into man's nostrils, so at the end of a human's life, the breath (רוּחַ) must return back to God from whence it came.

The rendering of "breath" (רוּחַ) as "spirit" in some translations reflects an understanding of life after death, concerning which Qohelet never expresses confidence (the closest he comes is "Who knows?"; see 3:21; see sidebar "Life After Death in Ecclesiastes" p. 108). Given the use of רוּחַ as "life breath" back in 3:19, the parallels to Genesis 2:7, and the many other passages where the term רוּחַ refers to "life breath" (e.g., Gen. 6:17; 7:15; Isa. 42:5), it would be contextually appropriate to understand it as such here, rather than "spirit." Qohelet sees human life as coming from and returning to God, a poetic symmetry that does not dampen death's power but at least shows God as the one in control. Modern believers encountering this verse may be inclined to read into it notions of heaven and dwelling with God, but such things were not universally understood by Old Testament saints. They had to trust God with the limited knowledge they had, and the overwhelming evidence in Scripture indicates that most did not think of the afterlife as part of their future. Certain passages may reflect the fuller understanding (Ps. 49:15 [HB 16]; Isa. 26:19; Dan. 12:2), but many others reveal little knowledge of this (see note on 9:5–6). Jesus confronted the Sadducean error of denying the resurrection by citing Exodus 3:6, proclaiming that God is the God of the living, not the dead (Matt. 22:29–32). Unlike the Sadducees, Qohelet does not outright deny a resurrection, but he stands in a position of limited knowledge and remains uncertain of the future, though confident that God will carry out justice.

## THEOLOGICAL FOCUS

Qohelet's final remarks to his pupils are filled with imperatives to live life freely and joyfully while they still can. The rapid-fire delivery of these admonitions gives off the impression that Qohelet himself is taking his last breaths and getting out as much wisdom as he can in the final moments. The content of the next several verses (12:1–7) portrays a physical decline that concludes in death in 12:7 and a return to the narrator in 12:8, followed immediately by 12:9 where Qohelet is spoken of in the past tense.

Life is short. There is not much time. All people are "lighter than a breath" when weighed on the scale (Ps. 62:9 [HB 10]). Humanity is but a "breath" (הֶבֶל; Ps. 39:5 [HB 6], 11 [HB 12]). Qohelet's anthem is that "everything is a breath" (הַכֹּל הָבֶל) or "an enigma" or "futile" depending on how the term is used throughout his teachings (1:2; 12:8). Everything Qohelet has taught so far has pointed to the transience and unpredictability of life, leading him to an impassioned plea that his pupils live their lives joyfully before God while they still have time (11:7–10). "Light is sweet," remarks Qohelet, but the coming "days of darkness will be many" (12:7–8). This time of darkness is portrayed in an extended metaphor in 12:1–7 wherein townsfolk prepare themselves for a looming storm. The imagery of these verses extends the imperative to "remember/dwell on your Creator while you are young!" throughout by the repetition of "before" (עַד אֲשֶׁר). Remember God "before" (עַד אֲשֶׁר) the time of evil (12:2) and "before" (עַד אֲשֶׁר) the storm clouds come (12:3) and "before" (עַד אֲשֶׁר) the lampstand (a symbol for the tree of life?; see note on 12:6) is broken and the light of life thereby removed (12:6). After that, the dust of one's body returns to the ground from which humanity was created and the breath of one's lungs expels upward to the God who first gave it (12:7; see Gen. 2:7).

The apostle Paul had similar imagery in mind (if not this very passage) when he wrote to the Corinthians that our human bodies are like "clay jars" (2 Cor. 4:7) and that our "outer self is wasting away" (2 Cor. 4:16). He thereby exhorts the Corinthian believers to look inward and remember that while the outer self is perishing, the inner self is undergoing renewal to prepare for the world we cannot yet see. So, while Qohelet has commented repeatedly on all the evil he has "seen under the sun," the apostle reminds us that we must "look not to the things that are seen but to the things that are unseen. For the things that are seen are transient, but the things that are unseen are eternal" (2 Cor. 4:18 ESV). Indeed, Qohelet has made this very point, in part: that everything under the sun is transient, a breath. And while Qohelet's faith in God's ultimate judgment of the righteous and wicked is secure, he does not yet know how that will happen after a person dies. In Christ Jesus, the answer to this question has been given: "For God so loved the world, that he gave his only Son, that whoever believes in him should not perish but have eternal life" (John 3:16). This proclamation to Nicodemus rings true for all people, who must recognize that now is the time—while alive and alert under the sun—to "dwell upon"/"reckon with"/"remember" (זכר) the Creator.

## PREACHING AND TEACHING STRATEGIES

### Exegetical and Theological Synthesis
In Qohelet's final section of teaching, he admonishes the young to live wisely before the Lord (11:7–12:7). Surprisingly, Qohelet asserts the goodness of youth and the fact that the young should take joy in their youthfulness (11:7–9). The young should enjoy their lives while they can for the "days of darkness" will eventually come (11:8). The enjoyment of youth, however, is not a license for sinful or pointless pleasures, for God will certainly bring all things into judgment.

Because of the goodness, yet brevity, of youth, the young must remember God early in their lives (12:1). Life is brief and, like an approaching storm, the threat of death rises and develops in the lives of all. In an extended metaphor, Qohelet describes the encroachment of death upon all people (12:2–7). Even before death finally arrives, the human condition deteriorates, leaving the elderly to long for death (cf. 12:1). The final state of humanity is the fulfillment of the curse of sin: "Then the dust will return to earth as it was" (12:7; cf. Gen. 3:19). The young, therefore, must not squander their precious years on earth, but rather, live joyfully and wisely before the Lord.

### Preaching Idea
Don't wait until it's too late. Remember God when you're young.

### Contemporary Connections

#### What does it mean?
Being young is a special blessing according to Qohelet. It is so special because it is so brief.

The young should enjoy their lives, for with age comes suffering (11:8). Enjoying one's youth is no excuse for foolishness, of course. What Qohelet teaches about enjoying youth must be understood in the context of fearing God and his future judgment (11:9). Qohelet poignantly reminds his young pupils: "You must give an account to God for everything you do" (11:9 NLT). Youthfulness is not an excuse for sinfulness. No matter what our age is, Scripture regularly warns us that we will give account before God for our lives (Matt. 12:36; Rom. 14:12; 2 Cor. 5:10).

Eventually, the young will run out of time to honor God. At a certain point, it may even be too late to remember God because the aging process has taken hold and decimated one's mental and physical faculties (12:2–5). Through an elaborate metaphor, Qohelet describes the physical effects of aging. The elderly shake and lose control over their limbs, their eyes don't work as well, and they can lose their teeth. They can lose their hearing and become fearful of risks, like slipping and falling. Sexual desire wanes. Human life becomes completely shattered by death (12:6). The only thing that a person can do in the face of death is remember God. All people—whether young or old—must seek the Lord before it's too late.

*Is it true?*
It can be tempting to delay figuring out what you believe about God. It can be very tempting to avoid going to church or getting involved in a ministry, especially when you're young. "I'll get around to all that spiritual stuff when I'm older," many people think to themselves. They believe that youth is about having fun, which usually involves illicit activities. If you think you will take God seriously when you are older, you are deceiving yourself. It can be hard to pay attention to God when you're young because there are so many fun opportunities to pursue, but it might be even harder to do so when you're older, for the responsibilities and the demands on your time increase. If it was easy to push God out of mind when you are young to go to a party, it is easy to push him out of mind when you are older because now your kids have soccer practice. Yet the longer you withhold yourself from pursuing God, the more perilous the situation you will find yourself in.

The plain fact is that the longer you live, the closer you are to death. And you never know when death may come. Do not delay believing in God and receiving his salvation, like the people of Israel did. The people of Israel could have entered into God's rest, his salvation, but they failed to enter it because they disobeyed him (Heb. 4:6). Yet God, in his mercy, set another time to enter his rest: the coming of the Lord Jesus. Now that Jesus has come, the author of Hebrews urges his readers to enter God's rest: "Today you must listen to his voice. Don't harden your hearts against him" (Heb. 4:7; cf. Ps. 95:7–8). In another place, the apostle Paul urges unbelievers to be reconciled to God because, "Now is the favorable time; behold, now is the day of salvation" (2 Cor. 6:2). Yet the opportunity to trust in God will not last forever. The Scriptures declare that this lifetime is our opportunity; we don't get another one: "It is appointed for man to die once and after that comes judgment" (Heb. 9:27). Do not waste your youth—or any more time for that matter. Trust in Christ today.

*Now what?*
What if you are already older? What if you totally disregarded God in your youth, but now you are here, desiring to know more about him? When then? In order to remember God when you are older, you must become younger. The gospel of Matthew records an instance where Jesus's disciples came to him and asked him who the greatest person was in God's kingdom (Matt. 18:1). Presumably, the disciples wanted to know either where they currently stood in the kingdom or how to climb the ladder to be number one. Jesus shattered their preconceived notions about God's kingdom by calling a child over to himself

(18:2). Jesus pointed out that "unless you turn and become like children, you will never enter the kingdom of heaven" (18:3). Childlike trust in God is the path to salvation according to Jesus. Jesus emphasized his point by declaring, "Whoever humbles himself like this child is the greatest in the kingdom of heaven" (18:4).

The path to being reconnected to God is through becoming young again. You cannot become literally younger, as if you could turn back the aging process. The point is to become young, like a child, in your *trust*. Children trust their parents implicitly and without need for explanation. They are wholly dependent upon them. It works the same way with you. You need to have a childlike trust in God. You must abandon all other options for trying to make your life "work." You must abandon all other attempts to save yourself, whether it's through your own obedience to a moral tradition or through adhering to your own developed moral code. Instead, you must cry out to Jesus as your Savior and find forgiveness in him alone.

*Creativity in Presentation*
In the sport of football, one play can change everything. In Week 17 of the 2022–2023 National Football League (NFL) regular season, the Buffalo Bills were playing the Cincinnati Bengals in an important matchup with playoff implications. After what seemed to be a fairly routine tackle in the first quarter, Bills safety Demar Hamlin stood up and then promptly collapsed on the field with cardiac arrest. The medical personnel rushed out onto the field and had to perform around nine minutes of CPR to save his life. One play changed everything. A stadium filled with more than 65,000 screaming fans at the beginning of the game fell eerily silent as they hoped and prayed for a miracle. Bills players broke down in tears. The NFL even canceled the game. Christian commentator Dan Orlovsky, who was covering the game for TV sports network ESPN, prayed live on the air for Hamlin, something that probably would have been unthinkable in American culture in the 2010s. In one moment, everyone watching the game was reminded of the fragility and brevity of life. We are not guaranteed another moment. We must remember God while we can before it is too late.

The big idea is "Don't wait until it's too late. Remember God when you're young." But why? Why is it so important to know and love God and follow him when we're young? Qohelet gives us three reasons:

- You will suffer as you age (11:7–8)
- You will have to give an account for your life (11:9–10)
- You will eventually run out of time (12:1–7)

## DISCUSSION QUESTIONS

1. Why should people rejoice in being alive (11:7–8)?

2. Why should the young rejoice in their youth (11:9–10)?

3. What should the young do while they have time (12:1)?

4. How is the decay of the human body described (12:2–6)?

5. What is the final destination for people this side of eternity (12:7)?

6. What does it look like to "remember God," whether we're young or old?

7. How does the gospel of Jesus Christ provide hope in the face of death?

# Ecclesiastes 12:8–14

**EXEGETICAL IDEA**
The narrator of Ecclesiastes returns to summarize the teachings of Qohelet, noting that while there is always more to learn under the sun, including many things that cause confusion and vexation, the simplest truth also happens to be the most profound: people must follow God.

**THEOLOGICAL FOCUS**
The legacy of the Hebrew sages is in their wisdom, as collectors of proverbs and teachers of life, but that wisdom finds its center in their admonition to fear God as the ultimate judge, whose commandments are the only lasting thing in a world otherwise plagued by *hevel*.

**PREACHING IDEA**
Fear God.

**PREACHING POINTERS**
In his final teaching, Qohelet instructed his students to remember God while they still lived. Old age and death would come upon them before they knew it, so Qohelet desired for them to have a strong foundation in God to face those things. In the final section of the book, the frame narrator summarized Qohelet's main teaching point: even though the world seems incomprehensible, irrational, and vain, the best thing someone can do is fear God and obey his commandments.

In a complex and often unpredictable world, it can be tempting to overcomplicate and overthink our existence. Human beings can undergo an endless search to figure out the mysteries of the universe and the meaning of life. The frame narrator of Ecclesiastes advises us to keep things simple. Instead of stressing ourselves out by attempting to know the unknowable, we must stay focused on the most important thing: fearing God and doing what he says. If we follow this simple, but hard, advice, we will make our way wisely through a world of vanity.

# HUMAN ENDEAVOR IS FUTILE, SO HEED THE WISE AND FOLLOW GOD (12:8–14)

## LITERARY STRUCTURE AND THEMES (12:8–14)

The final section in Ecclesiastes features the evaluative thoughts and concluding wisdom remarks of the book's frame narrator. Since the content of this section is consistent with Qohelet's teachings, though written by a narrator, it is included in the larger outline division of "II. The Admonitions of Qohelet (6:9–12:14)."

Some commentators start the new section at 12:9 (Seow 1997, 382), but we understand the structure of the text as following a biographical format (see Introduction) where the slogan of 12:8 ("'Vanity of vanities,' says Qohelet") does not belong to what comes before in 12:1–7, but actually marks the beginning of the narrator's final thoughts (see Longman 1998, 274). Minor divisions include the narrator's biographical summary of Qohelet as teacher and an admonition regarding sages and books (12:8–12), as well as a final admonition given in the spirit of Qohelet (12:13–14).

The first subsection (12:8–12) features praise for Qohelet and his wisdom, endorsing his pursuit of knowledge and truth. The implication of 12:8–10 is, at the very least, that Qohelet is an admirable figure and that his words are to be cherished and followed by his pupils. This is made explicit in 12:11–12 where sages are portrayed as shepherds that provide painful, but necessary and helpful, direction to those wise enough to heed it. The second subsection (12:13–14) features the final directive of the book of Ecclesiastes, also given in the spirit of Qohelet, that fearing God and keeping his commandments outranks every human endeavor and constitutes the one thing we can positively say is not "futile" or "enigmatic" (הֶבֶל) under the sun.

- *Heed the Wisdom of the Wise (12:8–12)*
- *Above All, Follow God (12:13–14)*

## EXPOSITION (12:8–14)

The epilogue of the text begins where the prologue ended (1:2), with the frame narrator's repetition of Qohelet's anthem: "'Vapor of vapors,' says Qohelet, 'All is vapor'" (12:8; see note on 1:2). This slogan bookends the teachings of the sage and functions as a sign that the narrator is now taking over. The text began with a brief introduction to Qohelet (1:1), followed by the slogan (1:2), and then a summary of Qohelet's teachings (1:3–11) leading up to the official starting point of his words in 1:12. For the many pages that followed, the narrator has been silent, with the exception of 7:27 where he merely injects, "says Qohelet." Here, however, at the conclusion of the text, following the requisite slogan (12:8), we have only the words of the narrator.

His final remarks begin with a brief biography, or perhaps eulogy, of the "wise" teacher's contributions to the fields of "knowledge" and "truth." The narrator's tribute to Qohelet does not reflect a heart of sarcasm but one of genuine adulation. Nor are these verses a kind of generous concession wherein it is implied, with a knowing wink and nod, that although Qohelet did his best to present wisdom about life, he ultimately failed. If that is true, why even bother preserving his words (Sneed 2015a, 341)? On the contrary, the narrator's efforts to preserve the teachings of Qohelet and to ascribe to him the motive of "writing uprightly the words of truth" tell a different story—one of admiration (so Bartholomew 2009, 363; Dell 2020, 151–52; M. Fox 1999, 372). This is played out in his commendation of the wisdom of sages whose words, though painful like the prodding of sheep, are valuable and reveal in the sage the heart of a shepherd. It is clear that Qohelet's own investigations cost him emotionally at times (e.g., 1:18; 2:17), and this is one consequence of too much consternation, so the narrator's admonition is for pupils of wisdom to be cautious of taking on much beyond "the words of the wise." The sages are the gold standard. This principle is explained in the very next line: there is no end to the amount of literature being produced, each book peddling its own wisdom and begging to be consumed. Thankfully, Qohelet has already demonstrated that the pursuit of wisdom as an ultimate treasure will only bring vexation and disappointment (1:18; 2:12–17).

The narrator marks his final admonition in 12:13–14 with the words "The end of the matter." If any part of his summative comments is intended to be cheeky, perhaps it is the notion that we have "heard it all" by this point. Qohelet has told us everything he has seen under the sun and claimed, ad nauseum, that it is all vaporous. So, to summarize all of life into what is most important for hungry pupils (who, though they stare lustfully at shelves of books, are nonetheless overwhelmed by the endless amount of wisdom they must conquer), the narrator looks to an admonition used repeatedly by Qohelet himself throughout the teaching: "Fear God." Obedience to God is the universal directive for "all of humanity." For all the uncertainty that life brings, one thing is certain: God will judge the deeds of all people, "whether good or evil" (12:14).

### Heed the Wisdom of the Wise (12:8–12)
The frame narrator lauds the wisdom and efforts of Qohelet, noting how he sought truthful words. The words of such a teacher may sting, but it is better to find one good teacher than to grow weary by following the advice of multitudes.

**12:8**. *Life is a vapor.* The text of Ecclesiastes began with a variation of this verse (1:2). The phrase traditionally translated "Vanity of vanities" is a way of saying "the most vain thing," but what is Qohelet identifying as the most futile and/or enigmatic thing (see note on 1:2)? It could be the very fact that "everything is futile and/or enigmatic." One is born into this world, quickly learns its basic rules and the traditions of culture, is taught to expect that things should make sense, but discovers (if they are wise) that nothing makes sense. *That* is the enigma—that everything is an enigma. The wise have the fortune (or misfortune?; see 1:18) of discovering that the world is an unsolvable puzzle, which will drive them away from coping delusions and into a state of valuing only what is most valuable: authentic living in the fear of God (2:24–26; 3:12–13, 22; 5:18–19 [HB 17–18]; 8:15; 9:4–5, 7–10; 11:1–10). The expression in 1:2 and here in 12:8 bookends the teachings of Qohelet. Now it is time for the narrator to speak from his own perspective.

**12:9–10**. Qohelet was a proper teacher, asserts the narrator; he was a realist who held onto both the fear of God and the severity of life in all its futilities, enigmas, and brevity. Not only were Qohelet's motives good, but his message was also joyful and truthful. To enhance our already positive view of the Teacher, the narrator adds that the sage "diligently sought to figure out joyful things," a search that resulted in him writing "the words of truth." Yet much of what Qohelet writes in the book is not joyful, but grim. He admits he could figure out next to nothing, but one thing he did manage to do was to set a few of life's joyful things, the *real* stuff of life, against the backdrop of life's futilities and incomprehensible darkness. His joy statements stood out like glimmering stars in the black space, like polished gemstones in a setting of rusty iron. They commended authentic living in the fear of God (2:24–26; 3:12–13, 22; 5:18–19 [HB 17–18]; 8:15; 9:4–5, 7–10; 11:1–10). Because of this, some even consider Qohelet a "preacher of joy" despite all the negativity he "sees" (Whybray 1982; see note on 2:24). The frame narrator knows that readers will be tempted to react negatively to what they falsely perceive as unhelpful pessimism in Qohelet's teachings, so he provides an endorsement that will cause his pupils to listen more carefully on their second read-through, looking for those diamonds in the rough (see sidebar "Qohelet as a Good Sage" p. 203).

Assyrian scribes. Public domain. The figure on the left writes on papyrus or animal skin; the figure on the right makes impressions on a clay tablet (see *ANEP* §235).

**12:11.** Good sages, such as Qohelet, are like shepherds who prod their sheep in the right direction, even if it causes pain. The line reads, "The words of the wise are like goads and sharp points [applied] by the masters of collections (sages). They (the prods) are given by any shepherd." Who is the "shepherd" mentioned about here? Is this referring to Qohelet? Does it refer to God? The term is certainly applied to God elsewhere in the HB: "He led his people out like sheep and guided them like a flock in the wilderness. He led them safely, and they were not afraid" (Ps. 78:52–53 CSB); and "Listen, Shepherd of Israel, who leads Joseph like a flock" (Ps. 80:1a CSB). Some English translations understand the figure to be God and indicate as much by capitalizing the term "Shepherd" in 12:11. There is, however, no need for this. The metaphor of a shepherd could simply refer to "a/any herder" (מֵרֹעֶה אֶחָד), as a way of indicating that this is how herders operate in general: they prod the sheep to move in the best/safest direction (see sidebar "Qohelet as a Good Sage" p. 203). Notes Gesenius, "Only in a few passages is a noun made expressly *indeterminate* by the addition of אֶחָד in the sense of our indefinite article," and though he does not list every instance, Ecclesiastes 12:11 belongs in that group (see also Judg. 13:2; GKC §225.b).

> **Qohelet as a Good Sage**
> In Ecclesiastes 12:9–12, Qohelet is identified as a sage. The ESV renders the opening expression in 12:9, "Besides being wise, the Preacher"; the NET reads, "Not only was the Teacher wise"; but Seow's suggestion is preferred: "Additionally, because Qohelet was a sage" (וְיֹתֵר שֶׁהָיָה קֹהֶלֶת חָכָם; 1997, 382). The words that follow do not comprise a list of Qohelet's extracurricular duties or hobbies, but serve as a description of his function as sage: "he taught knowledge," "he reasoned and deliberated," "he sorted out many proverbs." I do not mean here to imply that Qohelet held an official office as a sage, but that he was considered a wise figure in his society.

It should be noted that all three of the activities listed in 12:9 are the characteristic work of a sage, as Proverbs 1:1–7 makes clear. Some see the frame narrator's contribution at the end of Ecclesiastes as a rejection of Qohelet's teachings, contending that the narrator is being sarcastic in 12:9–10, and that he offers a criticism of the Teacher in 12:11–12 and finally a correction in 12:13–14. This interpretation is based on a number of assumptions about the nature of Ecclesiastes, which are discussed briefly in the Introduction. How a scholar understands the terms "vanity" and "under the sun," and how he/she addresses Qohelet's controversial statements are important factors for whether they see him as an unorthodox pessimist or an orthodox realist (or some other combination).

Our understanding is that Qohelet is an orthodox, though at times hyperbolic, realist, a point made in the commentary notes throughout. Accordingly, I do not see 12:11–12 as a rejection of Qohelet. Rather he is the good shepherd described in 12:11 who is willing to knock the sheep so that they will walk in the right direction. When the frame narrator refers to "any shepherd" in 12:11 (see note), he is not saying that *any and every* teacher is good or trustworthy, but that all shepherds prod their sheep; it is just what shepherds do. His point then would be that Qohelet's pupils should recognize sages as shepherds whose job it is to protect and provide, even though that at times requires a bit of painful jabbing. Hebrew sages do not exist to make people feel good about themselves, but to promote the spiritual well-being of the community, which may require the use of stinging words. This bit of information from the narrator makes good sense in light of Qohelet's bluntness and the many harsh realities he explores throughout his teachings. There were false teachers and prophets in ancient Israel and Jewish societies (e.g., Deuteronomy 13; Jer. 27:15), but those designations could be reserved for *other* so-called sages; as for Qohelet, he was one of the good ones.

**12:12**. In a sea of voices from countless so-called sages, be sure to heed only the good ones. Back in 4:13, Qohelet contrasted the poor, wise youth with a foolish king who does not know how "to be warned" (לְהִזָּהֵר), which is usually rendered in the English translations as "to take advice." The *niphal* of "to warn" (זהר) returns here in 12:12 in imperatival form: "My son, be warned!" (בְּנִי הִזָּהֵר). The narrator wishes to protect his pupil from the dangers of departing from the words of the wise just discussed in 12:11. To stay on the safe path, his son must be cautioned against receiving advice or wisdom "beyond these" (וְיֹתֵר מֵהֵמָּה; lit. "more than these")—that is, what he can get from the good shepherds, the sages of Israel who will prod him in the right direction. Referring to the Egyptian wisdom text Instruction of Kagemni, Seow points out its own warning that pupils should not go beyond what is written in it: "The warning not to go beyond the words of the text is formulaic: it is an affirmation of the completeness and sufficiency of the text" (1997, 388). This perspective is preferred for 12:12, but other scholars will assert that the narrator's warning is for the pupil to be guarded "from these" (מֵהֵמָּה), with "these" referring to the many teachings of the wise and especially the words of Qohelet himself (Longman 1998, 281). But as 12:9–11 demonstrates, the words of Qohelet and the words of the wise are a good thing the student should respect, not a dangerous thing the student should avoid. Nevertheless, not *all* sages are good, so discernment is required.

One reason to stick with the words of the wise and avoid too many teachers and teachings is that overexpanding one's list of things to figure out in life will certainly bring vexation and sorrow (see 1:18). The pupil, perhaps in an effort to excel in wisdom like his/her teacher, will attempt to do something their teachers never did themselves (because it is impossible): to consume everything, as in the endless stream of material constantly being written and/or copied (or write it themselves!; see Shields 2000, 125–26). But as Qohelet has demonstrated throughout his teaching (2:12–17; see notes on 7:25–29), this will only lead to disappointment and exhaustion. To think it can all be conquered is a delusion (2:12–17; 8:17).

### *Above All, Follow God (12:13–14)*

**12:13**. Follow God. The admonition to keep God's commandments is not so different from the rest of Ecclesiastes to justify the suggestion that verses 13–14 were written not by the frame narrator but by a later glossator (see Sneed 2015a, 343). Throughout his teaching, Qohelet has promoted wise living, affirmed righteousness, and admonished his readers to fear God. For the frame narrator to include "keep his commandments" is not such a radically new concept that we should think it foreign to the book (see Shead 1997, 90–91). So, the conclusion is not distinct from the teachings of Qohelet, only simplified even further so as to highlight the most important prescription given in the text—"fear God." Qohelet's many admonitions could be summarized by the insistence that his pupils live authentic lives, which includes pursuing wisdom, enjoying life's simple pleasures (food, drink, work, spouse, etc.), living freely (realizing you are not in control) and generously, and fearing God. It is this last admonition to "fear God" that appears most frequently in the text (3:14; 5:7 [HB 6]; 7:18; 8:12; 12:13), a principle also implied in many other places throughout Qohelet's teaching whenever God is mentioned. If a pupil could follow one life principle from all Qohelet has taught, it would be that he/she should be allegiant to the Creator, "for this is the entirety of human [purpose]" (כִּי־זֶה כָּל־הָאָדָם). Humans pursue many vain endeavors, but the duty of all of humanity is merely to fear God.

**12:14**. God will judge every person. One impetus for fearing God—and this has been clear throughout the teaching of Qohelet—is that God will judge evildoers (3:17; 8:12–13; 11:9, and elsewhere implied). Qohelet's faith in this principle remains, despite the fact that he has seen the wicked live to old age and go to their graves in honor, so while he does not have a clear understanding of what exactly happens after death (see Introduction and sidebar "Life After Death in Ecclesiastes" p. 108), he does believe that God will judge all wickedness. At the very least, the frame narrator agrees that judgment is coming, which is why he/she emphasizes the same point here. Qohelet has admitted his ignorance in places (e.g., 7:25–29), and surely human ignorance is why so much of the world is "enigmatic" (הֶבֶל) to us. That ignorance is occasioned in part by our natural limitations since we are left to judge the world around us by what we can "see" (רָאָה) under the sun, a term used frequently by Qohelet as parameters for his investigations.

But what about all the things humans cannot see? Surely those factor into why things are so hard to "figure out" (מצא). We can be assured of this: God sees everything under the sun, including "all that is hidden" (כָּל־נֶעְלָם). Nothing can escape his justice. This is both a great comfort to the pupil and a severe warning. While safety from life's unpredictable vanities can never be assured, the pupil who walks in the fear of God can rest confidently in the fact that he/she is safe from condemnation. The faith of Old Testament saints was expressed by fearing God, which meant believing God and keeping his commandments. In the new covenant brought by Christ, the imperative is not different at its core, though it has manifested more fully through his death and resurrection. One must still believe (Rom. 10:9–11).

## THEOLOGICAL FOCUS

The words of the wise will protect many from disaster. Even if those words at times hurt, they are for the overall health and well-being of the pupil who heeds them. The false prophets go about proclaiming "peace, peace, when there is no peace" (Jer. 8:11), but the prophet who fears God rightly proclaims God's judgment against sin. In like manner, the sages do not tell us what we want to hear but are like shepherds whose stinging prods lead their students into the path of safety. Qohelet is one of these sages; accordingly, his words are harsh and heavy and force his pupils to consider deeply whether their lives are being wasted on futilities. Such are delusions and false promises that are incapable of delivering the joy that comes solely from authentic living in the fear of God. Believers would be wise to drink in the bitter wisdom of the Hebrew sages and be careful what other sources of so-called knowledge they allow into their lives.

The book of Ecclesiastes serves as a theological funnel of wisdom, narrowing as it goes and preventing objects too large from passing through (e.g., the vain human pursuits of lasting satisfaction in pleasure, wisdom, work, wealth). The teachings of Qohelet depict most human pursuits as the symptoms of delusion and prescribe instead an authentic style of living marked by love for God's simple gifts (food, drink, work, spouse, etc.) and by the choice to live freely and generously (11:1–6). But Qohelet's list of legitimate joys can be narrowed further, as the narrator does, to simply fearing God and keeping his commandments (12:13). All the things Qohelet commends in the book of Ecclesiastes fall under this umbrella.

In the HB, the "fear of the Lord" is a reverence for him that is synonymous for the worshipper's love for him. When faced with the troubling news that Jerusalem was in shambles (Neh. 1:5), Nehemiah prayed to "the great and feared God" who protects "those who love him and keep his commandments." Jesus made this principle clear to his disciples in John 14:15: "If you love me, you will keep my commandments." In this way the believer's fear of God includes a love for God flowing from the heart of a human being who has left every empty idol under the sun so that they can "remember/dwell on" their Creator (12:1).

## PREACHING AND TEACHING STRATEGIES

### Exegetical and Theological Synthesis

Ecclesiastes ends the same way it begins: with the declaration that "all is vanity" (1:2; 12:8). The repetition of the phrase signals that now the frame editor of the book is taking over to commend and summarize Qohelet's teaching (12:9–14). The editor praises Qohelet as a wise teacher who spoke truthfully (12:9–10). Although Qohelet's words may be painful at times, they ultimately serve to make people wise, unlike much of the false philosophy out in the world (12:11–12). While Qohelet discoursed for twelve chapters on many different topics, the main content of his teaching consisted in admonishing his pupils to "fear God and keep his commandments" (12:13). Obedience to God is the wisest way to live because God is the sovereign judge to whom all people are accountable (12:14).

### Preaching Idea
Fear God.

### Contemporary Connections

*What does it mean?*
While Qohelet waxed eloquent on a variety of topics from justice to money to death, his teaching rests on the foundation of fearing God (12:13). If nothing else is remembered from Ecclesiastes, the one thing that should stand out is the importance of revering and worshipping the one, true, living God. Fearing God is so vitally important because without God, "all is vanity" (12:8). Even if you read Qohelet's words five hundred times, even if you attempt to plumb the depths of human existence, all is *hevel* without a relationship with God.

The teachings of the wise help us to fear God. A wise sage like Qohelet points students to the truth (12:9–10). He labors hard to communicate the truth of God effectively. His words—like any good teacher's words—work like "goads" or prods. Although painful at times, they move people to action (12:11). Yet, the editor reminds his audience that human wisdom still has its limits, a theme that runs throughout the book (2:12–16; 7:19–29; 8:16–17). The editor then explains that "the making of books has no end" (12:12). There is no end of those who have opinions about the meaning of life. Go online and search any place that sells books, and there is an almost endless stream of material on how to be happy, how to live a fulfilled life, or how to find meaning. Someone could go on and on, forever, studying these various opinions (12:12). Looking for fulfillment outside of God will wear you out, because it is not found there. There is a deeper wisdom found in the fear of God.

At the end of the day, fearing God expresses itself through obedience to his commandments (12:14). The Scriptures are clear that we are not saved by our obedience. We are only saved by grace through faith (Eph. 2:8–9). Yet the Bible is also clear that our obedience demonstrates the validity of our faith (James 2:14–26). "If anyone loves me, he will keep my word," Jesus teaches (John 14:23). Therefore, obeying God's commands is vital, for God will "bring every act to judgment." We will all stand before God one day to give account for our lives (Rom. 2:5–6; 2 Thess. 1:7–9; Rev. 20:11–15). Yet the future judgment that Qohelet acknowledges, the New Testament declares has already fallen decisively on Christ for those who trust in him: "There is now no condemnation for those in Christ Jesus" (Rom. 8:1).

*Is it true?*
Fearing God demonstrates that we have a relationship with God. Those who fear God are those who have been forgiven by God: "With you there is forgiveness, that you may be feared" (Ps. 130:4). The New Testament proclaims that the forgiveness of sin comes through the sacrifice of Jesus Christ (Heb. 9:15–28). The gospel demonstrates that "perfect love casts out fear" (1 John 4:18). The perfect love that Jesus has shown for his people by dying for their sins enables believers to come to God as a loving heavenly Father rather than a mere judge. Before someone has fear of God, they must embrace the forgiveness from God found in Jesus Christ alone. Do you believe in Jesus? Have you embraced his forgiveness? If you have, you can rightly revere the Lord.

Another way to fear God is to acknowledge his justice (12:14). While Qohelet is vexed by injustice throughout the book (2:18–23; 3:16; 4:1–3; 5:8; 8:10–11, 14; 9:1–3), he has hope that God will, one day, hold all people accountable. Why evil and wickedness prevail in this life has been a question that human beings have wrestled with from the beginning of time. Even the Bible records those who struggle with the wicked prospering (see the book of Habakkuk; cf. Ps. 73:1–28). The Bible is, of course, very honest—and Ecclesiastes very straightforward in particular—about the reality of suffering, injustice, and evil in this life. Why would God allow such things? While no exhaustive answer is given, the Scriptures do present some surprising reasons for why such things happen. The apostle Peter indicates that God does not bring immediate justice because "He does not want anyone to perish, so he is giving more time for everyone to repent" (2 Peter 3:9 NLT). God seems to allow injustice to occur because he is desirous that the wicked will turn to him. If God brought immediate justice as soon as a person sinned, no one would be spared for "all have sinned and fallen short of the glory of God" (Rom. 3:23). Is there not any better reason to fear God than to escape his justice?

*Now what?*
A wise person acknowledges God's power and justice. He or she does not play around with God but takes him seriously. According to the final verses in this book, one of the best ways that we can respect God is to stop searching

and start fearing (12:12–13). Sometimes the search for "truth" is really a way to avoid God. Sometimes we behave just like the ancient Athenians, who liked "telling and hearing something new" (Acts 17:21). Yet all other sources of fulfillment are "vanity" (2:1–26). Only God can satisfy.

The fear of God grows through heeding the counsel of wise people, and the wisest people we can listen to are the sages of Scripture. Wisdom literature, like Ecclesiastes and Proverbs, is given to us because "The fear of the Lord is the beginning of knowledge" (Prov. 1:7). Developing a truly reverential awe for the Lord requires diligence to read and ponder God's wisdom. Besides giving ourselves to consistent reading of God's Word, we can also grow wise by the counsel of godly and wise friends. Who are wise teachers in your life? Turn to them and learn from them.

Finally, the most important thing that we can do in response to these verses is to believe the gospel. Ecclesiastes clearly pronounces a future judgment (3:17; 11:9; 12:13–14). How could we ever hope to endure God's judgment when we have given ourselves over to so many vain pursuits instead of loving him completely? The good news is that Jesus has taken on our sin for us (2 Cor. 5:21). Jesus was the perfect human being who always pursued God instead of the things "under the sun." He willingly went to the cross to die and receive the judgment of God for our sins (Rom. 3:26; 1 Peter 3:18; 1 John 2:2). Jesus did not stay dead, however. On the third day he arose from the grave, victorious over Satan, sin, and death. Now, Jesus stands ready to save all who would trust in him. Turn from your sin and trust Christ today. For the end is not the end with Christ; it is just the beginning. The vanity of this life melts away for those who are in Christ, and everything we do can matter: "Therefore, my beloved brethren, be steadfast, immovable, always abounding in the work of the Lord, knowing that your toil is not in vain in the Lord" (1 Cor. 15:58).

### Creativity in Presentation

Some refuse to believe the gospel because they see the wicked prospering in this life. Their objection often gets framed in the famous question, "How can God allow bad things to happen to good people?" Yet the most shocking answer to injustice is found in the gospel itself. Andrew Wilson, in his book *God*Stories* (2009, 112), proposes God's answer to suffering:

> Imagine all humanity had a committee meeting to establish what God would have to go through to truly understand human suffering. The poor would say he should be homeless, frequently hungry, and constantly moving from place to place. Bereaved people would say he should lose a parent and perhaps a close friend as well. Holocaust victims might insist he be Jewish; those who lived in occupied territories, that he should live his entire life in subjection to a brutal empire. Outcasts would insist he face a major social stigma: accusations of illegitimacy or drunkenness or demon-possession. The abused might demand he face physical violence, ritual humiliation, abandonment, and betrayal by those closest to him, and yet with the perpetrators never punished. I don't know what you would throw in—never having children, being murdered in his prime, or perhaps facing extended torture and slow death. Maybe those who had felt the silence of heaven, like Job, would add that to the list, to form the most profound and wide-ranging suffering imaginable. Then and only then, humanity might say, could God be regarded as being able to understand our suffering. Only if God had lived through the worst this life had to offer and been perfect throughout could we say he had provided Suffering's Answer.

Sound like anyone we know?

The gospel of Jesus Christ reveals a God unwilling to be disengaged from the suffering of the world. God did not content himself to forever reside in the heavens while humans suffer on earth. God entered our broken world in the person of Jesus Christ, and Jesus suffered the injustices of our world. But Jesus did not merely suffer. Jesus suffered *for* us: "Christ also suffered once for sins, the righteous for the unrighteous, that he might bring us to God" (1 Peter 3:18). The Perfect One bore the sins of the imperfect. The Righteous One took on the sins of the unrighteous: "[God] made Christ, who knew no sin, to be sin on our behalf, so that we might become the righteousness of God in him" (2 Cor. 5:21). That is good news! No one has to face the judgment of God any longer, for an escape has been made through the death and resurrection of Jesus. Come to Jesus. Believe in him. Find the true meaning of life in him.

The big idea for this section is "Fear God." A proposed outline for this section focuses on answering the question, "How?" How do we grow in our fear of God? The outline suggests three ways:

- Heed the teaching of the wise (12:9–11)
- Avoid the counsel of the foolish (12:12)
- Obey the commandments of God (12:13–14)

## DISCUSSION QUESTIONS

1. What qualities make Qohelet a good teacher (12:9–11)?

2. What warning does the editor give to his readers (12:12)?

3. How could Ecclesiastes be summarized (12:13)?

4. When will God bring justice to the world (12:14)?

5. In what ways have you lacked appropriate fear of God in your life?

6. How does the gospel drive out fear or judgment and replace it with awe-filled wonder?

# INTRODUCTION TO SONG OF SONGS

> ## OVERVIEW OF SONG OF SONGS
>
> **Title:** The Song of Songs
>
> **Authorship:** An inspired scribe in the tradition of Solomonic wisdom
>
> **Date:** Uncertain; possibly eighth to sixth centuries B.C.
>
> **Readers (Hearers):** The average Israelite
>
> **Historical Setting:** Uncertain; possibly late monarchic Judah
>
> **Occasion for Writing:** To celebrate and inform about romantic love in the Israelite context
>
> **Genre:** Love poetry with ties to the wisdom genre
>
> **Literary Structure:** A collection of poems united by recurring themes and a loose storyline
>
> **Theological Emphases:** Romantic love informed by the wisdom of God's creation; romantic love as an analogy for other types of love relationships, chiefly the relationship between God and his people

## TITLE

There are a couple of possible meanings for the book's title, "The Song of Songs." The construct relationship in Hebrew between "Song" (שִׁיר) and "Songs" (הַשִּׁירִים) could suggest either that the text is a "song made up of several songs" (option 1) or that it is "the best of all songs" (option 2). Some may use the collective sense (option 1) to support their argument that the text is an anthology of songs grouped together in a kind of "erotic psalter" (see Longman [2001, 1], who actually sees both options working). But the nature of the construct relationship is best understood as a grammatical superlative in light of others known elsewhere in the HB (option 2; e.g., קֹדֶשׁ קָדָשִׁים "holy of holies," meaning "the most holy" in Exod. 29:37; הֲבֵל הֲבָלִים "vanity of vanities," meaning "the most vain" in Eccl. 1:2; see Arnold and Choi §12.2.13). The songwriter makes the bold claim that this collection of poems makes up the world's greatest song.

## AUTHORSHIP

The issue of authorship is not as pressing for the Song as for other parts of the Bible, such as the New Testament epistles. Ambiguity regarding the authorship of the book begins with its first line where the prepositional phrase (לִשְׁלֹמֹה) could be translated as "by Solomon," "concerning Solomon," or even "for Solomon." For example, the MT of Psalm 72 begins with the authorial stamp "by/of/for Solomon" (לִשְׁלֹמֹה) but proceeds to speak about Solomon in the third person, with the final verse stating that the psalm was part of a larger collection of "the prayers of David." For this reason, some translations of Psalm 72:1 read "for Solomon" (e.g., KJV, NET), and others "of Solomon" (e.g., ESV, NASB), the latter of which leaves room for the interpreter to decide whether "of" means "concerning/about" or "by." Due to the semantic range of such biblical superscripts, the question of authorship for the Song cannot be settled by a preposition alone.

The suggestion that Solomon wrote the book is based on indications from the text of 1 Kings that, under Solomon, Israel was flourishing economically and politically. Once Solomon's reign was established and there was peace and safety, there would have been ample time and resources for impressive literary works to be composed (1 Kings 4:25). Moreover, Solomon is said to have an interest in writing songs (v. 32). One difficulty, however, in viewing Solomon as the Song's author also comes from 1 Kings 11:3, where he is described as having seven hundred wives and three hundred concubines. Several scholars indicate that this would make Solomon unfit for the task of writing on the topic of monogamous love. Others retort that Solomon's wicked lifestyle later in life may mean he wrote the Song at some earlier point. He was a complex character, after all, like his father David who, though he was "a man after God's own heart," was still capable of sin (Garrett and House 2004, 24).

Indeed, a biblical character's disobedience to God does not disqualify them from having been used by God at various points in their life, but the nature of the Song insists that if Solomon, who was in full-blown, unrepentant rebellion by the end of his life—a rebellion marked specifically by his indulgences in "foreign women" and idolatry (1 Kings 11:1–8)—wrote the Song, it *must* have been very early on in his reign. However, the view of Solomon presented in the Song is one of established opulence with a harem and great wealth (3:6–11; 6:9; 8:11). For this reason, it would be better to understand the vision of Solomon portrayed in the book either as (1) a foil (to be contrasted with the simple but authentic living of the ordinary, country couple; Provan 2001, 198; see Eccl. 1–2) or as (2) an idealized model of royalty embodied by the male of the Song. This commentary follows the second approach.

There are several other indicators that the author of the Song was not Solomon. First, the only references to Solomon are in the third person (1:1, 5; 3:7–11; 8:11–12). While songwriters in Scripture may elsewhere speak of themselves in third person (e.g., the repeated use of "your servant" in the Psalms to refer to the author), it is typically in the form of direct address; the references to Solomon in the Song possess a noticeable level of abstraction. Furthermore, at no point is it clear that Solomon is speaking in the Song; rather, the speakers appear to be an anonymous man and woman. Others point out that the brief mentions of Solomon in the Song are negative in nature, or at the very least are meant to contrast the humble countryside dwelling of the couple with the elaborate, conspicuous consumption of an overpowered king (see Eccl. 2:1–11; Provan 2001, 198; this view follows Provan's reading of the Song as a three-character drama). Finally, the presence of later linguistic features may suggest a composition after the lifetime of Solomon. The prevailing view among scholars is that the book was written later, but ascribed to Solomon, like other well-known texts (e.g., the first-century B.C. Greek text of "The Wisdom of Solomon"; see "Authorship" in the Ecclesiastes section). A later attribution does not change the fact that the book was received by Jewish and Christian communities as canonical, even if most saw the references to Solomon as part of the justification for its canonicity; modern scholars' inability to resolve such matters does not change the movements of God through his people in shaping the canon of Scripture.

The circumstantial evidence often cited in defense of Solomonic authorship (e.g., Solomon's opulence and his known writing career in 1 Kings 4:32) does not sufficiently account for objections to it. Such evidence could fit just as easily with the reign of a later Judean king, like Hezekiah (as Solomon's reign was not the only time of economic and potential literary flourishing). The migration of northerners into Judah after 722 B.C. could explain the several northern references, though these would have been known to any scribe in the royal court of Jerusalem. The presence of Aramaic in the Song may also be the result of northern influence, given Israel's proximity to Aram. Perhaps Tirzah is mentioned (6:4) specifically because the mention of Samaria, which had been ransacked by the Assyrians, would be too painful a memory (Keel 1994, 4–5).

While absolute certainty on the issue of the Song's authorship is not possible (nor necessary to affirm the book's canonical status), a tentative proposal could be put forth. The designation "of Solomon" in 1:1 may represent a later author's presentation of an old series of poems passed down about the life of Solomon. Since the time of Hezekiah was a time of flourishing for Israel, it certainly could have been a scribe within Hezekiah's royal court who did this (on the roles of scribes, see N. Fox 2000, 94–110.

In all, a post-Solomon authorship could account for (1) the third-person references to Solomon, (2) the lack of direct speech from Solomon, (3) the overt monogamy promoted by the text, (4) the incursions of later linguistic features (see "Date"), and (5) the proposed polemic against Solomon's excesses (though this commentary does not follow the three-character drama and rather sees the portrayal of Solomon as an idealized figure embodied by the male of the Song). Furthermore, though the prevailing view throughout later Jewish and Christian history was that Solomon composed the text, there were first-century A.D. rabbis who believed that the songs had been collected and written down by someone within Hezekiah's court (Keel 1994, 1). Whether Solomon, Hezekiah, or some other nameless scribe penned the text, its status and usefulness as inspired Scripture in the Christian community remain unchanged.

## DATE

The timelessness of the Song, a feature of its unanchored beauty, has had many readers question the importance of dating the text in real time and space, and understandably so since "the time of singing" (2:12) never ceases, appearing year after year (Exum 2005, 67). For biblical scholars, however, key terms such as place names, possible loanwords from other languages, and detailed references to extravagant luxury (among other clues) have stirred the waters of investigation and produced a number of interesting options. Still, some have wisely taken "an agnostic stand on the issue of date" since issues of language and authorship appear too fraught with subjectivity to arrive at a clear conclusion (Longman 2001, 19; Provan 2001, 198–99). That the text was written in or around Jerusalem seems apparent, given its constant references to the capital city and to royalty (e.g., 1:5; 2:7; 3:5, 10–11; 5:16; 6:4).

Interpreters have had an on-again, off-again love relationship with dating biblical texts based on linguistic clues, like the presence of particularly archaic or late forms. Some suggest that the Aramaic terms and the Persian terms אַפִּרְיוֹן ("carriage-bed"; 3:9) and פַּרְדֵּס ("orchard"; 4:13) found in the book argue for an exilic authorship (Davis 2000, 231; Murphy 1990b, 4–5). While the presence of supposedly later terms certainly *could* serve as evidence that the Song was written during the Persian period or after, their presence does not necessitate such, especially since the original manuscripts of the Song are unavailable to us and their copying over the centuries would have doubtlessly seen the insertion of anachronisms and later linguistic developments. Also, given Aram's close contact with Israel, the presence of Aramaisms in Hebrew may not indicate later writing. Garrett and House argue, citing Young, that, "Classical Hebrew coexisted side by side with a colloquial Hebrew that often used Aramaisms. Preexilic Hebrew was already very diverse and included many Aramaic elements" (Garrett and House 2004, 17; they note, furthermore, that the lack of the *wayyiqtol* form is also not good evidence for lateness since this is typical of lyric poetry elsewhere in the HB). Young has written that the references in the Song that point to an older time in Israel's history are not undone by the suggestion of later loanwords, which themselves have questionable provenance (Young 1993, 165). For each of these rebuttals, though, there are matching rebuttals from the late-date crowd. Shaky linguistic debates complicate scholarly attempts at arriving at a satisfactory conclusion regarding the date of the Song. For these reasons, many commentators, including some of those just mentioned (e.g., Garrett and House 2004; Longman 2001; Murphy 1990b; Pope 1977; Provan 2001) caution against viewing linguistic features in a text as airtight evidence for dating.

Given the uncertain value of language for dating the Song, others have pointed to circumstantial evidence. Certain indicators in the text hint at the well-known phenomenon of literary development accompanying times of economic flourishing, like the songwriter's intimate knowledge of exotic goods, such as spices, that come from large-scale international trade. In this case, the beauty of the Song may be attributed to the humanistic renaissance or enlightenment of a Solomonic-like era (Murphy 1990b, 4, citing von Rad and Gerleman). Of course, these factors could easily be applied to other periods of economic flourishing in Judah, like the late eighth and early seventh centuries during the reign of Hezekiah.

Related to economic flourishing and the mixing of cultures are the strong similarities between Egyptian love poetry and the Song, with their affinities being too close to be the mere consequence of incidental contact. In other words, the author or compiler of the text was clearly influenced by Egyptian poetry (M. Fox 1985, xix–xxvii). Such Egyptian poetry was composed in the late second millennium and would not have entered the consciousness of the fledgling Israelite tribes, at least not prominently, until they were established under the monarchy, when stability allowed for literary flourishing.

The many striking similarities between Israelite and Egyptian love poetry demonstrate not just that the two countries existed within the same cultural milieu, but that there was some kind of direct exchange or sharing of literature, at least from Egypt to Israel (M. Fox 1985, xix–xxvii). This was certainly the case in Solomon's day, when Israel traded abundantly with international superpowers like Egypt and welcomed foreign dignitaries to engage in an exchange of wisdom (1 Kings 10). When national entities are brought together in close contact, normally for military or financial reasons, it is inevitable that there will be a transference of culture across borders. But this does not necessitate that the Song was composed during Solomon's lifetime; there were several moments during the Judean monarchy when cultural exchange was high and the influence of poetry from Egypt very likely. Against the notion of a late date, Othmar Keel argues that the similarities between Egyptian love poetry and the Song are so much stronger than between the Song and later Greek poetry (1994, 5): "In my opinion, the collection most nearly fits between the eighth and sixth centuries B.C. At that time ancient Egyptian love literature was still flourishing (a fact that has not been demonstrated for the Hellenistic era; but see n. 42), and ancient Near Eastern (ANE) motifs were enjoying a final heyday in Israel." For this reason, Israelites (esp. the cultural elite) would have known of Egyptian poetry during that age of flourishing. Egyptian poetry would have made its way into the cultural canon of Israelite thought and become known to the best scribes for many generations.

Place names are also not very helpful for this discussion. Some consider the Song's mention of Tirzah in 6:4 (instead of the later northern capital, Samaria) as evidence that the text was written in Solomon's day, but the inclusion of Tirzah could just be a demonstration of the author's familiarity with northern territories and his conscious effort to make the Song consistent with Solomon's time. Furthermore, the mention of En Gedi in 1:14 may push the timeline away from Solomon and toward the seventh century and beyond (Keel 1994, 5), but how far beyond is difficult to say.

In sum, the evidences for and against Solomonic authorship and early dating are too shaky to arrive at a dogmatic conclusion. However, the arguments cited for a later composition along with the author's keen knowledge of Israel and older ANE references (as opposed to a heavy Greek influence) suggest that the Song may have been composed in the late monarchic period, perhaps the eighth to sixth centuries B.C. and possibly in connection with the works of Hezekiah.

## READERS (HEARERS)

The Song was likely intended both for entertainment and instruction. Since the place of its writing is most likely Jerusalem, it would follow that the Song's readers/hearers would be the people of that region, especially of the royal court, though there is no reason to think the average Israelite did not have the songs committed to heart. The author may have intended for the work to circulate and become well known internationally, a realistic possibility since texts within the Solomonic corpus (Proverbs, Ecclesiastes, Song of Songs) and Job discuss matters that are highly transferable between cultures.

The original readers likely would have understood the text to be a collection of romantic love songs, related by its characters and plot movements, not an allegory for God's relationship to Israel (an interpretation that appears to have arisen later, possibly in the first century B.C.). We should not rule out the possibility that the Song was also meant to be understood as a useful *analogy* for God and Israel (Provan 2001, 202, 212); however, "analogy" is distinct from "allegory," and the sexually explicit language of the Song makes the latter less likely; such highly erotic terminology does not fit well with the God/husband–Israel/wife metaphors found elsewhere in Scripture.

The original readers would likely have been *hearers* since there is no evidence of widespread literacy in Israel outside of professions that required it, like that of scribe (Rollston 2010, 134). The singing of the Song may have taken place at weddings, festivals, or various banquet settings.

## HISTORICAL SETTING

The section on date suggests that the Song may have been composed around the time of Hezekiah or perhaps later, but pre-Alexander. This would mean the historical setting is Judah late in the divided monarchy. The broader historical setting of the Song is the ANE, which included not only the cultural influences of Mesopotamia, Hatti, Canaan, and Egypt, but also the literary corpora from these places, which certainly had an impact on how Israelites thought and wrote. Moses, for example, was learned "in all the wisdom of Egypt" (Acts 7:22; cf. Exod. 2). While the literature from surrounding cultures crafted the styles and genres of writing known to Israelite scribes and later used by them, the ethical and religious nature of Biblical Hebrew texts contrasted sharply with that of Israel's neighbors. For example, there are a great many similarities between the Song and Egyptian and Akkadian love literature, like the motif of lying awake in bed: "I was asleep, but my heart was awake!" (Song 5:2) and "My heart is awake though I am sleeping" (Wasserman 2016, 135; other such connections are cited throughout the commentary). However, romantic love and sex are presented very differently in ANE literature than in the Song. In the mythologies of Egypt, Canaan, and Mesopotamia, the gods regularly engaged in sexual acts with other gods, humans, and aspects of creation. Of course, Scripture does not portray the God of Israel as engaged in any such activities. While the legal material of the ANE is vast and not uniform in its approach to sexual issues, and while there is some sense of sexual propriety (e.g., adultery being forbidden in several texts), there is general approval for fornication (see Greengus 2011, esp. his examples from Neo-Assyrian and Middle Assyrian legal texts). Hittite law even made provisions for certain forms of bestiality. Of these ANE sources, the greatest influence on Israel was the love poetry of Egypt, and it likewise promotes fornication.

The worship of Yahweh alone as God, however, mitigated how literature and shared thinking in the ANE intersected with Israelite thought. While the nation as a whole regularly engaged in syncretistic thinking that drew flimsy lines between their own religion and that of others (a behavior for which they were repeatedly rebuked by God), the prophets of Israel and scribes of Scripture better represented how influential thought from the broader world could be helpfully incorporated, but more often confronted, by Yahwistic thought. Israel was never an isolated nation; rather, it was a superhighway where the flow of foreign ideas rarely slowed. But starting with Abraham, the Israelites were called to step away from their former religious contexts in order to make a covenant with Yahweh, the only true God. He would then use the known constructs of their world to reveal new truths to them. This reality is all too apparent when ANE legal material on sex, which again at times allowed for various forms of fornication and bestiality (Greengus 2011, 29–30, 84), is contrasted with laws from the Bible that are couched within the context of personal and corporate holiness (Lev. 19:2) and prohibit all such loose sexual behavior (e.g.,

Lev. 18–20). Similarly, the Song of Songs can be contrasted with Egyptian and Mesopotamian love poetry and Ugaritic narrative poetry, all of which celebrate the kind of immorality that clashes with Yahwistic law.

Too often the Song of Songs is not viewed within the HB's larger statement on sexuality, leaving some scholars to see the Song as portraying sexual promiscuity. But both the broader cultural statement on sex coming from the Torah, and the extent to which the Song is an instructive text (see notes on 2:7; 3:5; 8:4, 6–12), lean in the other direction. They indicate the text has something to contribute to the conversation on sex within its broader cultural context, and that what it contributes is in keeping with Yahwistic standards of sexuality. Since the Song is poetry, and not a legal text nor a straight narrative written by the prophets, it unsurprisingly lacks direct propositional teaching on the topic. Nevertheless, the text's plot points and the movements of its monogamous characters expose the incredible contrast between its ethics and the ethics of Egyptian poetry and the ANE, broadly (see notes throughout commentary).

While later allegorical interpretations of the Song certainly helped settle the rabbinic debates over whether it should *remain* in the canon, the text was already included in the first place (Provan 2001, 199–200). And we cannot know that the literal reading was not how the text was understood from the time of its composition (note the LXX's literal, nonallegorical, rendering of the Song). In sum, while the form of the Song of Songs frequently matches the form of Egyptian love poetry, and while the cultural marks of its ANE context persist throughout, its ethical and religious content is consistent with what we find in Torah.

## OCCASION FOR WRITING

The universal occasion for the creation of lyric love poetry is to celebrate life, freedom, love, and passion (Hess 2005, 33). The Song both exalts the passion of romantic love and acknowledges its role in confronting death; "Perhaps all literature is a defense against mortality," as J. Cheryl Exum puts it (2005, 3). If so, then love is literature's most formidable weapon. This principle is not difficult to see in Scripture, where death is the enemy of human existence and ultimately an opponent defeated by Christ, who himself represents the love of God made manifest (1 John 4:9). The Song of Songs was written to show that love is the only force on earth comparable to death (8:6), and that by observing its rhythms in nature humans have the opportunity to experience its raw, inimitable, glorious power.

The local occasion for the Song's writing depends on how one interprets the text as a whole. Over the millennia, the Song has been interpreted along the spectrum of highly allegorical to highly literal. It seems the earliest known interpretations of the Song were literal; the LXX, copied in the first to second centuries B.C., treats the text literally and does not make an effort to avoid its sexual language (e.g., consider the LXX's literal rendering of "your two breasts" in Song 7:3 [HB 4] as contrasted with the Targum's "your two redeemers"). Since the LXX acknowledges the text's language of intimacy, it can be argued that the major interpretation before this time was also to take it literally. It was not until the second half of the first century B.C. that the rabbis were known to allegorize the text, which meant moving it from its originally intended meaning to an extended metaphor of the covenant relationship between God and Israel—the former being represented by the man in the text, and the latter by the woman. Such interpretations may have been prompted by Roman rule in the first century B.C., inspiring Jews to preserve national identity and a strong separation of sacred from profane, connecting all texts by the common thread of Yahweh's relationship to Israel (Keel 1994, 7). In any case, the Song was reinterpreted in innumerably strange ways throughout the centuries, ignoring its natural setting as lyric love poetry in order to make it fit within emerging Jewish, and subsequently Christian, thought.

While some scholars are intent to remind us of the Song's complex history of interpretation in faith communities (Hendel 2019, 60–83), prompting great appreciation for the plethora of allegorical scholarship leading up to the present, it is ultimately unfair to the Song to surrender it to a state of interpretive paralysis as if its meaning is totally unrecoverable to us or, even worse, is subject to whatever we want to make of it. Not all ideas about the Song are equally valid or defensible, even considering the multiplicity of contexts in which those ideas were written. Ultimately, we must consider how we might best recover the earliest intended meaning of the text, practicing humility as we go. For nearly two thousand years the Song was subjected to a host of interpretations that attempted to hide its clearly sexual meanings. At times it was wed to contemporary circumstances (e.g., the reformer Martin Luther's political interpretation), or reinterpreted altogether as a history of salvation (e.g., the Targumim) or as an allegory of Israel and God (for Jews) or Christ and the Church (for Christians). How the Song should be read, whether literally or allegorically, has sparked heated debate among interpreters since one's approach bears implications for how other biblical texts should be read. An example of this passion can be seen in Keel's remark that it was not until the twentieth century that "the Song's captivity under the capricious rule of a spiritualistic Babylon" began to see a gradual end (1994, 11; by that, he means the death of the allegorical approach). This interpretation of the Song contrasts sharply with that of certain twenty-first-century scholars who argue that the Song should be read allegorically (Davis 2000) or typologically (Hamilton 2015), the latter approach being considered by some grammatical-historical leaning scholars as another way of reintroducing allegory through the "back door" (Garrett 1993, 358 n. 57).

## Introduction to Song of Songs

In contrast to the allegorical approach, the Song emphasizes the equality of the couple; however, God and Israel are not equals (M. Fox 1985, 237). Furthermore, the abundance of erotic language in the Song makes this allegory a strange option, especially since other metaphorical language in the HB about God and Israel as husband and wife lacks such erotic content. The suggestion that there is Yahwistic language hidden in the Song's oath formula of 2:7 and 3:5 (בִּצְבָאוֹת אוֹ בְּאַיְלוֹת הַשָּׂדֶה), such as "hosts" for "gazelles" and "Shaddai" for "field," all immediately following the mention of Jerusalem, is not evidence for allegory (see the allegorical reading in the Targumim for Song 2:7); if such subtle references to God are intended, they would only be indicative of the Yahwistic context in which the Song was written, elevating the statement to the level of divine oath. In this case, the creatures by which the maidens swear may refer to the God who made both creatures and sexuality, nature standing in as his representative (see note on 2:7).

The allegorical approach at least seeks to view the text as part of the canonical-theological whole of Scripture in the face of certain other approaches that attempt to rid the text of any spiritual significance whatsoever (those who go beyond the literal approach to assert that the Song has no connection to Yahwistic faith). Davis has attempted to strike an appropriate balance between the theologizing allegory of medieval Christians and Jewish scholars on the one hand, and the hyper-secular interpretations of modern scholars who deny the Song any religious import on the other (2000, 235; cf. Grossberg [1989, 59], who sees no religious significance). Still, the rabbinic and Christian allegorical approaches should not be considered ideal ways to read the Song. Any suggestion that the original author only intended for the text to be read allegorically is indefensible. Equally indefensible is the hyper-secular interpretation of the Song that strips it of any contact with religion or the covenant of Israel. Is there really any ANE text that is not religious (even Mesopotamian legal texts, letters, and sales receipts bear marks of religion)? For example, treating the Song as a collection of bar songs celebrating pornography is as sensational a thought as it is unsubstantiated.

Many interpreters have suggested that Solomon's marriage to the daughter of Pharaoh occasioned the composition of the Song (1 Kings 3:1; Song 1:9). Other scholars, most notably Marvin Pope (1977), have connected the song to the Mesopotamian fertility cults, written in Sumerian and Akkadian. These cuneiform texts praised the love relationship between a specific god and his consort goddess. The Levantine peoples likewise engaged in their own parallel fertility cult honoring Baal and Anat, leading some to see the Song as an Israelite version of the same (Pope, 1977). This theory breaks down in the text where the connecting points between the Song and proposed cuneiform parallels are revealed to be too superficial to claim descendance. It is in the particular contexts and styles of these two genres that the comparison falls apart, and contrast rises. As discussed in "Historical Setting" and "Genre," the Song is stylistically similar to the love poetry of Egypt, though distinct in its ideological presentation of romance. It is possible that the similarities between the Song and Egyptian love poetry occasion its writing since there are ways in which the two can be *contrasted*. In other words, the author of the Song could have intended not only to express the beauty of love poetically as the Egyptians had but also to provide a distinct vision for love within the Israelite context, a superior vision. However, the Song is not an outright polemic nor a sex and marriage manual, and while principles regarding romantic/marital love can be observed in the Song (as this homiletical commentary attempts to do throughout), its poetic, storytelling form should be contrasted with the propositional forms known from other biblical texts that discuss marriage (e.g., 1 Cor. 7; Eph. 5:22–33; etc.).

The Song is love poetry composed within the covenantal context of ancient Israelite Yahwism, influenced in part by the wisdom of the Solomonic tradition. As such, the occasion of its writing was likely to extol the merits of romantic love, loosely analogous to how Solomon praises wisdom in Proverbs or Qohelet commends joyful, authentic living in Ecclesiastes. We say "loosely" to distinguish the Song's overall tone from the overtly didactic tone of the other two texts, though instruction should not be totally ruled out as a function of the Song (2:7; 3:5; 8:4, 6–12). In application, the Song could conceivably have been used to celebrate marriages within Israelite communities (cf. Ps. 78:63). Perhaps the man would, in such a setting, take on the imaginary role of Solomon and his bride the Solomon-ness (the Shulammite) as they together, with their community, sing of love's glory and its reflection of the glorious Creator.

## GENRE

The Song is love poetry with some connections to the wisdom genre. Regarding the Israelite genre of wisdom, Keel writes: "The wise ones did not gain their knowledge like the priests, through patriarchal instruction and contact with the holy, or like the prophets, through God's personal address, but rather through their own alert minds, through observation of the course of everyday affairs, and through attention to the experiences of earlier generations" (1994, 3). While this observation properly orients wisdom toward observation and thought rather than direct revelation, we would add that the Holy Spirit is at work enabling the sages to see God's wisdom in God's creation (2 Peter 1:21). While the law, covenant, and temple inform the boundaries of the Israelite belief system, the scribes for their purposes prioritize Yahweh's natural revelation (see Ps. 19:1–6). Metaphorically, nature has assumed the roles of temple, priest, and prophet, with its intrinsic holiness instructing humanity. Though classifying the Song as "wisdom literature" would be too strong, it bears some semblance to the wisdom genre and belongs in discussion with other more overtly pedagogical texts like Proverbs (Dell 2005). Wisdom texts seek to instruct their readers in skillful living in the world. The brand of wisdom-lite found in the Song is essential for understanding the passions of romantic love in a Yahwistic context. What can be learned about romantic, sexual love from this ancient poem is most naturally applied to the male-female marital bond, a bond that further informs the Christian reader, by analogy, of the extent and power of God's love for his creation and especially for those with whom he shares a covenantal bond. In Ephesians 5:22–33, the apostle Paul makes the *analogical* connection between Christ's relationship to the church and a spousal relationship. When approaching the Song, interpreters likewise ought to say, "the intensity and singularity of the Song's love *reminds us* of Christ's love for the church," or "the Song teaches us about romantic love, which can be generally (as in abstractly) applied to our understanding Christ's love for the church." It is a mistake, however, to proceed as though the Song is speaking firstly or only about Christ's relationship to the church. Like the rest of the Solomonic corpus, the Song informs our understanding of God's world and, in turn, the gospel. But our reading of Old Testament texts should prioritize their historical, literary, and original spiritual contexts so that we can recover first the intention of the biblical author, knowing that all Scripture ultimately points us to Jesus.

The Song of Songs is ancient Israelite love poetry divinely inspired and intended to exult the glory of God in the romantic marital union between man and woman. As ANE love poetry, it bears the familiar marks of its genre and is comparable in many ways to Egyptian love poetry, though catered to the romantic concerns of Israelites within a Yahwistic context. While Egyptian love poetry exults sexual union in contexts contrary to the biblical law (e.g., prostitution), the Song promotes monogamous marriage, thus concentrating the full romantic energy of the one man for the one woman, and the full romantic energy of the one woman for the one man. As love poetry, the Song validates the goodness of love and sex, and the importance of passion in a relationship. As Holy Scripture, it provides the guardrails to harness the power of such love (see the refrains and 8:6–12). Though the various sections of the Song are distinctly beautiful, only as a collective whole can the text be understood to carry the above-stated function—to exalt love in the marriage union, a union designed by God.

## LITERARY STRUCTURE

The structure of the Song has received much attention in scholarly writing. It is best understood as a literary whole united by common themes and a loose storyline, though not a perfectly sequential narrative. Common language, themes, and the presence of the *wasf* (an Arabic-style ode to a lover's body) in places contribute to viewing the text as a unified composition (Hess 2005, 27–34). Some break down the text into poems that are related thematically, but not sequentially, that is, related only by the motives and language one would expect to see in any love poetry (e.g., Hess 2005, 34; Grossberg 1989, 58; Longman 2001, 55). They view the Song as having no discernable plot or forward movement. While the loose storyline of the Song is not presented in an easily discernible style (even as clearly as the narrative poetry of Ugarit), some story elements cannot be denied. While the introductions of some commentaries deny an overall story structure, their individual notes on key story points cannot help but concede that there is forward movement in the drama. Garrett notices that there is a certain kind of "transformation" that occurs for the bride in the story, which is more apparent when a loose sequence is assumed to the ordering of the chapters (he even suggests a sophisticated chiasm; Garrett and House 2004, 30–35).

While story elements cannot be denied altogether, the Song is less interested in communicating a plot and more interested in foregrounding the motifs of separation, longing/pursuit, and embrace. For example, what we have in the Song is a country love saga that has been boiled down to its most essential parts and rearranged in such a way that the primary themes and motifs of that story have now become the driving focus of the piece. Yet there are still the elements of a narrative form in the Song: there is the longing and pursuit of a relationship, obstacles that get in the way, the overcoming of said obstacles, and the moment of consummation (5:1). The story then repeats itself in an imprecise way in chapters 5–8, returning to the themes of longing and pursuit as the marriage progresses and encounters difficulties common to human experience. The sexual union in 5:1 is the climax of the story, no doubt, but the message of the Song is embedded in its many poems of longing scattered throughout.

The Song does not read like a typical story in precise chronological order, one scene right after the next—there are many gaps; nevertheless, it does appear to have a discernible beginning, middle, and end (though missing many of the pieces that might otherwise appear in an expanded narrative). Cyclical themes of relational pursuit build until they crescendo at its climax in 5:1, after which those themes cycle through again. These themes are by no means strict divisions. While the Song has observable themes and patterns, these frequently overlap. The Song invites readers into its dramatic movements, which it presents as distinct, but it resists readers' attempts to strictly categorize its parts; in fact, as Exum beautifully puts it, "Part of the Song's artistry, and its artifice, is the way it draws us in while seeming to keep us out" (1999, 58). Still, for purposes of discerning these themes of relational pursuit, the following pattern may be observed:

|  | Separation | Longing and Pursuit | Embrace |
|---|---|---|---|
| Introduction | | 1:1 | |
| Sequence 1 | 1:2–8 | 1:9–3:11 | 4:1–5:1 |
| Sequence 2 | 5:2–9 | 5:10–6:13 (HB 7:1) | 7:1 (HB 2)–8:5 |
| Conclusion | | 8:6–14 | |

Sequence 1: separation (1:2–8), longing/pursuit (1:9–3:11), and embrace (4:1–5:1); Sequence 2: separation (5:2–9), longing/pursuit (5:10–6:13 [HB 7:1]), and embrace (7:1 [HB 2]–8:5). The Song concludes with lessons of love (8:6–14). Again, these divisions are imperfect and could be construed differently, but the fact that these themes exist in the Song is undeniable.

We must ask how we can properly understand parallel language placed at corresponding points throughout the poem (2:10–13 and 7:12 [HB 13]–8:1; 2:14–17 and 8:13–14; 3:1–5 and 5:2–8; 3:6–11 and 5:9–16; 4:1–7 and 6:4–10; Johnston 2009, 299–305; see Garrett and House 2004, 30–35). For such a coincidence to occur in sophisticated biblical poetry with no authorial forethought is highly doubtful. Others, however, rightly dispute the presence of a *mechanically* precise chiasm where one line or stanza perfectly corresponds to the other; indeed, that is lacking. It would be appropriate to think of the text as possessing an imperfect mirror of parallel themes, thoughts, and, at times, even words from one end of the story to the other.

This commentary understands the Song to present a bare-bones storyline such that all chapters and songs within it are necessary parts of the whole. It should be read as a loose storyline in poetic form, providing some basic storytelling components throughout while lacking many of the details and logical connection points typically found in straight narrative prose or even epic poetry. In consideration of the homiletical purposes of this commentary, the thematic divisions and story elements of the Song are brought together and rendered as the following preaching units:

- The Lovers Invite One Another (1:1–8)
- The Lovers Affirm One Another (1:9–2:7)
- The Lovers Anticipate One Another (2:8–17)
- The Lovers Pursue One Another (3:1–11)
- The Lovers Embrace One Another (4:1–5:1)
- The Lovers Renew Their Pursuit (5:2–6:13 [HB 7:1])
- The Lovers Renew Their Embrace (7:1 [HB 2]–8:5)
- Love Is Supreme (8:6–7)
- Love Is Rewarding (8:8–14)

## THEOLOGICAL EMPHASES

One of the main questions asked of the Song is "Why is God never mentioned?" Though the other texts of the Solomonic corpus mention God in several places, the terms typically used to refer to him ("God" or the divine name, Yahweh) appear to be missing in the Song (a possible exception might be 8:6). It still reasonable, though, to assume the presence of God in the background of the Song given its relationship to the Solomonic corpus, its creational themes, and the potential allusions embedded in the refrains (2:7 and 3:5) and in 8:6. Wisdom texts like Proverbs are concerned with what can be learned from observing natural phenomena. The sages were more interested in what they could learn from the lesser *torah* of God's creation than directly from the scroll of Deuteronomy, for example. Their observations do not contradict Torah; rather, they expose the fact that God's Torah is woven into the fabric of creation. This is consistently the case in the Song, which is even further removed from references to the Law than are the books of Proverbs and Ecclesiastes. While not properly wisdom literature in the old nomenclature, the Song is still the kind of text that exalts the work of creation and, by that, the Creator. Noting this, the theological themes emerging from the Song include romantic love informed by the wisdom of God's creation and romantic love as an analogy for all types of legitimate relational love, chief among which for Christians is the relationship between Christ and the church.

To begin, romantic love informed by the wisdom of God's creation looks differently than the type of love celebrated in ANE love poetry (see "Historical Setting," above). The basic human experienes of separation, longing, pursuit, and consummation appears in both biblical and nonbiblical comparative literature, but the context of love is markedly different in the Song than in Egyptian or Mesopotamian love songs that feature promiscuity and cultic applications of sex. In the Song, one woman and one man pursue each other for marriage. Scholars who deny any notion of chastity must interpret the explicit lesson on chastity in 8:8–10 at the Song's conclusion as something else (contra M. Fox 1985, xxiii). Egyptian love poetry, while literarily brilliant and filled with many of the same wonderful themes found in the Song, does not approach sexuality with the same concerns for sexual propriety—concerns that stem from the Yahwistic covenantal context in which the Song was written. Certain Egyptian love songs can be described as "pornographic" and even feature prostitution (M. Fox 1985, 72–73). Love that is shaped by God will exalt all of the mysteries and enticing pleasures of romance but within the context of a couple's pursuit of marriage. To this first theological emphasis we could add the topic of romantic love in conversation with God's creation. As discussed in "Genre" above, nature testifies not only to the creative power of God but to the truths of God (Ps. 19:1–6). Not surprisingly, the creation narrative of Genesis 1–2 is alluded to in several places. In the Song, love follows the rhythms of nature and seeks to learn from it the way disciples might sit at the feet of a rabbi.

Second, the romantic love featured in the Song can serve as an analogy for love's power and worth (8:6–7) in any human relationship, but especially the relationship between God and his people (e.g., Isa. 54:5; Jer. 2:2; Hos. 2:19). In the new covenant, this is construed more specifically as a relationship between Christ and his church. In this union, Christ is pictured as the groom, and the church as his bride (e.g., 2 Cor. 11:2; Eph. 5:25; Rev. 19:7–9). Certain principles of love derived from the Song can be applied to our understanding of the indomitability of God's love for us, that not even death can overcome it (Song 8:6–7; Rom. 8:38–39). The Song, however, should not be understood as an allegory whereby any part of it is taken as an intentional symbol for God and/or the church; rather, priority should be given to the contextual reading before drawing analogies. For example, in the odes, the lovers exalt each other's bodies in obvious sexual language, from which we could draw the following principles:

1. Literally, the text demonstrates the benefits of one spouse showering affection on the other, which has applications in marriage.
2. Analogically, the text reminds us that in our loving relationship with Christ, we find ourselves praising him rather than exalting ourselves.

## OUTLINE OF THE SONG OF SONGS

### THE RUDIMENTS OF LOVE (1:1–2:17)

- The Lovers Invite One Another (1:1–8)
  - Title of the Song (1:1)
  - The Woman's Invitation (1:2–7)
  - The Man's Invitation (1:8)
- The Lovers Affirm One Another (1:9–2:7)
  - The Man and the Woman Affirm Each Other's Beauty (1:9–17)
  - The Man and the Woman Affirm Each Other's Uniqueness (2:1–3)
  - The Woman Rests in the Man's Love (2:4–6)
  - The Woman Warns the Daughters of Jerusalem (2:7)
- The Lovers Anticipate One Another (2:8–17)
  - The Woman Witnesses the Man's Efforts (2:8–9)
  - The Man Actively Anticipates the Woman (2:10–14)
  - The Woman Actively Anticipates the Man (2:15–17)

### THE ACTS OF LOVE (3:1–5:1)

- The Lovers Pursue One Another (3:1–11)
  - The Woman Pursues the Man for Marriage (3:1–5)
  - The Man Prepares for the Wedding (3:6–11)
- The Lovers Embrace One Another (4:1–5:1)
  - The Man Woos the Woman by Praising Her Body (4:1–7)
  - The Couple Invite One Another to Join in Sexual Intimacy (4:8–16)
  - The Couple Embrace One Another in Sexual Intimacy (5:1)

### THE RENEWAL OF LOVE (5:2–8:5)

- The Lovers Renew Their Pursuit (5:2–6:13 [HB 7:1])
  - The Woman Pursues the Man Again (5:2–6:3)
  - The Man Pursues the Woman Again (6:4–6:13 [HB 7:1])
- The Lovers Renew Their Embrace (7:1 [HB 2]–8:5)
  - The Man Again Woos the Woman (7:1–10 [HB 2–11])
  - The Woman Again Invites the Man to Join Her in Sexual Intimacy (7:11 [HB 12]–8:4)
  - The Couple Again Embrace One Another in Sexual Intimacy (8:5)

### THE LESSONS OF LOVE (8:6–14)

- Love Is Supreme (8:6–7)
  - Nothing Is More Powerful Than Love (8:6)
  - Nothing Is More Valuable Than Love (8:7)
- Love Is Rewarding (8:8–14)
  - The Reward of Peace (8:8–10)
  - The Reward of Pleasure (8:11–12)
  - The Reward of Longevity in Love (8:13–14)

## FOR FURTHER READING

Davis, Ellen F. *Proverbs, Ecclesiastes, and the Song of Songs.* WeBC. Louisville: Westminster John Knox Press, 2000.

Garrett, Duane. *Proverbs, Ecclesiastes, Song of Songs: An Exegetical and Theological Exposition of Holy Scripture.* NAC 14. Nashville: Broadman & Holman, 1993.

Garrett, Duane, and Paul House. *Song of Songs/Lamentations.* WBC 23B. Nashville: Nelson, 2004.

Keel, Othmar. *The Song of Songs.* Translated by F. J. Gaiser. CC. Minneapolis: Fortress, 1994.

Longman, Tremper III. *Song of Songs.* NICOT. Grand Rapids: Eerdmans, 2001.

Murphy, Roland E. *The Song of Songs: A Critical and Historical Commentary on the Bible.* Edited by S. Dean McBride Jr. Hermeneia. Minneapolis: Fortress, 1990.

# THE RUDIMENTS OF LOVE (1:1–2:17)

The beginning of the Song introduces readers to its main characters, the woman and the man, as well as a chorus of others whose lyrics will serve to move the themes forward. Following the Song's title, the woman opens with an invitation for the man to pursue her romantically while confronting those who are critical of her appearance. The man responds in 1:8 by accepting the call and offering a veiled invitation of his own. Song of Songs 1:9–2:7 suggests the lovers are now together, though not yet sexually, as they convey for the first time their affirmations of one another's beauty and uniqueness.

This first major section, The Rudiments of Love (1:1–2:7), is broken into three preaching units: The Lovers Invite One Another (1:1–8), The Lovers Affirm One Another (1:9–2:7), and The Lovers Anticipate One Another (2:8–17).

# Song of Songs 1:1–8

**EXEGETICAL IDEA**
The lovers' desires for one another lead them to initiate the process of courtship through invitation, welcoming all subsequent joys the courtship may bring.

**THEOLOGICAL FOCUS**
Truthfully acknowledging one's affections and initiating the process of courtship can echo and affirm, when done in accordance with God's standards, the divine authorship of love.

**PREACHING IDEA**
Cultivate a passionate relationship.

**PREACHING POINTERS**
The author of this book did not just write a song, but he wrote the "Song of Songs," the best song. He wrote the best song on the best theme: love. He was not shy in extolling the beauty and passion of human love. He carefully constructed an intricate song detailing the exploits of a man and woman in love. He began his song by showing how the man and the woman longed for and pursued each other.

The message of the Song of Songs is desperately needed in the church today. The enticements of a culture awash in sexual immorality can lure believers away from the purity God demands. On the other hand, some believers may see the licentiousness of the culture and respond by unintentionally denigrating God's good gift of marital sexual intimacy. Consequently, the beauty and power of God-sanctioned romance needs to be emphasized. The Song provides the proper understanding of love, romance, and sexual desire for the church. Strong desire comes from God and should be cultivated for marriage. When the Holy Spirit directs our desires, we can experience the wonders of God's love both in our marriages and in our churches.

# THE LOVERS INVITE ONE ANOTHER (1:1–8)

## LITERARY STRUCTURE AND THEMES (1:1–8)

The first line of the Song provides the title, "The Song of Songs," and indicates that the text has to do with Solomon but provides no further information. Immediately after is the woman's open invitation for courtship (1:2–4a), followed by a chorus affirming the man's value in the eyes of young maidens (1:4b). Then comes the woman's subsequent proclamation and defense of her beauty against critics (1:5–6). Her first instance of separation suspense prompts her to ask her lover where he can be found (1:7). The man directly answers her insecurities but does not reply to her question with an exact location (1:8); rather, he invites the woman to pasture her flock where he can easily find her and where her beauty, as verses 9 and following demonstrate, will be on full display against the backdrop of other shepherds and shepherdesses.

- *Title of the Song (1:1)*
- *The Woman's Invitation (1:2–7)*
- *The Man's Invitation (1:8)*

## EXPOSITION (1:1–8)

By attaching the Song to King Solomon, the songwriter drew the attention of an ancient audience intrigued with the history and later legends of the wise king and his reputation as a master songsmith and sage (1:1; cf. 1 Kings 4:32). The songwriter then composed introductory poems that introduced the main characters and created an initial cause for both romantic excitement and suspense. The songwriter caused readers to ask timeless questions found in many stories of romance where obstacles keep lovers from coming together in oneness and embrace.

Following the Song's title, the woman confesses her desire to be loved by the man whom she hopes will kiss her "with the kisses of his mouth," while admitting his popularity among all the maidens of Jerusalem. She then addressed what she sees as her inadequacies, which sets up the man to both extol her and respond to her invitation with one of his own.

### Title of the Song (1:1)

The songwriter titled the Song in such a way as to draw the attention of ancient readers, indicating that it related somehow to Solomon, the renowned king of Israel.

**1:1.** The scroll begins with, "The Song of Songs, which pertains to Solomon" (concerning the book's title in the first half of the verse, see "Title" in the Introduction). The latter half of 1:1 contains the relative clause "that refers to Solomon" (אֲשֶׁר לִשְׁלֹמֹה), which could be taken in a number of ways. Traditionally, the addition of the preposition *lamed* (לְ) to a proper noun (in this case, שְׁלֹמֹה) in the heading of a poem has been understood as a sign of authorship (see, e.g., CSB, ESV, NASB), which is why so many of the psalms containing the superscript "of David" (לְדָוִד) are thought to have been written by King David himself. However, this need not always be the case since the construction can have the unspecific meaning "with respect to David." Such a *lamed* of specification occurs in a few places where it appears with a proper noun, as in Genesis 17:20, "And with regard to Ishmael" (וּלְיִשְׁמָעֵאל; cf. Num. 8:24; see "of Solomon" and "of David" in Ps. 72:1, 20; see Arnold and Choi §4.1.10h)

The preposition *lamed* could mean "belongs to" or "refers to" or "[is composed] by" Solomon. These categories may not be totally distinct, meaning that more than one may apply. There is a lack of adequate internal evidence to come to any conclusion dogmatically, but it seems that the songwriter at the very least intends the meaning "which refers to Solomon." This conclusion is reached by considering evidence that suggests a different author and a later date of composition, such as the unlikelihood of a biblical author writing such braggadocious material about himself and the repeated mention of Solomon in the third person (1:1, 5; 3:7, 9, 11; 8:11, 12). For more on this topic, see "Author" in the Introduction.

> **Canonical Placement of the Song of Songs**
>
> When we consider the layout of the books in the Hebrew canon, there may be implied connecting points between Proverbs 31, Ruth, and the Song, the three immediately following one other. It could be that the faith communities that arranged the Hebrew canon intended for the "woman of honor" (אֵשֶׁת־חַיִל) of Proverbs 31:10–31 to be is modeled by the Moabitess in the novella that immediately follows. Ruth was a foreigner, a female, and a widow, which in Iron Age Israel would make her a woman of little worth, at first (חַיִל can refer to worth or virtue), socioeconomically speaking. Nevertheless, her diligence and faith resulted in favor from God, as evinced both by her improved state at the end of the story and her role in the ancestry of David. In other words, she proved to be a "woman of honor" (אֵשֶׁת־חַיִל) both in character and in her eventual socioeconomic status.
>
> The exceptionalism of such a woman is extended from Proverbs 31:10 through the book of Ruth to the Song, where the female protagonist, a mere country maiden, is described by the man as "the most beautiful of women" (1:8) and "a flower among thorn bushes" (2:2). Reading the HB in the traditional canonical order would make us less surprised by the forwardness of the woman in initiating this pursuit. She, like Ruth and the "woman of worth," will not be impeded by the roadblocks and criticisms that threaten to disqualify her from her pursuits, as 1:5–7 will show.

### The Woman's Invitation (1:2–7)

The female protagonist begins with an invitation for her lover to kiss her passionately, while justifying her own beauty before potential critics.

**1:2a.** The woman's invitation is direct and unmistakable—at the very least, she wants her lover to kiss her. She states, "Let him kiss me" (יִשָּׁקֵנִי), a jussive expressing the desire of the woman in the form of an overt invitation (see the NET: "Oh how I wish you would kiss me passionately!"). While the verb "to kiss" (נשׁק) is used in a variety of contexts such as nonsexual familial affection or a greeting between friends, both here and in 8:1 the sense is clearly romantic (see Jones 2019, 110–14).

She invites the man to "kiss me with the kisses of his mouth" (יִשָּׁקֵנִי מִנְּשִׁיקוֹת פִּיהוּ), a cognate accusative where the verb and its object (here the object of a preposition) form a construction intended to intensify or emphasize the action. Parts of the human anatomy are referenced frequently throughout the Song as the lovers describe one another, but the "mouth" (פֶּה) is the first to be mentioned, likely because it is a typical starting point for physical affection. The fact that the woman is taking the lead on this relationship may seem countercultural, though it is not unprecedented in Scripture (cf. Ruth). The clear force of the entire first clause is that the woman craves immediate affection from the man and is able to state it boldly. The second clause of this poetic line provides her rationale.

**1:2b.** In the second clause the woman switches pronominal suffixes from third to second person. While in the first colon she appeared to be speaking *about* the man, now she speaks *to* the man. While on the one hand this person-switching type of "morphologic parallelism" is a known feature of biblical poetry (Berlin 2008, 40), readers are still left wondering how such a switch affects our understanding of who is present at this moment in the text. Since the woman is speaking to the man, the most reasonable assumption is that they are in one another's presence, perhaps in a social setting or passing in the street. Otherwise, the woman could be daydreaming about a hypothetical conversation she is having with the man. A potential explanation for how the woman can speak *about* the man in one colon and *to* him in the next (as happens again in 1:4 below, though in reverse order) is to understand them as being physically together while the woman continues an internal monologue reflecting her deepest desires. (See note on 1:4 below for further explanation. If our interpretive response to such questions as this, i.e., the person switching in 1:2, is always to throw up our hands and say, "Who knows? It's poetry," then we are not being honest about the fact that such questions linger in our minds as we read. Hence, we offer up soft suggestions in this commentary, which may aid in forming a somewhat coherent reading of the text.)

She reasons "for your loving essence is better than wine" (כִּי־טוֹבִים דֹּדֶיךָ מִיָּיִן). And here may be the first metaphor of the Song, where the man's "lovemaking" or "loving essence" is brought into close relationship with the idea of drinking wine. This is not the only time wine is used in association with lovemaking (1:2, 4, 10; 7:9 [HB 10]). The meaning of the term "love" (דּוֹדִים) in the plural typically refers to sexual intimacy or the potential for it (cf. Prov. 7:18; Song 1:2, 4; 4:10; 5:1; 7:12 [HB 13]; Ezek. 16:8; 23:17). The woman is here affirming what she perceives to be the man's sexual prowess, though it does not seem yet that the two have been together when we compare chapters 1–4 with the heightened sexual tone following 5:1.

The mention of wine is a reference to the physical side effects of consuming alcohol, so the clause is contrasting the superior euphoria and excitement of sexual stimulation/arousal with what the woman deems to be the inferior euphoria of drunkenness. In this case, the power of sexual stimulation is superior to the power of alcohol, which the lovers acknowledge is considerable (otherwise why use it for contrast?). The excitement of two lovers is heightened by the mere anticipation of sex. She is intoxicated with the man's "love" and wants her feelings validated by his kisses, so she invites him.

Amenhotep IV posturing to kiss his wife (see Song 1:2a and sidebar "The Kissing Gesture" p. 317). Due to the lack of human representations in Israelite art, imagery from Egypt, Mesopotamia, and Canaan is commonly employed to illustrate what the biblical text is describing. Public domain (see Wiedemann 1920, 93, §9).

**1:3**. In continuing her adulation of the man, she reverses the order of 1:2, here providing the man's qualifications first, then asserting affection. This time, she states that "as a fragrance, your perfumes are pleasant" (or "your anointing oils are fragrant," ESV), continuing the intoxicating notion started in 1:2. The theme of "scent" (רֵיחַ) recurs throughout the Song as a trigger for sexual pursuit (e.g., 7:8 [HB 9]).

The presence of *lamed* (לְ) at the start of 1:3 presents a few options to translators. It can be understood as emphatic ("indeed!") or as a continuation of the comparison in 1:2, though the latter does not fit well with the syntax. Here I have taken the *lamed* as a dative of reference, "with reference to scent/smell, your perfumes are pleasant." The term for "perfume" (שֶׁמֶן) is usually translated "oil" elsewhere, but the addition of the noun "fragrance/scent" allows for a more specific designation.

The second clause extends the idea of perfume as the woman provides the next metaphor of the Song: "your name is perfume poured out" (שֶׁמֶן תּוּרַק שְׁמֶךָ). The verb "poured out" (תּוּרַק) appears in a few places, notably Ecclesiastes 11:3 where the clouds "pour out" rain. The translation difficulty in Song 1:3 is due to the feminine imperfect (תּוּרַק), which doesn't match either of the two masculine nouns in the clause. The initial letter (ת) may be a scribal copying mistake, where the letter (מ), similar in appearance, was original, creating "poured out" (מוּרָק), a *hophal* participle, matching the sense of the LXX for Song 1:3.

It affects everyone standing nearby. Just the mention of the man's name or the thought of his presence or reputation, all of which is implied by the Hebrew term for "name" (שֵׁם), brings young women the same delightful feeling one gets when a fine perfume or cologne wafts by. As stated in Ecclesiastes 7:1, "A good name is better than fine oil." So she concludes, "Therefore the young maidens love you," a reference to young women in general as potential suitors and possible competitors. They could be equated with the "daughters of Jerusalem" in 1:5 and elsewhere, who will function as pupils to the woman's wisdom, as a chorus that moves the story forward, and as an indirect foil to the woman's pursuit of her beloved (see 1:5–6; 6:1). They too take note of his attractive aura.

### Poetic Elegance in the Song of Songs

The Song begins with a masterful display of the songsmith's literary skill. Straight away in 1:2 the invitation "Let him kiss me with the kisses of his mouth" (יִשָּׁקֵנִי מִנְּשִׁיקוֹת פִּיהוּ) features the alliterating sounds "sh," "q," and "n" and the near-alliteration of "m" and "p" along with the assonance of "i" and "e." The sounds "sh-q"-"sh-q"-"p" may form an onomatopoeia, which is to suggest that the words themselves simulate the sound of kissing (Watson 1986, 235). Similar features continue into 1:3 where the Hebrew syntax rolls off the tongue as smoothly as the man's name: "like oil poured out." The plural term "oils/perfumes" at the beginning of the verse parallels the single "oil/perfume" in the following clause. The singular "your perfume/oil" forms a word pair with "poured-out oil" (שְׁמָנֶיךָ // שֶׁמֶן תּוּרַק; Berlin 2008, 45, 71). The woman then equates the man's "name" *shem* (שֵׁם), which sounds similar to the term "oil/perfume" *shemen* (שֶׁמֶן) just used, with the overwhelming sensation of a room filled with sweet aroma after a bottle of perfume is poured out—*that* is how his presence makes her feel. That is what she means when she says that he is intoxicating. As elegant poetry, the Song is filled with similar word pairs, alliteration, assonance, metaphors, clever syntax, and specialized vocabulary. While such features are typically unobservable in English, it is helpful for the preacher and teacher to at least be aware that they exist so that the Song's brilliance can be conveyed to others.

**1:4.** The woman now speaks more forcefully. The imperative "Draw me!" is followed by the imploration "Let us run!" She goes on to say, "The king has brought me into his chambers" (הֱבִיאַנִי הַמֶּלֶךְ חֲדָרָיו). As in 1:2 above, here again the woman switches person, though now from third to second person. The king spoken of here is the same as the lover addressed in 1:2 and throughout the Song (see Exum 2005, 96; contra Provan 2001, 225, who sees them as two distinct characters throughout the Song). The Syriac version attempts to resolve the person-switching problem by treating "The king has brought me" as an imperative with the vocative sense of the definite article on "king" and a second person suffix on "chambers"; hence, "Bring me, O King, to your chambers!" While this may seem to nicely parallel the imperative at the beginning of the line, it is not necessary. As in 1:2, it is possible to understand third-person incursions as the woman's inner monologue wherein she expresses her deepest desires. Such an interpretation fits well here, where she longs to be brought into the king's bedroom. The NET suggests reading "brought me" as a precative perfect, "May the king bring me," which would echo the jussive in 1:2. Ending this section in the third person would parallel how the section opened in 1:2: the woman is daydreaming (expressing internal monologue) about the potential for making love with the man. Her request to enter the "chambers" (חֲדָרָיו) of the king is part of a larger theme of the lovers' desires to isolate themselves from the world and to one another.

In the chorus that follows, of which the woman appears to be a part, the three verbs function as synonyms, all meaning some form of "praise," though the final such verb (נַזְכִּירָה), usually "remember" in the *qal*, here in the *hiphil* can mean "praise" with a nuance of remembrance. One good option is the ESV's "extol," though a better rendering would be the JPS and NJPS translation of "savor," which makes sense with the mention of "wine" (see NET note on 1:4).

All of the woman's statements about the man serve to justify or explain why women are so smitten with him. She joins the chorus in proclaiming, "rightly do they love you," but she alone appears to have the inside track to the man's heart. The term "rightly" (מֵישָׁרִים) is actually a noun, "righteousness," but is functioning adverbially. The subject "they" refers to the maidens referenced at the end of 1:3 (and perhaps maidens, generally) and implied by the cohortative verbs in 1:4 ("We will praise . . . exult . . . extol").

**1:5.** The woman states confidently, "I am dark, but lovely" (שְׁחוֹרָה אֲנִי וְנָאוָה). Most translations take phrase "and beautiful/lovely" as a disjunctive, making it "I am dark, but lovely." Regarding her complexion, the LXX reads, unmistakably, "black" (Μέλαινά) rather than the traditional English translation "dark"; however, this should not be understood in any way as a racial designation, which is an obscurity occasioned by modern readings that do not prioritize the ANE context of the Song (regarding the NRSV's "black," see Bellis 2021, 91, 110; on race as irrelevant to her description here, see Exum 2005, 104; Provan 2001, 225).

The conjunctive "dark *and* beautiful" reading is unlikely given the surrounding context and the fact that fair skin was preferred in most ANE cultures (Gault 2019, 67; contra Fischer 2018, 305–24, who sees the expression as a boast from the woman). It should be pointed out that this is an issue of cultural preference for what was considered physically attractive in Iron Age Israel and later and has nothing to do with the woman's ethnicity. What matters is that she is lovely in spite of how roughly she has been treated by her brothers. The woman indeed seeks the affirmation of her lover, but she will suffer no fools while she waits, confronting any criticism others may have of her appearance. There is a reason why she is so dark, which she gives while making the point that her sun-wrought complexion is an insufficient disqualifier from the designation "lovely/beautiful," a label the man will later apply to her in 6:4.

She then illustrates her two qualities, "dark" and "beautiful." She compares her dark complexion—something she considers unattractive—to "the tents of Qedar," a reference to a South Arabian tribe located in the desert between Egypt and Edom (K/Qedar is mentioned in a few places, notably Ps. 120:5; see *HALOT* s.v. "קֵדָר" 1072). The term "curtains" (יְרִיעָה) appears also in Exodus 26:7 where a tent or curtain of goats' hair is to be placed over the tabernacle. Though she is dark like the course, matted tents of the desert, she is beautiful like the "curtains of Solomon." It is also possible that the tents of Qedar and the curtains of Solomon were considered both simultaneously "dark, but lovely" (Exum 2005, 101).

**1:6**. The woman's confidence in her own beauty does not make her utterly impervious to criticism. She orders that the maidens "not glare" (אַל־תִּרְאוּנִי) at her judgmentally just because she is dark, for the sun has already fixed its "gaze" (שֶׁשֱּזָפַתְנִי הַשָּׁמֶשׁ) on her, changing her complexion. The verb in "the sun has looked/gazed" (שׁזף) at her connects to the previous verb where she commands the girls not "to look" (ראה) at her and to the following verb where her brothers "burn" against her (חרה) just like the sun did. In all, "Stop staring at me!" Ironically, the notion of "look away" is reversed later in the Song after the woman's status has changed from country maiden to glorious queen; at that time, it will be the man who begs that she turn her face away as the beauty of her eyes overwhelms him (see note on 6:5).

No explanation is given for why her brothers made her the keeper of the vineyards, but the consequence of this appointment was that she was unable to keep her own vineyard, a reference to her body and appearance. In any case, this sets her up as a kind of underdog protagonist who will experience a rags-to-riches journey as the Song progresses and her relationship to the king develops.

Before proceeding, we should note that the postbiblical relative pronoun שֶׁ appears throughout the Song but is otherwise rare in the Hebrew Bible (113×). It is combined with the preposition *lamed* to form the extremely rare postbiblical genitive particle שֶׁל (Waltke and O'Connor §9.7c). As mentioned in the Introduction, some scholars point to late lexical items like these to argue that the Song is postexilic (Davis 2000, 231), but many deny the usefulness of scant lexical clues for dating any biblical text that has been transmitted for centuries, noting the possibility of later insertions or updates (see "Date").

**1:7**. The woman's invitation for the man's kisses, her praise of his excellence, and her self-expression of both confidence and insecurity, are now followed by a direct question that demands a response: "Where are you?" Before asking, she calls him "the one whom my soul loves." Her actual question is stated, "Where do you shepherd?," followed immediately by the poetic parallel, "Where do you make the flock lie down at noon?" The imagery of the man vacillates between that of king and shepherd. He is both.

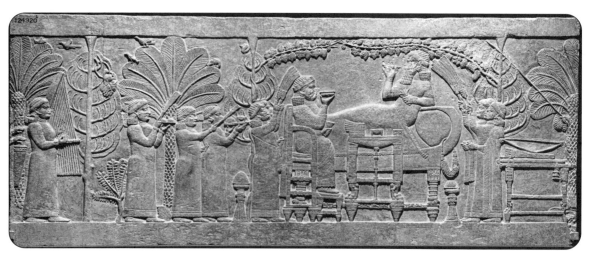

King Ashurbanipal and his queen dining at their vineyard, surrounded by servants (see 1:4, "The king has brought me into his chambers." See also the banqueting scene in 2:4). Public domain (see *ANEP* §451).

232

He must respond, "or else" (שַׁלָּמָה) she will become like one who "veils" herself beside his companions. In her mind, this is the only alternative since she is determined to go looking for him whether he answers or not, but the thought of veiling herself around others, an act that may signify her availability as a prostitute (as Tamar did in Genesis 38:14), is an unwelcome one (M. Fox 1985, 103). There are other possibilities (see sidebar "Ambiguity in the Song" p. 233). No matter how we interpret "veil," the suspense of the verse is felt.

> **Ambiguity in the Song**
>
> There are many places in the Song of Songs where the meaning of the text is unclear, even intentionally so it seems. Many scholars of the Song have commented on its ability to draw readers in while simultaneously keeping them out. Readers have the privilege of participating in the beauty of the Song, as if we were counted among the onlooking maidens of Jerusalem in 1:4, or the gazelles, does, and other aspects of creation mentioned throughout. We behold the saga of the couple's love not exploitatively nor critically, but as students of love and enthusiasts of the beauty of God's creation. But there are limits to reader participation, and part of that is experienced in the Song's ambiguity. Abstraction is typical of Hebrew poetry, in general (and a known feature in poetry cross-culturally), but the level of abstraction achieved in the Song is perhaps unparalleled by the rest of the HB.
>
> Examples of this persist throughout, but one of the earliest encountered appears in 1:7 where the woman inquires about the man's location, noting that if she does not find him, something bad will happen—she will become like a woman who is veiled in the presence of other men. Many commentators have suggested that the veil is a symbol for prostitution (see note on 1:7 and Gen. 38:14); Garrett (Garrett and House 2004), Longman (2001), Murphy (1990b), and others, however, see this interpretation as unlikely since that would bring her chastity into question (a valid objection considering the Jewish community who produced and preserved the text). Exum (2005) likewise notes the absence of sufficient evidence to defend that interpretation. They instead list the possibilities that the term עטה may refer to swatting at lice or wandering about (which would require transposing the Hebrew letters) or covering oneself to avoid identification or to create mystery (see the discussion in Emerton 1993, 127–40). It may be, however, that the term "lest" (שַׁלָּמָה) is opening the door for the woman to create, playfully, a hyperbolic alternative if the man does not answer quickly enough: "If you don't tell me where you are, I'll have to wander around giving others the wrong impression!" It is clear from her singular focus on this one man that she is not interested in prostituting herself or in marrying anyone else (see Giszczak 2015, 58–70, who points to "ancient Near Eastern wedding rituals that entail a veiling ceremony"), but she presents an absurd hypothetical in order to draw a response from the man who has thus far been silent.
>
> This passage is, again, one of many with which the exegete must wrestle. And it is difficult to say for certain when an enigmatic feature of the text is unclear due to modern scholars' insufficient familiarity with ancient customs or to the author's intention to remain vague. It is, however, in perfect keeping with the Song's style of poetry to draw its readers in while holding them at arm's length.

### The Man's Invitation (1:8)

The male protagonist finally responds, and his response does not disappoint. He not only echoes her invitation from 1:2, but profoundly confronts the insecurity of her heart with two qualifying words.

**1:8**. Finally, the man speaks, and the two words he uses to describe her are appropriately accented by the Masoretes with an *athnach* that brings the Song to a screeching halt—one could hear a pin drop as he calls her "the most beautiful among women" (הַיָּפָה בַּנָּשִׁים). Instantly, her insecurities expressed in 1:6 and her anxiety over finding him in 1:7 are confounded by the sound of his voice and the lyrics of his verse: she is beautiful, and he is here to say it. With this, he echoes her invitation in 1:2. One might expect him to give an exact geographic location where he can be found, but instead he perpetuates the chase, further building their anticipation and setting them up for an exquisite discovery. By beckoning her to pasture her young goats by the other shepherds and their sheep, he positions her as a "lily among thorns," which is how he intends to find his flower, his "darling among the maidens" (2:2).

The only other occurrences of the expression "most beautiful among women" are spoken by the maidens of Jerusalem in 5:9 and 6:1, but this does not preclude the man from using that same title for her. If the maidens are also the speakers in 1:8, what would this verse mean? Some suggest the maidens are mildly rebuking the woman who ought to know the answer to her question in 1:7 (e.g., Garrett and House 2004, 138), but others identify the man as the speaker (e.g., Exum 2005, 108). The former say that if she ever wants to find him, she will have to leave the homestead. This is an interesting possibility, but no more defensible than the idea that 1:8 represents the man's immediate response to her question (see Verde and van Hecke 2017, 211). The verse should be understood as coming from the man who is telling her to do the very thing she fears (1:7): pasture among the other shepherds. When she does so, she will stand out as a royal mare among them (1:9).

## THEOLOGICAL FOCUS

By mentioning Solomon at the start, the author intends not only to pique the interest of ancient readers but to bring them into the world of Yahwistic wisdom with which Solomon has always been associated (1 Kings 3:1–15; this is not the same as saying the Song fits perfectly in the wisdom literature category; see "Genre"). The songwriter presents the true, raw expression of the woman's love and attraction to the man: never is an attempt made to hide how she truly feels. Her invitation to love is for a singular person, seeking out the man and him alone. She does not bother to mention other potential male suitors. His "name" has an intoxicating aroma that turns the maidens' heads in his direction. They all want to be with him, but none of them will surpass her in this pursuit. She beckons him to "draw" her to himself (1:4), already imagining their future life within the king's palace and in his bedroom chambers.

In keeping with God's wisdom, her affection is truthful (Prov. 24:26), does not conceal or seek to harm the man through insincere kisses (Prov. 27:6), nor attempts to lure him into immorality (Prov. 7:13). The woman's language conveys a high view of the man's worth, reveals her own confidence mixed with insecurity, and demonstrates an uncut passion buried deep within her to actualize the affection she feels for him. Her life has not been one of royal luxury, but one of hard labor under the scorching heat of the Middle Eastern sun. Her brothers did not seek to protect her appearance for marriageability, and her life as a farmer meant that she could not prepare herself to be with a man in the way, one imagines, certain other "daughters of Jerusalem" could. While critics may decry her dark complexion, she affirms her own beauty and proceeds with her investigation regarding the man's whereabouts. She is undeterred by what others say, even if she is somewhat affected by them, heeding instead to the beckoning of love within her that exclaims, "Let him kiss me!"

Her undaunted affection echoes, by analogy, the great love of God for Israel in the Old Testament and for the church in the New. It reflects the potential power of love, an affection emanating from God and extending to his creation. Love's expression, exercised in the context of

Yahwistic order, is an acknowledgment of its Creator. Hence, this passage affirms that truthfully acknowledging one's romantic desires and initiating the process of courtship can, when done in accordance with God's covenantal standards for sexuality, echo and affirm the divine authorship of love.

## PREACHING AND TEACHING STRATEGIES

### Exegetical and Theological Synthesis

The Song of Songs extols the richness and beauty of human love through intricately constructed Hebrew poetry. Yet the opening reference to King Solomon, the wisest of Israel's kings (1 Kings 3:9–12), calls to mind the necessity of wisdom when pursuing romantic relationships. The Song not only seeks to delight but also to instruct. Since the Song is poetry, the man and the woman are probably not intended to be literal, historical people. Instead, they are most likely idealized representations of a man and woman in love. Though lowly, they view each other as royalty (1:4, 9–10, 12; 3:9; 4:1–7).

As the first poem opens, the woman is desiring the man (1:2–4). While the woman expresses confidence in her own beauty, she still struggles with feelings of insecurity over her appearance (1:5–6). She wrestles with obstacles getting in the way of her love, namely, the burdens laid on her shoulders by others (1:6). Undeterred, the woman desires the separation from the man to end, using strong language to provoke a response from the man (1:7). She does not want to resort to extreme measures to gain his attention. To her relief, the man responds to her invitation and immediately calms her fears by calling her "most beautiful among women" (1:8). He loves her. But his love is not to be coerced and so he invites her to respond to his invitation (1:8). She must seek him out too.

The back-and-forth nature of love makes it both exhilarating and terrifying. One moment, star-crossed lovers are experiencing the best moments of their lives because they are together. Then the date ends and they go their separate ways, and it feels as if a dagger was driven through their hearts. The beauty of God's design is that such passionate desire moves men and women to pursue one another for a lifetime of marriage. The normative pattern laid down in Scripture is for one man and one woman to be united for one lifetime under the rule of the one God (Gen. 2:22–24). And as Song of Songs demonstrates, love is the powerful and magnetic force that binds two people together.

### Preaching Idea

Cultivate a passionate relationship.

### Contemporary Connections

#### What does it mean?

The Song of Songs is love poetry and has ties to Wisdom Literature. As love poetry, the Song invites its readers into a world of passion and romance. As wisdom, it seeks to instruct its audience in God-glorifying relationships. The complexity of the Song enables it to speak to the full range of human experiences concerning love.

The Song uses poetry to narrate a basic storyline of a man and woman falling in love, getting married, and renewing their love. The man and the woman intensely long for each other and their longing motivates them to build a dynamic, passionate relationship. The woman clearly esteems the man very much (1:2–4). His love is better than wine (1:2). Nothing can compare to it. She does not allow anything else to get in the way of his love. She also upholds his good name and character, noting that even others recognize it (1:3). Her uttermost desire is to be with the man, away from the demands and crowds of life (1:4). But as much as she wants to be with the man, she must deal with her insecurities, otherwise, such things could derail the relationship. She knows she is beautiful: "I am dark but lovely" (1:5). Sometimes self-affirmations aren't enough, as she is still beset with insecurity over her looks (1:6). Her looks are likely not her only concern. She may wonder if she will even be able to pursue a relationship amid the responsibilities heaped upon her shoulders by others (1:6). As a later verse instructs, the couple must deal with the "little foxes" that can spoil the vineyard of love (2:15).

Frustrated by life, the woman wonders where her lover is (1:7). It's easy to imagine the woman pining to spend time with the man after she worked a long day in the sun only to be let down by the fact that he is not to be found. Does he even care? Desperate times call for her desperate measures, so she gives him an ultimatum: "Why should I be like a veiled woman beside the flock of your friends?" (1:7 NIV). "Do you really want me spending time with other men?" she seems to be saying. She playfully provokes him because she longs for a response. And respond he does! The man attempts to banish her fears in this moment by praising her as "most beautiful among women" (1:8). But even though he loves her, he won't let her off the hook that easily. If she really wants to spend time with him, she will have to put in some effort too. She will have to chase him just as much as he chases her.

God never intended marriage to be the end of passion. If anything, God intended marriage to be the driver of passion for human beings. But the suffering of life and responsibilities of adulthood can eat away at the passion in any relationship. Therefore, a passionate relationship must be cultivated.

*Is it true?*
The Bible speaks of the goodness of passionate, romantic love. According to the Scriptures, sexual desire—the fulfillment of romantic love—is a good thing if it is channeled toward God's design of marriage. The goodness of passionate relationships is directly tied to the goodness of the created order. Five times God saw that his creation was good (Gen. 1:10, 12, 18, 21, 25). On the sixth day, God created humanity as male and female so that they could be fruitful and multiply through sexual intercourse (Gen. 1:27–28). After creating these two sexes with their capability for intense longing and capacity for sexual intercourse, he declares the world "very good" (Gen. 1:31). Sexual desire is a good gift from God, which is a message the Song reinforces.

Besides the creation account and the Song, other Scriptures exhort married couples to be enthralled with each other. Husbands should take great joy in their wives (Prov. 5:18)—a husband should be "satisfied" with his wife's breasts. More shockingly, the author of Proverbs recommends that couples be "drunk" on love (Prov. 5:19). Love should make us stagger! Even the seemingly dour Qohelet in Ecclesiastes advises that men should "enjoy life with the woman whom you love" (Eccl. 9:9). In no place do the Scriptures advocate for a passionless, sexless marriage.

Of course, Scripture warns of the trouble that sexual passion can bring if it is not channeled into a covenant of marriage. When warning against adultery in the book of Proverbs, Solomon asks, "Can a man bring fire near his chest and his clothes not be burned?" (Prov. 6:27). Solomon wonders whether unbridled desire can have any other effect except destruction. The answer is clearly "no." Unbridled sexual desire destroys marriages, rips apart families, and harms children. It even damages the person engaged in illicit activities: "Every other sin a person commits is outside the body, but the sexually immoral person sins against his own body" (1 Cor. 6:18). Therefore, Christians must cultivate passionate relationships under the authority of God's word, guarding against sexual temptation.

*Now what?*
How do we cultivate a passionate relationship? We do so by prioritizing the other person. Relationships do not thrive on their own. Like

plants, they must be actively tended to and given ample attention. The woman in the Song sets the example for us as she declares the man's love is better than wine. In the Scriptures, wine is often used as a symbol of God's blessing (Deut. 11:14; 14:23; Ps. 104:15; Isa. 25:6). In this way, the woman identifies the man's love as a good blessing from the Lord. Even amid the busyness of her life, all she wants to do is run away with the man (1:4). Do you prioritize your spouse? Do you ever give him or her the best of your time or merely the leftovers? Do you invest significantly in continuing to get to know your spouse?

Couples can prioritize one another by dealing with their insecurities. Even women long ago struggled with societal expectations of beauty, just as the woman of the Song expresses dismay about her looks (1:5–6). Husbands should be inspired by the man in the Song to remind their wives that they are "most beautiful among women." Husbands must be the real mirror for their wives.

We can also cultivate a passionate relationship by injecting some "chase" into it. The woman declares she may have to resort to veiling herself in front of others (1:7). No matter what the exact meaning of her declaration is, she is trying to provoke a response from the man. The man responds but doesn't necessarily make it too easy on her either. He reaffirms her beauty but also invites her into pursuing him (1:8). She should follow the path to where he is. How many times do relationships dry up and die because there is no longer any excitement or "chase" involved? What can you do this week to invite your spouse to "chase" you? What can you do this week to provoke a response of love from them?

Since the Song speaks primarily to married couples because of its emphasis on romantic love, does the book have anything to say to those who are single? Yes, it does. For those who are single but desiring to be married, the examples of cultivating a passionate relationship provide a paradigm from which to learn. Singles preparing for marriage can learn what a healthy marriage looks like. For those God has called to singleness (1 Cor. 7:7–8, 17, 20), the text still provides principles for cultivating healthy relationships even if they are devoid of a romantic element. Friends must still prioritize one another or a friendship will falter. Dealing with one's own insecurities is good practice no matter what one's relationship status. And while those called to singleness should not entice one another to the chase of romantic love, they can still pursue others in friendship and ministry.

### Creativity in Presentation

What comes to mind when you hear the word "priority"? Do you think deadlines, obligations, or responsibilities? What about rocks? A common illustration about prioritization is known as the "big rocks" illustrations. In the big rocks illustration, you take a large mason jar and fill it mostly with sand. You then fill it another quarter of the way with pebbles. Finally, you fill it with some big rocks. The point of the illustration is that the big rocks won't fit. But could they? To demonstrate that they could, you would put the big rocks in first *then* the pebbles and *then* the sand. The point of the illustration is to encourage the congregation to prioritize their relationships. God created us for community. Therefore, our relationships, especially if we are married, must be big rocks. But do we make time for them? Or do the sand and pebbles of distraction crowd out time for cultivating a real relationship with someone? The woman in the Song clearly prioritizes her relationship, especially when she extols the man's love as better than wine. Could your spouse say the same thing about you?

Many popular songs, both modern and classic, can help convey the depth of emotion and passion in the Song. Using contemporary songs can be an especially powerful way to illustrate the text since the Song is, well, a song. "Perfect" by Ed Sheeran is a song that expresses deep and enduring love. It speaks of a couple who met while they were young and grew in their love together. "All of Me" by John Legend speaks of the total self-giving that love engenders. "Unchained Melody" by the Righteous Brothers is a classic song, speaking of the intensity and love associated with romance. These are but a sampling of the songs that can bring the Song to life for contemporary congregations.

The big idea of the passage is "Cultivate a Passionate Relationship." Taking cues from how the woman and the man conduct themselves, we can learn different ways to build a more passionate relationship.

- Prioritize the other person (1:2–4)
- Deal with your insecurity (1:4–6)
- Engage in the chase (1:7–8)

## DISCUSSION QUESTIONS

1. How does the title of the book affect our interpretation of the Song (1:1)?

2. How does the woman express her desires? What kind of man is she pursuing (1:2–4)?

3. What insecurities does the woman have? How does the man attempt to calm her fears (1:5–8)?

4. How can we acknowledge the goodness of sexual desire without abandoning God's guidelines (chastity before marriage and fidelity within marriage)?

5. How can our desires motivate us toward maturity and marriage?

# Song of Songs 1:9–2:7

**EXEGETICAL IDEA**
The man and the woman affirm one another with elegant language, further intensifying their desire to be together.

**THEOLOGICAL FOCUS**
Verbal affirmation in romantic relationships engenders confidence, vulnerability, and intimacy.

**PREACHING IDEA**
Use words wisely to build flourishing relationships.

**PREACHING POINTERS**
The man praised the woman as if she were royalty, although she was a humble worker of the land. The woman reciprocated his affirming words by proclaiming he was royalty too. The man and the woman continued to trade compliments back and forth, demonstrating that the bond of their love had led them to a blossoming and fruitful relationship. Yet the woman recognized the power of romantic love and encouraged others to wait until the right time to fulfill the desires for romantic love.

The characters of the Song provide the paradigm for how we can improve our relationships. We must speak words of affirmation to one another, generally, in both marriage and friendships. For married couples, these words will include comments about one another's beauty. For those who are not married, these words will include affirmation of the work God is doing in each other's lives. In romantic relationships, though, we must be careful not to stir up desires for love before the appropriate time. Couples who pursue courtship before they are ready for the commitment of marriage invite considerable difficulty into their lives.

# THE LOVERS AFFIRM ONE ANOTHER (1:9–2:7)

## LITERARY STRUCTURE AND THEMES (1:9–2:7)

After the opening section where the lovers playfully invite one another into the pursuit of love (1:1–8), they then affirm one another in their beauty (1:9–2:7). In this unit, the lovers hold nothing back in their adulation of each other's desirability. Their back-and-forth praise of the other's attributes even seems competitive in nature as one attempts to outdo the other. Commentators differ on how to group the sections together. One could divide the units based on smaller themes, like the metaphor of the mare (1:9–11), the poem about fragrance (1:12–14), the "how beautiful" poem (1:15–16), and so on. Or one could acknowledge these smaller divisions while observing larger themes, such as affirmations of beauty (1:9–17), affirmations of uniqueness (2:1–3), the woman resting in the man's love (2:4–6), and the oath (2:7). Since the Song is poetry, it does not always conform to a tidy literary structure, and many sections overlap. There are enough indications, however, to group sections together in the following manner:

- **The Man and the Woman Affirm Each Other's Beauty (1:9–17)**
- **The Man and the Woman Affirm Each Other's Uniqueness (2:1–3)**
- **The Woman Rests in the Man's Love (2:4–6)**
- **The Woman Warns the Daughters of Jerusalem (2:7)**

## EXPOSITION (1:9–2:7)

Having invited one another into the pursuit of love (1:2–8), the lovers proceed to affirm one another's character, beauty, and uniqueness (1:9–2:3). The man begins by comparing his darling to a decorated royal mare among the chariots of the Pharaoh, irresistible to the stallions and singularly powerful. As future descriptions from the man will show, the woman's beauty in no way diminishes her intimidating power (6:5, 10). The woman returns the compliment as the two trade metaphors for one another's uniqueness. In 2:4–6, the woman imagines (or reports) a banqueting scene wherein the couple embraces, which prompts her warning to the maidens in 2:7 to not awaken love until "it pleases."

Certain early passages of the Song are debatable as to whether they are describing a courting scene, the woman's imagination, or the act of sex itself. Given the clear references to sex and the more explicitly sexual descriptions of the lovers that appear in the second half of the Song following 5:1, it is our opinion that these earlier passages are portraying the woman's imagination and/or the rhythms of courtship leading up to the moments of fuller sexual embrace that come later (e.g., 5:1; 8:5). If these earlier scenes are descriptions of sexual consummation, we have to ask why later passages are so much more explicit. The Song seems to present a movement from near intimacy in earlier passages to unrestrained sexual embrace in later passages. One objection to our approach would be that in both 2:6 and 8:3, the woman says, "His left hand is under my head, and his right hand embraces me," which is unmistakably sexual. The first example (2:6) occurs before the wedding language of chapters 3 and 4 and the proposed act of consummation in 5:1. But would an Israelite community espousing chastity (8:8–10) compose a Song celebrating sex before the couple is wed?

Some scholars would note that this problem is only a problem when interpreters choose to see a storyline unfolding in the text. It is more appropriate, they argue, to see the Song as an anthology of loosely related love poems (see Introduction), implying either that there is no chronological order or that things will necessarily be out of order. This is possible, but as our notes reveal throughout the commentary, the couple appears to be experiencing a progression from one chapter to the next; for that reason, a chronological sequence is not out of the question. Hence, the reference to the couple's encounter and "embrace" in 1:12–2:6 may merely refer to the wishful imagination of the woman, a feature paralleled later in 8:3. This follows the symmetry of the Song where elements from the beginning are paralleled at the end (see notes on 8:8–14).

### The Man and the Woman Affirm Each Other's Beauty (1:9–17)

Both the man and the woman tell one another how beautiful they are. They use their words to heap praise upon one another.

**1:9.** The man elaborates on the contrast begun in 1:8, further proving his point that she is "the most beautiful among women." He compares her to a stunningly beautiful mare in the royal precinct of Egypt. She is "as a mare of Pharaoh's chariot corps" (לְסֻסָתִי בְּרִכְבֵי פַרְעֹה). The man sets the woman apart as incomparable, something he will do again in 2:2. He furthermore calls her "my darling" (רַעְיָתִי), a feminine form of "friend" (רֵעֶה) appearing only in the Song (1:9, 15; 2:2, 10, 13; 4:1, 7; 5:2; 6:4).

> **A Military Stallion or a Distracting Mare?**
> There has been some confusion over the man's description of the woman as a mare among Pharaoh's chariot corps, especially since Pharaoh's chariots were drawn only by stallions (Keel 1994, 56). It may be sufficient to say that metaphors allow for this kind of flexibility, but this does present some interesting options. The man could be calling her a mare simply because she is a woman, though he intends for her to be elevated to the status of one of Pharaoh's stallions. However, it is not necessary that the mare pull a chariot to be "among" (בְּ) chariots; mares were used in other martial contexts, like carrying soldiers in battle (Cantrell 2011, 24). Either the man is (1) contrasting the beauty of a royal, procession-ready, Egyptian military horse with the mundane appearance of ordinary horses; or (2) he is asserting that she is like a beautiful mare who distracts the male horses, sending them into a frenzy (cf. the man's comparable role in 1:3–4).
>
> To the first point, there are good reasons, linguistic and conceptual, for understanding this description of the woman as "a military mare" (Verde and van Hecke 2017, 212). To the second point, scholars frequently cite an Egyptian text describing a battle wherein "the Prince of Kadesh sent out a mare, which [*was swift*] on her feet and which entered among the army" in order to disrupt Pharaoh's stallion-drawn chariots (*ANET*, 241; Cantrell 2011, 23; Murphy 1990b, 131). The mention of chariots in the verse is sufficient to elicit military imagery and support the second of the two options, originally posited by Pope (1977, 336–41). She is bejeweled with ornamentation as if prepared for public presentation and use by royalty. This description of her may be a reference not only to how the man sees her in her present state, but how he imagines she will appear on the day of their wedding.

**1:10.** He describes the ornamentation referenced in 1:9, calling her cheeks "lovely" (נָאווּ), a rare verb appearing also in Isaiah 52:7 to describe the feet of a messenger of good news and peace (cf. Ps. 93:5). The added imagery of a string of jewels about her neck is not difficult for modern readers to envision, as battle and/or processional horses from various historical periods have often been depicted in film and period art with such adornments. Egyptian art reflects this very feature in royal monumental inscriptions that have accompanying images of a pharaoh on a horse-drawn chariot. The prominence of the neck as a symbol of pride is well attested, and the rounded jewels (תּוֹרִים) would bring special attention to this enticing part of the woman's body (cf. Song 4:4; 7:4 [HB 5]; also Job 15:26; Ps. 75:5 [HB 6]; Isa. 3:16–27). These descriptions of the woman greatly contrast with her lived-in reality as a country gal, a shepherdess, which lends further to the theory that the metaphors themselves are set within daydreams whereby the couple idealize one another's beauty.

Pharaoh Tutankhamun hunting wildlife while riding his horse-drawn chariot. Note the ornamentation on the horses (see 1:9–10). Public domain (see Pritchard 2011 §41).

**1:11.** It is not obvious who is speaking, but the intent of the line is clear. The chorus of girls (and/or the man and his companions?; see note on 6:13 [HB 7:1]) break in to express their intent to contribute to her beauty by fashioning the very things magnified by the man's imagination in 1:10. It is as if they heard his idealization of her and now intend to make it a reality, possibly in preparation for their meeting or their wedding. Otherwise, this is simply the man speaking of what he and his companions will do. In either case, they will create ornaments of gold laced with "studs" of silver; in other words, they will adorn her with jewelry befitting of royalty.

**1:12.** There is a sudden change of scenery in what may be a daydream where the king is now pictured resting at his "round" (מֵסַב) dining table, perhaps surrounded by a divan of couches (Murphy 1990b, 131). The Song mixes countryside imagery with royal imagery, back and forth (Exum 2005, 110), making it difficult to know whether certain verses represent reality or wishful thinking. Our approach is to take these early, scattered images in the book as daydreams, much like the end of the book where the woman conjures up scenarios wherein she could draw close to the man (8:1–2).

The imagery from Esther 1 may be appropriate here, where King Ahasuerus is in the company of his royal entourage when he demands the presence of Queen Vashti. Here in the Song, however, the woman is not being exploited by the king before his guests; rather, she is alluring him by the scent of her strong perfume. Such role reversals are common in the Song's portrayal of the woman whose beauty, passion, and aura (6:4, 13) make her a formidable presence in the man's life.

**1:13.** The woman wants to secure the man in an intimate way, and the metaphor she has chosen to express this emotion is a small pouch of myrrh that could be stored in her bosom, a "popular perfume in the ancient Near East" (Murphy 1990b, 132). Myrrh was used in the Persian court to prepare the young women of the harem for their first night with the king (Esther 2:12; see Exum 2005, 111–12). The meaning of the metaphor is simply that she considers him precious and wants to hold him close. This connection between the woman's breasts and perfume/spices is one of several in the Song, though in later places her breasts are pictured as mountains (2:17; 4:6; 8:14).

**1:14.** En Gedi is a lush oasis in the Judean desert wilderness, and throughout recorded history has been home to plants and wildlife, fed by its abundant spring water. A vineyard in its midst would be even more special in such an arid, lifeless climate. This magnifies the rarity, value, and uniqueness of the man, who is described as "a cluster of henna in the vineyards of En Gedi." Henna was a well-known plant in Palestine, used to dye hair red (Longman 2001, 106) and known for its pleasant smell. The "vineyard" is used as a symbol for various things within the Song. It can refer to the responsibilities of life (1:6), the woman's body (1:6b), the relationship between the man and the woman (2:15), and the status of one's life or body (8:11–12). One interesting possibility is to understand (עֵין גֶּדִי) to mean "the eye/spring of my good fortune/delight," for which a good case can be made (Strawn 2020, 122). However, the text appears to present a concentric progression of the man's rarity, beginning with the largest sphere and moving to the smallest: "En Gedi" > "vineyard" > "henna blossom." The point is that he is a jewel *within* a jewel *within* a jewel—a truly rare find, like the (אֵשֶׁת־חַיִל) "woman of great worth" in Proverbs 31:10 who is nearly impossible to find (מִי יִמְצָא) since "her value is far above that of jewels" (וְרָחֹק מִפְּנִינִים מִכְרָהּ).

**1:15.** In a burst of praise, the man exclaims: "Look at you! You are beautiful, my darling!" He proceeds to compare her eyes to a dove. This metaphor is repeated in 4:1 and 5:12. Many suggestions have been made for the meaning of this comparison, like the perceived softness of a dove's eyes, its glistening green-blue neck (species *columbia livia*), the oval shape of its body, or, as Gault suggests, the notions of timidity and being a love-messenger, both of which are associated with doves in comparative literature (2019, 138–44). One difficulty is that the three occurrences of the term in the Song are different enough that no one designation fits perfectly. Regardless, all major suggestions are positive in nature, which we would expect since the metaphor is used to describe something good or desirable about the woman.

**1:16–17.** The woman repeats the language of the man from 1:15, extolling his exceptional beauty. In the scene-switching nature of the Song, the couple is now pictured lying on a grassy forest floor, as if in bed together, looking up at the cedars around them as if they were pillars to a mansion, with tree branches spreading across to form rafters. She imagines their future together as they pour the energy of their affections into one another.

> **Cultic Imagery in the Song**
> At times the Song employs language normally reserved for cultic settings. This is done in order to raise the stakes of what is happening in the text, elevating the description of the couple's love to the level of otherworldly experience, which is itself an attempt at conveying heightened emotions through words (see sidebars "The Woman's Glorious Appearance" p. 302 and "The Song and Mt. Carmel" p. 331). Words are often inadequate for telling how a person feels, which is where hyperbole, metaphor, and imagery become useful.
>
> One example of this is seen in 1:16–17, where the woman imagines her future with the man, their backs against the grass, looking up at an impossibly tall cathedral ceiling of cedar surrounded by walls of pine. This is their palace of love, of escape. Their bed is "green," a color associated in Scripture with the trees under which the Israelites would engage in idolatrous worship, including ritual sex, to invoke the blessing of the Canaanite fertility god Baal (Keel 1994, 75). The Israelites were commanded to tear down such "high places," which included profane areas, "under every green tree" (Deut. 12:2). This imagery is marshalled by the Song perhaps to invoke a sense of ritual worship, not in an effort to turn the couple themselves into gods, nor to invoke the worship of a false god, but to reflect

their heightened feelings concerning their relationship. The couple uses cult imagery to describe what is actually lovemaking (or the hope for it) in a non-idolatrous context. The mention of "house" (בַּיִת) and "cedars" (אֲרָזִים) may likewise allude to the temple in Jerusalem, which was also called God's "house" (2 Sam. 7:5–6) and made with "cedar" (1 Kings 1:8–9; recall that flora and fauna imagery were also associated with the Temple of Jerusalem—1 Kings 7:18–19, 24–26, 29, 36, 42–44, 49). The implication is that the couple's relationship is *like* a sacred space, set apart.

## The Man and the Woman Affirm Each Other's Uniqueness (2:1–3a)

The lovers describe each other as one of a kind.

**2:1**. The woman describes herself as "a flower of Sharon, a lily of the valleys." Sharon refers to the stretch of land between the Mediterranean coast of Israel moving eastward to the Shephelah, or foothills, after which comes the hill country. The traditional translation "rose" is unlikely since the flower did not come to Israel until much later (Longman 2001, 110). The term could mean something like "crocus," "lotus," or "lily" (Garrett and House 2004, 148). The valley described is not like the dry, treacherous valleys of the Grand Canyon, but a flat plain of fields separating distant hills or mountain ridges, such as can be seen throughout Israel today. The lily is a lovely flower and used in positive contexts, but here the woman describes herself as one among many lilies in a valley plain (contra Suderman 2005, 42–58, who considers שׁוֹשָׁן a "lotus" and an expression of beauty rather than mundanity; however, the "one among many" interpretation fits better with the immediate context, esp. the man's response in 2:2). She does not think of herself as unlovely (cf. 1:5), nor does she think she is unique. This self-deprecation sets the man up for a complimentary rebuttal, which he delivers in the next verse.

**2:2**. The woman describes herself in pleasant but unexalted terms, but the man takes things much farther. His lover is like a "lily among thorns," with the thorns representing "the daughters" (הַבָּנוֹת) or "young women" (ESV). The woman looks around the valley and sees other lilies, but the man sees just her, surrounded by thorns. It would seem strange to refer to the maidens of Jerusalem in a negative way, but when they are contrasted with the beauty of "my darling," such is the case. The emphasis is on the exceptional beauty of the woman. His hyperattention is placed on her, whom he sees in vivid color against the drab backdrop of the masses (see notes on 1:8–9).

**2:3**. Now it is the woman's turn, and she uses the image of an apple tree to point out the uniqueness of her beloved against the backdrop of common, less-appealing trees in Israel. Apple trees were not native to the land and, as such, would need to be imported (Garrett 1993, 149). Apples were known in Mesopotamia and were referenced in Sumerian literature in conjunction with romantic and even erotic descriptions of a man (Keel 1994, 82–83). She delights to sit in his "shade." The term "shade" (צֵל) or shadow often refers to safety and protection in the HB (Pss. 17:8; 36:7 [HB 8]; 57:1 [HB 2]). Just as a shady tree provides relief in the middle of a hot day, so the relationship that she has with the man provides rest and refreshment for her.

The woman is also said to "delight" in it/him. The woman not only rests under the shade of this "tree," but also tastes its fruit. Now that the imagery has switched to the tree, it would be appropriate to translate the remaining pronouns as "its" instead of "his" (they are grammatically identical in Hebrew, so the translator must decide which is best). Enjoying the shade and eating apples are the common ways in which people experience an apple tree, so on one level the woman is expressing how he makes her feel—secure and sated. On another level, the reference to an apple tree is sexual in nature ("an unmistakable erotic image"; Exum 2005, 114; see note on 8:5). It should be noted, though, that claims of eroticism in the Song are sometimes overstated (see sidebar "Sexual Metaphors and Innuendo" p. 312). This verse is spoken by the woman and is an expression of her imagination, not his, perhaps making the tree metaphors primarily a way of conveying feelings of security rather than the fulfillment of male pleasure (though the sexual reference cannot be denied). Furthermore, the line about "taste" serves as a bridge between the present poem and the banquet scene that follows (2:4–6), a poem that is all about the woman's satisfaction and not the man's.

### The Woman Rests in the Man's Love (2:4–6)

The woman employs banquet imagery to describe her fantasy of being enraptured with her beloved.

**2:4.** "He brought me into the house of wine, and his gaze on me was loving." The man not only protects and refreshes the woman (2:3) but also brings her to "the house of wine." The house of wine probably refers to something like a banquet hall of feasting and celebration. The man's love is intoxicating, making her "sick with love" (2:5). The enigmatic expression "his banner over me was love" could be using the term "banner" (דֶּגֶל) the way the term is used throughout Numbers and elsewhere in the Song (6:4, 10) to refer to a military banner signaling a division of troops. However, this may not make the best sense. The expression may rather be that the man's "gaze" upon her was love. The Akkadian term *diglu* means "a look, a view," and may serve as cognate here (*CAD* D s.v. "*diglu* A" 136). A verbal form of דגל appears in 5:10 to refer to the man as visually "outstanding" or "distinguished," likely also a cognate to Akkadian *dagālu* (this view is contested, however, by Danilo Verde who makes a case for retaining the military sense of "banner" [2016, 194]; though martial references do appear in the Song, the "view/gaze" interpretation of דֶּגֶל fits better with the context of 2:4). Furthermore, looking back at 1:6, the sun and the brothers "look/gaze" at her in a hurtful way; she also orders the daughters of Jerusalem to not "look" at her disdainfully. That would be contrasted with how the man "looks" at her with love in his heart here in 2:4. Hayim Tawil translates the line, "his gaze toward me (was of) love" (2009, 72, s.v. "דֶּגֶל").

**2:5.** She describes herself as "sick/exhausted with love," which is why she needs refreshment. She is experiencing the intoxicating effects of love and exclaims that she is "lovesick"! She cannot get enough of him, but his presence is also overwhelming for her (cf. 6:5 where the man expresses a similar sentiment). She longs to be refreshed with raisin cakes and apples. Both apples (see note on 2:3) and raisin cakes are affiliated with fertility and sexuality (cf. Hos. 1:3). With the present poem set in "the house of wine," a reference to the intoxicating effects of the man's love, the woman's love hangover requires that she be mended by even more love (apples and raisin cakes, both symbols for love), which may refer to the behavior of a drunkard who turns to more drink to mend his drink-related wounds (Prov. 23:35; see note on 5:8). This may not seem like an attractive picture for modern readers, but the woman's goal here is not to appear poised and under control—quite the contrary! She intends to show how very smitten she is with the man.

**2:6.** Continuing her description of the man's actions, the woman says that his "left hand is beneath my head and his right hand embraces me." Keel points out an Old Babylonian terra-cotta image of a nude couple embracing in exactly the fashion described here in 2:6 (Keel 1994, 90, fig. 44). The embrace here may be taking place in the woman's imagination (see exposition above). The language of "embrace" (חבק) here parallels the cognate Ugaritic term "embrace" (*ḥbq*) in descriptions of sexual embrace and conception (see the activities of Ilu in *COS* 1:281; see also the relief depicting lovers from Ugarit embracing in Pritchard 2011 §246 [*ANEP* §818]).

The building up of affection results in a moment of embrace and then a warning to the daughters of Jerusalem (2:7). A variation of this pattern repeats in 3:4–5 and 8:4, though the contexts are distinct. In each case, there is a heightened sense of urgency in the lines immediately preceding the refrain.

## The Woman Warns the Daughters of Jerusalem (2:7)
The woman urges the daughters of Jerusalem to wait until the right time to pursue love.

**2:7**. In favor of viewing the Song as having some kind of connection to wisdom are the woman's instructional statements here and in 3:5 and 8:4, 6–12. Her direct exhortation is that the maidens (and any wise young men listening) not "arouse love until it pleases." In other words, there is a better way to engage in love than simply to trust human instinct. Love has *its own* timing. The woman's objective is not to say that there are precise, clearly defined rules one must follow (though there may be in the broader scope of Scripture), but that there is surpassing value in waiting until the right moment to engage in romance.

An argument can be made that the adjurations in 2:7, 3:5, and 8:4 are a plea for privacy, that the maidens should not disrupt the couple during their times of intimacy (Gault 2011, 93–104; see also M. Fox 1985); however, the abstract notion of "love" (הָאַהֲבָה) in the refrain, as opposed to "lovemaking" (דּוֹדִים), fits well with the universal appeal at the end of the book in 8:6–12 (Exum 2005, 118). The very fact that it is a refrain argues in favor of it being part of a larger, global message from the Song, written after the fact and from the perspective of the already-wed woman who is recounting her experiences (similar to how the expression "all is vanity" recurs in Ecclesiastes). This suggests the injunction is not so specific as to refer only to the couple's lovemaking, nor even to lovemaking as a category; rather, the tone of the refrain and its topic of "love" is broader and, like 8:6–12, contributes to the overall message of the book. While scholars are divided on whether the author of the Song intends to teach anything, the approach of this commentary is that he/she does.

The oath speaks against engaging in romantic love recklessly or in an untimely fashion (Longman 2001, 115–16). By itself, the oath is not more specific than this. In other words, the oath cannot be reduced to a statement on chastity alone; rather, when viewed in conjunction with the lessons of love in 8:6–12, which include an appeal for chastity, the refrain can be understood as an umbrella injunction against all kinds of impropriety regarding love. Thus, the woman is using sexual terminology ("stir up" and "arouse," both forms of עוּר) to symbolize romantic love in general (not her specific engagement with the man), dissuading the maidens of Jerusalem from rushing headlong into such a weighty endeavor.

In all three places (2:7; 3:5; 8:4), the adjuration comes at a moment of heightened sexual language, which is precisely the time one would expect Israelite Scripture to issue a warning (cf. Prov. 5:7–14). It has been argued that the sensual context of the whole Song, and especially of the texts wherein the oaths occur, does not allow for such a romance-prohibitive oath, and that if interpreters see in the oath a call for chastity (or in our case, a broader appeal for proper timing and decision-making regarding love), then they are ignoring the sensual context in favor of applying biblical principles of sexual ethics from elsewhere in Scripture. However, it is especially in a sensual context that we might expect an adjuration to unmarried maiden-pupils. The woman wishes for them to observe the seasons, the signs, and rules of love, some of which are observable in nature (e.g., 2:10–13), and others they may know from God's law (e.g.,

Exod. 22:16–17; see notes on Song 3:4 and 8:8–10). In sum, the oath of 2:7, 3:5, and 8:4 is not merely a call for chastity, but a universal call to heed love's natural rhythms and timing while acknowledging its fierce power. There may be a corollary for the Song's refrain and lessons of love in Proverbs where, typical to the style of wisdom, the specific words of the Torah are not commonly cited; rather, the sages turn primarily to how the rules of life and love are observable in creation itself (Prov. 5:15–19; 7:21–23). In other words, nature is already in league with its Creator, and its rhythms reflect his truth; accordingly, whenever a person receives the Creator, he/she aligns with the natural order (Job 5:23). The Song never goes so far as to explain things theologically like this, but by adjuring the maidens to swear by nature, she appeals to its intrinsic truth (see note on 7:11 [HB 12]).

### The High Stakes of Love

In 2:7 and 3:5, the woman makes her pupils swear on something sacred, like testifying under oath, only instead of placing one's hand on the Bible as in a modern courtroom, the maidens must swear by "the gazelles or wild does of the field" (however, Exum sees the inclusion of these animals as a sign that the oath is "lighthearted" [2005, 119]). But these creatures, in their natural beauty, instinctual innocence, and symbolism as figures of sexuality (as seen on countless depictions in ANE art where they are taken very seriously), are both bearing witness to this oath and are themselves the sacred symbol of love upon which the oath is taken. She does not call upon the women to swear on love *itself*, but on a symbol of love. In the same way, one does not swear by God *himself*, but "by heaven as the throne of God, or by the earth as his footstool, or by Jerusalem as the city of the great King (Matt. 5:34–35)" (Keel 1994, 94).

The terms for "gazelles" (בִּצְבָאוֹת) and "field" (הַשָּׂדֶה) bear resemblance to the terms "hosts" and "Shaddai" used in reference to God elsewhere in the HB. One possibility is that these aspects of nature by which the maidens are to swear are subtle allusions to the God who created sexuality and has imbued nature with his love. This should not, however, serve as evidence for an allegorical reading (see Introduction; cf. the targumic reading of 2:7). Weighty spiritual terminology appears in various places in the Song where it is intended by the author to draw upon the cognitive religious framework of readers/hearers in order to emphasize the fact that love itself and the unique beauty of the couple are enshrouded in a sense of otherness. It is in no way an assertion that her status is anything bordering on divine (they are merely human); rather, the employment of these terms is meant to stretch the limits of human imagination such that love is understood to be superior to all other forces on earth, and this couple sees each other as more appealing than all other men and women (see notes on 4:6, 7, 15; 7:5 [HB 6]).

## THEOLOGICAL FOCUS

It was the woman who first praised the man and invited him to join her in love (1:2–4). Her words of affection spurred on his own, and now each lover is fully engaged in affirming the other's beauty. She is unique like a royal mare (1:9) and a lily among thorns (2:2). He is unique like an apple tree standing alone in the forest (2:3). In the elegant, scene-switching imagination of the woman, the two are drawn together in their love-palace (1:12–13), are found lying beneath a canopy of trees (1:16–17), and feast in the banqueting hall of love (2:4–6). There, in "the house of wine," the woman is pleasantly afflicted by love's embrace. Nevertheless, through the haze of intoxication, the woman has not forgotten her other purpose, so she sternly warns the maidens of Jerusalem to never submit to love's spell before the appropriate time. This is not merely a warning to remain chaste (cf. 8:8–10), but a recognition that love is bigger than any two lovers. Its power and truth are evident in the fabric of God's creation, love having emanated from him, as had wisdom (Prov. 8:22–23).

It can be observed in the rhythms of nature all around them, so it should not be entered into frivolously but only at the right time.

When words of affirmation are spoken, relationships of fruitfulness and blessing result. The man affirms the woman's beauty and uniqueness (1:9–10, 15; 2:2). She likewise praises him and expresses her longing for him (1:12–14, 16–17; 2:1, 3–6). As they heap up praise, they exhibit an understanding of love that is lost to most people at some point in life. Early in a relationship, this type of exaltation seems easier and more obvious to most, but over the years there are competing forces that interfere with these rudimentary, essential components of a loving relationship (see notes on 8:7, 12). The lovers of the Song challenge the people of God to praise their spouses in public and in private. This is an important step toward deeper intimacy.

In their relationship, there are no rivals. They look exclusively at one another as incomparable, as unique (1:9; 2:2–3). By analogy, Israel's praise was to rise exclusively to Yahweh; and while he is indeed Lord of all the earth, his covenant was reserved for Israel and for all who would call upon his name in faith (Exod. 24; Isa. 56:3–5; Hos. 2). Just as a man and a woman should be solely devoted to one another in marriage, so believers should be solely devoted to worshipping the one, true God. Such a devotion led Moses and all Israel to sing, "Who is like you among the gods, O Lord? Who is like you, glorious in holiness, greatly praised, performing wonders?" (Exod. 15:11).

## PREACHING AND TEACHING STRATEGIES

### Exegetical and Theological Synthesis
In the face of the woman's insecurity, the man reassures her of her beauty (1:9–10). Yet the woman also reassures the man by speaking of her exclusive devotion to him (1:12–14). The back-and-forth praise they give one another leads the woman to proclaim the goodness of their relationship (1:16–17). The opening of chapter 2 has the woman expressing insecurity again, believing she is no one special, just one flower among many (2:1). But the man knows better: she is his unique lover while all others are like thorn plants (2:2). The woman then extols the man (2:3–6). He is the fruitful tree among dead pines in the forest (2:3). He embodies the wealthy king who showers her with love and affection (2:4). He is the affectionate lover who drives her wild with love (2:5–6). Because of the power of words to cultivate desire, the woman warns her friends to "not awaken love until it pleases" (2:7). She knows the power of love and is ready for it (cf. 8:10), but for those who are not ready, arousing desires of romance before the appropriate time can bring terrible consequences.

The Song implicitly acknowledges that our words carry weight. Both characters in the Song must have known the power of their words. While the woman is depicted as a peasant farmer, burdened with work and scorched skin, to the man she is a queen. Even though the man is depicted as a lowly shepherd, working out in the fields with smelly sheep, he is regal in her eyes. They both use their words to create a new reality. Their speeches give credence to the idea that speaking the right kinds of things, like affirmations of beauty and love, build flourishing relationships (1:16–17). The lovers in the Song provide a paradigm for how believers can use their words. Yet these words of affirmation must be used appropriately and wisely so as to not arouse romantic desires outside of the proper timing and context.

### Preaching Idea
Use words wisely to build flourishing relationships.

### Contemporary Connections

#### What does it mean?
The Song of Songs might surprise modern readers with its praise of romantic desire. The

Scriptures are not prudish about sexual intimacy; however, because God created romance, sex, and marriage, he wants his people to experience the full depth of these good gifts. Enjoyment of these things is not always easy in a world now broken by sin. Insecurity often stands in the way. For example, even though the woman expresses some confidence in herself, she still feels insecure about her looks (1:5–6).

The man makes sure to affirm the woman by calling her the "most beautiful among women," as well as likening her to a queen (1:8–10). He provides the affirmation she is longing for. Clearly, the man and the woman have been putting in work to build their relationship into something impressive. The woman likens their relationship to a blossoming forest, filled with strong and stately trees (1:16–17). Such a relationship could not occur through cutting one another down with negative words. Instead, the man and the woman use their words to construct a beautiful relationship.

When the woman again feels insecure—like a nobody—the man interjects and builds her up by noting her uniqueness (2:1–2). In response, the woman builds up the man (2:3–6). Her man is utterly unique like an apple tree in the forest (2:3). He is fruitful and strong. He provides her rest and refreshment. He is also like a wealthy king, bringing her to a banqueting hall to enjoy a lush meal (2:4). He is affectionate to her, embracing her in love (2:5–6). I've heard it said before that men desire to want while women desire *to be* wanted. But men too want to feel desired by their wives. And the woman in the Song clearly expresses her desire toward him.

The woman knows, however, of the power of her words as well as the power of romantic desire. She exhorts the maidens around her to wait for the right time of love (2:7). Therefore, the example of the woman for us today is to use our words *wisely*. We should not indiscriminately use romantic language. Instead, we must wait for the proper time like being in a committed relationship. Yet even if we are not in a romantic relationship currently, we can still gain guidance from this couple by appreciating the power of words to contribute—positively or negatively–to a relationship or friendship.

*Is it true?*
Our words can either build up or tear down: "Death and life are in the power of the tongue" (Prov. 18:21). Our words can drive people toward either insecurity and doubt, or assurance and confidence. For example, the devil insidiously used his words to create doubt in Eve's mind concerning God's word: "Did God really say . . . ?" (Gen. 3:1 NLT). The doubt grew large enough in Eve's mind to move her to succumb to the devil's temptation and eat the forbidden fruit (Gen. 3:2–6). Words are powerful, especially when spoken to those we are closest to. Therefore, one way to use our words for good is to do our best to assuage the insecurities of those around us, especially if we are in a romantic relationship.

In the Song, the man praises the woman's beauty (1:9–10). His words would have surely had a positive impact, for what woman would not want to hear that her beloved thinks she is beautiful? The man's commitment to his woman's beautification reminds us of a husband's responsibility to minister the word of God to his wife (Eph. 5:26). Husbands should be committed to the outer and inner beautification of their wives. Church members can similarly use their words in a positive way by encouraging one another daily (Heb. 3:13). We can all point out and praise the good things that others within the body of Christ are doing.

The woman lets the man know how precious he is to her (1:13–14). The man is likened to a "pouch of myrrh" between her breasts (1:13). In other words, the man is close to her heart. He is her one and only love. He is also unique, rare, and exquisite, like finding a vineyard in an arid desert (1:14). The woman reminds the man of how much he means to her, and in doing so she provides an important lesson for us. It is so easy to take those closest to us for granted, whether a spouse, parent, child, or friend; yet, we can use our words to build up our relationships by letting them know how much they mean to us.

Because words are powerful, we must exercise wisdom when speaking: "Those who guard their mouths and their tongues keep themselves from calamity" (Prov. 21:23 NIV). Using romantic language with one's spouse can help a marriage flourish, as exemplified in the Song. Yet, using romantic language outside of marriage can lead to confusion and pain. Leading others on by flirting, using intimate or sexualized language with those not one's spouse, or making inappropriate comments can indicate an "unguarded" mouth and bring horrible consequences into one's life.

## Now what?

Husbands, how do you talk to your wives? Do you express how beautiful they are to you? Do you communicate with them clearly and directly? Do you tell them that you love them? Follow the lead of the man in the Song who praises his woman's beauty and uniqueness. Our words can cause our wives to feel insecure and doubt their place in the relationship, or they can provide assurance and confidence. Seeing how the man speaks to the woman in the Song challenges the notion that our wives always feel loved by us without being told. We must not assume they know they're loved solely by our actions. We must tell them.

Wives, how do you respond to your husband's words? Do you cringe and blush, telling him to "stop it," or do you receive the praise and compliments he gives you? Do you take comfort and solace, finding security in the relationship like someone could take cover under a tree in a storm? And do you affirm him, praising his physical attributes and character? Unfortunately, modern stereotypes often characterize men as not needing verbal affirmation. Yet, if Scripture commands us to encourage one another, how much more should wives encourage their husbands with their words?

Singles, how do you use your words among your family and friends? Do you encourage others and build them up, or do you tear others down? Do you point out what's right in the relationship, or do you typically point out the negative? Too often, Christians get caught up in pointless discussions about profanity, debating the merits of whether this or that word is profane. Such discussions miss the larger point about our words. Someone could *never* use profanity and yet still speak the most cutting, hurtful, and cruel words imaginable. Of course, some words are offensive and crude depending on the culture and should not be used. Yet the attitude and disposition of the heart matters significantly for how we are using our words (Luke 6:45). As believers in Jesus, we must use our words to build up our brothers and sisters in Christ.

### *Creativity in Presentation*

*Married at First Sight* is an American reality TV series that debuted in 2014. As the name implies, the participants in the show get legally married to someone they see for the first time at the altar. While there's an intense screening process at the beginning of the show by marriage experts to create a good match, there is still so much for the newly married couples to learn about one another. In season 9, two well-matched participants, Greg and Deonna, struggle communicating with each other. Deonna complains about how many compliments she receives from Greg. She was just not used to receiving so much verbal affirmation! While Deonna's reluctance to accept compliments may have been unique to her personality, I suspect her experience is probably much more universal than many people may care to admit. Many people can struggle to take compliments because they have never been in a household or relationship where verbal affirmation was commonly spoken.

In February 2020, the Christian satire website *The Babylon Bee* ran a humorous article for Valentine's Day, imagining how "sweetheart" candies would read if they had quotes from Song of Songs. Some of the candies might say:

- Hey, tower neck!
- Ur breasts = fawns
- Ur teeth are sheep
- You have goat hair
- Ur legs = marble pillars
- Pardon me but your goblet is showing
- Ur tower nose is hawt

While we may laugh at some of the language that the Song of Songs uses, the challenge for married couples is to praise our beloved as much as the Song does. We should strive to hand out as many "sweethearts" as we can. Are we giving short and sweet affirmations to our spouse regularly? For those who are not married, are we encouraging those around us regularly? Encouragement should not be in short supply within the church.

The big idea for a sermon could be, "Use Words Wisely to Build Flourishing Relationships." The following outline might be helpful to preach through the passage:

- Express affection with joyful words (1:9–17)
- Nurture love with positive words (2:1–6)
- Recognize the power of invitational words (2:7)

## DISCUSSION QUESTIONS

1. How does the man pacify the woman's insecurities (1:9–11; 2:1–2)?

2. What qualities does the woman praise about the man (1:12–17; 2:3–6)?

3. Why does the woman warn her friends about the power of love (2:7)?

4. Why is it difficult to graciously receive compliments sometimes?

5. How can you become a better affirmer or encourager, in your marriage or other relationships?

# Song of Songs 2:8–17

## EXEGETICAL IDEA
The man and the woman eagerly anticipate one another as they seek to remove every obstacle to their love.

## THEOLOGICAL FOCUS
Healthy romance involves both longing for the other person as well as a willingness to address known obstacles that could hinder the relationship.

## PREACHING IDEA
Overcome alienation through intentional effort.

## PREACHING POINTERS
The lovers encountered many different obstacles during their relationship. At times, the relational alienation between them seemed like they were separated by a vast mountain range. Even when in close physical proximity, the lovers sometimes felt as if there was a wall between them. In other moments, they were vexed by smaller problems. While these smaller issues might have seemed insignificant, if left unattended, they could have wreaked havoc on the harmony of the relationship, just as foxes can destroy an unattended vineyard. They had to put forth intentional effort to overcome the relational isolation and separation they felt.

The existential alienation people feel is rooted in their estrangement from God through sin. Even the best relationship has times when each person feels estranged from the other. Human beings can feel isolated and lonely even when sitting in a crowded room. Therefore, we should not be surprised when we experience relational distance from friends, relatives, and even our own spouses. The reality of relational separation should lead us to take action to overcome the distance and be close to those we care about.

# THE LOVERS ANTICIPATE ONE ANOTHER (2:8–17)

## LITERARY STRUCTURE AND THEMES (2:8–17)

How this section is divided depends on whether interpreters choose to treat the entire speech event as one unit (since even the man's speech is actually a quotation from the woman) or force a break at the man's words in 2:10b–14. Garrett (1993), for example, breaks up the unit based on separate speakers, but some prefer a more simplistic approach to this particular poem since (1) the man is merely quoted here, and (2) there is an apparent *inclusio* in 2:8 and 17 where the man is portrayed as a gazelle leaping over the hills to reach his darling (see Longman 2001; Murphy 1990b). For preaching purposes, it is possible to discern within the longer poem of 2:8–17 three distinct movements that drive the story forward. The first (2:8–9) describes the man's efforts to reach the woman; the second (2:10–14) is the man's recorded speech to the woman, a contained poem (2:10–13) with an additional plea at the end (2:14); the third (2:15–17) shows the woman responding to the man agreeably, beckoning him to approach her.

- **The Woman Witnesses the Man's Efforts (2:8–9)**
- **The Man Actively Anticipates the Woman (2:10–14)**
- **The Woman Actively Anticipates the Man (2:15–17)**

The adverb "actively" is used to acknowledge that while the couple is looking forward to the chance to meet and embrace, they are doing so wisely by anticipating obstacles and taking the appropriate measures to remove them. By the end of the poem, little is left standing in the way of their marital union.

## EXPOSITION (2:8–17)

The Song presents romantic love in the most true-to-life way, by engaging with the language of desire while acknowledging the threats of separation. Despite all the emphatic longing encountered in these lines, the couple is still either experiencing alienation or anticipating threats to their relationship. Romantic love is presented here as a glorious pursuit worthy of all the passion the human heart can muster, but it is also rife with potential difficulties and occasions for separation. This theme of separation is recurrent throughout the Song. In the first chapter the woman could not find the man but was driven forward by her desire. Here in chapter 2 the man waits behind a "wall" (2:9), perhaps representing the social barrier of the woman's status of belonging to her parents (3:4), a status that could be changed through marriage. Nevertheless, the couple acknowledges that the time is right for love as "the rain has passed and gone" and "the time of pruning and singing has arrived" (2:12). The winter weather is no longer a hindrance; instead, it now invites the couple to proceed in lovemaking. Nevertheless, there is still a threat of "foxes" that could ruin the lovers' vineyard.

### The Woman Witnesses the Man's Efforts (2:8–9)

The woman surges with excitement as she notices her beloved gazing at her longingly.

**2:8.** The physical senses of sight, smell, hearing, taste, and touch are recurring features of the Song. The section begins in 2:8 with the woman hearing the sound of her lover rushing to her from afar. Her interjection is "Here he comes!"—the generally terse nature of these short lines speaks to the sense of urgency she feels. The scene feels like it is unfolding right now as the reader encounters it in the text, for the author has created "an illusion of immediacy" to thrust readers into the lovers' anxious state (Exum 2005, 3–6). The woman witnesses how no distance nor obstacle (here, mountains) can hold him back. He has "superhuman power" (Keel 1994, 96) generated by his love for her. What would normally be a setback for the two (distance, mountains) has been completely obliterated by the man's passion, which gives him both speed and agility (see sidebar "Strong Legs, Firm Feet, and Virility" p. 256). The comparison to a gazelle in the following verse is an appropriate metaphor to describe the man's actions here in 2:8.

### Strong Legs, Firm Feet, and Virility

ANE authors connect the idea of strong, stable legs and feet to concepts of heroic abilities in the arenas of warfare and love. A hero's ability to climb mountains and leap is occasioned by the presence of an enemy, some divine purpose assigned to them, or the promise of romantic love. Here in the Song, the woman refers to her beloved as a gazelle or young stag (2:9, 17; 6:2–3; 8:14), animals known for their ability to climb impossibly steep cliffs and remain sure-footed. In Hebrew, Akkadian, and Egyptian texts, firmly planted feet represent strength, stability, and/or righteousness (Deut. 32:35; Neh. 9:21; Job 12:5; Pss. 17:5; 18:33, 36 [HB 34, 37]; 26:12; 31:8 [HB 9]; 38:16 [HB 17]; 56:13 [HB 14]; 66:9; 73:2; 91:12; 94:18; 116:8; 119:105; 121:3; 140:5 [HB 5]; Prov. 3:23; 4:26; Jer. 13:16; for examples from Egypt and Mesopotamia, see Jones 2019, 43–45). Other connotations related to feet have to do with the path one takes in life (1 Sam. 2:9; 2 Kings 21:8; 2 Chron. 33:8; Job 18:8; Pss. 9:15 [HB 16]; 25:15; Prov. 1:15–16; 5:5; 6:18; 7:11; 19:2; Isa. 59:7; Jer. 14:10; Ezek. 32:13).

The woman of the Song further describes the man's legs as solid and strong, like "pillars" of alabaster stone (5:15). In Assyrian military campaigns, a king may describe his versatility in the roughest terrain. Sennacherib brags, "Like a wild ox I journeyed before them— moats, gorges, gullies, and difficult high

Naram-Sin featured on a high plateau or mountain ridge, towering over his enemies. Public domain (see *ANEP* §309; see also the sculpted calf muscles of men featured on the Black Obelisk of Shalmaneser III in *ANEP* §351–55).

mountains I surmounted on my throne. Where for my throne it was difficult, I would jump out on foot like a mountain goat" (my trans.; for text, see Grayson and Novotny 2012, 178). In Psalm 18:29 (HB 30), God empowers the king with the ability to leap over a wall (וּבֵאלֹהַי אֲדַלֶּג־שׁוּר). M. Fox cites an Egyptian text wherein the female states, "If only you would come to (your) sister swiftly, like a gazelle bounding over the desert" (1985, 66). In the late Egyptian tale of the Doomed Prince, a young prince escapes his imprisoned childhood to face a number of fates. He learns of a challenge issued by the prince of Nahrin that whoever is able to leap up into the window of his daughter's bedroom (seventy cubits high) will win her as his wife. The traveling prince successfully reached the window, at which point the princess "kissed him, she embraced him on all his body" (Lichtheim 1973b, 201). In sum, the man of the Song possesses a supernatural strength fueled by his love for the woman.

**2:9.** Sound gives way to sight. Here the man is compared to a gazelle, last mentioned as the object by which the maidens must swear in 2:7 (also later in 3:5). The comparison of the man to a gazelle comes up again in 2:17 at the end of this section (as an *inclusio*) and again in 8:14 at the close of the Song. The hurried language continues from 2:8: "Look! He's standing there!" She sees him through an opening in the wall, through the lattice, as if hiding or somehow restrained. The contrast between his urgency in 2:8 and the halted nature of his final approach in 2:9 points to his awareness of the delicacy of the moment, and reaches back to 1:8 where the man does not give her perfect directions on how to find him but instead places her in a setting where she stands out as exceptionally beautiful against the backdrop of others.

Interpreters may find it sufficient to say that "These descriptions of separation are the romantic motif of cat-and-mouse," going no further into why the man is stopping short of embracing the woman. And while that is true, the Song assumes readers intuitively know what is going on here or will interpret the behavior of the couple. In other words, the man's action of stalling by the wall not only serves a motif but represents some kind of real cause for hesitation. What might that be? Could it be the foxes of 2:15? We know there are dangers in the city street (5:7). Could it be something more culturally embedded, like the separation occasioned by the woman's status as unmarried (if one understands chapters 3–4 to follow sequentially from this point)? She appears to be in her parents' home (considering that single, young women did not own homes). If so, his halted approach is not just to perpetuate the tease but recognizes a cultural boundary line. To seduce her before marriage would be inappropriate and have potentially humiliating consequences (Exod. 22:16–17). As with Jacob's pursuit of Rachel, there are expectations from the girl's father (or other relevant guardian), and there are customs to observe. The same phenomenon is featured in Ruth whose proposal is accepted only tentatively by Boaz, who first followed guidelines before joining her in marriage. Prior to that, Naomi's consent for her to pursue Boaz is important for Ruth, regardless of custom. We cannot be certain about such things in the Song, and we should not be dogmatic, but thinking through the couple's actions creates interesting possibilities to consider.

### The Man Actively Anticipates the Woman (2:10–14)

The man beckons the woman to join him in nature's celebration of springtime, which is marked by various expressions of fertility among the flora and fauna.

**2:10.** At the beginning of 2:10, the woman introduces the man's speech, and most of the speech is a contained poem (2:10b–13) since it begins and ends with the same lines: "Arise my darling, my beauty! And come!" The beauty of the poetic arrangement is seen in its alliteration, assonance, wordplay, and archaizing terminology, revealing it to be "crafted in a combination of learned choice of vocabulary, skillful exploitation of technical devices and neatly balanced structure" (Watson 1986, 368–71). The next verse (2:14) continues the theme of the man's speech, but itself may be the start of a new, brief poem (2:14–15); it is difficult to say with certainty. In any case, there is no subtlety nor mixed messaging in the man's address—he wants to take things further. The man's exhortation to the woman in 2:10b opens his discussion of the spring season, which concludes in 2:13 when he again proclaims, "Come!"

> **Urgency in the Song**
> The dialogue of the couple repeatedly creates a sense of urgency in the Song. That phenomenon is featured in the man's speech in chapter 2, quoted by the woman in 2:10b–14, one feature of which will serve as our focus here. In several verses throughout the Hebrew Bible the imperatives "arise" (קוּם) and "come" (לֵךְ) appear side by

side (asyndetically) to form the hendiadys "get going!" or "go immediately!" as in Jonah 1:2 (קוּם לֵךְ), though in a few examples, the conjunction (וְ) joins the verbs (e.g., 2 Kings 8:1; Mic. 2:10). Two of the fourteen occurrences may appear here in the Song (2:10, 13), but that would require emendation of the MT since, instead of placing the imperatives side by side, the MT of 2:10 follows the first imperative "rise" (קוּמִי) with the reflexive prepositional phrase "for yourself" (לָךְ; Arnold and Choi §4.1.10m). Several manuscripts read this (לָךְ) as a scribal typo for the imperative (לֵךְ) or (לְכִי), which would retain the hendiadys. The same issue appears in 2:13 where the lines are repeated. The tight ABBA structure of the line appears as follows: A "arise" B "my darling" B "my beauty" A "come," and though the imperatives are clearly meant to parallel one another semantically, the otherwise attested close relationship of these verbs suggests the force of the hendiadys be retained, which only amplifies the hurried nature of his invocation. Hence, we could still paraphrase the MT without emendation, "My darling, my beauty, come immediately!"

**2:11.** Anticipating objections she or anyone may have to his overture in 2:10b, the man begins his nature-based apologetic by making the point that spring is the season for love! The winter has passed (Israel's rainy season), so the rain is also gone. Not only have the darker, heavier clouds moved from the sky, but they have nourished and prepared the way for new plant and animal life. Israel's greenery is fed by a combination of natural springs, winter rains, and the waters descending from Mt. Hermon in Syria down to the Hula Valley basin and into the Chinnereth (Sea of Galilee), exiting southward to form the Jordan River. The Banias Springs and Tel Dan in northern Israel look like a jungle, even in the summer, especially when contrasted with the Dead Sea region to the far south and into the Negev. The Galilee is also verdantly lush, especially after the rainy season, and the hill country where Jerusalem is situated receives ample rain cover. Though the summers are very hot and dry, in the rainy season the desert wadis (valleys/ravines) can overflow and turn the regions near Masada and Qumran into a spectacle of rushing floods and miniature waterfalls bursting through the dry rock, looking for a place to escape. What is left over in April/May is a light coating of green on what is normally a sea of dry limestone hills and plateaus. The blooming of flowers in all the northern territories is a sight of beauty to behold. In the Song, the man's appreciation of this beauty is both amplifying his excitement to be with his darling and justifying his appeals that they come together soon.

**2:12.** Trees, vines, and flowers are blooming all over. The earth itself is in love and beckons love between humans. Here, God has ordained nature to preach its own sermon to humanity, something it is known to do: "The heavens declare the glory of God and the earth below proclaims his handiwork" (Ps. 19:1 [HB 2]). The title of the sermon is "Love!" The man uses these clear signs around him as proof that not only is there no rain or chill to impede their countryside romance, but the new season is also actively inviting the couple to join in the act of love, for "the time of pruning and singing has arrived." Birds are making their mating calls and going through the motions, doing what they must to attract a mate. The man sees a truth outside of himself, in nature, that cannot be denied, and it affirms what he feels internally.

The physical sense of hearing is brought up again here thanks to the turtledove. The absolute noun in the construct chain may be "pruning" (*HALOT* s.v. "זָמִיר II" 273) or "singing" (*HALOT* s.v. "זָמִיר I" 273), but both meanings may be intended (see note in NET). The mention of "blossoms" is followed by "pruning/singing," which is followed by the "voice of the turtledove," offering the possibility that the "pruning/singing" serves as a hinge between the first part of the verse and the second part. It may be, though, that this degree of subtlety is too inconspicuous for ancient readers to catch, forcing a choice of one reading over the other. Commentators have also noted that the time for pruning does not coincide perfectly with the end of the rainy season (see also Keel 1994); nevertheless, the dual interpretation offers an interesting possibility (see note on 3:10). Lastly, the repeated "o" sound of "voice" (קוֹל) and "dove" (תּוֹר) may be an example of onomatopoeia, simulating the sound of a dove cooing (Watson 1986, 369).

> **Physical Senses in the Song**
> The five physical senses are engaged throughout the Song. There is repeated mention of perfumes, spices, fragrant flowers, beautiful colors, visual splendor, pleasant sounds, singing, delightful tasting fruit, and the enticement of touch. It is difficult to read through more than two verses of the Song without encountering phenomena with which humans engage physically. While the body and senses play an important role in other biblical literature, none other compares to the Song. In chapter 2, the man makes a case for why the woman should come out from her house and participate with him in the rhythms of nature. He cites strong evidence with which she could easily relate, having experienced all of these through her own physical senses. He argues that the woman can see the bright colors of the season (2:11–12a), hear the turtledove (2:12b), and smell the fig trees and grapevines (2:13), implying the senses of both touch and taste. All of these beckon her to join him in the chorus of spring. So he repeats the invitation from 2:10b, "Arise! Come, my darling! My beauty! Come!"

**2:13–14.** The ode to spring concludes with further mention of plants that blossom and give forth a fragrance (the physical sense of smell; see 2:8–9 above for other senses; see also sidebar "Physical Senses in the Song" p. 259). The song of spring ends with 2:13, but the man offers one final plea to the woman based on his experience of her majesty since the beauty of her face is "delightful" and the elegance of her voice is "lovely."

Just as the man was hidden behind the wall of her house, so she is depicted here as a dove hiding in the crevices of a rock face, in "the hidden places of the cliff." The rock dove (*columba livia*) is said to hide in the cliffs of Edom (Keel 1994, 106, citing Jer. 49:16 and Obad. 1:3). Her hiding reflects her timidity (Gault 2019, 141). Still, we ask why she is timid. Are his overtures too intimidating? It would not seem so, given her already-expressed passion for him. Perhaps she is waiting until the appropriate time to leave her parents' home, not daring to awaken love "until it pleases" (see notes on 2:7, 3:5, and 8:4). He sped to her in 2:8–9a, but then halted in 2:9b, standing behind the wall. She remains temporarily inaccessible, like a dove tucked away in the pitted face of a cliff. Accordingly, he must draw her out so that she comes of her own volition from behind the wall of her parents' house to join him in the love chorus of nature.

### The Woman Actively Anticipates the Man (2:15–17)
The woman implores the man to remove both the dangers and distance that impede their love.

**2:15.** The man's speech appears to be over at 2:14, despite the quotation marks provided at the end of 2:15 by the ESV (see Exum 2005, 128–29). It is the woman's turn to respond. She speaks of a vineyard, the mention of which is part of a larger theme of the "garden of delight" spoken of throughout the Song (1:6; 2:15; 3:12–13, 16–5:1; 6:2, 11; 7:13 [HB 14]; 8:12–13), which has parallels in Egyptian and Mesopotamian love literature; but in the Song, may be a callback to the original garden where the first two lovers met in Genesis 2. Much has been written about the possibility of a connection between the Song's garden of delight and the purity of the garden of Eden. When consideration is given to the Song's subject (romantic, sexual love; marriage in 3:11), setting (the garden), and the Israelite/Jewish community in which it was composed and received as canonical, it is difficult to deny such connections or God's original directives about romantic relationships (Gen. 2:24). The Song also lacks any sense of prudish shame about the lovers' bodies, which reflects the sense of Genesis 2:25: "The two of them were naked, the man and his wife, but they were not ashamed."

The masculine plural imperative "Catch!" (אֶחֱזוּ) has led to some confusion since the woman is speaking to the man, who is singular. It is possible that she is, as Murphy (1990b, 141) and others have suggested, responding in a coy way by reciting a song that itself has the plural form. She wishes to address another potential obstacle to their love. Foxes (sometimes translated "jackals") were despised pests that were known to destroy crops (cf. Judg. 15:5; Lam. 5:18; Ezek. 13:4). There's been considerable discussion, based on Egyptian parallels, that these foxes represent other young men who may pursue her sexually or even attempt to assault her, though Longman acknowledges a lack of satisfactory evidence for this view and prefers to view the foxes as any and all obstacles (2001, 124–25; cf. M. Fox 1985, 11). However, the Egyptian parallel is compelling, since as Keel points out, in such texts "the 'fox' or especially 'young fox' is a metaphor for the great lover or womanizer" (1994, 110). If the foxes do represent potential lovers who could upset the couple's vineyard, then the woman is making the man aware that such obstacles—like the mountains, the winter, and the wall of her parents' house—must be resolved for their love to fully manifest itself. The active anticipation of the woman is a coupling of her excitement for the man's arrival with a recognition of a potential problem.

**2:16**. The woman expresses resolve in the face of obstacles when she recites the elegant expression "My beloved is mine and I am his" (דּוֹדִי לִי וַאֲנִי לוֹ) (cf. 6:3; 7:11 [HB 12]). The long o-vowel of *dôdî* "beloved" is followed by three long i-vowels (making the sound "eee") and concludes with the long o-vowel to create *dôdî lî waʾănî lô*. Like Adam's exclamation in Genesis 2:23 ("bone of my bone and flesh of my flesh"), this exclamation from the woman "expresses the feeling of deepest and most intimate connectedness" (Keel 1994, 114). There are in fact many threats to their love, as the remainder of the Song will show, but if the lovers can face these obstacles with the confidence expressed by the woman here in 2:16, they will succeed. The maidens of Jerusalem desire the man too (1:3–4), and the woman's beauty attracts the "foxes," but the lovers know that they belong to each other. After all, no scurrying, den-dwelling pest could ever compare to a majestic gazelle that gracefully "grazes among the lilies." Some suggest that the man's grazing activity is an indication of eroticism (cf. 6:3; Case 2017, 171–86), but scholars vary. Our approach in this regard is to interpret metaphors in the simplest way (here, that the man is a gazelle) unless eroticism is clear, in which case one could posit a second level (grazing gazelle = erotic activity; see sidebar "Sexual Metaphors and Innuendo" p. 312).

**2:17**. The woman concludes by stating explicitly what was implied in 2:16: her beloved is a gazelle. So she exhorts him to continue his undaunted pursuit of her "until the day breathes and the shadows flee," most likely a reference to sunrise. His pursuit is to be relentless now in the day and through the night until the new day breaks. The new day may be the symbol of their marital consummation as well as their life spent together. He is to be like a "gazelle or a young stag in the crevice of the mountains." The term "crevice" (בֶּתֶר) has been variously interpreted as a real place (Bether) or as the woman's breasts, in which case it would refer to a mountain ravine (cleavage) between two peaks (*HALOT* s.v. "בֶּתֶר II" 167). She had stated previously in 1:13 that her beloved is a pouch of myrrh between her breasts, and in 4:5–6 he describes her breasts as "the mountain of myrrh" and "the hill of frankincense." This is echoed in 8:14 where the man is beckoned to hurry over like a gazelle to the "mountains of spices" (1:3; 4:14–5:5). The association of her breasts with mountains may imply that the man considered her bosom to be large, which, based on the discovery of hundreds of large-breasted Judahite pillar figurines as well as literary descriptions of large breasts in Mesopotamian literature, suggests that this was a preferred physical feature for women in Iron Age Israel (Ben-Shlomo and McCormick 2021; Gault 2019, 105–10; see note on 7:7 [HB 8]). So, is the image of man at the end of 2:17 one of heroism and virility (as in 2:8–9)? Or is it a picture of him engaging with her sexually? As with many such conundrums in the Song, the answer is "Yes" (even if one argues that the intimacy is merely imagined at this point rather than actualized).

## THEOLOGICAL FOCUS

The motif of separation starts gaining traction in 2:8–17, and the circumstances will grow with intensity in the following chapters. The lovers find themselves between two worlds: one of intense desire and one of constant obstacles. Ancient love stories are well aware of this true-to-life dichotomy, so they employ it regularly in storytelling (see Jacob's pursuit of Rachel being interrupted by Laban's guile in Gen. 29). The lovers in the Song reveal no shortage of passion for one another as they eagerly anticipate the time when they can be together in the fullest sense, but they are likewise painfully aware that there are hindrances to such a union, hindrances they must address. The man's heroic efforts as a gazelle bounding over hills is noticed by her, and she prefers to envision him in this way (2:17). There is no hint that the obstacles are so great the lovers will not attempt to supplant them; even so, they pursue one another with an awareness that there are greater forces at play that will not relent until the proper time.

Healthy romance involves both longings for the other person and a willingness to address known obstacles that could hinder the relationship. For ancient Israelites living within the covenant framework of Yahweh, sex cannot be pursued legitimately through passion alone; wisdom must intervene to guide a couple in their choices. By itself, the wall of the woman's home (2:9) may seem like nothing more than a wall, but when taken together with the mention of her mother in 3:5 the wall may symbolize her status as a virginal daughter of Jerusalem in the protective care of her parents. They may recognize that the season is right, that nature beckons them, and that mountains cannot hold them back, but there is work to do. There are foxes, which, even if they do not represent other potential suitors, at least represent further obstacles. Marriage will break down the wall that divides them and render all threats neutral. While the ANE legal traditions allow for various forms of illicit sexual activity, and ANE love poetry and mythology promote promiscuity in pornographic language that surpasses the erotica of the Song (see Introduction), the biblical legal tradition and the Song of Songs offer a better path—one that glorifies God and honors those made in his image.

For Christians, those who likewise seek to honor God within the new covenant framework of the gospel, there is a call emerging from the poetry of the Song to eagerly anticipate one's beloved with a willingness to both recognize and address obstacles that threaten the relationship.

## PREACHING AND TEACHING STRATEGIES

### Exegetical and Theological Synthesis

As the passage opens, the man and woman find themselves separated. A mountain range stands in their way! The man bounds over them like a supernatural gazelle to reach his beloved (2:8). He finally reaches his lover yet still finds himself separated from her (2:9). The man attempts to woo his beloved to come out from her house, the place of separation. The two of them should be together because the time is ripe for love (2:10–13). The man desires the woman to leave behind her cares and concerns and to come and join him on the journey of love (2:14).

The woman responds to the man's effort by calling for further action on his part. The woman wants the man to pay attention to the relationship, possibly pushing away any rival suitors (2:15). Yet one person was not responsible for all the work to maintain the relationship. Through their mutual efforts, the man and the woman were able to achieve harmony and unity in their relationship (2:16–17). Although experiencing alienation from one another, the couple is able to overcome their relational separation through intentional effort.

### Preaching Idea
Overcome alienation through intentional effort.

### Contemporary Connections

*What does it mean?*
When Adam and Eve sinned in the garden, relational estrangement entered the world. They were not only separated from God, being banished from the garden, but their own relationship was frayed as well (Gen. 3:16, 24). Song 2:8–17 demonstrates the persistent reality of relational estrangement, even among those who deeply love each other. Yet the lovers are not content to allow such distance to stand between them. When the man faces the seemingly impossible odds of connecting to his beloved (symbolized by the mountains), he climbs and runs over them (2:8). Even after putting forth strenuous effort to draw near to his beloved, the man still finds himself estranged from her when he reaches his destination. His beloved is in her house, sequestered away from him (2:9). Sometimes, after trying to build closeness, couples will still feel like a wall is between them. In this instance, the man uses his words to coax his lover from timidiy into relational intimacy (2:10–13). He points out that winter is gone and the time for joyful love has come, symbolized by the springtime imagery.

Nonetheless, the woman is still hiding in the cleft of the rock. And seeing her there, the man requests her to climb down. Presumably, the woman acquiesces to the man's request given her statement of relational unity with the man (2:16–17). Before she comes down, the woman calls the man to further responsibility, asking him to be proactive in getting rid of nuisances in the relationship (2:15). Both put forth significant effort to achieve relational closeness.

The Song indicates that relationships are not meant to be 50/50 as if they are a contract with each person performing a predefined set of responsibilities. Healthy relationships are to be 100/100 with each person fully giving of themselves to the other. The use of intentional effort to overcome alienation not only applies to married couples but to all Christians since the Bible likens the relationship the church has with Christ to a marriage (Eph. 5:22–33). Unfortunately, indwelling sin causes continued estrangement between the believer and Christ (Rom. 7:14–25; 1 John 1:8–10). While salvation is completely a gift of God's grace received through faith, the growth (sanctification) process of the believer requires Spirit-driven effort (Rom. 8:1–4; Phil. 2:12). Believers must lay hold of the ordinary means of grace, such as hearing the word preached and partaking in the sacraments, to stay close in their communion with Christ.

*Is it true?*
Author and psychotherapist Bruce Tift has joked that he no longer experiences problems in his marriage because he *expects* problems in his marriage. There is wisdom in such an attitude that should not be ignored. The human condition is one in which we all desperately need relationships, yet they are often out of reach for us. Even worse, when we enter a relationship (whether a friendship or a romantic relationship), we may find ourselves still separated from the other person. One of the reasons why we struggle so much in relationships

is because, unlike Tift, we do not anticipate and expect problems. Expecting a problem-free life should be foreign to the Christian, for sin still afflicts believers (Rom. 7:14–25; Gal. 5:16–26). It is important to look on the bright side of such a sad truth, however. Knowing that separation continues in all relationships (even friendships) reminds us to continually embrace the process of getting to know others. If we knew everything about someone right away, there would be no mystery, no passion, no pursuit, and no effort needed to get to know them. It is often in the struggle that we learn best. It is often in conflict, disagreement, and argument that we come to a deeper level of knowing someone. Of course, these challenges produce good fruit in us and our relationships only if we are willing to put forth the effort to overcome the gap between ourselves and the other person. Otherwise, the gap will remain, and we will be left standing isolated and lonely on the other side of a relational mountain.

Growing wise in relationships means embracing the fact that problems will arise in relationships, yet we must always be hopeful that these problems can be overcome. Both naivete and cynicism can cripple even the healthiest relationship. Being naive and expecting that conflicts will never happen can lead you to pull back and isolate yourself when they inevitably do arise. You may even be tempted to give up on the relationship, thinking, "It's not supposed to be like this!" On the other hand, accepting the inevitability of problems and believing they are impossible to solve can destroy relationships too. Having no hope of a turnaround leads to despair. And despair rarely contributes to the healing of a relationship. Hope and realism must reign for relationships to flourish.

## Now what?

What intentional efforts do you need to make to get close with your beloved? Consider the number of repeated actions of love the man takes to reach the woman on his mountain journey. Certainly the journey would require great persistence and endurance. It would also involve taking one step at a time, day after day. While making large gestures of love for someone can be appropriate, healthy relationships are often built by repeating loving actions consistently. If the man is willing to traverse snow-capped mountains for his beloved, certainly putting the toilet seat down or refusing to call out your spouse when they do something not to your liking for the millionth time is warranted.

Notice the wise, wooing word the man uses. After his mountain journey, the man winds up in the place of his lover, only to find a wall still between them. When faced with continuing separation from his beloved, the man uses his words to beckon her to come down to him. The man is not manipulating the woman but seeking genuine connection. He provides compelling reasons for why they should be together. It is the right time for love. They have done everything the right way, God's way, and now is the time to enjoy their relationship. What wise, wooing words do you need to speak to your beloved? How can you encourage them to be vulnerable? Often, encouraging vulnerability in others first requires vulnerability in ourselves.

While the man puts forth significant effort to bound over mountains and use many wonderful words, all the responsibility does not rest on him. The woman responds to the man and climbs down to him. Embrace mutual accountability in your relationship. Relationships turn toxic when there are unspoken expectations and unkept responsibilities. It is not healthy for someone to give 110 percent in the relationship while the other person is only giving 50 percent. Relationships grow and flourish when each person takes on the responsibility to pursue the good of the other. Marriages, after all, are covenants, not contracts (Mal. 2:14).

The separation that continues to exist between human beings should signal to us the deeper separation from God that all of us experience. Because of our sin, each person is "separate from Christ" and "without God in the world" (Eph. 2:12). But, in Christ, those who were far away from God have now been brought near (Eph. 2:13). Jesus overcomes the alienation we have with God by dying for our sins. Now, we can be reconciled and brought into the closest possible relationship with our Creator. Although remnants of the estrangement still exist in believers' lives, they can be overcome through consistent confession and repentance so that they can grow closer and closer to the Lord (1 John 1:9).

### Creativity in Presentation

One of the best books on growing closer in relationships is Peter Scazzero's *Emotionally Healthy Relationships* (2017). In the book, Scazzero provides different skills that people can learn that enable them to love others well. One of the foundational skills presented in the book is called the Community Temperature Reading (CTR). The CTR is a tool that helps couples, friends, and church members have conversations with one another. To really get to know someone, you must be able to talk with them on a deeper level. The CTR is a helpful tool for facilitating deeper conversations.

Unfortunately, our culture provides us with many examples of persistent alienation and estrangement between married couples, especially in movies and media. They illustrate what happens when someone no longer seeks to overcome the separation in a relationship but instead desires to go their own way. Public figures have at times explained openly in interviews why they chose divorce, and sometimes the only reason given is unhappiness and falling out of love with their spouse. They may even clarify that their ex-spouse had not been unfaithful, neglectful, or abusive. Of course, people are not perfectly forthcoming in a public forum like that (not that they should be), and there's always more to the story than what's being told. However, if our reasons for divorce are truly so paper-thin, then such disunions do not glorify God (Matt. 19:6). They demonstrate why so much estrangement and alienation continue today between people: we pursue our own happiness at the expense of others. But real happiness is found in sacrificing our lives for the benefit of others. As Jesus says, "Whoever wishes to save his life will lose it; but whoever loses his life for my sake will find it" (Matt. 16:25). The intentional effort we must make to grow in intimacy with others requires real sacrifice.

The big idea for this passage is, "Overcome Alienation through Intentional Effort." We look to the couple as a paradigm for practices to conquer obstacles in our relationships. An outline might detail the various ways to overcome relational estrangement:

- Persevere in acts of love (2:8–9)
- Use wooing words (2:10–14)
- Deal with the nuisances in the relationship (2:15)
- Enjoy unity together (2:16–17)

## DISCUSSION QUESTIONS

1. What does the man do to overcome the separation between himself and his beloved (2:8–14)?

2. How does the woman respond to the man's words and actions (2:15)?

3. What "little foxes" do you need to watch out for in your relationships (2:15)?

4. Where do the actions of the man and the woman lead them (2:16–17)?

5. How can you grow closer to others in the body of Christ this week?

# THE ACTS OF LOVE (3:1–5:1)

In this central portion of the Song, the lovers graduate from the rhythms of courtship in the first two chapters to an intensified pursuit and eventual embrace in the two that follow. Their pursuit of one another (3:1–11) includes dramatic story points that show the woman searching fervently for the man, finding him in spite of danger, and bringing him to her mother's house (perhaps to finalize marriage arrangements). Immediately following, a royal wedding procession is described wherein the man is portrayed as glorious in appearance, approaching her from a distance. Then, to initiate the rhythms of embrace, the man sings an eloquent ode to the woman's beauty and irresistibility, a song that concludes with the mutual agreement from the couple and the chorus that now is the time to make love (4:1–16). The very next verse (5:1) may feature the first real (as in not daydreamed) instance of sexual intimacy in the Song.

This second major section, The Acts of Love (3:1–5:1), is broken into two preaching units: The Lovers Invite One Another (3:1–11), and The Lovers Embrace One Another (4:1–5:1).

# Song of Songs 3:1–11

**EXEGETICAL IDEA**
The lovers seek and find one another to make preparations for their wedding.

**THEOLOGICAL FOCUS**
God honors the honest pursuit of a mate at the right time, which at the very least includes being guided by the wisdom of his word and the witness of his word in creation.

**PREACHING IDEA**
Channel intense desire toward marriage.

**PREACHING POINTERS**
The Song has captured the intense desire of love through its poetic descriptions of a man and woman who have pursued one another in a romantic relationship. The intoxicating power of love has caused the woman to warn others against awakening love until the right time. She understood that the intense desire that moved her toward her beloved needed to be directed toward an appropriate end. The proper end of sexual desire in the Song, as in the rest of the Scriptures, is marriage.

Both the church and the world need to hear the message that marriage is the proper destination for the fulfillment of intense romantic longing, particularly sexual longing. While all manner of sexual activity outside of marriage is promulgated by the culture, the church can provide a picture of true human flourishing by pointing to God's design. The Bible teaches us that the safest and most liberating context for true sexual fulfillment is the covenant of marriage. Therefore, all people should channel their intense sexual desires toward the pursuit of marriage.

# THE LOVERS PURSUE ONE ANOTHER (3:1–11)

## LITERARY STRUCTURE AND THEMES (3:1–11)

The unit can be broken into two main sections, one describing the woman's search for her beloved and the other describing the man's preparation for the wedding. First, the woman tirelessly seeks her beloved and brings him to her mother's house (3:1–4). Then a break occurs in 3:5 where the woman once again adjures the maidens of Jerusalem as she had done in 2:7. Immediately following, in 3:6–11, the man is depicted as gloriously adorned and approaching the woman in what could be described as a royal wedding procession.

Scholars who see a connection between 3:1–5 and 3:6–11 (a unit I identify as loosely describing wedding preparation) typically affirm that there are story elements at play throughout the Song. Those who deny any connection between these units, however, adopt an interpretive approach that sees the Song of Songs as an anthology of nonsequential, unrelated poems that are united primarily through common themes. It is the detailed, sequential activities described in 3:1–11, however, that give the impression of a story arc.

- The Woman Pursues the Man for Marriage (3:1–5)
- The Man Prepares for the Wedding (3:6–11)

## EXPOSITION (3:1–11)

Here a familiar stress returns—the woman longs for the man but cannot find him. Now that stress has heightened, giving a more desperate sense than what the woman's search in chapter 1 indicated. Then, she was longing to be kissed by him, but now that longing has become more visceral and raw—she must have him! This drives her to do something radical. And while some commentators argue that 3:1–5 describes a dream (since it is unthinkable that a young woman would wander the city streets at night), it is precisely for this reason that the passage is filled with anxiety; she is actually doing it. Her desperate longing for her beloved compels her to do something dangerous. Love can drive someone to take bold actions. Ruth's nighttime adventure to the threshing floor of Boaz was risky, but she was driven by a purpose that was larger than herself, which was sufficient to motivate her actions.

It is possible that strict curfew expectations were not placed on women in ancient times, but only in early Judaism (Keel cites a number of HB passages where women are seen out in public encountering men [1994, 120]). However, those cited by Keel are not particularly dangerous encounters, and the general principle of needing to protect the virginal status of a young woman is evident throughout the HB (e.g., Deut. 22:28–29). Hence, the passage presents an anxious sequence of events, but one that ends successfully when she brings him to her mother's house (3:4). Since the passage is lacking the vivid sexual descriptions that come later in the Song, it may be that the mother's house represents an attempt to finalize plans for marriage with her family. It is in keeping with biblical and ANE traditions to arrange this kind of contractual agreement between a bridegroom and his father-in-law.

It comes as no surprise then, that the circumstance of the beloved going "to my mother's house" is immediately followed by a reminder of the Song's chief lesson in 3:5, that love not be awakened until it pleases. This is not to say that there are no sexual overtones since this house and "the chamber of her who conceived me" may be where the couple join sexually in 5:1; however, the mention of the woman's mother and her conception emphasize the theme of love's perpetual cycle through the generations (cf. 8:2 where these same sentimental and sexual overtones appear). Young women engaged in illicit sexual behavior were not quick to mention their mother positively in such contexts since their deviant activity would bring shame on their parents (consider how, in Sumerian texts, Inanna seeks to deceive her mother so that her parents do not discover that she is lying with Dumuzi while they are still unmarried; Pritchard 2011, 407; see note on 8:2). For this reason, and others stated in the Introduction and throughout the commentary, I do not view 3:4 as more than the woman's imagination.

The second unit (3:6–11) in this section flows naturally from the first (see the case made by Provan 2000, 151). It is an idealized portrayal of her beloved as King Solomon, arrayed in all the trappings of a royal wedding procession, approaching in majesty from the forest with his assembled host.

### The Woman Pursues the Man for Marriage (3:1–5)

The woman describes a stressful sequence wherein her restless longing for her beloved drives her to take dangerous measures.

**3:1.** The passage opens with the woman's nighttime longing in her bedroom. "Night after night" (בַּלֵּילוֹת) she seeks him. In only ten verses is "night" (לַיְלָה) plural in the Hebrew Bible, two of which appear in this chapter (3:1, 8). Psalms 92:2 [HB 3] and 134:1 also appear with the preposition בְּ as here in Song 3:1. We are left wondering how she could be seeking him night after night *while* lying on her bed. A simple explanation could be that she was looking/waiting/hoping for his arrival (see the semantic range of the verb in *HALOT* s.v. "בקשׁ" 152). She was looking for him to show up.

One can imagine the scene: A young woman is pacing nervously, mistaking every stray sound for a knock on the door. She is looking out the window to see if he is coming. She is asking her sisters if they have seen him. The man never comes. Finally, driven mad by waiting for his proposal, she goes out to find him herself. Some commentators consider 3:2–4 a dream the woman is having (e.g., Provan 2000, 151), which is certainly possible, but the arrangement of scenes stretching from 3:1–5:1 appear as a logical sequence of events that suggest forward movement in the story: (1) At 3:4 the couple arrives at her mother's house, (2) 3:6–11 portrays a royal wedding procession of sorts, (3) chapter 4 features the most elevated language of longing and eroticism so far in the Song, and (4) the beginning of chapter 5 shows the couple together in intimacy. Is all of this merely imagined by the woman and none of it real? It certainly seems real. We cannot be dogmatic, though, and merely offer the possibility that these things are all actually happening.

> **Lovesickness**
> The activity of lovers longing for and/or searching for one another is a recurrent theme in love poetry from Egypt and Mesopotamia. Strong desires often leave the lovers "sick" (Song 2:5) such that they need physicians, but the doctors prove unhelpful since the love of their beloved is the only cure (Egyptian: Papyrus Harris 500:A:6 in M. Fox 1985, 13; and, tragically, 2 Sam. 13:5–14). Lovers at times set out on journeys (sometimes treacherous) to find their beloved (Song 3:1–5; Sumerian: Descent of Ishtar in Matthews and Benjamin 2016, 367–70; Egyptian: P. Harris 500:A:4, 8 in M. Fox 1985, 11, 14). Solomon's personal bodyguards in Song 3:7–8 are prepared for "the dangers of the night" as his procession marches through the forest to reach his darling. Such longing results in lovers finding ways to overcome obstacles that separate them, like deceiving their parents about their whereabouts (see Pritchard 2011, 407).

**3:2.** She takes matters into her own hands, leaving the house to find him in the streets. Only desperation would drive a young woman of this time period away from the safety of her parents' house and into the streets at night (cf. Ruth 3). The horrifying images of the city square of Sodom come to mind, where it was not safe for anyone, man or woman, to be wandering around at night. The setting here may not be as fraught with danger as Sodom (Gen. 19), but common sense dictates that an unprotected young woman is unwise to put herself in such a position. Safety, however, is not her concern. She is smitten with love, and if the previous unit (2:8–17) is any indication (where several barriers to their love were dispensed with), there is little left to prevent them from taking the next steps.

One of the two nouns for "street" (שׁוּק) appears in only four verses in the HB, one notable occurrence being Proverbs 7:8 where the naive young man is walking along the street at night near the house of an immoral woman who beckons him to come in (the image of Judah willingly engaging a prostitute in Genesis 38, his own daughter-in-law Tamar, comes to mind). Of course, the young man of Proverbs 7 obliges the woman, but tragically, it costs him his life. Such imagery would likely come to mind for an ancient reader familiar with the broader corpus of Hebrew Scripture, but the contrast between the motivation of the immoral women and that of the woman of the Song (and Ruth who sneaks into Boaz's compound at night) is apparent and perhaps intentional irony. She is not searching for just any man, offering sex in exchange for temporary financial security; she is not seeking just any tree of the forest, but the unique "apple tree" that stands out in the crowd—her beloved (2:3). So, she is searching "all around repeatedly" (וַאֲסוֹבְבָה) for him, a *poel* verb that suggests an iterative or cyclical action.

**3:3.** She runs into the watchmen who are patrolling the city at night. They are said to be moving about "inside the city," not merely walking along the top of the city wall; in 5:7 she calls them "watchmen of the walls," but this might merely be an attempt to satisfy an *inclusio*—in other words, watchmen from every post could be in view. It is not clear whether the woman is in violation of some kind of curfew since later on in the Song the watchmen attack her (5:7), but here there is no mention of assault. As with most things in the Song, the presence of the watchmen is assumed rather than explained. Since there is no reason to view them metaphorically, they should be understood literally, as town guards one might encounter in a city street at night.

In Middle Assyrian laws there were specific guidelines for how women should present themselves in the city street (with or without a veil depending on their social class and sexual/marital status). Prostitutes were not to be veiled since they could be confused for a virginal, unmarried daughter of a man. If a veiled prostitute was found out, she was to be seized, defrocked, and physically punished in a severe way, including fifty blows (Roth 1997, 167–68, §40). Could there have been some comparable rule in Israelite towns that would have resulted in the guardsmen assuming evil of the woman in 5:7, which states, "They beat me, they bruised me, they took away my veil, those watchmen of the walls"? The woman is nowhere presented in the Song as an actual prostitute, though it is possible that the imagery of a prostitute in danger is being marshalled to convey the heightened sense of desperation felt by the woman as she searches (see note on 1:7 and consider a potential parallel in Ruth 3:1–7).

Here in 3:3, however, the sentinels do not seize her. Rather, she poses the question, "Have you seen the one whom my soul loves?" There is no response given, so presumably the answer is "no." In Judges 7:19, Gideon takes one hundred men to the edge of a Midianite camp at "the beginning of the middle watch," which was an opportune time since that was when there was a turnover in the "guards" (the same term as here in the Song: הַשֹּׁמְרִים). The woman, however, is not trying to avoid the guards; rather, she seems to consider it fortunate that she has run into them since they are the most likely to have seen her beloved. There is a noticeable pattern between 3:2 and 3:3. In 3:2 she begins by "patrolling" the city (סבב) but cannot "find" (מצא) her love, and in 3:3 the watchmen "find" (מצא) her since they were "patrolling" (סבב) the city.

**3:4.** She had "hardly passed from them" when she found her beloved, whereupon she "seized him and would not let him go." What the reader may have expected to happen to the woman in the previous line (that the guards would seize and detain her), she does to the man. She takes him to the house of her mother, to "the chamber of her who conceived me." For scholars who take earlier references to the couple's encounters as real sexual encounters rather than daydreams, the woman has not been a virgin for some time and 3:4 here is another reference to sex; however, a necessary distinction should be drawn between the passages occurring before 4:1–5:1 and after (4:1–16a is the man's sexually heightened speech to the woman which results in her consent [4:16b] and their intimacy in 5:1). Prior to chapter 4, the metaphors and expressions of longing are not as explicitly erotic in nature, nor terribly specific; but after chapter 4 the descriptions become unmistakably sexual. This shift warrants hesitation in identifying earlier passages as clear signs of intercourse.

In keeping with the interpretation that the Song features a loose storyline, one logical reason why the woman would bring the man to the house of her mother would be to somehow ratify the marriage with her parent(s). Aside from the overarching objection to this approach—that readers should not be looking for logical story-point explanations in the Song (though I would retort that these vignettes expect that from the reader)—objections to this approach could be: the father is not mentioned and it is he who would have to ratify the marriage arrangement; and the other occasion where a mother's house is mentioned is in 8:2–5, where sexual activity is clearly implied. There is good reason, though, for the father to be absent here (see sidebar "The Expertise of the Mother" p. 270). And the awakening of the man she effects in 8:5 takes things a bit further than what we see here in 3:4.

> **The Expertise of the Mother**
> It may seem odd that the woman's father is never mentioned, given all we know about marriage arrangements in the ANE. Is the father foreign, as in the book of Ruth? Is he no longer living? Perhaps the father is not mentioned in the Song because his presence could interrupt the romantic flow of the passage, impeding it with thoughts of legality. The importance of legality cannot be denied, but it can be ignored to an extent, especially if doing so serves the romantic tone of the Song. The lack of focus on the girl's father may also be a decision to view wisdom as feminine (cf. Prov. 1, 8), meaning that the woman's mother is taking the lead as the resident expert on romance, as the appropriate one to "teach" her child (8:2). Naomi tells her daughters-in-law to return to their mothers' houses (1:8), the preferred place for young women to receive the best wisdom regarding love. Egyptian love poetry also mentions the importance of the mother's house, and Mesopotamian love literature features Inanna consulting her mother (Exum 2005, 137). It is the mother, better than anyone else, who understands "the passion that now controls the daughter" (Keel 1994, 124).

**3:5.** For a second time (the first appearing in 2:7), the woman makes the daughters of Jerusalem swear that they will not awaken love "until it pleases" (see note on 2:7). The oath formula is identical in both places. In both passages, there were expressions of longing that concluded with the lovers finally meeting before the oath formula is given. Of course, in the first instance, the lovers embrace (2:6) just before the oath, but in this latest example, the couple is meeting at her parents' house. The woman's warning to the daughters of Jerusalem is that they follow the rules of love, which at the very least involves a sensitivity to wisdom as taught by nature but may also include shared cultural understandings regarding propriety and even legal considerations. That last bit (about legal concerns) may seem tonally inimical to the Song, and I would agree that it is not the first level of consideration, but it is hard to imagine an ancient Israelite context in which there was absolutely no concern for such things in the minds of maidens and their suitors. The oath will return for a final time in 8:4.

## The Man Prepares for the Wedding (3:6–11)

The man is portrayed as arriving from afar in a glorious procession that captures the attention of the woman.

**3:6**. If this passage follows sequentially from 3:1–5, where the couple is located at her parents' house (and I suggest it does), then one would think some kind of arrangement was made for the couple to wed. Typically, the bridegroom would bring a "bride price" as a gift to his father-in-law in exchange for the man's daughter in marriage (cf. Gen. 34:12; Exod. 22:16; 1 Sam. 18:25). See 1 Samuel 18:25, where King Saul required as a bride price that David slaughter one hundred Philistines, or Judges 1:12 where Caleb promises to give his daughter as a gift to any man who "attacks Kiriath-sepher and captures it." In the Song, what would be the man's bride price for the woman? The following section in 3:6–11, which appears to be a royal wedding procession, may be an indication of this very thing (the Amarna letters feature large financial gifts between kings as forms of international trade and alliance, often featuring the sending of royal daughters from one king to another; see sidebar "To Retrieve a Princess" p. 272).

On three occasions in the Song, the question is asked, "Who is this?," the precise expression (מִי זֹאת/זֶה) of "who" with the singular demonstrative appearing only fourteen times in the Hebrew Bible, three of which appear in the Song (3:6; 6:10; 8:5). A notable example from outside of the Song includes Isaiah 63:1 where Yahweh is depicted as marching up from Edom where he has trampled the wicked—"Who is this coming up from Edom in bright red garments from Bozrah? Who is this in glorious apparel, marching forth in the multitude of his strength?" This is is reminiscent of the description of the man here in Song 3. A militaristic royal procession coming up from Edom after a battle mirrors the ceremonial march portrayed in Song 3, though there is no indication that a battle has taken place; rather, this is a show of the man's prowess and may indicate the preparation for a wedding or even the presentation of a bride price. Another notable example appears in Psalm 24:8: "Who is this king of glory? The LORD who is strong and mighty! The LORD who is mighty in battle!" (ESV). Here again a military context is supplied. And finally, in Job 38:2 and 42:3, God responds to Job's lamentation with, "Who is this who darkens counsel with words without knowledge?" It seems clear from the examples shown here as well as others left unmentioned that this feature is a literary device intended to tantalize the reader with an important question that bears special significance for the passage in which it appears. In Song 3:6, that question precipitates the hymn to King Solomon's glory that follows. The song itself may have been sung at the occasion of a royal procession.

Murphy offers that the question "Who/what is this?" represents the cry of a watchman from the wall, demanding the identity of the one who approaches (Murphy 1990b, 149). If the woman's hometown is not Jerusalem (her eventual destination and the context in which she addresses the maidens throughout the Song), perhaps Solomon is portrayed here as approaching the walls of her town, which would occasion the question. The problem with the question, grammatically speaking, is that "this" (זֹאת) is feminine, which leads some to think it is a reference to the carriage-bed that is described below (in which case it would be, "What is this?"). If not that, then could "this" refer to the woman of the Song who is being retrieved by Solomon and brought to Jerusalem in royal fashion? (see note on 8:5 and a discussion of this issue in Dirksen 1989, 219–25). There is another possibility: Song 3:6–11 has parallels with Psalm 68 where God is portrayed as a warrior whose enemies can see his "processions" (הֲלִיכוֹתֶיךָ), a feminine noun, from afar—perhaps the "processions" are the referent for the demonstrative "this" (זֹאת).

Psalm 68 interestingly offers two possibilities for how we should understand "columns of smoke" (כְּתִימֲרוֹת עָשָׁן) in Song 3:6. The smoke could represent the fires of a battle just won (Ps. 68:2), or it could be a reference to the desert dust kicked up by Solomon's march in from the wilderness (Ps. 68:4, 7 [HB 5, 8]). The "rider of the clouds" (לָרֹכֵב בָּעֲרָבוֹת) reference in Psalm 68:4 (HB 5) could, beyond the mythopoetic reference to Yahweh's chariot, also serve as a metaphorical description of dust kicked up by the approach of his procession (in which case the MT עֲרָבָה "desert" would be followed rather than the assumed interchange of פ for ב forming "clouds," as in the Ugaritic description of Baal as *rkb ʿrpt* "rider of the clouds," though other passages in the HB clearly apply such imagery to Yahweh—Deut. 33:26; 2 Sam. 22:11; Pss. 18:10 [HB 11]; 68:4, 34 [HB 5, 35]; 104:3; Isa. 19:1; Hab. 3:8). Finally, the columns of clouds could represent the burning of the incense mentioned at the end of the verse.

Given the information immediately available in Song 3, it seems likely that the scene features Solomon approaching in a grand, royal procession, perhaps to retrieve the woman (an image alluded to later in 8:5) with the columns of smoke referring to the burning of fragrant incense. Annette Schellenberg argues that the description of Solomon in 3:6–11 is a later insertion meant to mock him, repudiating any notion that Solomon stands as a cipher for the male shepherd of the Song (2020, 177–92). The idea of ridicule, however, is either so indirect in the Hebrew text of 3:6–11 that it is nearly impossible to discern, or it is simply absent (for the interpretation that Solomon is a foil, see Provan 2001 and Introduction). Nevertheless, significantly differing views are symptomatic of the Song's ambiguity and should be approached humbly.

### To Retrieve a Princess

It is possible to understand Song 3:6–11 as a description of Solomon retrieving his soon-to-be bride from her home country to join him at the palace. Ramses II, for example, once sent a large procession of soldiers and dignitaries to escort a Hittite princess back to Egypt for their wedding. The relevant text recounts a treaty between Egypt and Hatti (which Egypt of course interpreted as a surrender on the part of Hatti) wherein a Hittite princess was sent from the distant north and brought down to join the harem of Pharaoh Ramses II in Egypt. The Hittite king "caused to be brought [his] eldest daughter, with noble tribute before her: gold, silver, many great ores, horses without limit to them, cattle, goats, and sheep by the ten-thousands, without limit to the products of their [land.]" When the royal procession from Hatti drew near to Egyptian territory, an Egyptian herald proclaimed to the pharaoh: "Behold, even the Great Prince of Hatti! His eldest daughter is being brought, carrying abundant tribute of everything. They cover the [valleys with] their [numbers], *the daughter* of the Prince of Hatti and the [*daughter of the*] Great Princess of Hatti *among* them. They have passed difficult mountains and wicked ravines. *Ramses II. They have reached the frontier of his majesty. Let (35) *our* [*army*] and the officials [*come*] to receive them" (*ANET*, 257). Is Song 3:6–11 a description of the man (imagined as Solomon) and his royal entourage approaching the woman to retrieve her for marriage? Or, is the man still at home while he sends a large procession to get her (as in the case of Ramses II mentioned above)?

**3:7.** "Look! The carriage-bed of Solomon!" The fact that his bed is surrounded by dozens of soldiers while he is "coming up" from the wilderness suggests that he is being transported, hence the interpretation of this passage as describing a procession. Exum notes how, from the perspective of the speaker, the traveling party appears closer and closer as the passage progresses (2003, 311). In 1 Kings 10, the queen of Sheba is described as arriving in a processional of "glorious splendor" with great quantities of camels, spices, gold, and gems. Here in the Song, sixty of Israel's mightiest warriors, Solomon's personal guard, accompany the carriage-bed as it approaches. Following David's swan song in 2 Samuel 23 is a listing of his "warriors" in 23:8, which total thirty in number, matching the number of soldiers sent by the Philistines to Samson's wedding (Judg. 14:11; note the interesting lines in 2 Sam. 17:1–3 where Ahithophel plots a raid on David's armed procession and the comparison of a bride returning home to her husband). In sum, the mention of sixty armed guards "means to imply a superlative force" (Keel 1994, 128).

**3:8.** The sixty men are not donning merely ceremonial costumes devoid of any real wartime relevance; rather, they are *bona fide* soldiers who are "trained in warfare," each of them amply equipped with a sword on his side prepared for the "dread of night." It is assumed, given the other descriptions of Solomon's procession in this passage, that the soldiers are serving both as presentational ornaments in the parade and as literal protection, if needed. At one point Solomon had made three hundred "shields of hammered gold" (1 Kings 10:17), so presentational attire is possible here. The modern equivalent for their appearance could be the various traditional or dress uniforms donned by soldiers around the world, such as appear at military graduation ceremonies or palace guard stations.

Psalm 91:5 is the only other occurrence of "the dread of night" which gives a very helpful listing of potential terrors from which God will protect his chosen one. The notion that the wedding party needs to be protected from demons is absent in both Psalm 91 and Song 3, though it is mentioned by some commentators in reference to Tobit 3:7–17 (Murphy 1990b, 152). There is a lack of spiritual terminology in the Song in general, though. Hence, the likely dangers of the night involve what anyone might expect: wild animals and bandits.

Medes and Persians (alternating) marching in procession for the New Year's festival while wearing traditional costumes, which include weaponry. Public domain (see *ANEP* §28).

**3:9.** The carriage-bed (אַפִּרְיוֹן) is rendered "palanquin" or "carriage" in several translations, and "sedan-chair" in the NET. The term is understood to be a Persian loanword and, as such, is used by some commentators as evidence that the Song was composed much later than traditionally thought (see Introduction). Keel mentions Egyptian use of such "litters" or carriage-beds as early as the third millennium B.C., being made of wood and covered in gold plating (1994, 130). Solomon's carriage-bed is made of the cedars of Lebanon, a type of wood used regularly in his building projects (1 Kings 7:2). In a military context, the king would ride a chariot, but here his chariot is symbolically represented by an ornate carriage-bed.

**3:10.** The most interesting material chosen for the construction of Solomon's carriage-bed is mentioned last—"love." This could actually be a reference to the Arabic term "leather," which in Hebrew would be spelled the same as "love" (אַהֲבָה), but just as זָמִיר ("pruning/singing") in 2:12 may have a dual meaning, perhaps the description of materials used in construction of the carriage-bed concludes with an element (leather/love) that serves as a transition to the mention of the maidens (see note on 2:12). The interior of the carriage-bed was constructed with leather/love "by the daughters of Jerusalem." Keel doubts the adverbial sense of "with love" or "lovingly" is necessary here and prefers to see this as a reference to love scenery either carved or painted on the interior of the carriage-bed (1994, 134; symbols of fertility in Semitic cultures included ibexes, nude female figures, fruits, etc.). Another interesting possibility is to understand "inlaid" (רצף) as "paved" in light of Akkadian *raṣāpu*, a verb used in numerous cuneiform texts to describe royal structures that were paved with impressive decorations (Tawil 2003, 267–70; see also Tawil 2009, 371 s.v. "רצף").

**3:11.** The final verse of the processional song is a beautiful piece of poetry, filled with the internal rhyming of alliteration and assonance. The first four words form a unit, the first two being verbs accented on their respective e-vowels (*segol-yod*) with a recurring *nun*, and the last two are accented on their respective o-vowels (*cholem*); the first and last words of the set contain the consonant *tsade*. At the *athnach*, stands "Solomon" (שְׁלֹמֹה), after which is the nominal form of "crown" (עֲטָרָה) accompanied by its verbal form (שֶׁעִטְּרָה) and followed by a dominance of o-vowel assonance for the remainder of the poem. The writing is as elegant as what it describes.

The injunction to the maidens of Jerusalem is, "Come look at Solomon!" They are instructed to gaze on the crown with which his mother crowned him on his wedding day. The king's mother held a significant role in his life, though her act of crowning Solomon on his wedding day may be more an expression "of poetic imagination than actual custom" (Longman 2001, 139). The term "wedding" (חֲתֻנָּה) helps contextualize the entire processional song. The term has a cognate noun in Akkadian *ḫatnūtu* for "marriage," and the verbal expression "makes marriage" is represented by *ḫatnūtam epēšu* (*CAD* Ḥ, s.v. "*ḫatnūtu*" 150). Hebrew renders this verbal expression with (לקח) and (אִשָּׁה) as in "to take a wife" (Gen. 24:3), or with the verbal form (חתן) "to marry" (Gen. 34:9). The *Comprehensive Aramaic Lexicon* lists the verb *ḥtn* in the D stem "to join in marriage." The point is that this term, though it appears only here in the Song, is attested in cognate Semitic languages and known to us thanks to the work of comparative philologists; hence, we can feel confident about its usage here. The broader context of the previous verses (3:1–5), where the woman is taking the man to her mother's house, also suggests more than just a desire for intimacy; it suggests a desire to move the relationship in an official direction. In the very next chapter, the man refers to the woman as "bride" (כַּלָּה) five times (4:8–12), concluding with 5:1 where he says it again and the two make love. It is more difficult exegetically to deny any notion of marriage in 3:4–5:1 than it is to affirm it since the reference to her mother's house and the terms "wedding" and "bride" point so evidently to marriage. The Song's poetry is often enigmatic, so it would be odd to see a more detailed, almost narratival description of marriage than what is provided in these verses.

The wedding is seen as occurring here at the end of the procession. Solomon's wedding day happens to be "the best day of his life" (וּבְיוֹם שִׂמְחַת לִבּוֹ more literally, "the day of the joy of his heart").

## THEOLOGICAL FOCUS

Psalm 45 contains features strikingly similar to Song 3. In verses 1–9 (HB 2–10) of Psalm 45, the bridegroom is described as a mighty king of glory and valor riding forth in military procession. Likewise, in verses 10–17 (HB 11–18) the bride is adorned with the most precious robes interwoven with gold as her attendants lead her in procession to the palace where she will join her king forever. In much shorter space, Psalm 45 effectively shows the transformation that takes place for the woman as she departs from her hometown and people to become a queen. Reading texts like Psalm 45 and Song 3 conjures up grandiose images of storybook proportions, but in poetic form.

This is because the Song of Songs is a love song that speaks to the wonder of human romance within the covenantal context of Yahwism. The regal imagery packed into the processional song is a testament to the glories God intends for marriage. This is not an objective prescription for how a couple should arrange their wedding day, with precious metals and the finest clothes and imported incense; rather, the poem is a statement regarding the value placed on marriage by ancient Israelites. In light of such examples, we could imagine a poor Israelite couple assuming the roles of Solomon and the Shulammite by arraying themselves in the finest attire their families can reasonably afford. Garrett discusses examples from early Jewish literature that suggest bridegrooms wore garlands and brides rode on palanquins (Garrett and House 2004, 181). Such customs further imbued a couple's wedding day with the degree of royal significance they imagined it to have. Such practices, like the Song of Songs itself, reflect a weighty spiritual understanding of the significance of marriage.

By analogy, it is not difficult to see how the Scriptures frequently refer to God as Israel's husband and the people as his bride. This analogy is carried forward in the New Testament with the identification of Christ as the bridegroom of the church (Eph. 5). The images of royal wedding procession in Psalm 45 and Song 3 bring to mind the celestial majesty awaiting those who are in Christ. Such glories cannot be fathomed against the backdrop of our current state (Rom. 8:18). Nevertheless, the woman's voice in Song 3 is one of future hope in her groom. Likewise, we are called by Christ to live not in despair, but in hope of our eternal union with him. Such hope is possible when we consider that God's love and provision for us is greater even than his care for the lilies: "even Solomon in all his glory was not arrayed like one of these" (Matt. 6:29).

In the book of Revelation, a multitude of heaven's hosts cry out, "'Hallelujah, because our Lord God, the Almighty, reigns! Let us be glad, rejoice, and give him glory, because the marriage of the Lamb has come, and his bride has prepared herself. She was given fine linen to wear, bright and pure.' For the fine linen represents the righteous acts of the saints" (Rev. 19:6b–8 CSB). It is important for believers to keep in mind that the serene majesty of the Song of Songs, with its odes to human love, is merely a glimpse of what lies ahead.

## PREACHING AND TEACHING STRATEGIES

### Exegetical and Theological Synthesis

The Song recounts how the man and the woman long for each another yet find themselves separated from one another (1:6–9; 2:8–14). It is no different in this passage. As the woman lies on her bed longing for the man, she is unable to find him (3:1). Her desire moves her to search for him, even putting herself in harm's way as symbolized by her nighttime trek through the city (3:2–3). Eventually, she finds the man and never wants to let him go again (3:3). But she cannot truly be inseparable from him because they are not yet married. She realizes the power that her intense desire has over her and so warns the daughters of Jerusalem not to unleash such a powerful force until the right time (3:5).

Immediately upon giving her warning, the scene shifts to her wedding (3:6–11). The man comes up from the wilderness, arrayed and guarded like King Solomon (3:8–9). He is crowned and ready for his bride (3:11). In places throughout the Song, the man and the woman seem quite ordinary. He is a shepherd; she is a worker in a vineyard. Yet, on their wedding day, they are king and queen. Their wedding day is "the best day of [their] life" (see comments on 3:11). It is important to note that the Song depicts that the joy of union is found primarily in marriage, not necessarily the act of sexual intercourse itself (Ortlund 2014, 500).

Celebration, pageantry, and joy are all the most appropriate attitudes and actions for a wedding. Marriage is celebrated and sanctioned by God himself as it was his creational design even before sin entered the world (Gen. 2:23–25). Because God created and blessed marriage, it is to be "held in honor among all" (Heb. 13:4). Marriage is especially important in the biblical storyline for it points beyond itself to a greater reality, the union of Christ and his church (Eph. 5:22–33). It is not surprising then that the second coming of Christ is described as the return of the groom in his royal processional for which we wait as his bride (1 Thess. 4:16–17; Rev. 19:7–8).

### Preaching Idea
Channel intense desire toward marriage.

### Contemporary Connections

*What does it mean?*
The Song is a jubilant celebration of human love, even sexual love. Love is a powerful force; it is even as "strong as death" (Song 8:6). Love moves us in profound and surprising ways. It makes a man, who was initially afraid of commitment, pledge his whole life to a woman. It gives a woman the courage to drop everything and move halfway across the country to follow the lead of the man.

Love, when not guided by God's word, can also move us in damaging and sinful directions. Unguided love can lead a young woman to give herself away to a man who should not have her. Unguided love can mess with a man's head so that he jumps into a marriage where he inflicts deep emotional wounds upon his wife because he is spiritually and emotionally immature. The intense desire of love makes us "lovesick" like the woman (2:6; 5:8). When we have not heard back from the one we love, we end up tossing and turning on our bed all night (3:1). Love drives us to risk everything. Therefore, the intense desire of love must be channeled toward the right time and the right context.

The Song clearly shows us the only context that can appropriately handle the torrent of romantic love: marriage (3:6–11). Within marriage, we see a celebration of the couple's love for each other. Finally, a man and a woman can be fully united. The Song makes a surprising admission, however. As erotic as the Song can be, it speaks of "joy" primarily in the context of marriage (3:11). The man derives his joy from being in a relationship with his wife, not necessarily through the act of intercourse itself. Of course, the Song will have much to say about the pleasure and beauty of sex in the coming poems. But we must not miss the point: relationships are far more than sex.

Under the influence of surging hormones and a desire for romance, Christian adolescents often ask the question, "How far is too far in a dating relationship?" In other words, they want to know how much physical affection they can give someone without falling into sin. But "How far is too far?" is the wrong question. Instead, the Song invites us to ask a better question: "When is the right time?" When is the right time to awaken the mysteries and passions of love? When is the right time to pledge your whole being to someone? The Song answers these questions with one simple word: marriage. Marriage is the God-ordained context for the fulfillment of intense desire and sexual longing. In marriage, sex is not shameful but joyous. In marriage, emotional connection is not stunted but finds safe parameters in which to operate.

## Is it true?

Philosopher Alasdair MacIntyre argues in his book *After Virtue* (1981) that one of the reasons why we have such trouble discussing moral issues in American society is that we do not have any notion of a common *telos* for human life. No one agrees on the proper purpose and end goal of human existence. A similar dynamic, I believe, is at work in our society's discussions of sexuality. As a culture, we largely have no idea what sex is *for*. Culturally, we do not know what the purpose of sex is. And so, our culture has built its current sexual ethic on the sole foundation of *consent*. If those involved in a sexual encounter consent to it—the argument goes—then it is morally acceptable. Having the morality of a sexual encounter rest solely on consent, however, is difficult, as evidenced by discussions of what counts as consent (vocal and explicit vs. implied).

Christians can certainly agree on the goodness of consent for sexual activity: no one should be coerced into sex, even a married spouse (1 Cor. 7:3–4). But the Scriptures provide a more robust foundation for building a sex ethic, and it is the foundation of another term: covenant. In the Bible, a covenant bonds people together as family. In the marriage covenant, two people, who were previously unrelated to one another, are now bound together in the deepest possible human relationship. Since the foundation of marriage is love and covenant, and *not* sex, the Bible encourages us to never get physically naked with someone we are not getting spiritually "naked" with (Keller 2013, 256). The Bible clears up the confusion about the purpose of sex: it is for marriage.

Marriage is the only appropriate context for sexual desire and expression. It is in the safety of a marriage where real consent can occur because the two partners are not just consenting to a one-time sexual encounter, but instead, consenting to give all of themselves away to the other person. Ironically, it is only in a Christian marriage in which the power dynamics of the world are inverted. In marriage, both the man and the woman hold authority over each other's bodies, diffusing any notion of a power differential between the couple (1 Cor. 7:3–4). Sexual intimacy outside of marriage, however, is a display of raw power. Without the safety of a whole-life commitment, the encounter merely becomes about one's own pleasure: "What can I get out of it?" Such a sentiment is just an exercise of power: How can I assert myself over the other person to get what I want? Christian marriage, on the other hand, is a complete giving of oneself.

## Now what?

Intense desire is a very common aspect of human life. While the Song certainly calls for a stewarding of desire, it does not condemn the man or the woman for having strong desires, even sexual ones. In fact, the Song recognizes that sexual longing exists in people even before they are married (1:2–2:17). God created sexual desire and it is, therefore, good. Sexual desires become twisted, however, due to our sinfulness. People need to know about the goodness of sexual desire, but that it must also be channeled toward God's appropriate end, marriage.

Yet the building up of the relationship does not end when the minister pronounces a man and a woman husband and wife. There must be continual cultivation of the marriage relationship. It is also important to know that marriage, not sexual intercourse, is what gives "Solomon" joy (Ortlund 2014, 500). While sexual intercourse is obviously a very important piece of marriage, it is only a piece. The marriage covenant encompasses so much more than sex. It is to be the context for holistic flourishing in every area: mentally, emotionally, spiritually, and yes, sexually. But it requires great effort and persistence to continue to build a God-glorifying marriage.

What about those who are single? What relevance does this text have for them? The text puts intense desire and sexual longing in proper perspective. While the Song celebrates the goodness of marriage and sex, both of those things are not the most important things in human existence. The storyline of Scripture indicates that human marriage instead points to a relationship that is far greater: the relationship between Jesus and the church (Eph. 5:22–33). While human marriage is important and deserves a lot of attention, Jesus himself relativizes its importance. "In the resurrection," Jesus explains, "[people] neither marry nor are given in marriage" (Matt. 22:30). Therefore, singles should not feel like second-class citizens in the church.

Pastors must be sensitive not to oversell marriage. It does not fill the human soul, and it is not the point of a person's life. No amount of sex, or companionship, can fill the place in the human soul that only God can fill. Singles can be encouraged to channel their intense desires toward loving the Lord with all their heart, soul, mind, and strength (Deut. 6:5; Matt. 22:37). Without the burden of marital responsibilities, singles can also be encouraged to be more devoted to service in the church (1 Cor. 7:32–35). Pastors would probably do well to remind singles, however, that if they are unable to control their desire, it is better to marry than to burn with passion (1 Cor. 7:8–9).

### *Creativity in Presentation*

Every Sunday morning is an opportunity to build a culture of marriage within the local congregation. What message does your church communicate about marriage? Consider your church website. What pictures of the staff are displayed? Are they corporate-like headshots or pictures of the pastor's family? Think about the broader implications of the kind of representations that adorn the church building. Do they present marriage as something good and right? Or are only the young and cool displayed? Another opportunity to build a culture of marriage is through how we speak about it outside of the pulpit. Do you make jokes about your spouse? Do you speak as if marriage is a drag? Do you make it seem like your wife is the real authority in the relationship and you are dictated by her whims? These things can subtly denigrate marriage.

Within the worship service, think about different ways to communicate the beauty and value of marriage. A great video clip to play for the congregation is "This Is About That" by an English church, King's Church Eastbourne. The video explains the significance and meaning of marriage, but also the deeper spiritual realities that it points to. Getting diverse voices to speak about marriage can be helpful for the congregation as well. Consider interviewing some married couples during the service or the message. Or host a panel discussion on marriage with your elders and their wives.

Sexual desire is like a blazing fire (cf. 8:6). When placed in the proper context, fire is enormously helpful and good. In a fireplace, it warms the house. In a fire pit, it roasts marshmallows. But unleashed in a bone-dry forest, it is destructive. Christians must therefore guide their sexual desires toward marriage and their love for God. If the big idea is "Channel intense desire toward marriage," then a potential outline for the text could be:

- Understand the power of desire (3:1–5)
- Pursue the context for desire (3:6–11)

# The Lovers Pursue One Another (3:1–11)

## DISCUSSION QUESTIONS

1. What drove the woman to seek the man in the city? What was she risking by doing so (3:1–4)?

2. What warning does the woman give to the daughters of Jerusalem (3:5)?

3. How is the man described on his wedding day (3:6–11)?

4. Describe a time in your life when an intense desire drove you in a good direction.

5. Describe a time in your life when an intense desire drove you in a bad direction.

6. Why is it important we submit all our desires to God's will and standards?

# Song of Songs 4:1–5:1

**EXEGETICAL IDEA**
The lovers embrace one another in marital intimacy.

**THEOLOGICAL FOCUS**
Sexual intimacy in marriage is a good gift from God that is designed for human pleasure and for God's glory.

**PREACHING IDEA**
Enjoy God's gift of marital intimacy.

**PREACHING POINTERS**
The man and the woman pledged themselves in marriage to one another. Then, on the verge of their wedding night, they continued to pursue each other with lovely words. The man repeatedly reminded his wife how beautiful she is. He worked his way down her body with dramatic metaphors to express his desire. He beckoned her to come down from her place of isolation and be joined to him in body and soul. His pure bride responded to him, making herself accessible so that they might enjoy all the fruits of intimacy together in unashamed joy.

Sexual intimacy is a very important aspect of a godly marriage. While many outside of the church may believe that God is against sex, the reality is that God created sex as a gift to be enjoyed within marriage. Only within a committed covenant marriage can a couple experience being naked but not ashamed. Married couples can enhance the intimacy of their sexual encounters by complimenting one another's beauty.

# THE LOVERS EMBRACE ONE ANOTHER (4:1–5:1)

## LITERARY STRUCTURE AND THEMES (4:1–5:1)

In this unit (4:1–5:1) the lovers embrace one another, but the encounter begins with two long speeches from the man, who expresses his utter fascination with her beauty and goodness—she is irresistible. Readers encounter three sections of a song that features increasing degrees of intimacy the further one reads. The first poem (4:1–7) already begins with a passionate description of the woman's body, using all manner of metaphor specific to the couple's own cultural experiences and references. This is followed by 4:8–16 where the couple invite one another to join in sexual intimacy, beginning with the man's description of her as intoxicating, after which the woman invites him to "his garden" (her body). Finally, in 5:1 the couple engage in sexual intimacy, an act described through the metaphor of a banquet. Murphy (1990b) follows the same divisions for the entire unit (4:1–5:1); and while others subdivide the first section similarly to how we have done here with 4:1–7 (Keel 1994, Longman 2001; though Garrett ends it at 4:6 [Garrett and House 2004]), they typically divide the remainder of the text into several smaller units based on perceived textual breaks and debates over who is speaking. The love song concludes with the chorus of maidens (the likely identity of the singers) inviting the couple to become "drunk with love."

- *The Man Woos the Woman by Praising Her Body (4:1–7)*
- *The Couple Invite One Another to Join in Sexual Intimacy (4:8–16)*
- *The Couple Embrace One Another in Sexual Intimacy (5:1)*

## EXPOSITION (4:1–5:1)

In the previous unit (3:1–11), the woman sought the man in desperation, her heart committed to seeing them wed. She found him in the streets and brought him to her parents' house (3:1–5), perhaps so that the man can speak with the woman's parents. Culturally, such a sequence makes good sense, but other interpreters view 3:4 as a sexual encounter and deny the proposal of a loose storyline. The refrains of 2:7, 3:5, and 8:4 serve as the woman's lesson about love. Following the refrain, the text then immediately flashes forward to a poetic vision of the man portrayed as Solomon, entering on a portable carriage-bed made of the most luxuriant materials, itself inlaid with "love." With him comes a grand procession of attendants and warriors, approaching the maiden's city and prompting the tower guards to shout, "Who is this?" (The other possibility is to see the woman approaching Jerusalem on the carriage-bed sent by Solomon to retrieve her; see sidebar "To Retrieve a Princess." p. 272) The text closes with references to the king's mother and the crown placed upon his head on the day of his wedding, "the most joyous day of his life" (3:11).

This has led the couple into the realm of intimacy, a process that begins not immediately with sex, but with the man wooing his "bride" by praising her physical attributes (4:8, 9, 10, 11, 12; 5:1). Prior to this passage, the man has not called her his bride, which leads to the likely conclusion that an official union has occurred in the poetic lines of 3:6–4:16. Moving from the top of her head down to her breasts (anatomical descriptions typically descend: e.g., Prov. 6:16–19; see Watson 1986, 353; see note on 1:2a), the man describes her appearance as "flawless" (4:7). So, he beckons her to leave her distant dwelling place, symbolized by mountains, and join him in love. In the height of their excitement for one another, the woman unlocks the garden (her body) for intimacy (4:16b) so that the couple can fully embrace one another sexually. The passage concludes with the man and woman sated with love (5:1).

### The Man Woos the Woman by Praising Her Body (4:1–7)

The bridegroom exults in his bride, beginning with an exclamation of her beauty.

**4:1.** In a burst of excitement, the man praises her beauty. The exclamation serves as a soft *inclusio* for the metaphorical description of her body that follows, concluding in 4:7 with a restatement of the original sentiment from 4:1, that she is "beautiful!" In 1:15, the man described her eyes as doves, and in 2:14, she was seen as a dove hiding in a rock crevice (see discussion on 1:15). Here again he notes how her eyes possess that intrinsic dove-like quality (perhaps their shape and color; cf. 1:15) as they hide behind her veil (cf. 2:14). Rebekah is said to wear a "veil" (צָעִיף) prior to her marriage (Gen. 24:65), but the term here in the Song (צַמָּה) appears only elsewhere in Isaiah 47:2. There is too little known about women wearing veils in Israel at this time to be assertive about the circumstances in which this was customary and whether that practice changed over time. The example of Rebekah in Genesis 24:65 may be sufficient to say that women wore some kind of covering prior to marriage, if only just prior. The verb "to veil" in 1:7 is עטה, though it may be a transposing of letters for "to wander about" (טעה) according to several manuscripts. In 4:1, 3; and 6:7 the noun "veil" (צַמָּה) appears, but in 5:7 the term "veil" (רְדִיד) is used. Again, there is much uncertainty regarding these terms that are assumed to be related to "veil," but the context of each of these passages suggests that it consisted of some kind of fabric wrap.

The following description of her hair is a clear example of how culturally specific references can be lost on modern readers, especially those from non-agrarian contexts where sheep and goats are not being raised. Even farmers who raise such livestock may not have witnessed how a flock can blanket a section of hillside and then run downward. The term "descending" or "leaping down" (גָּלַשׁ) appears only here and, as such, has resulted in debate as to its meaning, but a helpful suggestion is to adopt a facet of both interpretations (Gault 2019, 155). This may mean that the woman's hair is tied up and then let down in an "undulating flow" created by descending waves over the top of her back (Murphy 1990b, 159), much like a slow-motion shampoo commercial. Steven Tuell prefers "flowing in waves" to reflect the relationship of Hebrew גלש to Ugaritic *glṯ* (1993, 103). In sum, she has great hair and a lot of it.

> **Hair as a Feature of Beauty**
> Hair is an evident symbol of feminine sexuality throughout ANE literature (cf. *COS* 1:554; Lichtheim 1973b, 190). Both the description of the woman's hair in 4:1 as well as iconography from Egypt and Mesopotamia suggest a preference for long hair on women at this time (examples abound: see the Asiatic women in Pritchard 2011, 30 §2, and the Egyptian women in figure §32; certain passages suggest that Israelite women also had long hair that could be tied up, e.g., Num. 5:18; cf. Bollinger 2018, 56 n. 57, 179–80). Men's hair is usually depicted around shoulder length or shorter (see also *ANEP* §2), but there were exceptions like Absalom (2 Sam. 14:25–26; Mesopotamian kings may be depicted with slightly longer hair, as in the case of Ashurbanipal in Pritchard 2011 §122 and Shalmaneser III in §247; see a discussion of long hair in the Nazirite ritual in Bollinger 2022). In both Song 7:6 (HB 7) and 5:11, the lovers' hair is mentioned as a facet of human beauty. The man chooses Gilead for the

setting of pasturing goats, a northern, well-watered territory in keeping with the images of springtime and the floral descriptions of 2:10–13.

**4:2**. Keeping with the sheep and goats metaphor from 4:1, the man switches to describe her teeth, which are "like a flock of sheep about to be shorn" that are ascending from a watering hole. Evidence from other Near Eastern texts suggests that common practice was to wash the sheep before shearing them, which would result in the glistening appearance of their wool, an apt comparison to shining teeth, a desirable trait in several texts (Gault 2019, 157 n. 85, 158). Perhaps the ascent of the flock and their great number are a reference to how the woman's teeth are revealed in a smile. The pairs of matching ewes could be a recognition of how her teeth match from one side to the other (Murphy 1990b, 159).

**4:3**. The association of the color "crimson" with lips is readily understandable to modern readers, especially in cultures where red lipstick is popular. Lipstick is not a modern invention, as "archaeological evidence from Egypt indicates that females used red color to enhance the beauty of their lips" (Gault 2019, 160). Duguid and others have made the interesting connection to Joshua 2:18 where Rahab also lets down a "crimson thread" (חוּט הַשָּׁנִי) to mark her dwelling for the spies, perhaps otherwise an invitation to her services as a prostitute (Duguid, 2015, 111–12). That the color is considered luxurious is apparent from its usage in Proverbs 31:20 where the virtuous woman is said to clothe her family in "crimson." This holds true for the following description of the woman as having cheeks like the slit of a pomegranate, which are also crimson in color. Again, we have examples from Egypt of the application of red makeup to the cheeks of women (Gault 2019, 165). These descriptions of the woman are not only a reference to makeup, but to the natural features of her beauty that may be enhanced by such applications. Whether she's born with it or not, he does not care—she is stunning to him.

**4:4**. This is the first of two references to the woman's neck as a tower (7:5 [HB 6]). Here, her neck is compared to a tower with stacked layers of stone upon which all the shields of the mighty hang. The association of her neck with the tower of David suggests dignity and invulnerability (cf. Ps. 48:12 [HB 13]), while the shields could represent ornamentation, like a necklace (Murphy 1990b, 159). It is difficult to know precisely whether a physical attribute or a conceptual attribute is primary, or if both are primary. Rows of necklaces about her neck could bear resemblance to rows of stacked stones used to construct a tower, and Keel even suggests that crowns worn by Assyrian queens in seventh-century B.C. "might symbolize an unconquered city" (1994, 147). If the conceptual attribute is emphasized, then the woman's neck could represent pride and dignity. And though the women of Jerusalem were condemned by Yahweh for going about with "outstretched necks," this would not be the first time a positive attribute of the woman in the Song could be contrasted with the improper use of that same attribute elsewhere (Isa. 3:16; see note on 4:1).

Conceptually, it could be argued that the symbols of war ornamenting her "tower" represent peace, security, and confidence. These metaphors could also serve as symbols that she is as yet sexually inaccessible, a sentiment that would fit with the "locked garden" metaphor that appears in 4:12 and the "wall" of 8:10 (and possibly, 2:9, though with a different Hebrew term). This long description of her attributes in 4:1–5 is centered on positive observations made by the man. To use a metaphor of our own, the woman is like an ornate stained-glass window in a medieval church—everywhere the man looks he is enraptured with the stories told by her beauty.

**4:5**. He began with her eyes and hair but now draws his own eyes downward to her breasts, which he describes in terminology bewildering to nearly every moderner upon first hearing it: "like a pair of fawns." They are also "the twins of a gazelle." She had previously told the man to be like a gazelle on the "split/Bether mountains," a reference to her breasts (see note on 2:17). Here in 4:5, it is more likely that the man is making a comparison of image rather than concept. Gazelles are regularly featured in imagery related to fertility and sexuality. There is no shortage of seal impressions and other artistic representations of such creatures (Pritchard 2011 §2). The man is overcome with sexual desire for the woman. That the image of breasts need not match the image of fawns/gazelles is apparent in the other references to gazelles in the Song (the oaths in 2:7 and 3:5; the descriptions of the man in 2:9, 17; and 8:14). In sum, her breasts are a symbol of natural beauty, as reflected in Proverbs 5:18b–19: "Take pleasure in the wife of your youth. A loving deer, a graceful doe—let her breasts always satisfy you; be lost in her love forever" (CSB).

**4:6**. We last encountered this elegant bit of poetry back at 2:17, where the woman used the expression when speaking to the man. She stated, "Until the dawn breathes and the shadows flee, turn my beloved, and be like a gazelle or a young stag on the divided mountains." Here he responds to that specific request by repeating the introduction and resolving to "go to the mountain of myrrh and to the hills of frankincense." That there has been a shift since 2:17 to now (in terms of the woman's availability) is evident both by the sequence of songs moving in an increasingly more intimate direction and by the resolve expressed by the man here in 4:6. Again, the day breathing is likely a reference to the morning (contra Keel 1994, 151), when the shadows indeed depart away from the direction of the rising sun. This does not mean, though, that the lovers are not joined together at night; rather, the suggestion is that he is to pursue her all night long until morning. Keel suggests that the mention of these spices (to which we could add the mention of mountains) evokes sacred imagery: "the combination of the two conjures up an intensity characteristic of something totally other or holy" (1994, 153; see notes on 4:7 and 7:5 [HB 6]; see sidebar "Cultic Imagery in the Song" p. 244). She keeps myrrh between her breasts, which is where she wants him to be (1:13). He also desires this deeply and it has motivated him to sing a song of her beauty to prepare their hearts for that very moment.

**4:7**. The song concludes similarly to how it began, with an exclamation of her beauty. After describing her from "head to toe" (though technically he stopped at the breasts) he adds, "All of you is beautiful, my darling. And there is no blemish in you!" The term "blemish" (מוּם) is the same term used in the law to describe the physical flaws of a human (Lev. 21:17) or a sacrificial animal (Deut. 17:1). Such humans and animals were restricted with respect to the holy things of God. The man's use of this term in the Song continues the religious undertones mentioned in the note on 4:6 above, suggesting that the woman's status is elevated and uniquely qualified for their vineyard of love.

### *The Couple Invite One Another to Join in Sexual Intimacy (4:8–16)*

The man explains why he cannot restrain himself—she is irresistible.

**4:8**. The change of tone is noticeable right away. In 4:8–15 that follows, there is an urgency in the man's voice. He has no time to waste, so he makes his final approach. His exhortation is bold and direct, that she emerge from her hiding places, like the rock crevice of the dove (2:14), the dens of the lions, and hilltops of the panthers. She cannot hide behind her veil (4:1) any longer, and he would add that his own time of flirtatious sneaking has come to an end (see note on 4:9–10a). Lebanon to the north is where Mt. Hermon, Mt. Senir, and Mt. Amana are located. She is not literally hiding in a cave like a feral beast (an unromantic thought, indeed); rather, the mountains are merely part of a "trope of alienation that the lover wants the woman to overcome so that they may be united in intimate bliss" (Longman 2001, 148). The lions and leopards/panthers are, like the foxes (2:15), representative of abstract threats to the woman's pure status, though it is possible they could represent false suitors. He beckons her to come out of her country town and join him at last.

**4:9**. He is transfixed with her and cannot hold back any longer, "you have captivated me, my sister, my bride" (לִבַּבְתִּנִי אֲחֹתִי כַלָּה). The denominative "heart" (לבב) in the *piel* stem is used by the man to claim that his heart has been stolen (see NET). Calling her "my sister" is only a means of expressing an even deeper level of closeness, suggesting that they are as inseparable as family (see sidebar "Familial Language in the Song" p. 287). From the perspective of the man, the woman has not had to put in much effort to totally incapacitate him—just one glance has accomplished this. After all, he considers every part of her to be flawless, so even the smallest feature of her essence is sufficient to steal his total focus. Keel's creative translation reads, "You drive me crazy!" The man tells her why this is the case in 4:9–11, using "three repetitive parallelisms, each with three members, produc[ing] a rhythmic undulating, bringing one new high point after another" (Keel 1994, 161). All he has to see is a mere "jewel" or "bead" (Murphy 1990b) from her necklace to be smitten with love.

> **Approaches to Jewelry, Makeup, Perfume, and Style**
>
> At times, the lauded attributes of the woman are condemned elsewhere in Scripture when they are used to describe a sinful woman. For example, the adulterous woman of Proverbs has lips that "drip honey" (Prov. 3:5; cf. Song 4:11) and she owns fine fabrics (Prov. 7:16; cf. Song 4:11) and perfumes that match those of the woman in the Song (Prov. 7:17; cf. Song 4:14). This wayward woman insists she and her victim "indulge in love until morning," which can be compared to the couple in Song 4:6 and 5:1 (Prov. 7:18). The woman's flowing/wavy hair is praised by the man of the Song, but the women of Jerusalem will be shaved bald when Babylon comes to exile them (Isa. 3:24), likely a symbolic action indicating that their trust was placed in their beauty, which had led them to sin.
>
> The lesson for each of these comparisons is that accoutrements like hair, spices, linens, and jewelry, along with physical descriptions like glistening eyes, a proud neck, and so on are not intrinsically evil for any woman but *can* become symbols of avarice and rebellion if the heart of the woman strays from Yahweh. The tragedy of this sin is seen also in Jezebel, who worshipped fertility deities, and who "painted her eyes and adorned her head and looked out of the window," presumably to seduce Jehu who had been sent to exact God's judgment on her (2 Kings 9:30; for the "woman in the window" motif in art, see Pritchard 2011 §28). This principle is carried forward in the New Testament with 1 Timothy 2:9–10 and 1 Peter 3:3–4, where a proper interpretation is *not* that such facets of beauty are evil, but that a misprioritization of such accoutrements over godly character can indicate a problem of the heart.

**4:10**. He continues giving reasons for why he has lost his mind over her. Just as she began the Song in 1:2–3 with "Let him kiss

## The Lovers Embrace One Another (4:1–5:1)

The jewelry and headdress of a Sumerian queen. Public domain (see Song 1:10–11; 4:9; *ANEP* §72).

me with the kisses of his mouth" followed by an explanation "for your lovemaking is better than wine; your fine perfumes are fragrant," so here the man repeats to her in 4:8 "Come down with me" for "how beautiful is your lovemaking . . . how much better than wine! And the fragrance of your perfumes is better than any spice" (4:10). What began in the heart of the woman has come full circle to the point that he cannot resist her as much as she could not resist him. Longman notes the high value of the particular "spice" mentioned here; it was one of the finest gifts brought to Solomon from the queen of Sheba (1 Kings 10:2), used in the temple as anointing oil (Exod. 25:6), and served as part of the beautification process for the Persian harem (Esther 2:12; Longman 2001, 154).

**4:11**. In his final explanation for why he is helpless in her presence, he remarks that her "lips drip honey" and that her garments bear the scent of Lebanon. This is evidently appealing since the forbidden woman of Proverbs uses the honey-on-lips tactic to lure her prey (Prov. 5:3). The "honey and milk" description of the woman's lips and/or mouth is the reverse order of the "milk and honey" description of the Promised Land (Exod. 3:17). "The woman is a landscape," writes Exum, "a promised land, and, particularly, an Edenic garden flowing with honey and milk" (2005, 173). Her scent is reminiscent of the legendary glory of the forests of Lebanon.

**4:12**. In his final approach, he speaks more directly about her sexuality and his desire to be with her. Just as in 2:8–17 where the couple anticipated one another by removing every obstacle from love's path, so here the man addresses the final block in the road: "My sister, my bride, is a locked garden." He may be expressing concern, for how will he access her unless she becomes available? She is a "sealed fountain," and he finds that problematic in light of his burgeoning desires. The term "fountain" (גַּל) here may be a scribal typo for "garden" (גַּן) according to several manuscripts; however, it could be argued that by (גַּל), the MT is preserving the sense of a "stone heap" that could be used to seal up a well (Rogland 2013, 648; cf. Gen. 29:2b–3, 8–10).

He may be praising the fact that she is "locked," as it makes her special, likely a reference to her chastity. Nowhere in the Song has the man praised her for being sexually open to every man; rather, he delights in the fact that she is different, unique. Later in 8:8–10 she will call herself a "wall," which also should be understood as a reference to chastity. This is not merely a case of the heart desiring what it cannot have since her other attributes are what have brought him to her, but her inaccessibility only adds to her mystique and desirability. Ultimately, it is not just that she is off-limits that makes her appealing, but that she has been chaste.

> **Familial Language in the Song**
>
> Familial language is used in a number of contexts in the ANE to connote closeness between two people who are not real siblings. Consider the friendship of David and Jonathan (2 Sam. 1:26) who could call one another "brother." This is comparable to the strong bond between Gilgamesh and Enkidu (*ANET*, 76). In the Amarna letters, kings engaging in international trade (or treaty-making) also wrote to one another with familial and affectionate language that would seem strange if it showed up in modern political correspondence. A king of Mitanni writes to the Pharaoh: "Since you were friendly with my father, I have accordingly written and told you so that my brother might hear of these things and rejoice. My father loved you, and you in turn loved my father" (*COS* 3:240). The man of the Song refers to the woman as "sister" to connote closeness, but in the context of romance. Later she will daydream about him being her brother just so that she could be physically in the same space with him, but free from public scorn (see note on 8:1).

**4:13–14.** Here the man lists all the rare and exotic produce cultivated in this garden, likely to make the point that no garden like this exists in the world (Murphy 1990b, 161). She is one of a kind. The garden seems to refer generally to the woman's body and perhaps abstractly to her sexuality, but it would be hard to deny the more specific erotic implications of an expression like the one made in 4:16: "May he enter" (יָבֹא), the verb being used throughout the HB to refer to the act of coitus (e.g., Gen. 29:23).

The man's description of the woman does not focus overtly on her ethical traits, but the positive imagery he uses is consistent with descriptions of high moral value found elsewhere in Scripture and the Near East. In an analogy from Egyptian wisdom literature, the Instruction of Amenemope describes two men as trees, one grown indoors (the unwise) and the other outdoors (the wise). The tree that grew indoors is like an angry man who cannot survive because he lacks sunlight. As for the tree that grows in the garden: "The truly silent, who keeps apart / He is like a tree grown in a meadow / It greens, it doubles its yield, / It stands in front of its lord. / Its fruit is sweet, its shade delightful, / Its end comes in the garden" (*COS* 1:117; cf. the man planted by streams of water in Ps. 1:3). The woman has been like this wise person, protected and nourished by the sun into flawless beauty that the man cannot live without.

**4:15.** Like the springs of En Gedi (1:14), the woman is a perpetual source of life, a "well of living water." Keel mentions the mountain streams of Lebanon that do not "run dry" (Jer. 18:14), stating, "nor does the beloved—a garden of wonders with a miraculous fountain—ever lose her power to refresh and enchant, even in the Near Eastern heat" (1994, 181). For the man, her vibrancy and appeal will never end.

In Song 4:15, the man describes the woman as a well of "living water" (מַיִם חַיִּים). The LXX renders "living water" as ὕδατος ζῶντος, the same construction used in the LXX version of Genesis 21:19 when God rescued Hagar by causing her to see "living water" in the wilderness after she had been exiled by Sarah (cf. Gen. 26:19; MT: בְּאֵר מָיִם). The same expression appears elsewhere in the LXX where it may refer variously to "living water," "spring water," or "running water." The expression has theological significance in Jeremiah 2:13, where God refers to himself as "living waters" (מַיִם חַיִּים/ὕδατος ζωῆς) that the people have rejected. The prophet Zechariah foresaw a time in the eschaton when "living water" (ὕδωρ ζῶν) would flow from Jerusalem (Zech. 14:8). The reference to "living water" in Song 4:15 may be merely a description of desirable spring water, but the terminology could also carry spiritual undertones employed for the purpose of heightening the significance of the woman and love in general (see notes on 2:7; 4:6, 7; 7:5 [HB 6], and sidebar "Cultic Imagery in the Song p. 244").

**4:16**. The verse is divided into two emphatic proclamations. First, the man calls upon nature to unlock the garden and make his darling fully available for love's delights. Winds from the north and the south stir up the mounds of ground spice (her sexuality) to create an aromatic cloud that engulfs the lovers. No man could unlock her garden, so an appeal had to be made to powers from without. This should not be taken literally as if there is a spiritual component to nature that must activate the woman sexually, nor is this a direct reference to God's power. Rather, this is a poetic association between truth and nature (a frequent association in wisdom texts). Just as the authors of Proverbs appeal to nature for life's lessons, and as the psalmist interprets nature as a witness to God's power God (Ps. 19:1–6), so the man is making a poetic summons to a greater authority on the subject of love, God's creation. Associations like this between nature and sexual intimacy are not relegated to the Song. In Psalm 19:6, God makes "the sun rise like a bridegroom exiting his chamber." The man understands nature's authoritative knowledge of love, and, therefore, appeals to this knowledge. She responds, "Let my beloved enter his garden and eat of its choice fruit!" The metaphor is self-evident at this point in the Song (see note on 4:13–14)—a banquet of love awaits them!

### The Couple Embrace One Another in Sexual Intimacy (5:1)

The man describes his delight in making love to her, while the chorus of maidens affirms their union.

**5:1**. The long i-vowel sound pervades these lines as the man describes their marital consummation in terms consistent with enjoying the fruits of a garden. He calls her "My garden, my sister, [my] bride," and then identifies the produce of this exotic gardens as, "my myrrh," "my spices," "my honeycomb," "my honey," "my wine," and "my milk." Lest everything that came before 5:1 be lost on the reader, remember that the couple has pursued one another relentlessly, and it has resulted in her not only consenting to this sexual engagement but craving it as badly as he had (the Song actually begins in 1:2 with her desires, but one might argue they have heightened throughout the dialogue and especially the *wasf* of ch. 4). So, when he calls the produce of the garden his own, he is not exerting some kind of domineering oppression on a hapless Israelite virgin. The evidence from the Song moves clearly in the opposite direction. By claiming the produce of the garden as his own, he is receiving what she is willingly giving to him, just as she is receiving from him. The chorus (presumably, of maidens) uses the metaphor of a banquet to insist that the couple hold nothing back.

In the end, the goal of the first four chapters of the Song is achieved—the two are joined in love. At this point the reader may begin to wonder what the couple's future could entail. Will it always be this good?

## THEOLOGICAL FOCUS

The reader of the Song assumes the role of a Jerusalemite maiden who is instructed by her wise teacher, the woman of the Song, not to awaken or stir up love before its time. As her pupils, we have witnessed the great benefits of observing love's pure timing. The sequences of nature, the movement of birds and creatures, and the experience of the senses have all been influential in our lovers' journey together. Their hearts may have run wild with excitement, but they were patient to observe the course of nature. And when the time was right, they called upon their teacher to blow forth the winds of love. Nature is in no sense God; rather, it is his creation, and as his creation, it testifies to his glory (Ps. 19:1) and instructs all living creatures in the mysteries of his wisdom. The rhythms of the natural world bear witness to the love of God for the universe he created and called "very good" (Gen. 1:31).

For believers viewing all of Scripture through the lens of Christ's finished work on the cross, we observe how the majesty of human intimacy looks forward analogously to a relational joy that cannot be expressed with words. While the Song celebrates intimacy between a man and a woman who pursue love within the bounds of God's covenant, it also gives a glimpse into the potential for ultimate human fulfillment in the Creator.

Jesus refers to "living water" (ὕδωρ ζῶν) in John 4:10 when speaking with the Samaritan woman at the well. Could he be referring to God's provision of "living water" to Hagar in the wilderness (Gen. 21:19)? Could he be alluding to Jeremiah 2:13 where God is described as a "fountain of living waters" (מְקוֹר מַיִם חַיִּים). If so, would the Samaritan woman have understood this? Jesus's conversation with her was about her many marriages, and if the Song of Songs survived as a wedding anthem in Jewish culture, then perhaps it would have come to mind when Jesus used this expression. We cannot know for sure. Regardless of the specific allusion being made by Jesus, it was used to teach the Samaritan woman that the fulfillment she sought from elsewhere could only really be achieved through knowing "the Christ" (John 4:25–26). The "living waters" appear again in eschatological language describing Jerusalem and the throne of God (Zech. 14:8; Rev. 22:1). Later, in Revelation 22:17, an invitation is issued to all who are thirsty, that the one who desires to do so take "the water of life" (ὕδωρ ζωῆς) without price. The powerful language of the Song both encapsulates the passion of the couple and causes us to look ahead to the fulfillment of all things beautiful in God.

# PREACHING AND TEACHING STRATEGIES

## Exegetical and Theological Synthesis

After the grand processional of the wedding in 3:6–11, the Song depicts the man and woman alone together on something akin to their wedding night. The man's intense longing for the woman issues forth in ecstatic praise for her body (4:1–11). She is the woman of his dreams! They are at last alone together as the separation and alienation between the couple has finally been overcome. The distance between them has not yet fully been dismantled, for the woman is still a "locked garden" (4:12). One final barrier exists for the couple: lack of physical intimacy.

What will happen? Will the woman become accessible to the man? Yes, the woman freely gives herself away to the man (4:16). The man now enters the garden of her love, consummating the relationship (5:1). The prevalent use of garden imagery speaks to the fruitfulness and vitality of their relationship. The imagery also calls to mind the garden of Eden when the first man and woman were "naked and were not ashamed" (Gen 2:25). A relationship built on God's Word, pursued God's way, and consummated in God's timing leads to human flourishing.

## Preaching Idea

Enjoy God's gift of marital intimacy.

## Contemporary Connections

### What does it mean?

Even before sin enters the world, God declares that there was something "not good": man being alone (Gen 2:18). To remedy man's loneliness, God creates the institution of marriage (Gen. 2:24–25). God creates marriage not merely as some kind of contractual arrangement, but as a place for passion, desire, and enjoyment of sexual intimacy. If marriage is the proper context to enjoy sexual intimacy, then it behooves followers of God to build intimacy his way, under his covenantal standards.

The Song points us to the primary way to experience sexual intimacy: marriage (3:6–11). While marriage is supposed to be a relationship of celebration and relational intimacy, there can still be difficulty being intimate within marriage. To combat drifting apart, every couple must build increasing levels of trust in their relationship. Within the Song, the man contributes to building trust by praising the woman's body with "carefully composed words" (4:1–7; Garrett 1993, 379). He selects culturally appropriate metaphors to highlight the beauty of his wife's body. The man describes her love as if it is a life-giving river of water (4:12–15). The woman reciprocates by making herself available to the man (4:16). While sex is to be reserved solely for marriage, it should be uninhibited within marriage. Sex is to be the most joyous expression of love and intimacy a married couple can engage in. In some sense, all the desire, longing, and words spoken by the couple up to this point are for the purpose of moving them to be physically joined together.

*Is it true?*
Countless movies, TV shows, and songs teach that sex is best enjoyed outside of marriage. The impression one could get from modern media is that the most exciting and passionate sex happens between total strangers. But that is not the case in reality, nor according to God's holy Word. Rather, as the man and woman's relationship in the Song grows, so grows the intensity of their romance. What makes the sexual intimacy of the Song so wonderful is the safety of marriage.

The woman is clearly chaste before her marriage, as the man describes her as a "locked garden" that he will enter (4:12, 16). According to God's design, the gate should only be unlocked for one person. The commitment to fidelity within marriage builds a thick and strong wall of protection around the cultivated garden of sexual intimacy that a husband and wife can enjoy. Once inside the garden, there are no inhibitions for the couple! In the Song, the man and the woman partake in all the delights of sex without the shame or stigma of violating God's standards because they are married.

While sex is a good gift to be enjoyed in marriage, a thriving sexual relationship will not happen for some married couples. There may even be difficult periods in the sexual relationship of the happiest couples because of sin. Since human beings live in a broken world, getting married is no guarantee the world's brokenness will not find its way into the most intimate parts of life. Nevertheless, God's design typically leads to a passionate and enjoyable intimate relationship. The reason why marriage is so important for a thriving sexual life is because sex is more than a physical act. According to the Bible, the act of sex unites two people together in some mysterious way (see 1 Cor. 6:15–16). Therefore, couples will maximize their ability to have a fulfilling sex life by enjoying the gift of intimacy within the safety of a committed covenant marriage.

*Now what?*
Married couples must work hard to continue to build sexual intimacy within their marriages. The man's praise of the woman's physical appearance should challenge Christian husbands to praise their wives as well. Husbands can often struggle verbalizing praise to their wives, devolving into a generalized statement of "You're so hot." The Song challenges every husband to extol the virtues of his wife, both creatively and appropriately. The Song likewise invites every wife to pursue and respond to their husband eagerly. Just as wives want to be pursued, so men want to be wanted; so, one of the best things a wife can do to cultivate intimacy is tell her husband how much she wants him.

Within the Song, there is a heavy emphasis on mutual invitation to sexual intimacy. Contrary to some conservative stereotypes of women being almost a-sexual, the woman in the Song expresses intense sexual desire for her husband (1:2–4, 12–14; 2:5; 3:1–5). She is not shy telling the man what she wants! Likewise, the man genuinely desires his wife and does not guilt, cajole, or manipulate her into sex. They are both fully and freely giving of themselves to one another.

Since this section speaks at length of the joy and passion of married sex, how does the text relate to those outside the marriage covenant? The text reiterates a foundational truth in Scripture about sexual intimacy: it is best enjoyed in marriage. Single people must not be deceived by the world and think that marriage kills desire or leads to an unsatisfying sex life. The opposite is true. Following God's way leads to the most satisfying sex possible. The text also provides some implied standards for choosing someone to date. How do they use their words? Is there mutual affection in the relationship, or is it all one-sided? Are they committed to reserving sexual intimacy for marriage as well? These questions can help single people have the right frame of mind when they enter the dating pool.

## Creativity in Presentation

A great depiction of marriage in the media is on the TV show *Friday Night Lights*. The show follows the story of a high school football coach in a small town in Texas. While much of the show naturally focuses on the football team, the marriage of the coach Eric Taylor and his wife Tammy holds the narrative together. Not only does it hold the story together, but it also holds the community together. While all manner of family dysfunction rages around them, from divorce to infidelity, the marriage of Eric and Tammy is the one constant in the lives of their students. Even more encouraging, their marriage is not an uneventful, joyless affair, but one of deep passion and commitment to one other.

Pastors should think creatively as to how to highlight the goodness and joy of married sex without using cringy gimmicks like speaking of one's "smoking hot wife." Scripture is not calling us to "out-sex" the world but instead to present a different story of sexuality. One way to present a different story is to emphasize the stories of long-time married couples. Consider filming the stories of your three longest-married couples for the church and incorporating them into your worship services.

One illustration to use concerning the balance of chastity before marriage and enjoyment of sex within marriage could be Christmas. To fully enjoy Christmas, we must wait. Christmas would lose its power if we celebrated it every month of the year. Once Christmas comes around, it is appropriate to celebrate with full gusto. No one likes a killjoy on Christmas! So it is with marriage. If we violate God's design and transgress his word by engaging in sexual relations before marriage, we harm our own heart and the heart of the other person. Guilt and shame can infect our lives. If we wait for the right time of marriage, we can enjoy the gift of sex with unabashed joy. Married couples must shake out any timidity and prudishness. Marriage is the couple's own little kingdom, or to use the imagery of the Song, their cultivated garden, to be enjoyed.

A big idea for the text is, "Enjoy God's gift of marital intimacy." The outline for the sermon could focus on ways that married couples could cultivate enjoyment of God's gift of intimacy:

- Praise one another's physical appearance (4:1–7)
- Invite one another into intimacy (4:8–16)
- Embrace one another in intimacy (5:1)

## DISCUSSION QUESTIONS

1. How does the man show his affection and desire for his wife (4:1–7)?

2. What effect does the woman have upon the man (4:7–11)?

3. How can you use your words wisely to build someone up (including your spouse) this week?

4. If married, how can you build intimacy with your spouse?

5. If single, what is encouraging to you about the Song's depiction of marriage?

# THE RENEWAL OF LOVE (5:2–8:5)

The Song's cyclical nature can be seen in how the themes of separation, longing/pursuit, and embrace encountered between 1:2 and 5:1 repeat in the second half of the Song (5:2–8:5; see "Literary Structure" in the Introduction). Song 1:2 began with the couple's separation during their initial courting relationship, wherein they pursued one another for the first time. This pursuit crescendoed, reaching its highest point in 5:1 when the lovers embraced sexually. In keeping with the pattern of separation, 5:2 abruptly departs from the excitement of the previous verse in anticlimactic fashion. From here, the lovers must overcome their latest case of separation—a feat they will accomplish through relentless pursuit, first from the woman (5:2–6:3), and then from the man (6:4–13). Their embrace begins with the man wooing the woman in 7:1 (HB 2), just as it had in 4:1 leading up to their sexual union in 5:1. This continues until 7:10 (HB 11). Then, in 7:11 (HB 12)–8:4, the woman once again invites the man to join her in sexual intimacy (just as she had in 4:16b after his first round of wooing her). The final moment of embrace is referenced in 8:5, which contains a poetic reminder that the cycle of love will continue for generations.

This third major section, The Renewal of Love (5:2–8:5), is broken into two preaching units: The Lovers Renew Their Pursuit (5:2–6:13 [HB 7:1]), and The Lovers Renew Their Embrace (7:1[HB 2]–8:5).

# Song of Songs 5:2–6:13 (HB 7:1)

**EXEGETICAL IDEA**
The lovers renew their pursuit of one another in the face of obstacles.

**THEOLOGICAL FOCUS**
When believers experience marital hardships that create distance, they must passionately renew their pursuit of one another to restore the relationship.

**PREACHING IDEA**
Perseverance and commitment are necessary to build lasting love.

**PREACHING POINTERS**
Even after the man and the woman are married, they still find themselves separated from one another. The man knocked on the door of the house to be with his wife, but when she answered, she found that he had already left. The woman embarked on another nighttime search to find the man. The journey was treacherous, however, as the guards of the town physically assaulted her. The woman beseeched others to send a message to her beloved if they found him: she was lovesick. She then praised the man, likening him to a great statue. After an exchange with the chorus again, she came to realize where he was: in his garden. She returned to the man and he was delighted to be with her, for he spent considerable time praising her beauty again.

Getting married does not solve all of a couple's problems, as this portion of the Song shows. And while we cannot know the reason for the couple's separation in this passage, we do know the kinds of things that impede our own marriages. After the honeymoon, couples must continue to work on their relationship. One area of struggle for couples can be a difference in libido. Generally, men desire sexual intimacy more frequently than do women, although this varies among couples. One spouse may approach the other for intimacy, only to feel like they are being rejected. The pain of rejection, whether it manifests as emotional neglect or denied sexual advances, can cause rifts between couples. No matter what the problem is, however, perseverance is needed to build long-term, healthy relationships.

# THE LOVERS RENEW THEIR PURSUIT
## (5:2–6:13 [HB 7:1])

**LITERARY STRUCTURE AND THEMES (5:2–6:13 [HB 7:1])**

The present unit covers nearly two chapters, from 5:2 to 6:13 (HB 7:1; the Hebrew text of ch. 6 ends at v. 12 and treats v. 13 as 7:1). There are interpretive difficulties in reconstructing the end of the unit (6:11–13 [HB 7:1]), on which commentators differ, but our view is described below.

There are two main sections in the present unit, each of which could be broken down into several parts; but for the sake of simplicity, and in consideration of practical concerns related to preaching the material, it is sufficient to divide the text as follows: (1) the woman pursues the man again (5:2–6:3), and (2) the man pursues the woman again (6:4–6:13 [HB 7:1]).

The first section begins with the the couple's separation, which leads to a harrowing pursuit once again through the city. In desperation, she calls upon the maidens to aid her in her manhunt. They ask her a fair question: "What's so great about him that we should help?" (5:9 paraphrased). This prompts the woman to give a long, exalting description of her beloved's body (which is really a description of how he makes her feel; Sun 2022), a response to the maidens and a defense of his incomparability (5:10–16). Finally, after she is finished answering the maidens' question, they ask her where he has gone (6:1). She knows the answer and gives it (6:2–3).

The second section begins with the man's voice in 6:4, who proceeds to praise his bride for her incomparability, mirroring much of the language from his description of her in chapter 4. At the conclusion of his ode, he pictures her as more than just a personification of beauty, but as a figure of awe-inspiring power (6:4–10).

- *The Woman Pursues the Man Again (5:2–6:3)*
- *The Man Pursues the Woman Again (6:4–6:13 [HB 7:1])*

**EXPOSITION**

A major shift of tone and emotion has taken place between 5:1 and 5:2. While in 4:1–5:1 readers witnessed wave after wave of the couple's passion for one another (climaxing in 5:1 when they are finally intimate), there is a sudden shift in 5:2. The woman is pictured lying in bed (echoing 3:1). While in bed, her heart is alerted by a sound. The man has arrived home and attempts to enter the house, but for some reason, he cannot. When she opens the door, she finds that he has left. His absence reignites her longing, driving her into the streets where she is confronted by the watchmen (echoing 3:2–4), but this time they assault her. She appeals to the chorus of maidens to help her in her pursuit of her beloved. In response, they cleverly ask her "What is so great about him anyway?" (my paraphrase). Why is he better than any other man that the maidens should feel any urgency here? She responds and she finds him. He then reacts startlingly to the aura of her beauty. Though he describes her in second person, it is not apparent that they have found one another yet.

The unit concludes with the man going into an orchard (6:11–12) to see if the season is right for love (see note on 6:11–12 for why the man is the likely speaker; 6:12 is, however, one of the most difficult verses in the Song to interpret). Upon discovering that love is in the air, he mounts a chariot to go find her. He calls out to her to "return" so that "we" (the man and his entourage from 6:12) "may look upon you." This mirrors 5:8 where the woman was searching frantically for the man and, in her desperation, enlisted the maidens' help. And just as the maidens responded with "How is he better than any other man?," so here in 6:13b (HB 7:1b) the maidens ask the man, "Why should you look upon the Shulammite?" This prompts him (as it had for the woman in 5:10–16) to sing yet another ode to her beauty, but that will be reserved for the discussion on 7:1–10 (HB 7:2–11).

### The Woman Pursues the Man Again (5:2–6:3)

The couple's love is confronted by obstacles, which occasion separation and, consequently, a renewed pursuit for one another.

**5:2.** As in 2:10–14, so here the man appears to be beckoning her with his "voice" or perhaps the "sound" of his approach (the same Hebrew term: קוֹל). The language of this passage uses sexual euphemisms, but not for the expected reasons. The couple does not appear to be having sex; rather, the double entendres express both the man's literal inability to enter into the house and what that symbolizes sexually for the couple—that she has become temporarily inaccessible. Both the literal and figurative readings must be kept in view since rejecting the figurative/sexual reading would mean ignoring the clever double entendre, and rejecting the literal reading (that he is locked out of the house) would not serve the story points that follow in 5:6–8. The ordinary problem of being locked out and having to go elsewhere is the real situation into which the sexual metaphor is woven. We are not given the reason for why she does not at first open the door. The euphemistic language includes the expression "open to me" in 5:2, the mention of her "feet" in 5:3, the woman's restless body in 5:4, among other things.

To start, the woman recounts that she was sleeping, "but my mind awoke" (וְלִבִּי עֵר). The Hebrew term is "heart," but can mean "mind." It may simply indicate that her heart started racing when her beloved began knocking on the door, as happens whenever someone is startled awake. It is possible to take this as describing a dream (as some do for 3:1–4), but we read the events as real story points. She was startled awake by the sound of her beloved knocking on the door. The verb "knocking" (פדק) is elsewhere used to describe men pushing one another (or beating repeatedly) on a door (Judges 19:22). The noun "sound" stands by itself at the front of the clause, creating a sense of abruptness. This can be contrasted with the gentle, almost timid approach of the man hiding behind the lattice in 2:9 (Murphy 1990b, 165). Back in chapter 2, the woman was anxiously awaiting him, but now her response seems different. Perhaps his abruptness has occasioned hesitancy from her. Having achieved the union for which he longed in 5:1, has he now become cold and assuming in his own pursuit of her? Has this coldness occasioned a coldness from her? Do these questions even matter? It is not appropriate to apply blame to either the man or the woman because the text does not provide enough information for that (Longman 2001, 167). The sudden shift from extreme passion in 5:1 to a sense of distance in 5:2 is radical. It is an intentional shift by the author to show both extremes of a romantic relationship, the point being here that they are once again apart.

The phrase "but my mind awoke" is the first of three disjunctive *waw* clauses, the others appearing in 5:4, "but my body groaned/was excited," and in 5:5, "but my hands dripped." These three clauses, along with her concerns about getting dressed and washing her feet in 5:3, may convey a sense of hesitation on the part of the woman. This, again, comes in stark contrast to what readers just witnessed in 4:16–5:1, and, as such, likely serves as a clever literary device to show how even the most passionate romances can experience a lull.

Unable to get in the house, the man calls out to the woman, using several of his most affectionate epithets for her, to let him in: "Open to me, my sister, my darling, my dove, my perfect one." The line features a repetition of the long i-vowel six times for internal rhyming. He goes on to explain that his hair is wet with dew, likely an indication that he has been out very late. Keel notes that "Palestinian dew could occasionally be as heavy as rain," reminding readers also of the large amounts of moisture on Gideon's fleece (1994, 189; Judg. 6:33–40). Perhaps the man was out late, working by torchlight.

**5:3**. She seems hesitant and provides reasons for why she cannot rise. It is not clear whether she is responding to him out loud or just thinking to herself. For the woman to answer the door would mean she must get dressed and soil her feet again, which may be too much trouble. Another possibility is to see her reply as verbal foreplay in order to delay their meeting and thereby intensify the passion between them (see Exum 2005, 195). The Song is not bothered to present these experiences as logical or understandable, just as it is not interested in explaining why the man was out late (or any number of details). Rather, its focus is to convey the ordinary human experience of romance, noting accurately that there are many ups and downs, and our lovebirds are experiencing an unexpected low moment.

**5:4**. "My beloved sent his hand through the latch, but my body was in turmoil within me." This reading is quite different than the ESV's "my heart was thrilled within me," but what if the woman has been unpleasantly awakened and does not desire to answer the door (see Ps. 42:5 [HB 6] for a similar expression to connote stress: "my soul is distressed within me" [נַפְשִׁי וַתֶּהֱמִי עָלִי]?). The term "womb" (מֵעֶה) here is often taken for her area of sexual excitement, but it could refer to the seat of her emotions (see Duguid 2015, 126, though most take it to be unmistakable sexual arousal—e.g., Exum 2005, 195). In Job 30:27 and Lamentations 1:20 and 2:11, the noun is used in connection with groaning accompanied by grief. In the other passages related to emotion, the noun is used in connection with longing for someone or having compassion on them. If the conjunction is disjunctive here, then when he reached for the latch, instead of feeling excitement she may have felt frustration—"but my insides/heart groaned." This is not to deny that a euphemism is at work. It is possible that both meanings bear relevance here; in other words, the euphemistic/sexual language is being used ironically to describe story points that actually show the couple experiencing an impasse. The terminology is sexually suggestive: the man reaches for the "hole/latch," a euphemism for her genitalia, by means of his "hand," a euphemism for his genitalia (Isa. 57:8). While the euphemistic terminology is intentional on the part of the author, and literarily brilliant, the tenor of such language is contradicted by the fact that the lovers do not actually join together, but are again separated.

**5:5**. When she rose to answer the door, she anointed her hands with perfumes, "but my hands dripped with myrrh. Myrrh ran over my fingers onto the handles of the bolt." She rises to consent to his overtures and prepares herself with perfumes. If the *waw* is read as a disjunctive "but" instead of "and," then this could be another explanation for her hesitancy, though couched in romantic language—due to these last minute preparations, she now literally has a mess on her hands. It is also in keeping with the disjunctive *waw* clauses in these verses. Murphy argues that the man is responsible for pouring myrrh on the lock as a potent reminder of his presence just before disappearing (1990b, 171), but the man is not shown doing any such thing here (see Exum 2005, 195, and her citation of the oft-cited Lucretius's *De rerum natura* where the man is locked out but leaves gifts at the door).

**5:6.** Back in 3:1, her longing for him while in bed led her to search for him in the streets. This time around, there are obstacles preventing a quick response from her, and now he is gone. When she finally opened the door for him, he was nowhere to be found. Her "soul went out," which could mean that she was distressed or that she followed after him (see explanation below). Keel understands the expression to mean that she completely lost her will to live (1994, 194). Perhaps a better option would be to read "when he spoke" as the verb (I-דבר) "when he turned," in which case her soul going out could simply mean she chased after him: "When he turned, I went out," rather than the ESV: "My soul failed when he spoke" (after all, at this point the man is gone). This is apparent with what follows in the remainder of 5:6–7. An identical expression appears here as in 3:2, "I sought him but did not find him."

**5:7.** On this occasion, when the watchmen found her, they proceeded to beat her, but no explanation is given for why. It is unclear whether they are simply reprimanding her, though violently, for breaking a law (being out past curfew?), or if they are sexually assaulting her. The fact that they took her "veil" (רְדִידִי) could be an idiom for such an assault, but we cannot be certain. Isaiah 3:16–26, in a proclamation of judgment on Jerusalem, describes the haughty women who have outstretched necks (see notes on 4:1 and 4:4), jewelry, perfumes, and more. In this passage the Lord vows to remove their accoutrements, such as their robes and "veil" (וְהָרְדִידִים), but we cannot be certain of the term's meaning since there are several synonyms for "cloak" and "shawl" crowded together in Isaiah 3:22–23. Here in Song 5:7, the term רְדִידִי could be translated "cloak," an item of clothing the city guards took from her to reprimand her for being out in the streets at night. If this is a legal violation, then she is a repeat offender. She may have gotten a "pass" on her first offense in 3:3–4, but not this time. Keel points out the Middle Assyrian law against a prostitute wearing a veil in public. If caught, she would lose her clothing and suffer a terrible beating (1994, 195). If these laws had parallels in the setting of the Song, it is possible the woman was mistaken for a prostitute. Whether she was (1) violating some kind of curfew law, (2) being punished for supposed prostitution, or (3) simply being wrongly assaulted by wicked city guards, her end state is the same: she has been physically harmed and she has lost something of value. This is what she was willing to risk to find her beloved.

**5:8.** In 2:7 and 3:5 the woman made the daughters of Jerusalem swear that they would not awaken love until it pleases. In this latest adjuration, she is making them swear that if they find her beloved, they will tell him that she is "sick with love"—she has the bruises to show for it, too! The woman used this same expression to describe how she felt in 2:5. The sages also use this same verb to declare that "hope deferred makes the heart sick, but a desire realized is a tree of life" (Prov. 13:12). The verb similarly appears in Hosea 7:5 where the wicked princes of Judah become "sick with the heat of wine," evidently the way to say "hangover" in Classical Hebrew. The woman has been with the man and longs to be with him again. Indulging in any pleasure may result in painful withdrawals that pull the person back into deeper consumption of the same, like the experience of fictional music producer Bruce Dickinson (played by Christopher Walken) and the "fever" he had, the "only prescription" for which was "more cowbell" (as seen on an episode of *Saturday Night Live* that aired April 8, 2000). Given the other associations between love and intoxication in the Song, it is no leap to suggest here that she is hungover with love, and that the only cure is more love.

**5:9**. In response, the maidens ask an appropriate question. One may assume they have been privy to all that has gone on in the Song thus far, and if so, they have heard her describe him as "an apple tree among the forest," meaning that he's one of a kind (2:3). One may also assume these maidens are among "the virgins" of Jerusalem who "love" him (1:3). They have also heard her description of his sexual prowess, that he is a "young stag on the cleft mountains" (2:17). In light of this, perhaps their question is occasioned by the couple's confusing separation in 5:2–4. They need to be reminded why he is better than the rest.

It is helpful to remember that there are larger structural forces at play in the Song beyond the fact that the maidens have just asked a question that needs answering. Based on the previous cycle, it is at this point that the reader could expect another ode to the man following the pattern of separation and pursuit in chapter 3. The Song cycles twice through a sequence of separation, longing/pursuit, and embrace in 1:2–5:1 and again in 5:2–8:5. The conclusion of the Song (8:6–14) shares the lessons learned from love along with some of these features from the cycle.

> **The Body in the Song of Songs**
> In the Song of Songs, the human body as a whole is praised for its beauty, not just those parts most commonly associated with sexual intimacy. The lovers mention the following: mouth (1:2; 4:36; 5:16; 7:9 [HB 10]), skin color (1:5–6), cheeks (1:10; 4:3; 5:13; 6:7), neck (1:10; 4:4; 7:4 [HB 5]), breasts (1:13; 4:5; 7:3 [HB 4], 7–8 [HB 8–9]; 8:1, 8, 10), eyes (1:15; 4:1, 9; 5:12; 6:5; 7:4 [HB 5]; 8:10 idiomatically), hands (2:6; 5:4, 5; 8:3), head (2:6; 5:2, 11; 7:5 [HB 6]), face (2:14), hair (4:1; 5:2, 11; 6:5; 7:5 [HB 6]), teeth (4:2; 6:6; 7:9 [HB 10]), lips (4:3, 11; 5:13; 7:9 [HB 10]), tongue (4:11), feet (5:3; 7:1 [HB 2]), fingers (5:5), arms (5:14; 8:6), body/stature (5:14; 7:7 [HB 8]), legs (5:15), thighs (7:1 [HB 2]), navel (or "vulva," 7:2 [HB 3]), belly (7:2 [HB 3]), nose (7:4 [HB 5]), and the abstract concept of the heart (4:9; 5:2, 4; 6:6). There are also elements related to parts of the body, like the woman's necklace (4:9), her sweet breath (7:8 [HB 9]), or references to kissing (1:2; 8:1). Unlisted here are the numerous references to physical anatomy that may occur in metaphors since their interpretation is debated; rather, these are being treated individually throughout the commentary.

**5:10**. In answer to the maidens' question above, the woman calls her beloved "gleaming and ruddy/red, distinguished from 10,000 (the multitude)." The term for "gleaming" (צַח) is an adjective appearing only once in the Bible, though its verbal form is used in Lamentations 4:7 to refer to clear or healthy skin. Lamentations 4 is actually a helpful parallel to the woman's description of the man just as Isaiah 3:16–26 was a helpful parallel to his description of the woman (see notes on 4:1, 4; and 5:7). Unlike Isaiah 3, where judgment is being pronounced against Jerusalem due to the gaudy arrogance of its inhabitants, Lamentations 4:7 mourns the once opulent state of these inhabitants and how they have now been reduced to dust. At one time, their princes were "whiter/shinier than milk" (צַחוּ מֵחָלָב), just like the man of the song is "gleaming" (צַח); their bodies were "ruddier than coral" (אָדְמוּ עֶצֶם מִפְּנִינִים), just like the man of the song is "ruddy" (וְאָדוֹם); other parts of their body were like lapis-lazuli (סַפִּיר), just like the man's body is covered with "lapis-lazuli" (סַפִּירִים; Song 5:11). The man's head is made of "pure gold" (כֶּתֶם; Song 5:11), but the "pure gold" (הַכֶּתֶם) of Jerusalem has become contaminated through judgment (Lam. 4:1). In both Isaiah 3 and Lamentations 4, the language of opulence is brought out in the context of judgment and mourning, but in the Song those same descriptors are used by the lovers to praise one another's beauty. What may be observed from this contrast is that exceptional beauty and opulence, in general, are not evil. It is rather the heart of the individual that concerns the prophets of Israel (see note on 4:1).

The meaning of "red" (אָדֹם) for his skin tone could be broad in application, as in shades of brown. His radiance and ruddiness make him "distinguished" (דָּגוּל) among the multitudes, but given the man's use of the root דגל in 6:4 and 6:10 to describe the woman as awe-inspiring, the woman's use of the root here may convey a comparable kind of adulation. His appearance among the multitude is glorious, even "unnerving" and "intimidating" (see Andruska's helpful discussion [2018, 1–7]).

**5:11–12.** His hair is black like the "crow/raven" (עֹרֵב). His dove-like eyes are white spots, like doves floating about the water (see notes on 1:15, 4:1, and sidebar "Hair as a Feature of Beauty" p. 282).

**5:13.** His cheeks are like "towers of spices," which could be understood to mean "towers of aroma." Perhaps the image is that his face and beard had been perfumed and emit a strong, pleasing aroma to the woman like scent billowing up from a pile of ground spices in the marketplace. His lips are like the petals of a flower, also richly aromatic (for more on scent in the Song and comparative evidence from the ANE, see Gault 2019, 202).

**5:14.** Several translations read "bars of gold" in consideration of the two other places where the noun occurs, in Esther 1:6 (a curtain rod) and in 1 Kings 6:34 (hinges on a door). If "bars" is maintained, then we must take יָד to mean "arm" rather than "hand" since that fits better with the imagery of the verbal root גלל "to roll." Murphy asserts, "there is no evidence in the Old Testament for such elaborate ornamentation of the male arm" (1990b, 172); however, there is comparative evidence from Egypt for such descriptions (Keel 1994, 202).

Longman takes מֵעָיו to be "his member," as in his penis, and translates עֶשֶׁת שֵׁן as "ivory tusk." It seems more likely to understand the term מֵעָה as "belly," like the cognate Aramaic term for "belly/midsection" (מְעָה) appearing in Daniel 2:32 where we have a similar description of a man's body: "The head of this image was of fine gold, its chest and arms of silver, its middle [מְעָה] and thighs of bronze" (ESV).

The woman could be making veiled geographic references in this verse. The term "bars" is similar to "Galilee," a region covered in mounds of hills and, at times, adorned with flowers. The woman could be describing the curves, knuckles, and musculature of his hands. In the very next colon, she mentions "topaz" (NET: "chrysolite"; ESV: "jewels"), which is identical in spelling to the word for "Tarshish," the place to which Jonah was fleeing (Jonah 1:3) to avoid going to Nineveh. It is hard to say for certain, but these images could be references to locations associated with exotic goods or the colors associated with such goods.

**5:15.** His strong legs are compared to the cedars of Lebanon. Interestingly, the man had noted that the woman's scent was like the fragrance of Lebanon (4:11). In 5:10 she had referred to his head as "gold," and here she refers to the base of his legs as "gold"; "The woman's beloved is gold from head to foot" (Keel 1994, 205; see sidebar "Strong Legs, Firm Feet, and Virility" p. 256). The description of the man in 5:10–16 raises a fascinating discussion on the interplay between poetic description of the body and statuary art in the ANE (See Dobbs-Allsopp and James 2019, 297–323).

**5:16.** The expression "*all of him* is totally desirable" (וְכֻלּוֹ מַחֲמַדִּים) aligns with 4:7 where the man stated, "*all of you* is beautiful" (כֻּלָּךְ יָפָה). The plural noun מַחֲמַדִּים is rendered "desirable" because it parallels the descriptive noun "sweetness" (מַמְתַקִּים; also plural) in the previous colon. The two plural nouns do not make good sense unless they are understood as plurals of "intensity" (GKC §§396–97). At the same time, "desirable" (מַחֲמַדִּים) literally means "precious objects," which would, while also serving as a plural of intensity, echo her description of his body as being made up of precious metals and jewels in 5:14–15. This concludes her answer to the maidens' question back in 5:9, which apparently is enough to convince them to help.

**6:1–3.** The maidens ask where he has gone, and she does not hesitate to place him in "his garden," typically a reference to her body (4:16). Having located him, she offers reposefully, "I am my beloved's and my beloved is mine." Chalk it up to poetry that the woman suddenly knows where to find him since she was just looking for him all over and they still do not seem to be together in 6:13 (HB 7:1). In concluding that he has gone down to the garden, she is resolving that just as she has been looking for him, so he has been looking for her. Since their purposes are united, they end up in the same place.

### The Man Pursues the Woman Again (6:4–13)

The man now turns to praise his beloved.

**6:4–5a.** Back in 1:6 she told the maidens, "Do not look at me because I am dark, for the sun has stared at me." Ironically, that has all changed now. The man's love has brought about a transformation in her that goes beyond beautification to near glorification. It is the man who begs her to look away lest her glory burn holes through him! He describes her as beautiful, lovely, and "terrifying" (אֲיֻמָּה), a term only elsewhere used to describe the awe/fear-inspiring power of the Chaldean army (Hab. 1:7). She is not just a delicate flower, but a force of nature. She is as "terrifying/awesome as rows of army banners" (אֲיֻמָּה כַּנִּדְגָּלוֹת). Her eyes "bewilder" (שֶׁהֵם הִרְהִיבֻנִי) him. He tells her to turn away her eyes because he cannot withstand the power of her beauty—he is intimidated. He begins his ode here by describing her as "terrifying" and will conclude with the same description in 6:10.

Why does the man parallel Jerusalem to Tirzah and not Samaria, Israel's northern capital? This may be the result of the Song being written after the Assyrian destruction of the northern kingdom in 722 B.C., so perhaps Samaria is destroyed and too painful a memory to mention (see Introduction and Keel's suggestion that the Song was written in Hezekiah's day; also, Long 1996, 705).

The term typically translated "banners" (נִדְגָּלוֹת) could refer to a bannered army (Verde 2016, 194) or could come from the Akkadian verb *dagālu* "to look" and related noun *diglu* "a look/view/sight" (see notes on 2:4 and 6:10), leading to the possible translation of the last line in 6:4 and 6:10 as "overwhelming/breathtaking like the[se] sights," referring to the items that precede this expression in both verses: Tirzah, Jerusalem, the moon, and the sun (Long 1996, 708).

**6:5b–7.** Here the man repeats some of his descriptions of her from 4:1–3 and adds that the appearance of her rosy cheeks between the lattice of her veil is like looking into the webbed arrangement of pomegranate fruit (see note on 4:3).

**6:8–9.** All the maidens "call her blessed" and all the royal women "praise her," adulations reminiscent of 1:3–4 where the maidens were praising the man. It is not so heartwarming to modern sensibilities, however, to hear a man say that a particular woman is his *favorite*, as in *better than all his other wives and concubines*! In the context of ancient Israel, though, this likely would have been a well-received compliment by the woman if told to her by a royal figure (or in this case perhaps a man portraying royalty). The mention of an active harem, though, simply serves the "royal fiction" motif (Exum 2005, 221) and is not taken as a threat by the woman, for whom the man has a singular focus. Rather than insist that Solomon himself wrote the Song, it is better to understand this as a legendary tale *"about Solomon"* (לִשְׁלֹמֹה), but likely adopted by ordinary Israelite men and women as a means by which to express their own experiences of romance and marriage (see Introduction and note on 1:1). One imagines that when they sing the Song, they assume the roles of a king and queen; he is thought of as the mighty Solomon, and she as a country maiden whose beauty outshines a host of royal women. In such a metaphorical adoption of roles, it is not crucial to resolve the problem of Solomon having innumerable wives and concubines alongside the Shulammite.

**6:10**. In 3:6, the question was asked, "Who is this?," which was followed by a description of Solomon that focused on his glory and might. Here, the question is repeated, but now the woman is the one portrayed as powerful. The speaker up to this point has been the man and the language of this verse echoes his description of the woman in 6:4–5, so there is no reason to insist that the speakers here are the chorus of maidens or the harem mentioned in the previous verse. The man began his song in 6:4–5a, referring to her as "terrifying," and here he compares her glow to the impressive light of a full moon or the scorning blaze of the sun. She is again "terrifying/awesome as rows of army banners." The man of the Song sees his darling as not just another pretty face, but a unique power with which to reckon. She is incomparably beautiful, yes, but there is also something so rich and pure about her that he turns his face away from her gaze (6:5) because it is both as awe-inspiring as the moon and as piercingly bright as the sun. There is truth in her so brilliant that it exposes him, like the sunlight of King David's justice nurturing the people and scorching the wicked (2 Sam. 23:4–7). So, he says, "Turn your eyes away from me, for they bewilder me!" (6:5).

### The Woman's Glorious Appearance

The language used by the man to describe the woman in 6:4–5a and 6:10 is an example of how the couple at times describe one another with terms typically reserved for divinity. Elsewhere, the songwriter emphasizes her otherworldliness by alluding to divine imagery (see notes on 2:7; 4:6, 7, 15; 7:5 [HB 6]). For example, the language of 6:10 directly parallels awe-inspiring images of the goddess Inanna and other such deities in Mesopotamian literature, though the comparison of beautiful women to celestial bodies is part of a broader pattern in ANE literature that does not always suggest deification (Gault 2019, 190–92).

David Musgrave's 2010 dissertation on the phenomenon of viewing deity in the ANE provides examples of the fear or awe felt by a supplicant when in the presence of a god, feelings that resulted in worshippers hiding their faces, such as in the Sumerian hymn An Adab to Nergal for Šu-Ilīšu: igi ḫuš u₃-ni-gur₃-u₃ igi nu-bar-re kalam-ma, "when you lift your furious face, upon it people cannot look" (Musgrave 2010, 22). A similar passage refers to the deities being unable to view the face of Enlil: mùš-za digir igi nu-bar-re-dam, "no god can ever see your face," this passage being spoken of a person (Šulgi; Musgrave 2010, 22 n. 36). The man of the Song likewise directs the woman to turn away her eyes because they "overwhelm" him (6:5). In many places humans (or lesser deities) could look directly at the face of a god, so the Song's adoption of this language in 6:4 along with the majestic description of the woman in 6:10 are intentional allusions to divine imagery for the purpose of elevating the woman (terminologically) to the category of "otherworldly"—literally, though, she is still understood as a mortal woman.

The terminology of 6:4 and 6:10 also reminds us of the prophets' and apostles' visions of God throughout Scripture (e.g., Daniel, Ezekiel, Isaiah, and the apostle John; see also the blinding light of Christ in Saul's journey to Damascus in Acts 9). The imagery of celestial bodies in Song 6:10 also reminds us of the transfiguration of Christ: "And he was transfigured before them, and his face shone like the sun, and his clothes became white as light," after which the voice of God was heard, and Peter, James, and John "fell on their faces and were terrified" (Matt. 17:2, 6 ESV). Modern fiction also captures the imagery of Song 6:10. For example, in *The Fellowship of the Ring*, the powerful elf Galadriel describes what she would become if she possessed the Ring of Power:

> And now at last it comes. You will give me the Ring freely! In place of the Dark Lord, you will set up a Queen. And I shall not be dark, but beautiful and terrible as the Morning and the Night! Fair as the Sea and the Sun and the Snow upon the Mountain! Dreadful as the Storm and the Lightning! Stronger than the foundations of the earth. All shall love me and despair! (Tolkien 1954, 366)

A cylinder seal impression depicting the goddess Ishtar arrayed in glorious splendor. A worshipper gazes at her with his hand raised in a symbol of awe and deference. Public domain (see *ANEP* §526; see notes on 6:4–5a, 10).

In sum, the man of the Song has employed language that effectively conveys how she makes him feel—helpless and in awe—and this style of description has had lasting impact on ancient and modern literature and art.

**6:11**. Commentators differ on whether the man or the woman is speaking here. In the Song, the first person "I" is not reserved for the woman only; the man also speaks in the first person (see 1:9; 7:8 [HB 9]), and he refers to himself in third person (7:5 [HB 6]). The man was the speaker in the verses immediately preceding (6:4–10), so what reason could we give for the woman being the speaker in 6:11, the very next verse? In favor of the man being the speaker, we see him engaging here in an activity he had performed in 2:10–13, observing the signs of the seasons. While doing so, something happens suddenly.

**6:12**. Song 6:12 is perhaps the most enigmatic verse in the Song. The phrase begins with לֹא יָדַעְתִּי נַפְשִׁי שָׂמַתְנִי, literally, "I did not know, my soul set," which several versions take as "before I knew it" in an attempt to make sense of the strange Hebrew syntax. There are nearly three dozen occurrences of לֹא יָדַעְתִּי in the Hebrew Bible, and none of them are typically translated as "Before I knew it" except for here in Song 6:12 (e.g., ESV, KJV, NASB, NIV, NLT). But the expression could be a way of conveying a sudden feeling of bewilderment, perhaps better captured by "I didn't know what was happening to me" (CSB). The expression could be compared to a medical expression in Akkadian texts that indicates a partial loss of consciousness: *ramānšu la īde* "he did not know himself" (Paul 1978, 545). Regardless of what it means, upon realizing that the garden had indeed bloomed (meaning that the time for love had come), he was instantly swept away on a quest to find his darling.

The term עַמִּי־נָדִיב is not likely a reference to "Amminadab" (LXX and Vulgate), whose name is a strange one to invoke at this juncture, but something to do with "noble people." Just as the woman had enlisted the maidens of Jerusalem to help her find her beloved in 5:8, so here the man has set himself among the chariots of his nobles, enlisting their help to find his darling.

### The Shulammite

The female protagonist of the Song is named only once, and she is called (הַשּׁוּלַמִּית) "the Shulammite," though the definite article may be understood as vocative, as in *"Oh*, Shulammite" (Arnold and Choi §2.1.3). The term has received considerable attention in scholarship, with some identifying it with a Mesopotamian goddess (Albright 1931–1932; and Pope 1977), others a woman from the town of "Shunem" (like Abishag in 1 Kings 1:3), or as a way of saying "Solomon-ness," this last option being the most likely of the three (Longman 2001, 192; Murphy 1990b, 181 see Frolov, who makes a connection between the Shulammite and Bathsheba [1998, 256–58]). The ending -*i* or -*it* normally designates a person's place of origin, but here in the Song it may be that the implicit affinity is not to a place but to a concept. Given the relationship between the name "Solomon" and the Hebrew term for "peace/completion" *shalom* (שָׁלוֹם), the term may imply that she brings "wholeness" to Solomon: "I was in his eyes as one who finds peace" (8:10). The implication could be that as the "Peacetress," she completes him. Some scholars will argue that the woman should not be referred to as "the Shulammite" when discussing other parts of the Song since he views the various songs as a loosely related anthology. However, since I read the Song as a loose poetic storyline (see Introduction), the woman can rightly be called the Shulammite throughout, though she perhaps comes more into the role as the story progresses.

**6:13 (HB 7:1)**. This final verse is divided into two speech acts. Commentators have struggled with how to interpret it, but our view is explained below. The first includes the words of the man and his search party, "Return! Return! O Shulammite. Return, that we may look at you!" This is followed by a question from the maidens, "Why do you look at the Shulammite like a dance between two armies?" A similar sequence appeared back in 5:8–9 where, in the first speech act (5:8), the woman is calling for help from the maidens, and in the second speech act they are responding to her with a question (5:9). Here in 6:13 (HB 7:1), the situation is reversed as the man is seeking the woman, and so the speakers are likely himself and his search party of nobles from 6:12.

In 5:9, the maidens asked the woman, "Why is your beloved better than others?" Here the maidens ask the man and his search party, "Why do you all look at the Shulammite as a dance between two armies?" Several manuscript traditions make "two armies/camps" (הַמַּחֲנָיִם) plural rather than dual, so just "camps/armies." It may not change the overall point. This "dance" (מְחֹלָה) could be a battle, though there are no other examples in Scripture of battles being described as a dance. The expression may be a reference back to 6:4 and 6:10 when the man described the woman as "awesome as army banners," the banners of course representing the presence of an army or armies. The maidens see the look of wonder in his eyes and they hear him say how she is otherworldly, so they ask him why he looks upon her in this way (again, cf. 5:9).

The man's following ode to the woman parallels that of the woman in 5:10–16, but the man's song also serves as his final approach, which I see as a form of verbal intimacy leading directly into physical intimacy, included for that reason in the following section, "The Lovers Renew Their Embrace." Looking back to 4:1–16, we saw that this final song from the man precipitated the woman's invitation and then their lovemaking. This pattern will repeat in the following chapters.

## THEOLOGICAL FOCUS

Romantic love can run cold and experience difficulty. Elsewhere in Scripture, there are examples of couples expressing love to one another, such as when Isaac loved Rebekah and she deeply comforted him after his mother's death (Gen. 24:67). Also, Jacob loved Rachel, which led him down a sacrificial path to get her (Gen. 29:18). Love, however, can be complicated by multiple spouses (Gen. 29:30; cf. Deut. 21:15; 1 Sam. 1:5; 2 Chron. 11:21, to name only a few). It can be rife with deception (Judg. 16:15) and be born out of complex circumstances wrought through sin (2 Sam. 12:24). For all the power of romantic love between men and women, there is great potential also for pain. Sometimes this pain is tragic, and at other times it simply represents a time of cooling down and a need for renewal. This is a fact of life that the Song explores. The lovers become separated from one another, but the longing they experience drives them to renew their relationship, a relationship now matured through suffering.

Several features of this passage could be understood analogously with reference to both Israel's relationship with Yahweh and Christ's relationship with his church. While the Song does not attribute fault to the man or woman for the separation experienced in 5:2–7, we do find ourselves culpable for the sin that separates us from God. Scripture is filled with references to Israel's love for Yahweh running cold, leading them to false worship—either directly in the form of idolatry, or indirectly by trusting in their wealth and military might. In those times, Yahweh often turns the people over to their own devices, which leads them to desperation when they discover that their strength is insufficient. Being joined in covenant means that they cannot both thrive as a people and remain independent of the other covenantal party, the Lord God.

The prophet Hosea was used by God to demonstrate this very point. Israel had abandoned the Lord, committing spiritual adultery. This would result in tremendous suffering for the covenant people, often driving them back to him in repentance (e.g., Isa. 65:1, 12; Jer. 7:27; 29:13; Hos. 2:7; 5:6). In spite of their sin and the punishment that followed it, God would not utterly abandon them: "Yet the number of the children of Israel shall be like the sand of the sea, which cannot be measured or numbered. And in the place where it was said to them, 'You are not my people,' it shall be said to them, 'Children of the living God'" (Hos. 1:10 ESV).

Christians find themselves in an analogous situation. Though we are under the new covenant of Christ's blood, we are easily allured by idols and experience seasons of rebellion that not only "grieve the Holy Spirit of God" (Eph. 4:30) but deeply distress our own souls (Rom. 7:14–25). The covenant faithfulness of God never fails, though, and what he accomplished through his Son means that "there is no condemnation for those who are in Christ Jesus" (Rom. 8:1). Those who are in Christ are allegiant to Christ, and while they may sin and bring grief into the relationship, they are compelled by the Holy Spirit to run after Christ out of thankfulness in their hearts for all God has done through the gospel (2 Cor. 5:14–15). In sum, we love because he first loved us (1 John 4:19).

## PREACHING AND TEACHING STRATEGIES

### *Exegetical and Theological Synthesis*

On their wedding night, the man and the woman experience the thrill of total unity: emotional and sexual intimacy (5:1). Their relationship faces a challenge as their love runs cold for a moment and necessitates the need for reconciliation. The man, coming home late at night, desires to be intimate with his wife, but for reasons not provided in the text, she does not reciprocate (5:2–4). Meanwhile, the man leaves. When the woman does answer the door, it is too late (5:6a)! She now runs off and searches for him, once again putting herself in harm's way under the influence of love (5:6b–7). The text attributes no fault to either the man or the woman for this outcome, but the tension of their separation is felt nonetheless.

While the couple is apart, both the man and the woman praise the other (5:10–16; 6:1–10). Underlying any temporary disinterest is the deeper commitment to and interest in the other person. Feelings may come and go, but the passions of love run deeper and stronger. Therefore, the lovers renew their pursuit of one another in the face of potential hurt and rejection in the midst of their separation.

### *Preaching Idea*

Perseverance and commitment are necessary to build lasting love.

### *Contemporary Connections*

#### What does it mean?

The couple had just experienced the thrill of total vulnerability consummating their relationship (5:1). But now, they must navigate feelings of mismatched expectations and rejection. The scene is one that many long-time married couples might resonate with. The man is coming home from a long day away, being amorous for his wife (5:2). He is knocking on her door and wants to enter, a euphemism for a sexual encounter. The woman does not jump to reciprocate his overtures; after all, she is snuggled up in bed (5:3)! When she checks the door, she finds he has departed. Again, details are lacking in the text to explain the separation—the text appears to be uninterested in why they are apart, being solely concerned with the fact that they are apart.

She jets out of the house to search for him. She again finds herself in the city, looking for him. Only this time, the people she runs into are not helpful but hostile, physically assaulting her (5:7). Undeterred, she calls on the other maidens of the city to pass along a message to the man if they happen to find him: she is sick with love and wants to be with him (5:9). The maidens ask the woman what kind of man he is, and she describes him as a stately statue (5:10–16). Eventually, she figures out that the man has gone to his garden, and she goes to meet him there (6:1–3). While the man is waiting in the garden, he praises her beauty again (6:4–9). She is one of a kind and someone altogether perfect for him. At long last, they have overcome their estrangement and are together once again (6:10–13).

The man and the woman in the Song testify to the fact that every relationship will have ups and downs. Even the most "in love" couples will eventually have a disagreement, tiff, or full-blown argument. It is not a matter of if seasons of difficulty will come into our relationship, but when. While the man and the woman experience the "high" of the relationship in 4:1–5:1, a thriving relationship cannot be built solely upon ecstatic feelings. Every couple instinctively knows that the "honeymoon phase" does not last forever. After the "shine" of the relationship wears off, couples must learn new skills to keep the relationship thriving. Due to the ongoing effects of sin upon relationships, perseverance and commitment are necessary to build lasting love. A healthy marriage must have a stronger foundation than merely being built upon feeling "in love." Instead, a marriage that lasts will be built upon covenant commitment. Each spouse must be utterly committed to "'til death do us part." The unwavering commitment to one another will help couples weather the storms of disagreement and hurt that will come. The quality of a relationship is not found in the good times but when it is tested in the difficult times.

## Is it true?

Relationships falter when founded on feelings. Of course, real love contains feelings! The apostle Paul indicates that love, solely consisting in actions without feelings, is pointless (1 Cor. 13:1–3). Nevertheless, the Scriptures also indicate that a commitment—a covenant commitment—undergirds marriage, for God always intended marriage to be permanent. Certainly, the Bible allows for the concession of divorce in certain circumstances. Even Jesus himself agreed with allowing for divorce in particular situations (Matt. 19:9). But the allowance for divorce was based on human sin, not God's design. "From the beginning it has not been this way," Jesus reminds us (Matt. 19:8). God has always desired for marriages to last.

The permanence of marriage necessitates perseverance within marriage. There will be times, just like in 5:2–8, when one spouse will say "no" to the other spouse's sexual advances. Such an experience could make the amorous spouse feel rejected and he or she could be tempted to pull away from the other person. The text seems to indicate that the man turns and leaves just as the woman begins to warm to him (5:6). The incident leaves the couple at a crucial point: Will they isolate themselves from each other or renew their pursuit of one another? Both partners renew their pursuit for the sake their relationship. The woman undertakes a dangerous journey as she searches throughout the city at night. She even suffers physical harm just to be close to the man again (5:6–7). She goes on to praise his excellencies to her friends (5:8–16). She also apparently knows her beloved well enough to know where he would have gone (6:1). The man, for his part, also renews his pursuit as he praises the woman, even though she has previously rejected him (6:4–12). The man does not give up his pursuit as he beckons the woman to himself once again (6:13 [HB 7:1]).

## Now what?

The text invites spouses to evaluate their commitment to the marriage relationship, especially if they have been hurt by their spouse. When you are hurt by your spouse, do you back away, giving him or her the silent treatment or sulking in another room in the house? Do you allow resentment and bitterness to grow in your heart? Or are you committed to moving toward your spouse in forgiveness and reconciliation? Are you willing to be transparent and vulnerable with him or her? Will you renew the pursuit or give up?

One of the best tests of any marriage is to consider what happens when your spouse says "no" to your sexual advances. It may be even worth taking a step back and considering whether he or she even feels comfortable enough to say no. Is your relationship filled with enough trust, safety, and honesty to have real conversations about your sex life? How do you react if your advances are rejected? Do you sulk, cajole, or try to manipulate your spouse into sex? Or do you listen with an understanding ear? Have you clearly communicated your expectations for frequency of sexual intimacy?

Managing expectations in relationships is a crucial skill, especially in the realm of sexuality. Many couples have different levels of sexual desire and drive in the relationship and, therefore, different expectations concerning sex. Pastor and author Peter Scazzero talks about how many expectations we have are unconscious, not spoken, not realistic, and/or not agreed-upon (2017, 47). When expectations are "invisible" to us, they can wreak havoc on our relationships. Therefore, we must work hard to make our expectations "visible."

Scazzero points out that an expectation can only be valid if it is conscious, agreed-upon, realistic, and spoken (2017, 48). Do you even realize that you have expectations surrounding sex (conscious)? Have you and your spouse agreed to these expectations? Are they realistic? Most importantly, have you spoken to your spouse about these things? Maybe one of the first things you need to do is schedule a time for a private conversation with your spouse to speak openly and honestly about these things.

For those who are not married, the text still speaks to the need for perseverance in all kinds of other relationships. Just because you may not be married does not mean you will be free from conflict! Even good friends can hurt one another (Prov. 27:6). The text again challenges our level of commitment to the closest relationships we have with our parents, siblings, children, friends, and church members. Are we willing to persevere in these relationships or let them crumble?

### Creativity in Presentation

Love is like a voyage on the waters of life. Sometimes spouses will sail smoothly together, with the sun shining and wind at their back. Communication is easy; lovemaking is thrilling. At other times, nasty storms arise, battering the vessel mercilessly. External circumstances, like the increasing responsibilities of work or the relentless demands of childrearing, can eat away at the passion a couple once had. Even worse, it may not only be gales and winds that sink the boat; sometimes, the boat may take on water due to self-sabotage from those inside! As author Timothy Keller has said, the greatest threat to our marriages is our own self-centeredness (2013). Our selfish desires and demands can erode trust and feelings of goodwill in the relationship.

Major caveat: the song I'm about to suggest is probably not appropriate to recommend in a public setting. Nonetheless, to get inside the mindset of the man in the passage, it may be worth listening to the song "Locked Out of Heaven" by Bruno Mars. In the song, the singer is pleading with his lover to "open up [her] gates" and allow him in because her "sex takes me to paradise." But for some reason, the woman is rejecting him and he feels "locked out of heaven." Compare the desperation in the song with the desperation in the Song as the man pleads, "Open to me, my sister, my darling, my dove, my perfect one" (5:2). Another song that captures well some of the themes in the text (and one probably much more appropriate for a public setting) is Mat Kearney's song "Ships in the Night." It describes a couple that keeps missing each other like ships passing each other in the night. They want to connect, but despite their best efforts they keep talking past each other and misunderstanding one another. But the singer is determined: "I'm gonna find my way / Back to your side."

One way to encourage the congregation would be to share stories of perseverance in the marriage covenant. *The Notebook* is a classic modern love story that features a man caring for his aging wife with Alzheimer's. It could also involve sharing true-life stories of couples that have been divorced but then had their marriage restored through the gospel of Jesus Christ.

The big idea for the text is, "Perseverance and commitment are necessary to build lasting love." The outline of the text could explore why couples need perseverance and commitment.

- The dilemma of distance and miscommunication (5:2–8)
- The power of words to foster reconciliation (5:9–6:9)
- The beauty of renewed unity (6:10–13)

## DISCUSSION QUESTIONS

1. How can miscommunication or unstated expectations occasion distance in a marriage (5:2–6)?

2. What does the woman do when she fails to find the man (5:7–16)?

3. What is the man's attitude toward the woman (6:4–13)?

4. Why is perseverance so important in any kind of relationship?

5. How can you use your words to build up the relationships around you?

# Song of Songs 7:1 (HB 2)–8:5

### EXEGETICAL IDEA
The lovers renew their embrace of one another.

### THEOLOGICAL FOCUS
Believers ought to renew their embrace of one another throughout the many seasons of marriage.

### PREACHING IDEA
Pursuing sexual pleasure with your spouse has no expiration date.

### PREACHING POINTERS
After their time of separation, the couple renewed their pursuit of each other. Their pursuit for one another did not stop there; they renewed their embrace in sexual intimacy. The man praised his wife's beauty once again and determined to make love to her. The woman responded to the man by expressing her own feelings of sexual desire. She took the initiative to think of exciting ways to make love to him. She intensely desired him, even longing to cast off all ancient societal norms so that she could be close to him.

No matter how long a couple is together, pursuing sexual pleasure with one's spouse never expires. Of course, older couples will face challenges that come with aging. But even older couples can still be exclusively devoted to one another and pursue each other in a myriad of ways. Nothing is greater than an enduring love.

# THE LOVERS RENEW THEIR EMBRACE
# (7:1 [HB 2]–8:5)

## LITERARY STRUCTURE AND THEMES (7:1 [HB 2]–8:5)

The versification of the Hebrew text differs from the English here. The Hebrew of chapter 6 ends at verse 12, meaning that 6:13 of the English text actually is 7:1 of the Hebrew text; so, for the entirety of chapter 7, the Hebrew text is one verse ahead of the English. This commentary follows the English divisions while providing the Hebrew in parentheses or brackets.

Commentators differ considerably on the divisions that make up 7:1 (HB 2)–8:5. This is due primarily to the switches back and forth between speakers as well as certain syntactic signals (e.g., the parallel expressions in 7:1 [HB 2] and 7:6 [HB 7] as well as the imperative in 8:1 and the adjuration in 8:4). These divisions are based on what I perceive to be a pattern observed in a previous section of the Song. This section (7:1 [HB 2]–8:5) loosely parallels the unit "The Lovers Embrace One Another" (4:1–5:1). In that unit, we observed the following divisions:

- The man woos the woman by praising her body (4:1–7)
- The couple invite one another to join in sexual intimacy (4:8–16)
- The couple embrace one another in sexual intimacy (5:1)

The divisions we drew for 4:1–5:1 are, admittedly, too tidy for the Song (putting the untamable Song of Songs into preaching units is a challenging task, to say the least). Likewise, the divisions of the present unit may appear even more conveniently construed. It should be acknowledged, though, that this is an attempt to organize the text for the purpose of teaching while remaining fully aware that the poetry of the Song at times resists strict boundaries. Technically, there are several places in this unit of text where one could justify making divisions. For example, the man delivers two poems, the woman interjects, and then she delivers two poems of her own. The unit is then concluded in a single verse by an interjection from the maidens of Jerusalem followed by the woman's description of the couple's lovemaking.

- The man's first poem (7:1–5 [HB 2–6])
- The man's second poem (7:6–9a [HB 7–10a])
  - The woman's interjection (7:9b–10 [HB 10b–11])
- The woman's first poem (7:11–13 [HB 12–14])
- The woman's second poem (8:1–4)
- The maidens' interjection and the couple's act of love (8:5)

To simplify things further, we note that 7:1–10 (HB 2–11) is all part of the man's speech, including the woman's interjection in verses 9b–10 (HB 10b–11). This is followed by the woman's speech (7:11 [HB 12]–8:5a), including the maidens' interjection in 8:5a. Finally, the couple once again embrace in 8:5b. Altogether, the section is broken up as follows:

- ***The Man Again Woos the Woman (7:1–10 [HB 2–11])***
- ***The Woman Again Invites the Man to Join Her in Sexual Intimacy (7:11 [HB 12]–8:5a)***

- ***The Couple Again Embrace One Another in Sexual Intimacy (8:5)***

## EXPOSITION

If the Song of Songs seeks to communicate a loose storyline, as I suggest it does, then what happens next in the Song is predictable and portrayed in the most elegant fashion. The renewal of the couple's embrace is occasioned by their time of separation beginning in 5:2. Just prior to the stressful events of that chapter, the man had eloquently wooed the woman, she had accepted his overtures, and the two made love. In the present unit, the couple seeks to renew this experience. Once again, the man will woo the woman (7:1–10 [HB 2–11]), the woman will again accept his overtures (7:11 [HB 12]–8:4), and the two will again make love (8:5).

The patterns do not match perfectly, though. Both the fact that the Song is poetry and the fact that the Song is portraying romantic love—which itself can be fraught with unpredictable changes—place readers in a position to simply receive the text rather than forcibly wrangle with it at every point. While it is the duty of exegetes and expositors to present the text of Scripture in understandable and applicable ways, it is also fair to admit that some texts (esp. the Song) resist such structured predictability. The Song is a work of art, but it is instructional with regard to love; it means to teach its readers (2:7; 3:5; 8:4, 6–12), but it does not attempt to do so in a simple, propositional way like the book of Proverbs. The raw artistry of the songwriter is on full display in his/her description of the couple's love.

### Sexual Metaphors and Innuendo

ANE descriptions of sex and the body may seem crass to modern sensibilities (see Inanna's description of her own body in *COS* 1:522). And while the Song is full of its own sexual language, it does not engage in quite the same degree of graphic description (it tends to be more "tasteful" in its terminology; Longman 2001, 195). The Song often refers to reproductive anatomy in metaphors that are at times more enigmatic to modern readers (e.g., 7:2 [HB 3]), and at times less so (e.g., 7:7 [HB 8]). Commentators fall along a spectrum of sexually explicit interpretation when it comes to just how graphic and specific they believe the Song to be when referring to human anatomy. A survey of scholarly publications reveals that some see more innuendo and sexual metaphor than do others (see note on 7:2 [HB 3]).

Our approach is to only make these connections when the comparisons are more obvious, either because a word like "breasts" is specifically stated, or because the metaphor is apparent (the palm tree of 7:7 [HB 8]). We take less obvious comparisons to be a reference to some attribute of the woman's character or the pleasant experience of being in her presence. Not *everything* needs to be a metaphor for sex or genitalia; the Song does not require that approach. That said, 7:1–9a (HB 2–10a) is the most detailed physical description of the woman. Her feet, legs, navel (or vulva?), belly, breasts, neck, mouth, nose, eyes, and hair are explicitly mentioned.

### *The Man Again Woos the Woman (7:1–10 [HB 2–11])*

In his final ode, the man describes her from toe to head as an irresistible delight.

**7:1 (HB 2).** The man responds to the question at the end of the previous verse by wooing the woman. Just as in 4:1–16, the "highly erotic nature of this particular poem" and the poem that follows "suggest his movement toward sexual intimacy" (Longman 2001, 193). Both here and in 7:6 (HB 7) below, the man will begin with the laudatory expression "How beautiful!" He will describe her beauty *from toe to head* just as she had described him *from head to toe* (5:10–16). As with much of the language of the Song, the metaphors employed by the man here in chapter 7 use imagery foreign to modern readers and must be elucidated the best we can on the basis of comparative evidence.

His attention is first drawn to her feet "in sandals" (בַּנְּעָלִים). The term is not uncommon, its most famous usage appearing in Ruth 4:7 where Ruth's kinsman-redeemer revoked his duty by removing his sandal to give it to Boaz (cf. Deut. 25:5–10). At the beginning of the Song, the woman appears to be an ordinary, though beautiful, country maiden, but her status has now changed; she is now beautifully sandaled and called a "noble daughter," a callback to 6:12 when the man enlisted the help of his noblemen to find her. The term "noble" (נָדִיב) certainly refers to wealth here, but it is possible that there is an implication of virtue (like how the term חַיִל in Proverbs 31:10 contains both the ideas of wealth and virtue). In Proverbs 17:26, the term is used in parallel to "righteous" (צַדִּיק), suggesting that "noble" could, in certain contexts, also connote righteousness (see Isa. 32:5). The very next line continues the notion of wealth, however, as her round thighs are as smooth as jewels. The term "curves" (חַמּוּק) could also just mean that the shape of her legs is as perfect as a professionally cut gem or gold ring: "the work of the hands of a craftsman." The thighs were an alluring part of the female body in ANE texts as well see the Love Lyrics of Nabu and Tashmetu in *COS* 1:445).

**7:2 (HB 3).** He has moved upward from her feet and legs to her mid-torso. The noun for "navel" (שׁ֫רֶר) appears in Exodus 16:4, referring to the umbilical cord. In Proverbs 3:8, the term seems to be a reference to the belly. It is possible that the term can refer to the vulva (based on Pope 1977, Murphy 1990b, and others, comparing it to Arabic *sirr* "pudenda" or "secret"), but Gault settles for "navel" based on the other passages (2019, 122), though he agrees that double entendre may be possible. Longman suggests that שׁ֫רֶר should be translated "navel," but that it is symbolic for the "vulva": "This indirect reference to the vulva is in keeping with the poet's strategy of tasteful, though erotic allusions to the woman's body" (2001, 195). The fact that the man is starting at the feet and working upward would suggest that he encounters the vulva before the "belly" (בֶּטֶן) of the next line; however, the man's description is not in perfect ascending order throughout the poem (see 7:4 [HB 5] where the eyes are mentioned before the nose). It could be, then, that man is thinking of the naval and belly as two parts that exist on the same plane.

Conceptually, the navel as endless wine and her belly as endless wheat is the man's way of saying that she is ever-satisfying, never lacking in her ability to create pleasure for him. The association between sexual gratification and fine dining goes back to the banquet language of 4:16–5:1. It is also possible that the heaps of wheat in references to her waist area suggests that she is fertile, fit for childbearing. The term is used elsewhere to refer to a woman's womb (e.g., Judg. 16:17; Ps. 22:10 [HB 11]). Visually, the curvature of a heap of wheat along with its flesh-tone color may contribute to the imagery (Gault 2019, 182–83).

**7:3 (HB 4).** He moves upward to her breasts, which are flawlessly alike, as beautiful as fawns in a meadow. This verse is an exact copy of 4:5.

**7:4 (HB 5).** In 4:4 the man had compared her neck to the "tower of David." The imagery is paralleled here where her neck stands tall and proud, though not in any negative sense (see sidebar "Approaches to Jewelry, Makeup, Perfume, and Style" p. 285). The "pools of Heshbon" is a reference to an Amorite city (Num. 21:26) and perhaps refers to the crystalline shine of her eyes. Bodies of water are considered special in biblical imagery, in general, but there may be something else unique about the pools of Heshbon that is unknown to us. Keel points to Numbers 21:16–25 where the Israelites sing a song to a well before pressing on through a number of other cities until they reached Amorite land (1994, 236). They requested to pass through peacefully, but instead the Amorite king dwelling in Heshbon attacked them and was defeated. In Song 5:12, the woman had compared his eyes to "doves on streams of water," another description of sparkling eyes. The geographic references continue, though we cannot be certain about "Bath-Rabbim" (the town of Rabbah has been suggested, but not convincingly; Brenner 1992, 113–15). We do, however, know plenty about Lebanon and Damascus. The tower of Lebanon that overlooks Damascus may be a reference to Mt. Hermon (Murphy 1990b, 183). All of these images would have been known and adored for the male singer to have included them.

**7:5 (HB 6)**. In favor of the tower of Lebanon referring to Mt. Hermon in 7:4 is the reference in this verse to Carmel. The imagery evoked is one of majesty, dignity, and divine mystery. Again, this is not an association between the woman and any goddess; rather, this is the author's way of co-opting divine language to express the otherworldliness of the lover's beauty (see sidebars "Cultic Imagery in the Song" p. 244, "The Woman's Glorious Appearance" p. 302, and "The Song and Mt. Carmel" p. 331). More literally, though, it is a recognition that her head sits "upon" her body in the same way that the mighty Mt. Carmel crowns the Jezreel Valley, a fertile plain rich with all the best kinds of flora and fauna mentioned throughout the Song. Mountains, in general, are associated with God's mysterious presence (e.g., Exod. 19:11; Ps. 68:15–16 [HB 16–17]) and that of the gods (1 Kings 20:23), so the man's reference to Mt. Carmel evokes a sense of divine mystery surrounding the woman (see *HALOT* s.v. "הַר" 254–55, for the many references to mountains and divinity). There is something totally different about her (see notes on 4:6–7).

Her hair is purple, a difficult dye to produce and, hence, an expensive color of fabric to purchase. It was extracted from a particular snail in the coastal areas beneath Mt. Carmel (Keel 1994, 238). Longman remarks that her hair is rare and royal, fit for temples and palaces (2001, 195; Exodus 25–39; Judg. 8:26). The king is "held captive in the courses" or "in the tresses"

An ivory carving of a crowned woman (the front is missing) found at Megiddo. Public domain (see *ANEP* §126 and note on 7:5 [HB 6] and the description of the woman throughout 7:1–9a [HB 2–10a]).

(בָּרְהָטִים). Regardless of which translation is chosen for "courses/tresses," the sense is the same: flowing locks of hair as in 4:1. Scholars point out an Egyptian love poem where the woman's hair captures the man like a "snare" (e.g., Keel 1994, 238). The verb "capture" (אסר) here in Song 7:5 (HB 6) is also used to describe Joseph's imprisonment (Gen. 39:20), Samson's binding (Judg. 16:6), and numerous passages related to military restraints and captivity. When referring to humans, the verb is never used in a positive context except the setting free of captives (Isa. 61:1) or a person binding themselves by pledge (Num. 30:4). The man of the Song is also willingly bound to the woman. He is delightfully impeded by the ensnaring power of her allure, just as her piercing eyes had afflicted him earlier in Song 6:5. The king is entranced with the beauty of her hair, and the image the man uses is of Solomon tangled in an overabundance of the rarest and richest fabrics, as if he is having to push tapestries out of his way in order to walk freely in his own palace. In as much as it is possible for one's wealth to be so great that it becomes a burden, so the man is no match for the wealth of beauty contained in the woman—she overwhelms his senses.

**7:6 (HB 7)**. This verse is either concluding the present song by way of *inclusio* (notice the "How beautiful" of 7:1 [HB 2]) or introducing the next song unit (7:7–10 [HB 8–11]). In either case, the point made here is easily understood. Back in 1:16 the man had made a similar proclamation: "Look! You are beautiful my beloved! Indeed, delightful/pleasant!" The final expression in this verse may seem a little strange, "O Love, with [its] pleasures!" (אַהֲבָה בַּתַּעֲנוּגִים). The man could be (1) using "love" appositionally by referring to the woman as "love," or (2) he may be letting out an exclamation regarding the power of love—"O love!" Option 1 is more likely and could be enhanced by reading "with [its] pleasures" (בַּתַּעֲנוּגִים) as a haplography (an accidental pushing together of the words "daughter of delights" into one word). In favor of option 2, love is also spoken of abstractly in 8:6.

**7:7 (HB 8)**. The man compares the woman to a palm tree (a date palm), which is tall and slender, though the metaphor should not be taken too far here. There is mixed evidence regarding the preferred body type for women in ANE societies, but most depictions (especially from Egypt) are of slender women (Gault 2019, 182). Large breasts, hips, and thighs were also preferred, all symbols of fertility in the minds of ancient people. The clusters of dates hanging at the top of a date palm are used as imagery for the woman's breasts here. The large-breasted pillar figurines discovered in Judah, thought by some to be goddesses or perhaps fertility tokens, highlight this physical feature (see Dever 2014, 129–41; see note on 2:17).

**7:8–9a (HB 9–10a)**. The Hebrew verb "to say" (אמר) means "to think" in many contexts. The man is actively using his imagination, so to begin with "I declare" is less natural than "I think" or "I imagine." He pictures himself ascending the date palm to take hold of these large "fruit-laden clusters" (on סַנְסִנָּיו, see Viezel 2014, 751). Elsewhere in the Song, the man is pictured clambering over mountains and demonstrating his physical prowess as an expression of his strength and virility (see 2:8, 17). Her stature is so intimidating that he will have to call upon the same kind of powers to ascend the heights of her beauty. At the conclusion of his speech, the man expresses three desires related to the woman's body: that her breasts be like date clusters, her breath like apples, and her mouth like fine wine. Apples, date clusters, and wine are tied to fertility imagery throughout the ANE (see notes on 2:3–5; 7:13 [HB 14]; and 8:5).

**7:9b (HB 10b)**. The woman now jumps in to affirm this desire, hoping expectantly that the pleasantness of her mouth be like wine "flowing freely/rightly for my beloved"

(לְמֵישָׁרִים לְדוֹדִי הוֹלֵךְ); see Prov. 23:31 for "rightly" as "smoothly"). She then says, "flowing over lips and teeth" (וְשִׂפְתֵי), following various textual witnesses. The MT renders the line "flowing [over] the lips of those who sleep" (דּוֹבֵב שִׂפְתֵי יְשֵׁנִים), which could be understood, "He causes to pine the lips of sleepers," taking the participle as a *polel* of דוב and emphasizing the theme of the lovers' longing (Pfenniger 2010, 300). The *polel* reading is an attractive option, but "flowing over lips and teeth" fits best with all the other references to body parts just mentioned by the man, especially those in the region of the face in 7:8–9a.

**7:10 (HB 11)**. Versions of "I am my beloved's" appear in 2:16 and 6:3. The conclusion of her line is the new element here: "his desire is for me" (וְעָלַי תְּשׁוּקָתוֹ). Interestingly, the term "desire" (תְּשׁוּקָה) appears in only three places in Scripture: (1) in Genesis 3:16 it refers to the woman's desire for the man; (2) in Genesis 4:7 it refers to sin's desire for Cain; (3) here in Song 7:10 (HB 11), it refers to the man's desire for the woman. The first two examples are given in negative contexts that indicate that the desire spoken of is one of domination or control (the notion that the woman's desire in Genesis 3:16 is sexual does not fit with the line that immediately follows regarding the man's domination of her; the sexual sense also does not make sense in light of Genesis 4:7). Here in the Song, however, the "desire" of the man for the woman should not be understood in a negative way. The key may be the preposition used with the noun, the negative connotations appearing as "to" (אֶל) in Genesis 3:16 and 4:7, and the positive connotation appearing as "on" (עַל) in Song 7:10 (HB 11). A. A. Macintosh has further argued convincingly that "desire" (תְּשׁוּקָה) should be understood, based on his review of its scant occurrences in the MT and DSS, as "concern, preoccupation, (single-minded) devotion" (2016, 365). She is confident about how he feels concerning her.

The image of the garden of Eden from Genesis 1–3 is not far from the mind of the Song's author, so it is possible that the mention of this term for "desire" is an intentional insertion meant to reverse the painful reality of God's statement to the woman in Genesis 3:16 and sin's evil desire in Genesis 4:7. The man and woman of the Song do not desire to dominate one another, but to return to the idyllic conditions of the garden before evil entered the heart of humanity.

### The Woman Again Invites the Man to Join Her in Sexual Intimacy (7:11 [HB 12]–8:4)

Following the man's affectionate wooing of the woman, she now invites him to join her in intimacy as she had in 4:16.

**7:11 (HB 12)**. The imperative creates an unmistakable tone. She is ready to join him in love. She leads the charge by urging him to "come" so that they can "go out" and "lodge" in the countryside, undoubtedly expressing a desire to be surrounded by all the trappings of nature, springtime, and the signs of fertility mentioned throughout the Song. Though her appeal is not ethical in nature, the language from Eliphaz captures this sense of union with nature. In the countryside is where the couple will be "in league with the stones of the field, and the beasts of the field shall be at peace" with them (Job 5:23; in context, Eliphaz is describing how receiving reproof from God aligns one with the created order, which is already in covenant with its creator). Relatedly, from the perspective of the songwriter, love seems best pursued in nature, in the environment of love. There, the so-called experts, who often demystify love through their many explanations, cannot be heard (self included); instead, the "voice of the turtledove" preaches its truth (2:12). The couple will spend the night in the natural ambiance of love (see note on 2:7).

**7:12 (HB 13)**. She wants to spend the evening with him (the previous verse) and the morning with him. They will go to the garden of love to see if it is the proper time for lovemaking (see 6:2, 11), and "there" she will "give my love to you" (שָׁם אֶתֵּן אֶת־דֹּדַי לָךְ). The term "love" (דּוֹד), when plural, always refers to "lovemaking" throughout the HB, but here it has the same meaning in the singular.

**7:13 (HB 14).** The "mandrakes" (הַדּוּדָאִים) or "love fruits" (*HALOT* s.v. "דּוּדָאִים" 215–16) or "love apples" (Keel 1994, 257) were an aphrodisiac and had a close connection to the concept of fertility (Murphy 1990b, 184). In Genesis 30, Reuben is said to have found mandrakes and given them to his mother, Leah. Rachel, who had been unable to have children, desperately wanted these mandrakes, but Leah was not keen to give them to her since Rachel had already "stolen my husband." So, the two women struck a deal that Rachel would give up Jacob for the night so that Leah could sleep with him in exchange for the mandrakes. That night, Leah reports to Jacob: "You must sleep with me because I have paid for your services with my son's mandrakes" (Gen. 30:16 NET). There is an abundance of irony in the narrative driven by the theme of faithlessness in the covenantal promises of God. The woman of the Song has stored in her house and at/above/beside their doors all the best fruits ("new and old," meaning "all kinds") that would occasion their lovemaking.

### The Kissing Gesture

The kissing gesture is well attested in the Bible. It occurs primarily as an expression of non-sexual, familial acceptance or friendship (e.g., Gen. 27:26–27; Ruth 1:9; 1 Kings 19:20). The same holds for Egyptian and Mesopotamian texts, where a mother may kiss her child, where friends kiss in greeting (e.g., Gilgamesh and Enkidu), or a supplicant kisses the earth before a deity or king. However, kissing does have its place in sexual contexts, as when the woman of folly seizes an unwitting fool "and kisses him" (Prov 7:13), or in positive romantic encounters (Gen. 29:11; Song 1:2; 8:1). Sexual descriptions of kissing of course appear in ANE literature. From Ugarit, see The Birth of Šaḥru-wa-Šalimu: "their lips are sweet, sweet as pomegranates. When he [El] kisses, there is conception, when he embraces, there is pregnancy" (*COS* 1:281; cf. Aqht in *COS* 1:344). Examples from Mesopotamian literature abound (see *ANET*, 181, §9; OB marriage contract, *ANET*, 544; Enki, *ANET*, 39–40; Nergal and Ereshkigal, *ANET* 104; *CAD* N.2 s.v. "*našāqu*" 59; Sumerian love poetry in *COS* 1:541).

Egyptian love poetry also features romantic kissing (*COS* 1:129; 1:130). The Middle Egyptian term for "to kiss," *sn*, only rarely includes the mouth sign, and instead focuses on the nose. Bruno Meissner proposes that kissing in Egypt was first a nose kiss (rubbing noses) and only gradually became a mouth kiss (1934, 915–16). Robert Schlichting, however, clarifies that the action of smelling or inhaling was the primary meaning before the term was used more frequently to refer to the kiss, and that both occur simultaneously when one approaches a male or female friend, as if the beloved person is recognized by their smell (1979, 902 n. 4). This interpretation is interesting considering the mention of "scent" and "nose" in Song 7:8–9a (HB 9–10a; for more on the gesture of kissing, see note on 1:2a; see also Jones 2019, 110–25).

**8:1.** As the man had expressed hope that her breasts be like clusters of grapes, her breath like the scent of apples (7:8 [HB 9]), and her mouth like fine wine (7:9 [HB 10]), so here she wishes that the man were as close to her as a brother. What we can be certain of is that these verses fit well within the Song with their motifs of separation and desire, but if we consider the possibility that the ordering of its chapters reflects authorial intent, then one may conject about how 8:1–5 fits as a sequential point in the story. The entire set of verses (8:1–5) is an expression of the woman's imagination, but why is she resorting to imagination if the couple is married now and does not need to fantasize like they once did? After all, what is left that prevents them from engaging in romantic behavior? The expression "Who is this coming?" in 8:5 echoes 3:6 and may be the clue needed to understand this sequence of verses in 8:1–5. It appears the woman is reliving the past feelings of excitement she experienced in 1:2–3:5, immediately after which came 3:6 and the phrase "Who/What is that coming up?," which kicked off the royal procession scene that was followed by the man's *waṣf* in chapter 4 and their eventual consummation in 5:1. Of course, this paradigm for reading the Song is not provable and should not be held dogmatically, but I present it as a possibility.

She wishes he were like a brother to her. Modern readers may misconstrue this metaphor for incest, but that would be taking the woman's figurative language too far. She does not wish he was literally her brother, but that he was "like" (כְּ) her brother, understanding נתן idiomatically (cf. Judg. 9:29; see helpful note in NET at Song 8:1). In other words, she is using her imagination to construct a scenario in which she could kiss the man free from public shame, but the only way that would be possible is if they were siblings (see sidebars "Familial Language in the Song" p. 287 and "The Kissing Gesture" p. 317). To kiss a nonrelative romantically "in the street" (בַּחוּץ) would have been taboo. However, if he were her brother, then "they would not despise me!" In the notes on 3:3 and 5:7, I mention Middle Assyrian laws regarding women's behavior in public. Though these laws do not specifically mention kissing, it seems clear enough that kissing a nonrelative of the opposite sex in public would result in shame.

> **Reality-Bending Love**
>
> Egyptian love songs feature lovers concocting unrealistic scenarios that would place them within close proximity of the one they love, which requires circumventing socioeconomic norms. In the love songs from Cairo, a boy fantasizes about a girl he admires: "If only I were her Nubian maid, / her attendant in secret! / She brings \<her\> [a bowl of] mandragoras. . . . / It is in her hand, / while she gives the pleasure. / In other words: / she would grant me / the hue of her whole body" (M. Fox 1985, 37). In these lines, the boy expresses a lustful fantasy of being the female maid of a girl he fancies. The fact that this imagined scenario has forced him to switch genders is no bother to him—it was the only way he could realistically place himself in close physical proximity to her. He imagines bringing her fruit, whereupon she pleasures him sexually with her whole body in the secrecy of her bedroom. For any couple to engage in that level of romantic behavior in public would be considered shameful. The shame would only magnify if the couple were unmarried. Similarly to the Egyptian text, in Song 8:1 the woman suspends reality in imagining she and her lover were siblings just so that she could be close to him.

**8:2**. She continues reliving her old feelings of desire through imagination (see note on 8:1). Unlike the lustful imagination of the Egyptian boy of the Cairo love songs, the woman here is not imagining an illicit tryst performed apart from her parents' approval. She is not sneaking off to a secret location to avoid shame from her mother; rather, she imagines all this taking place within the context of her parents' home. In the Sumerian texts about the romance of Dumuzi and Inanna, the goddess Inanna knows that if she stays the night with her lover, her mother will be angry, so she asks, "What shall I say to deceive my mother![?]" Dumuzi comes up with a plot that Inanna should tell her mother that she was spending time with one of her friends, saying, "Thus deceitfully stand up to your mother, / While we by the moonlight indulge (our) passion, / I will [prepare] for you a bed pure, sweet, (and) noble . . ." (Pritchard 2011, 407). The woman of the Song, however, expressly mentions her mother (and his; 3:11) only positively and imagines what it would be like for her to take her beloved straight to her mother's house.

The woman of the Song imagines that the only way for the two of them to become intimate would be for the man to be brought out to her mother's house "who taught me," so that he could "drink spiced wine from the nectar of my pomegranates." References to the woman's mother conjure up the notion that love is cyclical from generation to generation (see note on 8:5). Presumably, her mother had taught her the ways of love to prepare her for intimacy with a man one day. Perhaps part of that instruction involved the importance of aphrodisiacs like drinking the juice of the pomegranate (Keel 1994, 262; see sidebar "The Expertise of the Mother" p. 270). There may be double entendre, though, with the pomegranates representing her breasts.

**8:3–4**. Song 8:3 is identical to 2:6, following which came the adjuration to the daughters of Jerusalem in 2:7. The same pattern follows here in 8:4. This points readers to the symmetry of the Song, where elements from chapters 1–2 are paralleled near the conclusion (see notes on 8:8–14). The formula is similar to 2:7 and 3:5. One of the things missing in the MT of 8:4 is the object upon which they swear: "the gazelles or does of the field." Another difference is that the the oath formula of 2:7 and 3:5 has been replaced with the interrogative "Why?" (מַה). Nevertheless, the translation in all three places is identical in the ESV: "that you not stir up or awaken love until it pleases." Perhaps the absence of the sworn-upon object in 8:4 is due to the fact that the woman can now speak experientially about sexual intimacy and has no need to appeal to nature, and as a result the oath has turned into a question at this point: "Why bother arousing love since it will appear when it so desires?" (my paraphrase; see Exum 2005, 248).

## The Couple Again Embraces One Another in Sexual Intimacy (8:5)

The lovers return to a state of enraptured embrace.

**8:5**. The woman's exercise of reliving the golden years of love comes to a conclusion here in 8:5 (see note on 8:1). The maidens of Jerusalem are the presumed speakers in the first part of the verse. They ask a question that perfectly mirrors 3:6, "Who/What is that coming up from the wilderness?" In 3:6 the answer to that question was King Solomon on his royal carriage-bed (possibly including the woman; see note on 3:6 and sidebar "To Retrieve a Princess" p. 272). Here the answer to that question is the woman, for she is said to be "leaning on her beloved." Just as the man went out to the countryside to retrieve her in 3:6, so now she relives the experience as the couple is pictured returning to the palace together in 8:5.

The expression "under the apple tree" (תַּחַת הַתַּפּוּחַ) takes readers back to 2:3 where she compares him to a rare apple tree among the other ordinary trees of the forest. She sat there in the shade of that tree. Two verses later, in 2:5, she desires to be refreshed with apples. Here at 8:5, under the apple tree, she "stirs" (עוּר) him, a verb she has used repeatedly in her admonishment to the maidens of Jerusalem that they not "stir up" love until the right time (2:7; 3:5; 8:4). In 4:16 the verb was used to welcome the act of sex in the verse that immediately followed (5:1). In 5:2–3, the verb was used euphemistically when the man was trying to enter the house but she would not rise to open the door. In this final appearance of the verb, the woman has determined this is the right time for love, just as in 4:16, so she "stirs" him. Given the other uses of the verb in the Song, this is an unmistakable reference to sexual arousal and the consequent act of sexual intercourse.

The woman says that she arouses the man "there" (שָׁמָּה) where his mother conceived and bore him. The imagery of the apple tree conjures up an idyllic countryside scene, and it serves as double entendre to refer to the reproductive regions of the couple's bodies. Modern readers may find the repeated mentions of the couple's mothers odd in the context of romance (1:6; 3:4, 11; 8:1–2, 5; the man mentions her mother in 6:9), but for the young woman, her mother represents all she knows of this mysterious world of lovemaking. She had taught her daughter the ways of love (8:2).

The woman's references to mothers also speaks to the rhythms of love within the circle of life. Motherhood is where life begins, and this couple's lovemaking will likely make motherhood the destiny of this woman. The fact that generations of lovers repeat the cycle of love gives at least one level of legitimacy and purpose to the lovers' act (though becoming "one flesh" alone is sufficient for that; Gen. 2:24). This pattern of life is larger than the couple's relationship. Romance is not merely untethered passion between two people, but the perpetuation of a pattern of life—a pattern reflected in the seasons of the year, in the flora and fauna of the earth, and in the "wonderful" way of a man with a maiden (Prov. 30:19b). The Song presents sex as an emblem of something much larger than fleeting feelings of lust. The Song continually makes references to universal principles that supersede the romance of any one couple. There is no greater testimony to the universal power of love than the section that follows (8:6–7).

## THEOLOGICAL FOCUS

The Song is filled with imagery and it, perhaps more than any other text of Scripture, invites the reader to activate their own imagination based on concrete realities. We know, for example, that King Solomon was involved in the design of his royal palace and the Lord's temple and was familiar with the finest materials, such as purple fabric (2 Chron. 2:6). He commissioned that such materials be used in the adornment of the temple. It is not difficult, therefore, for readers to imagine King Solomon surrounded by hanging fabrics and tapestries brought to him by his artisans so that he could exercise his famous wisdom in choosing only the best for his palace and for the temple of God. The description is of a king encumbered by such great luxury that he gets caught in a sea of purple fabric, an apt analogy for his darling's long, flowing hair (7:5 [HB 6]). He is rendered immobile by the overabundance of the world's rarest and richest spices, jewels, textiles, wines, and food. He is one of only a few in his time who must say "no" when offered more and more of the best his world has to offer.

The innumerable facets of the woman's beauty likewise paralyze him. There are not enough metaphors to adequately describe just how marvelous she is. From the bottom of her feet to the top of her head she is remarkable (7:1–5 [HB 2–6]) and he is rendered "captive in the tresses" (7:5 [HB 6]). Her beauty ensnares him like a prisoner of love, so he is helpless in her presence. This is the type of affection promoted by the Song. And while the couple focuses on the outward features when describing the other, we know that the Song points, by analogy, to a love far more profound than what makeup, jewels, the best clothing, and an ideal physique can evoke (Song 8:6–7). After all, outward "beauty is a vapor" (Prov. 31:30); it is transient and it does not speak to a person's inner beauty. Physical beauty tends to fade, but those who "fear the Lord" are to be highly favored (Prov. 31:30).

Believers ought to renew their embrace of one another throughout the many seasons of marriage. The woman's imagination in 8:1–5 may have taken her back to those early feelings of romance, but those memories were activated so that they could be put into the service of the couple's real, present-day relationship. So, we can say that 8:5b represents another real occasion of sexual intimacy. The Song has shown how love cycles through times of wonderful excitement and times of difficulty. These occasions of renewed embrace are times of open and spoken affection from one lover to the other. The man and woman must speak with unrestrained affection to one another and be willing to back it up with action. The man will climb whatever mountain to get to his beloved. She will deny all suitors in waiting for him. They both will restrain their bodies until the time that love has arrived; and when it has, they will embrace it with the fullest passion.

Just as romantic love between a couple experiences seasons of excitement interspersed with seasons of difficulty, so an analogy can be made to the relationship between Christ and his church. As believers, we can often become cold to the calling of God for our lives. We can lose sight of the gospel and its transformative effect on our hearts and the world around us. Sadly, we can fall "in love with this present world," like Demas, and let our affections for Christ run cold (2 Tim. 4:10). To battle this, we must regularly renew our pursuit of him through prayer and repentance, in the Word of God and on our knees. In so doing we may be "transformed by the renewal" of our minds, able "to discern what is the will of God, what is good and acceptable and perfect" (Rom. 12:2). This cannot be the listless duty of a religious drone, but the passion of a heart longing for something "not of this world," a joy attainable only through the full, vibrant indwelling of God in our hearts, the Holy Spirit (John 18:36; Eph. 5:18). Throughout seasons of rebellion in our hearts toward God, if we listen, we can hear the voice of his Spirit speaking to us:

> Awake, O sleeper,
> and arise from the dead,
> and Christ will shine on you. (Eph. 5:14)

# PREACHING AND TEACHING STRATEGIES

## Exegetical and Theological Synthesis

The lovers have not given up on their relationship, even though they have experienced the difficulty of separation. Pushing past the pain, they continued to pursue one another. Their renewed pursuit, however, has a *telos*, a goal: sexual union. The lovers begin to renew their embrace of one another by praising one another's physical and relational prowess as well as beckoning each other toward lovemaking. Both partners took action to renew their sexual embrace. Both partners felt sexual desire for one another.

The renew of sexual embrace is the logical conclusion to the renewal of pursuit for a couple. It is very difficult to have a thriving relationship with a dysfunctional sex life. And just because some couples have been together for a long-time does not mean that sexual intimacy must wane. In fact, the apostle Paul seems to suggest that married couples should not go for long periods of time without being intimate (1 Cor. 7:5). Pursuit of one's spouse never becomes optional just because the couple has been together for a long time.

### Preaching Idea
Pursuing sexual pleasure with your spouse has no expiration date.

### Contemporary Connections

#### What does it mean?
The man and the woman must renew their sexual passion for one another again. They had already experienced the pain of "missing" each other earlier in the text (5:2–6). Yet they did not give in to the hurt. They persevered in their relationship, fueled by an underlying love and commitment for one another. Now together once again, the man and the woman entice one another toward sexual union. The man allures his woman with wonderful words (7:1–6 [HB 2–7]). He is not satisfied with merely bland compliments like "You look good." Instead, he uses intriguing word pictures. He likens his beloved's hair to an enticing labyrinth of rich purple fabric that could trap a king (7:5 [HB 6]).

The man expresses his determination to make love to his wife (7:7–8 [HB 8–9]). The man does not give in to self-pity because he did not get his way earlier in the text (see 5:2–6). He does not sulk nor feel that he has been rejected forever. No, he gets up and is determined to make love to his beautiful wife. No matter how far along in the relationship, the man must continually pursue his woman. The desire of the man is matched by the woman's own desire (7:11–13 [HB 12–14])! She beckons him to a private place for lovemaking. She earnestly desires to give herself to him. She even thinks of new ways to "spice up" their love life.

The expression of the woman's desires in the Song challenges certain Christian viewpoints on marriage and sexuality. Some pastors present the marriage union as if it is the man's job to pursue the woman for sexual pleasure and the woman's job to receive his overtures. Some Christians make it seem like any sexual advance or overture by the woman would be inappropriate or, at the very least, contrary to her role as a woman. But Scripture presents the woman's desire much differently. She pursues her husband by beckoning him to a place of lovemaking (7:11 [HB 12]). She earnestly desires to make love to him and has even saved up resources to enhance their lovemaking (7:12–13 [HB 13–14]). She longs to be affectionate to the man in public (8:1). She is going to lead the man to a place where they can make love (8:2). She longs to be in sexual embrace with her husband (8:3). In contrast to our culture's typical view of marriage, the man and the woman still have an exciting and alluring sexual life.

*Is it true?*
Sex is not just for the honeymoon. Scripture makes it clear that a husband and a wife are to "fulfill their duties" to one another consistently (see 1 Cor. 7:3). The apostle Paul advises that a husband and wife should only abstain from regular sex if they both agree to for a limited time (1 Cor. 7:5). Married couples must be passionate lovers, not just efficient roommates. The Song puts a poetic spin on what the apostle Paul teaches in 1 Corinthians. In Song 7:1–8:5, the couple is already married. They have gone through the pain of relational dysfunction, but they have also demonstrated their commitment to one another. After the pain of estrangement, they do not merely emotionally reconcile; they also seek to please one another sexually. There is no expiration date on the sexual aspect of a couple's relationship.

Of course, different seasons in a couple's life call for different expectations surrounding sexuality. A couple with a young child, or many young children, may not have as active of a sexual life as a couple without children or with children who are a little bit older and sleeping through the night. The responsibilities of caring for children are not the only thing that can get impede a couple's sex life. Work, countless responsibilities, and other important commitments, can eat into the time and energy couples may have for one another. The march of time presents a challenge as well, for the longer a couple is together the more they know about each other. The more a couple knows one another, the more work it takes to keep things exciting. Of course, not every sexual encounter must feel like the honeymoon all over again. The larger point is that couples must fight *for* each other and prioritize one another. If a couple does not work to renew their embrace, they may find themselves in a very difficult relationship. Furthermore, as you could probably expect, as a couple ages, their frequency of sexual encounters drops as well. Ecclesiastes seems to indicate that sexual desire wanes as people age (Eccl. 12:5). Yet for most couples, their sexual relationship does not end completely. The work to renew a lover's embrace is also set before the married couple.

## Now what?
How are you going to pursue your spouse? Sexual pursuit, according to Scripture, is not reserved only for the early years of a relationship. It is not God's intention that all sexual passion disappear once we have been married for a long time. The couple in the Song goes through extraordinary efforts to return the "spark" to the relationship. The man uses his words and his intention to spark sexual chemistry. He "woos" his wife. How are you speaking to your wife? Do you come up with creative compliments? Are you the "mirror" for her body, praising her physical attributes and making her feel "sexy" no matter her physical condition? Are you actively "romancing" your wife, or do you only do romantic things for her when you want sex? Growing in romance requires planning and forethought.

For the married woman, do you desire your husband? Are you pursuing him like the woman in the Song is pursuing the man? The woman in the Song does not want that aspect of their relationship to fall into a rut but saves up all kinds of things to enhance their lovemaking (7:13 [HB 14]). The responsibilities and demands upon each spouse can be great, especially if they have children, care for extended family, or have other such commitments. But the responsibilities of life must be put in their proper place so that the marriage relationship can flourish.

While couples must pursue renewal in their marriages, it is incumbent upon all believers to pursue renewal in their relationship with the Lord. Salvation does not end with accepting Jesus as Lord and Savior. In fact, turning to Christ in repentance and faith is just the beginning of salvation. All Christians then commence on the long walk home toward the kingdom of God (Rom. 8:28–39). Therefore, singles may clearly see something that married couples may not: the point of human existence is God, not marriage. The concern that the couple pours into each other in this passage mirrors the concern that single people can pour into their relationship with God. Singles are not missing out on God's best by not getting married if they are pursuing him and seeking renewal. So, while the text more directly applies to married couples, it can still instruct singles and warn those who are married to not lose sight of the ultimate relationship all believers have with God.

## Creativity in Presentation
The challenge of creatively presenting the text is how to speak about sex in the way that the Song speaks about sex. While commentators routinely debate how much euphemism is present in the earlier parts of the Song, there is no debating that 7:1 (HB 2)–8:5 concerns sex! Pastors should not seek to be overly graphic nor overly prudish when preaching the Song. They need to be especially sensitive to how such a passage would be communicated if children are going to be present in the worship service.

Here are a few suggestions for how to creatively present on sex without being crass. First, assume that children, or at least teenagers, will be present in the audience. If you have, or had, or are going to have teenagers one day, think about how you would want a pastor to address them. Thinking through what you'd want your own kids to hear in a sermon can help shape what you would say to your congregation. Second, recognize that the Song is sensual and erotic, but not so explicit on the surface. In other words, the Song cloaks the sexual act in metaphor. The Song is a sensual and erotic poem because it speaks of sexual intimacy. But unlike pornography, the Song often keeps a veil of metaphor between the reader and what is being described. Pornography, on the other hand, is the opposite of the sensual and erotic; it is explicit. It rips down the veil and literally exposes the sexual act for all to see. Therefore, as pastors, we must labor diligently to keep the veil up.

Third, immerse yourself in the Song to get over feelings of awkwardness. I am assuming that if you're reading this commentary, you're probably already investing in an intense study of the Song. One of the best ways to get over the awkwardness of preaching about sex is to continually read and reread the Song. If we feel awkward talking about a subject, our audience will feel awkward. But if we allow the Song to reshape our imagination and perspective on sexuality—that it is good and right and should be celebrated within marriage—then we will become more confident when preaching on sex. Sex is a great gift within marriage and should be celebrated. So, we need the Song to recalibrate—or, to use Richard Lovelace's term, "disenculturate"— our view of sex so that we are shaped by a thoroughly biblical view of sex, not one beholden to an overly prudish subculture if we find ourselves within one.

The big idea of the text is, "Pursuing sexual pleasure with your spouse has no expiration date." The outline of the text can focus on how the couple in the Song renews their embrace of sexual intimacy and how Christian couples can as well:

- Woo your spouse with words (7:1–10 [HB 2–11])
- Invite your spouse to exciting places (7:11 [HB 12]–8:5a)
- Embrace your spouse in intimacy (8:5)

## DISCUSSION QUESTIONS

1. What can we learn from how the man uses his words (7:1–10 [HB 2–11])?

2. How does the woman express her desire for the man (7:11 [HB 12]–8:5)?

3. What admonition does the woman give to her friends (8:4)? Why?

4. How can you become better at romancing your spouse?

5. How does this passage shatter the stereotypes about marriage we often hear in the world?

# THE LESSONS OF LOVE (8:6–14)

The Song's conclusion features the woman's lessons on the raw power of love, on chastity, and on love's surpassing value. Up to this point, the woman has exhorted the maidens of Jerusalem to not awaken or stir up love until it pleases (2:7; 3:5; 8:4). Here in the final lines of the Song, there are still allusions to the couple's relationship, but the lessons are more centered on universal principles of love that the student of love must heed. First, in 8:6–7, her pupils will discover that love is the preeminent force in the universe, as powerful as death itself. Love is a fire that cannot be snuffed out by opposing powers, nor can it be rendered irrelevant through wealth. Second, in 8:8–14, the student will learn of the rewards of love both when encountered within the context of chastity (8:8–10) and as a treasure more valuable than any possession (8:11–12). The Song concludes with two verses that draw the reader back into the couple's love saga as a reminder that love never ends.

The entire section is labeled The Lessons of Love (8:6–14), which is broken into two preaching units: Love Is Supreme (8:6–7), and Love Is Rewarding (8:8–14).

# Song of Songs 8:6–7

## EXEGETICAL IDEA
The woman proclaims that love is more powerful than any earthly force, even as powerful as death itself.

## THEOLOGICAL FOCUS
Believers should acknowledge the inimitable power of romantic love, driving them to revere it as divinely given rather than as a mere tool for manipulation and pleasure.

## PREACHING IDEA
Love is supreme.

## PREACHING POINTERS
After writing many chapters of imaginative poetry, the author provided the clearest exposition of love in the whole book. The author explained that love is a force as strong as death, backed up by the repeated lovesickness the woman felt when separated from the man. The power of love crashed over the woman like a wave. Love burned in their lives fierce like lightning. Love was so valuable as to be priceless, such that if anyone tried to buy it they would be criticized as a fool.

If love is the most important thing in the world, believers should do everything in their power to grab hold of it. Human love provides a dim picture of God's fierce love for his people. As great as human love is, human life becomes meaningless without the love of God. Once people experience God's love, they learn to love everything, and everyone, properly.

# LOVE IS SUPREME (8:6–7)

## LITERARY STRUCTURE AND THEMES (8:6–7)

This is the shortest unit in all the Song. Both verses deal with the subject of love's insurpassability—its supremacy over all things (8:6), including wealth (8:7). Song 8:6 concludes by asserting that love's power burns like heavenly fire, and 8:7 begins by stating that no waters can quench it. In the latter half of 8:7, these opposing "waters" are embodied through "wealth," one means by which humans may attempt to quench love's fire.

The two verses, beginning in 8:6b, may form a loose parallel structure as well. There is a theme line in 8:6a where the woman asks the man to make her a permanent fixture of his heart, following which is her explanation for why this is important:

Set me like a seal on your heart / like a seal on your arm (6a)
  A For love is as mighty as death, as severe as Sheol (6b)
    B its burnings are the burnings of fire, the fire of the Lord (6c)
    B′ many waters are not able to quench love, and rivers cannot drown it (7a)
  A′ If a man gave all the wealth of his house for love, they would certainly despise him (7b)

The structure can be observed as: A power; B fire; B′ water; A′ wealth. The A and A′ lines are more abstractly related and speak to love more broadly rather than describe love's qualities, which are featured in B and B′. Furthermore, the attributes of love featured in 8:6 cannot be thwarted by its opponents in 8:7. This point is further illustrated in the verses that follow (specifically, 8:11–12).

- *Nothing Is More Powerful Than Love (8:6)*
- *Nothing Is More Valuable Than Love (8:7)*

## EXPOSITION (8:6–7)

The text has a proverbial tone. This passage and the oaths recited by the woman throughout the Song (2:7; 3:5; 8:4) lead us to believe that the text was intended to communicate to an audience that is broader than just the maidens of Jerusalem. The term "didactic" is typically reserved for works traditionally classified as "wisdom literature," especially Proverbs and Ecclesiastes, and is not an appropriate label for the Song as a whole. If, however, the Song is at all instructional, then that attribute is seen most clearly in the refrains and here at the conclusion.

Song 8:6–7 is not a summary of the entire Song, but it addresses the elephant in the room: the fact that love is not always marked by sunrises, sunsets, fruit blossoms, and flowers. Rather, love is raw, powerful, and undaunted. Song 8:6 and 7 present two fundamental truths about love. In 8:6 we learn that love is untamable, uncontrollable, and fierce. In 8:7 we discover that this power cannot be avoided. The chief means by which the human race dispenses with problems is through the overlapping forces of power and wealth, neither of which can compare to or in any way sidestep the might and value of love.

### Seals in the Ancient Near East

The "seal" (חוֹתָם) referenced by the woman in 8:6 is likely an engraved signet of some kind, like a cylinder seal. Cylinder seals were small (about one to two inches long) and bore a specific image and/or inscription that, when rolled onto soft clay, could be used to authenticate documents like a modern signature (Nemet-Nejat 2002, 53). Other kinds of seals were also in use in the ANE, like stamp seals, rings, or scarab seals (a type of stamp seal in the shape of a scarab beetle). In Genesis 38:18 Tamar takes Judah's seal, cord, and staff as collateral for her prostitution services; these were used by her later to prove his identity. In 1 Kings 21:8 Jezebel uses Ahab's seal to ratify a letter conspiring against Naboth. In the first colon of Song 8:6 the woman requests that he set her as a seal on his heart, like a necklace, but in the parallel colon the seal is around his "arm," which could simply mean wrist, as in a bracelet. For these reasons it seems a cylinder with a hole for a leather strap or a string is the most natural image.

### Nothing Is More Powerful Than Love (8:6)
The woman attributes to love the power of death, the grave, and the very flame of God.

**8:6.** The woman exclaims that the man should take her as a seal on his heart and on his arm (see sidebar "Seals in the Ancient Near East" p. 327). Valérie Kabergs points out that the construction "set on heart" (שִׂים עַל־לֵב) elsewhere means "take to heart" as in "take very seriously" (Isa. 42:25; 47:7; 57:1–11; Jer. 12:11; Dan. 1:8; Mal. 2:2); thus, the line could be rendered, "Take me to heart, as a seal" (2014, 263; see her further discussion of זְרוֹעַ). Both the literal (an actual seal) and metaphorical (take me seriously) readings make good sense in this context. But why should the man do this? She explains that "love is as strong as death." She compares love to death in order to elevate the status of love in the minds of her hearers, for nothing otherwise can compete with the insatiable appetite of death/the grave (Hab. 2:5; see sidebar "The Power of Death" p. 329). As several have so eloquently stated, the act of lovemaking is itself an act of defiance toward death (Exum 2005, 3; Watson 1997, 386).

"Jealousy" is a good translation option for קִנְאָה, given the implication of competing forces that rise up against love, including the explicit mention of wealth as a rival distraction to the human heart (8:7). The term "difficult/severe/jealousy" (קָשָׁה) has a similar sound to the Hebrew term "bow" (קֶשֶׁת), which opens the door to understanding "its flashes" (רְשָׁפֶיהָ) in the next line to mean, metaphorically, "its arrows." In Psalm 76:3 (HB 4), the term "flashes" is a stand-in for "arrows" in the phrase "the flashes of the bow." The translation "its flashes are the flashes of fire" seems rather redundant in English, but the construction is known elsewhere in Hebrew (a plural subject with a pronominal suffix followed by plural predicate nominative of the same root, which is itself in construct with an absolute noun that qualifies the preceding nouns). For example, in Deuteronomy 32:32 we have the expression, "their grapes are the grapes of poison" (עֲנָבֵמוֹ עִנְּבֵי־רוֹשׁ). Others come from Isaiah 59:6–7: "their deeds are the deeds of evil" (מַעֲשֵׂיהֶם מַעֲשֵׂי־אָוֶן) and "their thoughts are the thoughts of evil" (מַחְשְׁבוֹתֵיהֶם מַחְשְׁבוֹת אָוֶן). Finally, Proverbs 3:17 states, "her ways are the ways of pleasantness" (דְּרָכֶיהָ דַרְכֵי־נֹעַם). The syntactical function appears to be one of emphasis. In each of these instances, the initial noun is a known entity and readily understandable: "grapes" (Deut. 32:32), "deeds" (Isa. 59:6), "thoughts" (Isa. 59:7), and "ways/paths" (Prov. 3:17). The absolute noun carries the adjectival/qualifying sense, producing the understanding "poison" grapes, "evil" deeds, "evil" thoughts, "pleasant" ways.

The problem in the Song 8:6 expression is that the lead noun (רֶשֶׁף) is very rare and its meaning is elusive—what is a "flash"? The gloss "flash" is uncertain and is based on uses of רֶשֶׁף in the Samaritan Pentateuch and Jewish Aramaic. Comparative evidence points scholars to the god Resheph, a Canaanite deity of war and plague (see *HALOT* s.v. "רֶשֶׁף I" 1297–98). One possibility could be to see רֶשֶׁף as "plague" (cf. Hab. 3:5). Plagues are known, and comparative evidence suggests this as the strongest possibility, one that also happens to fit well with the context of Song 8:6 where love's ferocious attributes are described. It could be that the "flashes/

plagues" refers to a burning physical sensation. There are different kinds of burning: a person can be burned by fire, lightning, poisons, and other things. The implication from this would be that love can cause an unrelenting emotional burning of one's heart that can lead to a level of desperation suggestive of death. If, on the other hand, the expression is understood as "its flashes are the flashes of fire," we might ask how "fire" qualifies "flashes" in any way similar to the examples of this type of construction above. Noting the connection of "flashes" with arrows (Ps. 76:3 [HB 4]), perhaps this is a reference to "flaming arrows" such as might correspond with storm imagery and remind us of the scene atop Mt. Carmel in 1 Kings 18.

The woman tells the man to make her like a seal around his neck or arm, a permanent signet of his identity, because her love for him is powerful, unrelenting, jealous, and even potentially harmful. These words from the woman fly in the face of any suggestion that the Song is promoting "free love" (Longman 2001, 209). A flippant attitude about romantic love is rejected by the Song. Love is consequential and dangerous. The danger comes from love's nature as a consuming fire, even the "fire of Yah" (שַׁלְהֶבֶתְיָה). Based on conflicting manuscript evidence and the contexts of these verses, commentators debate whether the name of God is present at the end of this word or if the ending is merely an intensifier, making it "almighty flame" (see discussion in Exum 2005, 253–54). However, the divine imagery used throughout the Song, the particularly high volume of cultic terminology appearing here in 8:6–7 (and thematic connections to 1 Kings 18 and the "fire of Yahweh" אֵשׁ־יְהוָה), and the subtle allusions to the "Almighty" in the refrain (see sidebar "The High Stakes of Love" p. 248) suggest that here we have another subtle reference to God that has suffered from haplography, its original perhaps being "flame of Yah" (שַׁלְהֶבֶת־יָהּ). There may be a conceptual connection here to God's right as judge to avenge the spouse spurned by adultery (Lev. 20:10; Jer. 29:23). The sages warn all men (and by implication, all women):

> Can a man carry fire next to his chest
> and his clothes not be burned?
> Or can one walk on hot coals
> and his feet not be scorched?
> So is he who goes in to his neighbor's wife;
> none who touches her will go unpunished.
> (Prov. 6:27–29 ESV)

Such stern warnings are for those who toy carelessly with love's raw power. This, of course, does not mean though that there is no potential for healing and restoration; "a broken and contrite heart, O God, you will not despise" (see Ps. Ps. 51:17 [HB 19]).

### The Power of Death

For the speaker in Song 8:6 to equate the power of love to the power of death is no small claim. Death is often portrayed in biblical and Ugaritic literature as the single most threatening force on earth. It is spoken of in this way abstractly in Scripture, but death is identified with an actual god in Ugaritic mythology. In Scripture, death is personified as a monster with an insatiable appetite: "Therefore the grave/Sheol has enlarged its appetite and opened its mouth beyond measure, and the nobility of Jerusalem and her multitude will go down" (Isa. 5:14). Death is also personified as an enemy nation coming to devour all people: like greed, "death never has enough. He collects for himself all nations and gathers as his own all peoples" (Hab. 2:5). Similarly, "Sheol and Abaddon are never satisfied" (Prov. 27:20; cf. Prov. 30:16). In Ugaritic literature, the term "death" is also a god by the same name ("*Môtu*"). In these texts, *Môtu* says this about himself: "My throat is the throat of the lion in the wasteland, and the gullet of the 'snorter' [some think "whale"] in the sea" (*COS* 1:264). He goes on to say that he swallows up everything, even other gods. Ancient people of course understood the all-encompassing power of death, that *nothing*

> was stronger. In Ecclesiastes, death forms a basis for Qohelet's vexations over the futility of human endeavor in light of the transience of life; it is what inspires him to say, "All is vanity!"
>
> This broader cultural understanding of the unmatched power of death occasions the Song's use of the concept to elevate the status of love in the mind of the reader. The incomparable power of death is also the backdrop against which Scripture writers describe God's power to "swallow up death forever" (Isa. 25:8), which is picked up by the apostle Paul in his ode to the surpassing power of the resurrection (1 Cor. 15:54–55; cf. Hos. 13:14).

### Nothing Is More Valuable Than Love (8:7)

The woman lists the opponents of love and their inability to undermine its power and value.

**8:7.** Not only is love as powerful as death, as jealous as the grave, and capable of severe affliction—its worth is immeasurable. It cannot be suffocated by "many waters" or by "floods." This image of a fire so intense that it cannot be quenched by water brings to mind 1 Kings 18 when, atop Mt. Carmel, Elijah challenged the prophets of Baal by declaring that the deity "who answers by fire" on the altar is truly God. To demonstrate the true power of God, Elijah dug a trench around the altar and ordered three times that jars of water be poured over the sacrifice, until "the water surrounded the sacrifice such that even the trench was filled with water." Then "the fire of the LORD" (אֵשׁ־יְהוָה) fell and consumed every drop of water, including the burnt offering, wood, stones, and dust. This type of imagery certainly came to mind for ancient readers when hearing Song 8:7. The "flame of the LORD" (שַׁלְהֶבֶתְיָה) mentioned at the end of Song 8:6 suggests an allusion to the story of Elijah and Mt. Carmel, but the "many waters" (מַיִם רַבִּים) of the very next line confirms it.

The god Baal holding in his left hand a spear stylized as lightning. Public domain (see *ANEP* §490).

## Love Is Supreme (8:6–7)

No river deluge can choke out the flame of love. For a real-world example of this, the songwriter presents "wealth" (הוֹן) as a competing power sometimes used by people to supplant love (as when one attempts to bribe a jealous lover in Proverbs 6:34–35). Scripture speaks frequently about the limited power of wealth and its inability to compete with superior forces like love or wisdom (e.g., Ps. 39:6 [HB 7]; Prov. 3:13–18; 11:4; 29:3; 30:15; Hab. 2:5). The Song states here that even if someone gave away his entire estate "for love . . . they would certainly despise him" (בּוֹז יָבוּזוּ לוֹ). A survey of this verb's use (and the related verb בזה) in the Hebrew Bible reveals that it almost always means "to look down on" or "be disgusted with" someone or something (e.g., 2 Kings 19:21; Prov. 1:7; 6:30; 15:20; 23:22). It is almost always used to describe how the wicked despise the vulnerable, the righteous, or God. Only rarely is God the subject, and even then, the verb is used to describe what he does *not* despise (Pss. 22:24 [HB 25]; 51:17 [HB 19]; 69:33 [HB 34]; 102:17 [HB 18]). A physical manifestation of this emotion is seen in the act of literally pointing a finger at someone in disgust in order to unjustly accuse or harm someone (Isa. 58:9; possibly Prov. 6:13), to legitimately accuse someone of evil in Akkadian texts, to decry taboo behavior (like gluttony) in Egyptian texts, or to mock someone openly (like when they pass through the city gate) in Sumerian texts (Jones 2019, 19–31). Anyone who mistakenly elevates the inferior value of money to the level of love will be, as the woman of the Song insinuates, the object of such finger-pointing derision.

Why is the man of Song 8:7 despised? He has given up all of his accumulated wealth in exchange "for love" (בְּאַהֲבָה). The preposition "for" (בְּ) here represents the thing being purchased (cf. Gen. 23:9; Song 8:11). The man is attempting to buy love. In his own mind, the man is making a huge sacrifice in exchange for love, which seems like a noble act on the surface. However, the currency of wealth is not accepted here; only love can be used to acquire love. Speaking idealistically, the Song claims that this man's potential lovers (and others in society in general) will utterly despise him for attempting to gain by monetary means what can only be truly won through love. Certainly, a man in Iron Age Israel could offer a bride-price to a woman's father in order to acquire her as wife, and she may go willingly or begrudgingly (cf. Gen. 24:52–59; 25:15–30; Judg. 1:12–13), but this is quite different from winning the woman's love. The man and woman of the Song, however, are infatuated with one another. His affection pours from his lips at every opportunity. There is no doubting his love for the woman, and while he may adorn her with many riches in keeping with cultural norms, the true currency of this exchange is not gold, purple, or prestige, but love.

### The Song and Mt. Carmel

Song 8:6–7 shares themes with the Elijah-Elisha narratives and the Bible's polemic against Baalism. Several Elijah-Elisha passages contain implicit or explicit references to how Baal's supposed powers are proven to be false and are actually powers possessed only by Yahweh. Polemical texts of Scripture such as these make many subtle references to the stories of Baal known to us through the Ugaritic text corpus. In those ancient myths, Baal is depicted as battling with other gods associated with death and the river. This motif of battling against chaotic flood waters (or a dragon/serpent) is well known in ANE mythology and has echoes throughout the HB where Yahweh is depicted as the victor against all such forces (e.g., Pss. 68; 104:1–9; and many others related to the *chaoskampf* motif). The language of Song 8:6–7 mentioning "death," "rivers," "fire," and "flood" would evoke cosmic, cultic imagery known throughout the ANE and elsewhere in Scripture: "Sheol, the barren womb, the land never satisfied with water, and the fire that never says, 'Enough'" (Prov. 30:16). To this we could add biblical passages where the mighty "waters" fled at the rebuke of God (Ps. 104:6–7).

> Here in the Song, however, love is the subject of the cosmic motif, not Yahweh directly, though both are present in the imagery of these verses (Wilson-Wright 2015, 333; see also Kaplan and Wilson-Wright 2018, 334–51). Just as the man compared the woman's head to "Carmel" in Song 7:5 (HB 6), drawing out a similar sense of divine wonder and majesty (see note on 7:5 [HB 6]), here the woman draws upon other cultic references to evoke a sense of love's otherworldly power. Love is not a god but its power originates in God, as it is described by the woman to be simultaneously the most wonderful and terrifying force on earth. Such cosmic, mythopoetic language is therefore appropriate for the subject of love (see sidebars "Cultic Imagery in the Song" p. 244 and "The Woman's Glorious Appearance" p. 302).

## THEOLOGICAL FOCUS

This brief text (8:6–7) is an elegant summary of the Song's main subject: love. While there are many places throughout the Song that could be compared to the high style of love poetry from ANE texts, particularly those of Egypt, "the beauty of these biblical lines remains unsurpassed" (Murphy 1990b, 196). The Song is both a divinely inspired product of its environment and, at the same time, incomparable in its literary brilliance.

Throughout, the Song has demonstrated the power of romantic love. It causes men to leap over mountains to reach their darling (e.g., 2:9). It sends women into the heart of danger at night to find their beloved (3:2–4; 5:6–7). The gravity of 8:6–7 is seen throughout the lovers' story in the many poems leading up to this epic speech from the woman. Having witnessed these truths throughout, we now hear the sage voice of the woman teaching the maidens (and by proxy, teaching us) the lessons of love. Love is supreme. Nothing matches the price of love. Wealth is ultimately man-made and artificial, but love is God-made. Anyone attempting to use wealth to overcome or buy love will fail and "be utterly despised" (8:7). Such an attempt would represent a fundamental failure to understand the ineffable nature of love, a force powerful enough to inspire both awe and terror in human hearts.

The severity of love calls to mind other places in the Song where the woman is described in terms of her raw and intimidating power (1:9; 6:4–5, 10) or the man's majesty (3:6–11) and prowess (2:8, 17). Love is not all sunshine and roses; rather, it can be emotionally paralyzing and awe-inducing, like Christ's transfiguration where the disciples witnessed how "his face shown like the sun, and his clothes became white as light," causing the men to fall on their faces and become "terrified" (Matt. 17:1–6). Love bears the imprint of its creator, who himself is both glorious and dangerous. In C. S. Lewis's *The Lion, the Witch, and the Wardrobe*, it is said of Aslan the lion (the story's allegorical Christ-figure) that "he isn't safe. But he's good." Love likewise cannot be reduced to a passing feeling that, if acted upon carelessly, would result in pleasure without consequences. Rather, real love is richer and longer-lasting than a spontaneous tryst that does not survive the summer. It is fierce—true love goes to war against apathy, lust, distractions, and every competing power that assails it. Real love "never ends," because it is the "greatest" of the affections (1 Cor. 13:8, 13).

We see an analogy between the love of the Song's couple and the love of God for humanity. Here also, in the gospel of Christ, we observe love's unassailability and undaunted strength: "For I am sure that neither death nor life, nor angels nor rulers, nor things present nor things to come, nor powers, nor height nor depth, nor anything else in all creation, will be able to separate us from the love of God in Christ Jesus our Lord" (Rom. 8:38–39 ESV). For all who put their faith in Christ, forgiveness for all sin, including every sexual sin, has been purchased through his death on the cross, and justification through his resurrection (Rom. 4:25). The message of the gospel is sometimes abused in

Christian culture when it is reduced to a perverse, populist understanding of love devoid of any power. In this way, it is often used as an antidote to any talk of God's judgment against sinners, as if his love has made him ambivalent to the sin that corrupted the world, marred his created image, and required the sacrifice of his only Son. In this way, a message of sin without consequences is deceivingly promoted, a kind of antinomian Christianity that is foreign to the Old and New Testaments. In Scripture, however, the message of the gospel never lessens the severity of love's power nor the harsh reality of what love requires; in fact, the gospel only magnifies it.

# PREACHING AND TEACHING STRATEGIES

## Exegetical and Theological Synthesis

After continued back-and-forth dialogue between the man and the woman (7:1 [HB 2]–8:5), the woman then provides what amounts to the clearest exposition of love found in the book. She longs for permanent union with the man: "Put me like a seal over your heart" (8:6a). The woman desires the man to be fully committed to her because love is fierce, undaunted, even potentially destructive. Love is a powerful force that should not be treated lightly. Only the marriage covenant is a "container" big enough to corral the unbridled power of love.

But love must be freely given; it cannot be purchased. Those who try to manipulate their way into love end up with nothing. They are ultimately pitied by the world because of their foolishness; love cannot be coerced. Therefore, love is the most valuable thing in the world. To be truly loved by someone is worth more than all the riches in the world. When oriented toward God, it is even better than life itself as King David declares: "Because your love is better than life, my lips will praise you" (Ps. 63:3).

## Preaching Idea
Love is supreme.

## Contemporary Connections

### What does it mean?
Love is the most valuable thing in the universe because, in the words of singer Deon Jackson, "Love makes the world go 'round." Human existence was knit together by love because God himself is love (1 John 4:16). God's love for himself in the Trinity precedes all acts of creation or redemption. Therefore, God created the world not to get love, as if he were lonely, but in order to give love. He created the world out of the overflow of his love. Therefore, human beings were built to exist on love.

As human beings, we crave love and subsist on it. Love is the highest of the virtues for Christians, as the apostle Paul articulates: "Faith, hope, and love, abide these three; but the greatest of these is love" (1 Cor. 13:13). Of course, Paul is not speaking of romantic love, per se. Romantic love, however, cannot be shorn away from the full-orbed view of love that Scripture gives. Even from the very beginning, it was not good for man to be alone (Gen. 2:18). And the answer to man's loneliness was marriage (Gen. 2:22–24).

If the world was made through God's love, and human beings need it, then we must ask the question: What is love? Debate over the definition rages in both the broader culture and the Christian church. Due to our current cultural moment where love is often defined solely in terms of feelings, many in the church have overreacted and have come to define love solely as an action. But the Scriptures recognize that actions of love without affections or love are pointless (1 Cor. 13:1–3)! What Scripture holds together (actions and affections), we must not separate. Love is both a deep affection for something and actions of sacrifice done for the good of that thing/person.

Love is not just a feeling or an action, however. The Song of Songs describes love as a powerful force. It is like a burning fire that rages, an enduring bulwark that can tame the crashing waves, and an unstoppable force like death (8:6). Therefore, love must be handled with care (2:7; 3:5; 8:4). Unhitched from the guiding principles of God's Word, love, with its powerful desires, can wreak havoc on our lives.

*Is it true?*
Love is supreme because no matter how much wealth we have accumulated as a culture, we are not any happier. In fact, our happiness is declining almost in proportion to the amount of wealth we are accumulating. It is almost as if we have done culturally with happiness what the foolish person has done in 8:7 with love: tried to purchase something that cannot be bought. Furthermore, in our highly individualistic culture, we are lonelier than ever. As Robert Putnam pointed out in his book *Bowling Alone* (2000), the American experience is becoming more isolated from community. If we are becoming more isolated from community and relationships, we are, in turn, cutting ourselves off from real love. Love can only exist in relationships. While America may not be a place of material poverty, it is becoming a place of relational poverty. Relational poverty is the bankruptcy of love.

What the Song, and the Scriptures as a whole, teaches us is that it is far better to have love with little else than to gain the whole world but lack love. What the Song presents through poetry, the Proverbs teach through maxim: "Better is a dish of vegetables where love is than a fattened ox served with hatred" (Prov. 15:17). The Song shows the utter beauty of two ordinary individuals (a woman who works in the fields and a man who is a shepherd) who are in love. With love, they are kings and queens in their own minds, and that's all that matters. Together, they can get through anything.

*Now what?*
If love is so important, then we must pursue it. But unlike the fool in 8:7, we must pursue it the right way. One way to rightly pursue love is to wait for the right time (see 2:7; 3:5; 8:4). Rushing into a romantic relationship is a recipe for disaster. While some people get married to their high school sweethearts, most teenagers are not emotionally, financially, and spiritually ready for dating. The high school years are hard enough to navigate with surging hormones, difficult social dynamics, and the soul-crushing ubiquity of smartphones. Adding a romantic relationship into the mix could prove disastrous.

On the other hand, when the time is right, believers should not postpone marriage. People are marrying later than ever now. It seems that one of the narratives our culture preaches is that young people must first "establish" themselves financially, and then pursue marriage. While such a life plan may seem prudent, it could be a veiled form of attempting to purchase love. Furthermore, marrying later provides complicated life dynamics. For the woman, it can create an urgency to have children as quickly as possible before her window of opportunity closes. It can be more difficult to adapt to another person because you are both set in your ways. It can be hard to prioritize one another when both are deeply embedded in a demanding career. Love is elusive and often fleeting. So when you find someone you love, hold on to them! If you're young, it is possible for both of you in the relationship to pursue careers; you just have to pursue them together.

For those who are single, the greatest love comes from the Lord. We do not derive value from our marital status or fertility. We derive our value from being in Christ. While marriage shows the depth of God's love, singleness allows us to demonstrate the breadth of God's love (Scazzero 2015, 87). Single people are able to be involved in more ministry opportunities and are often more attentive to the needs, hopes, and fears of those around them. Too often, the vision of married couples, and especially parents, gets clouded by the immediate responsibilities of married and family life that presses in on them.

### Creativity in Presentation

A song to consider is, as mentioned before, Deon Jones's classic song "Love Makes the World Go 'Round." It is a good illustration of the power of love and the fact that it is the fabric of society and human flourishing. Taking a slightly different direction is the song "Ring of Fire" by Johnny Cash. The song vividly illustrates the burning power of love: "Love is a burning thing / And it makes a fiery ring / Bound by wild desire / I fell into a ring of fire." The singer understands the immense power of love, and the dangers of allowing unbounded desire rules one's life.

If love is so valuable, we must seek to embrace it and overcome loneliness. The United Kingdom even recently hired a "Minister of Loneliness" to help the country grapple with its loneliness epidemic. What would it look like for a church to have a "minister of loneliness"—or, at least, a ministry to the lonely? This could look like implementing small groups in your church. Small groups are one of the best ways to provide a context for building and maintaining close relationships in the body of Christ. Ministering to the lonely may also mean leveraging technologies to reach out to people. Calls, text, and emails, while not a replacement for in-person conversation, could be a way to supplement the care ministry of the church.

Another important ministry in the church would be to have couples preparing for marriage go through premarital counseling. Rob Green's book *Tying the Knot* (2016) provides a very helpful curriculum. Tim Keller's book *The Meaning of Marriage* (2013) is also a helpful resource to use when counseling couples preparing for marriage. If love is so powerful, we must equip couples with ways to harness it in the marriage covenant.

The big idea of the text is, "Love is supreme." Why is love the most important thing in the world? The outline points could answer such a question:

- Nothing is more powerful than love (8:6)
- Nothing is more valuable than love (8:7)

## DISCUSSION QUESTIONS

1. What desire does the woman have (8:6a)?

2. How is love described in the passage (8:6b–7)?

3. Why is a person who tries to buy love despised (8:7b)?

4. When have you experienced the power of love in your life?

5. How can you become a more loving person?

# Song of Songs 8:8–14

**EXEGETICAL IDEA**
The woman proclaims the ways in which love is rewarding.

**THEOLOGICAL FOCUS**
Those who pursue love honorably, prioritizing the romantic relationship over competing forces, are granted pleasure, longevity, and peace.

**PREACHING IDEA**
Pursue love the right way and reap the rewards.

**PREACHING POINTERS**
Wrapping up the Song, the woman provided poetic lessons on how to handle love. She spoke of the importance of proper sexual conduct and its resulting rewards. She described how love works. Love must be freely given. She emphasized the important role community played in the preparation for love. After her lessons on love, the man beckoned the woman away to himself again, indicating that the cycle of longing, estrangements, and pursuit never ends.

The Song is love poetry that bears some resemblance to wisdom literature since at least part of its purpose (see most clearly in 8:6–14) is to instruct others in how to rightly navigate the power and complexities of love. As the book ends, the woman rightly reminds us to pursue love the right way. If we abide by God's standards and follow his will, certain rewards will come to us. They may not be worldly rewards of sexual fulfillment or a life of ease and prosperity; instead, we will receive a harvest of peace, contentment, and a lifelong partner to pursue.

# LOVE IS REWARDING (8:8–14)

## LITERARY STRUCTURE AND THEMES (8:8–14)

Readers once again are confronted with options when deciding the structure of this unit. Those who focus on the four speech acts of this final section will see divisions at: (1) the maidens (8:8–9), (2) the woman (8:10–12), (3) the man (8:13), and finally (4) the woman again (8:14). A broader scope considers that some of these speech acts are part of larger conversations, in which case the woman's words in 8:10 should be joined with those of the maidens in 8:8–9 due to similar themes, and 8:11–14 might be considered a confined unit based both on similar themes and on the use of the imperative and second-person pronominal suffixes. Keel (1994), Murphy (1990b), and Longman (2001) also consider 8:8–10 a confined unit, but they separate 8:11–12 and 8:13–14 into distinct units based on the change of tone at the beginning of 8:13. I take the same approach, dividing the entire unit of 8:8–14 into three sections reflecting love's rewards.

Having learned from 8:6–7 that love is supreme, unstoppable, and undaunted, readers now discover in 8:8–14 that love is rewarding, a point made by the three sections that comprise this unit:

- *The Reward of Peace (8:8–10)*
- *The Reward of Pleasure (8:11–12)*
- *The Reward of Longevity in Love (8:13–14)*

## EXPOSITION (8:8–14)

The final section of the Song has elements of all that has come before, both the saga of 1:2–8:5 and the sermonette on love in 8:6–7. The excitement of the couple's chase, their exaltation of each other's bodies, and the painful reality of temporarily losing one another (5:2–8) all inform these final verses of the Song. Added to this is what has been learned from the message of 8:6–7, where love is described as an all-consuming fire, unquenchable, as powerful as death, and greater in value than all the world's wealth. Love's indomitability and surpassing worth should lead the man to make his darling a permanent fixture of his identity—"Set me like a seal on your heart" (8:6).

The current unit (8:8–14) brings these lessons forward by applying the principle of chastity to the love lives of future marriageable maidens (8:8–10), by demonstrating that the supremacy of love taught in 8:6–7 must overcome the temptations of wealth (8:11–12), and by conveying the permanence of love through the couple's continued pursuit of one another (8:13–14). The Song, therefore, concludes on a powerful note of hope, one that seeks to acknowledge that the seasons of life and love will continue into perpetuity. And though romantic love is portrayed as an indefatigable force, the woman is no less urgent when she exclaims, "Hurry away, my beloved! And be like a gazelle or a young stag on the mountains of spices!"

### *The Reward of Peace (8:8–10)*

Love rewards those who honor it—a point made by the woman in 8:10 following the short life lesson of 8:8–9.

**8:8**. The woman was just speaking in 8:7, so it seems natural that she has continued speaking here in 8:8 where she quotes a proverb of chastity, but the first-person plural "we" may represent the maidens again. The proverb itself presents the perspective of older siblings who have a younger, prepubescent sister. The woman then addresses this proverb in 8:10 and relates it to herself.

With portions of chapter 8 somewhat mirroring portions of chapter 1, the presence of siblings in 8:8–9 is reminiscent of the brothers in 1:5–6; however, the two texts are only superficially connected. In other words, 8:8–9 is not a continuation of the theme in 1:5–6 (for an opposing view, see Spencer 2019, 423–28). The sister is "little," meaning young or prepubescent, a detail confirmed by the fact that "she does not [yet] have breasts." The moment a young woman was born in ANE cultures, it was assumed that her main future role would be to marry, bear children, and keep the home. Women could, of course, have other roles as well, such as prophet, scribe, entrepreneur, etc. Fundamentally, though, young women functioned, through marriage, as means to form bonds with other families, resulting in financial and social protections afforded by such alliances (see note on 3:6 and sidebar "To Retrieve a Princess" p. 272). While in a patriarchal society, fathers typically had the final say, it is evident that whole families could be involved in the process of finding a suitable mate; hence, the need for siblings to protect their marriageable sisters (on the benefit of family alliances, see Gen. 24; Deut. 2:25; the protective vengeance of brothers, Gen. 34).

While examples of brutality toward young women abound in biblical and ANE texts (consider the horror of Gen. 19:8), the preciousness of a young woman in healthier households and less danger-fraught circumstances should not be understated. Consider Nathan's rebuke to David, when the prophet describes the proverbial poor man's pet lamb as precious, "like a daughter to him." The siblings of the young woman in Song 8:8–9 have a duty to protect their kid sister, both for her own sake and for the sake of the family's honor. The proverb reads, "What should we do on the day when she is spoken for?" (מַה־נַּעֲשֶׂה לַאֲחֹתֵנוּ בַּיּוֹם שֶׁיְּדֻבַּר־בָּהּ). The phrase "when she is spoken for" (שֶׁיְּדֻבַּר־בָּהּ) is literally "when it is spoken on/concerning her," a reference to betrothal. This refers to when a man approaches the girl's father and states his intentions to marry her (cf. Gen. 29:18; 1 Sam. 25:39). In 1 Samuel 25:39 the same basic construction (דבר + בְּ) appears where David "speaks on Abigail in order to take her as his wife" "spoke on/concerning" (וַיְדַבֵּר בַּאֲבִיגַיִל לְקַחְתָּהּ לוֹ לְאִשָּׁה).

The answer to this question of what the siblings should do will depend on whether their kid sister remains chaste while waiting for the day of her wedding. The implication is that there is a span of time between betrothal and the marriage consummation. It is important to the siblings that their sister remains chaste in the waiting. While the practice was likely common, there is no clear example of it in the Hebrew Bible (the Jacob and Rachel arrangement in Genesis 29:18–20 has more to do with needing a bride price). However, in the New Testament, Joseph fears the shame of his community since he was "betrothed" (μνηστευθείσης) to Mary, who was suddenly found to be pregnant (Matt. 1:18–19). Of course, in his mind this would mean that she must have been with another man, for which a severe punishment was warranted (Deut. 22:23–24), but to the broader community, her pregnancy may have suggested that Joseph himself did not exercise restraint leading up to the day of marriage. The verb "to betroth" (μνηστεύω) "indicates a firm commitment, normally undertaken a year before marriage. During that year the girl remained with her own family, but the tie established was a strong one and was really the first part of marriage" (Morris 1992, 26–27). At the very least, the siblings in Song 8:8–9 are concerned with their sister's status as "virgin" leading up to her wedding (Deut. 22:13–21). For her to sleep with her betrothed husband would be a dishonor, and for her to sleep with another man during the betrothal would be even more severe.

**8:9.** The protasis "if she is a wall" refers to her commitment to remain chaste during her betrothal, in which case they will fortify that wall by building upon it a "battlement" (טִירָה), meaning an "encampment fortified by a stone wall" (*HALOT* s.v. "טִירָה" 374). It will be made of silver, possibly suggesting that the siblings are rewarding their sister with adornment that further reinforces her decision to remain chaste. If, however, "she is a door" (walls do not open, but doors do), then the siblings will board her up with cedar planks (נָצוּר עָלֶיהָ לוּחַ אָרֶז). They will not allow her to bring upon herself or her family the dishonor of sexual promiscuity while she is in a state of commitment to another man.

The imagery in 8:8–10 may suggest that other rival suitors or unsafe men are seen as invaders who seek to conquer the woman (a city) through siege (James 2017, 448–57; see the "foxes" of 2:15 and the "lions" and "leopards" of 4:8 as possibly referring to such men). She needs the protection of others to help her just as Ruth was granted the protection of Boaz, who told his young male workers not to touch her (Ruth. 2:8–9). The woman of the Song will prove in 8:10, however, to be unassailable (the nature of the attack she suffered in 5:7 is unclear. In any case, it did not disqualify her claim in 8:10).

### Chastity in the Song of Songs
Song 8:8–9 may seem like a strange departure from the tone of the Song up to this point, which has been all about sexual pursuit and embrace. So, to step away from that intense momentum to talk about chastity comes across as jarring. However, it should be noted that the Song has been repeatedly preaching the message that the virginal daughters of Jerusalem ought not awaken love prematurely (2:7; 3:5; 8:4), which we have taken to be a reference to observing the appropriate time to pursue love (see note on 2:7). When the principle of proper timing was not being specifically stated by the woman, it was being demonstrated by all the references to the couple going to the garden to see if the fruits and other flora were in bloom (2:10–13; 4:12–5:1; 6:11–12; 7:11–13 [HB 12–14]), the timing of which is a crucial indicator of whether or not they should make love. To this we could add the references to the woman's mother and home, all suggestions that cultural propriety (which included the concept of chastity) was understood by the couple.

**8:10.** As the woman explains here, her own patient chastity paid off in that when she became sexually mature or marriageable (signaled by "my breasts were like towers"), she was able to find favor in the eyes of her beloved: "then I was in his eyes like one who has found peace" (אָז הָיִיתִי בְעֵינָיו כְּמוֹצְאֵת שָׁלוֹם). The mention of "peace" (שָׁלוֹם) is likely a play on her status as the "Shulammite," or Solomon-ness (הַשּׁוּלַמִּית), as well as the name "Solomon" (שְׁלֹמֹה), which appears in the next colon at the beginning of 8:11. The term "peace" is better understood as "wholeness" or "intactness" (*HALOT* s.v. "שָׁלוֹם" 1507), as in the feeling of being "complete." She acknowledges her role as "Peacetress" (see sidebar "The Shulammite" p. 304 and note on 6:13).

The verb "find" (כְּמוֹצְאֵת) in the MT may actually be a *hiphil* of יצא "to go out" (כְּמוֹצֵאת) producing "like one who brings forth peace." The idea that the woman is bringing peace/wholeness to her husband as a result of her chaste behavior seems more likely than the more convoluted "I was in his eyes as one who *finds* peace." Even so, the idea of "finding" peace is not far off conceptually. In Proverbs 3 a blessed and happy person is one who "finds wisdom" (מָצָא חָכְמָה), a force created by God (Prov. 8:22) and personified as Lady Wisdom (Prov. 3:13). Lady Wisdom is more valuable than gold, jewels, riches, and honor, "and all her paths are peace" (וְכָל־נְתִיבוֹתֶיהָ שָׁלוֹם; Prov. 3:14–17). Throughout the Song, the young couple has sought to honor the laws of love that were embedded in nature by its Creator, leading them down a path of inevitable peace.

### *The Reward of Pleasure (8:11–12)*

The supremacy of love is seen in the superiority of the woman's garden to the man's wealth.

**8:11**. Song 8:11 begins like a parable, meaning that it is less concerned with relaying facts the way a historical narrative would, and more interested in communicating a lesson of some kind; however, unlike a parable, 8:11 should not be understood metaphorically but literally. The king kept a vineyard in Baal-Hamon, a place about which we as yet know nothing for certain.

Solomon entrusted his vineyard "to keepers" (לַנֹּטְרִים) who were to sell its fruit and return to him one thousand shekels of silver. Only a few verses ago, when the lessons of love began, a stark contrast was drawn between the limited value of wealth and the surpassing value of love (8:7). In application, a similar contrast is drawn here between Solomon's business ventures and the woman's free gift of love, the worth of which is vastly superior to anything the king's vineyards could produce. Murphy suggests that the vineyard in 8:11 is a reference to Solomon's harem, but too many of the verse's details are grounded in reality for this to be likely: the mention of a specific place name (Baal-Hamon), what is known of Solomon's wealth and property (1 Kings 4:20–28), and the task assigned to the vineyard's keepers—this would require a confusing application if the men represent eunuchs who oversee the harem (Murphy 1990b, 200; cf. Keel 1994, 283). Longman points out that Solomon had a thousand women in his harem (1 Kings 11:3); but there is also a passage in Isaiah describing how a profitable vineyard could yield a thousand silver shekels (2001, 219; Isa. 7:23). Given the financially focused context starting in 8:7 and picked up again here in 8:11, the reference is likely not to the king's harem, last mentioned in 6:8. Rather, the focus is on the value of money as contrasted with the value of love (8:6, 11–12). Solomon's real-world business ventures required great investment and labor, but the woman's "vineyard" is free.

We cannot ignore the parallels between Song 8:11–12 and Isaiah 5:1–7, the latter being a parable about the faithless deeds of the Judeans, which begins with "I will sing to my beloved a song of my beloved regarding his vineyard" (אָשִׁירָה נָּא לִידִידִי שִׁירַת דּוֹדִי לְכַרְמוֹ), followed by the same construction that appears here in Song 8:11, only replacing the name "Solomon" with "my beloved" (כֶּרֶם הָיָה לִידִידִי). The song in Isaiah goes on to talk about a vineyard (representing Judah and its people) the Lord had laboriously constructed with all the necessary elements to succeed, but instead of producing good grapes, it produced "wild ones" (בְּאֻשִׁים). In Song 8:11, the woman appears to be raising an image known to readers from parables (e.g., Isa. 1:8; 3:14; 5:1–7; Jer. 12:10), metaphors (throughout the Song), and proverbs (Job 24:6, 18; Prov. 24:30; 31:16) to supply a new and shocking application that will be revealed in 8:12.

> **Geography in the Song of Songs**
> Just as nature imagery is an important part of how the Song grounds its abstractions in reality, so place names serve as reference points that contextualize metaphors. They appear throughout: Kedar, 1:5; Jerusalem/Zion, also implied throughout the Song, 1:5; 2:7; 3:5, 10–11; 5:16; 6:4; En Gedi, 1:14; Sharon, 2:1; Lebanon and various mountain peaks, 3:9; 4:8, 11, 15; 5:15; 7:4 (HB 5); Gilead, 4:1; 6:5; Tarshish (wordplay?), 5:14; Galilee (wordplay?), 5:14; Tirzah, 6:4; a possible reference to Shunem, 6:13 (HB 7:1); Heshbon, Bath-Rabbim, and Damascus, 7:4 (HB 5); Carmel, 7:5 (HB 6); Baal-Hamon 8:11. We could add to this the many references to mountains, vineyards, forests, and gardens. These locations are spread throughout the northern and southern territories, though the majority of them appear in what was once northern Israel. This is likely because there is a much higher concentration of floral beauty in the northern territory, due to its abundant irrigation from Mt. Hermon.

## Love Is Rewarding (8:8–14)

Egyptian harvesting scene.
Public domain (see *ANEP* §91).

**8:12.** This is one of several allusions to chapter 1 (or just poetic echoes) that appear here in the final verses of the Song (see note on 8:13). The woman offers Solomon a vineyard he did not plant or maintain; rather, this vineyard (her body) is a free gift to him, and he can have it all. Some think the man is speaking here and is contrasting the high value of his vineyard (the woman) with Solomon's literal vineyard (Exum 2005, 260–61). This is a tantalizing possibility, and it would maintain the contrast (and resolve the problem of figuring out why the "keepers" are still mentioned in 8:12). However, our approach has been to see Solomon as a cipher for the male figure of the Song, not a foil. And the last time we encountered the expression "my own vineyard" (כַּרְמִי שֶׁלִּי) was back in 1:6 when the woman regretted that she had not been able to focus more on her beauty since her brothers had made her "the keeper." In our approach, the woman is speaking and is contrasting Solomon's business enterprises in 8:11 with the superior thing she offers—her love. If the man is speaking, then he too would be contrasting the value of the woman ("my vineyard") with Solomon's vineyard. Either approach makes the point well enough.

Our approach does leave us with a potential problem: Why are the "keepers" of the literal vineyard in 8:11 still mentioned in 8:12, now that the vineyard has become a metaphor for her body? Also, why should the keepers receive two hundred shekels? It is possible to overthink the woman's metaphor by trying to find a corollary for every element presented in 8:11. It seems she is simply making the point that her vineyard is freely his for the taking and that it is guaranteed to generate the desired produce.

### The Reward of Longevity in Love (8:13–14)
The couple conclude their most excellent Song by echoing its most pertinent themes: separation, longing/pursuit, and the promise of embrace.

**8:13.** The final two verses of the Song are not a "lesson" in any way comparable to the contents of 8:6–12. However, there is a lesson implicit in the couple's return to the most prominent motifs of the Song.

The mention of "keepers" (נֹטְרִים) in 8:11–12 and "companions" (חֲבֵרִים) here in 8:13 reminds us of the verse pair at the beginning of the Song, in 1:6–7, where the woman's brothers were angry with her and made her "the keeper" of the vineyard. When she was searching for the man she asked, "Why should I be like one who veils herself beside the flocks of your companions?" (1:7). Perhaps the shared concepts between 1:6–7 and 8:11–14 are meant to demonstrate how far things have come, and yet how cyclical love is. The terms "keeper" and "companions" are merely poetic echoes, showing a symmetry of thought and emphasizing that while things seem to have changed for the woman, love must still run its course and follow the predetermined pattern that finds the lovers apart, then together, then apart, then together again.

She dwells in the gardens surrounded by "companions" (the maidens? a royal entourage?), who are "listening intently" (מַקְשִׁיבִים). Song 8:13–14 may be simply a flashback to her status as an unclaimed maiden, but who is to say her status remained unchanged here? Perhaps she should be viewed now as queen, surrounded by attendants. If the latter, we imagine the maidens waiting with bated breath for what she will say next, but they are not alone—he exclaims, "Let me hear!" (הַשְׁמִיעִנִי). With the callbacks to 1:6–7, this imperative could correlate with 1:8 when he directs her to "follow" (לְכִי־לָךְ; also imperative) in the tracks of the flock and let her goats pasture beside the shepherds' tents. In the note on 1:8, I suggested that this is the man's way of placing the woman where she can be easily found. Here in 8:13, he likewise wishes to bridge the spatial gap between himself and his darling.

**8:14**. Her response to him is in keeping with the whole Song, and especially 8:6–12 where love is shown to be as indestructible as death and taxes (8:6–7). Love will return again and again throughout the many chapters of the couple's life. Life is short, and their passion is strong, so she beckons him to "hurry away!" and "become like a gazelle or a young stag on the mountains of spices" (cf. 2:17). She wants him to run after her as he had done before and arrive at the comfort and aromatic delight of her bosom (cf. 1:13; 2:17; 4:6).

The Song need not continue beyond 8:14 for the reader to know what will happen next between the lovers. They will go to the garden, check to see if the vines have bloomed, find that they have, and then sing of each other's beauty until they are fully enraptured by love's embrace.

## THEOLOGICAL FOCUS
The lessons of love in these verses teach that love is supreme (8:6–7) and rewarding (8:8–14). The supremacy of love (8:6–7) is observed in the way that love rewards those who listen to its rhythms and follow them (8:10), and in how love prevails over every distraction (8:11–12) in order to return to itself, season after season, in a never-ending current of affection (8:13–14).

The couple has learned much in their journey, and the learning will continue throughout their lives and for the generations that follow them, reaching successions of lovers who themselves will have to encounter love's mysteries and demands. There is no mistaking the importance of chastity in 8:8–10 for how the couple was rewarded with "shalom." This is the lesson to the protective siblings who ask in 8:8 how they must guide their kid sister through to marriageable age. Furthermore, we discover that love cannot be bought (8:7, 11), but is only freely offered (8:12) and then must be eagerly pursued (8:13–14).

These lessons of love are important for those who claim Christ as Lord. To experience love's supremacy, believers must sift out perverse cultural ideologies of sex and intimacy that are inimical to love's divinely appointed rhythms. As such, the apostle Paul vehemently exhorts the believers of his day to "flee sexual immorality," knowing that its cost extends far beyond the disapproval of others into the realm of self-harm and sin against God (Rom. 1:24; 1 Cor. 6:18; 1 Thess. 4:3–7). The adjuration of the woman to the maidens can be heard also in the command of the apostle to the fledgling church of Corinth, that they heed the warnings of the past, knowing how "being immoral" (πορνεύωμεν) cost their forefathers far more than they were prepared to pay (1 Cor. 10:8). The sexual permissiveness of the modern age offers immediate gratification to those who will embrace it, but only after tasting its fruit again and again do most eventually realize that what it offers is not love at all, but a gradual draining of one's energy and a depletion of one's hope.

By contrast, the woman had become "like one who found peace in his eyes" (Song 8:10). This wholeness is quite different from the cheap, fleeting, self-centered, and shame-inducing sexual passion of Judah with Tamar (Gen. 38), or the forbidden love of Samson and Delilah that turned Israel's herculean antihero into a blind martyr (Judg. 16:30). These patriarchs and heroes are left on the pages of Scripture not to immortalize their greatness, but to demonstrate the grace and power of the Lord through broken vessels—men and women who more often than not went against the current of his will.

The conclusion of the Song is hopeful for the couple's continued love. By analogy, we see that the conclusion of the gospel is likewise hopeful—that one day those who call upon Christ will stand in a renewed Eden, with the "river of the water of life" (Rev. 22:1; cf. Song 4:15; John 4:10) flowing through the city and the "tree of life" (Rev. 22:2; cf. Gen. 2:9) bursting with twelve kinds of fruit. There the "servants" of God "will worship him. They will see his face, and his name will be on their foreheads" (Rev. 22:4; cf. Rev. 3:12; 7:3; 14:1). Like the woman of the Song who longed to be sealed upon her beloved's heart, the servants of the Lord will be sealed with his name, forever secure in the identity of their Bridegroom (Song 8:6; cf. John 3:29). But until that time, the seasons will continue to change and the rhythms of life will go on. This is in keeping with the Lord's decree: "While the earth remains, seedtime and harvest, cold and heat, summer and winter, day and night, shall not cease" (Gen. 8:22).

## PREACHING AND TEACHING STRATEGIES

### Exegetical and Theological Synthesis

The woman exposits the power and supremacy of love in 8:6–7. Love is the most valuable commodity in the world, and those who try to manipulate their way to it will end up despised. Those who pursue love the right way, on the other hand, will be rewarded (8:8–14). Through a proverb-like aphorism, the woman speaks of the importance of chastity (8:8–10). Using her own experience, she teaches families, who may have younger daughters, how they can guide them into mature love.

The book closes with a mysterious scenario, using it to exemplify the back-and-forth nature of love (8:11–14). "Solomon" may have been successful in business, but the love of his woman is worth far more (8:11–12). The supremacy and greatness of love never ends in a relationship because the ongoing cycle of separation, beckoning, and union continue on and on in an ever deepening and strengthening of love (8:13–14). Just as romantic love follows a cyclical pattern, so our own growth of love with Christ follows the same pattern: sin, confession, repentance, and renewed closeness.

### Preaching Idea
Pursue love the right way and reap the rewards.

### Contemporary Connections

#### What does it mean?
The Song exhorts people to pursue love the right way; specifically, it must not be pursued until the right time (2:7; 3:5; 8:4). Love must also be corralled by the commitment of marriage (3:6–11). Love must be respected for its power and passion; it is not to be trifled with (8:6–7). As the Song finishes, the woman continues to instruct us how to pursue a romantic relationship the right way. Romantic love must be coupled with chastity. The woman speaks of her own experience: she was a "wall," that is, she was chaste until she was married (8:10). Her choice to remain chaste contributed to the feeling of peace between the couple. Furthermore, she avoided the pain that sexual promiscuity can inflict. This same kind of peace can accompany the union of couples who wait for marriage. There is a joy, a peace, a shalom (wholeness) of waiting until marriage for sexual intercourse and only having intercourse with one's spouse.

The other way to pursue love is to freely give oneself to one's beloved. The woman freely gives herself to her "Solomon." She holds nothing back from him. There is complete vulnerability and transparency. The whole Song testifies to the fact that she has pursued love the right way. And because she has done so, there is a corresponding blessing to those who helped her get ready and journeyed with her along the way: the two hundred shekels (8:12). There are spillover benefits to doing things God's way. The reward of doing things the right way means that one will always be engaged in the never-ending story of love. It will grow deeper and more beautiful and will continue to beckon us to regions unknown.

*Is it true?*
Even though our world is flooded with endless choices and options for how to do things in life, there is still a right way and a wrong way to go about things in the realm of love. The plain reality of life is that those who go about doing things the wrong way usually create trouble for themselves (cf. Ps. 73:15–20). Of course, there is a reality where the wicked do end up more successful than the righteous because we live in a world broken by sin. Things are not the way they are supposed to be, especially with the wicked on top sometimes.

Yet the Song is related to the wisdom tradition in that it aims, in part, to teach us how to navigate life well through immersion in an alternative universe. In the world of the Song, the man and the woman who pursue each other the right way are blessed. They are blessed with passion for one another. They are blessed with fierce commitment to each other. Following God's design generally results in blessing, but the blessing may be different than we expect. God does not promise that couples who save themselves for marriage will have perfect sexual intimacy; he does not promise couples who wait to awaken love until the right time a relationship free of difficulty. The Song clearly testifies to the fact that obstacles to love and relational distance between the couple is an ongoing reality. Instead, what God promises in the Song is that when you find someone and pledge yourself to them and they pledge themselves to you, you will face life together, with all of its ups and downs, with all of its highs and lows, and with all of its passion and hurt.

*Now what?*
The primary emphasis in this text can come on those who are younger or preparing for marriage. There is great blessing in chastity. God calls us to abstain from sex outside of the marriage covenant (1 Cor. 6:15–20; 7:1; 1 Thess. 4:8; Heb. 13:4). There are consequences for those who disregard such instructions. Paul talks about sex as a special class of sin where we sin "against our body." Furthermore, he speaks of sinning against our brothers in the church as well when we don't live in sexual purity. Sexual sin has wide-ranging consequences. While certain ministries in "purity culture" have tended to focus on the biological consequences of premarital sex (STIs, unplanned pregnancy, etc.), the biblical authors focus primarily on the spiritual consequences: alienation from God and our brothers and sisters in Christ.

There is a blessing to abstinence before marriage. God's commands are good and they are not burdensome, which includes the call to abstinence (1 John 5:3). Again, following God's will concerning sex will not necessarily lead to perfect intimacy. But it will bring a closer relationship with God, no sense of shame, and the ability to freely give yourself to your spouse in wholeness. Even if your body is not healthy or able to function properly for the kind of physical intimacy portrayed by the Song, that does not obliterate romance or emotional intimacy. As the Song teaches us, while sexual passion is a great thing, the joy of marriage is grounded in a couple's loyal love for one another.

Married couples must continue to pursue the growth of their relationship the right way. Just as the woman gave herself away freely and wholly to her "Solomon," so every spouse must also continue to do so to their spouse, even as the years roll on in marriage. In marriage, every couple should push to deeper levels of intimacy with one another, which means being even more vulnerable and more transparent with age. A couple that accumulates secrets and locks away parts of their lives from each other is an affront to the Song's call to unbridled love.

### Creativity in Presentation

One of the clearest illustrations for love is that of a journey. You could use the metaphor of a cross-country road trip to illustrate the issues of love. Love is a long trip. It is not a jaunt to the grocery store five minutes away. It requires patience and perseverance, just like making your way to the opposite coast. Most road trips feature times when the road is clear and you are able to cruise along. There will be seasons of life when the relationship is easy and the sex is great. Other times on the road, you may hit potholes, traffic, or bad weather. There will be seasons of difficulty in the relationship. You may not be communicating well and sex may feel like a duty. Sometimes it is helpful on a road trip to pull over and be refreshed by stopping at a hotel for a night to get some needed sleep. So too, in a marriage, it is important to schedule times away from the normal business of life to be refreshed. Vacations, even for just a weekend, can help married couples recalibrate their relationship.

Since the text aims to instruct those getting ready for marriage, it could be used to speak to the teenagers in the congregation about the importance of chastity before marriage. Preparing for marriage is a lot like preparing for standardized tests in school. There are important things to know, and it requires a great deal of effort and patience to succeed. Some students will be very dedicated to passing the test. They will study at home and enroll in specialized classes to give themselves an advantage. Like these students, some younger people in the church will take God's instructions on sexual purity before marriage very seriously. But some won't. Some may even come into the church, having already violated God's standards. The good news of the gospel is that even if we have failed the test, we can have a fresh start, a clean slate through Christ. He took the test for us. He bore God's wrath against our sins, yes, even our sexual sins, to provide forgiveness for each one us. Now, no matter who we are or what we have done or where we come from, we have been received into a relationship with God like a pure bride awaiting her husband (Rev. 21:2).

The sermon could take shape with the following outline. The big idea would be "Pursue love the right way and reap the rewards." The outline points would explain how to pursue love the right way and its corresponding reward.

- Pursue chastity and reap favor (8:8–10)
- Pursue commitment and reap blessing (8:11–12)
- Pursue your spouse and reap deepening intimacy (8:13–14)

## DISCUSSION QUESTIONS

1. What blessing did the woman receive for maintaining her chastity before marriage (8:10)?

2. Why did the woman freely give herself to "Solomon" (8:11–12)?

3. What do the man and the woman continue to do, even though they have been married for a while now (8:13–14)?

4. How can we build a culture in the church that promotes sexual purity, yet without legalism?

5. How can you pursue your spouse for a deeper relationship this week?

# REFERENCES

Aḥituv, Shmuel. 2008. *Echoes from the Past: Hebrew and Cognate Inscriptions from the Biblical Period*. Translated by Anson Rainey. Carta Handbook. Jerusalem: Carta.

Albright, W. F. 1931–1932. "The Syro-Mesopotamian God Sulman-Esmun and Related Figures." *AfO* 7:164–69.

Alter, Robert. 2010. *The Wisdom Books: Job, Proverbs, and Ecclesiastes*. New York: Norton.

Anderson, William H. U. 2014. "Ecclesiastes in the Intertextual Matrix of Ancient Near Eastern Literature." In *Reading Ecclesiastes Intertextually*, edited by Katharine Dell and Will Kynes, 157–175. LHBOTS 587. New York: Bloomsbury.

Andruska, Jennifer Lynn. 2018. "The Strange Use of דגל in Song of Songs 5:10." *VT* 68, no. 1:1–7.

Arnold, Bill T., and John H. Choi. 2003. *A Guide to Biblical Hebrew Syntax*. Cambridge: Cambridge University Press.

Atkinson, Tyler. 2015. "Contemplation as an Alternative to Curiosity: St. Bonaventure on Ecclesiastes 1:3–11." *SJT* 68, no. 1:16–33. DOI: 10.1017/S0036930614000878.

Bartholomew, Craig G. 2009. *Ecclesiastes*. Baker Commentary on the Old Testament Wisdom and Psalms. Grand Rapids: Baker Academic.

Bellis, Alice Ogden. 2021. "I Am Burnt but Beautiful: Translating Song 1:5a." *JBL* 140, no. 1:91–111. DOI: 10.15699/jbl.1401.2021.5.

Ben-Shlomo, David, and Lauren K. McCormick. 2021. "Judean Pillar Figurines and 'Bed Models' from Tell En-Naṣbeh: Typology and Petrographic Analysis." *Bulletin of the American Schools of Oriental Research* 386 (November): 23–46.

Berlin, Adele. 2008. *The Dynamics of Biblical Parallelism*. Rev. ed. Grand Rapids: Eerdmans.

Bialik, Hayyim Nahman, and Yehoshua Ḥana Rawnitzki, eds. 1992. *The Book of Legends: Sefer Ha-Aggadah; Legends from the Talmud and Midrash*. Translated by William G. Braude. New York: Schocken Books.

Blomberg, Craig. 1992. *Matthew*. NAC 22. Nashville: Broadman & Holman.

Bollinger, Sarah Elizabeth. 2018. "Ritual Manipulation of Women's Hair in the Hebrew Bible." PhD diss., Hebrew Union College–Jewish Institute of Religion.

———. 2022. "Hair as Ritual Symbol in the Nazirite Vow: A Study of Biblical Hair Manipulation in Numbers 6:1–21." In *The Body Lived, Cultured, Adorned: Essays in Honor of Nili S. Fox*, edited by Kristine Henriksen Garroway, Christine Elizabeth Palmer, and Angela Roskop Erisman, 239–70. Cincinnati: Hebrew Union College Press.

Bonaventure, Robert J. Karris, and Campion Murray. 2005. *Commentary on Ecclesiastes*. Works of St. Bonaventure 7. New York: Franciscan Institute Publications.

Borger, Rykle. 1963. *Babylonisch-assyrische Lesestücke*. Rome: Pontifical Biblical Institute.

Breasted, James H. 1906–1907. *Ancient Records of Egypt*. 5 vols. Chicago: University of Chicago Press.

Brenner, Athalya. 1992. "A Note on Bat-Rabbîm (Song of Songs VII 5)." *VT* 42, no. 1:113–15. DOI: 10.2307/1519125.

Brown, William P. 2000. *Ecclesiastes*. IBC. Louisville: John Knox.

Buhlman, Alain. 2000. "The Difficulty of Thinking in Greek and Speaking in Hebrew (Qohelet 3.18; 4.13–16; 5.8)." *JSOT* 25, no. 90:101–8. DOI: 10.1177/030908920002509007.

Burkeman, Oliver. 2022. *Four Thousand Weeks: Time and How to Use It*. London: Vintage.

Burkes, Shannon. 1999. *Death in Qoheleth and Egyptian Biographies of the Late Period*. SBLDS 170. Atlanta: Society of Biblical Literature.

Cantrell, Deborah O'Daniel. 2011. *The Horsemen of Israel: Horses and Chariotry in Monarchic Israel*. HACL 1. Winona Lake, IN: Eisenbrauns, 2011.

Case, Megan L. 2017. "Cunning Linguists: Oral Sex in the Song of Songs." *VT* 67, no. 2:171–86. DOI: 10.1163/15685330-12341277.

Clemens, David M. 1994. "The Law of Sin and Death: Ecclesiastes and Genesis 1–3." *Them* 19, no. 3:5–8.

Crenshaw, James L. 1987. *Ecclesiastes: A Commentary*. OTL. Philadelphia: Westminster.

———. 1998. *Old Testament Wisdom: An Introduction*. Rev. ed. Louisville: Westminster John Knox.

Davis, Ellen. 2000. *Proverbs, Ecclesiastes, and the Song of Songs*. WeBC. Louisville: Westminster John Knox.

Debel, Hans. 2014. "Stones of Contention? A Critical Evaluation of the Erotic Interpretation of Qoh 3:5a." *VT* 64, no. 4:554–60. DOI: 10.1163/15685330-12341162.

Delitzsch, Franz. 1982 [1877]. *Commentary on the Song of Songs and Ecclesiastes*. Grand Rapids: Eerdmans.

Dell, Katharine J. 1994. "Ecclesiastes as Wisdom: Consulting Early Interpreters." *VT* 44, no. 3:301–29. DOI: 10.1163/156853394X00321.

———. 2005. "Does the Song of Songs Have Any Connections to Wisdom?" In *Perspectives on the Song of Songs / Perspektiven Der Hoheliedauslegung*, edited by Anselm C. Hagedorn, 8–26. BZAW 346. Berlin: de Gruyter.

———. 2016. "Ecclesiastes as Mainstream Wisdom (Without Job)." In *Goochem in Mokum/Wisdom in Amsterdam: Papers on Biblical and Related Wisdom Read at the Fifteenth Joint Meeting of The Society of Old Testament Study and the Oudtestamentisch Werkgezelschap, Amsterdam July 2012*, edited by George J. Brooke and Pierre Van Hecke, 43–52. OTS 68. Leiden: Brill.

———. 2020. "A Wise Man Reflecting on Wisdom." *TynBul* 71, no. 2:137–52.

———. 2021. "Solomon and the Solomonic Collection." In *The Oxford Handbook of Wisdom and the Bible*, edited by Will Kynes, 321–35. Oxford Handbooks. Oxford: Oxford University Press.

Dever, William G. 2014. "The Judean 'Pillar-Base Figurines': Mothers or 'Mother-Goddesses'? In *Family and Household Religion: Toward a Synthesis of Old Testament Studies, Archaeology, Epigraphy, and Cultural Studies*, 129–41. Winona Lake, IN: Eisenbrauns.

Dirksen, Peter B. 1989. "Song of Songs III 6–7." *VT* 39 (2): 219–25. DOI: 10.1163/156853389X00093.

Dobbs-Allsopp, F. W., and Elaine Theresa James. 2019. "The Ekphrastic Figure(s) in Song 5:10–16." *JBL* 138, no. 2:297–323. DOI: 10.15699/jbl.1382.2019.555597.

Dominicus, Brigitte. 1994. *Gesten und Gebärden in Darstellungen des Alten und Mittleren Reiches*. Studien zur Archäologie und Geschichte Altägyptens 10. Heidelberg: Heidelberger Orientverlag.

Driver, S. R. 1913. *An Introduction to the Literature of the Old Testament*. New York: Scribner.

Duguid, Ian M. 2015. *The Song of Songs: An Introduction and Commentary*. TOTC 19. Downers Grove, IL: IVP Academic.

Elayi, Josette. 2018. *Sennacherib, King of Assyria*. ABS 24. Atlanta: SBL Press.

Ellis, Maria deJong. 1989. "Observations on Mesopotamian Oracles and Prophetic Texts: Literary and Historiographic Considerations." *JCS* 41, no. 2:127–86. DOI: 10.2307/1359912.

Emerton, John A. 1993. "Lice or a Veil in the Song of Songs 1:7." In *Understanding Poets and Prophets: Essays in Honour of George Wishart Anderson*, edited by A. Graeme Auld, 127–40. JSOTSup 152. Sheffield: Sheffield Academic.

Estes, Dan. 2014. "Seeking and Finding in Ecclesiastes and Proverbs." In *Reading Ecclesiastes Intertextually*, edited by Katherine Dell and Will Kynes, 118–29. LHBOTS 587. London: Bloomsbury.

Exum, J. Cheryl. 1999. "How Does the Song of Songs Mean: On Reading the Poetry of Desire." *SEÅ* 64:47–63.

——— . 2003. "Seeing Solomon's Palanquin (Song of Songs 3:6–11)." *BibInt* 11, no. 3:301–16. DOI: 10.1163/156851503322566741.

——— . 2005. *Song of Songs: A Commentary*. OTL. Louisville: Westminster John Knox.

Fikkert, Brian, and Kelly Kapic. 2019. *Becoming Whole: Why the Opposite of Poverty Isn't the American Dream*. Chicago: Moody Press.

Fischer, Stefan. 2018. "Schwarz bin ich und schön: Retorische ironie im Hohelied." *AcT* 26:305–24.

Forti, Tova. 2014. "Of Snakes and Sinners: An Intertextual Reading of *Baʿal Ha-Lashon* in Ecclesiastes 10:11 in Light of *ʾIsh Lashon* in Psalm 140:12[11]." In *Reading Ecclesiastes Intertextually*, edited by Katherine Dell and Will Kynes, 84–93. LHBOTS 587. London: Bloomsbury.

——— . 2021. "Ecclesiastes." In *The Oxford Handbook of Wisdom and the Bible*, edited by Will Kynes, 515–32. Oxford Handbooks. Oxford: Oxford University Press.

Fox, Michael V. 1977. "Frame-Narrative and Composition in the Book of Qohelet." *HUCA* 48:83–106.

——— . 1985. *The Song of Songs and the Ancient Egyptian Love Songs*. Madison: University of Wisconsin Press.

——— . 1989. *Qohelet and His Contradictions*. JSOTSup 71. Sheffield: Almond Press.

——— . 1999. *A Time to Tear Down and a Time to Build Up: A Rereading of Ecclesiastes*. Grand Rapids: Eerdmans.

——— . 2004. *Ecclesiastes: The Traditional Hebrew Text with the New JPS Translation*. JPS Bible Commentary. Philadelphia: Jewish Publication Society.

——— . 2009. *Proverbs 10–31: A New Translation with Introduction and Commentary*. AB 18B. New Haven, CT: Yale University Press.

Fox, Nili S. 1995. "Clapping Hands as a Gesture of Anger and Anguish in Mesopotamia and in Israel." *JANES* 23 49–60.

——— . 2000. *In the Service of the King: Officialdom in Ancient Israel and Judah*. Cincinnati: Hebrew Union College Press.

Fowler, Donald. 2008. "Introduction to Old Testament Backgrounds." BIBL 373: Old Testament Backgrounds. Class lecture at Liberty University, Lynchburg, VA, February 2, 2008.

Fredericks, Daniel C. 1988. *Qohelet's Language: Re-evaluating Its Nature and Date*. ANETS 3. New York: Mellen.

Fredericks, Daniel C., and Daniel J. Estes. 2010. *Ecclesiastes and The Song of Songs*. ApOTC 16. Downers Grove, IL: InterVarsity Press.

Frolov, Serge. 1998. "No Return for Shulammite: Reflections on Can 7,1." *ZAW* 110, no. 2:256–58.

Garrett, Duane. 1993. *Proverbs, Ecclesiastes, Song of Songs: An Exegetical and Theological Exposition of Holy Scripture*. NAC 14. Nashville: Broadman & Holman.

Garrett, Duane, and Paul House. 2004. *Song of Songs/Lamentations*. WBC 23B. Nashville: Nelson.

# References

Gault, Brian P. 2008. "A Reexamination of 'Eternity' in Ecclesiastes 3:11." *BSac* 165, no. 657:39–57.

———. 2010. "An Admonition Against 'Rousing Love': The Meaning of the Enigmatic Refrain in Song of Songs." *BBR* 20, no. 2:161–84. DOI: 10.2307/26424294.

———. 2011. "A 'Do Not Disturb' Sign? Reexamining the Adjuration Refrain in the Song of Songs." *JSOT* 36, no. 1:93–104. DOI: 10.1177/0309089211419412.

———. 2019. *Body as Landscape, Love as Intoxication: Conceptual Metaphors in the Song of Songs*. AIL 36. Atlanta: SBL Press.

Giszczak, Mark. 2015. "Song of Songs 1,7—What Kind of Wrapping?" *RB* 122, no. 1:58–70.

Gordis, Robert. 1971. *Poets, Prophets, and Sages: Essays in Biblical Interpretation*. Bloomington: Indiana University Press.

Grayson, A. Kirk, and Jamie Novotny. 2012. *The Royal Inscriptions of Sennacherib, King of Assyria (704–681 BC), Part 1*. University Park: Pennsylvania State University Press.

Green, Rob. 2016. *Tying the Knot: A Premarital Guide to a Strong and Lasting Marriage*. Greensboro, NC: New Growth Press.

Greengus, Samuel. 2011. *Laws in the Bible and in Early Rabbinic Collections: The Legal Legacy of the Ancient Near East*. Eugene, OR: Cascade.

Greer, Jonathan S., John W. Hilber, and John H. Walton. 2018. "Introduction." In *Behind the Scenes of the Old Testament: Cultural, Social, and Historical Contexts*, edited by Jonathan S. Greer, John W. Hilber, and John H. Walton, xvii–xix. Grand Rapids: Baker Academic.

Grossberg, Daniel. 1989. *Centripetal and Centrifugal Structures in Biblical Poetry*. SBLMS 39. Atlanta: Scholars Press.

Hamilton, James M. 2015. *Song of Songs: A Biblical-Theological, Allegorical, Christological Interpretation*. Focus on the Bible. Ross-shire: Christian Focus.

Heim, Knut Martin. 2019. *Ecclesiastes: An Introduction and Commentary*. TOTC 18. Downers Grove, IL: IVP Academic.

Hendel, Ronald S. 2019. "The Life of Metaphor in the Song of Songs: Poetics, Canon, and the Cultural Bible." *Bib* 100, no. 1:60–83. DOI: 10.2143/BIB.100.1.3286050.

Hernandex-Murillo, Ruben, and Christopher J. Martineck. 2010. "Dismal Science Tackles Happiness Data." *Regional Economist* 18, no. 1. https://www.stlouisfed.org/publications/regional-economist/january-2010/the-dismal-science-tackles-happiness-data.

Hess, Richard. 2005. *Song of Songs*. Baker Commentary on the Old Testament Wisdom and Psalms. Grand Rapids: Baker.

Hilber, John W. 2020. "Prophecy, Divination, and Magic." *Behind the Scenes of the Old Testament: Cultural, Social, and Historical Contexts*, edited by Jonathan S. Greer, John W. Hilber, and John H. Walton, xvii–xix. Grand Rapids: Baker Academic.

Holmstedt, Robert D., John A. Cook, and Phillip S. Marshall. 2017. *Qoheleth: A Handbook on the Hebrew Text*. Baylor Handbook on the Hebrew Bible. Waco, TX: Baylor University Press.

Homan, Michael M. 2002. "Beer Production by Throwing Bread into Water: A New Interpretation of Qoh. XI 1–2." *VT* 52, no. 2:275–78. DOI: 10.1163/156853302760013893.

Jacobson, David M., and Shimon Gibson. 1995. "A Monumental Stairway on the Temple Mount." *IEJ* 45, nos. 2–3:162–70.

James, Elaine Theresa. 2017. "A City Who Surrenders: Song 8:8–10." *VT* 67, no. 3:448–57. DOI: 10.1163/15685330-12341274.

Johnson, Dru. 2021. *Biblical Philosophy: A Hebraic Approach to the Old and New Testaments*. Cambridge: Cambridge University Press.

# References

Johnston, Gordon H. 2009. "The Enigmatic Genre and Structure of the Song of Songs, Part 3." *BSac* 166:289–305.

Jones, Jordan W. 2019. *She Opens Her Hand to the Poor: Gestures and Social Values in Proverbs*. Perspectives on Hebrew Scriptures and Its Contexts 30. Piscataway, NJ: Gorgias.

_____. 2022. "An Embodiment of Silence: The Hand-on-Mouth Gesture in the Hebrew Bible and Ancient Near East." In *The Body Lived, Cultured, Adorned: Essays in Honor of Nili S. Fox*, edited by Kristine Henriksen Garroway, Christine Elizabeth Palmer, and Angela Roskop Erisman, 49–80. Cincinnati: Hebrew Union College Press.

Kabergs, Valérie. 2014. "Lovely Wordplay in Canticles 8,6a." *ZAW* 126, no. 2:261–64. DOI: 10.1515/zaw-2014-0018.

Kaplan, Jonathan, and Aren Wilson-Wright. 2018. "How Song of Songs Became a Divine Love Song." *BibInt* 26, no. 3:334–51. DOI: 10.1163/15685152-00263P03.

Keefer, Arthur. 2019. "The Meaning of Life in Ecclesiastes: Coherence, Purpose, and Significance from a Psychological Perspective." *HTR* 112, no. 4:447–66. DOI: 10.1017/S0017816019000233.

Keel, Othmar. 1994. *The Song of Songs: A Continental Commentary*. Translated by F. J. Gaiser. CC. Minneapolis: Fortress.

Keller, Timothy. 2013. *The Meaning of Marriage: Facing the Complexities of Commitment with the Wisdom of God*. New York: Penguin.

_____. 2016. *Every Good Endeavor: Connecting Your Work to God's Work*. New York: Penguin.

Knapp, Andrew. 2015. *Royal Apologetic in the Ancient Near East*. WAW Supplement 4. Atlanta: SBL Press.

Krüger, Thomas. 2004. *Qoheleth*. Hermeneia. Minneapolis: Fortress.

Kynes, Will, ed. 2021. *The Oxford Handbook of Wisdom and the Bible*. Oxford Handbooks. Oxford: Oxford University Press.

Lichtheim, Miriam. 1973a. *Ancient Egyptian Literature, Volume 1: The Old and Middle Kingdoms*. Berkeley: University of California Press.

_____. 1973b. *Ancient Egyptian Literature, Volume 2: The New Kingdom*. Berkeley: University of California Press.

_____. 1980. *Ancient Egyptian Literature, Volume 3: The Late Period*. Berkeley: University of California Press.

Linafelt, Tod, and F. W. Dobbs-Allsopp. 2010. "Poetic Line Structure in Qohelet 3:1." *VT* 60, no. 2:249–59. DOI: 10.1163/156853310X489089.

Loader, J. A. 1986. *Ecclesiastes: A Practical Commentary*. Grand Rapids: Eerdmans.

Lohfink, Norbert. 2003. *Qohelet: A Continental Commentary*. CC. Minneapolis: Fortress.

Long, Gary Alan. 1996. "A Lover, Cities, and Heavenly Bodies: Co-Text and the Translation of Two Similes in Canticles (6:4c; 6:10d)." *JBL* 115, no. 4:703–9. DOI: 10.2307/3266352.

Longman, Tremper, III. 1991. *Fictional Akkadian Autobiography: A Generic and Comparative Study*. Winona Lake, IN: Eisenbrauns.

_____. 1998. *The Book of Ecclesiastes*. NICOT. Grand Rapids: Eerdmans.

_____. 2001. *Song of Songs*. NICOT. Grand Rapids: Eerdmans.

Macintosh, A. A. 2016. "The Meaning of Hebrew תשוקה." *JSS* 61, no. 2:365–87.

MacIntyre, Alasdair. 1981. *After Virtue: A Study in Moral Theory*. Notre Dame, IN: University of Notre Dame Press.

Magarik, Larry. 2000. "Bread on Water." *JBQ* 28, no. 4:268–70.

Matthews, Victor H., and Don C. Benjamin. 2016. *Old Testament Parallels: Laws and Stories from the Ancient Near East*. 4th ed. New York: Paulist.

Maul, Stefan M. 2019. *The Art of Divination in the Ancient Near East: Reading the Signs of Heaven and Earth.* Waco, TX: Baylor University Press.

McCarthy, Cormac. 2005. *No Country for Old Men.* New York: Knopf.

McCullough, Matthew. 2018. *Remember Death: The Surprising Path to Living Hope.* Wheaton, IL: Crossway.

Meek, Russell L. 2013. "The Meaning of הבל in Qohelet: An Intertextual Suggestion." In *The Words of the Wise Are Like Goads: Engaging Qohelet in the 21st Century*, edited by Mark J. Boda, Tremper Longman III, and Cristian Rata, 241–56. Winona Lake, IN: Eisenbrauns.

Meissner, Bruno. 1934. *Der Kuss im Alten Orient.* Sitzungsberichte der Preussischen Akademie der Wissenschaften phil.-hist. Klasse 28. Berlin: Verlag Akademie der Wissenschaften.

Merchant, Brian. 2017. *The One Device: The Secret History of the iPhone.* New York: Little, Brown & Co.

Morris, Leon. 1992. *The Gospel According to Matthew.* Pillar New Testament Commentary. Grand Rapids: Eerdmans.

Murphy, Roland E. 1990a. "The Sage in Ecclesiastes and Qohelet the Sage." In *The Sage in Israel and the Ancient Near East*, edited by John G. Gammie and Leo G. Perdue, 263–71. Winona Lake, IN: Eisenbrauns.

———. 1990b. *The Song of Songs: A Critical and Historical Commentary on the Bible.* Edited by S. Dean McBride Jr. Hermeneia. Minneapolis: Fortress.

———. 1992. *Ecclesiastes.* WBC 23A. Waco, TX: Word.

Musgrave, David. 2010. "Viewing Deity in Ancient Near Eastern and Biblical Literature." PhD diss., Hebrew Union College.

Nemet-Nejat, Karen Rhea. 2002. *Daily Life in Ancient Mesopotamia.* Peabody, MA: Hendrickson.

Newport, Cal. 2021. "Why Do We Work So Much? *The New Yorker* August 30, 2021. https://www.newyorker.com/culture/office-space/why-do-we-work-too-much.

Niebuhr, Reinhold. 2012. *Man's Nature and His Communities: Essays on the Dynamics and Enigmas of Man's Personal and Social Existence.* Eugene, OR: Wipf & Stock.

Ogden, Graham. 1987. *Qoheleth.* Readings. Sheffield: JSOT Press.

Ortlund, Eric. 2014. "Laboring in Hopeless Hope: Encouragement for Christians from Ecclesiastes." *Them* 39, no. 2:281–89.

Pascal, Blaise. 1958. *Pascal's Pensées.* New York: Dutton.

Paul, Shalom M. 1978. "An Unrecognized Medical Idiom in Canticles 6, 12 and Job 9, 21." *Bib* 59, no. 4:545–47.

Perkin, Hazel W. 1988. "Family Life and Relations." In *Baker Encyclopedia of the Bible*, edited by Walter A. Elwell, 767–73. 2 vols. Grand Rapids: Baker.

Peterson, Jesse M. 2022. "Times as Task, Not Timing: Reconsidering Qohelet's Catalogue of the Times." *VT* 72, no. 3:444–73. DOI: 10.1163/15685330-bja10039.

Pfenniger, Jennifer. 2010. "Speaking or Smouldering Lips in Song of Songs 7:10 (Eng. 9)?" In *The Bible as a Human Witness to Divine Revelation: Hearing the Word of God Through Historically Dissimilar Traditions*, edited by Randall Heskett and Brian Irwin, 285–301. LHBOTS 469. New York: T&T Clark.

Pope, Marvin. 1977. *Song of Songs: A New Translation with Introduction and Commentary.* AB 7C. New York: Doubleday.

Pritchard, James B. 2011. *The Ancient Near East: An Anthology of Texts and Pictures.* Princeton, NJ: Princeton University Press.

Provan, Iain. 2000. "The Terrors of the Night: Love, Sex, and Power in Song of Songs 3." In *The Way of Wisdom: Essays in Honor of Bruce K. Waltke*, edited by J. I. Packer and

Sven K. Soderlun, 150–67. Grand Rapids: Zondervan Academic.

———. 2001. *Ecclesiastes, Song of Songs*. NIVAC. Grand Rapids: Zondervan.

Putnam, Robert. 2000. *Bowling Alone*. New York: Simon & Schuster.

Quackenbos, David Allen. 2019. "Recovering an Ancient Tradition: Toward an Understanding of Hezekiah as the Author of Ecclesiastes." PhD diss., Southeastern Baptist Theological Seminary.

Rainey, Anson F. 1964. "Study of Ecclesiastes." *CTM* 35, no. 3:148–57.

Rendsburg, Gary A. 1990. *Diglossia in Ancient Hebrew*. American Oriental Series 72. New Haven, CT: American Oriental Society.

Rindge, Matthew S. 2011. "Mortality and Enjoyment: The Interplay of Death and Possessions in Qoheleth." *CBQ* 73, no. 2:265–80.

Rogland, Max Frederick. 2013. "גל נעול in Canticles 4,12." *ZAW* 125, no. 4:646–49. DOI: 10.1515/zaw-2013-0040.

Rollston, Chris A. 2010. *Writing and Literacy in the World of Ancient Israel: Epigraphic Evidence from the Iron Age*. ABS 11. Atlanta: Society of Biblical Literature.

Roth, Martha. 1997. *Law Collections from Mesopotamia and Asia Minor*. 2nd ed. WAW 6. Atlanta: Scholars Press.

Routledge, Robin. 2008. *Old Testament Theology: A Thematic Approach*. Downers Grove, IL: IVP Academic.

Rudman, Dominic. 2002. "Determinism and Anti-Determinism in the Book of Koheleth." *JBQ* 30, no. 2:97–106.

Ryken, Philip Graham. 2014. *Ecclesiastes: Why Everything Matters*. Preaching the Word. Wheaton, IL: Crossway.

Samet, Nili. 2019. "How Deterministic Is Qohelet? A New Reading of the Appendix to the Catalogue of Times." *ZAW* 131, no. 4:577–91.

Scazzero, Peter. 2006. *Emotionally Healthy Spirituality: Unleash a Revolution in Your Life in Christ*. Grand Rapids: Zondervan.

———. 2015. *The Emotionally Healthy Leader: How Transforming Your Inner Life Will Deeply Transform Your Church, Team, and the World*. Grand Rapids: Zondervan.

———. 2017. *Emotionally Healthy Relationships: Discipleship That Deeply Changes Your Relationship with Others*. Grand Rapids: Zondervan.

Schellenberg, Annette. 2020. "The Description of Solomon's Wedding: Song 3:6–11 as a Key to the Overall Understanding of the Song of Songs." *VT* 70, no. 1:177–92. DOI: 10.1163/15685330-12341433.

Schlichting, Robert. 1979. "Kuß, küsse." *Lexikon der Ägyptologie* 3:901–2. Wiesbaden: Harrassowitz.

Schreiner, David B., and Lee Compson. 2022. *1 & 2 Kings: A Commentary for Biblical Preaching and Teaching*. Kerux Commentaries. Grand Rapids: Kregel Publications.

Schoors, Antoon. 2004. *The Preacher Sought to Find Pleasing Words: A Study of the Language of Qohelet Part II: Vocabulary*. OLA 143. Leuven: Peeters.

———. 2013. *Ecclesiastes*. HCOT. Leuven: Peeters.

Seow, C. L. 1996. "Linguistic Evidence and the Dating of Qohelet." *JBL* 115:643–66. DOI: 10.2307/3266347.

———. 1997. *Ecclesiastes: A New Translation with Introduction and Commentary*. AB 18C. New York: Doubleday.

———. 1999. "Qohelet's Eschatological Poem." *JBL* 118, no. 2:209–34. DOI: 10.2307/3268004.

Shead, Andrew G. 1997. "Reading Ecclesiastes 'Epilogically.'" *TynBul* 48, no. 1:67–91.

Shelley, Percy Bysshe. 2012. *The Complete Poetry of Percy Bysshe Shelley*. Vol. 3. Baltimore: Johns Hopkins University Press.

Shields, Martin A. 1999. "Ecclesiastes and the End of Wisdom." *TynBul* 50, no. 1:117–39.

———. 2000. "Re-Examining the Warning of Eccl XII 12." *VT* 50, no. 1:123–27. DOI: 10.1163/156853300506152.

———. 2006. *The End of Wisdom: A Reappraisal of the Historical and Canonical Function of Ecclesiastes*. Winona Lake, IN: Eisenbrauns.

Sneed, Mark. R. 2015a. *The Social World of the Sages: An Introduction to Israelite and Jewish Wisdom Literature*. Minneapolis: Fortress.

———, ed. 2015b. *Was There a Wisdom Tradition? New Prospects in Israelite Wisdom Studies*. AIL 23. Atlanta: SBL Press, 2015.

Spencer, F. Scott. 2019. "Feeling the Burn: Angry Brothers, Adamant Sister, and Affective Relations in the Song of Songs (1:5–6; 8:8–12)." *CBQ* 81, no. 3:405–28. DOI: 10.1353/cbq.2019.0138.

Strawn, Brent A. 2020. "עין גדי in Song of Songs 1,14." *Bib* 101, no. 1:114–23. DOI: 10.2143/BIB.101.1.3287518.

Suderman, W. Derek. 2005. "Modest or Magnificent?: Lotus versus Lily in Canticles." *CBQ* 67, no. 1:42–58.

Sun, Chloe. 2022. "'My Beloved Is Dazzling': Reading Song of Songs 5:10–16 for the Church." Paper presented at the Annual Meeting of the Evangelical Theological Society. Denver, CO, November 16, 2022.

Suriano, Matthew, 2017. "Kingship and *Carpe Diem*, Between Gilgamesh and Qohelet." *VT* 67, no. 2:285–306. DOI: 10.1163/15685330-12341276.

Taleb, Nassim Nicholas. 2012. *Antifragile: Things That Gain from Disorder*. New York: Random House.

Tawil, Hayim. 2003. "Paved with Love (Cant 3,10d): A New Interpretation." *ZAW* 115, no. 2:266–71.

———. 2009. *An Akkadian Lexical Companion for Biblical Hebrew: Etymological-Semantic and Idiomatic Equivalents with Supplement on Biblical Aramaic*. New York: KTAV.

Tolkien, J. R. R. 1954. *The Fellowship of the Ring: Being the First Part of The Lord of the Rings*. Boston: Houghton Mifflin.

Tuell, Steven Shawn. 1993. "A Riddle Resolved by an Enigma: Hebrew גלש and Ugaritic *GLT*." *JBL* 112, no. 1:99–104. DOI: 10.2307/3267867.

Verde, Danilo. 2016. "War-Games in the Song of Songs: A Reading of Song 2,4 in Light of Cognitive Linguistics." *SJOT* 30, no. 2:185–97. DOI: 10.1080/09018328.2016.1226047.

Verde, Danilo, and Pierre van Hecke. 2017. "The Belligerent Woman in Song 1,9." *Bib* 98, no. 2:208–26.

Viezel, Eran. 2014. "סַנְסִנָּיו (*sansinnāyw* Song of Songs 7:9) and the *Palpal* Noun Pattern." *JBL* 133, no. 4:751–56. DOI: 10.15699/jbibllite.133.4.751.

Waltke, Bruce K., and Michael O'Connor. 1990. *An Introduction to Biblical Hebrew Syntax*. Winona Lake, IN: Eisenbrauns.

Wasserman, Nathan. 2016. *Akkadian Love Literature of the Third and Second Millennium BCE*. Leipziger altorientalistische Studien 4. Wiesbaden: Harrassowitz.

Watson, Wilfred G. E. 1986. *Classical Hebrew Poetry: A Guide to Its Techniques*. JSOTSup 26. Sheffield: JSOT Press.

———. 1997. "Love and Death Once More (Song of Songs VIII 6)." *VT* 47, no. 3:385–87. DOI: 10.1163/1568533972651243.

Weeks, Stuart. 2012. *Ecclesiastes and Scepticism*. LHBOTS 541. New York: T&T Clark.

———. 2020. *A Critical and Exegetical Commentary on Ecclesiastes*. Vol. 1. ICC. New York: T&T Clark.

Weinberg, J. P. 2003. "Authorship and Author in the Ancient Near East and in the Hebrew Bible." *HS* 44:157–69.

Whitwell, Christopher. 2009. "The Variation of Nature in Ecclesiastes 11." *JSOT* 34, no. 1:81–97. DOI: 10.1177/0309089209346354.

Whybray, R. Norman. 1974. *The Intellectual Tradition in the Old Testament*. BZAW 135. Berlin: de Gruyter.

———. 1982. "Qohelet, Preacher of Joy." *JSOT* 7, no. 23:87–98. DOI: 10.1177/030908928200702305.

———. 1989. *Ecclesiastes*. NCB. Grand Rapids: Eerdmans.

Wiedemann, Alfred. 1920. *Das Alte Ägypten*. Kulturgeschichliche Bibliothek 2. Heidelberg: Winter.

Wilson, Andrews. 2009. *God*stories: Explorations in the Gospel of God*. Colorado Springs: Cook.

Wilson-Wright, Aren M. 2015. "Love Conquers All: Song of Songs 8:6b–7a as a Reflex of the Northwest Semitic Combat Myth." *JBL* 134, no. 2:333–45. DOI: 10.15699/jbl.1342.2015.2810.

Wood, Carrie. 2022. "Sabbath and Time Management." In *Scribes for the Kingdom*, edited by Corné J. Bekker and James T. Flynn, 89–101. Dubuque, IA: Kendall Hunt.

Young, Ian. 1993. *Diversity in Pre-Exilic Hebrew*. FAT 5. Tübingen: Mohr Siebeck.